HARVARD HISTORICAL STUDIES · 165

Published under the auspices
of the Department of History
from the income of the
Paul Revere Frothingham Bequest
Robert Louis Stroock Fund
Henry Warren Torrey Fund

— THE —
CONSERVATIVE
TURN

Lionel Trilling, Whittaker Chambers,
and the Lessons of Anti-Communism

MICHAEL KIMMAGE

HARVARD UNIVERSITY PRESS

Cambridge, Massachusetts
London, England

2009

Library of Congress Cataloging-in-Publication Data

Kimmage, Michael.

The conservative turn : Lionel Trilling, Whittaker Chambers, and the lessons of
anti-communism / Michael Kimmage.

p.   cm.

Includes bibliographical references and index.

ISBN 978-0-674-03258-3

1. Trilling, Lionel, 1905–1975—Political and social views.   2. Chambers, Whittaker—Political and
social views.   3. Right and left (Political science)   4. Communism—United States—History.
5. United States—Intellectual life—20th century.   I. Title.

PS3539.R56Z83 2009

818'.5209—dc22   2008029729

for my mother and father

Petersburg, 1913. A lyrical digression: the last reminiscence of Tsarskoe Selo. The wind mumbles, perhaps a recollection, perhaps a prophesy:

Bonfires warmed the yuletide,
   Carriages fell from the bridges,
      A whole city floated in mourning.
Unknown to what end,
   With, or against, the flow of the Neva,
     But away, away from its graves.
An archway crouched dark on Galernaya,
   In the Summer Garden a weathervane hummed
      And brightly over the silver age,
        The silver moon grew cold.
Because, along all the roads,
   Up to all the thresholds,
      A shadow slowly crept.
The wind tore posters from the wall,
   Smoke danced about the roof
      And the graveyard smelled of lilac.
Cursed by Tsarina Avdotya,
   Dostoevskian and demonic,
      The city shrank into fog.
A rakish old Petersburg playboy,
   Peered out once again from the darkness,
      And the drum beat before the hanging . . .
The darkness before the war,
   Frigid, prodigal, dreadful,
      Filled with some future din,
The din was more muffled then,
   It hardly troubled the soul
      And sank into snow banks along the Neva.
Like a person, mirrored in a dreadful night,
   Who rages and refuses
      To recognize himself.
Along the embankment of legend,
   It drew near—not on the calendar—
      The real Twentieth Century.

—ANNA AKHMATOVA, FROM "POEM WITHOUT A HERO"
(TRANSLATED BY DANIEL KIMMAGE)

CONTENTS

ACKNOWLEDGMENTS

From my early years in graduate school, when *The Conservative Turn* took shape, to the completion of this book, I have many people and institutions to thank.

I first read Lionel Trilling's *The Middle of the Journey*, the novel that is the keystone of this book, in a seminar with Ruth Wisse; in so many ways, my book would not exist without her help and her example. James Kloppenberg shared his erudition, his enthusiasm, and his eye for small details and big questions. Lizabeth Cohen stewarded this project from start to finish, tendering advice that was invariably right, if resisted at times in the short term. She was exceptionally generous with her time and expertise, doing what she could to rein in the abstraction and vagaries of intellectual history.

I would also like to thank the late Geoffrey Blodgett, my professor of American intellectual history at Oberlin College, whose teaching was the point of departure for this book. At Oberlin, Tom Newlin and Vladimir Golstein taught me to read and write about literature; their instruction in Russian culture was invaluable when it came to conceptualizing this not-entirely-American project. The same is true for Richard Pipes, with whom I had the privilege of studying Russian history in graduate school.

Crucial assistance, and much kindness, came from Christine McFadden, administrator of the History of American Civilization program at Harvard. Many of this program's students and alumni were valuable interlocutors and friends: Peter Becker, Mark Hanna, Chris Schmidt, Suleiman Osman, Talaya Delaney, Yael Schacher, George Blaustein, and Noam Maggor. Ali Yaycioglu brought his great eagerness to discuss American history to the writing of this book. Werner Sollors read chapters with great care, sharing with me his fascination with Trilling. I am only one of many American studies scholars who owe a great deal to Werner and his ebullient, scholarly spirit. Profligate with his curiosity, John Stauffer offered a wealth of bibliographic suggestions and much good conversation. Nathan Glazer read and critiqued several chapters, invaluable help from someone who knew firsthand the milieu of my protagonists.

I would like to thank those who have read parts the book manuscript as the chapters emerged. Sam Tanenhaus has generously shared his mastery of the Chambers story and of the ideological landscape around it. Neal Kozodoy offered questions and support, especially helpful since his connection to my subject is not entirely academic. Alex Star shared his expertise with Trilling and much else while speculating about the content of my argument. Through his books and his company, Neil Jumonville offered his deep store of knowledge about the New York intellectuals and American liberalism. Michael Gordin, youthful scholar of Richard Nixon, read and vibrantly discussed much that I have written. David Greenberg read early chapters; his own scholarship and our long-running conversation about history and politics have been an inspiration. The late Richard Rorty read and commented on Chapter 6; Louis Menand commented on this chapter as well. Susanne Klingenstein provided detailed commentary on the early chapters of this book. Michael Kazin read the manuscript in its entirety, offering suggestions and criticism from a perspective that is both scholarly and personal where my material is concerned. An anonymous reader of this manuscript for Harvard University Press did a careful and spirited job critiquing it.

At Harvard University Press, Lindsay Waters gave generously of his curiosity and support. In discussions that moved between high-toned philosophizing and the rough-and-tumble of political debate, very much in the spirit of my subjects, he helped me to think of this project as a book. Phoebe Kosman has patiently helped with many questions relating to publication, and I am grateful for the fine editorial assistance of Melody Negron and Jennifer Seifert. I owe a particular debt of gratitude to Thomas Leitch and his splendid annotated bibliography of Trilling; it was a pleasure to meet the man behind the book in Lafayette, Louisiana.

With intellectual flair, Karl Borromeus Murr, Max Müller-Härlin, and Anna Plodeck have invited me into Germany's rich historiographical world, as has Tim Müller. Rajesh Vedanthan and Prabal Chakrabarti keep the flame of political disputation alive—the heart of this project—as do Antonio Battaglia and Shilpa Prasad. Gary Shteyngart, a writer who handles my themes in the domain of literature, gave his encouragement to my scholarship. Angela and Patricia Banks have kept track of this project for years, lending their intellectual companionship along the way. Jonathan Beere was among the first of my peers to look far beyond the liberal weltanschauung, giving me questions that preoccupy me still.

At Harvard I received financial support from the History of American Civilization program, from the Graduate School of Arts and Sciences, and from the Charles Warren Center; a Whiting fellowship and a Javits fellowship were similarly invaluable during graduate school. I would also like to thank the Gilder Lehrman Institute in New York for a summer research grant and to express my continuing gratitude for a British Marshall Scholarship: without my two years at Oxford, where I was fortunate to study with Leslie Mitchell and Hartmut Pogge von Strandmann, this would be a substantially more provincial book. The same could be said about the Humboldt Foundation for the year at the Ludwig-Maximilians Universität (LMU) in Munich it made possible, and for its continuing support I would like to thank Steffen Mehlich, a Russianist and an Atlanticist, for his help and also Maria-Bernadette Carstens-Behrens for her help. Thanks to the Humboldt Foundation, the Amerika Institut of the LMU is my second academic home: its former director, Berndt Ostendorf, is a transatlantic scholar with a transatlantic purview, a genuine cosmopolitan in the republic of letters; Michael Hochgeschwender has given the gift of his scholarship, with his book *Freiheit in der Offensive*, and the gift of his friendship; Peter Schneck, Meike Zwingenberger, Klaus Benesch, Thomas Greven, Christa Buschendorf, Andreas Etges, Britta Waldschmidt-Nelson, Markus Hünemörder, Kerstin Schmitt, Sascha Pöhlmann, and Julia Apitzsch are all esteemed colleagues in Germany; and Christof Mauch is a fellow traveler on the Washington-Munich bridge, an intellectual, and a helper of intellectuals.

At the Catholic University of America my colleagues make the history department a congenial place. They understand the high ideals and the practical demands of scholarship and could not be more helpful to new faculty, which is what I was when I began teaching here. Jerry Muller is deeply versed in my field of research; he is a role model and a highly discerning critic of whatever I give him to read. Leslie and Tom Tentler have taken an avid interest in my research since my arrival in Washington, D.C. Tom Cohen and Lisa Fuentes may be perplexed by my involvement with conservatism but, with their signature exuberance, they encourage my interest in literature and ideas. Owen Stanwood is far enough away, in historiographical time, to see the strangeness of my subject and close enough, in sensibility, to see my aspirations for it. Catholic University has supported my work with summer research grants and in many nonfinancial ways.

Finally, I would like to thank my family, for whom communism and anti-communism have never been dull subjects. *The Conservative Turn* is unthinkable without a family trip taken through the East bloc at the height of the Cold War, and it is equally unthinkable without a tradition of political and historical reflection that runs through generations. Alma Dirzyte can tell me exactly how American my perspective on Soviet communism is; for this, and other things, I am very grateful. My parents and brother have taught me to regard communism and anti-communism not simply as political phenomena but as matters of humanistic significance. My book is the product of their teaching.

THE CONSERVATIVE TURN

INTRODUCTION

The first televised spectacle in American history began in 1948. It came to be known as the Hiss case because it involved Alger Hiss, president of the Carnegie Endowment for International Peace when the case began and a former State Department bureaucrat in the era of Franklin Delano Roosevelt. The essence of this spectacular case was a battle of words waged by two men, Alger Hiss and Whittaker Chambers. An editor at *Time* magazine, Chambers was overweight and poorly dressed; he had confessed to being a Soviet spy in the 1930s. It was his word against the word of Hiss, and the arbiter was the House Un-American Affairs Committee (HUAC). British journalist Alistair Cooke titled an eyewitness account of the Hiss case "A Generation on Trial." If it was a generation on trial, then Hiss and Chambers were from opposite sides of their generation. Or so it must have seemed in 1948 to those first confronted with the case. On one side was Hiss—a successful, handsome, well-connected civil servant, owner of a fine resume; on the other was Chambers—a man on the margins. Chambers was an ex-communist, an ex-spy, a homosexual perhaps—someone as un-American as the affairs the House Committee was supposed to investigate. Yet it was Chambers who accused Hiss of disloyalty, of being a communist, a charge that Hiss categorically denied. Each against his will, Hiss and Chambers stood on the national stage, objects of mystery, bluntly contradicting each other. After countless dramatic twists and turns, Hiss was convicted of perjury in 1950 and sent to jail. Chambers, the ostensible victor, was not declared a hero in the wake of the Hiss case. Many loathed him and continued to believe passionately in Hiss's innocence, as they would for decades. With Chambers's unfinished victory, a new anti-communist mood settled on the United States.

The Hiss case contributed to three major political developments. The first was the end of the New Dealers' preeminence in American politics, the second was the postwar rise of the Republican Party, and the third was the ascendancy of Richard Nixon within the Republican Party. An icon of New Deal ambition, Alger Hiss had worked in various federal agencies, coming into government with recommendations from Harvard Law School, as if recruited to personify Roosevelt's brain trust. Hiss knew Franklin Roosevelt personally and although his conviction for perjury and implied treason did not destroy the New Deal, they did challenge the moral authority of New Dealers. If Hiss was a communist, who else from his world—from within the government, from within the Roosevelt administration—might be a comrade? The Democrats had held the White House since 1932; they would lose it in 1952. Senator Joseph McCarthy, for whom every Democrat and not a few Republicans were potential Alger Hisses, exploited the advantage the Hiss case handed to the Republican Party. A far cannier politician than McCarthy was Richard Nixon, without whom there would have been no Hiss case at all. A junior representative from California, Nixon was a member of HUAC in 1948. He never wavered in his belief that Hiss was guilty and that Chambers was a hero. At the outset, and possibly with the help of a tip-off, Nixon's persistence kept the Hiss case alive.[1] Nixon's efforts were abundantly rewarded when he became vice president in 1952, the credentialed anti-communist on the Eisenhower ticket and a prophylactic against McCarthyism. Nixon would serve two terms as vice president, proceeding to win presidential elections in 1968 and 1972.

The Hiss case inaugurated a new division between Left and Right in the United States, changes that were registered and at times anticipated in intellectual life. The 1950s witnessed the emergence of conservative intellectuals who were politically minded. The aesthete conservatives of the 1920s—T. S. Eliot, for example—might have been monarchists or fascists, but they all stood (proudly) on the fringes of American politics. A conservative intellectual of the 1930s and 1940s, Albert Jay Nock acknowledged the lonely status of conservatives in his 1943 autobiography *Memoirs of a Superfluous Man*, more the protagonist of a nineteenth-century Russian novel than a hero in the American vein. In the 1930s intellectual dynamism and self-confidence had belonged largely to the Left. The Great Depression, coupled with the growing power of fascism in Europe, had left American conservatives confused and unpopular. The conservative intellectuals of the 1950s were ideologically astute in a way that earlier conservatives were not. Several of these new conservatives had mastered the intricacies of

Marxism-Leninism, either as fellow travelers or as communists in the 1930s, and they lent the fruits of their ideological training to the anti-communist cause. A wave of conversions from the Left strengthened the Right, giving it new life and new ideas. On the Left, the prestige of Stalin's Soviet Union had helped to paint the 1930s Red. Even before the Hiss case, however, the intellectual Left was splintering into anti-Stalinists and a dwindling band of enthusiasts for the Soviet Union. In the late 1940s a group of anti-Stalinist intellectuals, subsequently known as the New York intellectuals, began to coalesce, and they would prove that one could be both liberal *and* anti-communist. From Harry Truman to John F. Kennedy to Lyndon Johnson, the Democratic Party would prove the same. This was no less significant a development than the elaboration of a politically relevant conservatism on the Right.[2]

When examined together, developments on the Left and the Right outline a twofold conservative turn after World War II. The Right turned to the center, as many of its intellectuals rejected the neofascist conservatism of the early twentieth century, challenging conservative American traditions of isolationism and anti-Semitism and embracing elements of modernity—the industrial revolution, capitalism, democracy, and the need for a rational bureaucratic state or at least a bureaucratic national security state. The Left turned away from radicalism; it, too, moved toward the political center. In both cases, the crucial issue was that of communism or, rather, anti-communism. Anti-communism spurred the Right to unify, to gain intellectual respectability, and to think strategically—to overcome the division between traditionalists, who objected to the modern world, and capitalists, who wanted the business of America to remain business. These two rival factions would gradually grow together in the campaign against communism, an atheist ideology that promised a state-planned economy. At the same time, anti-communism taught the Left to proceed cautiously after the excesses of the 1930s, to dispense with revolution and, most generally, to define commitment to the Left as liberal or moderate rather than radical.[3] Karl Marx's ideas had been applied to America in the 1930s, if not his doctrines in full then at least his vocabulary. After the 1930s Marx would fade away and the Soviet Union, official guardian of Marx's legacy, would be transformed for many on the Left from a Popular Front ally to a Cold War enemy. Anti-communist liberals and anti-communist conservatives could support similar Cold War means in the pursuit of sharply divergent political ends.[4]

In the years between the 1930s and 1950s, anti-communism was not the sole impetus for change in America's political and intellectual life. Nor was it the only cause of the conservative turn. The New Deal and World War II restored American capitalism, if not to its laissez-faire glory days then at least to a renewed sense of confidence in itself; the postwar economic boom heightened this sense of confidence. The growth of American military power, culminating in the Cold War, followed from old trends dating back to the nineteenth century when the United States amassed extraordinary territory and wealth. Furthermore, Right and Left, as argued about by intellectuals, were not synonymous with the fate of the Republican and Democratic parties. These parties might at times benefit from the help of intellectuals, but they were also beholden to forces other than ideological debate and controversy, and they were transformed by principles other than those devised by intellectuals. The hard calculus of electoral college votes matters more in American politics than does any idea or theory of politics. The postwar political climate did not emanate from the pages of intellectual magazines such as *Partisan Review*, *Commentary*, or *National Review*. Likewise, the opportunism of politicians such as Nixon and McCarthy threw into question the political importance of anti-communist intellectuals. Intellectuals' ideas were valuable but rarely in the way they were intended to be. Often, anti-communism was politically useful without any relation to ideas at all. Intellectuals did not single-handedly determine political change, and anti-communism was valid for reasons other than its intellectual substance. As far as the conservative turn of the postwar period is concerned, the writing of intellectuals is only one piece of a large and complicated puzzle.

Nevertheless, midcentury intellectual history illuminates a peculiar political circumstance. The cardinal experience of American intellectuals in the 1930s was their encounter with Soviet communism, and a central problem facing the American polity in the 1950s, from its culture to its foreign policy, was that of domestic and foreign communism. This peculiar circumstance can be conveyed in a single vivid example. In the 1930s, as Irving Howe, Irving Kristol, and Daniel Bell were coming of age, they furiously debated questions of communism—parsing the words of Marx, Lenin, Trotsky, and Stalin—in alcove one in the cafeteria of the City College of New York. They were honing the ideas and arguments of the anti-Stalinist Left by analyzing the trajectory that led from Marx to Stalin and investing their collegiate high spirits in one of the most important intel-

4

lectual problems of their generation. The cafeteria's next alcove belonged to the Stalinists, and it was presided over by Julius Rosenberg, who would become an icon of postwar American radicalism when he and his wife were executed for atomic espionage. The Rosenberg case is at the heart of twentieth-century American history. Intellectuals such as Howe, Kristol, and Bell, all of whom were public voices by the 1950s, could comment on the significance of Julius and Ethel Rosenberg not as disembodied observers of the political scene but as those who knew the milieu, ideas, dilemmas, and personalities of their era—personal, firsthand knowledge that drove their ideological passions. This was a circumstance that sharpened the intellectual history of the period, making it relevant and giving it its high degree of specificity, energy, and bitterness.[5]

The point at which the anti-communist intellectual and political worlds met was less the Rosenberg case than the Hiss case, which raised questions of interpretation that intellectuals, schooled in the radicalism of the 1930s, were exceedingly good at answering—or, when answers were hard to come by, at speculating about and discussing. Intellectuals knew why people became communists (for many of them had) and why people became anti-communists (for many of them had gone in this direction well before the Hiss case). An analogous situation involved progressive intellectuals, such as Herbert Croley or Louis Brandeis, who had addressed themselves to the underside of industrial capitalism before World War I. They left a legacy of progressive social-democratic thought that could be applied to the economic dislocations of the 1930s. One can and should draw a line from these progressive intellectuals to the New Deal. Similarly, one can draw a line from the intellectual anti-Stalinism of the late 1930s to the anti-communism that established itself in Washington, D.C. after World War II. In the same way that the Great Depression gave credence to the work of progressive intellectuals and power to the New Dealers, the Cold War gave credence to the work of anti-Stalinist intellectuals. Politicians did not pass up the chance to augment their power by putting this work to use and aligning themselves with the conservative turn. Ideas that would wind their way through the Cold War, from 1948 to 1989, had their debut in the late 1930s and early 1940s. An anti-Stalinist education was invaluable when the Cold War transformed debates about theory into debates about policy.

Exemplars of the conservative turn, Lionel Trilling and Whittaker Chambers met at Columbia College in the early 1920s. Chambers was born on Long Island in 1901 into a declining middle-class family that was formerly Protestant and effectively atheist. Trilling's family was Jewish. He was born in New York City in 1905 but his parents had immigrated to the United States from Poland. Both men were communists for a time and, after considerable turmoil, they became anti-communists. Trilling would take the lessons of anti-communism to the Left or, to use his word of choice, to liberalism. Chambers would do the same on the Right. Side by side, their careers reinforced the congruence between the intellectual preoccupations of the 1930s and the political configurations of the 1950s.

A rough parallelism in experience connected Trilling and Chambers. They got their intellectual start at the same literary magazine, *The Morningside*, which was published by Columbia undergraduates. Of the two, Chambers was the first to become a communist, joining the Communist Party around 1923 and eventually entering its underground. Chambers was as deeply involved as he could be: he was a spy for the Soviet Union. Trilling and most other *Morningside* contributors followed suit—with their sympathy for communism, not by becoming spies—in the early 1930s, although Trilling never joined the Party. By the mid-1930s Trilling had broken ranks before he could ever become an enthusiast of the Popular Front. In 1937–1938, Chambers moved precipitously from the radical Left to the Right, ending up as an outspoken conservative editor at *Time* magazine; his decision to abandon communism has been called (hyperbolically) "one of the most significant events of the twentieth century."[6] Trilling's magazine of choice in the late 1930s was not *Time* but *Partisan Review*, the scourge of pro-Soviet communists and very much an initiative from the Left. By 1940, both Trilling and Chambers were anti-communist intellectuals of note, translating anti-communism into the vocabulary of American culture. They took it upon themselves to preach the anti-communist gospel in the 1940s, and in this decade they devoted most of their energy to the practice of anti-communism. They strove to convince their readers that the Soviet Union and communism were a menace, a threat to Western civilization as well as to the American republic.

After breaking with communism, Chambers dedicated himself to the modernization of the Right. Conservatives might admit that the West was "this sick society," as Chambers described it in *Witness*, his autobiography, but before they could heal a sickly West they would have to accommodate themselves to it.[7] The stakes were too high for failure. If the United States were to fail the Soviet Union would surely succeed, and this was what Chambers wished to prevent at all costs. Chambers focused on anti-communism with a pragmatic eye and a willingness to compromise his own more extreme convictions. Although he did not gladly enter the maelstrom of the Hiss case, the event greatly helped his cause. Chambers's friendship with Nixon, which followed from the Hiss case, lent him the ear of a vice president as of 1952 and of a senator before that. Chambers argued against William F. Buckley Jr., a young admirer of his and founder of the conservative magazine *National Review*, who considered Eisenhower too centrist to be a conservative statesman. A powerful, if pessimistic, theorist of American conservatism, Chambers promoted the modernization of the Right via the Republican Party, claiming that mass politics, rather than subtle ideas, was crucial to political action. If the Right could fend off the Soviet Union and the philo-communist Left in America, then it could address itself to the evils of a godless modernity. In the meantime, anti-communism would have to do.

The anti-Stalinist Trilling presided over the moderation of the intellectual Left. Author of an essay collection titled *The Opposing Self*, Trilling's thoughts often went in circles. He questioned himself repeatedly, making use of his self-doubt in essays that exposed the dangers of facile self-confidence and rigid political posturing. If Trilling doubted his own position after rejecting Soviet communism, he did not doubt the pernicious influence of Stalinism, a complex of radical attitudes toward art, culture, and politics that he attributed to the intellectuals of the 1930s. One need not adore Stalin to be complicit with Stalinism, Trilling believed, for Stalinism had become an organic part of American culture in the 1930s. From the 1930s onward, Trilling was one of the subtlest critics of Stalinism, but his subtlety did not temper his zeal: in his short stories and one published novel he depicted Stalinism in the harshest possible light. In his essays of the 1940s, several of which were gathered into his 1950 book *The Liberal Imagination*, Trilling contrasted an urbane liberal imagination to the vulgar radicalism of the 1930s, advocating the replacement of a philo-communist ethos with one that combined conservatism and liberalism. With Trilling, anti-communist liberalism acquired intellectual depth and a kind of bourgeois respectability about which Trilling had his own characteristic doubts. He was not one to join a movement, not even one of his own making. In his combination of liberalism and conservatism Trilling was sui generis.

The image of liberalism versus conservatism, of Chambers locked in battle with Hiss, has remained iconic for the American Right. In 2003, conservative ideologue Ann Coulter published *Treason: Liberal Treachery from the Cold War to the War on Terrorism*, an extended reflection on the Hiss case, on *Witness*, and on the relationship between liberalism and treason. In *Treason*, the Cold War is more or less contemporary; that is, its political meaning is contemporary, making Chambers a prophet of the war on terrorism. At its most interesting, *Treason* illustrates Coulter's close identification with Chambers, her association of all conservatives with Chambers, and her sense that bearing witness is the essence of conservative experience.

> Liberals waged a conscious conspiracy [against Chambers] directed from the White House, and it took forty years to prove Chambers was telling the truth. Liberals wrote the history of McCarthyism and to this day no one knows that McCarthy was right. Liberals wrote the history of Watergate and consequently, no one has the first idea what that even was. Already liberals are trying to rewrite the history of the Cold War to remove Reagan from its core, to make him a doddering B-movie actor who happened to be standing there when the Soviet Union imploded. They have the media, the universities, the textbooks. We have ourselves. We are the witnesses.

In *Treason*, Coulter repeats one of Chambers's main theses, arguing that "the fundamental difference between liberals and conservatives is: conservatives believe in God's image; liberals believe they are God. All their other behavioral tics proceed from this one irreducible minimum." She then states baldly what Chambers never directly said but often seemed to imply: "the inevitable logic of the liberal position is to be for treason."[8]

Chambers's conservative logic was less one-dimensional than Coulter's polemic would suggest. Chambers, the Eisenhower Republican, was both normal and abnormal in the context of 1950s conservatism. In his private life he departed from the mainstream. He and his wife, Esther, repudiated the modern world by raising their children on a remote farm in Maryland. Chambers's cultural conservatism was unusually stark: he repeatedly predicted the collapse of the West, which lacked all conviction, he believed, while the Soviets were full of passionate intensity, as were Western intellectuals enamored of the Soviet Union. Hope resided in the common folk of America, undefiled by the liberalism and socialism of the educated middle class. Chambers was a supple political thinker, but behind his fascination with the play of power politics was a highly moral vision of the world in which evil seemed always to have the upper hand. Chambers was a conventional American conservative in that he was a devout Christian, and his Christianity was his way back to America after some fifteen years as a Marxist revolutionary and employee of the Red Army. Although Chambers did not write about American political history, the tradition into which he fell was that of Christian republicanism, more the engaged, pious conservatism of John Adams than the alienated, ironic conservatism of Adams's great-grandson Henry. Thrown in was a bit of Thomas Jefferson and a bit of Henry David Thoreau. Chambers had the farmer's suspicion of cities and manufacturing that Jefferson considered the guiding spirit of American republicanism. Chambers's farm was his anti-communist Walden.

Unlike Chambers, the agrarian anti-communist, Trilling was self-consciously an urban, bourgeois intellectual—a professor of English literature at Columbia University and a resident of Manhattan. Even as a young man, Trilling had rebelled against rebellion, against the intellectual's occupational dislike of the middle class. When Trilling employed his signature "we" in his essays, he was referring to his fellow liberals, but "we" were also the educated middle class to which Trilling belonged and for whom he wrote. As early as the 1920s Trilling detected an "adversary culture," a term he would popularize in the early 1960s, tracking its expansion with the radical insurgency of the 1930s. The infatuation with Bolshevism left a permanent mark on the American intelligentsia, he believed, setting the middle class against itself. Trilling, suspicious of modernist literature already in his college years, became an odd kind of social critic in the 1930s. The object of his criticism was not so much American culture or society per se but the often malign role of intellectuals within this culture. Trilling found an alternative to the adversary culture in the writings of Victorian poet and intellectual Matthew Arnold. Arnold, in his social criticism, had urged the English middle class to educate itself, a lesson that Trilling took to heart and applied to America. Trilling could act on Arnold's injunction as a Columbia professor and as a sponsor of the Readers' Subscription and Mid-Century book clubs, the aim of which was to make great books available at low prices to provide the means for mass self-education.[9] Trilling was an ambivalent spokesman for bourgeois enlightenment. He never forgot Arnold's characterization of the bourgeoisie as philistine, and he adored Freud's *Civilization and Its Discontents*, which informs many of Trilling's essays. Freud taught Trilling that no amount of bourgeois respectability could reverse the drives, appetites, and discontents that imperil civilization.

Anti-communism, a bipartisan persuasion, went in two separate directions after World War II. Harry Truman was an outspoken anti-communist leader and so too was John F. Kennedy, who had a brilliant galaxy of liberal anti-communist intellectuals behind him. The Kennedy White House glowed with their enthusiasm, with the energy of a decade's thinking on the subject of communism and anti-communism, and with the cultural prestige anti-communism had gathered by the 1950s. However, the Kennedy mystique masked the precariousness of liberal anti-communism, just as it obscured the many opponents of liberal anti-communism in the early 1960s. After Kennedy's assassination in 1963, the liberal anti-communist cosmos would lose its luster; and under Kennedy's successor, Lyndon Johnson, it would start to decline. Richard Nixon, Kennedy's Republican rival in the 1960 presidential election, was a frequent houseguest at Chambers's farm in Maryland, but Nixon was never the ideal anti-communist for Chambers. Barry Goldwater's insurgency in 1964 tilted the Republican Party more toward Chambers's ideals than Eisenhower's administration ever had. First, Goldwater made conservatism an explicit theme in American politics when, in 1960, he published his campaign book *The Conscience of a Conservative*. Goldwater was also a populist—populism being a cherished predisposition of Chambers even before he was a communist. Chambers would probably have approved the merger of the Christian Right and the Republican Party, and he would have delighted in Ronald Reagan's unequivocal anti-communism in part because Reagan had learned a great deal about communism from reading Chambers. Liberal anti-communism declined in the 1960s while conservative anti-communism was on the rise: the history of American anti-communism is robustly nonlinear.

If Chambers and Trilling left a common legacy at all, it was in their posthumous influence on a group of intellectuals for whom anti-communism was a tradition and conservatism a new discovery. This group would come to be known as the neoconservatives.[10]

Many of the neoconservatives of the 1970s—Norman Podhoretz and Irving Kristol, for example—had known or studied with Trilling, and they had an important role model in Chambers, someone radically new to conservatism in the late 1930s. Chambers was the archetypal American neoconservative. Like Chambers, the neoconservatives would use their autobiographies to describe and recommend a conservative turn. For them, politics had an autobiographical dimension, each autobiography a chapter in the collective conservative turn. Chambers began *Witness* with a letter to his children, a personal appeal to the next generation. A student and friend of Trilling's, Podhoretz echoed Chambers's "Letter to My Children" in his own antiradical memoir *Breaking Ranks*. Podhoretz prefaced his Chambers-esque confessions with "Prologue: A Letter to My Son."[11] For Podhoretz the paradigm was no longer the intellectual as revolutionary or reformer but rather the intellectual as parent, impressing conservative wisdom on an immature younger generation. Chambers was the first to establish this narrative paradigm in American political writing. David Horowitz, another neoconservative intellectual, would compare himself with Chambers in his autobiography *Radical Son*, a title that evokes paternity in reverse. Horowitz is clearly proud to be in Chambers's company.

> I was like Whittaker Chambers in their generation [the generation of the New Left]—a young man inspired by the high-minded passions of the Left who had broken through to the dark underside of the radical cause. Like Chambers, I had encounters with totalitarian forces that involved betrayal and death, and even a Soviet spy. Like him, I had been demonized for my second thoughts by a culture sympathetic to the Left and hostile to its adversaries. I, too, had to face the same personal attacks by my former comrades that were designed to warn others to remain in the fold. Like Chambers, I had become the most hated ex-radical of my generation. And like him, I had discovered that the enemies against whom I battled so furiously were more fantastic than real. I also discovered that I was not alone.[12]

Chambers offered his neoconservative followers the precedent of an openly conservative persona, a feel for political strategy, and a frank sympathy for religion, qualities that were not to be found in any of Trilling's books or essays. Chambers's mysticism and world-historical pessimism were absent among the neoconservatives, who were far closer to Enlightenment reason and Enlightenment optimism than Chambers ever wished to be.[13] Yet the neoconservative movement, with its many Jewish voices, did not eschew the legacy of Chambers the Protestant. Religion was often promoted by the first neoconservative generation as it has been by the second—by William Kristol, the son of Irving Kristol and Gertrude Himmelfarb, by David Brooks, and by many others. Religion is good in its own right, and it is the ideal antidote to radicalism, a shield against the Left and its seductive secular utopianism. The Jewish neoconservatives and the Christian Chambers could agree on this point.[14] As for political strategy, Chambers's advice throughout the 1950s was for conservatives to work through the Republican Party. On the merits of this advice, a neoconservative such as Podhoretz and an older conservative such as Chambers's friend William F. Buckley Jr. could join hands, as they eventually did, fellow admirers of Chambers's student, Ronald Reagan. Chambers recommended using practical means to achieve ideological ends.[15] In the 1970s and 1980s many neoconservatives refused to align themselves with a splinter party, one more in harmony with their ideas than the imperfect Republican and Democratic parties. Under Ronald Reagan, the Republican Party was a populist force and a vehicle for anti-communist conservatism to which neoconservative intellectuals could and did contribute.[16]

The path from Trilling, a lifelong Democrat, to Reagan is anything but straight. Once a student at Columbia, David Horowitz has likened himself to Chambers, and he has also paid tribute to Trilling by calling him "one of the most perceptive liberal thinkers."[17] Trilling had scrutinized the psychology of the Left in ambitious essays and reviews; he was important to neoconservatives for his cool intellectual style, his sophistication, his awareness of cultural nuance, his vast erudition. Trilling ushered conservative ideas into his essays and books with the aim of expanding the liberal imagination and widening the parameters of American intellectual culture, opening the door to conservative ideas without ever walking through to the other side. He wrote appreciatively about the (reactionary) politics of T. S. Eliot, about the moral vision of the Victorians, about the merit of hierarchy, and of stable ethical values. He championed the sincerity of eighteenth-century culture by contrasting it to the destructive modern search for authenticity. Trilling's critique of liberalism—intended as an internal liberal affair—could be used for other purposes. Indeed, the literary scholar Ruth Wisse understands Trilling's 1947 novel *The Middle of the Journey* as "a blueprint for the cultural reversal that became known as neoconservatism." Wisse argues that the neoconservative implications are latent in Trilling's writing—latent but crucial. They needed only the right set of architects to build upon the blueprint. In a similar vein, Cornel West has called Trilling the godfather of neoconservatism.[18]

One architect working off the Trilling blueprint was historian Gertrude Himmelfarb, who was a friend of Trilling's together with her husband, Irving Kristol; both Kristol and Himmelfarb were central figures in the neoconservative movement. Himmelfarb's 1994 essay collection *On Looking into the Abyss* is so close to Trilling in style and subject as to be almost a dialogue with him. "Rereading Trilling's essay ["On the Teaching of Modern Literature"]," Himmelfarb writes at the beginning of *On Looking into the Abyss*, "I was struck by how pertinent it is to the present state of the academic culture; indeed, it is more pertinent now than it was in his own day." Himmelfarb continues: "Trilling was troubled by the ease with which the great books were emasculated (a word one hardly dares use today), the way passionate affirmations were reduced to rote formulas and subversive ideas were banal and respectable. But his students were at least reading those books and confronting those ideals. One cannot say that now with any confidence."[19] The light cast by Trilling's example makes even his dilemmas enviable. As a historian of Victorian Britain, Himmelfarb has continued the comparison between nineteenth-century Britain and modern America that Trilling explored throughout his career as simultaneously a scholar of English literature and an American intellectual. Himmelfarb respects Trilling for his moral imagination, which was touched with something conservative; she has titled one of her books *The Moral Imagination: From Edmund Burke to Lionel Trilling*. Lionel Trilling's wife, Diana, was emphatic about her husband's liberalism, but her defense of his liberalism is couched in curiously retrospective language: "I am of the firmest belief," she wrote in her memoir, "that he [Lionel] would never have become a neoconservative . . . his own stand was in the traditional liberalism of the nineteenth century and, complicate though he does, he remained a traditional liberal until his death."[20]

The neoconservatives came out of an anti-communist intelligentsia, which Trilling and Chambers had helped to create in the 1940s and 1950s. Its cultural side was in New York and in western Europe and its political side in Washington, D.C. It was united by a single assumption: not just that communism was a moral disaster but that communism was a living threat to America and to Western civilization. American power was the last resort against this threat, and the anti-communist intelligentsia—whether

Democrat or Republican, liberal or conservative—existed in some favorable relation to American power, defining its aims and worrying about its limits. From the vantage point of their radical youth, only a conservative turn could have taken Trilling and Chambers to positions of esteem and influence within this intelligentsia. The anti-communist intelligentsia was of essential importance to America's war of ideas, waged from the 1950s to the 1980s. It was the kind of war that intellectuals such as Trilling and Chambers were most adept at fighting.

If Trilling and Chambers tried to apply their anti-communist lessons in America, with the medium of American power in mind, they had as their larger context the twentieth century, a temporal geography they regarded as a metaphor for crisis.[21] Their purview was not global: they cared mostly about Europe, the United States, and the Soviet Union. They cared, in other words, about the West, as they understood the term, and about the West as a civilization more than as a political entity. Here their Columbia education in great books left its intended mark, as did their youthful interest in Oswald Spengler's *The Decline of the West*, published in America in 1926, which explained more of the twentieth century to them than Marx's *Das Kapital* ever did. In her "Poem without a Hero," Anna Akhmatova—who lived literally in Stalin's shadow—distinguished between "the calendar twentieth century" and "the real twentieth century." The real twentieth century was a time of troubles that happened to fall in the calendar twentieth century. To their shame, Trilling and Chambers both felt personally implicated in the troubles of Stalinism, in Stalin's "murderous madhouse," and, to borrow a phrase from Irving Howe, in "the ghastly large-scale infatuation with a totalitarian regime which disgraced the thirties."[22] If there was any single thing they wished to conserve as anti-Stalinists, it was Western civilization. They wanted to prevent this civilization from becoming yet another casualty of the real twentieth century. It was an ambition that Trilling and Chambers shared not because they were similar but because they had a similar education and had lived through similar intellectual and historical cataclysms. In turning toward communism and then toward anti-communism, they never turned their backs on Western civilization, the golden thread for these two lovers of it, connecting beginning to end and end to beginning.

1

SONS OF THE BOURGEOISIE

Portrait of Lionel Trilling and Whittaker Chambers as Young Men

Herodotus—Sophocles—Plato—Aristotle—Demosthenes—
Cicero—Vergil
Horace—Tacitus—St. Augustine—St. Thomas Aquinas
Cervantes—Shakespeare—Dante—Milton—Voltaire—Goethe

—NAMES ON THE FAÇADE OF COLUMBIA UNIVERSITY'S
BUTLER LIBRARY, COMPLETED IN 1934

The Sea of Faith
Was once, too, at the full, and round earth's shore
Lay like the folds of a bright girdle furl'd.
But now I only hear
Its melancholy, long, withdrawing roar,
Retreating, to the breath
Of the night-wind, down the vast edges drear
And naked shingles of the world.

—MATTHEW ARNOLD, "Dover Beach"

Radical times called for radical measures or at least for radical gestures. Whittaker Chambers first achieved notoriety as a college undergraduate when he wrote an atheist play "A Play for Puppets," which
he published in Columbia College's literary journal, *The Morningside*.
His adviser, the celebrated literary scholar Mark Van Doren, described the
play as "brilliant." A journalist at the *New York Tribune* observed that the
play had "a distinctly Wildean flavor." Others were less impressed. Professor John Erskine, doyen of humanities at Columbia and creator of its
"great books" program, found Chambers's play immoral. Erskine deni-
grated "A Play for Puppets" as "cheap," and he engineered Chambers's resignation as editor of *The Morningside* in October 1922. In one of several

newspaper articles about this academic episode, *The Morningside* was identified as having "a reputation for being radical." With the Red Scare in the very recent past, the alleged radicalism of *The Morningside* may have frightened Erskine: atheist today, communist tomorrow.[1] This was not a ludicrous fear. Many of the magazine's contributors—Herbert Solow, Lionel Trilling, Clifton Fadiman, Meyer Schapiro, and Chambers himself—would later become deeply involved with radical thought and movements. Whittaker Chambers was the most conspicuous communist ever to attend Columbia, although in 1922 the radicalism of *The Morningside* had little to do with socialism or communism, little to do with politics per se. The scandal of Chambers's undergraduate play, according to those who were scandalized, was the insult it gave to Christian honor.

Radical Columbia as embodied in *The Morningside* was more bohemian—more Wildean—than Bolshevik. In the early 1930s Chambers's Columbia classmate Lionel Trilling reflected in print on the radicalism of *The Morningside*: "1921 saw the issue of radicalism terribly sharpened," Trilling reported, " 'Law and Order,' Ku Klux Klan, the Red Raids and A. Mitchell Palmer, exportation of aliens on putative 'ships of stone with sails of lead.' Yet we were not excited by the real reign of terror that was going on." *The Morningside* contributors "sneered at law and order shriekers from the intellectual height." These collegiate intellectuals had no sympathy for the perpetrators of the Red Scare; they were more exercised by a disdain for vulgarity than by a fear of political persecution. To them, "the world was a place of stupidity and grossness." Their weapon was irony. To this effect, Trilling quoted Clifton Fadiman's "valedictory comment: 'We departed from everything that was esoteric and futile and ephemeral . . . there is nothing we can reform. We have no power beyond ourselves. We must bear the order of things as we find it.' " The order of things, Trilling explained, was vulgar: " 'Babbitry' was the word" for it. Opposition to vulgarity could be woven into an avant-garde sensibility, carrying with it an aura of aristocratic scorn for the masses.[2] Hence, *The Morningside* was not " 'radical' but it was advanced."[3] "A Play for Puppets" was an attempt to create an advanced work of art, and the vulgarity of the middle-class American preoccupied Chambers as well as Trilling, products of bourgeois families who affirmed their status by attending Columbia, where there were many paths leading out from the sundry middle class into the open plains of civilization.[4]

Trilling and Chambers began their lives in civilization through a singular dilemma, to which literature was more central than politics. This was the dilemma of despair, concentrated for them in the figure of Henry Adams and in Matthew Arnold's "Dover Beach"—"the melancholy, long, withdrawing roar." Henry Adams had exposed the emptiness at the heart of the modern world. According to Adams, an absence of religious faith ensured the triumph of a commercial bourgeoisie over a Christian aristocracy. By neglecting the Virgin and by harnessing the dynamo, the West might acquire greater and greater power, but in doing so it was corrupting its soul and degrading its culture. The disaster of World War I made the West's decline obvious, lending Adams the mystique of a prophet. The evidence of modernist literature, which contributors to *The Morningside* routinely championed, extended Adams's cheerless argument. Beneath a veneer of vulgar exuberance—the Roaring Twenties, the Jazz Age—lay a terrible despair. Such was the condition of the modern world; such was the condition of the modern world in the 1920s. One had only to read a novel of Theodore Dreiser or F. Scott Fitzgerald, Thomas Mann or Franz Kafka, whose difficult literature was discovered after his death in 1924, to know the despair that burdened "modern man." To be either radical or advanced was to be aware of this burden, which made Chambers and Trilling the sons of a despairing bourgeoisie or despairing sons of a vulgar bourgeoisie. In their minds there was little guarantee that their bourgeois world would endure.[5] Perhaps it was a world that did not deserve to endure.

As young intellectuals filled with melancholy, Trilling and Chambers refused to adopt the standard attitudes toward despair. Over time, Chambers would move to the Left of *The Morningside*, and in a sense Trilling would move to the Right of it. Chambers rejected his bourgeois patrimony, suffering from a sense of personal dislocation, which he interpreted as the decline of the bourgeoisie in Western history and culture. Not long after leaving Columbia in 1923, Chambers joined the Communist Party, a radical answer to a crisis that Chambers perceived as radical, his joining both an expression of despair and an effort to overcome this despair. Trilling's despair was softer, more literary. He wished to attack "stupidity with the critical attitude."[6] The bourgeoisie was irredeemable, but perhaps it was also educable in a way that the polity as a whole was not. Trilling hoped to see America's vulgar middle class transform itself into a *Bildungsbürgertum*, an educated force for cultural and political good. Trilling stayed in college until graduation, choosing an eminently bourgeois profession, a life of literary scholarship, to buttress his career as a critical intellectual. To the despair of modernist literature, Trilling preferred Jewish humanism, an elevated ideal for assimilating into America, or he preferred the self-confidence and vigor of the Victorians, who had tasted Arnold's despair without succumbing to it. For both Trilling and Chambers, despair was a powerful intellectual catalyst and not simply a mood to be indulged.

Trilling's family was resolutely bourgeois, while the Chambers were a middle-class family in decline.[7] Nominally Episcopalian, Chambers's family was not religious; there was very little in American life to which it did belong. The aspect of his childhood Whittaker most cherished was the unspoiled nature of rural Long Island, an endangered commodity. In his love of nature as well as his love of poetry, his wide-ranging erotic longings, and his radical politics, Chambers resembled a twentieth-century Walt Whitman. Lionel Trilling had no such precedent in American life or letters. His parents were Polish Jews who immigrated to the United States, via England in his mother's case. Like the Chambers, the Trillings were intellectually inclined, but they were religious—Orthodox, in fact. The attitudes of the Chambers and Trilling families converged in the ambitions held for their sons, who were to be educated gentlemen, versed in Western civilization, and successful in the upper reaches of America's middle class.[8] There was a reason why they met at Columbia.

The Trillings were hardly stereotypical Jewish immigrants from Eastern Europe. What separated them from other Eastern European Jews was their Anglophilia. Trilling's mother and his grandmother "had been born and schooled in England," experiencing there "the curiously quick and thorough acculturation that seems to be the characteristic effect of England on foreigners," Trilling wrote in 1972. Although he never lived in England, Trilling's father loved "England as the land of liberty." His mother's affection may have been more conservative; her mind was "suffused by the English mythos." As Trilling recalled, "among my earliest memories are the things she used to say about Queen Victoria and the Royal Family." The Trillings' Anglophilia was reinforced by the fact that their name sounded more English than Jewish or Eastern European: "I don't know what the origin of the strangely un-Jewish name is," Trilling wrote toward the end of his life, "but that it *was* un-Jewish made, I have no doubt, a significant fact in my life."[9] There was no socialist enthusiasm in his household; Trilling did not grow up on the Lower East Side of Manhattan; he did not have Yiddish-speaking parents. Through his parents, he had a purchase on English-language culture that was highly unusual for a child of immigrants. He did not Anglicize a foreign-sounding last name as so many of his Jewish contemporaries did, although the Trillings' Anglophilia was by no means the only constituent of Lionel's cultural inheritance. His parents were pious Jews, and they were patriotic Americans. Trilling's father came from a family that was, as Lionel recalled in 1972, "intellectually distinguished in Bialystock, Poland, which was also the birthplace of my mother's father, a city in which there was a flourishing Jewish culture." An affection for England and its literature did not translate into a repudiation of Judaism: "The family religion was orthodox and was taken very seriously, with quite strict observance, but in a spirit of conscious enlightenment."[10] The bridge between the Trillings' Orthodoxy and their allegiance to America was their piety. Trilling remembered his parents' joy that their son was born on the fourth of July: "my parents' piety towards their adopted country had been rewarded." The piety was not political in any specific way but it was civic minded: "both parents had a strong explicit feeling for traditional civility and were remarkably accurate in knowing what constituted it in America." In an unfinished memoir Trilling wrote of "the circumstance that my boyhood was suffused by the sense of its being specifically American."[11] The Anglophilia, the Judaism, and the American patriotism reinforced each other, and all three were harmonized by a fervent commitment to "the idea of 'culture,' of a life shaped to several kinds of amenity."[12]

Trilling and Chambers grew up among conservative influences. Chambers's parents were Republicans, and Trilling would later define the ideals of his parents as conservative, ascribing to them the conservative tendency in his own character. "The conservative tendency is, I feel sure, to be traced to my family and not least to what I think can be called its piety in the good sense of the word," Trilling wrote to a graduate student in 1972. Piety, the bridge to America, was also Trilling's link to Judaism: "this [piety] was rooted, I think it can be said, in religion, even when it manifested itself in specifically social ideals." Once again, Judaism contributed to civility: "the emphasis my parents put on manners was, it has long seemed to me, in accord with the orthodox Jewish insistence on ritually precise behavior." Finally, "religion reinforced my curiously vivid consciousness of the past and the authority it had in my imagination." The Judaism that Trilling outlined in this letter was rather ethereal; it was not a matter of law or dogma or belief. As such, Judaism could easily be assimilated into a secular culture. If he chose, Trilling could dispense with the ritually precise behavior and keep the manners that followed from it, as he traveled further and further into America. With a culture shaped to various kinds of amenity, upheld by an "ancient ethos of bourgeois self-esteem," Trilling was prepared for Columbia as an institution.[13] At the same time, he was prematurely alienated from the cultural and political radicalism percolating at Columbia, which shaped his generation of intellectuals. At college the conservative tendency would be modified by a liberal tendency. However they modified each other, Trilling's various pieties would help keep him within the world of his bourgeois, Anglophilic parents. His career as a professor of English literature would realize the ideals of their world.[14]

The ancient ethos of bourgeois self-esteem was not the spirit that animated the Chambers family. Later in life, Chambers saw his family as representative, as participants in a historical trajectory that was making a mockery of bourgeois self-esteem. He titled the second section of his autobiography, *Witness*, "The Story of a Middle Class Family." This bland title was a polemic against the inadequacy, hopelessness even, of the suburban middle-class family. By the early twentieth century, Chambers's polemic went, the bourgeois ethos had become one of self-loathing. This was a conviction that Chambers developed in his adolescence and never discarded. It shaped his communist sympathies, convincing him that the proletariat was destined to replace an exhausted, decadent bourgeoisie. The horror of bourgeois life also informed his conservatism, especially the religious and pastoral qualities of his ultimate conservatism, to which he opposed the secular and urban ethos of the bourgeoisie.[15] For Chambers these political positions derived their force from the example of his actual family, "rock-rib Republicans from way back." His parents were also "the intellectuals of that period; that is, were aware of the new ideas and read the latest books."[16] Their culture was their undoing: "our house was a peeling outpost of what both my father and mother would have summed up as 'culture.'" Perhaps it was their intellectuality, perhaps their culture that singled out the Chambers from the other families in Lynbrook, Long Island, for they were known locally as "the French family."[17] This family of rock-ribbed Republicans was also profoundly alienated from the country around them. As Chambers described his younger self: "I am an outcast. My family is outcast. We have no friends, no social ties, no church, no organization that we claim and that claims us, no community."[18]

The Chambers were representative in their failure, although it was an ambiguous failure. When reading *Witness*, one is never quite sure whether the Chambers failed as a middle-class family per se or whether they failed to be a middle-class family at all. Chambers's parents were themselves ambivalent about the middle class. His father wished to escape it, and his mother wished to rise above it. Chambers's father "regarded himself as an artist . . . and he had no intention of surrendering to middle-class standards of comfort." His mother on the other hand came from a mildly patrician background and "some day, she hoped, the children would find their way back, translating her with them, to that upper-middle-class world which was, for her, the earthly paradise." She educated her sons to conduct themselves as gentlemen. For Chambers's father, paradise was to be found in fin-de-siécle aestheticism and, for his mother, in the assurance and style of the upper middle class. For neither parent was paradise to be found in Christianity. Hence, as educated people, they were genuinely representative figures: they "belonged to a generation of intellectuals for whom the word God was already a little embarrassing." Nor was this a matter of social convention. They did not believe in God. Chambers's mother taught him that "the world was formed by gasses cooling in space."[19]

Chambers regarded his family as cause of disillusionment but not of shame. The boy Chambers wondered whether his family was exiled from a world to which it was not worth belonging. At age nine he read *Les Misérables*, which "gave me my first full-length picture of the modern world—a vast, complex, scarcely human structure, built over a social abyss of which the sewers of Paris was the symbol, and resting with crushing weight upon the wretched of the earth." Chambers made the radical overtones of this description explicit by labeling *Les Misérables* "a Summa of the revolt of the mind and soul of modern man against the materialism that was closing over them with the close of the Middle Ages and the rise of industrial civilization—or, as Karl Marx would later teach me to call it: capitalism." *Les Misérables* helped Chambers to articulate his instinctual suspicion of all things bourgeois, and, as such, the novel was a tool of self-understanding. The suspicion crystallized around the moment in *Les Misérables* when a respected Bishop rides a donkey. " 'My bourgeois friends,' said the Bishop pleasantly, 'I know why you are smiling. You think that it is pretty presumptuous of a poor priest to use the same conveyance that was used by Jesus Christ.' Thus I first learned the meaning of the word bourgeois, so that, unlike most Americans, I was quite familiar with it when I came across it later in the writings of Marx and Lenin." An outsider in the eyes of others, Chambers willingly became an outsider to the bourgeois ethos. He resolved never "to live a life in which money, comfort, appearances and pleasure mean success."[20]

If Chambers's animus against the bourgeoisie was rooted in his family, it had another source in his homosexual leanings. Chambers may not have had any homosexual experiences until the 1930s, but he expressed his desires in homoerotic poetry, which he published in the 1920s.[21] Chambers knew first-hand the threat that homosexuality posed to the family. His father had lived for a time with a male lover, and Whittaker's childhood was punctuated by his father's absences. In a 1924 letter, Chambers described his sensuality as "gaining on me and [it] may be fated to overthrow whatever high fantasy of hope and beauty I may uprear. Curtailment does no good; desire battens on unsatisfaction; and in the end I surrender myself to what is destined before the event to waste me and make me unhappy."[22] Homosexual tendencies could only have contributed to Chambers's image of himself as on the margins of the respectable bourgeois world.[23] However, if his sensuality struck him as destructive, it was not to be curtailed for the sake of preserving the declining middle-class family. He was not going to defend a lost cause. The legacy, then, of his troubled family was almost entirely negative, a series of shortcomings and failures that amounted to a painful vacancy. *Les Misérables* may have helped him understand this vacancy as a modern phenomenon with a modern vocabulary. Chambers would have to look elsewhere if he hoped to fill it.

Throughout their lives, literature was the strongest link between Chambers and Trilling; they were to be literary intellectuals, moving back and forth between the world of politics and the world of literature. *Les Misérables* was a favorite novel of Trilling's father, described by Diana Trilling, Lionel's wife, in her memoirs as "his secular Talmud."[24] Trilling's parents taught him to revere literature and art. In Diana Trilling's description, art served as a substitute for religion, or an extension of it, in the Trilling household. Significantly, Trilling's mother wanted her son to become a professor, not a rabbi, the operative image derived from the English mythos. In the words of Diana Trilling, Lionel's mother "had early decided that Lionel was to have an Oxford Ph.D.; he said he could not have been more than four or five when she first announced this to him."[25] Lionel might thus extend the pieties of his family into the modern world, which was indeed the world of bourgeois success. For Chambers, *Les Misérables* was no secular bible, and it offered no avenue for the preservation of religious piety in the modern world. It was a mirror of this shattered world, a record of bourgeois smugness. A devoted reader of literature from his childhood onward, Chambers was not inclined to experience salvation in art. Trilling may not have looked for salvation, but in art he had a spiritual resource that Chambers would find only in politics and religion. So much was clear before they arrived at college.

These dissimilar sons of the bourgeoisie made their way to Columbia, where each of them received two discreet educations. One was in the classic works of Western civilization, as determined by the Columbia great books curriculum. The other was at *The Morningside*, among a coterie of passionately intellectual undergraduates who were affiliated with the magazine. The university curriculum, combined with the unofficial curriculum of *The Morningside* circle, familiarized Trilling and Chambers with both sides of "the great earthquake crevice between Paul Elmer More and H. L. Mencken."[26] With these words, Edmund Wilson characterized the dichotomy between the genteel humanists of the academy, like Paul Elmer More or John Erskine, and Mencken, the red-blooded satirist of 1920s journalism, between a humanism that looked back to nineteenth-century certainties and a modern sensibility colored by skepticism, mordant irony, and urbane sophistication. It was not simply Mencken's gift for satire and sarcasm that distinguished him from the academic humanists. It was his involvement with Friedrich Nietzsche and with Nietzsche's radical assault on the Enlightenment.[27] If Columbia's curriculum encouraged Chambers and Trilling to identify with the recognized masterworks of Western civilization, with Western civilization as achievement, members of *The Morningside* circle tended to assume that this same civilization was synonymous with crisis. From their cherished modern writers—Dostoevsky, Nietzsche, André Gide, James Joyce, and T. S. Eliot—*The Morningside* circle assimilated "our immediate modernity of explicit despair," in Trilling's evocative phrase.[28] Trilling and Chambers considered despair the mark of their generation and of their moment in history.

Columbia's general honors course had been instituted to impart classical learning by modern means. From the mid-eighteenth century to the 1870s, Columbia College had demanded that its students learn Greek and Latin, pillars of its *studia humanitatis.* By 1917, Greek and Latin had been eliminated as requirements for graduation, and, when the United States entered World War I, Columbia was educating future soldiers in "war issues." After the war, there was a call for coursework in "peace issues," satisfied in part by a program called Contemporary Civilization, a combination of natural sciences and social sciences intended "to make students citizens who can participate in national affairs with clear judgment and intelligence." Meanwhile, Erskine took it upon himself to develop a similar program in the humanities, the general honors course, with the aim of rectifying "the literary ignorance of the younger generation." Academic expertise in classical languages and comprehensive knowledge were subordinated to the direct encounter with canonical texts, read, if necessary, in translation. Assigned reading included Homer, Aeschylus, Dante, Shakespeare, the Bible, Plato, Aristotle, Saint Augustine, and Spinoza, suitable education for the "acropolis on Morningside" that Nicholas Murray Butler, the university's president, wanted Columbia to be.[29] The general honors program could contribute to what in 1955 Trilling would describe as an established and conservative ideal at Columbia, "the Renaissance ideal of the whole man, and . . . the ideal of the gentleman, of the honorable and responsible citizen of enlightened and gracious mind."[30]

Erskine's general honors course and the more avant-garde *Morningside* circle were not wholly separate. A reverence for master texts touched them both, and the general honors course could inform the discussion of modern despair. For Trilling one of the representative figures of this despair was Matthew Arnold. At the same time classical and modern, Arnold bore a genealogical relationship to Erskine, who "had been a pupil at Columbia of George Eliot Woodberry, who at Harvard had been the pupil of Charles Eliot Norton, who had been the friend of Carlyle, Ruskin, and Matthew Arnold," Trilling wrote in the autobiographical mode. *The Morningside* circle had about it a prevailing sense of alienation, while Erskine's honors course emphasized connection to the polity, something that Trilling attributed to Erskine's intellectual genealogy. The Victorian lineage that went from Arnold to Erskine "makes clear the provenance of the idea that was at the root of the General Honors course—the idea that great works of art and thought are a decisive part in shaping the life of the polity."[31] One might use art and thought to transform the polity—they had that power—and because of this power there was no need to wallow in despair, to wring one's hands because the vulgar masses were neglecting the life of the mind.[32] Chambers, too, had clearly assimilated its spirit. Throughout his career he would treat art and thought as agents that shape the polity. This notion frames Chambers's autobiography, *Witness*, and Trilling's collection of essays, *The Liberal Imagination*, the two most famous books of these general honors alumni.

Trilling's liberal imagination was intimately connected to Columbia. Indeed, "the liberal-democratic tendency was the mark that Columbia put upon me," Trilling later explained. He defined this mark as "a sort of Bertrand Russell view of life," going on to say that "a considerable part of my expectation of life was shaped by Wells and Shaw." It was a signature assumption of Trilling's that writers of fiction supply political labels with their cultural content. The liberal-democratic tendency was a tradition at a university where "part of the . . . legend was the reactionary moves that had been made by the President and the Trustees against certain faculty during war, and all intelligent students were conscious of this." However, the historians "[Charles] Beard and [James Harvey] Robinson were already in the past; they were martyr figures in the legend," lost to the past partly because they were so robustly political and not at all literary. With the students who had arrived on campus after World War I, things were quite different: "I can recall virtually no explicit political concern, only a feeling that conservatism was stupid—not intelligent—and the sense that the world was changing, that modernity was upon us. Whittaker Chambers was radical—I.W.W.—but this was thought of as merely an interesting idiosyncrasy."[33] The feeling that conservatism was stupid did not banish a certain dread of the new: modernity was "upon us."

For Trilling, Columbia's liberal-democratic tendency was more of an attitude than a considered philosophical position, not that its mark was in any way superficial. Trilling, the archetypal intellectual, recalled that "as an undergraduate I made no claim to intellect." Trilling saw himself as "*literary*, that is to say intuitive, perceptive, sensitive, etc." Trilling's life-long skepticism regarding orthodoxies and absolutisms might be linked to the liberal-democratic tradition Columbia impressed upon him and, in turn, to the pragmatism of John Dewey, but his literary mindset was almost unphilosophical. Trilling's reluctance to align himself with intellect came from an inability to understand philosophy and in particular the philosophy of John Dewey. For the undergraduate litterateur, pragmatism was an atmospheric, not a formal, influence. Trilling writes that "John Dewey was an admired figure for many of us [at Columbia], and some of my friends attended his lectures; for me he was a revered and shadowy figure, a wise man; I knew nothing of his doctrine and heard him lecture only once at the insistence of a friend, and found him incomprehensible."[34] For Trilling and *The Morningside* circle, John Dewey and Bertrand Russell could not compete with the great modernist masters.

Trilling's liberal impulse was troubled by his reading of literature. The modernist masters voiced dark and often illiberal truths, which *The Morningside* circle comprehended sympathetically. Proust and Nietzsche fueled their undergraduate disdain for vulgarity. From Proust and Nietzsche and many others, these young intellectuals formed a composite attitude of irony, pessimism, and contempt for middle-class America. "A high school teacher or two, certain culturally alert fellow-students," Trilling recalled in 1974, "were passing the word of modernity, which in the America of that time meant a principled uneasiness about American life as such as was expressed in the *Smart Set* of [H. L.] Mencken and [George] Nathan, in *The Freeman, The New Republic, The Dial.*"[35] It was not an attitude that Trilling accepted without question, nor could it be, given his parents' pieties. Rather, Trilling followed the evolution of the modern sensibility closely without ever giving it his allegiance. Between him and *The Morningside* circle was a significant distance: "the members of the set I admired had their own purposes of ideality, but these didn't relate to—perhaps didn't countenance—my primitive or naïve notions of the heroic, and they had no taste for reading which invited them to temporize or look backward."[36] The distance between Trilling and modernism, as he understood it, would only develop over time, as would his own taste for looking backward. Literature invited him to temporize, and his literary criticism would encourage others to temporize with him. (Later in life, Chambers would write a magazine piece titled "To Temporize Is Death.")

The book that codified the melancholic modernist tenor was *The Education of Henry Adams*, privately printed and then published in 1918. It would be difficult to exaggerate its influence on either Trilling or Chambers.[37] *The Education of Henry Adams* embodied a crucial set of paradoxes. It was modern in tone as well as ironic, pessimistic, and antimodern in argument; Adams scorned the world of bourgeois capitalism that had emerged in the second half of the nineteenth century.[38] One might adopt Adams's tone or his argument, or one might look to *The Education* more generally as evidence of the intellectual's plight in America—lacking tradition, lacking an avenue to power, lacking the esteem of fellow citizens. For those passing the word of modernity, it was an intoxicating book. As Trilling recalled, "to the gradually cohering body of dissenters from the orthodoxies of American life, *The Education of Henry Adams* was a sacred book . . . despite, or because of, its hieratic esoteric irony and its reiterated note of patrician condescension. More than any other book that I can remember it threw around the state of personal alienation—to use the word of a later day—the aura of high pathos."[39] In *The Education*, Adams was not conservative in any programmatic way. The weight of his patrician condescension did not fall behind a party or movement of reaction, although Adams gave voice to unmistakably conservative doubts about progress. His alienated persona made him a citizen of the twentieth century rather than of the nineteenth, when he came of age, or of the eighteenth, where he thought his family belonged.[40]

The undergraduate Trilling was a passionate reader of Henry Adams but not a passive one. He revised the antimodern arguments of *The Education* to suit the education his parents had given him, audaciously comparing the Adams family with the Trilling family. Adams's lament for the decline of aristocracy was at the same time an expression of contempt for bourgeois success. "Upon his [Adams's] failure's significance he took his stand," Trilling observed in his unpublished memoirs.[41] Trilling read Adams with the consciousness that he was himself an American bourgeois. On reading the book for the first time at Columbia, Trilling wondered whether Adams's failure (as a Boston-born, aristocratic WASP) demonstrated Trilling's own potential for success (as a New York City–born, middle-class Jew). The question came from a serendipitous correspondence between the opening of *The Education* and the actual name of Trilling's grandfather.[42] Trilling used Adams to understand the grammar of success in America.[43] There was Henry Adams, "an Adams born in 1838, grandson of the fifth President of the United States and great-grandson of the third President . . . as little fitted for the American life of his day as if he had been born into the family of the High Priest at the time of the (presumably Second) Temple." And there was Lionel Trilling, "an actual member of the Cohen tribe . . . grandson of an actual

Israel, a first generation American born in 1905, the year in which Adams completed *The Education*, was I fated to account myself a failure, as Adams did?" The question was "splendid and exhilarating . . . because it offered the thought that I might—that I must—view myself in relation not merely to my familial and social circle but to the vast totality of the nation."[44] Here was an irony that even a master ironist like Adams could not have predicted: that a twentieth-century Jew might use Adams's solitary ruminations to connect himself to the American republic. Trilling put *The Education* to exactly this use, aligning it and its sporadically anti-Semitic author with an ascendant *Bildungsbürgertum* in America, a social category that could just as well be Jewish as Anglo-Saxon.

Trilling made such eccentric extrapolations from *The Education* because he read it through the eyes of his parents, a frame of reference that yielded unexpected insights. "My parents, if they read the book would have been much distressed that any one as well endowed as Adams was should take such a [pessimistic] view," Trilling wrote in his memoirs. Rather than excoriating American society, as Adams did, his parents "would have concluded that this is his business, by which they would have meant that his perverse and self-destructive view of the American situation had no bearing on the way they saw it." They would have challenged Adams's gloom where their son was concerned, their son "to whom they had given the explicit assurance that his being president was entirely within the range of possibility." In addition to being perverse and self-destructive, Adams was curiously deficient in patriotism. The Trilling parents, on the contrary, had benefited from "the love they bore the nation, [and] the trust they reposed in it." From the Trillings' perspective, there was no modern crisis and to invent one was to distract oneself from the work of culture and professional success. Either Adams refuted the Trillings, or the Trillings refuted Adams. Trilling's sympathies were with his parents. In his unfinished memoirs, he says as much: "I understood success and its importance, having learned it from my parents' teaching, to which I offered no resistance." Success, for his parents, was not a question of competitiveness. It was another of their pieties. "They believed that the proper respect for society implied that one should value and desire the things that society could provide, the things that society had been contrived for the express purpose of providing—security, comfort, the good use of one's neighbors which might advance toward respect and admiration and even reach the point of fame," Trilling wrote. To place oneself above society's rewards was unforgivable arrogance. It was "to belittle the social providence. And it wasn't merely to society in general as in the abstract but to a specifically American society that my parents felt their obligation—they must give all credence to the promises they understood the nation to be making." As a young man, Trilling had to make sense of these bourgeois convictions, and he had to do so in the critical atmosphere of *The Morningside* circle. The recollection of his encounter with *The Education of Henry Adams* shows the degree to which Trilling retained the bourgeois teaching of his parents, however much the advanced opinions of his Columbia classmates militated against it.[45]

Columbia made a liberal mark upon Chambers as well, although his submission to the liberal ethos was nothing if not traumatic, canceling beliefs he had brought with him to Columbia. As an adult anti-communist, Chambers would allege an organic connection between liberalism and communism. It was a connection that he had lived: in absorbing the liberalism of Columbia, Chambers took his first fateful step toward the Communist Party. Unlike Trilling, Chambers's memories of *The Morningside* circle centered on politics, not literature. He remembered the circle as "a leftist intellectual group" with whom he did not so much discuss Joyce and Mann as "Marxism and social revolution."[46] Perhaps this was because of Chambers's anomalous status within the circle: he was not Jewish like the rest of the circle and he was a conservative from Long Island, the political progeny of rock-ribbed Republicans. In Mark Van Doren's 1927 essay, "Jewish Students I Have Known," Chambers figured as "the Gentile student," yet again a foreign element (in context).[47] The thread of piety that runs through Trilling's thought was a sustaining continuity, while Chambers's early years were rife with discontinuity. Such was the story of Chambers's journey from conservatism to communism, which was also his journey out into the world. If Trilling remained aloof from the modernism of *The Morningside* circle, uncomfortable with the completeness of its rejections, Chambers adopted the modernist mood of despair and almost immediately tried to act on it politically.

Chambers had entered Columbia a conservative. "I was a conservative in my view of life and politics," he recalled in *Witness*, "and I was undergoing a religious experience."[48] He was an enthusiastic supporter of Calvin Coolidge, and his conservatism was not unexamined.[49] "I was reading widely and constantly in the lives of the Federalists," he wrote. To the Federalists' political sobriety he added a handful of classic conservative tenets: "the family is the basic unit of history . . . the father is the ultimate authority in the family. But the source of all authority is God." Coolidge conservatism could also be applied internationally, which, for Chambers, meant that he "detested and feared the Russian Revolution. I saw in it a threat to civilization . . . and I felt that threat precisely in its religious form." There was nothing original or novel about Chambers's collegiate conservatism. What was unusual was the intersection of his conservatism with avant-garde intellectual ambitions. In the "zone of earthquake that I stepped into on 116th [street]"—Columbia University, that is—here were two reigning schools of thought: liberalism and advanced or radical modernism. They were not compatible schools, but they both conspired to undermine Chambers's conservatism. The first dissolvent of Chambers's conservatism was liberalism, which amounted to a "bland, emollient, persuasive climate [in which] the bond of my frail ideas was gently to leach and melt away until they crumbled in absurd ruins." Chambers immediately realized the threat his liberal advisor Mark Van Doren posed to his conservative political stance: "I perceived that in Mark Van Doren's world . . . people thought that Coolidge was something much worse than bad. They thought he was funny."[50] Van Doren challenged both sides of Chambers's conservatism, the political and the religious. When Chambers submitted some religious poetry to Van Doren (as he recalled in an autobiographical document written for the FBI), his adviser "said it was very interesting but that it contained 'a pathological fallacy,' which I had never heard of until then. This fallacy, according to VAN DOREN, was that 'God operates in nature.'" In retrospect, Chambers was emphatic about his advisor's influence: "I think that was the beginning of my pulverization in college," he wrote. "VAN DOREN was at that time 'a liberal rationalist.'"[51]

Once wounded by liberalism, Chambers's conservatism could no longer protect him from the radicalism of *The Morningside* circle. They designated themselves the *ernste Menschen*, the serious or earnest men.[52] They were Jewish and especially so in their worship "of education and things of the mind," although "most of these men were intellectually irreligious." They were exemplars of a European high culture that was modernist in caste, and their ideas were more disturbing than Van Doren's liberal rationalism because to Chambers they were more compelling. "Without knowing it," he wrote in the 1950s, "I was in the presence of a new way of life, a new culture, which I felt to be deeply antagonistic to my own and which I lunged out against. I brashly asserted my own religious, conservative and anti-socialist views."[53] Their culture was revolutionary, and it was overpowering. The revolution came to Chambers "first in literary form" in the works of Hauptmann, Ibsen, Chekhov, Gorky, and Tolstoy, who were anything but comforting champions of Western civilization. They wrote books in which "the soul of man uttered its cry against the suffering of the twentieth century, and that cry echoed in my soul."[54] *The Morningside* circle won its argument with Chambers. Needless to say, the Columbia liberals lost theirs. The Coolidge fan who had stepped into the earthquake zone that "might as well have been called Harvard (see John Reed) or Princeton (see Scott Fitzgerald)" abandoned the Republican Party for the revolution. Impatience with liberalism smoothed his way: "long before I would admit a change, my viewpoint had shifted [because] of my growing susceptibility to my opponents' insistence that political democracy is not enough."[55]

Chambers gravitated towards radicalism, while Trilling vacillated between old–fashioned humanism and the anguished mood of advanced, modernist writers. By 1927, Chambers was contributing regularly to the *Daily Worker*, a communist paper, and Trilling was an editor at the magazine *Menorah Journal*, a Jewish magazine for which Chambers was the in-house German translator. The *Menorah Journal* dedicated itself to such classically, almost stereotypically, bourgeois pursuits as cultural elevation and humanism, while mocking the middle class as Mencken did; but by the time the stock market crashed, the ideal of Jewish humanism began to fade in the light of more radical ideals. In the pages of the *Daily Worker*, the bourgeois appeared in grotesque caricatures—corpulent, cigar-smoking men straddling the world with their capital. The *Menorah Journal* and the *Daily Worker* were points of entry, the former into the world of bourgeois self-criticism and bourgeois self-improvement, the latter into the world of the anti-bourgeois. Typically, the *Menorah Journal* was a circle as well as a magazine. The leader of these young Jewish intellectuals was Elliot Cohen, described by Trilling as "the greatest teacher I have ever known," a brilliant editor with a very particular editorial mission. Cohen devoted himself to the "dream of arranging a marriage between the intellectuals . . . and American culture, and at the same time a reconciliation between them and the Jewish community." In Trilling's opinion, Cohen succeeded at his mission, teaching "the younger men around him that nothing in human life need be alien to their thought and nothing in American life, whether it be baseball, or vaudeville, or college tradition, or elementary education, or fashions in speech, or food, or dress, or manners."[56]

Cohen's Jewish American editorial mission guided Trilling's early intellectual career, although Trilling moved toward Judaism, or Jewish life, only to move away from it over time.[57] The *Menorah Journal* resolved a dilemma of Trilling's education in Judaism as a boy and in European high culture as a young man. "I recall my college days as an effort to discover some social entity to which I could give the credence of my cause, as it were," he wrote in 1966, "and with whom I could be in some relation."[58] This entity was emphatically not the Jewish community in America, whether defined by religion or by secular commitments.[59] It was America itself, and the *Menorah Journal* was the impetus to discovery.[60] It "made America available to my imagination, as it could not possibly be if I tried to understand it with the categories offered by Mencken or Herbert Croly or, for that matter, Henry Adams," Trilling recalled in 1966.[61] Trilling did not move from particular to universal but from particular to larger particular, from a Jewish to an American world suffused with European culture. A striking feature of the *Menorah Journal* was the tone of cultural despair, often imported from Europe, that manifested itself beneath the self-improving surface of its formal intentions. Underneath the humanism, the celebration of Jewish cultural history and the mockery of the "Jewish booboisie" was a kind of Spenglerian gloom.[62] An anecdote in Max Eastman's memoirs pinpoints a shift in cultural mood to which the *Menorah Journal* contributors were very sensitive. In 1926, Eastman gave F. Scott Fitzgerald the manuscript of his radical novel *Venture:* "of his [Fitzgerald's] praise the only thing I remember is his allusion to 'that wonderful era of liberal enthusiasm' through which I had lived, and of which for him my novel was a 'beautiful record.' This jolted me, for I thought that my novel was concerned with proletarian revolution, and that the revolution was still engaged in building a new world in Soviet Russia."[63] To this one might add the memory Trilling himself had of 1926: "we were living in a time of the 'machine'—an abstraction which, with another, 'the mob,' was made out to be the cause of cultural imperfection . . . (Spengler came along in 1926 to crystallize this hyper-realism.)."[64] In his writing from 1926 to 1929, Trilling took on the subject of Spenglerian despair repeatedly.[65]

Trilling held cultural despair up to critical scrutiny. He learned the latest Spengler-inflected theses about mob and machine and was bold enough to reject them. Reviewing Proust's *In Search of Lost Time* in 1928, Trilling identified its theme as the "triumph of unworth over worth."[66] Trilling had in mind the triumph, traced so meticulously by Proust, of a vulgar bourgeoisie over a decadent but still alluring aristocracy. Behind this Proustian theme was the unworth of mob and machine elevated to power by democracy. Also in 1928, Trilling praised a novel of Count Gobineau's *The Pleiades* as "lovely and moving," one of the rare books that "deal wisely, serenely, logically, maturely, with modern confusion." In *The Pleiades*, continued Trilling, the protagonists "regard the spectacle of the democratic West with its 'bestial stupidity, destruction, and death.' " The bestiality, stupidity, destruction, and death of recent history have remade modern artists who must protect their protagonists from modern society: "the activity of the hero is now not the fight against evil for society, but a fight against society itself."[67] Only by an adversarial attitude can the protagonist escape despair. America, for Trilling, was a milder version of Gobineau's democratic West: "America, where it is considered best that color be whitewashed, civilization taught quaint new purposes, and freedom and creation shown their limits."[68] In their battle with America, Trilling and the writers at the *Menorah Journal* had the weapon of Jewish humanism, which was starting to yield to another ideal—political radicalism. With the Great Depression, the *Menorah* circle would "stop thinking of themselves first as Jews and only secondarily as members of their nation," in the words of Diana Trilling. "They were suddenly catapulted into citizenship."[69]

Trilling was intrigued by literature's civic resonance. Culture should confirm citizenship and vice versa, Trilling believed, in harmony with his parents' pieties. Trilling attacked Ludwig Lewisohn, a Jewish American novelist in search of a Jewish homeland, for presenting America and the Jew as at odds with each other. Appalled by the association of Judaism with self-removal, Trilling wanted to see the Jew ensconced in the American scene. Yet Trilling considered self-removal representative of Jewish fiction: "as soon as the Jewish writer gets his hero to be a Jew, he wraps him up in a *talith* and puts him away."[70] A coda to Trilling's sharp disagreement with Lewisohn was Lewisohn's Zionism and Jewish piety, for Trilling and his colleagues at the *Menorah Journal* "were not religious . . . [and] we were inclined to be skeptical about Zionism."[71] They were seeking a secular Judaism anchored in America and in Western civilization. If Lewisohn's novels offered an unrealistic, evasive set of options for American Jews, the *Menorah Journal* itself provided the alternative. Trilling outlined his vigorously secular vision of Judaism in a letter to Elliot Cohen in December 1929. "It seems to me," he wrote solopsistically, "that the whole practical purpose of Jewish endeavor is to create a community that can read the *Menorah Journal.*" Then he specified: "the purpose is to construct a society that can consider its own life from a calm, intelligent, dignified point of view; take delight in its own arts, its own thoughts, the vagaries of its own being." To be Jewish is to aspire to cultural ennoblement. "The purpose of Jewish life is cultural," Trilling asked, "is it not?" For "if the Journal is chucked, then Judaism has also to be chucked and made over into a Benevolent Association."[72] For Trilling, what distinguished Judaism from the Elks Club was not religion but the arts that bring delight as well as the occasion for calm, dignified reflection.

By equating Judaism with a culture of intelligence and delight—with a kind of Jewish Hellenism—Trilling paved the way for his own departure from Jewish concerns. By 1929, modern problems claimed Trilling's attention to a far greater extent than did Jewish problems. Trilling was captivated by the two demigods of the modern intellectual world, Marx and Freud, who happened to be assimilated Jews. They "taught the intellectual classes that nothing was as it seemed, that the great work of the intellectual was to strike through the mask."[73] Trilling never sought to unmask the bourgeoisie for the sake of destroying it, continuing the work of cultural renewal to which the *Menorah Journal* had been dedicated. Trilling's ideal of cultural renewal led him back into the past—not to the Jewish or the American past but to the Victorians, who had as much to say to the contemporary crisis, Trilling felt, as did their brilliant (Jewish) critics, Marx and Freud. Already in 1928, Trilling was troubled by the modern veneration of despair. Modern literature, American or European, drove the contempt for modern society to excess: "it becomes ridiculous in the intelligent American," Trilling complained, "to discuss life in terms of an American Tragedy."[74] In a review published in 1929 and titled "Stendhal Made Valiant War on Vulgar Boredom," Trilling reviewed what had become a well-rehearsed argument. "Vulgarity is the functioning of the individual as though he embodied all the characteristics of the mob—its generality, its lack of the time and ability to distinguish, its heavy arrogance," Trilling wrote, explaining that "as democracy spread, [consciousness of the mob] became perhaps the most important fact of the modern world." Trilling united writer, critic, and reader in a single pronoun: we intellectuals, we the educated middle class, we the creators and reformers of our culture. "In Stendhal, there is a spiritual impotence, one feels, that needed the arousing lash of violent deed," Trilling wrote. "Nowadays, we tend to ascribe that pretty prevalent impotence to our civilization."[75]

Trilling juxtaposed the modern and the Victorian sensibilities, criticizing the new by comparing it to the old. In a 1929 review for the *Menorah Journal*, "Despair Apotheosized," Trilling recapitulated the machine-mob exposé only to arrive at an unexpected conclusion. Despair demands our attention because "it is too deeply identified with the spiritual structure of the nineteenth and twentieth centuries to be dismissed." The hero, reduced by modernity, may succumb to a widening sense of despair: "for the past two years [impotent despair] has returned, concomitant with a new anti-democratic philosophy," Trilling observed. "In A *Portrait of the Artist as Young Man*, in *Ulysses* . . . in the *Wasteland*, to mention but a few of the better known monuments, this misery and despair and impotence make the dominating matter." Yet antidemocratic despair suffers in comparison with the Victorians' energy and activity: "one looks back upon the Victorians, and one remembers with refreshment that they had muscles and the willingness to live, even by the deep error of willful blindness."[76] Trilling devoted increasing attention to the modern intellectual as false prophet. We intellectuals, he wrote in a 1930 essay titled "Necessary Morals for Art," "are a little too apt in America to lay our spiritual difficulties on our environment," clouding moral judgment and contributing to "a stupid habit of mind current among us, which preciously but vigorously bars the use of the word 'moral' from talk of art." This was not a Victorian problem. American writers and their propagandists, the intellectuals, do not "make the ultimate, the hard affirmation." They are too caught up with negation, and they are responsible for "the amazing sterility of American literature."[77] "We" lack the necessary muscles and willingness to live.

By praising affirmation, Trilling was not urging American intellectuals and writers to celebrate the status quo in America. From thinkers such as Ortega y Gasset, author of *The Revolt of the Masses* published in English in 1932, Trilling had learned that the modern tendency was nothing less than the "dehumanization of art."[78] With the Great Depression one could expand the point: the dehumanization of art augured a more massive dehumanization; Trilling's father, a furrier, was a victim of the Great Depression. As Trilling wrote in October 1930, "the mass of personal

35

misery and crippled talent that marked our artistic life for so many years [must be laid] at the door of a stupid, ruthless civilization."[79] Nor were the machine and the mob adequate explanation for this stunted civilization. Poverty, too, was at issue: "we are living in an environment that is befouling and insulting. Only the very wealthy do not live in such an environment and only the very blind do not know it." Trilling saw first-hand "an America of insanity and dissolving souls, of weariness and hate."[80] Alive to the crisis in his midst, Trilling still could not sanction the adversary culture gathering under the dual influence of modernist literature and the economic crisis. "Joyce, Mann, Lawrence, Eliot, Gide, and Proust have all written in the travail of opposition to their world," Trilling wrote in a 1930 essay "Portrait of an Artist as American." Although "we have a sense of injustice, decay, desperation, frightful confusion of soul, the probable eventual triumph of these things does not invalidate them for art." American writers have come to prefer modernist formulae to an engagement with the terrible truths of the modern era. Trilling implicated himself for the sake of a more persuasive Jeremiad: "we have been using the whipping-boy of the mechanism-mob a little too long. It has indeed many outrages to account for, but the inferiority of American art in the last fifteen years is not one of them. The fault for this must lie with the American artist himself." Modernism has inspired the modernist pose. The more this pose became entrenched, the more the adversary culture of artists and intellectuals induced complacency and blindness. Trilling denounced the countless books "marked by a sort of half-intelligence and artistic aplomb that could not exist were not the writers fairly sure of their place in their environment. One will seldom find that these writers succumb to the dangers of their milieu." The problem of such rebellious literature is, ironically, that it "resists [its environment] much too successfully—resists by evading it or by looking at it with a careful half-an-eye."[81]

Trilling renounced modernist posturing, as he saw it, in order to deal more candidly with the reality of a disintegrating bourgeois society. In a biographical essay Trilling asked: "How could one read Yeats or Joyce or Eliot or Proust or Mann or Kafka without understanding that the culture of humanism was at a point of crisis? The society which had sustained this culture was in dire straits." Unlike the American realists, the best European writers applied artistry and intelligence to the crisis descending upon them. "The works that mark the artistic heights of the modern

36

world," Trilling argued in "Portrait of the Artist as American," "have consistently been those that have undertaken the philosophic issues and emotional confusions of that world."[82] The urge to undertake philosophical issues and emotional confusions without succumbing to despair drove Trilling back, once again, to the Victorians—to their civic sense and to their unembarrassed moralism. At Columbia, he sought as his dissertation advisor Emery Neff, known for his scholarship on Carlyle and Mill—two eminent Victorians.[83] But in distancing himself from the modern style and educating himself in the nineteenth century, Trilling was not avoiding the modern intuition of despair. "All I knew about Matthew Arnold," wrote Trilling about the decision to begin a dissertation on Arnold, "derived from an affection for some of his poems whose melancholy spoke to me in an especially personal way. I thought it would be interesting to discover and explain in historical-cultural terms why he was so sad."[84] When he turned his attention to Matthew Arnold, Trilling bid farewell to the cause of Jewish humanism.[85] As he wrote to Elliot Cohen in 1929, resorting to metaphor but discussing his family, "I see its Jewish gestures as the swing of the clapper of a bell: while the clapper hung in the bell it was intended for, it struck the sides and gave forth a sound. But now the clapper had been hung in a bell that was too big for it. It swung but it could not reach the side of the new environment. No sound came."[86] Trilling's environment was not inevitably Jewish. In Trilling's view the Left was still a distant point of orientation, obscured by an amorphous liberalism, to which Jews owed their emancipation. In an essay written in 1930 for the *Menorah Journal*, although unpublished until 1966, Trilling detailed "The Changing Myth of the Jew." This myth had proven "a useful instrumentality in the hands of conservative, chauvinistic, anti-democratic powers. Under its cover, they could fight the forces of democracy, the forces working for an extended franchise, emancipation of the lower orders, liberation of oppressed minorities." These forces were none other than "the middle-class liberals."[87]

Meanwhile, Chambers was rushing as fast as he could toward a communist rejection of middle-class liberalism. Chambers was unusually cosmopolitan in his reading of history, from which he derived a political program. The movement of history that had resulted in World War I was cause enough for despair, a mood Chambers enthusiastically adopted and never outgrew. In Chambers's memory, World War I was the cardinal event of the early twentieth century, a refutation of Trilling's generalization that "the war was not very real to us who had entered college in 1921."[88] Nor did Chambers draw the conclusion of the historian Arthur Schlesinger Sr. that after World War I "the [American] republic would breathe a new spirit of internationalism on behalf of world democracy."[89] As a tourist, together with his Columbia classmate Meyer Schapiro, Chambers traveled throughout Europe not long after World War I. He "was particularly concerned with the aftermath of the war and formed the definitive opinion that there was something basically wrong with the conditions of the world."[90] A dedicated student of German culture, Chambers was particularly horrified by Weimar Berlin, where "behind these impressive appearances [of modernity] life had gone mad." In a phrase that bears the mark of the older man, Chambers wrote that World War I "ended after leveling Europe to a ruin that could not be measured merely by its physical wreckage. For the ruin took place in men's souls before it was made visible in the rubble of cities."[91] This was the despair apotheosized that Trilling considered such an unsettling quality of modern culture. Chambers embodied this despair, cultivated it, and regarded it in others as a sign of intellectual seriousness.

What prevented Chambers's reflections on World War I from slipping into a *Morningside* cliché about modern vulgarity was their political edge. At college, he was a young communist in the making. "I was not satisfied to seek the human condition only in literature," as to a great extent Trilling was, "but sought it also in political manifestations," Chambers later wrote. The crisis of the West was not merely a matter of mob and machine, much as Chambers detested both, but of international politics: "even I could see that with the destruction of the great dynastic empires—Germany, Austria, Russia, Turkey—was destroyed the stability of the West."[92] Back in the United States, Chambers placed on his private curriculum socialist and left-wing thinkers such as Sidney and Beatrice Webb, R. H. Tawney, and G. D. H. Cole, theorists of capitalist crisis who further exposed the weaknesses of the West. To Chambers's mind they offered nothing prescriptive: "these works went into great detail as to what was wrong with world conditions, but, so far as I could see, they did not offer any real solutions to the problem."[93] In a 1924 letter to Meyer Schapiro, Chambers described the path that led away from socialism and toward communism. In the beginning was hatred for the world that the industrial revolution had created.[94] Yet this hatred was self-defeating. In a confessional mode, Chambers wrote about convictions that could be called conservative: "in my heart of hearts I hate machines, and I hate a mechanistic civilization. And if, at times, I seem resigned I am never acquiescent. But neither am I of the eighteenth century of Henry Adams. Perhaps I adumbrate a type of the future, that is to say the present." The present demands radicalism: "my secret quarrel with socialism of the Webb, Cole type is that it aims to utilize and exploit and augment the exiting mechanism; my secret sympathy with the Sorel brand of radicalism is that it promises to subvert the present order."[95] By 1924, Chambers was drifting away not only from Columbia in person but also in spirit.[96]

Chambers's path to communism was gradual. His reference to Sorel, rather than Lenin, was telling. *Reflections on Violence*, published in 1908 by the French syndicalist Georges Sorel, was a pre-Bolshevik piece of Chambers's radicalization. Although he did not "lean towards violence myself," Chambers recalled that "SOREL's book seemed to be a solution because it dealt with violence in the revolutionary movement."[97] Sorel's importance for Chambers was three-fold: a Henry Adams-esque hostility toward all things modern and bourgeois, a belief in action as the logical culmination of thought, and an appeal to violence as a necessary aspect of revolution.[98] Lenin's writing and leadership helped crystallize for Chambers the teachings of Sorel. Still, the move to Bolshevism required a suppression of the antimodernism to which Sorel was prone. Chambers's life changed when he happened upon the writing of Vladimir Lenin. Some time in 1923, Chambers had "obtained a pamphlet written by LENIN, published by the Rand School, and entitled 'A Soviet at Work.'"[99] Revolution may have come first to Chambers in the form of modernist literature, but the Bolshevik revolution came to him, appropriately enough, through the figure of Lenin, the first revolutionary intellectual to rule a great power.[100] In Edmund Wilson's metaphor, Lenin had used his intellect, his grasp of Marxist theory, to turn the key in the lock of history.[101] Lenin's pamphlet "dealt directly with daily problems that confronted a Soviet, and appeared to me the most realistic writing I had ever read to date in connection with the revolutionary movement." Lenin led Chambers back to Marx, but it was Lenin the tactician who inspired Chambers's political devotion more than Marx the high priest of communist theory: "I reached the conclusion that the theories of KARL MARX and the tactical directions of LENIN offered the best explanation and solution for the social crisis."[102] Lenin extricated Chambers from the compromises of the socialists and the political irrelevance of the literary modernists. If Lenin was indeed right about the social crisis, one could act on his intelligence, substituting constructive action for despair. In *Witness*, Chambers wrote that "A Soviet at Work" gave him "what nothing else in the dying world had power to offer at the same intensity—faith and a vision, something for which to live and something for which to die."[103]

Chambers, "the foreigner," had an un-American relationship to communism, arriving at the Communist Party through European and Russian texts. There were not many American texts to convert a young intellectual to Marxism in the early 1920s and no splendid history of communist agitation in America. Marxist ideology supplied an alternative to capitalism, but for Chambers the Soviet experiment was not the final blossoming of the Enlightenment as it was for many, perhaps most Western intellectuals.[104] Part of Bolshevism's appeal was its rootedness in Russia's non-Western soil. The communalism of the Russian past struck Chambers as superior to the atomized Western present. Russian history encouraged the "belief that peasant collectivism represented a form of life higher than the society of the West whose hallmark was secular individualism in all fields." The peasant *mir'* (commune) presaged the *soviet* (council), and a Slavic "collectivism would carry Russia to a new height, and thereby redeem all mankind by skipping entirely the historical form known in the West as capitalism."[105] Chambers was not a Slavophile in the sense of being a Russian nationalist—this would have been ridiculous for someone born on Long Island to WASP parents—but the fact that "the Russian people are almost organically anti-middle-class" was sufficient to lend them a messianic aura in his eyes.[106] Late in life, Chambers would attempt to situate his anomalous communism in Russian intellectual history: "unlike most Western Communists, who became Communists under the influence of Social Democracy, I remained under the influence of the Narodniki long after I became a Marxist."[107] Chambers's indifference to the Enlightenment, to the revolution as a product of reason, made him appear un-Western: "to the Russians, it [my identification with the *narodniki*] made me seem a freak of nature—an American who was almost a Russian."[108] Whatever the inflection of his communism—Sorelian or Leninist, Russophile or Marxist—Chambers left Columbia for good in January 1925, by which time he was a committed member of the Communist Party.[109]

A family tragedy completed Chambers's journey. Chambers understood his brother's suicide (in September 1926) as the consequence of nihilism, of the nihilism to which bourgeois civilization had fallen prey. In addition to alcoholism, Chambers's brother had before his suicide "developed an interest in reading and an admiration for the 'French Rationalists.' He had become an atheist and was a complete skeptic in every field. He was also a devout Darwinian." It was as if he had chosen to live out the melancholy described in "Dover Beach," without having the strength to do so. Chambers could find only one conclusion to draw: his family represented "in miniature the whole crisis of the middle class."[110] For Chambers, Lenin's revolutionary message acquired even greater personal resonance in light of his brother's suicide. Lenin proved to him that the old bourgeois world was dying. The old world was a "haunted house," in which "the mother and the father are divided . . . the household has been split for years. The father is incapable of love. The mother seeks to dominate through sacrificial love," Chambers wrote in the 1950s.[111] The metaphor was more a recounting of family history than a figure of speech: "one son will kill himself in clear perception of the truth, but first he will die of despair. The other son? If he remained in that house, he will die with it. He can only live by fighting it and everything it stands for to its dying breath." In more direct language, Chambers wrote that "my brother's death stunned me . . . this is the point at which I became a thorough Communist. I felt that any society which could result in the death of a boy like my brother was wrong and I was at war with it. This was the beginning of my fanaticism."[112]

Despair had driven Chambers to communism. The "thorough communist" he thought he became in 1926 was certainly in the throes of terrible despair. The letters he wrote to Meyer Schapiro revealed a man caught between suicide and a religious crisis; communism could only be a partial solution to his personal dilemmas. "What shall I say, Meyer," he wrote in November 1926, "of what lies nearest to my heart? It is useless. While I am living I shall do what I can to change the face of life, the sad substance of life goes on. I shall sit in workers' councils, and maybe before I die in a Soviet [a communist administrative council], but all the activity, all the zeal, only encloses the quality of life itself." The Bolshevik resolve was missing, the concern with heart and soul dangerously close to bourgeois individualism and reactionary self-indulgence. Confidence in the revolution, the basic conviction of the communist, gave way at times to bottomless doubt: "the events one way or another, what mind can direct to any real degree? That they are trivial beside the inner man . . . the thing [life] was meant to rear is always underneath: the real thing is under it." Chambers even pondered the abandonment of urban life altogether. Might it not be better, he wondered, to become an American *narodnik*? "I have known the life of the earth for so long and loved it. Since I was a little boy with no one to urge me I have observed it. Shall I return to it?"[113]

In 1927, Chambers took an editorial position at the *Daily Worker* as a way to act on his despair. "I write good propaganda that reads unlike propaganda to the multitude," a concession to politics at a time when "the young men of our generation are going to pieces in America." Chambers quoted his comrade Mike Gold, a communist man of letters, to explain the current crisis: " 'there are only 2 positive philosophies in the U.S. today,—the philosophy of Capitalist Imperialism and the philosophy of the Communists; and the younger generation has been taught to scoff at both.' Of course it goes deeper than that," Chambers added, "but there is a grain of truth there." Like Trilling, Chambers recognized the temptation for critical intellectuals to dismiss everything, scoff at everything, and to seek solace in an "irritating nostalgia."[114] For Chambers, communism was an object of ambition, an escape from the bourgeois notion of career, and the highest example of civilization. On the one hand, Soviet civilization superseded a Western civilization tainted by liberalism and capitalism; on the other hand, the Soviet Union enlisted the best elements of Western civilization in its march toward communism. Chambers wrote to Schapiro that "Europe's energy and Europe's brain is all east of the Vistula [river]," suggesting that the Soviet Union was merely the eastern half of Western civilization. Perhaps the Soviet Union could renew the West, deformed as it had become in modern times, a missionary vision for the communist experiment: "the [communist] movement in this country [the United States], like everything else except industrialism, is weak, it is even pitiable, and to many intelligent people ridiculous. For me, I know it is here to stay, to err, to fortify and to multiply itself I have no fears for it, as I have no longer fears for the future of this [American] civilization."[115] American civilization is hopeless, and American intellectuals have no native civilization to serve; communism is their only exit.

Without communism, Chambers reasoned, the intellectual was mired in a dissolving bourgeois civilization. In poetry published in the *Daily Worker*, Chambers celebrated an undying devotion to revolution, the triumph of life over death, a triumph that only the Party can enact.

For the dead who died fighting for
Us in arms, for the imprisoned dead;
For those who died actively working in the factories
    or among the
Workers on the land, for these dead,
We march today, comrades,
Workers.[116]

The resolve of the revolutionist transcends the work of revolution. A hint of hopelessness draws attention away from the plight of the masses to the plight of the communist poet or intellectual, the proponent (in America at least) of a pitiable movement.

> But let our merciless steadfastness survive
> Our bodies at the end.[117]

Poetry did not satisfy Chambers's political ambitions, perhaps because his poetry was so personal, so much about his own need for communism, and so mediocre. As he observed to Schapiro in 1927, "I have made long poems [about the communist movement], but I do not think much of them, preferring acts at present more needed."[118]

At the *Daily Worker*, Chambers edited letters from workers so that he and his readers might know firsthand about the proletariat's struggle. His description of this in *Witness* recalls the sewers of *Les Misérables*, with workers writing in to describe "how it feels to lie unwanted and disabled on the human dump-heap of the modern world." To Schapiro Chambers evaluated his own editorial work in the following terms: "it is good journalistic training, and it keeps me somewhere near the center of the Party's affairs and gives me an experience in the day to day life of the Party." Such experience was not for the sake of mere journalistic ambition; it was, rather, "almost prerequisite for a leader." To Schapiro he wondered whether he might succeed as a communist leader. Even if he did not, he would not have a conventional career—"in fact I do not want a career, as you will know: I really have no will to it." Opposed to career, Chambers remained powerfully committed to the intellectual vocation. He saw intellect as a crucial part of political power, the means of combining theory and strategy, history and politics: "I am what is, in the Party, called a literate, and the literates willy-nilly, struggle as they may against it, make up a leading van, just as the Party as a whole leads the van of the labor movement: leads when it properly functions." Intellect, however, is only effective when it addresses itself to power, as Lenin's writing before 1917 had shown. In explicating the outlook of the communist intellectual, Chambers wrote that "faith to a certain extent is needed. More than faith, insight and understanding of economic facts and principles; and a hard, shrewd penetration of the process to the consequences of evolving materialism."[119]

However perfect the Party was for harmonizing the idea and the act in theory, it was painfully imperfect in practice.[120] Already in 1927 Chambers felt the need to add—"when it properly functions"—to his evaluation of communist leadership. The dysfunctional elements of the Communist Party had begun to overwhelm Chambers by 1929. At issue was the death of Lenin and the problem of succession, the "crucial yet byzantine battle, which ushered in more than a half-century of lies," in the words of the historian François Furet.[121] Chambers recalled the Stalinists' "fight to consolidate and control the party [as] one of the worst minor reigns of terror that he had ever known," causing a crisis of party affiliation.[122] What, he asked, did Stalin's conduct say about the Communist Party? Stalin had orchestrated the "expulsion of Comrade Trotsky from the Communist Party on grounds that I believed to be unjust if not wholly fraudulent." More generally, Stalin's repressive style was an ominous sign, for "a party which could conclude a decisive debate on strategy and tactics only by physically expelling an intelligent and very big minority group, betrayed a weakness that might be fatal," Chambers felt. Stalin ushered in a new communist style, inaugurating "the spectacle of the calculated degradation by lies and slander of the man [Trotsky] who, after Lenin, was undeniably the Communist Party's best brain."[123] Chambers was reacting to something that would come to be known as Stalinism: conformity to the Party line, the persecution of political opposition, and the stifling of intellectual dissent. Chambers suffered a crisis of confidence. He did not join ranks with Trotsky's followers, a common enough choice for disaffected radicals, but he felt compelled to break ranks with Stalin's Communist Party. At the *Daily Worker*, where Chambers was "somewhere near the center of Party affairs," he observed the fragmentation of the Party into Trotskyites, Lovestoneites, and Stalinists, regarding "the purge [of the Lovestoneites] with growing revulsion, though it did not touch me personally." Chambers was careful to stress his own volition in his departure from the Party in 1929: "I was never formally expelled by the Communist Party. I still considered myself a communist but other members of the

Communist Party refused to have anything to do with me. This was common treatment for heretics."[124]

Chambers, the son of the "French family," the WASP who appeared in an essay on "Jewish Students I Have Known," the Columbia drop-out, was now a heretic among revolutionaries. He was quite alone and not at all willing to return to the sickly world of the bourgeoisie. Better by far than being an adult bourgeois, he believed, was to be "an independent Communist oppositionist."[125] He had not been educated to be a communist at Columbia, but he had been educated in despair, and the informal education in despair, combined with the high intellectual seriousness Trilling and Chambers encountered at Columbia, would prove strangely helpful, more useful than Henry Adams's education at Harvard. Adams was always unprepared for the future, armed with the wrong ideas and the wrong convictions. *The Education of Henry Adams* is a biography of continuing failure. Trilling and Chambers were marginally better off because their world was poised to enter a decade less Red than deeply despairing—the despair of world war remembered and economic depression felt, of tyranny and military dictatorships forming, of world war in the making—and behind this the melancholy, long, withdrawing roar, as the Sea of Faith seemed to be drying up. Amidst a despair hardening into fanaticism or crumbling into indifference was the Soviet alternative, like a weapon to be picked up off the ground or "like the folds of a bright girdle furl'd," which was enticing even to an early exile from the Communist Party such as Chambers. Far from the American mainstream, the Soviet alternative was no novelty in the late 1920s and early 1930s. It had been there, in all its radical glory, since 1917.

2

RED YEARS IN THE RED DECADE

Pursuing Soviet Alternatives

> [T]he shell in which the cultural construction and self-education of Communist man will be enclosed, will develop all the vital elements of contemporary art to the highest point. Man will become immeasurably stronger, wiser, and subtler; his body will become more harmonized, his movements more rhythmic, his voice more musical. The forms of life will become dynamically dramatic. The average human type will rise to the heights of an Aristotle, a Goethe, or a Marx.
>
> —LEON TROTSKY, *Literature and Revolution*

In 1932, fifty-two American intellectuals publicly advertised their eagerness to vote for the Communist Party. For the signatories of *Culture and the Crisis*, a pamphlet explaining their position, the Soviet Union offered a model for American civilization, with the Great Depression as evidence of Soviet superiority.[1] Part of the Soviet Union's allure resided in the modernist élan of its culture, in the films of Sergei Eisenstein, the art of Kazmir Malevich, the poetry of Vladimir Mayakovski, and the short stories of Isaac Babel.[2] Starting in the 1920s and lingering into the 1930s the Soviet avant-garde tempted Western intellectuals to believe that the future was erupting from a revolutionary Moscow rather than an exhausted Paris or an impoverished New York; in *Culture and the Crisis* culture preceded crisis. Primarily, however, it was the Soviet Union as political fact that promised liberation. Only communism could forge ahead, leaving behind a bourgeois world mired in depression and nationalism, enervated by a liberalism without courage or confidence. Merely bohemian protest was passé by 1932.[3] Only "the overthrow of capitalism" and the Communist Party offered a "practicable solution of the crisis—a workers' and farmers' government."[4] The pamphlet touched on the ideals and stated program of the American Communist Party, leaving out a discussion of its leaders and its attitude toward the American constitution. It amounted to a literary "protest vote."[5] The authors arrived at a climax that was unexpectedly comical: "*Vote Communist—for Foster and Ford—on November 8.*"[6] These were intellectuals civil enough to vote for revolution. Whittaker Chambers and Lionel Trilling did not sign on to *Culture and the Crisis*, although neither was a stranger to its logic or its ambiguities. They wanted communism to work political magic and to enact the practicable solution. Yet they did not want to be subordinate to the Party.

In their radicalism as well as in their independence from the Party, Trilling and Chambers were emblematic of the Red Decade in America. There was nothing superficial about their radicalism, about the despair that America's shattered political economy had fostered in them, about the hunger for alternatives, about the fear of fascism, made immeasurably worse a year after *Culture and the Crisis* was published and Hitler seized control over Germany. Yet the salient political fact of America in the 1930s was the New Deal, the American alternative to the laissez-faire blunders of the 1920s; it was not the communist movement. What mattered was the vote for Franklin Delano Roosevelt (FDR) in 1932, not for Ford and Foster, although American radicalism could be stretched at times to include FDR, Ford, and Foster. In the years between 1935 and 1939 one could entertain radical dreams that included the New Deal *and* the Soviet experiment, American democracy and Soviet communism. This was the era of the Popular Front when the Party itself sanctioned a flexible commitment to communism. The radicalism of the 1930s was remarkably free: the Red Scare was over; no one could anticipate the price to be paid in the 1950s when Senator Joseph McCarthy would investigate the communist spirit of the 1930s; and in the pre-McCarthy era intellectuals were free to devise a communism of their own making, to join the Party or to sign a communist-tinged manifesto, a protest vote from afar. The Communist Party with its hierarchy and discipline had an innate disadvantage in democratic, individualist America. The more it tried to control the structure and content of the Left, the less American radicals wanted to belong to the Party.

Having left the Party in 1929 because of its Stalinist rigidities, Chambers returned to it in 1931, born again Chambers's return to the Party echoed the plot of a Hollywood movie, showing the triumph of dedication over adversity. He never had to humble himself for his earlier independence and opposition. Rather, he reentered the Party's ranks in a burst of celebrity, "a literary proletarian luminary," in Daniel Aaron's phrase, whose fiction had earned him accolades in Moscow itself.[7] Chambers's calling card with the Party was a quartet of short stories, which he would later describe as "stories that anybody might want to read—stories in which the correct conduct of the Communist would be shown in action and without political comment."[8] Each of them was published in the *New Masses* in 1931, satisfying his ambition to write readable communist literature and catching the attention of Mike Gold, a communist and the American impresario of proletarian literature. To Lincoln Steffens, a high-profile fellow traveler of the 1930s, the stories were exemplary works of proletarian fiction: "Whenever I hear people talking about 'Proletarian art and literature,' " Steffens wrote to Chambers in 1933, "I'm going to ask them to shut their minds and look at you . . . How you can write!"[9] The journalist Murray Kempton would describe Chambers as "the purest Bolshevik writer ever to function in the United States," although Joszef Peter, a Hungarian communist high in the leadership of the American Party, found the stories subversive, as Chambers recalled in *Witness*.[10] In fact, Peter "had fought fiercely to keep the State Publishing House [in Moscow] from translating and publishing them. I asked him why. 'They are against the Party,' he said."[11]

The varied critical responses to Chambers's stories were not necessarily contradictory. Socialist realism was a literary theory amenable to a communist such as Mike Gold. It might even be the official doctrine of Soviet literature: reason "combined with the ideological remolding and education of working people in the spirit of socialism. This method in literature and in literary criticism is what we call the method of socialist realism," as Andrei Zhdanov, Soviet commissar of socialist realism, defined the doctrine at the First Writers' Congress in 1932.[12] The formal dictates of socialist realism—the realism, the portrayal of class conflict, the indictment of the bourgeoisie, the heroic depiction of radical characters—did not require a glorification of the Party per se but this was taken for granted in Moscow. In retrospect, the anti-communist Chambers would agree with Peters: "The stories are scarcely about Communism at all," he argued in *Witness*, "what they are really about is the spirit of man in four basic commitments—in suffering, under discipline, in defeat, in death." The stories centered on the suffering, discipline, defeat, and death of communist protagonists. Peter's negative reaction—if Chambers's version of it in *Witness* is the entire story—must have stemmed from the expectation that the Party itself should be the protagonist. Chambers's stories developed out of the communist poetry he published in the late 1920s, consecrating the will to militancy, even (or especially) in face of impossible odds. At the center was the martyrdom of the communist rather than the rectitude of the Party. As an older Chambers observed: "in each [story], it is not the political situation, but the spirit of man which is triumphant."[13]

The first and most successful of the stories was "Can You Make Out Their Voices?" With quiet intensity, it tells of farmers on the brink of disaster. Superficially, the disaster has natural causes, but the story takes its readers to the heart of a society structured for disaster. The problem is inequality and a capitalist competitiveness that requires the exploitation of the poor. The problem is also political because the political system reflects and defends the travesties of the "free market." "Can You Make Out Their Voices?" deviates from Leninism in one striking way. The uprising of dirt farmers is spontaneous, led by the local communist Wardell who does not belong to a Leninist vanguard. He is simply a self-educated, decent soul from among the masses, and the story has a *narodnik* or populist spirit: the people awaken and strike out at the injustice of Washington and Wall Street. The farmers first attempt to save themselves and their families from starvation by taking milk from Purcell, the kulak among them, "the richest farmer in the district." Purcell, in turn, contacts Senator Bagheot in Washington, describing the situation as a "seizure of milk at a local farm by one hundred farmers, led by loafers." Bagheot promises to call the state's governor who is hard of hearing, a transparently symbolic detail. The senator asks for "even a very little relief," to which the governor responds, "I can't hear you."[14] The senator decides to send the Red Cross with two days' food supply. Wall Street figures in the unwillingness of local banks to give the poor farmers capital, and without capital they are helpless. They have neither the means of power nor the means of subsistence. The poor farmers must choose between death in the capitalist system and the life promised by Wardell, the story's communist hero.

Wardell is the story's big-hearted hero, showing exactly how romantic Chambers's idea of communism was. Wardell leads the farmers toward rebellion and, ultimately, toward the Party, but he must first reveal the actual workings of the capitalist system to them, penetrating the false consciousness of his fellow dirt farmers and turning their faith in the American system into a faith in communism. Wardell has read Engels's treatise *Socialism Utopian and Scientific* and his communist pedagogy is effective because he speaks the language of the other farmers. He argues that the crisis is not one of material shortage but of distribution: "you can eat like a hog—if you're a store keeper . . . we only *grow* the food—when we can: they *sell* it. But as I haven't got the money to buy and neither have you, I guess we'll take it or share." When asked, Wardell says that his being a communist "means that I'm for unlimited free groceries and meat to all poor farmers. No rent for two years. Free seed. Free milk for babies."[15] Wardell does not incite revolution, but his personal virtue is pivotal to the farmers' survival, no less so than his translation of *Socialism Utopian and Scientific* into the vocabulary of daily life. Communism triumphs in "Can You Make Out Their Voices?" because the spirit of man triumphs; there is no particular role for the Party to play.

In "You Have Seen Their Heads," the source of suffering is not twentieth-century capitalism but China's traditional, feudal society. The governor of a province has imposed heavy taxes on the protagonist's village. The protagonist's father explodes in anger at the tax collectors until he is subdued by the village elder, Fu fu ma. Fu fu ma dispenses a counterintuitive Confucian wisdom: " 'Actions are difficult, but understanding is easy.' He quieted my father and led him into our house." The protagonist's problem emerges as the story unfolds: he has internalized Fu fu ma's quietism. He is unable to act because he "reverenced Fu fu ma." To become a communist he must dissolve this reverence and endure great suffering. After his father's death, he marries and has three sons. When the army comes to take him into military service, Fu fu ma repeats the same statement about the difficulty of action and the ease of understanding. On hearing these words, the protagonist recalls his "father's face as Fu fu ma led him into our house, away from quarreling with the tax collectors. Honoring my father, I resigned myself and allowed them to push me into my place at the end of the line." In the army he learns that his wife has been killed during a communist uprising in their village. His grief induces him to escape from the army and devote himself to the communist cause. His first significant act as a communist is to kill Fu fu ma, murdering the ancien régime: "Fu fu ma was right: the spirit is stronger than the body. But not the spirit of Fu fu ma." Once again, the Party plays a marginal role; at the story's center is a conversion narrative without hope of easy political success: "We are harried among mountains. The march to victory is up the sharp side of mountains."[16]

The Party is central, but less than heroic, in "Our Comrade Munn." Its hero is a man much like Chambers himself, a well-intentioned communist at odds with the Party's pettiness. Munn is both American and "a shoe worker." He enters a branch of the Party held back by uninspired leadership and by an excess of foreign-born workers. One of them, Comrade Celensky, does not speak English. Munn pushes his branch to assist in a strike. At the picket line, a struggle ensues for the souls of the striking workers. Christianity plays a crucial role because "the larger share holder in the Atlas Mills, a member of the city council, F. X. Queeley, was the brother of Father Patrick Queeley, one of the best known Irish priests." Father Queeley's ideology is a restatement of Fu fu ma's, only with Christian rather than Confucian overtones: "he would attack the idleness of the rich, drawing a comparison in favor of the life of the poor, but happy, which has been the method in his church for several thousand years." Curiously, Comrade Munn does not attack Queeley for being a Christian but for being a bad Christian: "You are trying to stop them," Munn shouts, "because your brother, F. X. Queeley, owns the mill. The only God you serve is money!" To convince the workers not to break their strike, Munn calls on God to kill him, Munn, with lightening, but he dies when one of F. X. Queeley's guards shoots him. A martyr's death confers on Munn the heroism his comrades had failed to see. The strike fails and Munn dies, but the narrator senses victory. Because of Munn's dying request, Comrade Celensky learns English, "a general victory of our section in the objective field: it is part of the work of Comrade Munn."[17] The internationalism of Chambers's communist stories was conscious: if America and China stand at different distances from the ancien régime, the task and desirability of communism is universal.

The New Masses stories transformed Chambers into a communist success. "Can You Make Out Their Voices?" was turned into a play and performed internationally to great acclaim.[18] It was widely considered a "Communist classic," and Mike Gold's enthusiasm got Chambers an editorial position at the New Masses in 1931.[19] Chambers had joined the Party in 1925, and he could move in the non-Party intellectual world that many of his former Morningside colleagues such as Trilling were beginning to enter. His experience and education gave him the potential to exceed even Mike Gold as a leading communist writer, but Chambers shared Comrade

Munn's impatience with talk. Chambers's character and intellect recommended him to Max Bedacht, a high-ranking American communist who recruited him for underground work. On being asked, Chambers felt "a quiet elation at the knowledge that there was one efficient party organization and that it selected me to work for it."[20] In *Witness*, Chambers claimed that he turned down Bedacht's offer at his wife's insistence. They had recently moved to a farm in New Jersey, and both Chambers and his wife, Esther, wanted to have a family. Although underground work threatened these pastoral aspirations, Bedacht would not accept a negative answer. Were Chambers to decline the offer, his knowledge of the underground's existence would excommunicate him from the Party forever. Thus, Chambers was drawn into the "white-slave traffic whose victims were young idealists flirting with violence," as Arthur Koestler described the communist underground around this time.[21] In 1933 Chambers was sent to Moscow for training. Chambers's hesitation was surely genuine, but so, too, was the elation. As editor of the *New Masses*, he could serve the revolution with his intellect. As a Red Army spy who would be "the main link between the Party underground and Soviet intelligence," in the words of Christopher Andrew and Oleg Gordievsky, Chambers could serve the revolution directly.[22]

Underground work also afforded Chambers the option of trying on new identities. He had a penchant for pseudonyms that predated his career in espionage, and, as a spy, he would even get to play the role of the bourgeois.[23] Chambers's entry into the communist underground in *Witness* forms an anecdote of exquisite irony. He was notoriously sloppy, and when he became a communist spy, his superiors in the Communist Party told him to dress better. He had to buy new suits and attempt to look dignified. There was one thing in particular he was told to remember: "you're a respectable bourgeois now."[24] It was this outsider's job to blend in, and improbably disguised as a respectable bourgeois, Chambers finally acted on his homosexual urges. Beginning in 1933 and continuing "up to the year 1938, I engaged in numerous homosexual activities both in New York and in Washington, DC," he wrote in a letter to J. Edgar Hoover. He sought out such activities by going to "parks and other parts of town where these people were likely to be found." The Communist Party was no haven for homosexuals, and in a statement written for the FBI about his secret homosexual life, Chambers emphatically denied having relations with anybody "in the Communist Party or connected with Communist work of any kind. I kept my secret as jealously from my associates in the Communist Party as I did from everyone else." He was engaged in secret work, assuming manifold identities, using anonymity as a cover: "I am positive that no man with whom I had these relations during this period ever knew my true identity, nor do I at this time [1949] recall the names of any of them." Chambers also had affairs with women in his years in the underground. In the case of heterosexual infidelity, he later held the Party responsible: "immorality as such insofar as women were concerned, was openly accepted and engaged in by almost all members of the Communist Party at that time." As an espionage agent, he aspired to separate his life as a communist from his forays into the homosexual underground.[25]

Chambers's first assignment in the communist underground was unglamorous but satisfying. The turmoil of the Great Depression imbued underground members with a sense of purpose, even if Chambers's "first apparatus" lacked important connections and valuable material for espionage. The underground also put Chambers in touch with like-minded revolutionaries. Chambers reported to "Ulrich," a Russian "hero of the revolutionary world" and "the only Russian who was ever to become my close friend." Ulrich and his wife—known to Chambers as "Elena" or "Maria"—frightened Chambers at times. One of Ulrich's favorite expressions was: "I'll have you shot." Ulrich also inspired Chambers because he embodied Chambers's ideal of the revolutionary. Both Ulrich and his wife were versed in European culture, and in Ulrich's case "his humanity was greater than anything else." Elena was a Party member of unshakable dedication. Ulrich was more of a fellow *narodnik* or populist: he believed in revolution but was skeptical about the Communist Party, "a proletarian who read Byron as a boy." In Russia's prerevolutionary period he had belonged to the "left wing of the Socialist Revolutionary Party which, during the Russian Revolution, had gone over to the Bolsheviks."[26] Ulrich and Elena were the political soul mates Chambers could never find in the American Communist Party. Additionally, they did not sacrifice their critical intelligence to the greater glory of the Party. They were reflective, serious members—*ernste Menschen*—of its underground.

Keeping secrets within secrets, Chambers broke two rules of underground protocol. He maintained friendships outside the Party, and he did not force his wife to have an abortion. On October 17, 1933, their first child was born. Because children complicated underground work, reducing operatives' appetite for risk, the Party advocated abortion for Esther and

Whittaker.[27] Chambers wrote in *Witness* that "abortion was a common-place of party life [which] I then regarded, like all Communists, as a mere physical manipulation." The Chambers' decision to have a child did not follow from the "physical horror" of abortion that the anti-communist and Christian Chambers would later feel. Yet their decision was self-consciously rebellious, figuring in his journey away from communism: "if the points on the course of my long break with Communism could be re-traced, that is probably one of them."[28] A short section of *Witness* titled "The Child" stands vividly between a long chapter on the first espionage apparatus and a longer chapter on the second.

Chambers still suffered from some of his old doubts about the Party. Reports of terror in Stalin's Soviet Union might be dismissed by comrades in the open Party, waved away as further propaganda from the reactionary press, and Chambers would have liked to dismiss these reports in 1933; but he could not help noticing a new type of communist coming from the Soviet Union. "Herman," for example, was an early specimen of *homo sovieticus* and Chambers's superior for a time, a Bolshevik gangster of sorts, with no high spiritual aspirations for communism. Herman was susceptible to the baser seductions of New York City, and in *Witness* Chambers recalled Herman's habit "of taking from each trouser pocket a fat roll of bills which he weighed lovingly in each hand." Herman died in a confusing episode that was either a bar brawl or a murder set up to resemble a bar brawl. Chambers's encounter with Herman left him wondering, "Is this the kind of man communism is breeding?"[29] Chambers's other doubts concerned Stalin's statesmanship. Before Hitler's seizure of power in Germany, Stalin had believed that Nazi victory would provoke a Bolshevik-style revolution in Germany. Stalin stigmatized social democrats as "social fascists," in hopes of pushing the German proletariat behind the Communist Party. The Nazis capitalized on a divided Left, using their post-1933 power to crush communism in Germany. Thinking back to 1933 in *Witness*, Chambers recalled that he was "often in disagreement with Communist policy, which had turned Germany over to Hitler and led to the physical destruction of the second most powerful party in the International." Ulrich and Elena suspected Chambers of having doubts and got him drunk in order to divine his sincere opinions. He spoke his mind, and his opinions deviated from the Party line.[30] Chambers's contact with the outside world intensified his doubts about the communist movement under Stalin.

One such contact was Lionel Trilling, who invited his friend in the communist underground to lunch with a known communist heretic, Sidney Hook.[31] Trilling, too, was troubled by the Nazis' ascendancy in 1933. Diana Trilling remembered that Stalin's policy toward Germany "significantly contributed to our suspicion of Stalin [circa 1933] and thus to our impending break with the radical movement."[32] At a vegetarian restaurant somewhere near Madison Square Garden, Hook, Chambers, and Trilling debated the "social fascism" thesis—or, more precisely, Hook attacked the thesis while Chambers listened in silence.[33] In Hook's recollection, "Chambers sat as silent as a little Buddha [while Hook spoke], except for an occasional grunt and comments like 'Maybe!' and 'So you say!' "[34] Either Chambers's reservations about Stalin came after the lunch or he was being circumspect and keeping criticism of the Party to himself. Most surprising was Chambers's willingness to talk with nonaligned radicals: the lunch was an odd enough arrangement for Diana Trilling to argue in 1976 that it never happened at all.[35] Comparably intriguing was Trilling's eagerness to bring Hook and Chambers together; the lunch demonstrated Trilling's depth of emotional involvement with the Communist Party and with Chambers's position in it. "That night Trilling phoned," Hook remembered. "He seemed to be very distressed." Trilling said to Hook: "Sidney, I don't understand Whit at all. After you left, I turned to him and asked, 'Well, what do you make of what Hook said? It makes sense to me.' He didn't reply to any of your points. His only answer was, 'Lionel, I don't trust that man—he has a Social-Democratic face!' "[36]

Trilling was moving slowly away from the Party by the time of this lunch toward an ever greater independence of mind. As a communist he "accepted many of the current communist notions of post-1931—and lost some years of intellectual growth thereby—but never could believe that a communist book was a good book," Trilling wrote in a 1946 letter.[37] Before Trilling could assert his independence from communism, he had to assimilate the communist ideology, its interrelated scheme of attitude and explanation. Trilling's attraction to the Soviet Union was an attraction to revolutionary possibility, to the new era that communism augured, and he thirsted for "an art that would have as little ambiguity as a proposition in logic," not socialist realism but a "literature of the Revolution [that] would realize some simple, inadequate notion of the 'classical,' which I had picked up at college." In a 1955 essay, Trilling wondered whether he had been "drawn to this notion of the classical because I was afraid of the literature of modern Europe, because I was scared of its terrible intensities, ironies, and ambiguities."[38] The radical Trilling was not objecting to the apolitical quality of so much modern literature, the solipsism, say, that Edmund Wilson lamented in *Axel's Castle*, his influential study of modernism.[39] Trilling was seeking solace from the spirit of modern literature, from its ambiguities and negations and darkness. Perhaps communist art would be a precursor to classical order rather than to modern chaos.

Trilling's desire for a revolutionary literature was urgent, and he documented it in two book reviews from the summer of 1930. In the first, "A Transcendental Prude," he recapitulated an already well-established storyline for Western cultural history. His point of departure was malaise, for "a great part—perhaps the most relevant part—of the literature of these hundred years has been engaged in its description, from Arnold to de Vigny to Eliot, from Stendhal and Turgenev to Hemingway. Whatever its name, its kind and its causes, it [malaise] has manifested itself in the feeling that between the soul of man and the uses of this world there is a necessary and rigid divorce." The religious tenor of Trilling's language was conscious. The only recourse to the soul's alienation might be communion with God. In a secular era, however, the divorce between the "soul of man" and the "uses of this world" will not readily admit to theological aid: "in a more rigid age these manifestations would have been regarded as a normal part of the preliminary paraphernalia of religious conversion. This, indeed, they sometimes become, but on the whole sufferers from cosmic despair have adjusted their lives—if at all—without the ministrations of orthodoxy."[40] If one no longer had the ministrations of orthodoxy, one might find strength in the prospect of revolution, and Trilling's relationship to revolution was, essentially, a relationship to revolutionary literature. In "The Social Emotions," Trilling reviewed *The Nineteen* by Alexander Fadeyev, a Soviet hero who had both fought in the civil war and taken part in the suppression of a sailors' uprising at Kronstadt, an early instance of Bolshevik authoritarianism. By the time Stalin had consolidated power, a consolidation complete by 1930, literary activity was under state control. Fadeyev served as leader of the Russian Association of Political Writers from 1926 to 1932, and his novel, also known as *The Rout*, was a Soviet classic first published in 1927 and then filmed twice. An "outstanding work of socialist realism," *The Nineteen*'s protagonist "expresses the Bolshevik promise of Social change leading to a shining future."[41]

In "The Social Emotions," Trilling flirted with Soviet-style revolution. Fadeyev's heroes were refreshing, and "out of the novel emerges a set of ethical and emotional values so fine that, if revolution be necessary to achieve them, revolution becomes desirable." If literature creates its own political truths—forging values that might determine political affiliations—literature also derives from lived experience. Hence, Fadeyev's novel of Bolshevik heroism derives from "the difficulty and suffering with which the revolution was kept alive . . . this could never have been done without some spiritual force, however observed." Fadeyev fails to transform suffering into values because the glow of revolution can only do so much to redeem literature: "so touching and so pure are the deeds and motives of this novel that one almost distrusts it." Trilling concluded the review with a gentle critique of Fadeyev. The simplicity of Fadeyev's novel, as Trilling read it, casts doubt on its celebration of communist revolution. Excessive sympathy corrupts the novel's "important implication: that far from dehumanizing men into cogs of a communal machine, the communal ideal has given them a new and stronger individualism."[42] The success of the communal ideal—if it is truly a success—should itself be material for complicated, serious art.

The communal ideal had obvious appeal for Trilling in 1930. In a *Menorah Journal* review "Genuine Writing" Trilling even praised the prose style of Mike Gold, Whittaker Chambers's champion at the *New Masses*. Referring to Gold's 1930 book *Jews without Money* Trilling wrote apologetically that it "deals with filth and misery. But it deals with it so objectively," Trilling continued, "and so melodramatically that its stench becomes racy and Chaucerian, the scene becomes a little romantic and like a gypsy encampment."[43] More profound was Trilling's radical attack on Freud's *Civilization and Its Discontents*, Freud's essay on the irreconcilable tensions of civilized life. The attack was a book review written some time in 1930 for the *New Freeman* but never published and subsequently lost by Trilling. He summarized its argument in a 1959 letter. Trilling characterized *Civilization and Its Discontents* "as ridiculous and even offensive. I was just then beginning a period of Marxism and any explanation of the human condition by reference to anything else than economic and political injustice seemed to me morally indecent. And the discontents that Freud referred to *seemed* to me absurd and, indeed, really inconceivable."[44] *Civilization and Its Discontents* contained within it a polemic against communism, which Freud saw as an illusion.[45] "The communists believe that they have found the path to deliverance from our evils," Freud wrote. "According to them, man is wholly good and is well-disposed to his neighbor; but the institution of private property has corrupted his nature." Freud ventured no economic critique of communism, arguing instead "that the psychological premises on which the [communist] system is based are an untenable illusion . . . Aggressiveness was not created by property . . . it forms the basis of every relation of affection and love among people." An anti-communist Chambers would call this aggressiveness evil; an anti-communist Trilling would warmly agree with Freud; and as anti-communists, Chambers and Trilling would both see communism as a middle-class malady in the West, a symptom of bourgeois self-hatred. For this, too, there was a precedent in *Civilization and Its Discontents*. "It is intelligible," Freud wrote, "that the attempt to establish a new, communist civilization in Russia should find its psychological support in the persecution of the bourgeois."[46]

Lionel and Diana Trilling converted formally to communism in an atmosphere of bourgeois comfort. In the summer of 1931 they were at Yaddo, a writers' retreat in upstate New York. Given Trilling's attraction to Soviet Russia in 1930, his conversion must have been the confirmation of sympathy rather than the discovery of something new. According to Sidney Hook, "at the time we met at Yaddo, he [Lionel Trilling] was not a radical."[47] Trilling's reviews prior to Yaddo show him to have been on the way to communism when Sidney Hook converted him and Diana.[48] Hook was then an intellectual of note as well as a Jew in the philosophy department of New York University. For Trilling, who aspired to both academic and intellectual distinction, Hook's example could only have been heartening, a cause for emulation, although Hook's power of influence was strongest in the realm of ideas, ideas that were not literary but political. Hook's radicalism developed out of a commitment to democracy, which he associated with the Columbia philosopher John Dewey, someone Trilling had found "incomprehensible" as a student. Hook did not see liberalism as empty or foolish: liberalism was a political philosophy and a stage of history that needed to be reconsidered in light of Marxism.[49] Through Hook, Trilling might keep the liberal mark Columbia had made on him while responding fully to the crises of the 1930s. He might thereby become a communist.

Perhaps it was their pragmatism or perhaps their expansive notion of the word *liberal*, with all the American potentialities latent in this word, that kept Hook and the Trillings from joining the Communist Party. For whatever reason, membership in the Communist Party was optional for Hook and the Trillings, even if their general context for debate and thinking was revolutionary. Their radicalism was not genteel: "in America during this period to be a radical meant to be at least a Socialist," Hook recalled in his memoirs, "a revolutionary Socialist, at least a sympathizer or fellow-traveler, if not a member of a Communist Party or group—Stalinist, Trotskyist, or Lovestonite."[50] To ponder the achievements of the Bolshevik revolution was to speculate about a postbourgeois, nonbourgeois, or antibourgeois society possibly brought about by violence. Yet Trilling's dissertation had almost nothing to do with either communism or Marxism. He was at Yaddo to work on an intellectual biography of Matthew Arnold. Trilling hoped Arnold would show him "the personal changes in a man as he struggled to establish himself spiritually in the modern world."[51] Once again, Hook was a mentor who might help Trilling to write a dispassionate work of scholarship.[52] In the summer of 1931, Trilling wrote to Elliot Cohen that "the only way of treating [Matthew Arnold] is with great detachment. And probably that is an advantage for the particular thing I want to do. Hook is a most charming man . . . I expect I will get a few points from him."[53] The search for the "classical," adopted from the Columbia great books program, may have encouraged Trilling to praise Fadeyev's Soviet novel, although Soviet literature did little to satisfy the search. The "terrible intensities" of the avant-garde inspired a fear that could not be assuaged either by Soviet literature or by the revolutionary achievements of the Soviet Union. Such fear led Trilling not to speak in praise of the Victorians but to pay ever greater attention to these "terrible intensities," the origins of which lay in the nineteenth century.[54]

In the fall of 1931, when the Trillings returned to New York City from Yaddo, a group of radical intellectuals formed the National Committee for the Defense of Political Prisoners, which was dedicated to the cause of protecting political dissent. It was also a communist front with many of its members belonging to the Communist Party. They might direct the committee to assist the Party or to espouse the Party line while respectable "liberals" lent the committee their respectability. Lionel and Diana Trilling lent whatever respectability they had as well-educated liberal intellectuals, remaining fellow travelers until 1933 when Trilling arranged the lunch with Hook and Chambers. The devastation of the American world around him had entered the gates of Columbia University inducing "moral torture." To the undergraduate of 1924–1925, Babbitry, America's bottomless vulgarity, constituted "the order of things," as Trilling wrote in a short article on Columbia students.[55] To the undergraduate of 1932, the order of things "means misery and hardship, if not personal—and how often it has become that!—then so widespread as to be moral torture to all persons of good will."[56] America's misery created the need for a dynamic Soviet Union, and in 1932 Trilling's personal need was great. He disregarded the negative impressions of Soviet life passed on to him and Diana by friends who had recently returned from the Soviet Union and were shattered by what they had seen.[57] Even Hook, a philosophical opponent of absolutist convictions, kept his doubts about the Soviet Union at arm's length in 1932. It was fascism, in Hook's case, that shut his eyes to the possibility of a Soviet disaster, and Hook later recalled his antifascism as collective: "the terror of fascism helped to blur our vision and blunt our hearing to the reports that kept trickling out of the Soviet Union."[58]

In 1932, Trilling was sought after as a Marxist critic. He was invited to contribute to a proposed book of essays on radicalism by "bourgeois intellectuals who are working their way to a Marxist position."[59] It never materialized. In a review essay on the French literary critic Sainte-Beuve, the communist Trilling drew attention to Sainte-Beuve's lack of system. To possess system was to adopt a system from Marx, about which Trilling was guardedly optimistic: "in America, though Marxian (or its dilution, 'sociological') criticism may not yet have matured, and though it may still be used inflexibly and with insufficient scholarship, yet as a critical system it promises, in maturity, to provide emphases that are relevant, distinctions that are important, and assumptions that are effective and lasting tools."[60] Marx would educate the literary critic to whom all literature, even the most bourgeois, was available for study, but Trilling categorically avoided any connection between the needs of the critic and the demands of the Party. Party discipline was utterly alien to his experience of radicalism.

Relishing his independence, Trilling probed the contradictions of radicalism in 1932, his vehicle an essay on the Victorian thinker Thomas Carlyle. In Carlyle, who became a Calvinist conservative, Trilling observed a congruence of attitude between Tories and Marxists. Trilling argued that Marx regarded Carlyle with sympathy, as might the 1930s radical: "the ideology with which Carlyle combated it [liberal Whiggery] is in large part the ideology with which we today combat it. The realization of the failure of democracy and the recognition of the need to organize labor, to organize industry—these are the concepts which made Engels and Marx for a time so lenient to Tory opposition to the industrial liberals and especially to Carlyle."[61] Carlyle's life prefigured the dilemma of the bourgeois intellectual who advocates proletarian revolution, an age-old dilemma: "today, when so many of our middle-class intellectuals are swinging left, it is well to remember that the position of the bourgeois intellectual in any political movement has always been an anomalous and precarious one." The intellectual espouses mutually exclusive values such as economic equality on the one hand and a rarified modernist culture on the other: "however sincere he may be, the mind of the intellectual is so apt to be overlaid with conflicting values that it is impossible for him to be sure of his position; having so many values, he is likely to betray one to defend others." The Marxist Trilling beautifully exemplified the plight of the bourgeois-turned-radical intellectual. The swing to the Left is a fait accompli. Modern history has made a sham of the bourgeois virtues: this is what Carlyle did not understand and what Marx understood perfectly. Carlyle was an apologist for capitalism because he misconstrued "the pertinence (perhaps unconscious to Carlyle) of the virtues he had preached, of self-denial, obedience, unconsciousness, labor for labor's sake; under the light of the doctrine of morality of might, of imperialism, of the inferiority of the subject races, they become very clearly the capitalist virtues."[62] For all these reasons, the Left must prevail. Yet Carlyle's journey from Left to Right was "peculiarly relevant to our period," more so than Trilling could have known in 1932.[63]

Trilling took his radicalism furthest in "Forced Labor," an essay published in June 1933, in which he reviewed a pro-Soviet book on the American working class, *Forced Labor in the U.S.* Its premise was that all capitalist labor is forced labor. Trilling paraphrased Marx's theory of surplus value: "all labor, the product of which, with the exception of the sum sufficient to keep the laborer himself alive, accrues to others, which produces physical suffering, and which is terminable at the will of the employer, is obviously forced labor." Trilling praised *Forced Labor in the U.S.* for using the language of capitalist and anti-Soviet thinkers to further a radical agenda: "the major part of this excellent study accepts terms of forced labor as they are admitted by capitalist observers and as they are defined by those who have accused Russia of dumping on foreign markets the products of such forced labor." Trilling was making the most radical statements of his entire intellectual career based on the claim that "the modern prison is in effect a great factory," the factory a prison and the prison a factory. Therefore, "the only result of prison punishment is obviously terrorization of the working class." Even in the most communist of his reviews or essays, Trilling made no attempt to toe the American Party's pro-Soviet line. For Trilling, the book's unflattering comparison of the United States with Soviet Russia "has something of the propaganda quality of *The Soviet Union Today* where a smiling peasant face does duty for much exposition."[64] Trilling's objection was not at all anti-Soviet: "I do not question the facts that Mr. Wilson presents, but I feel that he would have clinched his contrast [between the U.S. and the Soviet Union] with far greater force had he written from a more intimate and analytical view of Russian labor. But perhaps this is quibbling over a very thorough book."[65] Trilling's critical instincts told him that the pro-Soviet passages of the book were tendentious, while his radical leanings made him regret this critical judgment.

At the height of their communist enthusiasm, the Trillings came close to Chambers and his not-so-secret underground world. This was in early 1933. On April 26, 1933, Whittaker Chambers came to see Diana Trilling about serving as a letter drop for the communist underground. Her involvement in a communist front must have encouraged Chambers to trust her. While attempting to persuade Diana, Chambers's appeal was interrupted by a telephone call. The caller informed Diana of the death of a friend, and, Diana remembered, "Chambers immediately suppressed his purpose in coming to see me in order to stay and comfort me." Although Diana was not inclined to accept Chambers's request, she was "enormously flattered that Whittaker Chambers thought me capable of such an assignment and I was ashamed to refuse him." He asked Lionel Trilling as well, requesting that Trilling "receive letters for him. He scarcely concealed that these letters were part of an espionage project," Trilling later recalled. In 1933, Diana was more deeply immersed in politics than Lionel, but her experiences and affiliations intertwined with those of her husband. In May 1933, Diana was outraged when the National Committee for the Defense of Political Prisoners (NCDPP), a communist front to which the Trillings belonged, urged her to write untrue letters, underscoring the Party line. She had hit on a dilemma of the fellow-traveling radical far more visceral than any Trilling had described in "Carlyle." What was one prepared to sacrifice to serve the Party? The incident with the letters was, in Diana Trilling's view, "decisive in my growing alienation from the Party and the radical movement."[66] Elliot Cohen, Herbert Solow, and both Trillings left the NCDPP.[67]

Leaving a communist front did not mean abandoning the revolution. In December 1933, Sidney Hook wrote to Lionel Trilling asking him to join an "informally organized revolutionary club . . . [that requires] no political commitments."[68] Other proposed members were Meyer Schapiro, George Novak, Elliot Cohen, Herbert Solow, Reinhold Niebuhr, and James Burnham, all distinguished intellectuals. In his letter Hook emphasized freedom from the Party as well as continued commitment to revolution, and Trilling aspired to be an independent radical like Hook. In a review indicting Victorian intellectual John Ruskin for obscurantism and incoherence, Trilling praised Ruskin for the cogency of his socialism. Ruskin, Trilling wrote, "attacked the assumptions of the classical 'scientific' economics, showed the fallacies of the Economic Man, of laissez-faire, or current theories of value, and reared a structure of social realism that the generality of economic theorists have yet to equal."[69] Trilling sympathized entirely with Ruskin's attack on the religion of laissez-faire and associated big business with fascism. Why, he asked, did the author of a book on Germany make "no mention of Fritz Thyssen and his mighty steel trust, now known to be the great power behind Hitler?"[70] Liberated from the need to bother about the Party and its troubling demands, Trilling could float free in the ether of revolutionary enthusiasm.

Trilling's freedom gave him license to map his own intellectual territory. He continued to examine the plight of the bourgeois intellectual, a subject he had first broached with some reluctance in "Carlyle." In a review essay, "The Comic Genius of Dickens," Trilling asked whether the literary techniques of Charles Dickens were sufficient to the task of writing revolutionary fiction. Was the literary darling of the nineteenth-century Anglo-American bourgeoisie a workable model for the communist writer of today? Trilling announced that the "necessity to think politically in terms of masses has been carried over with illegitimate literalness into art, and the creation of character is vaguely felt to be a sin. Yet it is a real question, whether the great revolutionary novel will not come close to Dickens' vital practice."[71] Trilling did not apologize for the hint of perversity in his question. In "The Coleridge Letters," Trilling offered another perverse insight: the combination of John Stuart Mill's liberalism and Samuel Coleridge's conservatism approximated the radical ideals of the 1930s. Coleridge's philosophy was one that "fascism, both in Italy and Germany, is now using to nationalize its fight against socialism." No worse thing could be said about any philosophy in 1933. Yet Trilling wrote, without disagreement, of Mill's belief "that the perfect state would be founded on combinations of the ideas of [the radical] Bentham and Coleridge—democracy and the centralized state, material well-being and cultural development, individual freedom and corporate loyalty."[72] However respectful Trilling was toward the pieties of his parents, he consciously and repeatedly mocked the pieties of the "radical mind."

Trilling's cherished independence did not go unnoticed among fellow independent radicals. He was coming to be known for his doubts and hesitations. In December 1933, Trilling wrote an angry letter to his Columbia colleague Meyer Schapiro, Chambers's close friend, responding to an allegation of professional opportunism. He stated that Schapiro had "ascribed my doubts and hesitations in political questions to a fear of losing my job." "If you really believe, as you seem to," he wrote sharply, "that there are no two ways of thinking about the particular form which the protest against Luther took, if you can really believe only practical-political considerations would make one hesitate to sign it, you are, to say the least, walking a very dangerous political path."[73] Written in anger, the letter is confusing. Was Trilling aligning himself with the Counter-Reformation of the Catholic Church, with "the protest against Luther"? If he was, it was an odd political analogy for the incipient anti-Stalinism of Hook and Trilling. Trilling defended the right to dissent from dissent, accusing Schapiro of radical dogmatism. If the only opposition to Luther could be "practical-political"—self-interest, in other words—then there is no need for intellectual doubt or hesitation. The "very dangerous political path" is submission to the accepted interpretations of the Communist Party. To assume that radicalism is necessarily good is to cede one's capacity for moral judgment. Trilling preferred to seem conservative (against Luther) than unthinking.

A more visceral dispute erupted at a rally in Madison Square Garden held on February 26, 1934. Socialists had organized the rally to protest the authoritarian policies of Austria's right-wing chancellor Engelbert Dollfuss whom they held responsible for murdering social democrats. Hook later conjectured that the "social fascism" thesis, not yet jettisoned in favor of the conciliatory Popular Front, "led the Communist Party violently to disrupt the rally."[74] Stalinists hurled chairs onto non-Stalinists.[75] The violence and brutality horrified many, including the Trillings. They signed a letter of protest to the *New Masses*, circulated by James Rorty, Herbert Solow, and Sidney Hook.[76] The signatories had undergone an important transformation. What had been kept private was now out in the open: the letter was, in Hook's estimation, "the first *public* protest against the Communist Party line by erstwhile fellow-travelers."[77] Leaving the NCDPP was a decision not to support the Party. Criticizing the Party openly—in the *New Masses* no less—was a far more radical step. Still, in breaking with the Party in 1934, neither Hook nor Trilling were abandoning the call of revolution.

As Trilling took his first public step away from the Party, Chambers went deeper into the communist underground. Trilling's discussions of revolutionary art were glib and unexamined compared with Chambers's total immersion in revolution. The moment revolution imposed itself on Trilling in the form of either propaganda (the NCDPP) or violence (the Madison Square Garden rally), he recoiled in disgust. Revolution was acceptable to him so long as he could remain a gentleman in its service. Chambers might have dressed like a "respectable bourgeois," but he knew himself to be in the service of a violent revolution. It was exactly this set of contrasts—between the revolutionary and the gentleman, between private conviction and Party membership—that described life in Chambers's "second apparatus." Joszef Peter, Chambers's boss in the underground, realized in 1934 that the radicalism of educated American professionals opened up spectacular new opportunities for espionage. Chambers also noticed a new breed of communists, "middle-class intellectuals who had gone directly underground without passing through the open party," and he was the ideal underground operative to work with them.[78] The idealism of the ineffectual "first apparatus" pleased Chambers; it was his first intoxicating taste of revolution. The second apparatus put Chambers where he had long dreamt of being, close to the levers of power. In Washington, D.C. he could be an actor on the historical stage with much to accomplish as the Popular Front was beginning to intersect with the New Deal and American radicalism was acquiring a touch of mainstream legitimacy.

The second apparatus was intimately bound up with the Popular Front. Hitler's consolidation of power had raised the prestige of the Soviet Union after 1933, and Stalin exploited the Soviet Union's popularity among

Western intellectuals by reversing the "social fascism" thesis: not all capitalist countries were equally fascist, America and the Soviet Union might jointly oppose European fascism, and American communists or fellow travelers did not have to choose between America and the Soviet Union. At the other side of the Popular Front was the New Deal, a new venture in American politics that was not socialist in theory or practice but that could be construed as proto-socialist. At the very least, the New Deal exposed the inadequacy of laissez-faire capitalism, and the New Deal brought a group of ambitious young radicals to Washington, D.C. The second apparatus, or Ware circle, used the Popular Front as camouflage. Harold Ware was the son of "Mother Bloor," a widely known Communist Party member and "a birthright member of the Communist Party," in Chambers's description.[79] Ware was passionately interested in agriculture and had served in the Department of Agriculture under Coolidge, leaving Washington in 1932 only to return in 1933 to "float" around the Department of Agriculture. He had also helped to organize a collective farm in Soviet Russia at Lenin's invitation.[80] Like Sidney Hook at Yaddo, Ware devoted himself to the work of conversion, recruiting promising government intellectuals to the communist underground in FDR's Washington. He edited *Facts and Figures*, a magazine about farm affairs that had a New Dealer readership as well as the backing of the Communist Party; one of its enthusiastic readers was Alger Hiss.[81] Other New Dealers who came under Ware's influence were John Abt, Henry Collins Jr., Lee Pressman, Nathan Witt, Victor Perlo, Charles Kramer, John Hermann, and Nathaniel Weyl.[82] They were New Dealers with sympathy for the Soviet Union, most of whom were at the Agricultural Adjustment Agency. According to Josephine Herbst, a novelist and the wife of John Hermann, members of the Ware circle "took great pride in their sense of conspiracy."[83] The Popular Front was sentimental and lazy by comparison with the Soviet underground.

Alger Hiss was a zealous member of the Ware circle, living out its many contradictions. He had excelled as an undergraduate at Johns Hopkins and excelled once again at Harvard Law School. Through working friendships with Oliver Wendel Holmes and Felix Frankfurter, Hiss entered early into the world of high politics. He did not confine himself to the conventional path of advancement within the Democratic Party. Instead, he joined the International Juridical Association, an organization dedicated to the discussion of labor law. It resembled the NCDPP in that its members were divided between liberals and communists.[84] As with Trilling in the early 1930s, Hiss was radical in part because his wife, Priscilla, was radical.[85] For a time, she belonged to the Morningside Heights branch of the Socialist Party. Often described as a kind of Popular Front archetype by admirers and detractors alike, Hiss thought of himself as a man of the 1920s. As he explained in his memoirs, "the avant-garde of the 1920s, in which I considered myself enlisted, was concerned chiefly with wit and iconoclasm." A charming detail from Hiss's memoirs is his introduction of Oliver Wendel Holmes (for whom Hiss clerked) "to T. S. Eliot, bringing him my volumes of Eliot's poems."[86] In the spring of 1933, Alger Hiss joined the Agricultural Adjustment Agency on the strength of a recommendation from Felix Frankfurter. A discussion circle with Harold Ware was the gateway from the iconoclastic 1920s to the radical 1930s.

Hiss and Chambers represented two distinct wings of the Party, both of which were secret. Chambers was known to the Ware circle as "Carl," a man with an identity so mysterious that, once again, he gave the impression of being a foreigner. Chambers's observation in *Witness*—that "Alger Hiss, like everybody else in the Washington underground, supposed that I was some kind of European"—is confirmed by the judgments of those who knew Chambers at the time.[87] Josephine Herbst met Chambers in Washington and believed "he was or might be, at least, European, perhaps Austrian."[88] If Chambers had various underground personae, Hiss also had multiple political identities—in essence, two. He was as an "exuberant recruiter" of others in government, persuading them to serve in one or another communist apparatus.[89] Yet Hiss also cut a dashing figure among non-communist New Dealers, someone who consistently impressed senior members of the political establishment, beginning with Holmes and continuing up to Franklin Roosevelt.[90] In 1935, Hiss worked on the Nye Committee at the Justice Department; in September 1936, he joined the State Department, working for Francis B. Sayre, then the assistant secretary of state. Hiss remained at the State Department, becoming head of the Office of Special Political Affairs, until he left for the Carnegie Endowment in 1946. He was also an assistant to Secretary of State Edward Stettinius. In *Witness*, Chambers wrote that Hiss held the New Deal establishment in contempt, as would make sense for a member of the communist underground. Hiss made "the most simple and brutal references to the President's physical condition as a symbol of the middle-class breakdown," and "Hiss's contempt for Franklin Roosevelt as a dabbler in revolution who understood neither revolution nor history was profound."[91]

Chambers's arrival in Washington as a courier for the Ware circle was the climax of his communist career. As an adolescent, Chambers had run away from home and worked as a day laborer in Washington, D.C., a bourgeois become proletarian overnight. The lowliness of his condition in 1919 made him feel exalted when he came to Washington in 1934, a Bolshevik revolutionary. He returned to Washington "as a secret agent of a revolutionary party which seemed conspicuously to embody in politics what, as a youth, I had unconsciously groped for in life." As in the first apparatus, Chambers found fulfillment in Washington because his work threw him together with educated, idealistic, and serious communists. His first friendship was with Harold Ware, the long-time communist of the group who, in Chambers's recollection, "had the same unromantic approach to conspiracy, the same appreciation of the difficulty of organizing intellectuals, and a common interest in farm problems." In 1934, the intent of the apparatus was not to commit espionage but to organize in secret with the eventual aim of influencing policy—"especially in the labor and welfare fields," Chambers recalled. The group Ware had assembled was formidable in educational pedigree, administrative experience, and—best of all—future political prospects. Ware's superior, Joszef Peter, could not resist bragging to Chambers: "Even in Germany under the Weimar Republic, the Party did not have what we have here."[92]

Joszef Peter may well have been right about the excellence of his apparatus. Hiss, for one, had much to offer his Soviet superiors. According to G. Edward White, "Hiss's placement, coupled with that of the British Soviet agent Donald Maclean, who held a high-level post in the British embassy in Washington from 1944 to 1949, meant that Stalin had a firm grasp of the postwar goals of the U.S. and Britain before the Yalta conference." Hiss would have had access to top-secret documents, and he requested "confidential information from the Office of Strategic Services on postwar atomic energy policy and the internal security of Britain, France, China and the Soviet Union. In this period Hiss had the sponsorship, with the State Department, of Hornbeck, Pasvolsky, Stettinius, and Assistant Secretary of State Dean Acheson."[93] As intriguing as it will remain elusive, the relationship between Hiss and Chambers flourished, according to Chambers.[94] One connection was a shared idealism. Like Chambers,

Hiss was drawn to the grandeur of revolution, and inwardly he was prone to an asceticism and simplicity that Chambers would label Quaker, "a profound suspicion of the pursuit of pleasure as an end in life, amounting to an antipathy merging with a deep distaste and distrust of materialism in its commonest forms of success and comfort."[95] Another connection between Hiss and Chambers was family. They were both fathers with young families, and, according to Chambers, their friendship entailed "the easy, gay, carefree association of two literate, very happy, fun-loving middle-class families."[96] One might infer two other connections between Hiss and Chambers: ambition and intellectualism. The rising bureaucrat who read T. S. Eliot as a law clerk was bound to appeal to Chambers; and the aspiring communist leader versed in Columbia's great books curriculum was bound to appeal to Hiss. The underground made possible their uncommon balance of respectability and revolution. In this manner, Chambers also participated in the disjointed spirit of the Popular Front.

By 1936, Stalin's Soviet Union had descended into the madness of purges and show trials.[97] No member of the underground could have remained impervious to the Moscow trials or to the purges that thinned the ranks of the Soviet underground, as they did the rest of Soviet society. In *Witness*, Chambers recalled a feeling of upset, although he saw "the Purge as the expression of a crisis within the group—the Communist Party—which I served in the belief that it alone could solve the crisis of the modern world."[98] He trained himself not to look. He simply did not read anti-communist books, "because I knew the party did not want me to read them." Even if he had read them, however, "I should not have believed them."[99] Chambers's intuition of disaster sustained his unwavering faith in communism. In a series of letters, written to Meyer Schapiro in the summer of 1936, Chambers espoused something like a theory of the future. America's backwardness in relation to world revolution would delay the inevitable reckoning or, as Chambers called it, "the final conflict." Reference to the final conflict was hopeful: "It will go very hard for us [communists] at first: all the sins of lost time and opportunity lost will have to be paid for in life: then the time will set for us, all that's decent in the world will begin to come to us." For Chambers, communist strategy had to be international, whatever Stalin had declared about "socialism in one country." Chambers predicted greater development in Asia than in the United States or Europe: "I still believe that in the end the East will be decisive for us; that the best we can hope for in the West will be to hold our own." To hold our own, it seems, was to avoid the loss of more West-ern countries to fascism. If defeating Japan "gives us [communists] China while we are still holding the West, we will be invincible—only, we must hold out in the West." When Chambers wrote about "we communists" to Schapiro, he meant those communists loyal to Stalin. He wrote about Trotsky without rancor and without high regard: "no battle could be won, I am confident; indeed, no serious fight can be fought under the leader-ship of LT [Leon Trotsky]."[100]

The first blow to Chambers's theory was the growing strength of Gen-eral Franco, and behind him of the Nazis, in the Spanish Civil War. Per-haps "we" could not hold out in the West. With the Spanish Civil War, Chambers's pessimism got the better of him. The thread of despair, to which communism was the only recourse, ran from his poetry in the late 1920s, to the short stories of 1931, to his letters in the summer of 1936. Spain proved once again that irreversible disaster was still possible: "what I read in tonight's papers makes me fear that the worst can happen." Yet it was precisely this despair that stimulated Chambers's desire to act. Like so many young radicals at the time, Chambers wanted to be in Spain: "I know that my child's future is being determined by our friends in those mountains [in Spain] and I would give a great deal to be there physically to help them." Here, "our friends" are presumably the republican forces or the Soviet elements within these forces. Whatever the outcome, the fi-nal conflict will elicit the heroism to which Chambers aspired as a com-munist: "we are isolated at least, we are surrounded. It may be terrifying, it is perilous, but it brings out the metal in us. I for one will go down fight-ing."[101] This could have been a line from one of Chambers's short stories.

Despising compromise, Chambers would find it difficult to understand the many compromises and "equivocal commitments" of the Popular Front, as experienced by those, like Trilling, who were not in the under-ground or the Party.[102] For Chambers, the Popular Front was a weapon in the Soviet arsenal, its concessions to bourgeois liberalism merely tactical. He did not believe that antifascism, in the words of François Furet, had rid "Soviet Communism of much of its antibourgeois aggressiveness," in perception if not in fact.[103] Therein lay the Popular Front's power of at-traction, although the embourgeoisement of the Left created its own problems.[104] The influx of middle-class intellectuals into the general am-biance of the Party, and the relaxed terms of this influx, dissolved the boundaries between liberalism and radicalism. The "Popular Front mind" was, therefore, many things. It was preeminently antifascist and pro-Soviet but its attitude toward America and the New Deal was muddled. How could Stalin's and FDR's aspirations be harmonized? One answer was in Sidney Hook's brand of Marxism, a tool to be used with pragmatism and the scientific method, an ideal philosophical underpinning for the Popular Front. One could be liberal and Marxist with help from Hook's pragmatist arguments, but by 1935, Hook was persona non grata among communists and an exile from the Popular Front because of his growing skepticism about the Soviet Union.[105] As liberals looked increasingly to the Soviet Union, Hook was shocked to discover "that hundreds of liberals . . . were prepared to turn their back on it [the American progressive heritage] when questions were raised about justice in the Soviet Union."[106]

Hook and other dissidents from the Popular Front had several reasons for their opposition. One was prior experience with communism of the sort that the Trillings had at the NCDPP. Another was the Soviet Union itself: the purges touching the underground were the stuff of daily newspapers in the mid-1930s. Hook described the Moscow trials and purges as a "turning point in the history of American liberalism, for it was irrevocably polarized by the controversies to which the trials gave rise."[107] To belong enthusiastically to the Popular Front was to deny either the existence or the importance of the purges.[108] In addition, the very popularity of the Popular Front engendered a counter-reaction. The Popular Front was chic, and its blending of fashion and politics had an air of hypocrisy about it. Mary McCarthy's memoirs contain two marvelous examples of this problem, the merging of downtown radicalism with uptown elitism. One was "at Dwight MacDonald's apartment near the river, on East 51st Street, I went to a cocktail party for the sharecroppers, wearing a big mustard-yellow sombrero-like hat from Tappé." Another was "a walkout in support of a waiters' strike at the Waldorf, which Johnsrud and I joined, also in evening dress—Eunice was wearing a tiara."[109] Finally, the Popular Front tended to attract an older generation of progressives against whom the youthful "New York intellectuals," striving for position and influence, defined themselves. In the mid-1930s no one could have known that the Popular Front was destined to collapse in 1939—the winds of opportunism could blow in any number of directions—but the sense of being against an errant establishment lent energy and purpose to the dissidents.[110]

Trilling, following once again in Hook's footsteps, was a skeptical dissident from the Popular Front, not a self-declared enemy. He tried to bore from within the world of progressive politics, lingering over the disturbing insight and writing to the gray areas of radical thought. He worked from the foundation erected in "Carlyle," probing the instability of radicalism as practiced by middle-class intellectuals. If he had hit upon his idea of the "adversary culture" in the 1920s, he refined and developed it in the early 1930s. Indeed, the Popular Front gave him wonderful material on the rising adversary culture. "The literate middle class caught up with the intellectual middle class," Trilling observed of recent cultural history in 1936. He meant that a middle-class readership was adopting the ideas and ideals of the intellectual avant-garde, a rapprochement that would have been hard to imagine in the vulgar 1920s. In the 1930s the Soviet Union was a bridge between the progressive middle class and the intellectuals. By 1935, Trilling was no longer writing with reference to Marxism or to the Soviet Union per se. When writing about the Soviet alternative, he was scrutinizing its attraction to educated middle-class Americans. The radicalism of "Forced Labor" had faded. He had changed, perhaps without even knowing it himself, from a mild-mannered devotee of the Soviet alternative to a kind of American Freud, reflecting on the illusions from which the bourgeoisie was taking its ethics.

Trilling's dissent from radical orthodoxy did not translate into a celebration of liberalism. History had exposed liberalism as too close to laissez-faire economics, too implicated in private property, and too connected to liberal "weakness" against the fascist enemy. Trilling's attitude indicated resignation, as if one had no choice but to go with the historical winners—not quite Stalin in 1935, and emphatically not Trotsky, but something loosely communist. In July 1934, Trilling published "Politics and the Liberal," a review of a biography written by novelist E. M. Forster. Goldsworthy Lowes Dickenson (1862–1932), the subject of Forster's biography, represented the liberal humanitarianism of his generation in England. Dickenson and his contemporaries "were men of good-will whose remoteness from reality, interests, and forces allowed them to serve unwittingly the predatory and the evil-willed." The predators were, presumably, the capitalists and imperialists who had corrupted the bourgeois ethos. Trilling brought up Dickenson's ethic—"based on individual 'understanding' and 'tolerance' "—to conclude that "history has proved them to be catchwords that becloud reality in the service of the worst 'passions and interests.' However, "in personal life these virtues are still real."[111] Liberal humanitarianism might remain a private code even after history damaged it beyond repair in politics.

Trilling had no lasting faith in the Soviet alternative. He was confused, a dissenter from the Party line, and a pessimist about the "liberal-humanitarian tradition." Trilling was also writing a dissertation on Matthew Arnold, and he fell back on Arnold's example when defending individual autonomy and responsibility—liberal principles par excellence—in a re-view of the Popular Front novelist James Farrell. Farrell elevated spiritual poverty above material poverty, Trilling felt, and "when we observe the de-feat of his characters we also observe the deterioration of communal institutions—the family, the school, the church." In Trilling's view such de-terioration implies the need for high culture; it is a "debasement [that] stands as the perpetual denial of the vaunt of culture and intellect." Trilling used Arnold's notion of literary adequacy to criticize Farrell. Adequate liter-ature is either comprehensive in the manner of Joyce's *Ulysses*, fully cap-turing the life of a city and a culture, or it is ethically alive. For the latter to be the case, characters must be "able to act, even mistakenly, and, by act-ing, to affirm the qualities essential to decent humans."[112] Farrell's charac-ters cannot "be engaged in morally significant action because the essence of the truth about them is that society has robbed them of the principles of free will."[113] Perhaps, as literature tells us, liberal autonomy is superior to radical determinism.

Trilling was not alone in feeling that literature should be set free from the constraints of radical dogma. *Partisan Review*, the magazine that would create the New York intellectuals, appeared in 1934, a communist magazine that belonged to New York's communist John Reed Club; the "first" *Partisan Review* would last from 1934 to 1936. Although initially a communist magazine, *Partisan Review* had communist ambitions that were doomed from the outset. The magazine's editors William Phillips and Philip Rahv were the victims of an illusion, Freud's indispensable word for the generation that came of age in the 1930s. Phillips recalled that "Rahv and I had the illusion that a new literary publication could be an organ for those radical writers who had no use for the party-line aes-thetics of the *New Masses*, and that it could be open to talent, regardless of politics."[114] Their primary allegiance was to literary modernism, which, in its hostility to bourgeois civilization, could be construed as con-tinuous with Soviet communism. The party-line aesthetics, however, were socialist realist, a retrograde and boring constraint in the eyes of *Partisan Review*'s editors. Socialist realism exposed as an impossibility the synthesis of political radicalism and high culture. Rahv and Phillips did not found *Partisan Review* to go against the Party, but almost immediately they "were coming to the conclusion that an independent literary movement could not exist within the orbit of the official Communist party."[115]

Like the editors of the first *Partisan Review*, Trilling remained within the world of radical politics even as he resisted the Party's version of radicalism, a subversive critic from within the fold.[116] He was still an intellectual of "good-will," emotionally sympathetic to the aims of the Left, but these aims became ever more distant after 1933. Meanwhile, conservative possibilities occupied his attention. Was it possible that the conservative Wordsworth was a better poet than the radical Wordsworth, the young poet who celebrated the French Revolution? It was indeed. In 1935, Trilling wrote to Malcolm Cowley that the Marxist critic cannot simply applaud Wordsworth's radicalism. "When Wordsworth was a revolutionary sympathizer," Trilling wrote, "he took up, along with his passion for mankind, a pretty shoddy philosophy."[117] Nor could one easily disdain Wordsworth's conservatism because "Wordsworth was writing very poor poetry during the time of his revolutionary sympathies and very good poetry when he gave them up."[118] Trilling was denying any simple connection between progressive politics and a worthwhile culture. Trilling understood disinterest in conservative ideas as an unfortunate corollary of radical commitment. While still a radical, Trilling read George Santayana's *The Last Puritan* with great appreciation, despite Santayana's indifference to socialism and his Henry Adams-esque contempt for the modern world. In 1936, Trilling wrote that he found Santayana's novel "so very fine and moving," explaining that "I still like *The Last Puritan* greatly and would like to undertake its exposition because I conceive that no one understands it right."[119] He did not mention the Popular Front, but it was obvious that the Popular Front's celebration of proletarian life and culture could not be reconciled with the aristocratic refinement of Santayana, who was so traumatized by American vulgarity that he lived in Europe. Trilling wanted an intellectual culture large enough to balance cogent progressive politics with antiradical, even conservative literature. This led him directly away from the Popular Front.

In a penetrating essay on Eugene O'Neill, Trilling fashioned a critical analysis of the Popular Front, using literary criticism as political commentary. Trilling wrote that "we do not read Sophocles and Aeschylus for the right answer; we read them for the force with which they represent life and attack its moral complexity." "We" may have misread O'Neill, seeing a genial progressive in him, while his spiritual biography is both conservative and terrifying. First O'Neill worshipped the power of nature, forging a "noble and realistic attitude" that allowed him to face the hard, tragic truths of life. Ultimately, he was unable bear these truths. He "lived for years in a torturing struggle with the rationalistic, questioning 'half' of himself which has led him away from piety to atheism, thence to socialism, next to unchastity and finally to the oblique attempt to understand his beloved wife." Like Carlyle, O'Neill chose not to remain a radical; O'Neill became a Catholic, a conversion that began for him in nihilism. Trilling emphasized the element of choice: "O'Neill feels that life is empty—having emptied it—and can only fill it by faith in a loving God." Trilling did not see O'Neill's journey away from radicalism as worth emulating, for it negated intellect and denied all but Catholic dogma: "the annihilation of the questioning mind also annihilates the multitudinous world."[120] In failing to keep up his "tragic affirmation," O'Neill lost his awareness of the multitudinous world. O'Neill's readers and critics would have to preserve their own resources of imagination if they were to avoid a similar fate.

Sponsors of the Popular Front, the middle-class followers of O'Neill, have substituted cheap reassurance for sincere terror. On the surface, O'Neill was an obvious enemy of the middle class. He was "an integral part—indeed, he became the very symbol—of that Provincetown group which represented the growing rebellion of the American intellectual against a business civilization." Such were the terms of opposition in the 1920s when Alger Hiss was reading T. S. Eliot. On the one side stood artists and intellectuals, armed with books and good taste, on the other stood a multitude of Babbits. By the 1930s many of the Babbits had taken note and were joyfully attending O'Neill's plays. The middle class had split in two—those trapped in a vulgar mainstream culture and those attuned to the avant-garde's critique of the middle class—and Trilling stressed the paradox of this division: "it developed, strangely, that the American middle class had no strong objection to being attacked and torpedoed; it seemed willing to be sunk for the insurance that was paid in a new strange coin. The middle class found that it consisted of two halves, bourgeoisie and booboisie."[121] If the booboisie was the object of satire and condemnation, the bourgeoisie warmly received and interpreted the art of the adversary culture, enjoying its artistic triumphs and admitting the truth of its harsh antibourgeois criticism. Yet this criticism was somehow true of others and not of themselves.

The adversary culture lost much of its seriousness through its popular currency, and the bourgeoisie did not allow O'Neill to trouble its idealism. Sounding like the Freud whom Trilling had dismissed only a few years ago, Trilling observed that "whoever writes sincerely about the middle class must consider the nature and the danger of the morality of 'ideals,' those phosphorescent remnants of dead religion with which the middle class meets the world." These ideals could be reinforced, paradoxically, through bourgeois condescension toward the booboisie. O'Neill was no longer truly radical for the bourgeoisie that "helped the Washington Square Players to grow into the Theater Guild."[122] Rather, his rebellion took on the curious guise of custom and convention, and "beneath the iconoclasm his audience sensed reassurance." The staged radicalism of the adversary culture insulated the middle class from the unsettling force of writers like Sophocles, Aeschylus, and O'Neill. It was this force that Trilling was defending, even when it joined hands with conservative Catholicism. In a highly rhetorical conclusion, Trilling returned to O'Neill's conversion. In becoming a Catholic, "O'Neill has crept into the dark womb of the Mother Church and pulled the universe in with him. Perhaps the very violence of the gesture with which he has taken the position of passivity should remind us of his force and of what such force may yet do even in that static and simple dark." O'Neill's cultural assault on the middle class took him not to communism but to a reactionary view of the world. He ended as someone who "finds the attack on capitalism almost an attack upon God, scorns socialism and is disgusted with the weakness of those who are disgusted with social individualism."[123] The "Popular Front mind"—and with it the progressive bourgeoisie—could only handle O'Neill if it twisted his ideas out of shape and denied him his genuine force.

As communists who came of age before the Popular Front, Trilling and Chambers wanted to help the masses, but their experience with American communism confined them to the progressive middle class, to O'Neill's self-congratulatory audience. Trilling and Chambers were drawn to the Soviet alternative out of a concern for economic dislocation, the crisis of forced labor at home, of capitalism gone awry, and the problem of Europe's future in an era of mass politics. While the Soviet

Union had answers, solutions, and visions on a massive scale, America deprived its communists of a radical mass movement. Neither Trilling nor Chambers worked with unions or with farmers; neither sat in endless meetings with working-class comrades, absorbing the Party's changing arguments and following its dictates; neither moved with the masses in demonstrations or in some great uprising, an American storming of the Winter Palace. Trilling's radicalism was expressed in book reviews that only the educated middle class could read. Chambers served the revolution directly, although he, too, was working with the educated middle class, with men like Alger Hiss and not with a grassroots movement. Trilling and Chambers were themselves sons of the bourgeoisie: their alienation from the American working class only intensified their involvement with communism in the 1930s, which captured only a small segment of the American working class.[124] The authors of *Culture and the Crisis* knew this all too well when they promised to vote communist in 1932. Had American communism been capable of revolution or civil war, the independence that Trilling enjoyed as a communist literary critic would have been constrained and ultimately impossible. Had Chambers become a commissar in a communist regime, he would not have founded a middle-class family, and he would not have lunched with independent-minded intellectuals who were not Party members.

From a national perspective, American communism was small-scale and ephemeral, but to Trilling and Chambers, and to many in their exotic world, the Soviet alternative mattered more than Franklin Roosevelt's New Deal. The 1930s, for Trilling and Chambers alike, were equivalent to the American encounter with communism, and, in the telling words of William Phillips, editor of *Partisan Review*, "the thirties were the cradle of our entire epoch."[125]

3

KRONSTADT

The Break

The time comes when each one of us has to give up as illusions
the expectations which, in his youth, he pinned upon his
fellow-men, and when he may learn how much difficulty and
pain has been added to his life by their ill-will.

—SIGMUND FREUD, *Civilization and Its Discontents*

At a 1938 Halloween party in Brooklyn, "masks, pumpkins, skeletons
were everywhere." The mood was jovial until an uninvited guest arrived. Soon after he entered the brownstone apartment, "a whisper,
'Whittaker Chambers is here!' spread to every corner of the house," recalled Sidney Hook, who was at the party. "Even those to whom the
name meant nothing were conscious of the sudden hush that fell on
the assemblage." The invited guests were there to celebrate the work of
the Commission of Inquiry, a mock trial of Leon Trotsky directed by John
Dewey. The Commission's conclusion—that Trotsky was innocent—flatly
contradicted the official position of the Soviet government, making the
commission's supporters into anti-Stalinists. All present were anti-
Stalinists, including Chambers, who had recently broken with the Communist Party. By attending the Halloween party he hoped to shake off the
obscurity of the underground. Having a public identity, he reasoned,
would inhibit the Soviet underground from killing him. Yet the anti-
Stalinists at the party did not welcome Chambers into their ranks. They
thought he was still a spy and, as such, an unwelcome representative of
Stalin's Soviet Union. "More than one guest mockingly greeted him:
'Whose ghost are you?' " remembered Diana Trilling, an invited guest.
About an hour after arriving, "Chambers left with the same fixed and
sickly smile on his face with which he entered," in Hook's recollection.[1]

Chambers inspired enmity where he had hoped to gain trust. It must have been especially painful to him that the wife of his college classmate, Diana Trilling, whom he had once asked for assistance in underground work, snubbed him at the party. On seeing Chambers, Diana "did not feel friendly to an agent of Stalin who could have the blood of innocent people on his hands." And so, "as Chambers came up to see me, I put my hand behind my back," she recalled, while "Chambers flushed and turned away." Diana's hostility was so palpable that Herbert Solow wrote to Lionel and Diana Trilling after the party. Solow was a fellow alumnus of *The Morningside* and *The Menorah Journal*, and he was Chambers's friend. It was Solow who brought Chambers to the Halloween party. "I was unaware that you guys had antagonism or distaste for Whit," he wrote to the Trillings, "though in any case I should, had I thought about the matter more carefully, have guessed in advance that there would have been discomfort among friends who do not know as much as I do about Whit's situation."[2] Solow's good intentions were in vain; the friends to whom Solow referred would retain their discomfort. Chambers would not forget the humiliation dealt him by Diana Trilling and others at the party. Liberating as the moment may have been for Chambers, signaling his reentry into polite society, it was also metaphoric of the schisms to come.[3] The break with Stalinism created no stable party of anti-Stalinists.

Lionel Trilling and Whittaker Chambers arrived at the same point, at their "Kronstadt," only to part ways forever. In the vicinity of Leningrad, Kronstadt was the site of a 1921 uprising that pitted sailors against the Bolshevik high command. The Bolsheviks' violent suppression of the revolt and their execution and imprisonment of the sailors caused some early fellow travelers to question their enthusiasm for the Soviet Union. The trauma of reckoning with state-sponsored violence at Kronstadt created the term, *Kronstadt*, shorthand for the disavowal of the Soviet experiment, a moment of psychological as well as political transformation. In *The God That Failed*, a compendium of Kronstadts, Louis Fischer observed that "what counts decisively is the 'Kronstadt.' Until its advent, one may waver emotionally or doubt intellectually or even reject the cause altogether in one's mind and yet refuse to attack it."[4] Trilling and Chambers wavered many times, enduring emotional and intellectual doubts about the communist cause, but they were only able to attack it toward the end of the 1930s. No single event precipitated their respective Kronstadts, nor can one say with precision when their moments of Kronstadt occurred. The Moscow trials and purges of the mid-1930s eroded their faith, eventually threatening Chambers's life. They prompted Trilling to sever an ever thinning band of affection between himself and the Soviet Union. When the Trillings and Chambers happened upon each other in Brooklyn—among the pumpkins, masks, and skeletons—the Trillings still regarded Chambers as a spy. Chambers considered Trilling a mere Trotskyite and, hence, no true comrade in anti-Stalinism.

The intellectuals' exodus from the camp of the Soviets began in 1936. *Partisan Review* reappeared in 1937, the heyday of the Popular Front, when the American Left had drawn as close as it ever would to the Soviet Union.[5] The Right was in disarray, held in especial disrepute among 1930s intellectuals whose Spenglerian gloom about the cultural consequences of democracy was in remission. To dissent from the orthodoxies of the Popular Front, the antifascist coalition par excellence, was to invite the dreaded label of conservatism. "To be critical of the Soviet Union, in that general climate [of the Popular Front]," recalled William Barrett, an editor at the second *Partisan Review*, "was to be immediately consigned to the Right, where in fact most of the doubts of the Soviet Utopia were being expressed."[6] United and powerful as the Popular Front might have appeared in retrospect, the emergence of the second *Partisan Review* in 1937 marked a fatal fragmentation in the Popular Front ethos. Instead of abandoning the Left, the *Partisan Review* anti-Stalinists were challenging the Communist Party's claim to it. "The Communists were more opposed to and more afraid of liberal and Marxist critics than they were of conservatives," wrote William Phillips in his memoirs, "and perhaps rightly so, for a challenge from the left tended to cut the ground from under their radical claims and pretensions while one from the right made them feel politically more virtuous." A formidable presence since its inception in 1937, the second *Partisan Review* would only grow larger in stature. "What I was witnessing was the breakup of the Party's virtual monopoly on the thought of the left," wrote Mary McCarthy, referring to the anti-Stalinist circle crystallizing around *Partisan Review* in 1937 and 1938. Kronstadts were cropping up everywhere, and *Partisan Review* was there to reap the harvest.[7]

Trilling's literary criticism was pivotal to the anti-Stalinism of *Partisan Review*. To a very great extent, the *Partisan Review* intellectual was a literary intellectual, and in the world of *Partisan Review* the brutality of Stalin had its echo in the philistinism of socialist realism and the aesthetic narrow-mindedness of the fellow-traveling critic. The hope of the second *Partisan Review* was that good taste in literature and wisdom in politics would reinforce each other. Hence, the "Editorial Statement" of December 1937, which implied that *Partisan Review* would forge ahead by going back to the modernist magazines of the 1920s: "the forms of literary editorship, at once exciting and adventurous, which characterized the magazines of aesthetic revolt, were of definite cultural value; and these forms *Partisan Review* will wish to adopt to the literature of the new period." The revolt against vulgarity might have been a-political in the 1920s or perhaps vaguely socialist, but in 1937 this same revolt was a move for political as well as aesthetic emancipation—an emancipation from the communist Left. "Formerly associated with the Communist Party," the "Editorial Statement" continued, "*Partisan Review* strove from the first against its drive to equate the interests of literature with those of factional politics. Our reappearance on an independent basis suggests our conviction that the totalitarian trend is inherent in that movement and that it can no longer be combated from within." In private correspondence, Trilling defended *Partisan Review* against the assaults of the fellow-traveling *New Republic* by calling *Partisan Review* "the only organ of the left to take culture seriously."[8]

Trilling had extensive training for such combat. The experience of communist sympathy followed by a Kronstadt was generally a prerequisite for the *Partisan Review* intellectual, and Trilling's Kronstadt was complete by 1936.[9] In August 1936, Trilling described his change of heart. "A letter isn't any place to talk about the Russian business: it needs a novel or an autobiography," he explained, as if anticipating his own novel, *The Middle of the Journey* (published in 1947), and Chambers's autobiography, *Witness* (published in 1952). "Everybody I know is very confused and dejected, I know that, though for long my feelings about Russia have been mixed enough to make me try to be philosophical." Trilling's language gives the impression of lost faith without anything very tangible to put in its place. "I feel now that I must completely overhaul all my ideas and my whole character," he confessed, "but all this settles nothing for me: except to convince me that I must always have a reservation of faith in anything." The Marxist dawn fades, as a kind of Freudian dusk sets in: "the revolutionary heroes—and they were certainly that—were disgusting; Russia was disgusting. Perhaps every revolution must betray itself. Perhaps every good thing and every good man has the seeds of degeneration in it or him."[10] A personal account of the "Russian business" would have to wait until long after the 1930s; the combat against Stalinism was to begin immediately.

Trilling leapt into the anti-Stalinist fray with a book review suggestively titled "Marxism in Limbo," an attack on the "Popular Front mind." Trilling addressed himself to a liberal audience rather than to a communist or a radical one, although the fallacies he was addressing were interrelated and not at all limited to radicals. As he wrote to the editors of the *Nation* in April 1937, correcting a misquote of Trotsky, Trilling felt that "liberals serve no good end at all when they cease to look for truth and, in the name of 'action' . . . substitute wish-thinking and rationalization for the functions of the critical intellect." However misguided, wish-thinking and rationalization might still be the consequence of good intentions. In "Marxism in Limbo," Trilling attributed malign intentions, an "authoritarian nihilism," to the progressive camp, which masked evil in an impermeable self-righteousness. This self-righteousness Trilling called the Angelic Fallacy, "which concludes that when a writer is, generally speaking, on the side of the angels—Mr. Briffault [author of *Europa in Limbo*, the book Trilling was reviewing] is a well known hater of chaos and injustice—he must for some reason be admirable and the expressed grounds of his partisanship sound." Briffault's stridency was proof, for Trilling, "that the angelic forces are in a state of desperation or irresponsibility: nothing could make them accept Mr. Briffault's authoritarian nihilism as intelligence or his spleen as anger."[11] Trilling's message was clear: liberals should absent themselves from the side of the angels.

Trilling's anti-Stalinist review was an appeal to liberal values, to reason and skepticism, and a pointed separation of these values from the communist movement.[12] With a touch of irony, he reversed a common lesson of Marxism: "if there is one thing the dialectic of history teaches it is an attitude on cultural matters the very opposite of the splenetic one. But that attitude is difficult and complex, while the attitude of spleen and vulgarity is simple and easy . . . rejecting all history, it believes that all good has been born with itself." The reduction of history and politics to a glorification of the Left is an abdication of intellectual responsibility. Complacent appeals to virtue offer no resistance to the practice of evil, and Trilling left little ambiguity about the evil of communism, which "wants not so much a liberated humanity as a sterilized humanity and it would gladly make a wasteland if it could call the silence peace."[13] Trilling hated the intellectual climate created by the Popular Front, which he described in a letter as "the greatest obfuscation going on under a cloud of seeming 'realistic' idealism." The Spanish Civil War was eliciting calculated distortions of the truth from fellow travelers: "The Spanish business, underneath, is the most depressing for those who, like me, know something about the situation, but I live surrounded by the clouds of complex and subtle misinterpretation," Trilling continued. Critical thought was subjected to censure, practiced not just by the Party but by liberals as well: "one has only to open one's mouth to have all the liberals, good, wise people feel that one is reactionary."[14]

Worst of all, for Trilling, many Stalinists were liberals and some liberals were Stalinists. By tethering themselves to the Soviet ideal, liberals had absorbed the political as well as the cultural assumptions of the radical Left. Trilling hoped to create a new type of liberal, armed with new assumptions; he was to be the first of the kind. He had already eschewed radicalism and revolution, as was clear from a 1938 letter to the *New Republic*. "Although my contempt for the cultural attitudes of the *New Masses* is perhaps even greater than Mr. [Malcolm] Cowley's [an editor at the *New Republic*], I am not a Trotskyist," he explained.[15] It is hard to say what he was. The disinterest in Trotsky placed him somewhat to the Right of *Partisan Review* in 1938. Yet he remained well within the magazine's ambiance. Terminology was becoming tangled. Liberals like Alger Hiss might have worked in government as respectable New Dealers, but they were liberal and pro-Soviet—Stalinists in the parlance of *Partisan Review*. Communist Party members and supporters were Stalinists by definition. Likewise, in 1938 conservatives were by definition anti-communists. Trotskyists might resolve their problem of leftist anti-Stalinism by repeating Trotsky's arguments about a revolution betrayed.[16] Trilling was an anomalous figure in 1938, a liberal anti-communist; but he was a subtle maverick, not an aggressive heretic, at a time of fluidity. Many lines that would later divide anti-Stalinists from each other had yet to be drawn.

Trilling presented the Popular Front as progressive and middle class, objecting to "that liberal-radical highmindedness that is increasingly taking the place of thought among the 'progressive-professional and middle class forces' and that now, under the name of 'good will' shuts out half the world." Writing in a tone of sarcasm and mockery that was as characteristic of his writing as detachment and irony, Trilling tried to demonstrate the inadequacy of mere purity: "it is hard to believe that the declaration of anti-fascism is nowadays any more a mark of sufficient grace in a writer than a declaration against disease would be in a physician or a declaration against accidents would be in a locomotive engineer." Purity leads to hypocrisy: "the progressive professional and middle class forces are framing a new culture, based on the old liberal-radical culture but designed now to hide the new anomaly by which they live their intellectual and emotional lives. For they must believe, it seems, that imperialist arms advance proletarian revolution, that oppression by the right people brings liberty." The imperialist arms and oppression, one gathers, are the aspects of American capitalism that Popular Front advocates have chosen to overlook. This was easy enough for middle class intellectuals who know "that within they are true proletarian men when they wrap themselves in Early American togas," but they are only deceiving themselves.[17] For the radical intellectual enamored of the Popular Front, "fascism is conceived not as a force which complicates the world but as a force which simplifies it"— harsh criticism from Trilling.[18]

The editors of *Partisan Review* also saw the Popular Front as a middle-class endeavor, reflecting a more conventional middle class than the one Trilling had in mind. For them, the middle class Left was vulgar and foolish in the way one might expect any bourgeoisie to be vulgar and foolish, and the *Partisan Review* committed itself to an adversary culture, aligned against this middle class. In the pages of the second *Partisan Review*, Edmund Wilson summarized Flaubert's *L'Éducation Sentimentale* in the following words: it inspires "the suspicion that our middle class society, and people who live and deal in investments, so far from being redeemed by its culture, has ended by cheapening and invalidating culture; politics, science and art . . . til the whole civilization has seemed to dwindle." This suspicion could be applied to Stalin's Soviet Union, with its growing bureaucracy, its materialism, its attachment to kitsch and other such petit-bourgeois vulgarity in culture. André Gide, a French man of letters and former communist, made this argument in *Partisan Review*, withdrawing his support for the Soviet Union in an essay titled "Second Thoughts on the U.S.S.R." He supplied his American readers with a capsule version of his political development: "I had come as an enthusiast [to the Soviet Union], I was totally convinced, I was prepared to admire a new world, and they offered me, as seductions mind you, all the prerogatives I abominated in the old . . . The new bourgeoisie forming there has all the faults of ours."[19] The revolution could not have been more bitterly betrayed than by yielding a Soviet bourgeoisie.

Philip Rahv and William Phillips decried the Popular Front for being bourgeois, not despite its pro-Soviet stance, but because of it. Such was the ugly truth behind "the People's front regime of ambiguity in politics and literature alike." It encouraged capitalism in the United States, Stalinism in the Soviet Union, and fascism in Europe. No amount of antifascist rhetoric could obscure the alliance between fascism and American capitalism, they argued. Wrapping oneself in the early American toga was foolish because America's political heritage was tied to the catastrophic legacy of John Locke and Adam Smith. By praising Jefferson and FDR, fans of the Popular Front ask us to "defend what we already possess, namely, our beautiful bourgeois democracy," Rahv wrote. The *Partisan Review* editors were still revolutionaries, and they were unsullied by commitment to either the United States or the Soviet Union. For them, the New Deal was grotesque and reactionary. "Even if the New Deal is heart and soul for the masses," they argued, "and we don't believe that it is— when capitalist decline has reached a certain point, it will have to decide whether to defend the capitalist state at all costs, or to overthrow it."[20]

After his Kronstadt, Trilling retained fragments of the 1930s radical ethos. He was, for example, unwilling to endorse any political entity complicit with capitalism or nationalism, which were understood to be the twin causes of fascism. In line with the editorials in *Partisan Review*, Trilling rejected the entry of the United States into World War II, accepting the editors' isolationist purview. The *Partisan Review* editors scorned prowar intellectuals for "tying themselves to the bourgeois war machine . . . [and giving] up their privilege—and duty—of criticizing ruling class values." The war was being fought by the wrong powers for the wrong reasons with the effect of "diverting us from the main task: to work with the masses for socialism, which alone can save our civilization." Trilling did not disagree: "I have very strongly the belief," he wrote in September 1940, "that if Roosevelt is elected there may well be war and the most enormous sabotage by the manufacturers." The *Partisan Review* position was painfully disassociated from any political party or constituency, a price paid for opposing the Soviet Union *and* the United States, not to mention the more moderate parties of the Left, like Norman Thomas's Socialists. Philip Rahv urged a "struggle against capitalism in all its modern guises and disguises, including bourgeois democracy, fascism, and reformism (social democracy, Stalinism)."[21] The hope was that the revolution would somehow swallow Stalin and move on, without

Stalin, to the worldwide eradication of capitalism. Until then, they would all be in the political wilderness.

As in the debate over World War II, Trilling adhered to the general position of the *Partisan Review* circle regarding Jewish questions. Jewish subjects and issues had receded from his writing since the *Menorah Journal* years (1924 to 1930). Communism was an internationalist persuasion, and the anti-Stalinism of *Partisan Review* was not in principle any less internationalist than the communism that had preceded it. In a 1937 review of *The Brothers Ashkenazi*, a novel by the Polish-Jewish writer I. J. Singer, Trilling conveyed his disillusionment with Stalin without embracing any distinctively Jewish alternative to communism, such as Zionism or a closer identification with Jewish life in America. For Trilling, the tragedy Singer outlines is essentially the tragedy of modern times. *The Brothers Ashkenazi* "is perhaps the basic story of our age—the story of the effect of industrialization on a traditional culture." Sounding a bit reactionary himself, Trilling mentioned as assumed knowledge the story "of how the machine impinges upon, then absorbs and destroys the old ways, breaking community bonds, negating tradition, attenuating religion. The old virtues—or many of them—become as pointless as the old methods of production and people give them up, or look about for new ones." Modernity impinges on Jews, in other words, in the way it impinges on all peoples.[22]

A defender of the old virtues, Trilling did not see Zionism as a worthy vehicle for modern political virtue. Trilling affiliated himself with a post-Jewish modernity, although he acknowledged "the contradictions of the organization of modern life." One such is capitalism, described in the review as "the struggle of rich Jew against poor Jew." Another is communism, "the belief that racial hatred will immediately disappear in the common struggle of Jewish and Gentile proletariat." No less illusory or dangerous is Zionism, that "mad parody of European nationalism, Jewish sectional pride." The organization of modern life is impossibly difficult, it seems, a difficulty Trilling attributed to Singer, although it was also implicit to Trilling's own sentiments. "If Mr. Singer seems to have some hope for Palestine," Trilling wrote wearily in conclusion, "we know that it will receive and perpetuate the contradictions."[23] Directed as the review was to the choices confronting European Jews, it was an essay that endorsed no single choice. There was no political solution to the anti-Semitic racial hatred that was then spreading across Europe. Trilling recognized that European Jews faced great adversity. Yet a world that offered only communist and capitalist answers was simply too contradictory to admit worthwhile solutions. Here Trilling was all too representative a member of the *Partisan Review* circle of the late 1930s. Without pro-Soviet blinders, they could diagnose the dilemmas of capitalism and communism with impunity and brilliance and still be at a loss for a usable way forward.

Trilling and the *Partisan Review* circle were politically disoriented as a result of their Kronstadts, progressives without a plan for progress. In "Realism and the Old Order," Trilling wrote, referring to the family at *The Brothers Ashkenazi*'s center, that "capitalism gave them more freedom and scope to injure more people."[24] Such was his position in 1937, and such was emphatically the position of the second *Partisan Review*. For both Trilling and the *Partisan Review* editors, the travesties of Stalinism did not add any luster to the capitalist system, even if, for Trilling, the loss of Marxist passion was liberating rather than stultifying. He had his mission. He was at war with those who, like him, claimed liberalism as their cause but who touted Stalin as their hero. He was less radical than Phillip Rahv, less involved with the radical Left, and at the same time less reactionary. The reactionary rejection of modern life and its historical protagonist, the bourgeoisie, had troubled Trilling since he was a college undergraduate. Perhaps there were unexplored resources in the bourgeoisie; perhaps there were resources within modern culture that might ultimately lead to decent political attitudes. To be a reactionary like Carlyle or Eugene O'Neill was easier than to look for affirmation in bourgeois life; it was also to admit defeat and to invite despair. Because it was antibourgeois, *Partisan Review* had proven that one could be anti-Stalinist while still being radical, with little need after 1937 to fear the conservative label. One risked the conservative label by betraying bourgeois proclivities, and an enduring suspicion would shadow Trilling in the *Partisan Review* circle: that for all his talk of liberalism this eminent bourgeois was at heart a conservative.

A reactionary element had been pronounced in Whittaker Chambers's character since his college years. He hated cities. He hated the culture made possible by machines and the world created by the industrial revolution. He preferred faith to reason. Reactionary leanings were problematic for a servant of the Bolshevik state, for the Bolsheviks aspired to create the most modern of all societies, cleansed of the corruption that was Russia's ancien régime. The Bolsheviks would liberate humanity with the factory and the tractor and the city, vowing, as Stalin put it, to be engineers of human souls. Soviet Russia would leave behind the church, the family, and the village as it built the socialist city on a hill. Chambers would never cease to dislike the bourgeoisie, and his Kronstadt involved the slow realization that Soviet society had the flaws of the Western bourgeoisie, that it, too, was beholden to the flaws of the modern world. As did the *Partisan Review* editors, Chambers held the modern qualities of Stalin's Soviet Union responsible for its fascist hue, and he was freed by his Kronstadt to pursue "reactionary options," to move out of the city forever. Chambers's Kronstadt and his turn to the Right were gradual developments more than they were abrupt decisions. There were stages along the way, and the way itself was complicated, at times tortuously so. Chambers had no common path to follow, unlike Trilling who operated within the *Partisan Review* circle. Chambers's Kronstadt had more than intellectual or even personal implications for him; it had a possible bearing on the relationship between the United States and the Soviet Union as well as on the tenor of domestic politics, sufficient reason to put his life in jeopardy.[25] Some time in 1936 Chambers read an obituary of Dmitri Schmidt, a Red Army general killed in the purges. The obituary stated simply that Schmidt had been tried and executed. In *Witness*, Chambers wrote that at the time he did "not know why I read and reread this brief obituary or why there came over me a foreboding, an absolute conviction, something terrible is happening."[26] In 1936, it was the second time he had felt such foreboding; the root cause, Stalinism, was the same.

One catalyst in Chambers's Kronstadt was his new superior, Colonel Boris Bykov, whose paranoia and brutality were better suited to an environment of show trials and purges than of revolutionary idealism. Furthermore, "Bykov was Jewish, but he was a violent anti-Semite," a circumstance of personal significance to Chambers, whose wife, Esther, was Jewish. In *Witness*, Chambers related an anecdote reminiscent of André Gide and his realization that Stalin was rearing a Soviet bourgeoisie. To thank the Ware circle for its brave service to the Soviet Union, Bykov ordered Chambers to deliver four Bokhara rugs from New York to Washington, an assignment for which Chambers enlisted the aesthetic advice of his friend Meyer Schapiro, by then a distinguished art historian. The rugs were a gift from a thankful Soviet people, but they were also intended by Bykov to compel further loyalty. "'Who pays is boss,'" Bykov explained to Chambers, "'and who takes money must also give something.'" Chambers saw in these words the philosophical betrayal of the revolution: "something in me more lucid than mind knew that I had reached the end of an experience, which was not only my experience."[27] Bykov inspired doubt in Chambers. Then, in 1937, Schapiro showed Chambers transcripts of the Moscow trials, to which Schapiro had gained access through the Commission of Inquiry, the same commission that would try Trotsky, exonerate him, and celebrate its labor at the 1938 Halloween party in Brooklyn. Chambers sensed in the transcripts—with their flagrant disregard for legal procedure and elementary logic—a terrifying signal from Stalin's Russia.[28] In *Witness* Chambers wrote that he "began to break with Communism in 1937." Chambers also feared for his own life, having been summoned to Moscow in July 1937. Sidney Hook believed that "sheer, stark fear for his life" motivated Chambers, "not the sudden vision of God that he retrospectively read into his break with Communism." Hook's claim is difficult to prove, but Chambers's fear was genuine; it would never quite leave him. In 1936 Igntaz Reiss, a Soviet agent, defected and was subsequently killed. On June 5, 1937, Juliet Stuart Poyntz, an American participant in the Soviet underground, disappeared after openly voicing criticism of the Soviet Union.[29] Chambers decided not to go to Moscow.[30]

The years 1937 and 1938 were possibly the darkest in Soviet history, approaching Solzhenitsyn's first circle of hell. Stalin's reign of terror was not a radical departure from Bolshevik precedent: Lenin had sanctioned the use of state terror against "enemies of the people," and the secret police had been a key element of Soviet governance from the revolution onward. Stalin radically expanded the scope of Bolshevik persecution, hunting old Bolsheviks and old aristocrats with equal zeal; anyone perceived to stand in his way could be killed or incarcerated, reduced overnight from citizen to slave. By 1929, Stalin had created an alternate world within the Soviet Union, an expanse of prisons, concentration camps, and labor camps through which an estimated eighteen million people would pass, most of them Soviet citizens. This has come to be known as the *gulag*, and its existence was an established fact outside the Soviet Union by the late 1920s.[31] The show trials, which usually resulted in a trip to the *gulag*, were not a secret or even a novelty by the time they assumed such manic dimensions in the mid-1930s. Historian Robert Service places their origins firmly in Lenin's Soviet Union: "show trials and the systematic fabrication of charges had been commonplace since the Socialist-Revolutionary leaders were arrested and sentenced in 1922," he writes. "The practice of accusing those who opposed the Bolsheviks of having direct links with foreign governments and their intelligence agencies had been rife since the suppression of the Kronstadt Mutiny in 1921."[32] By 1937, this logic was impossible to ignore, at least for someone as close to Moscow as Chambers had chosen to be.

Chambers's break with communism had two parts. One was the realization that communism, not just Stalin's Soviet Union, was evil. The other was that Christianity posed the only alternative to communism for him personally and for the American republic. Neither part was inconsistent with the fear that Soviet agents might do to him what they did to Trotsky in 1940—namely, kill him.[33] With the Schmidt obituary and the Commission of Inquiry transcripts still in mind, Chambers permitted himself in 1937 "to read books criticizing the Soviet Union."[34] One such was Vladimir Tchernavin's *I Speak for the Silent*, which documented the atrocities of the *gulag* system.[35] Whereas a year earlier he would have dismissed Tchernavin's book as necessarily false because it contradicted the Party line, "now for the first time, I believed that slave labor camps existed [in the Soviet Union]. I said: this is evil, absolute evil. Of this evil I am a part." If Tchernavin's book accurately depicted the Soviet prison system, then Chambers had no choice but to renounce the Bolshevik Revolution. His reasoning led him at first to nihilism: "If Communism were evil, I could no longer serve it, and that was true regardless of the fact that there might be nothing else to serve, that the alternative was a void."[36] The order of Chambers's realizations was less linear than he made it out to be. Still, the complete rejection, not just of Stalin or the Soviet Union but also of communism per se was the ultimate consequence of Chambers's break. Whatever his motivations, Chambers's Kronstadt was such that it made any commitment to revolution impossible. His Kronstadt quickly placed him to the Right of the second *Partisan Review*.

The alternative to the void was Christianity, which gave direction to Chambers's Kronstadt. He described his conversion in 1949 in a written statement to the FBI. The evil of communism follows from its rationalism, Chambers told the FBI, and in embracing the rationalism of the Enlightenment, communists had founded their ideas on atheism. Yet instead of achieving progress, as communists had hoped, they had fostered barbarism as soon as they acquired political power. "The vital defect in the Communist philosophy," Chambers concluded, "was the absence of God." It was a moral error to substitute history for God. In the Soviet Union, this error had sanctioned mass criminality in the name of history, for "man without God, no matter how intelligent he may be, or how dedicated, is inevitably a beast." The two parts of his Kronstadt had become one when Chambers realized that atheism spawned evil: "at this point I turned to God for the first time in my adult life and I found the strength to do what I never could have done without that guidance." This conversion narrative is an unusual FBI statement to say the least, and one wonders what the FBI made of Chambers's great-books language. Aspiring to the intimacy and intensity of Augustine's *Confessions*, Chambers was writing a rough draft of *Witness*: "the secret springs of my life, which had been lost so long in the desert of modernity joined their impulses, broke free and flowered unchecked."[37]

Chambers appended a singular renunciation to his break with communism. According to his own FBI testimony, with his Kronstadt Chambers put an end to his homosexual activities. His homosexuality had been made logistically easier by his life in the underground. In *Witness*, Chambers would attribute a general tolerance of promiscuity to the Communist Party, although his homosexual activities were his "darkest personal secret," never divulged "to any of my associates and friends, and particularly those in the Communist Party." Homosexuality and communism were related in Chambers's mind, if only as common aspects of a life that had to be transformed. He implied, although he did not explain, their interrelation in his statement to the FBI: "It will be noted that three things of some great importance happened in the year 1938. First, my cessation of my homosexual activities; my final break with the Communist Party; and my embracing for the first time, religion." In an another statement on the same subject, Chambers hinted at divine intervention: "Ten years ago, with God's help, I absolutely conquered it [homosexual activity]."[38] Divine intervention not only helped Chambers put his secret homosexual life behind him, in Chambers's version of events, but it also ensured that his new life would be militantly anti-communist. Chambers listened intently to a "voice [that] said with perfect distinctness, 'If you will fight for freedom, all will be well with you,'" taking the prophecy to heart, although it was unclear how he was to fight for freedom. By Chambers's account, he left the Party in April 1938, fleeing to Florida with his family, a bit of translation work as his sole means of financial support. At some point Chambers met with James Cannon and the Trotskyites. Cannon recalled that "after his break with the GPU [the State Political Directorate or Soviet secret policie], he [Chambers] came to us first . . . to see the Trotskyist group in Fall, '37, '38."[39] Whatever transpired in Chambers's meeting with Cannon, it led to no serious alliance. Chambers made no mention of this the meeting in *Witness*, either because the meeting was insignificant for him or because it disrupted the logic of his break, as charted in *Witness*. The break itself was a minor cause célèbre among intellectuals such as Herbert Solow and Sidney Hook. In May 1938, one month after Chambers had broken with the Party, Hook remembered that "Solow came to me with a startling piece of news. Chambers, he reported, with whom he had been in occasional touch, was 'breaking' with the Communist Party."[40] Already in 1938, Chambers's strange political biography was newsworthy.

In his "fight for freedom," Chambers sought out Hook, moving, as it were, from Trotsky to John Dewey. According to Hook, Chambers's ambition was to air his knowledge of the second apparatus, to make it a public fact. Chambers feared retribution from the underground on the one hand and public disbelief or indifference on the other. A man without an identity, Chambers was a former spy who would have to confess to practicing espionage, were he to reveal the truth about Alger Hiss and his accomplices. Chambers's idea, in Hook's words, "was to be received by John Dewey, to whom he was prepared to tell his story [about the second apparatus], and then under the protective mantle of Dewey's good name and reputation, he would give the whole story to the press." Chambers did not have to wait for the public's disbelief. Hook thought he was a liar, and he frowned on the idea of basing Chambers's story on Dewey's reputation. Hook believed that Chambers was still a Soviet agent involved this time in a plot to humiliate none other than John Dewey. Hook feared that Chambers might use Dewey's good name "to claim that they [Soviet agents] had received instructions from Trotsky, via John Dewey, to assassinate Stalin."[41] Dewey had a more prosaic reason for refusing to help. Regardless of whether Chambers's story was true or whether the American public would believe it, Dewey suspected that "his sponsorship of Chambers's return to public life would be seized upon by the Kremlin and its agents to discredit the work of the Commission [of Inquiry]."[42]

From the Trotskyites and the Deweyites, Chambers turned, according to his recollections in *Witness*, to the Democratic administration in his quest for recognition. In 1938, Chambers visited members of the Ware circle, trying to impress upon them the evil of communism. They were intransigent, and it was especially painful to Chambers that he failed to convince Alger Hiss, which put an immediate end to their friendship. At the urging of Isaac Don Levine, an energetically anti-communist journalist, Chambers met with Roosevelt's Assistant Secretary of State, Adolph Berle. Before he could meet with Berle, Chambers had to overcome his ambivalence about publicizing Soviet espionage in government. He might himself be tried for espionage, he would put his career at *Time* at risk, and the revelation of some secrets might end in the revelation of all secrets. Chambers was propelled toward the government by the idea that in 1939 communism and fascism were merging. Passionately antifascist, Chambers had "on the political side . . . broken with the Communist Party in large part because I had become convinced that the Soviet Government was fascist." The Nazi-Soviet pact lent credence to the argument that communism and fascism shared some powerful affinity for each other. More specifically, the Nazi-Soviet pact inspired in Chambers an anxiety that "the Soviet Government and the American Communist Party would at once put their underground apparatus at the service of the Nazis."[43] This the Trotskyites would be powerless to combat. Without Dewey's support, Chambers was unwilling to go to the press and he was too agitated by the continuing existence of the second apparatus to do nothing.

On September 2, 1939, Chambers went to Berle's Washington residence where Berle took copious notes, although Berle, like Dewey, chose not to champion Chambers's cause. Berle conveyed Chambers's disclosures to a White House in turmoil over World War II. Berle did not follow through on Chambers's allegations until 1941. Dean Acheson, Berle's colleague, and Felix Frankfurter, Hiss's law-school mentor, both dismissed Chambers's report as impossible. Chambers's efforts to gain a sympathetic audience on various sides of the Left—from the Trotskyites; from Hook, Dewey, and Berle—had failed, proving to Chambers that the Left was without a moral and political anchor. Trotskyists still favored revolution, although not the one Stalin had co-opted. Liberals might be more sober, and they had an established political party to express their views, but they had been seduced into identifying with communism or, at the very least, into seeing communism as benign and far away. In Chambers's eyes, "every move against the Communists was felt [by liberals] to be a move against themselves."[44] From his contact with communists such as Alger Hiss he had caught glimpses of the New Deal, knowing that Hiss and his comrades were a minority, a radical fringe. The mindset of a non-communist New Dealer like Berle betrayed a larger crisis of political understanding. Berle had little idea of communism and no idea of the communist presence in Washington. It was "with astonishment [that] I took my first hard look at the New Deal," Chambers recalled of the time after his meeting with Berle. This "revolution by bookkeeping and law-making," presided over by FDR, manifested the flaws of either a Berle or the flaws of a Hiss. It was mostly blind to the menace of communism, and those who were not blind were actively colluding with Moscow.

Having failed with the Left, Chambers had no immediate success with the Right. If there was a right-wing anti-communist campaign in the making in the late 1930s, it was not apparent to Chambers.[45] Not even J. Edgar Hoover was very interested in Chambers's allegations, when they first came to his attention in the early 1940s.[46] Right-wing anti-communism had a history going back to the Red Scare. In 1930 Representative Hamilton Fish investigated communism and attempted to make the American Communist Party illegal. In 1934 Elizabeth Dilling set up the Red Network with the goal of implicating New Dealers in communist subversion. Neither Fish nor Dilling had any notable success. In 1934 and 1935 the McCormack-Dickstein Committee in the House of Representatives studied political extremism, arriving at the conclusion that neither fascism nor communism had made deep inroads into American life.[47] Communism was an issue in the 1936 presidential campaign, with accusations beginning to surface about New Dealers who were closeted communists, but communist subversion was hardly the issue it would later become. In 1938 and 1939, the Dies Committee scored points against the New Deal by pursuing the question of communist subversion, without garnering national attention.[48] In 1939, the antiradical division of the FBI was brought back to life by presidential directive; it had been shut down in 1924 after the excesses of the Red Scare.[49] The various anti-communist demagogues of the 1930s, Father Coughlin most conspicuously, cast the anti-communist cause in a lurid light, associating it with the margins and not with respectable politics and parties. Republicans would have to wait until after World War II to promote themselves with an explicitly anti-communist attack on the New Deal.[50]

Chambers was disappointed with the low quality of political anti-communism in America, Right or Left. Like the liberal center, the Right lacked the militant character that communism possessed in abundance. "One is dismayed by the tatters or romanticism and excitement on the forces which are opposing themselves to evil [communism]," he wrote to Schapiro in 1938, "by their paucity of real knowledge, by their lack of firmness and deliberateness." Rather than preparing to lead an anti-communist campaign, the proponents of anti-communism "haven't got their feet on the ground, as we say, but until they have, the others will always win the game. It is the very presence of such firmness, deliberate thought and action, etc. which attract people to the others [communists] and hold them, even when such qualities are being perverted and misused for the worst ends."[51] Chambers's point was that the anti-communist cause needed resolve and strategy; and in 1938 it had neither. Chambers was himself politically confused. Doubt and anxiety pervade his correspondence with Meyer Schapiro in 1938 and 1939, as Chambers sought a stable relationship to political life, one that proved agonizingly difficult to find. The desire to weld history, ethics, and politics into a coherent position was a desire that Chambers took into his post-communist life from his years as a communist: "not to have a position is intolerable, especially for someone who had one." Chambers explained his intellectual disposition in the portentous language of his private correspondence: "intellectually, I am much more catholic than protestant: heresy at my stage of life and experience means more than schism, it could only be postulated on the basis of negation."[52]

Three circumstances helped to end the confusion that Chambers's Kronstadt had begun: his move to a farm in Maryland; his new job at *Time*; and his meeting with a former leader of the Soviet underground, Walter Krivitsky.

In Chambers's opinion, the moral corruption of his life as a communist was the fault of cities. The urban intellectuals who worshipped at the altar of Marx and Lenin—like the brilliant Columbia students gathered around *The Morningside*—had started Chambers on his way to the Communist Party. His disintegrating Long Island family left him with little or no defense against urban intellectuality and the radicalism to which it is prone. Chambers was concerned that his children not suffer the same fate. Farming offered "a way of bringing up my children in close touch with the soil and hard work, and apart from what I consider to be the false standards and vitiating influence of the cities." It was more a Jeffersonian than a Thoreauvian endeavor: the corruption of urban civilization did not compel Chambers to dissolve the bonds of citizenship. The retreat to the farm was a return to premodern notions of citizenship, unspoiled by manufacturing, for the soil, not the city street or suburban home, was to be the point of civic or national orientation for his children. Writing of his children's life on the farm, Chambers explained that his goal was "to root them in this way in their nation."[53]

Compared to the farm, Manhattan was a necessary evil. It was at *Time's* offices in Manhattan that Chambers could preach the anti-communist gospel to the nation, clarifying "on the basis of the news, the religious and moral position that made Communism evil . . . explaining simply and readably for millions the reason why the great secular faith of the age is wrong and religious faith of ages is right." In 1939, Chambers wrote three pieces for *Time:* "Intelligence Report" (May 1), "Night Thoughts" (May 8), and "The New Pictures: Ninotchka" (November 6). In "Intelligence Report," he reviewed a travelogue, which exposed the horrors of fascism. Chambers dwelt on the "heaped bodies on the road [and] . . . barbed-wire barricades," evidence of Japanese imperialism in China. "Night Thoughts" was a valiant attempt to help *Time's* readers through *Finnegan's Wake,* and in it Chambers was sharing the literary pleasures of *The Morningside* (or *Partisan Review*) with the masses, although in it he took a swipe at the cherished *Partisan Review* synthesis between literary modernism and political radicalism. He pointed out that Joyce liked to drink at Café Pfanen in Zurich. "Lenin used to frequent the same café," Chambers noted, "but the literary and proletarian revolutions never met," a terse way of deflating the *Partisan Review* hope that these revolutions were one and the same. "Ninotchka" was an exuberant review of Ernst Lubitsch's anti-communist romantic comedy, dubbed by Chambers "a literate and knowing satire, which lands many a shrewd crack about phony Five Year Plans, collective farms, communist jargon and pseudoscientific gab."[54]

Confident as Chambers had become in his anti-Stalinism by 1939, he was still a student, not yet a master. He disliked the anti-Stalinists of *Partisan Review* too much to learn from them. Most of them, he wrote to Schapiro, "are scared of their life that I may contaminate them. So much for their 'principles of conduct.'" Because the anti-Stalinists are so timid, they are in the end complicit with communism, Chambers argued. Because of their desire to remain progressives, they cannot organize politically against communism: "they are murderers—not of men only—they have destroyed the future of mankind for an incalculable time to come. It is all gone, and largely because not one man who could has resolutely stepped up to stop them at all costs. Oppositions won't do it: I will show them what will do it. I know what they are afraid of. From this moment, my friends will begin to drop away from me."[55] The men who can stop communism have confronted the truth about it, and the truth was a syllogism of sorts: communism is revolutionary, aspiring to Soviet domination of the world; communism is no better than fascism; and it must, therefore, be fought as resolutely as intellectuals and soldiers were fighting fascism. Opposition to Stalin of the kind that *Partisan Review* proposed was too weak, too abstruse, too intoxicated still by the elixir of revolution.

Chambers's teacher, Walter Krivistky, was a man who stood up to the Soviets at all costs. Krivitsky first came to Chambers's attention with a series of essays in the *Saturday Evening Post* published in April 1939, which the indefatigable Isaac Don Levine had helped bring into print.[56] Before defecting, Krivitsky worked for Soviet military intelligence; from 1935 to 1937, he was the chief of Soviet military intelligence in Western Europe. In 1939, Krivitsky published a book sensationally titled *In Stalin's Secret Service* (and no less sensationally *I Was Stalin's Agent* in the British edition).[57] Although an editor's note in the *Saturday Evening Post* described Krivitsky as "still a believer in the true communism of Lenin," Chambers appreciated Krivitsky's writings. The two met and became friends. Krivitsky argued that fascism and Soviet communism were subspecies of totalitarianism, although *totalitarianism* was not Krivitsky's word. "He [Krivitsky] believed, as I believe," Chambers recalled in *Witness*, "that fascism . . . is inherent in every collectivist form, and that it can be fought only by the force of an intelligence, a faith, a courage, a self-sacrifice, which must equal the revolutionary spirit that, in coping with it, it must in many ways come to resemble." Krivitsky's teaching was paradoxical, admitting no crude transfer of energy from Left to Right. According to Krivistky, all politics in the twentieth century is revolutionary. The defense of the status quo was an inadequate defense against Stalinism, even in bourgeois America. One must be counterrevolutionary: "in the struggle against Communism the conservative is all but helpless. For that struggle cannot be fought, much less won, or even understood, except in terms of total sacrifice. And the conservative is suspicious of sacrifice; he wishes to conserve, above all what he is and what he has."[58]

Krivitsky's teaching was untimely, and it set Chambers a difficult agenda. If interpreted as anti-communist, the American century could be accommodated to Krivitsky's theory of counterrevolution. The Republican Party would not just minister to the needs of Wall Street; but it would steer the United States to the summits of geopolitical leadership, and communist revolution could be kept at bay by promoting a revolutionary Americanism and by the spirited fight against communism. In 1939 Krivitsky's argument was both novel and marginal. President Roosevelt was perilously far from what Chambers and Krivitsky were seeking, and the Republicans were mired in isolationism, ignorant of communism, domestic or international, and unprepared for the sacrifices that communism would demand of its adversaries. Even the Nazi-Soviet pact did not convince Americans that they had to join in World War II and become a counterrevolutionary force in world politics. By 1941 the Soviet Union and the United States were antifascist allies, pushing Krivitsky's ideas even further from the mainstream. Krivitsky's teaching would take years to apply. His were ideas awaiting a war, the contours of which were unknowable in 1941. If Krivitsky taught Chambers the need for counterrevolution, Matthew Arnold instructed Trilling in the subtleties of revolution. It was Arnold's writing about the French Revolution that showed Trilling how to understand the Russian Revolution, much like Krivitsky helped Chambers to understand the Bolshevik Revolution.

Arnold's teaching—that a cultured, humane middle class could defend liberal principle, holding off the madness of revolution—was one that Trilling would take from his dissertation and convert into a program of liberal anti-communism. This was a highly improbable project, an unlikely use to find for Arnold, who appealed to the New Humanists, academic intellectuals such as Irving Babbit and Paul Elmer More trying to save the rigor and form of neoclassicism from the expressiveness and radicalism of the Romantic movement.[59] In the verdict of up-to-date intellectuals, Arnold belonged in the tradition of outmoded gentility and outworn nineteenth-century humanism. Arnold's father, Thomas, had earned a chapter in Lytton Strachey's *Eminent Victorians*, the book in which modern irony triumphed decisively over Victorian pomposity and self-deceit. Matthew Arnold drew a similar kind of ire in the twentieth century: in his diary, Edmund Wilson lamented Arnold's "dead impotent spot in his pulpiteering repetitions." Trilling knew that he was being "deliberately unfashionable" in researching Arnold. Trilling looked back on the year 1932, the year he began work on his dissertation, when he "was having a bitter time of it because it seemed to me that I was working in a lost world, and nobody wanted, or could possibly want, a book about Matthew Arnold." The Depression and countless other crises of the 1930s demanded a farewell to lost worlds: "there was at the time," Trilling later recalled, "a great deal of surveillance of the drilling places of the mind, and ivory towers were very easily imputed."[60]

Trilling's own position in the ivory tower was insecure, a position that had to be earned even if his ambition was not to stay within the ivory tower. In writing a dissertation on Matthew Arnold, and doing so as an American Jew, Trilling was audaciously claiming his place in Anglo-American academic high culture, a hard-won achievement. In 1936, the Columbia English department challenged Trilling's legitimacy as an as aspiring professor at Columbia. As a "Freudian, a Marxist and a Jew," Trilling was told, he might be more comfortable elsewhere. Trilling exposed these euphemisms for what they were, insisting that he was quite happy at Columbia. When Columbia's president Nicholas Murray Butler read *Matthew Arnold* and was impressed by it, Trilling's position at Columbia was assured. Just as significant as Trilling's victory in this battle was his willingness to wage it at all. Diana Trilling described the confrontation as among the most pivotal in Trilling's life: "the career by which we know him dates from the moment in which he refused to be dismissed from Columbia and was able to persuade his senior colleagues to value him as he wished to be valued."[61] *Matthew Arnold*, published in 1939, was the foundation of Trilling's career and something of a milestone for his generation: one could lay claim to Anglo-American high culture, even as the son of Jewish immigrants; one could stand where one wished in the world of American letters; one could succeed precisely the way Trilling's patriotic parents had hoped he would.

In the eyes of the downtown intellectuals, a dissertation on Matthew Arnold was retrograde, an obligatory, dull right of passage into the halls of academe. It was a subject not markedly Marxian, Freudian, or Jewish. In Sidney Hook's estimation, Trilling should have framed his portrait of Matthew Arnold's father, Thomas, with more criticism from the Left. The portrait struck Hook as "overgenerous. You don't bring out the English Tory, albeit an honest one, sufficiently," he wrote to Trilling in 1938. Jacques Barzun, a close friend of Trilling's and also on faculty at Columbia, detected a similar deviation from the standard intellectual attitude, which, for Barzun, was cause for praise. Trilling's dissertation was a "Stracheotomy," a reversal of the cultural tide that had been flowing against

Matthew and Thomas Arnold and the Victorians since the World War I.[62] The rise of a Marxist orientation among American writers and critics had distanced Trilling's dissertation from the intellectual center. As William Barrett observed about Trilling's *Matthew Arnold*, "the appearance of the book was all the more remarkable coming when it did in a period of debased Marxism with its plebian emphasis upon 'social consciousness' and proletarian literature."[63] The book would contribute to the notion of Trilling, not as a daring pioneer breaking ground but as an academic aloof from his generation, a well-mannered Victorian oddity among the modernists.

This was not at all what Trilling wanted. He understood his book on Arnold as modern in tone and subject, modern in its sensitivity to crisis, centering the modern era on an impression of loss. Whether one reads the pagan D. H. Lawrence or the Anglican T. S. Eliot, one cannot escape "the loss of the power to feel . . . this is one of the great themes of the last century and a half," Trilling wrote in 1954.[64] "An essential element of this loss was the elimination of the intensity of religious faith," Trilling explained, but no less essential were the machine and the city. "The 'mechanicalness' of the universe as conceived of by science seemed to be reflected in the mechanicalness of social life itself," and the backdrop to such troubled social life was "the great city as we nowadays know it, the overgrown, sordid sprawling city." Matthew Arnold the poet was alert to the modern crisis, giving something similar to religious feelings to secular readers "unable to accept dogma and orthodoxy, and yet impelled to conduct their moral commitment and their passion for human good and the vision of human fate with something beyond the merely temporal and wholly conditioned."[65]

Trilling identified personally with Arnoldian discomforts, living as he did amid the "naked shingles" of a secular modern world. He disclosed his spiritual disquiet in a letter, written while finishing the book on Arnold, in which he described himself as an atheist or agnostic who cannot dismiss theology. "As for Protestant theology," he wrote in September 1938, "I felt toward it what I feel toward all theology—a strong attraction as an intellectual exercise. It is the form of theology and puzzle that I am fondest of and scare myself often by my interest—by the ease with which I can translate its strange doctrines into the naturalistic realism I believe in." Yet intellectual exercise was not enough for Trilling in theological matters: this was his inner crisis. "I have not yet, I find, discovered the way

I want to shut up the subject of religion; I like nothing in it, almost, and it is not operative in me," he wrote. But he could not find the right way to shut it up, "and so a kind of humility keeps me from shutting it up." It was with reference to this humility that Trilling brought up Matthew Arnold. The letter contained an intriguing slip of the hand, which underscored the intellectual effects of Trilling's Kronstadt. Confusion "leaves me in a kind of Arnoldian position . . . Perhaps I can say this is a tribute to Arnold." After the word "Arnoldian" Trilling had written "or Feuerbachian" and then crossed it out. A necessary precursor to Marx, Feuerbach was a thinker in the radical canon, a path-breaking atheist who contributed to the secular radicalism Trilling had embraced as a communist. Matthew Arnold led in a different direction, toward a literary criticism that might itself be a source of spiritual guidance.[66]

For Trilling, Arnold's career coincided with the origins of the modern crisis. In *Matthew Arnold* Trilling divided Arnold's life into three phases, each of which was conditioned by developments in French and English history. The first phase was that of the despairing poet, the second of the skeptic toward revolution, and the third of the critic struggling to reconcile modern tensions. The pivotal event was the French Revolution, which created the modern spirit even while failing to solve the modern crisis in politics. Arnold's ambivalent relationship to this spirit lent drama to his thought because Arnold fell between the established categories of conservative and progressive. He was never merely for or against the French Revolution; he was, in Trilling's mysterious formulation, a "liberal of the future," and Arnold sought to balance the rationalist liberalism of Jeremy Bentham and John Stuart Mill with a culture that could plausibly replace religion as a source of moral and aesthetic excellence. If it achieved such balance, the liberalism of the future would realize the democratic promise of the French Revolution, without yielding to nihilism or anarchy or to the perils of untamed democracy. Political reform alone would not solve the modern crisis. A new age of liberty demanded the articulation of a new culture under the aegis of an educated middle class. Arnold believed that the English *Bildungsbürgertum* should harness its cultural resources and complete the work of the French Revolution. In the process, the best of the ancien régime could be interwoven with the best of modernity. Matthew Arnold's liberalism was very much an amalgam of conservative and progressive tendencies: his criticism "was, in effect, his refusal to move forward until Burke and Voltaire compounded their quarrel, bowed to each other and, taking him by either hand, agreed on the path to follow."[67] This is an image that would later suit Trilling himself.

The three phases of Arnold's life constituted three distinct responses to the modern crisis. In the first phase, Arnold registered the modern crisis in his poetry. In the second and third phases, Arnold confronted it, elaborating on the qualities modern culture ought to possess if it was to be both liberal and useful. This Trilling dubbed Arnold's "search for affirmation," and it brought Trilling full circle to his own youthful criticism, in which Trilling sought a connection to American society as opposed to a despairing rejection of it. Arnold's affirmative "liberalism of the future" was the antithesis of what Trilling saw around him in the late 1930s, most disturbingly in the pro-Soviet leanings of self-described liberals. Trilling wrote caustically of the present moment, "when intellectual men are often called upon to question their intellect and to believe that thought is inferior and action opposed to it, that blind partisanship is fidelity to an idea." To such sorry intellectual men, Trilling wrote, "Arnold still has a word to say—not against the taking of sides but against the belief that taking sides settles things or requires the suspension of reason." Liberals who forget this have unlearned the essence of liberalism.[68]

Trilling repeatedly emphasized Arnold's status as a modern man. By such emphasis, he could prove to his readers that Arnold did not belong in some museum of cultural history. Arnold was "one of the first modern literary men," Trilling wrote, modern not only in his intuition of despair but also in his realization that the modern artist's despair has a social dimension. "Arnold declared that the modern man was crippled and incomplete," but this declaration was not the extent of his insight. Never a Marxist, Arnold was able to connect religious and social crisis through the idea of alienation, the theoretical center of the Marxist system. The loss of God, according to Arnold, is also a loss of fraternity, a loss that the French Revolution had proven incapable of undoing. Trilling analyzed Arnold's early book of poems, *Empedocles on Etna* (1852), in exactly these terms: "without a God, fundamentally separated from Nature, there is nothing to bind him to life, strangely enough, little even to bind him to his fellow-man." The rootlessness of capitalism reinforces and to some degree reflects the emptiness of life without religious belief. Modern individualism is the melancholy link between atheism and alienation: "loss of a belief in a cosmic order requires men to retreat into their individual

selves, and the result of this philosophic act is confirmed by the individualism of a manufacturing society." In this fashion, Trilling showed that
Arnold's world was not a lost world; sadly, it was very much the world of
the twentieth century.[69]

As Arnold grew older, shedding the poet's garb and becoming a critic,
he tried to give the "spiritual dissolution of modernity" intellectual shape
and meaning. He did this by comparing the histories of France and England. The concerns of Arnold mirrored those of Karl Marx at least in the
broad outlines of Arnold's analysis. Arnold put the rise of the middle class
at the center of modern history, of which England was the leader in the
seventeenth and eighteenth centuries and France in the nineteenth. The
Puritan challenge to the Church of England marked the end of feudal-
ism in England—a splintering of authority and a loosening of tradition.
The Calvinist middle class espoused science, commerce, and freedom of
religion as a means of shifting authority away from Church and the
Crown and toward itself. Freedom of conscience blended together with
an attitude of economic laissez-faire: "the theories of religious freedom
and economic freedom were assimilated to each other and the rights of
the spirit became the rights of business enterprise." For Arnold, this was
not a salutary development. He did not thrill to the music made when
"the Economic Man and the Calvinist Christian sing to each other like
voices in a fugue." Arnold the literary critic did not decry capitalism per
se; he decried the cultural corruption engendered by this comingling of
capitalism and Calvinism. It was a problem in the present tense for Arnold,
who argued that "England is following a mistaken course in abandoning
herself to the middle class creed of Calvinism. For Calvinism is what
Arnold calls Hebraistic, which is to say that it is concerned with morality to
the exclusion of all other faculties."[70]

In Trilling's analysis, Arnold's changing attitude toward the French
Revolution defined the scope and limits of his liberalism. As historically
minded as Arnold, Trilling was not a historian so much as a critic struggling to situate the art and taste of his time in historical context. In the
preface to the first edition of *Matthew Arnold*, Trilling observed that
"what determined him [Arnold] to speak for or against the [French] Revolution at any particular time was his conception of how much the Revolutionary principle England at *that* time required."[71] As an intellectual
"concerned with establishing a Christian kind of conduct as against . . . a
revolutionary kind," Arnold was an agnostic with regard to the French

revolutionary legacy.[72] What struck him was the void left unfilled by the French Revolution, the achievements it had failed to realize. Trilling's prose turned purple in describing the situation as it appeared to Arnold: "the storm came—the fierce rationalism of the French Revolution. Yet the sun in the new-washed sky saw the race of man after the upheaval plying upon the chartless sea, clinging to the remnants of their dead faith." In 1866, Arnold changed his mind. In his own curious way he was "claiming to be continuing the work of the French Revolution," and in 1871 he warmly greeted the Paris Commune. Perhaps the proletariat would take up the call of culture along with its historical role. In these years, Arnold set himself against "the calloused betrayal by middle class liberalism of the best of modern Europe, the betrayal of the French revolutionary tradition, both in its rationalism and in its romanticism, its social good sense and in its spiritual aspiration."[73]

English and French history converged for Arnold on the question of the middle class. Whatever the grandeur of the French Revolution, Arnold did not read into it either a Marxist or a socialist program, whereby the middle class displaced the aristocracy only to itself be displaced by the proletariat. Perhaps some day the middle class would lose its hegemony, but "Arnold held that the immediate future lay not with the working class but with the middle class." Nor was this simply a matter of hegemony or brute power politics. The working class was not yet ready for leadership. It was ill-educated, culturally retrograde, and when it aspired to self-improvement, it aped the philistinism of the middle class. The "masses with vulgar tastes [are] corrupted by the Philistines [the middle class], the more substantial half of them in training to be Philistines themselves," Trilling paraphrased Arnold, "the rest a mere rabble." Once again, Arnold was modern in that "the world of bourgeois enterprise which arranged its own self-glorification in the Great Exhibition of 1851 would find little charm in Arnold. Inevitably—for Arnold would find little charm in the bourgeois world." Charming or not, however, the bourgeoisie was Western civilization's only hope if a culture that was neither Hebraic nor Calvinist nor commercial was to triumph. Arnold urged the middle class to create "a civilization into which the workers can 'grow.' "[74]

Trilling followed the subject of liberal culture with particular care. Arnold's writing was, for him, a storehouse of ideas that could be used to replace Marxism with a refined and relevant liberalism. An alien to the culture of socialism, with its celebration of the proletariat and its hopefulness about democracy, Matthew Arnold had a nervous pessimism about democracy, of the sort that Walter Lippmann (following Freud) and H. L. Mencken (following Nietzsche) had voiced in the 1920s. The chaos of democratic America in the Great Depression and Europe's descent into fascism in the 1930s were cause for pessimism, especially among those intellectuals who had rejected the Popular Front. With an audience of such intellectuals in mind, Trilling contended that Arnold was no dupe to nineteenth-century naiveté. Trilling's Arnold anticipated Reinhold Niebuhr in his grudging support of revolution: "it is the essence of revolutionary theory to insist on man's natural goodness," Trilling observed, and Arnold believed in no such thing. Likewise, Arnold's signature Hellenism, his sense that liberal culture rested on the culture of ancient Greece as much as it did on Christianity, made him ambivalent about democracy. Trilling noted that "the influence of Plato and Aristotle, clear enough through *Culture and Anarchy*, could scarcely have made him [Arnold] a partisan of democratic hope." Trilling's words were carefully chosen. It was not a chronic ambivalence on Arnold's part but rather a deficit of democratic hope. To the extent that the crises running from World War I to World War II were modern as well as democratic, Arnold's deficit of hope was a modern quality. One could only have so much hope for democracy, but a cultured liberal might also place hope elsewhere, outside of politics altogether. Pessimism demanded balance, and life itself, Arnold believed, "must be affirmative, interesting, complete, human."[75] If modern politics alone could not meet these imperatives, modern culture would have to assume the responsibility.

Arnold's creative ideal had both liberal and Hellenistic overtones. It was "reason experienced as a kind of grace by each citizen." Neither religion nor science could give grace and reason to the modern citizen, for "what is lacking [in modern life] is righteousness, and, with religion fallen on evil days, this too must be supplied by culture." To call for righteousness was, for Arnold, to call for moral order, and only the future could validate Arnold's affirmation. Trilling was both unconvinced and impressed: "Arnold falls, indeed, into 'rationalizations' and contradictions in his attempt to forge an affirmative attitude to modern life." Trilling accused Arnold of being unrealistic, but this shortcoming "does not diminish the truth of the basic insights . . . the nature of the full and healthy life of the spirit" that was Arnold's ideal for society. Trilling admired Arnold's will to be constructive. This was the glory of his criticism: "his poetry has probed the lacks of modern life; his critical effort undertakes to help the growth of a life molded to a nobler style"—better a doubtful solution than one that was incomplete, like democracy, or murderous, like fascism or communism.[76]

Arnold appealed to Trilling for his disassociation of liberalism from laissez-faire, from the "liberal" theory of economics. A New Dealer before his time, Arnold assigned the state two responsibilities: to regulate the needs of a liberal society, with its competing individual freedoms, and to further the cultural ideals that give individuals moral and aesthetic guidance. Arnold wrote *Culture and Anarchy*, Trilling explained, as a challenge to John Stuart Mill's *On Liberty*. Mill was overly hostile to the state, overly indifferent to the potential anarchy of individualism. Hebraism—the "concern with morality to the exclusion of other faculties"—needed to be held in check by the state. Otherwise, a rampant moralism might rend society in two, as it had during the English Civil War. Arnold conceived *Culture and Anarchy* to prove the superiority of Hellenism, with its sweetness and light, to Hebraism, with its dark moral passions. His other objective was to analyze the relationship between liberalism and the state. Liberalism needs the state, just as democracy needs the state. It was an argument that descended from Thomas Arnold to Matthew Arnold (through Dewey) right down to the political debates of 1939. "There is nothing essentially antagonistic between democracy and the State," Trilling wrote about Thomas Arnold, who believed "that, indeed, each does not imply laissez-faire, that organization does not imply repression. In this synthesis of the two dominant and seemingly opposed tendencies of his time and ours lies Thomas Arnold's political achievement. Matthew Arnold's, more complex, was not basically different."[77] Trilling's affinity for Arnoldian liberalism, as he defined it, was well suited to Franklin Roosevelt and the New Deal, which merged an activist vision of the democratic state with the ebullient style of the brain trust; it would be even better suited to the Camelot of Kennedy's White House, with its liberal American Hellenism.

After the state, the key Arnoldian institution was the university, and it was here that Arnold displayed his cultural conservatism. There was for Arnold "the theme of the 'whole man' who needs religion for his completeness." There was as well the political thought of the English romantics, for whom "society is of so organic a nature that it prohibits the interference of the analytical intellect." Between the "whole man" and the "organic society" stood the "reactionary possibilities of Arnold's vagueness," in Trilling's phrase. Such vagueness described Arnold's love for the university, which was expressed biographically in his cherished connection to Oxford. By reforming society from within, the state and the university might serve progress and tradition, and Arnold's admiration for the ancient customs surrounding Oxbridge and the English Parliament exposed the conservatism behind his liberal intentions. Trilling distinguished Arnold from many liberals, who "might see the university as merely vestigial. Arnold saw it as vital and important. To speak as an Oxford professor gave him a special right to speak of the nation's mind and soul."[78] In his longing for the whole man and the organic society, Arnold entertained reactionary emotions. Using the state and the university, the middle class could shepherd the working class toward the liberalism of the future, toward the ideal of reason "experienced as a kind of grace by each citizen."

Although Trilling did not formally adopt Arnold's program for the liberal middle class, he gave the impression of accepting it, and in doing so his Kronstadt was complete. In a perceptive 1949 review of *Matthew Arnold*, Trilling's friend Irving Kristol touched on the adversarial relationship between Trilling's literary study and the Popular Front. In *Matthew Arnold*, Trilling held "up to scorn the modern radical-liberal-progressive, with his casual optimism, his blind adulation of the 'common people,' his condescending good will, his failure to face up to the less tractable aspects of human nature."[79] Trilling wanted to be mature rather than aloof, and he wanted to imbue others with his maturity. Irving Howe accused Trilling in 1973 of "falling back with some didactic bravado on the moral assurances of nineteenth century writers," Matthew Arnold foremost among them. One might substitute the word *example* for *assurances*, for this is more of what Trilling took from Arnold and the Victorians. To have a Kronstadt was to grow up, Trilling concluded, and political virtue will only come when intellectuals value adult restraint above childish dreams and adolescent rebellion. In this the Victorians could teach the moderns something: "if the Victorians too much disregarded Rousseau and Wordsworth and thought of children as adults *manqués*, we today are perhaps too often tempted to think of adults as children *manqués*," wrote Trilling in *Matthew Arnold*. Trilling rooted himself in a liberal tradition that began with Arnold, and he did this to ensure his own political maturity. What Irving Kristol said of Matthew Arnold applied to Trilling as well: "Arnold was too serious a man to remain a critical intellectual, though he was too distraught a thinker, his own relation to tradition being that almost of an auto-didact, to be anything else successfully."[80]

One could say the same of Whittaker Chambers after his Kronstadt, with certain qualifications. Chambers could not remain a critical intellectual because he had never really been one. He had been an éngagé intellectual at least since the early 1920s, when he joined the Communist Party. Whether on the Left or the Right, Chambers calculated political ideas in terms of parties and powers. He was at every stage a distraught thinker, troubled by his own lack of faith until he found faith in communism. With communism, he had a tradition, replete with an epic story of revolutionary heroism, beginning in France and raised to new heights in Russia. Over time, however, communism made Chambers no less distraught, and without communism Chambers had no tradition at all. He became a Quaker, as his grandmother had been. He moved to a farm that reminded him of his Long Island childhood. He read Henry Adams, the *Federalist Papers*, and the Bible, drawing intellectual material from them for a conservatism that always had an air of autodidacticism about it. Chambers had no conservative tradition either in American thought or politics to support his passionate anti-communism. Nor did Trilling have a settled tradition of liberal anti-communism on which to draw. There were liberals who were anti-communist by the late 1930s, but there was not yet a coherent liberal anti-communism. Immediately after their Kronstadts, Trilling and Chambers were both in flux; and as the ill-fated Halloween party demonstrated, they were not destined to join hands, or even to shake hands, as anti-communists. Only gradually, as Americans moved en masse toward anti-communism in the 1940s and 1950s, did Trilling and Chambers find movements and parties—and with them traditions—that mirrored their convictions.

4

FIRST STEPS IN AN ANTI-STALINIST WORLD

> We Americans are unhappy. We are not happy about America.
> We are not happy about ourselves in relation to America. We
> are nervous—or gloomy—or apathetic.
>
> —HENRY R. LUCE, *The American Century*, 1941

The Kronstadt was not simply an end. It was also a beginning, resolving one question only to create a host of others. To undergo a Kronstadt was to reject the Soviet alternative, but it did not immediately answer the question of what Stalinism was, and anti-Stalinists construed Stalinism variously. Because of his life as an espionage agent, Whittaker Chambers saw Stalinism as innately political, although he located its cause in a crisis of Western civilization that extended far beyond political economy. Stalinism's sphere of influence, in Chambers's eyes, was the American intelligentsia as a whole, which looked favorably on communism even if it was not fully pro-communist. More important than the leanings of intellectuals, though, was the fact that the New Deal had given Soviet communism a foothold in American government, and of this Chambers had first-hand experienc e. Lionel Trilling confined his observations to the American intelligentsia whose culture, he believed, had gained a Stalinist inflection in the 1930s. When Trilling wrote of the corruption Stalinism had caused, he meant a corruption of American culture. Chambers, writing against Stalinism, had the corruption of both a culture and a polity in mind. Trilling's Kronstadt had put an end to his communist writing; Chambers's Kronstadt put an end to his affiliation with the Soviet Union.

The anti-communist wave that Chambers and Trilling helped generate in the 1940s was sufficiently powerful to foster a resurgence in American conservative thought. At the same time, much liberal thought was gradually reformulated to meet the moral and political imperatives of an anti-communist outlook. Trilling and Chambers did not set out in 1939 to make the Left and the Right anti-communist; these were roles and agendas they arrived at over time, thinking through the implications of their own heart-felt anti-communism without a clear sense of purpose or destination. Trilling would title his one published novel *The Middle of the Journey*, which he centered on the moment of Kronstadt and its consequences. This title suits Trilling and Chambers in their period of raw, early anti-communism, which began in the late 1930s and culminated with the Hiss case, in the tumultuous months between 1948 and 1950. The literary critic Leslie Fiedler would write about the Hiss case as an end to American innocence, a quality perennially being lost, and a curious postscript to the "low, dishonest" decade of the 1930s.[1] If there ever was a moment of American innocence in the twentieth century, it was lost in the many Kronstadts of the late 1930s and 1940s, long before the Hiss case began; but for Trilling and Chambers it was not as much innocence as youth that had been lost in the 1930s. Exiled from both innocence and youth, the mood of early anti-communism was self-consciously one of sober, worldly maturity, abetted by the outbreak of yet another world war. Whatever it was, anti-communism was not the beginning of the journey.

The early anti-communism of Trilling and Chambers had several interlocking components. Most obvious was the hostility toward the Soviet Union and the communism that it spearheaded internationally. Another component was a critique of the Left that went beyond Stalinism, penetrating to the Left's cultural and intellectual assumptions, to the conditions that had enabled support for Stalinism. The third component was a search for alternatives. This took Chambers to the Right and Trilling to a moderate liberalism. The final component was the most crucial, but it was not distinct from anti-Stalinism or from a critique of the Left: in their minds an intellectual triangle formed among the misdeeds of the Soviet Union, the miscues of the American Left, and the new possibilities they were making their own. It was not a static triangle but one that shifted over time. Any alteration at one point affected the status of the other two. Chambers in particular was a close observer of the Soviet Union, constantly reflecting on its global position and the steady encroachment of communism worldwide. A pioneering American leftist in the 1920s, operating in the literary and political avant-garde of the communist movement, Chambers ceased keeping up with the American Left in the 1940s, although he wrote with pleasure on the pro-Soviet delusions of leftist intellectuals. As an anti-communist, Chambers no longer responded to the arguments of the Left. Because Trilling remained on the Left, he was sensitive to its modifications and tensions. He had to be, for he wanted the Left to adopt his anti-communism as its animating spirit. As for the third point on the triangle—the ideals, aspirations, and possibilities—here Trilling and Chambers were entirely at odds with each other, charting territory that they did not want to share.

By the 1940s, Trilling and Chambers were living vastly different lives. They were out of touch with each other and would remain so until Chambers died in 1961. Settled with his family on their farm in Westminster, Maryland, Chambers would commute in to New York City several days a week to fulfill his editorial duties at *Time*; but the agricultural life claimed his sympathies, as did the Quaker meeting he attended with his family in rural Maryland. His pastoral conservatism was a lived conviction. If Chambers loathed New York, Trilling, in many ways, belonged to it. He had lived his adult life in Manhattan, in the vicinity of Columbia University, where he was a sought-after teacher. The cosmopolitan backdrop of New York was also crucial—more in a metaphysical than in a geographical sense—to Trilling's intellectual circle, whose spirit was not entirely defined by magazines like *Partisan Review* or *Commentary* but, rather, by the city of New York, with its immigrant energies and unembarrassed sophistication. Their group would for good reason come to be known as the New York intellectuals. Assimilated, urbane New Yorkers, often of Jewish background, the New York intellectuals did not consist of this intellectual type alone, but it was the dominant type among them and Trilling was a prominent example of it. Trilling was a respected, if never entirely representative, New York intellectual because some indeterminate conservatism separated him from many other New York intellectuals, whose anti-communism was unimpeachable but whose sympathies for radicalism had survived the 1930s. He was more bourgeois than the downtown intellectuals and vastly more bourgeois than Chambers, who would have liked to use his farm as a template for remaking American society. Trilling was mildly Jewish, while Chambers was very much a Christian intellectual, his political and personal life a reflection of his Christian conviction.

The distance between the liberal Trilling and the conservative Chambers showed itself in their journalistic homes—magazines. Trilling wrote for *Partisan Review,* and even when he published essays and reviews in *Kenyon Review* or the *Nation* or *The Contemporary Jewish Record,* he seemed to be writing for *Partisan Review.* In his essays, Trilling perpetrated *Partisan Review*'s in-house anti-Stalinism and wrote in the magazine's highbrow yet unacademic style. Chambers, meanwhile, was an editor at *Time,* which was not an openly conservative magazine; in fact, most of *Time*'s editors and writers had little sympathy with Chambers's conservatism or with his hard-line anti-communism. In the minority among his colleagues, Chambers was an ideological companion of Henry Luce, *Time*'s conservative editor, and Chambers did what he could to impress on Luce his conservative anti-communism. Chambers was also a contributor to the politically conservative *American Mercury.* The divide between *Partisan Review* and *Time* was fraught with political irony. Although a fair number of *Partisan Review* writers came from working-class, immigrant backgrounds, the company they kept at *Partisan Review* was elite. Its style was complicated, its outlook cosmopolitan, its taste schooled in the masterpieces of Western culture. Its contributors were generally dismissive of popular culture, if not actively suspicious of its complicity with capitalism, fascism, and communism. By comparison, *Time* was "conservative" because it was so vigorously commercial, its offices in Rockefeller Plaza symbolizing its home in capitalist America. *Time* was genuinely to the Right of *Partisan Review* when Luce used it to proclaim the American century in 1941. *Partisan Review*'s writers would have to wait for a 1952 symposium, "Our Country and Our Culture," to air patriotic sentiments that were even then rather tepid.

Time and *Partisan Review* were related, however, by a growing commitment to anti-communism in the 1940's, a growth that was certainly contested. A New York intellectual with a pronounced radical bent, Dwight Macdonald left *Partisan Review* in 1943 because he sensed that anti-Stalinism had driven the magazine's editors to outright anti-communism, and Macdonald rightly feared that anti-communism would imperil radical socialism. He founded the magazine *politics* in 1944, an early haven for anti–anti-communism, until it ceased publication in 1948. At *Time,* Chambers's anti-communism met with violent resistance, although Chambers succeeded, over time, in persuading Luce that anti-communism and the American century were morally at one with each other. Similarly, *Partisan Review*'s editors eventually agreed to an American role in World War II, asking themselves what the appropriate response was to the

Soviet Union's great power status and inching their way toward an anti-communist foreign policy. James Burnham, a former Trotskyite and an editor at *Partisan Review* in the 1940s, derived conclusions about American power that would by the 1950s take him to the Right.[2] For a short while in the late 1950s, Burnham and Chambers would both serve as editors at the conservative magazine *National Review* where Burnham espoused a much more aggressive program for the American century than Chambers ever did. In style, *Partisan Review* and *Time* had little in common; in political content, there were strong lines of connection between them.

Chambers at *Time* and Trilling at *Partisan Review* were both impatient with an insufficiently anti-communist Left. For Chambers, the damage communism had done to the Left was permanent, and he developed a two-fold critique of the Left: its complicity with Soviet crimes and its troubled philosophical and cultural origins. For Trilling, the damage philo-Soviet leanings had done to the Left was severe but potentially reversible. It was telling, however, that Trilling's term of choice as an anti-communist was *liberalism* and not the Left. Trilling had private reservations about the secular rationality of the Enlightenment, but in the political sphere he accorded pride of place to moderation, tolerance, and pluralism—the liberal, Enlightenment virtues that could be claimed as indigenously American. The potential chill of these virtues demanded the warmth of a vital culture, and Trilling sought out literature and criticism that would undo the stultifying, wanly optimistic culture he attributed to the Left of the 1930s, the attitudes and opinions that had encouraged American liberals to admire Stalin. Trilling turned his ire on any literature or criticism that struck him as a continuation of the Stalinist pattern. Trilling's anti-communist essays of the 1940s would give him the material for *The Liberal Imagination*, his most famous book. Often associated with the 1950s, the decade in which *The Liberal Imagination* had its deepest influence, the book's force derived from Trilling's Kronstadt and from the creative energy of his anti-communism. If *The Liberal Imagination* was of a decade, it was of the 1940s, recording the arc of Trilling's early anti-communism.

In the 1940s the immediacy of intellectual anti-communism derived from the increasing power of the Soviet Union. American communism did not disappear after the 1930s, but the Nazi-Soviet pact destroyed the capacious Popular Front radicalism, the sort of radicalism that could span the New Deal and the Soviet experiment. Public affection for the Soviet Union did return when the United States and the U.S.S.R. became allies in World War II.[3] Stalin even made inroads into American popular culture as "Uncle Joe," but Stalin made no comeback in the minds of Trilling and Chambers and he enjoyed no return to grace in the pages of *Partisan Review*. The anti-Stalinism Trilling, Chambers, and the *Partisan Review* circle had promoted in the late 1930s was impervious to these particular ups and downs. Accepting the Soviet Union as an ally in World War II was not the same thing as endorsing a Soviet alternative to the American system.[4] Whatever power communism continued to exert on the imagination of intellectuals, the Party was no longer a magnet for the gifted, ambitious young—in the United States, at least. In *The End of Ideology*, Daniel Bell wrote that "almost the entire group of serious intellectuals who had been attracted to Marxism [in the United States] had broken with the Communist Party by 1940," a situation that did not obtain in much of Europe until considerably later.[5] Well before the Cold War, the fate of the Soviet Union and the fate of the United States had become intertwined, and anti-Stalinism demanded a reconsideration of American power. Anti-communism, combined with the intense antifascism of the World War II years, prompted intellectuals to rethink their ideas about capitalist America, ideas they had formulated at the height of the Great Depression.[6]

Trilling and Chambers both came to see Stalin's Soviet Union as a regime that approximated fascism; for Chambers, approximation was more like correlation. In *Witness*, he described a discussion circa 1939 with Walter Krivitsky, his fellow anti-communist defector from the Party, during which Krivitsky asked him, "Is the Soviet Government a fascist government?"[7] It was a question that seemed to defy common sense. Yet Chambers replied to it in the affirmative. Trilling used the word *reactionary* rather than fascist when describing the Soviet Union. He wrote in 1946 that he had "for some years believed that Stalinist Russia was becoming a reactionary force in Europe." With a reactionary Stalin clearly in control of the Soviet Union, Trilling's concern was the cancerous influence of Stalinist reaction outside Soviet borders, an influence that "is growing and deadly—because it is not an 'influence' but often actually a domination." For Trilling, this domination was by no means negligible in the United States: Stalinist Russia's "manifestations in this country [the United States] through the agency of the Communist Party and the liberals who are intellectually and morally influenced by the Party," he wrote, "are almost always bad in the political sphere and always deathly in the cultural sphere."[8] A view of the Soviet Union as reactionary or fascist might have kept the flame of radicalism alive in other intellectuals. For Trilling and Chambers, political radicalism was eternally attached to Stalin's Soviet Union, too much attached for it to be worth saving. Having rejected the lost cause of radicalism, Trilling and Chambers embarked upon a search for liberal and conservative answers to a Bolshevism become reactionary and to a Soviet Union that was ever more powerful globally.

Chambers's was an insurgent anti-communist voice at *Time*, while Trilling was more the reluctant fellow traveler at *Partisan Review*. Chambers constantly pushed his editor and his colleagues to put out an anti-communist magazine, to dismiss any notion of the U.S.S.R. as an ally of the United States and to begin debating the nature of opposition to an emerging Soviet empire. It was an ambitious agenda even for Henry Luce and not one to which *Time* was ever subordinated in the 1940s. The editors at *Partisan Review* basically agreed with Chambers about the character of the Soviet Union. The distance they had traveled since 1935 was immense: from talk of revolutionary communism and open affiliation with the Communist Party, the *Partisan Review* editors had graduated to the recommendation that American foreign policy become more militantly anti-communist, asking whether socialism itself was a casualty of the Russian Revolution, although they still identified themselves as socialists. Trilling did not participate directly in such debates; he never wrote about foreign policy, and he was not drawn to speculating about socialism. It was the moral and intellectual influence of Stalinist Russia on American culture that worried him and not Stalinist Russia itself. Nevertheless, he strongly endorsed *Partisan Review*'s hard-line anti-communism, and it was an endorsement he never revised, a cardinal commitment for Trilling.

The *Partisan Review* intellectuals lacked political direction and purpose circa 1940. They were elated at the Nazi-Soviet pact, not for the diabolical alliance it brought into being but for the humiliation it handed their progressive antagonists. Only those blindly loyal to the Soviet Union could continue to march in step with the Party line. The anti-Stalinists at *Partisan Review* felt especially vindicated, for their anti-Stalinism predated the union between Nazi Germany and Soviet Russia. Yet the Nazi-Soviet pact did not emancipate *Partisan Review*'s anti-Stalinists from the status quo in America, the "conservative democracy" of the Western capitalist powers. As of 1940, the *Partisan Review* circle had no will to enter a second world war on anyone's behalf. Having grown up with the devastation of World War I, they had little desire to see human life expended on the defense of "conservative democracy." Trilling was nothing but pessimistic about the prospect of war in 1939, an exemplary *Partisan Review* intellectual. In "The Situation in American Writing," a *Partisan Review* symposium on literature, Trilling prophesied that war would bring disaster to American fiction. If war came, he contended, there was "every likelihood that the writer will be either silenced or enslaved."[9] The writer's responsibility in the face of the coming apocalypse was critical rather than political, the preservation of personal integrity rather than the taking of concerted action. The writer must try "to survive, to remain undeceived, to keep others from being deceived."[10] In 1941, Bruce Bliven, editor of the *New Republic*, sent Trilling a survey question about whether the United States should declare war on Germany. In a letter he never sent Trilling's answer was a self-doubting "no." War would adversely affect American politics; it would harm "liberal forces in England." Considering the adverse impact of war on American and British liberals did "not bring me to a position of opposing a declaration of war. But they keep me from urging it."[11] Politics, once the great elixir, was now a bitter drink.

Trilling's paralysis ended when he changed his mind about American involvement in the war. Already in 1940, Sidney Hook, Trilling's political mentor, had publicly declared his support for American entry into World War II, a reversal of his earlier antiwar position.[12] By 1942, Trilling wanted to serve in the military, and his wife, Diana, had to force him not to. His sense of duty was so strong that Diana worried in her memoirs about his never forgiving her "for exempting him from military service."[13] A warlike anti-communism arrived at *Partisan Review* in the form of James Burnham's essay "Lenin's Heir," published in 1945. Burnham's title was as polemical as one could be in context, given an audience that still identified themselves as radical. Lenin's heir was none other than Joseph Stalin, and "Lenin's Heir" telegraphed an attribution of guilt to Lenin for Stalin's crimes. The essence of Burnham's piece was an unapologetic repudiation of the Russian Revolution, an affirmation of "the truth—so weighty with consequence for our age . . . that under Stalin, the communist revolution had been, not betrayed, but fulfilled." Stalinism or communism—the distinction was irrelevant—was a quest for global domination. Because Stalin had brought Bolshevism to fruition, it followed that Bolshevism was "a conspiratorial movement for the conquest of a monopoly of power in the era of capitalist disintegration." The capitalist world was not a rag better left to rot but the only defense against an expanding Soviet empire. Burnham was thinking in the framework of the Cold War some time before the Cold War had formally begun.[14]

An editorial titled "The Liberal 'Fifth Column'" extended Burnham's Cold War analysis, positing American power as the vehicle of anti-communist opposition. Fellow-traveling liberals were at fault almost to the point of treason, *Partisan Review*'s editors believed, because they had alienated themselves from American power, trusting far too credulously in the benign nature of Stalin's Soviet Union. Throughout the editorial—which was the combined effort of Phillip Rahv, William Phillips, William Barrett, and Delmore Schwartz—the word *liberal* was put in quotation marks, emphasizing liberals' failure to see the illiberalism of the Soviet Union; hence, "the word 'liberal' now retains nothing but a denotative value." The *Partisan Review* editors worried about a conservative backlash that might bring fascism in its wake, yet they doubted that capitalism would be its cause. When it comes, political anti-communism "would be condemned to fall into reactionary hands by the 'liberals' themselves," for "they have failed to provide their own leadership." The editors did not equivocate. They wrote very much in the manner of Chambers when they remarked that "the Communists will be dealt with for what they are, outright foreign agents." Another Chambers-esque claim was that pro-Soviet intellectuals had achieved a high degree of cultural and political leverage in the United States. "Never during the disastrous period of fellow traveling in the Thirties were the Russian zealots so highly placed in American life [as today]," the *Partisan Review* editors declared.[15]

In their editorial, they did not mention Henry Wallace's extraordinary visit to Siberia. The progressive Wallace validated their suspicions of American liberalism with an official visit to a *gulag* that was somehow invisible to him. According to Ann Applebaum, "Henry Wallace, Vice President of the United States, made a trip to Kolyma [a stretch of Siberia later known as the Soviet "Auschwitz"] in May 1944—and never even knew that he was visiting a prison." The scene could be the climax of a twentieth-century *Divine Comedy*, if the cynicism and tragedy behind it could be adequately rendered. Wallace's Virgil was "Nikishov, the notoriously corrupt, high-living [regional] boss, [who] escorted Wallace around Magadan, the main city of Kolyma. Wallace, in turn, imagined Nikishov, a senior NKVD [Soviet secret police] officer, to be the rough equivalent of an American capitalist." Wallace toasted his environs in the following words: "'the people of Siberia are a hardy, vigorous race, but not because they are whipped into submission.'" A grotesque trip had its grotesque coda: "before Wallace left, Nikishov gave an elaborate banquet in his honor. Extravagant dishes, their ingredients carved out of prisoners' rations, were served; toasts were made to Roosevelt, Churchill, and Stalin."[16] Wallace was not alone in his incomprehension; but to the extent that his incomprehension deserved the label *liberal*, it disgusted the authors of "The Liberal 'Fifth Column.'" With "The Liberal 'Fifth Column,'" the rudiments of a sober anti-communist liberalism were being put in place. In 1946 Trilling noted the death of Trotskyism in American intellectual life, writing that he could not "think of a single person notable in our intellectual life now who can accurately be described as a Trotskyist."[17]

The *Partisan Review* intellectuals went in circles with their debates about socialism, rejecting utopia and the status quo in the same breath. Sidney Hook—among the most tireless of anti-communists—remained tireless as well in his commitment to socialism. He wanted a "mixed economy," and he hoped to see such an economy come about in a nonrevolutionary way, a "piecemeal socialism through the democratic process." With its revolutionary vanguard leading the proletariat to communism, Bolshevism had nothing in common with the socialism Hook envisioned. Neither was socialism to be combined with capitalism, whatever Hook said about a mixed economy. Hook confessed "to a certain skepticism concerning the reliability of organized capitalist groups in the struggle for democracy."[18] Yet it was not enough to celebrate socialism: Hook was still in search of some entity that could realistically thwart the Soviet Union, "a democratic analogue to Stalin's multinational Bolshevism." The best Hook could do was to pen appeals to "the West," imploring it to check Stalin's tyrannical and imperialist sway. The idealism of Hook's "democratic analogue" to the Soviet Union collided with his anti-Stalinist fears. Hook wrote gloomily of the fact that "if the Western statesmen don't understand that the world cannot remain half slave and half free, the Russians do."

The loss of radical socialism generated an outbreak of cultural pessimism at *Partisan Review* of the sort that came naturally to Whittaker Chambers. In a review of *The Long Dusk* by Victor Serge, Irving Howe, making his debut as an intellectual around this time, referred to Serge, a former communist, as "one of the few still responsive survivors of a destroyed generation." Howe competed in weltschmerz with Chambers himself, with whom Howe had otherwise little in common. An ardent anti-Stalinist and an ardent socialist, Howe allowed himself a Spenglerian flourish in his intuition of "a civilization at the end of its historic role." Howe's intuition was commonplace at *Partisan Review,* his gloom a standard assumption. "I do not say that Western Civilization is doomed," wrote Granville Hicks, the former doyen of communist literary critics, "but it is fatuous not to take the possibility of failure into account." Hicks pointed out the "return" to the despairing mood of the 1920s, the revival of talk about civilizational decline. The biography of a "destroyed generation" linked the sensibility of Chambers with that of the *Partisan Review* circle. "Many of us," Hicks recalled, "were weaned away from this belief [in progress] in the period after World War I, both by experience and by exposure to European pessimism." In this account, the Soviet alternative offered only a fleeting reprieve from a long bout of political pessimism. In the 1930s, at a moment of weakness, intellectuals "fell for the Marxian version of the idea" of progress, and anti-Stalinism was their rude awakening.[19]

In the 1940s a note of anxiety, of philosophical and moral doubt, sounded beneath the brash assertions and strident attacks of the *Partisan Review* circle. (As early as 1938, *Partisan Review* was said to be "based on political, cultural, and aesthetic disorientation" by no less an authority than Leon Trotsky.)[20] The overtones of doubt and anxiety coincided with the discovery of French existentialism, reported on in elaborate detail in the pages of *Partisan Review.* Existentialism provided a secular language well tailored to the mounting disillusionments of the 1930s and early 1940s. Jean-Paul Sartre, the guru of existentialism, was suspect by the anti-Stalinist standards of *Partisan Review,* an intellectual "well along the road to Stalinism," in William Barrett's judgment, "but he was the messenger who could not be ignored." Sartre's works, wrote Claude-Edmonde Magny in *Partisan Review,* are based on "the absolute subjectivity of values; this is the direct consequence of the fact that there is no God to guarantee them." Barrett made a similar point about Sartre, for whom "death (as elsewhere in modern life) becomes the agent of nihilism." The particular doctrines of Sartre

or of Existentialism were less powerful, one gathers, than the mood they inspired and sanctioned. This was the mood described somewhat archly by
Hannah Arendt, herself a student of Martin Heidegger and a friend of Karl
Jaspers, two existentialist demigods, as "that distinctive melancholy which,
since Kierkegaard, has been the hallmark of all but the most superficial
society."[21]

An editorial statement in *Partisan Review*, published in the early part of
1947, laid bare the origins of this melancholy and uncertainty. The Soviet
Union's descent into Stalinism had shattered the intellectual structure of
their world: "historical experience since 1917 has put the entire socialist
perspective into question," Hicks wrote. Since the midpoint of the nineteenth century, socialism had "provided both an optimistic view of history
and a confidence in the possibility of establishing a rational human
order." Socialism had extended the political promise of reason until it fell
into the hands of the Soviets in 1917, when a luminous Enlightenment
vanished into the Bolshevik void. Although the editors would still have
described themselves as socialists, they had succumbed to the paradoxical
conclusion that socialism could "no longer serve the Left as the basis of
its political life." The mood of defeat extended from politics to ethics.
The *Partisan Review* circle was in the throes of a political crisis, indicated
by the use of a negative term—anti-Stalinism—in place of socialism. Its
crisis was moral as well, a consequence not only of the moral compromises fellow traveling had entailed but also of Marxism itself. "Marx is by
no means solely responsible for our moral confusion," Hicks wrote of leftists in 1947, "but his guilt is large."[22] The Left must therefore strive toward
"the rehabilitation of morality." Gloomy as the ex-communist intellectuals at *Partisan Review* were about the Left in the late 1940s, they were not
gloomy enough to concede any territory to the Right or to conservative
intellectuals like Chambers. They did not intend the rehabilitation of
morality to be a conservative endeavor.

William Phillips, the archetypal *Partisan Review* editor, presumed a
stark difference between his "little magazine," put together in lower Manhattan, and *Time*, the mass-media behemoth in Rockefeller Center.
Phillips admitted to a modest pride in the recognition "that the little magazine is now accepted as a more or less permanent sideshow in our culture," upholding quality, while *Time* catered to the low standards of mass
culture. "We occasionally have to read a piece in *Time* twice," Phillips
complained, "to see how totally inadequate it is to its material." Phillips

went on to defame *Time*'s editor: shared anti-Stalinism did not mean that the *Partisan Review* circle had anything in common with "Wehrmacht generals like Louis B. Mayer or Henry Luce."[23] Chambers must have regarded Phillips's criticism with amusement, if he came across it. The scorn of the Left would have told him that *Time* was heading in the right direction. Yet to a remarkable extent, differences on the Soviet Union between Chambers and the *Partisan Review* editors were differences of degree or of sensibility: they all wrote articles on the need for combating Soviet communism globally, on the crisis of Western civilization, and on the moral crisis of the Left. "The Liberal 'Fifth Column'" placed the question of American power in an anti-communist context. Chambers spent much of his time in the 1940s exploring the political and moral implications of this question as well as its anti-communist context.

With his job at *Time*, Chambers put intellectual advocacy before political action for the first time since his days at the *Daily Worker* and the *New Masses*. Walter Krivitsky had inspired him with a program of counterrevolution; when Krivitsky died under suspicious circumstances in February 1940, Chambers believed that Soviet agents had killed him; and Krivitsky's death or possible murder encouraged Chambers to keep his knowledge of the Ware circle to himself.[24] He retreated from the political stage. For Chambers, the Left was worse than useless where anti-communism was concerned: it was evil because it weakened confidence in Western civilization, thereby strengthening Stalin's hand. It was evil as well because it was atheist, this being the essence of the divide between the communist East and the faltering West. A product of this divide, Chambers was baptized in September 1940 at the Episcopalian Cathedral of Saint John the Divine, a few blocks away from Columbia University where he had started on the path to the Communist Party. In 1941, Chambers would move to the Quaker denomination, a shift in allegiance that did little to change his ideas, as he wrote mostly about Christianity or simply about faith in God and not about interdenominational issues; faith was better than nonfaith and the details of faith were of more individual than political concern. Convinced that the Left was ethically bankrupt, Chambers pursued an anti-communism of the Right, and the task of his *Time* journalism was to make right-wing anti-communism accessible to the average American reader and citizen.

Chambers's status as a conservative intellectual was anomalous. As of 1940, right-wing anti-communism was tethered to an intellectual conservatism that was fitful and atomistic.[25] Anti-communism had begun to gain momentum in American politics: the Hatch Act (August 1939) and the Smith Act (June 1940) empowered the government to investigate, apprehend, and deport communists or subversives, as communists were coming to be known. The House Committee on Un-American Activities (HUAC) was created in 1938, and its political advocates were a consortium of Southern Democrats and Republicans, political constituencies not enlisted in the New Deal. A focal point of sorts, HUAC was an organization in which fear of communism and animus against the New Deal could converge.[26] Yet the avowal of anti-communism was not itself politically decisive, and often it was based on a thin body of knowledge. Communism might be identified as a domestic threat, but Soviet communism could still be regarded as a distant, obscure factor in the calculation of American national interest. Anti-communism's very utility as a proxy for criticism of the New Deal drew attention away from communism and the Soviet Union. Furthermore, the intellectual disorganization of conservatism was profound circa 1940. The Right did not have many political intellectuals after a decade of economic and political experience—the 1930s—that had moved the intellectual center so far to the Left. Conservatives had to rethink the antistatist, isolationist elements—traditionally prominent aspects of American conservatism—simply to consider participation in a "war" against the Soviet Union. If anti-communism had the potential to unify the Right, unity would only come at the price of transformation.[27] Chambers used his position at *Time* to encourage a transformation of the Right, working toward a conservatism of the future.

Chambers did not begin to articulate a Cold War mission for the United States until he became foreign news editor at *Time* in August 1944, the realization of a long-standing ambition. The job illustrated the respect Chambers had earned from Luce, vindicating Chambers in a longstanding argument with his boss and giving Chambers's anti-communism a foothold at *Time*.[28] Already in 1943 Luce had appointed Chambers to the prestigious Senior Group at *Time*, giving Chambers a role in shaping the magazine's journalistic agenda. By 1944, Chambers had persuaded a once reluctant Luce of Stalin's limitless thirst for dominion. In this campaign, Chambers had the help of John Chamberlain at *Life* and William Schlamm, an Austrian ex-communist who had made his way to an editorship at *Fortune*; Schlamm would later become an editor at *National Review*.[29] Chambers could publish his own articles and he could shape the foreign news that others wrote for *Time*, seeking to fracture a perceived Stalinist orthodoxy in the world of educated elites, which he described (in *Witness*) as "an impassioned, powerful and all but universal official and unofficial pro-Soviet opinion." The foreign policy wisdom of the "Popular Front mind" was that "World War III could be averted only by conciliating the Soviet Union." It was Chambers's journalistic mission to puncture this "willful historical self-delusion."[30] With the Cold War still to begin in 1944, Chambers was convinced that a state of war had been reached, at least as far as Stalin's intentions were concerned. Stalin was at war with the United States and the United States was at war with Germany and Japan, a sensible if incomplete list of enemies in Chambers's opinion. The United States had to realize that the Soviet Union was its enemy and the enemy whose ideological power was deepest, precisely because it was international.

Chambers's job at *Time* demanded the careful study of current events, and he tried to go behind them at times, assessing the causes of a totalitarian crisis that encompassed communism and fascism. In "The Anatomy of Fascism," published in the *American Mercury*, Chambers addressed himself to the instability of modern politics. The entrance of the masses onto the historical stage may lead inevitably to fascism because no one knows "how to stop the process. For nobody knows how to solve the chief political problem of the age—how to pacify the masses before they seize political control of the State."[31] American conservatives were among those without an answer. Chambers saw in Wendell Wilkie, FDR's Republican challenger in 1944, the same problem that characterized modern politics in general. Wilkie would have to work out a relationship with the masses to achieve political success and, in doing so, the masses might come to control him. Americans would have to guard against fascism in the United States, Germany, and Japan and, less obviously, in the Soviet Union. At his job, Chambers could educate the masses, and *Time* was undoubtedly a mass-circulation magazine. In 1945, *Partisan Review* had a circulation of 7,000; in the same period, *Time's* readership was 1.5 million; through other Luce publications such as *Life* and *Fortune* millions more readers could be reached.[32] Chambers worked tirelessly, to the point of endangering his health, in order to capitalize on the opportunity that Luce had given him. Chambers believed that an accurate rendering of the geopolitical situation, shorn of philo-communism, could yield only one conclusion in the years between 1944 and 1948. The West—and the United States as its de facto leader after World War II—had to marshal its power, military and spiritual, and check the advance of Stalin's Soviet Union.

For many of *Time*'s journalists, Chambers's anti-communism was eccentric and alarmist and his editorial inflexibility an outrage. These journalists were not communists; nor were they liberals enamored of the Soviet Union. Basically, they preferred to see the Soviet Union as an ally rather than an enemy of the United States. In early 1944 Richard Lauterbach, *Time*'s Moscow correspondent, attributed the Katyn massacre to the Nazis—the mass murder of Polish officers in the Katyn forest was then a mystery and has since been attributed to the Soviet Union. Troyan Pribichevich, another *Time* correspondent, saw political potential in Tito, the leader of communist forces in Yugoslavia against the non-communist Chetniks. In 1944, Theodore White, *Time*'s precocious foreign correspondent in China, was growing steadily more hostile toward the Nationalist Chiang Kai-Shek and progressively more curious about the communists centered in Yenan. As World War II seemed to be winding down, the hunger for peace was more palpable at *Time* than was genuine admiration for communism, Chinese or European. To identify the Soviet Union as an enemy was to deny that peace could still be obtained after years of catastrophic war. As a *Time* journalist, Fred Guin described the tension between editor Chambers and the journalists to his Left: "we had many anti-anti-Communists around—Chambers was charged by many of us as an evil influence trying his hardest to get us into war against the Russians even before the Nazis were completely licked."[33] The anti-Chambers camp looked out and saw possibilities corresponding to their hunger for peace. Chambers, gazing upon the same geopolitical political scene, saw an intractable communist menace.

In late 1944, the hostilities between Chambers and his opponents at *Time* reached their apex. Several foreign correspondents—John Osborne, John Hersey, Walter Graebner, and Theodore White—tried to unseat Chambers as editor of foreign news. They were angered by his anti-communist views but more so by the extreme editorial liberties he took with their reporting. They were also disturbed by factual errors and distortions that Chambers's editing had introduced into their writing. Luce did not want excessive anti-Soviet zeal to jeopardize himself or his magazine, and in 1944 anti-communism was hardly the official ideology of the United Sates government. Luce agreed with the anti-Chambers camp that Chambers "has to some degree failed to distinguish between, on the one hand, the general revolutionary, leftist or simply chaotic trends, and, on the other hand, the specifically Communist politics in various countries."[34] Yet Luce sided with Chambers, whose anti-communism impressed Luce less for its moral force than for its capacity to explain world politics. "The posture of events in January 1945," Luce wrote in a memo about Chambers, "seems to have confirmed Editor Chambers as fully as a news-editor is ever confirmed."[35] Luce kept Chambers on as foreign news editor until a heart attack forced Chambers to step down in the summer of 1945.

One can read this backroom drama into two *Time* articles written by Chambers, one on developments in Yugoslavia and the other on China. These articles are clearly Chambers's interpretation of events. In "Area of Decision," Chambers focused on the struggle between the anti-communist Chetniks and the pro-communist forces under Tito on the battlefield that was shortly to become communist Yugoslavia. Chambers reluctantly praised Tito as "a man of decision."[36] The future of Europe depended now on such struggles, Chambers argued, rather than on the soon-to-end struggle between the Allies and the fascist powers. Like James Burnham in "Lenin's Heir," Chambers was starting to think along the lines of the coming Cold War.[37] Through Tito, Chambers reasoned, the Soviet Union had the opportunity to control the southeast of Europe, an old ambition of the Russian empire. A Red Army presence in southeast Europe meant that "the Balkans had become a Russian sphere of influence. As such, it [the Soviet Union] undid the work of a hundred years of British statecraft and made Russia a Mediterranean power—poised massively about the artery of empire at Suez."[38] In the ruthlessness of its imperial designs, Soviet Russia was close to fascism. An argument about the fate of southeastern Europe, Chambers's piece was also an argument against *Time*'s Troyan Pribichevich, who had a far more benign impression of Tito.[39]

"Crisis" was an argument against Theodore White and at the same time an argument against the Chinese Communist Party. In May 1944 *Life* put out a critical article about Chiang Kai-Shek, and White, convinced of Chiang's corruption and military weakness, continued in a similar vein in his reports from China. Increasingly, White saw Mao and the Chinese communists as a viable opponent of the Japanese, an alternative to Chiang and to the nationalists behind him.[40] Published on November

13, 1944, "Crisis," very much the product of Chambers's thinking, made only sporadic use of White's reporting.[41] The crisis of the article's title concerned the American general Joseph Stillwell whom FDR had recently recalled from duty in China, setting off a rupture in the relationship between the United States and Chiang Kai Shek's nationalists. Chambers feared a shift away from the nationalists toward the communists. Were the communists to win, Chambers envisioned a massive communist bloc composed of China and the Soviet Union: "a Communist China (with its 450 million people) would turn to Russia (with its 200 million people) rather than to the United States (with its 130 million people) as an international collaborator." Journalists, like Theodore White, misunderstood the nature of communism, its expansionary power and its innate evil, so he could not comprehend the stakes of this particular crisis. Stalin had garnered Popular Front enthusiasm while terrorizing the Soviet world. Mao could potentially do the same, and Chambers feared the repetition of old mistakes on the part of Western observers: "touring U.S. correspondents have lauded Yenan's agrarian reforms, labor unions, well-fed troops, efficient guerilla organization. They have never reported Yenan's vigorous press censorship . . . its iron party discipline . . . secret police, other totalitarian features."[42] *Time* was not big enough to contain both Chambers and White and in 1946 White resigned from the magazine.

Apart from *Witness*, Chambers's most consequential anti-communist writing was without question "The Ghosts on the Roof," published in *Time* on March 5, 1945. A tone of hesitation colored the editorial preface to "The Ghosts on the Roof," as if the magazine were half apologizing for Chambers's intemperate anti-communism: "*Time* wishes to make clear that it admires and respects our heroic ally and recognizes great mutuality of interests between the United States and the U.S.S.R.—but that in any argument between Communism and Democracy, *Time* is on the side of Democracy."[43] Chambers's thesis in "The Ghosts on the Roof" was one that the Polish poet Czelaw Milosz, whom Chambers adored, would echo some eight years later in *The Captive Mind*: "Russia is effectively carrying out the precepts of the Tsars in regard to territorial expansion."[44] "The Ghosts on the Roof" was highly unconventional journalism, a combination of historical argument, op-ed polemic, and creative writing. Its form was a fictionalized dialogue between Russia's tsarist past and its Soviet present set above the roof of the Livadia Palace, where the Yalta conference had recently been held. The conference between Stalin and the Western powers, during which the Soviet Union secured its sphere of influence in Eastern Europe, had an ominous personal meaning for Chambers. Alger Hiss had attended on the American side. The proximity of Hiss to power, combined with the weakness Chambers attributed to Roosevelt's statesmanship at Yalta, confirmed Chambers's worst fears about American foreign policy in 1945.[45] Yalta might mean that Stalin was gaining the upper hand.

In "The Ghosts on the Roof," Chambers gave literary shape to his political anxieties. The irony of "The Ghosts on the Roof" is the unexpected admiration a ghostly tsar and tsarina feel for Stalin. "No Bolshevik was more tsar-like than he [Stalin]; but he was still a Bolshevik," Robert Service has written.[46] Building upon this insight, Chambers's literary conceit was a sly way of imputing the basest, most reactionary imperialism to Stalin. Although the Bolsheviks had murdered Nicholas II and Alexandra, the former monarchs cannot help themselves, as ghosts, from admiring the expansion of Russian power under Stalin. Nicholas II reconciles himself to Stalin "after the partition of Poland [in 1939], [when] Nicky insisted on returning to Russia. He began to attend the meetings of the Politburo." What Nicholas especially appreciates is the leverage twentieth-century ideology has given Stalin. Stalin can use Marxist language to justify his infiltration of a foreign polity, thereby drawing it into Russia's imperial embrace. Chambers has Nicholas say of Stalin: "He is magnificent! Greater than Rurik, greater than Peter! For Peter conquered only in the name of a limited class. But he [Stalin] embodies the international social revolution. That is the mighty new device of power which he has developed for blowing up other countries from within."[47] Nicholas' points of reference would not have been obscure in 1945: they were Soviet interference in the politics of Eastern Europe, Soviet exploitation of regional communist parties and the Red Army presence in Eastern Europe for imperial gain. Tsarist Russia had presided over its own partition of Poland, aiming for dominion in the east and south of Europe, and the Nazi-Soviet pact could be seen as a first step toward the recapitulation of a tsarist agenda. Only Stalin and the Bolsheviks were much more efficient and powerful than their monarchist predecessors. Tsarist Russia, the most reactionary of the European powers, had consistently offended advanced political thinking in the West, placing it at the margins of political fashion. Stalinism had the communist allure so fatal to many Western intellectuals.

Chambers leavened his depressing message with humor, ending "The Ghosts on the Roof" on an optimistic note. His assembly of characters from the afterlife was farcical. It was a world in which Nicholas II sat in Stalin's politburo. The muse of history, Clio, was comic in her "very slight grasp of historical dialectic," as Nicholas II puts it. Stalin has seduced even the muse of history, inducing her to confuse him with Woodrow Wilson. "All right-thinking people now agree that Russia is a mighty friend of democracy. Stalin has become a conservative," the muse contends. This was entertaining enough as an observation, a sanguine misunderstanding of Stalin's actual intentions from a muse who should have known better. The muse is assured of a democratic future: the Yalta conference will show "that the Soviet Union is prepared to collaborate with her allies in making the world safe for democracy." Against this deluded muse—a liberal muse, one gathers, from context—Chambers could indulge his own conservatism by giving the tsarina a sharper historical eye. The tsarina sees that the West and the Soviet Union are fundamentally at odds with each other. There can be no allies, she says, when one has "two systems of society, which embody diametrically opposed moral and political principles." The fictional mode offered Chambers the luxury of optimism. The muse makes a prediction about Anglo-American intransigence that follows from the tsarina's argument. Stalin will not win: "America and Britain, though they may undergo great changes, will not become communist states. More is at stake than economic and political systems. Two faiths are at issue."[48] In January 1948, *Time* reprinted "The Ghosts on the Roof" not as history but, in the words of Sam Tanenhaus, "as prophecy."[49]

The year Chambers published "The Ghosts on the Roof"—1945—was the same year that his personal knowledge of communist conspiracy was beginning to bear political fruit.[50] The testimony he had given Adolph Berle about the Ware circle was slowly starting to influence events, individuals, and institutions. In November 1945, Elizabeth Bentley spoke to the FBI about a communist cell in Washington, one much like the Ware circle, and the *New York Sun* went so far as to implicate Chambers in Bentley's revelations. Representative Karl Mundt wanted HUAC to subpoena Chambers, whose depositions to the FBI, together with Berle's memo about their meeting, were eliciting ever more excitement—at least among the select few who had access to them.[51] Already on May 10, 1945, the FBI had questioned Chambers at length. The political pieces of the great drama about to unfold in 1948 were falling into place, although in 1945 Chambers was content for others to pursue the Ware circle.[52] Chambers was not entirely secretive about his past, but with his family flourishing on the farm and an influential job secure at *Time*, he was not eager to let the public in on his story of espionage. An anecdote recalled by Arthur Schlesinger Jr. conveys Chambers's simultaneous openness and reticence regarding the Ware circle. In a private meeting with Schlesinger, Chambers casually dropped the names of Harry Dexter White and Alger Hiss. Chambers did not deny the communist affiliation of these august New Dealers, but he was evasive about their precise involvement with communism, sufficiently evasive to leave out the essence of the story: "the Hiss assignment, he [Chambers] said vaguely, was to provide information when needed. He made no allusion to Soviet espionage," Schlesinger recalled. Chambers's comments to Schlesinger, however incomplete, were still off the record. Washington had been informed, and there was nothing more to do. In Schlesinger's recollection, Chambers "had tacitly agreed with the communists to leave them alone if they would leave him alone."[53]

At this point, Chambers was content to confine his anti-communist activism to the realm of ideas. Pondering the Soviet-American conflict, Chambers drew inspiration from *A Study of History*, Arnold Toynbee's enormous history of civilization, which Chambers reviewed for *Time* in 1947. Toynbee, a British historian, claimed that history was a recurrent battle between a vulgar proletariat and a creative minority. The minority leads the proletariat, achieving victory at times—a victory that is always threatened with decay and overthrow. Toynbee put civilization rather than the nation-state at the center of historical change, "asserting God as an active force in history," in Chambers's paraphrase. Formerly, the British empire had stood guard over Christian civilization, and, as the British empire collapsed, the United States had no choice but to be the "champion of the remnant of Christian civilization against the forces that threaten it."[54] This was not at all the language of *Partisan Review*, but novel as such anti-communist language may have been coming from an intellectual, a former communist no less, it was a language that resonated with the public. *Time* received 14,000 requests for reprints of Chambers's review, approximately twice the number of people who subscribed to *Partisan Review.*[55]

At *Partisan Review*, Chambers's thesis about a reactionary imperialist Soviet Union had been conceded, leaving a vacancy that politics alone could not fill. What had been lost with the Soviet alternative and with the confusion of socialism could possibly be regained in the movement of Western culture, not back to Christendom, as Chambers hoped, but in the cultivation of the avant-garde. Perhaps the radical future was there to be discovered in culture, which might foster new forms of radical political life. Here Trilling, the student of Matthew Arnold, parted ways with *Partisan Review*. Trilling was no friend of the avant-garde—he never had been—and he was an enemy of radicalism, of radical culture and radical politics. One can see exactly how moderate Trilling was becoming by comparing him with Clement Greenberg, an art critic closely associated with *Partisan Review* who offered radicalism a second chance in his 1939 essay, "Avant-Garde and Kitsch." Greenberg turned his radical vision to art, hoping it would help revive a radicalism unsettled by the failures of the 1930s. Greenberg's essay on kitsch was a program for radicalism by other means.

"Avant-Garde and Kitsch" was a forthright repudiation of the Popular Front, the most original formulation of a common *Partisan Review* argument about the vulgarity of the 1930s: "the populist strain in the vulgar Marxism of the Thirties helped to prepare the ground for the later reconciliation with the commercial pressures of the mass market and its need for more conventional forms of art."[56] This was a development that had "conservative" overtones in Greenberg's essay. Knowing that he was inverting the conventional wisdom of the Popular Front, Greenberg allocated progressive virtue to the bohemian avant-garde and its centuries-old struggle to free itself from the clutches of the bourgeoisie. Kitsch illustrates the vulgar tendency of mass society, leaving its imprint on the culture of fascist, capitalist, and communist societies in the twentieth century. With his notes on kitsch, Greenberg took the thesis that Stalin's Russia was reactionary and extended it to the aesthetic realm: "kitsch has in the last ten years become the dominant culture in Soviet Russia." American kitsch points to the reactionary tenor of capitalism in crisis. Capitalism needs kitsch to hide its cultural bankruptcy, for "capitalism in decline finds that whatever of quality it is still capable of producing becomes almost inevitably a threat to its own existence." Greenberg's essay was the work of someone without viable political options. The industrial revolution had raised the masses to new heights, but in the process it had lowered much of culture to the level of kitsch, leaving a dwindling band of bohemians to create art of any quality. Greenberg had only the rhetoric of socialism, which may not generate a new culture, though socialism of some kind might preserve "whatever living culture we have right now."[57]

If Trilling agreed with Greenberg about the vulgarity of the Popular Front, his ideal culture was almost antiprogressive. High art did not need the shield of socialism, in Trilling's view; it needed artists courageous enough to transcend the pieties of the Left and not just the vulgarities of the Popular Front. The Left had to remake itself and to remake itself along liberal, not socialist, lines. Such was the exhilarating example of John Dos Passos, who both embodies "the cultural tradition of the intellectual Left" and operates as a "conscious corrective of the culture from which he stems," Trilling wrote in a 1938 essay. Fortunately, Dos Passos stands one step removed from the collectivist mentality of the Left. His affection for the individual, and reliance on individual conscience, distinguish him from the typical leftist to the point that "he is almost alone of the novelists of the Left . . . in saying that the creeds and idealisms of the Left may bring corruption quite as well as the greeds and cynicisms of the established order." For Dos Passos is to some degree an old-fashioned moralist, convinced that "the barometer of social breakdown is not suffering through economic deprivation but always more degeneration through moral choice." Rather than appealing to "socialism" of some not-yet-existing kind to calm the fever of the despairing intellectual, Dos Passos is simply despairing, and for this he earned Trilling's admiration. "I can think of no more useful political job for the literary man today," Trilling wrote in praise of Dos Passos, "than, by representation of despair, to cauterize the exposed soft-tissue of too easy hope."[58] To defy the Popular Front was to succeed, in Trilling's terms, and to succumb to it was to fail.

Dos Passos's *U.S.A.* was a literary success, while Hemingway's Popular Front persona was the reason for his artistic failure. Trilling criticized Hemingway for turning himself into a saint of the Popular Front. Upon Hemingway were concentrated "all the fine social feelings of the now passing decade [the Thirties]," the very ethos of "the liberal-radical movement." As Hemingway "the man" rose to the summits of radical esteem, Hemingway the writer lost his sense of purpose. The éngagé pose had disrupted Hemingway's literary talent, and the result was so disappointing to Trilling that "one is tempted to reverse the whole liberal-radical assumption about literature. One almost wishes to say to an author like Hemingway, 'You have no duty, no responsibility. Literature, in a political sense, is not in the least important.' " Hemingway had sacrificed his talent on the altar of the Popular Front, and not because the industrial revolution was forcing him to write Popular Front kitsch. Hemingway had accepted the crude standards of the Left's new culture in hopes of becoming its literary hero, safely expressing the fine feelings that his readers so enjoyed seeing in print, the interlocking self-indulgence of progressive writer and progressive reader.[59]

In turning away from this new culture, created under the auspices of the Popular Front, Trilling glanced back at the past, as if to reverse the forward-looking mindset of an avant-garde intellectual like Greenberg. The past contained instruction at a time when instruction was urgently needed. Avoiding the tone of nostalgia, Trilling observed calmly that we have "the practice of the past to guide us at least with a few tentative notions." Those on the Left would be well advised to bear these notions in mind—such as the space between art and politics. Consideration of the past yields an agenda for art: not quite art for art's sake but art that is at moral liberty to challenge political orthodoxy. From the past, Trilling concluded, "we learn not to expect a political, certainly not an immediately political, effect from a work of art; and in removing from art a burden of messianic responsibility which it never has discharged and cannot discharge we may leave it free to do whatever it actually can do."[60] Liberal culture should be composed of conflicting ideas, of a conflict contained within the culture and within the minds and souls of its adherents. Searching for the right metaphor, Trilling concluded that "a culture is not a flow, not even a confluence; the form of its existence is a struggle, or at least a debate—it is nothing if not a dialectic." A self-righteous monologue is only an impediment to the dialectic of culture. The critic's obligation is to celebrate "those writers who contain both the yes and the no of their culture," for "by that token they were prophets of the Future," writers who could evaluate utopian projects by the lights of a conservative imagination. One such writer was Nathaniel Hawthorne, who entertained "brilliant and serious doubts about the nature and possibility of moral perfection," which encouraged him "to keep himself aloof from the 'Yankee reality' and . . . [to] dissent from the orthodoxies of dissent and tell us so much about the nature of radicalism and moral zeal."[61] To dissent from the orthodoxies of dissent was a phrase that perfectly described Trilling's own ambition.

Trilling explored the space between literature and politics, where intellectual autonomy might thrive, with the intent of expanding this space.

Literature could enact "dissent from the orthodoxies of dissent" and American culture would be liberal rather than of the Left or the Right when it would be various and complex—to use adjectives Trilling would come to revere—rather than strident and self-righteous. A liberal culture would uphold no single orthodoxy. Trilling had reservations about what he termed "my position," on which he elaborated in a 1940 letter. Referring to a piece he published in *Kenyon Review*, "Literature and Power," Trilling described his intent as "an attack on the conception of literature as power, whether religious, social or scientific." He was "coming out for literature as contemplation, as an end in itself." Trilling worried about "whether certain of the deep modifications I'm making don't portend bad things for me." One is tempted here to fill in the word "conservative" for "bad things." Trilling comforted himself with the observation that the Right was now taking up the Left's dogmatic attitude toward literature: "the old idea of literature for power and responsibility which used to be a hallmark of radical thought, is now being used by the potential other side and first through the mouth of Archibald MacLeish." In an essay titled "The Irresponsibles," MacLeish had recently excoriated artists and intellectuals for their passivity in the 1930s. In the midst of their frenetic arguments, they had not done enough to reverse the advance of fascism and to defend Western civilization.[62]

Slowly, Trilling would disentangle his criticism of the Left, of the Popular Front and its legacy, from his aspiration to be present at the creation of a new, liberal culture in America. Trilling delved back into cultural history to understand what had produced the Popular Front, examining the psychological functions that radicalism served. In an essay on Sherwood Anderson, Trilling touched on the existential melancholy that led his generation to Marx and the Soviet experiment, a vision of life, in which "each individual is a precious secret essence, often discordant with all other essences." The progressive intuition was "that society, and more particularly the industrial age, threatens these essences; that the good values of life had been destroyed by the industrial dispensation; that people have been cut off from each other and even from themselves." Trilling himself had repeatedly addressed the discontents of the industrial society in the 1920s, when he was writing for the *Menorah Journal*. In "Sherwood Anderson," Trilling underscored the religious dimension to despair in America, although not in Europe. "Sherwood Anderson" anticipated the religious revival that would begin among intellectuals in the 1940s and last well into the 1950s, with Chambers among its most enthusiastic proponents. Trilling noted that "in Europe a century before, Stendhal could execute a bourgeois materialism and yet remain untempted by the dim religiosity which in American in the twenties seemed one of the likeliest of the new ways by which one might affirm the value of the spirit."[63]

The tragedy of the 1930s, in Trilling's thumbnail sketch of American cultural history, was that an intelligent despair found refuge in the unthinking pieties of the Popular Front. Progressivism compelled intellectual after intellectual, artist after artist, to succumb to the gratifications of the self-righteous ego. Yet again, Trilling criticized Hemingway—adding John Steinbeck and the playwrights Clifford Odets and Irwin Shaw to the list—in a review of *Let Us Now Praise Famous Men*, the book of photographs and prose that was a monument of the 1930s documentary style. Trilling concentrated on the psychological roots of the Popular Front, eschewing any simple equation of progressivism with a longing for social justice: "the 'social consciousness' of the Thirties which flowered in Hemingway and Steinbeck, in Odets and Irwin Shaw, which millions found so right, proper and noble, did indeed have a kind of passion, and perhaps it had the virtue of being better than nothing. But how abstract and without fiber of resistance it was, how much too apt it was for the drawing-room, how essentially it was a pity which wonderfully served the needs of the pitier."[64] In this final turn of phrase—about pity serving the needs of the pitier—lay an explanation for the obtuseness of so many radicals in the 1930s. Infatuated with their own pity and social consciousness, many radicals had refused to believe that the Soviet Union—which pitied the poor, the downtrodden, and the exploited so grandly in its official rhetoric—was rapacious and pitiless to a fantastic degree. Stalinism depended on such dishonest self-pity, and it was the lifeblood of the Popular Front.

Trilling's psychological insights drew on a pessimism he attributed to Sigmund Freud. As a radical, Trilling had identified Freud immediately as a threat to radicalism, fearing Freud's doubts about pity and idealism; as an anti-communist, Trilling used Freud to analyze the relationship between pity and the Left, to debunk pity, and to banish it from mature political thinking. To this end, Trilling attacked John Steinbeck, already a venerated statue in the pantheon of left-wing fiction, arguing that Steinbeck's problem is literary in part because Steinbeck "thinks like a social function, not like a novelist." Steinbeck's literary failure is less significant, however, than the popular success of *The Grapes of Wrath*, which Trilling ascribed to a distinct group of people—a class, even. "A book like *The Grapes of Wrath* cockers-up the self-righteousness of the liberal middle class," Trilling declared; "it is easy to feel virtuous in our love of such good *poor* people."[65] Again, this was an analysis that could explain the pro-Soviet sympathies of the Left in the 1930s. The actual goings-on in Stalin's Soviet Union were immaterial. The Moscow trials, the various Five Year Plans, and the purges had failed to complicate support for the good poor people of the Soviet Union. A personal sense of virtue and righteousness was at stake for the fellow traveler more than the actual condition of the Soviet people. The reception of Steinbeck's novel was symptomatic of a political condition in which the Left celebrated, more than anything, the heroic tribulations of its own conscience.

It was Freud who showed Trilling how to deprive the Left of its illusions.[66] Trilling broached the subject in "The Progressive Psyche," a book review in which he looked again at the problem of psychology and the Left. The book in question was *Self-Analysis*, by the psychoanalyst Karen Horney, which Trilling contrasted with Freud's psychological insights. Horney's book illuminated the "psychology" of liberalism in Trilling's reading of it, "these old, absolute simplicities of eighteenth-century liberalism," which amounted to an excess of optimism about human nature. Trilling went so far as to label the need for optimism "one of the great inadequacies of liberal thought." The liberal Horney must therefore disregard Freud, as Trilling himself had some ten years before, because she simply cannot accept the gravity of his wisdom. Hers is the shortcoming of the liberal middle class and her book the typical "response to the wishes of an intellectual class which has always found Freud's ideas cogent but too stringent and too dark."[67] For the purposes of criticism, Trilling placed himself outside the psychology of the liberal middle class, proclaiming his preference for Freud, whose pessimistic vision "demonstrates faith [in man] by daring to present man with the terrible truth of his own nature." Armed with such truth, one was insulated from the temptations of Stalinism.

In a review titled "The Lower Depths," Trilling once again lamented the "facile optimism" in the air, focusing on pity as a debit rather than a virtue. He made the factual statement that "almost every novel that tells me about poverty and degradation asks me to pity the people it describes. But I am enough of a Spinozist and Freudian to believe that pity is an

135

emotion much to be suspected." Trilling saw cause for concern and out-rage in poverty and degradation, but he distrusted high emotions flaunted in response to poverty and degradation. In "The Lower Depths," he was candid about his own confusion: "I am sure that the great fact of the mod-ern consciousness is the insupportable and inhuman existence of the larger part of humanity," Trilling began. "Sometimes this fact seems chal-lenging, sometimes desperately depressing, but I never find it confusing in the way I find life's response to it confusing."[68] The Popular Front's moral fervor was really a sign of its moral disarray. Trilling's progressive discontents had some resonance in the pages of *Partisan Review*. Less deftly than Trilling had, Sidney Hook tried to capture the psychology of the Left as of 1943: an "atmosphere of mysticism, of passionate sometimes sacrificial, unrealism, and of hysterical busywork." In practical political terms, the "unrealism" of the Left accrued to Henry Wallace, FDR's pro-gressive vice president and a Popular Front figure who had outlasted the Popular Front. Referring to recent developments in politics, Hook al-leged that a vote for Wallace was worse than a vote for the Republicans: "Wallace and his friends are much more threatening heralds of a totali-tarianism, in the mythology of liberal and democratic rhetoric, than con-servative democrats like Hoover and Gibson who do not, as yet, believe that our political democracy is excessive."[69] Wallace had learned nothing from the cataclysms of the 1930s; conservatives like Hoover were be-holden to no such false logic. This was as much a concession as a *Partisan Review* contributor could make to the Right, but a reader of Hook and Trilling, sensing their rejection of the Popular Front psychology, could le-gitimately ask whether conservatives were more astute psychologically— less encumbered by mysticism and unrealism.

Trilling's antiprogressive pessimism did not include a marked sensi-tivity to the persecution of European Jews. Even his reverence for Freud, who fled Vienna for London in 1938 to escape the Gestapo, did not precipitate extensive reflection on Hitler's designs for Europe. Trilling was hardly blind to the horror of Nazi anti-Semitism. Probably he perceived no need to augment an already rampant antifascism among American intellectuals, whereas there was a need to help along an embattled anti-communism. And yet, the lack of attention to Jewish subjects at a time of unthinkable crisis in Jewish history was a feature of Trilling's intellectual life—and of many Jewish intellectuals around him—that cannot be fully explained by their confidence in American antifascism. In a review of Stefan Zweig's anguished autobiography, *The World of Yesterday*, Trilling seemed more interested in repeating his points about liberalism than in responding emotionally to the crisis of European Jewry. Zweig was an Austrian Jew, a man of letters, who had emigrated to Argentina only to find his life there unbearable; he committed suicide in 1942. In Trilling's review, Zweig is a paradigmatic liberal, who "loved—but the word is inadequate; he adored—the liberal humanistic tradition and all his efforts were towards advancing its fortunes." Zweig had a passive and subservient "temperament, which responded too easily to something in his tradition which was at worst mortuary and at best academic."[70] Trilling could not have missed the more fundamental meaning of Zweig's pathos: the world of European Jewry was rapidly becoming the world of yesterday; but Trilling did not dwell on this pathos. Trilling's reserve was either too great or his battle against liberal shallowness too engrossing.

Trilling wanted to see liberals everywhere acquire philosophical and political toughness. He expressed this aim with greatest clarity in private correspondence: "I still feel furious with us liberals for being so pure and decent and human *impotently*," he wrote in 1947.[71] The "still" implies the duration of the fury, which long outlasted the Popular Front. Chambers's fury with liberals was intractable. He might grant them a certain brilliance, as he did Arthur Schlesinger Jr. in a review of *The Age of Jackson* for *Time*. Chambers titled his review "The Old Deal" and deemed Schlesinger's book "a brilliant justification of the New Deal disguised as a history of the age of Jackson."[72] Brilliance, however, was about all liberals had, in Chambers's view. They had no ethical sense whatsoever, only a myopia so extreme that evidence of Soviet crimes remained forever invisible. (This was Hook's frustration with Henry Wallace.) In a stinging review of the film made from Steinbeck's *The Grapes of Wrath*, Chambers attacked fellow travelers: "pinkos who did not bat an eye when the Soviet Government exterminated 3,000,000 peasants by famine, will go for a good cry over the hardships of the Okies."[73] It was not the impotence of liberals that bothered Chambers but their power and their ubiquity. The battle was not only a battle of words. When he could, Chambers used his editorial power to hinder the careers of fellow travelers. In 1942, for example, he manipulated evidence about Malcolm Cowley's communist past to prevent him from working at the Office of Facts and Figures, a small instance of the ideological battles on the horizon.[74]

Chambers took his criticism of the Left to radical extremes. Liberals and leftists were ignorant of the basic truths that Soviet history had to teach. "How should they [fellow travelers] know that Lenin was the first fascist," Chambers wrote with unforgiving sarcasm, "and that they were cooperating with the Party from which the Nazis borrowed all their important methods and ideas." The sickness of the Left was nothing other than the sickness of intellectuals, whose heyday was not the Roaring Twenties but the low, dishonest 1930s. Intellectuals' alienation from religion and tradition led them to love alienation as such and to mistake sickness for health. "Fundamentally skeptical, maladjusted, defeatist," Chambers wrote, "the intellectuals felt thoroughly at home in the chaos and misery of the '30s." Hence, the outpouring of enthusiasm for *The Grapes of Wrath*. The tragedy was the twisted decency of intellectuals: "fundamentally benevolent and humane, they loved their countrymen in distress far more than they ever loved them in prosperity"; it would be an abiding challenge for Chambers, in his later years, to promote American conservatism as an intellectual and to keep conservatism away from the intellectual's unhealthy influence.[75] Chambers did not recommend an abandonment of intellect, but his denunciation of the Left was so broad as to include "the intellectual" per se. For Trilling, the pro-Soviet Left was considerably smaller, an overgrown radical fringe that stalwart liberals could prune from the tree of genuine liberalism, which had its roots in the nineteenth-century world of John Stuart Mill and Matthew Arnold. Nor were intellectuals necessarily at fault for Trilling. Properly educated, they could even be the progenitors, not of socialism or of some new avant-garde but of a mature liberalism.

Trilling's and Chambers's early anti-communism is a clue to their later work. Trilling's 1939 book on Matthew Arnold was emphatically not a book of his generation, nor was it Trilling's own story; Matthew Arnold had been neither an American Jew nor a communist. Chambers did no introspective writing in the 1930s at all, with the exception of a few scattered letters. Through criticism of the Left, however, Trilling and Chambers were starting to think about their own lives in relation to politics and about politics in relation to their lives. The scales had fallen from their eyes, and never again could they see anything of merit in Soviet civilization. Their Kronstadts were not confined to a rejection of the Soviet Union but of communism and Marxism as well, and it was with communism and Marxism, not the Soviet Union, that their thinking became personal. Trilling and Chambers had internalized communism to the extent that their voyage away from it had immense inner meaning for them, giving their writing as anti-communists a new and complicated tenor, which was derived from their immersion in radical politics.[76] Long-standing experts in despair, their communist youth made them intimate with political tragedy, an intimacy audible in their two very different voices. The essays that would compose *The Liberal Imagination* were cool in tone but searingly first-person in substance—interrelated attempts to transcend the communist self that Trilling had once possessed and to fashion a viable liberal self. Likewise, Chambers's critique of "the intellectual" would take him to *Witness*, to the story of his life as an intellectual and as a communist, his voice the voice of a resourceful writer, a novelist of the self stained by communism and then liberated by Christianity. As anti-communists, Trilling and Chambers were learning not just to criticize but to find nuance and insight in self-criticism, balancing the abstractions of politics with the detail of lived experience. Had their anti-communism been merely a critique of others, of communists or of rival anti-communists, it would not have been much more than the transient polemics and political invective that quickly fade into obscurity. A studied, melancholic introspection gave their later anti-communist writing, the writing for which they would best be known, its breadth and force.

5

TOWARD AN ANTI-COMMUNISM OF THE LEFT AND AN ANTI-COMMUNISM OF THE RIGHT

In short, we have to open our minds to the whole question of causation in culture.

—LIONEL TRILLING, "The Sense of the Past"

Starting in the 1940s, the time had come to move beyond the failure of the Soviet Union, which was so obvious by then as to be almost uninteresting. In transcending simple anti-communism, Trilling and Chambers turned their attention to their homeland, discovering two separate countries, both of them American. Chambers found a Christian republic beyond the secular city, an agrarian life not yet corrupted by New York's decadence, and it was his task to link whatever remained of this America to an effective, anti-communist conservatism. What the anti-communist Trilling saw around him was, to his relief, a liberal society and polity. His America had resisted the totalitarian fanaticism of recent history and was susceptible, if grudgingly at times, to cultural elevation. This was the same country willing to grant him, the son of Jewish immigrants from Poland, a place in one of its great universities. America allowed Trilling to interpret—and even to shape—its culture, and from Trilling's perspective New York was the best place from which to do so. Washington, D.C. would provide the power and New York the culture for the anti-communist struggle. Whether in New York or on his farm in Maryland, Chambers thought apocalyptically. Only by saving its soul could America save itself from a communism poised to dominate the globe, and America was perilously far from saving its soul.

Chambers resolved more by becoming a conservative than Trilling did by aligning himself with liberalism. For one, Chambers made it immediately clear what he was not—not a New Dealer or a progressive of any kind, not an enemy of American power or American tradition. He was a Christian, an intellectual, and a man of the Right. Chambers never longed for a radically anti-communist, religious, or agrarian third party in the 1940s; only major political movements, capable of obtaining and exerting power, mattered to him. What Chambers had difficulty resolving was his status as a conservative intellectual. He was an isolate in the intellectual world of the 1940s, too steeped in European culture and global politics to be a provincial American populist, too centrist and moderate to tolerate the eccentricities of indigenous American conservatism, and too pragmatic, for example, to take seriously the pastoral fantasies of the Southern Agrarians. He was a conservative drawn to tradition and repelled by modernity, pushed repeatedly into the fray of modern politics by his ardent anti-communism. By nature he was a pessimistic man, and he was especially pessimistic about the capacity of his fellow intellectuals to understand the case for conservatism. A controversial figure at *Time*, recognized by Henry Luce as a talented ideologue, Chambers had no suitable conservative movement to give him hope or companionship. It became his ambition to create one.[1]

Trilling's anti-communist liberalism took him in several different political directions at once, toward FDR's New Deal, back in time to the liberalism of Victorian England, and to the margins of the non-liberal world. Trilling's "we," which he employed in essay after essay in the 1940s, had Arnoldian overtones, the voice of the educated middle class, vacillating between the achievement of enlightenment and the embrace of error and obscurantism. In these years, Trilling worked to separate his "we" from any vestige of Stalinism. If he wished at all for liberation as an anti-communist intellectual, it was undoubtedly a liberation *from* Stalinism or *from* the pro-Soviet Left.[2] The key difference between Trilling's liberalism and Chambers's conservatism was religion.[3] Whatever Trilling's sympathy for religious writers, and his sympathy was large, Trilling did not go back to the Orthodox Judaism of his childhood, nor did he convert to Christianity. He remained an assimilated American citizen in his personal life and, as it were, in his intellectual life. His writing on religious intellectuals concerned only Christian intellectuals. Sigmund Freud, the one intellectual of Jewish background who captured Trilling's imagination in this period, was avidly secular. Trilling's reading of Freud made him dismissive of utopian ideals in culture and politics. Freud's emphasis on tragedy and his pessimistic view of human nature resonated with the

Judeo-Christian notion of sin; but Freud dismissed religion as an illusion, unbecoming to modern adults. Reason and high culture were the ideals that Trilling took from Freud as much as from Arnold, while Chambers saw faith as the basis of civilization and the Judeo-Christian heritage as the basis of Western civilization. Anti-communism could not synthesize the ideas of Trilling the (mostly) secular liberal and Chambers the resolutely Christian conservative.

For both Trilling and Chambers, the modern spirit was sick, not exclusively—but poignantly—because of its association with political radicalism. In this, they resembled theologian Reinhold Niebuhr who stood between Trilling and Chambers, presiding over the articulation of Protestant neo-orthodoxy in the 1940s. Niebuhr applied traditional Protestant moral categories to modern thought and experience, for which Chambers admired Niebuhr immensely. A devout Christian, Niebuhr had moved far to the Left around 1930, although his Left was Norman Thomas's Socialist Party and never the Communist Party. During the Great Depression, Niebuhr was a radical because he was so passionately a Christian. He was a theologian conversant with the ideas of Marx and Freud, and his most explicit contribution to the literature of anti-communism was his 1944 book, *The Children of Light and the Children of Darkness,* an effort to balance Christian piety with moral realism, political idealism with modern pessimism. His high moral and intellectual stature among non-Protestant contemporaries lent prestige to Christianity and anti-communism alike. Despite Chambers's admiration, Niebuhr was a Christian anti-communist but not a conservative in the 1940s; nor would he ever become one. Niebuhr taught a few blocks away from Trilling at the Union Theological Seminary in Manhattan's Morningside Heights neighborhood and the two professors were acquaintances. For Trilling, Niebuhr's nonconservative anti-communism was exemplary, exactly what Trilling wished to promote in the secular language of literature and literary criticism. Niebuhr associated himself and his postwar popularity with Trilling, asking Trilling in a 1961 letter, "Are [you and I] supposed to be status symbols—what a curious destiny."[4]

According to Chambers, religion was the key to politics and the foundation on which any authentic conservatism must rest. In returning to the Christian faith he was repairing the damage Columbia College and its corrosive liberalism had done to him. He described the process in a letter to his friend and former Columbia classmate, Meyer Schapiro, with whom he had corresponded so exuberantly about communism in the 1920s. "I have [since 1938] been orienting myself away from all these influences which affected me most strongly from my youth into early middle age." The conversion to which Chambers alluded was also a return: "I felt an organic need to get back to being somewhat the kind of person I essentially was before I came to Columbia University," a return to his true self. As he explained: "especially important for me was the religious angle. I am first and foremost a religious person. This is a clue to my worst mistakes as it is to my final effort to outlive them." Chambers came back to his "true self" by becoming a Quaker, thus reliving his family history, in which there were several Quakers. As a Quaker, Chambers wrote to Schapiro that he "began to understand people in my family who had always baffled me and to recover great stretches of my boyhood Pennsylvania. The relatives I came to understand were Quakers and ex-Quakers in my line."[5] In his private life Chambers struck a workable compromise between Christianity and modern America: "It is the farm that I labored at *Time*, like Jacob with Laban, to support until it could support itself," he wrote in *Witness*. Chambers saw his family life on the farm as a kind of political statement: "by deliberately choosing this line of hardship and immense satisfaction, we say in effect: the modern world has nothing better than this to give us." Chambers's wording anticipated the cultural arguments of the next generation, of 1960s radicals whose discontents with modern civilization would prove strangely similar to Chambers's pastoral conservatism. "Its vision of comfort without effort," Chambers wrote of the modern world, "pleasure without the pain of creation, life sterilized against even the thought of death, rationalized so that every intrusion of mystery is felt as a betrayal of mind, life mechanized and standardized— this is not for us."[6]

Chambers considered it his responsibility to alert American conservatives to the revolutionary conditions of the modern world, from which the United States was not exempt. Only by knowing the truth of modern times could conservatives be effective. Trilling's "we" stood for the educated middle class in the United States and, less plausibly, in Britain. Chambers's "we" belonged to the generation that had built communism in Russia and China and fascism in Germany, Italy, Japan, and Spain, a generation positioned on the fault lines of twentieth-century history, armed with a powerful state and powerful technology, carried along by the recently empowered masses and indelibly marked by three disasters—World

War I, the Great Depression, and World War II. So far, the performance of this generation was disastrous. In Chambers's reckoning "we liquidated God. We developed the total state," he wrote in "Literary Autolysis," an article for the conservative magazine *American Mercury*, "the monolithic party, the political police organized as uniformed praetorian armies . . . Few other generations, I suppose, have ever been so unequal to so great a destiny." This "we" was not obviously the generation of the New Deal; it was hardly American at all. It could just as easily be Nazi or Soviet: "we destroyed the ghetto of Warsaw and liquidated the kulaks as a class."[7] We were culpable for the crimes of totalitarianism. Very few Americans on the Left or the Right thought in such cosmopolitan terms or were willing to project responsibility for Nazi or Soviet crimes onto *their* generation.

As a journalist, Chambers did not permit his readers to isolate themselves from the horrors of twentieth-century history, tacitly arguing for an engagé conservatism in America. To be a sentient conservative in America or anywhere else was to be aware of how revolutionary the present moment was: "those of us who are conservatives by force of conviction differ from those who are conservatives by force of inertia chiefly in the fact that we take the social revolution seriously." The social revolution was most extreme in Soviet Russia, but with the New Deal the United States had also embarked on a revolution of sorts. The widespread appeal of the Soviet Union in the 1930s, which Chambers connected to the New Deal via philo-communist New Dealers such as Alger Hiss, betrayed the New Deal's ultimate destination. The conservative had two potentially contradictory responsibilities: to take the social revolution seriously and at the same time to conserve something in opposition to this revolution. Here Chambers argued for conserving the pastoral ideal: "the landowning farmer, big and little, is the conservative base of every healthy society, no matter how many miles of factories may be required to keep the average city dweller in a state of civilized neurosis."[8] Chambers was pessimistic about the fate of the Christian and the pastoral ideals, which represented the best way to live. Fewer and fewer Americans wished to live on the farm or within the bounds of the church; the right path was no longer the popular path; all roads seemed to lead to a godless socialism. On the public stage of *Time* and *Life* magazines, Chambers struggled to rehabilitate religion in contemporary culture, writing on serious subjects for a mass audience, taking figures such as Franz Kafka, Marian Anderson, and Reinhold Niebuhr and welding them into a single argument:

Kafka, a European Jew, elucidated the nature of the problem, of life without God, while Anderson and Niebuhr were Americans who lived with God. Anderson was an artist, an African American vocalist whose people, in Chambers's view, were fortunate in their lingering Christian piety. Together, Anderson and Niebuhr demonstrated the vitality, perhaps even the centrality, of Christianity in American culture.

In December 1946, Chambers published "In Egypt Land" in *Time*, which appeared in *Time*'s Religion section and was meant to be read as a Christmastime article. It was about Marian Anderson, whom the Daughters of the American Revolution had barred from singing at Constitution Hall in Washington, D.C., in 1939, an egregious instance of racial prejudice. In the 1940s Anderson enjoyed a spectacular career, and Chambers's piece was a celebration of Anderson, not another commentary on the Cold War or on politics per se, although it shed light on his conservative thinking. Chambers presented Anderson as the product of a distinctly African American culture, which he lauded for its religious intensity. Anderson, in Chambers's words, "has taken to new heights the best that Negro Americans are. For the Deep River of her life and theirs runs in the same religious channels." Slavery had caused immense suffering, and from this suffering a Christian ethos had been born, making black Americans "the most God-obsessed (and man-despised) people since the ancient Hebrews."[9] The achievement of African American culture was religious, above all in music, and African Americans have consequently "enriched American culture with incomparable religious poetry and music, and its only truly great religious art—the spiritual."[10] Culture was not to be abstracted from politics. Chambers identified racial prejudice as a political problem that "could be explained (and must in part be solved) in political, social and economic terms. But it is . . . like all the great problems of mankind, at bottom a religious problem . . . the religious solution must be made before any other solutions could be effective."[11] It was a convenient rhetorical flourish on Chambers's part, leaving unsaid what the religious solution might be.

The spiritual illustrated the health of African American culture, which had transmuted suffering into art through religion. By comparison, Kafka's anguished fiction measured the spiritual poverty of a secularizing European culture. Kafka was in vogue among the *Partisan Review* and *Commentary* contributors, a modernist author of genius who spoke, in ways that Joyce and Proust did not, to the devastation of the 1930s and

1940s. Kafka seemed to have anticipated the moral universe of the concentration camp and the *gulag*, the tendency in twentieth-century history toward mass persecution of the innocent, accompanied by the rationalization of this persecution. Kafka's anguish demonstrated the crisis of "modern man," as a *Partisan Review* writer might have put it, with a nod to French existentialism, or the crisis of "man without God," which was how Chambers read Kafka. In a *Time* article titled "The Tragic Sense of Life," Chambers discussed Kafka as an index of contemporary culture.[12] Chambers defined Kafka's subject as "the nature of God and man's relationship to God," and the labyrinth of Kafka's novels and short stories, their traps and prisons, constituted a theological claim about secular life, about life without God. Kafka outlines "the bleak void in which man, like a rat in a laboratory maze, strives frantically (and often ludicrously) to approach God, while God (with the detachment of the scientific mind) observes the data of the frenzy and the fun."[13] It was immaterial for Chambers that Kafka was Jewish; Jewish blood made Kafka no less of a witness to the cataclysms awaiting the twentieth century. As a Christian conservative, Chambers did not share in the anti-Semitism endemic to pre–World War II conservatism, American or otherwise. "We" were responsible for destroying the Warsaw ghetto.

In a cover story for *Time*, Chambers lauded Reinhold Niebuhr for staring into the same bleak void that Kafka had, without losing his faith. In the 1940s Niebuhr appealed to the religious and the irreligious alike. He articulated "the angst that seemed to characterize the postwar West," in the words of Arthur Schlesinger Jr., himself an uncompromising atheist and a devoted reader of Niebuhr.[14] Chambers was virtuosic in his angst and unlikely to trust an intellectual who was not similarly inclined. In the 1950s, Chambers would write about the duty of intellectuals "to keep pointing out why the Enlightenment and its fruits were a wrong turn in man's history," and Niebuhr was one intellectual who honored this duty.[15] First of all, Niebuhr accurately read the past, when "under the bland influence of the idea of progress, man, supposing himself more and more to be the measure of all things, achieved a singularly easy conscience and an almost hermetically smug optimism." Progressives relied on a progressive vision of human nature, one that came to permeate twentieth-century thinking, although it was extravagantly contradicted by the hard facts of twentieth-century experience. How could one know of Hitler and Stalin, the *gulag* and Auschwitz, and still avow that "man is essentially good?" For this is what "20th Century liberalism [says], because he [man] is rational." In philosophy, Kierkegaard had undone the optimism of the Enlightenment; in literature, Dostoevsky had shown the abyss beneath socialist idealism; in history, "World War I ended the age of liberalism."[16] World War I, followed by Stalinism, followed by World War II, had cumulatively made this a "Lenten age." Chambers titled his article on Niebuhr "Faith for a Lenten Age," by which he meant to evoke the mood of the Easter holiday, the betrayal and murder of Christ coupled with the possibility of resurrection.

Chambers praised Niebuhr not just for affirming Christianity but for the neo-Orthodox manner in which Niebuhr voiced his affirmation. Chambers had little interest in liberal Protestantism, and he chose not to dwell on the fact that politically Niebuhr still traveled in the liberal orbit.[17] Chambers extracted the most "conservative" elements from Niebuhr, the emphasis on tragedy and sin. Niebuhr's writings suited a generation—Chambers's "we"—that was guilty, and his tone suited a political moment rich in catastrophe. Chambers seconded Niebuhr in the conviction "that the pursuit of happiness loses measure, just as optimism loses reality, if neither is aware of what Wordsworth called 'the still sad music of humanity.'" One is reminded here of Trilling's reason for writing a dissertation on Matthew Arnold: he wanted to know why Arnold was so sad. In relating the "still sad music of humanity" to the grim realities of the twentieth century, Niebuhr had made himself a model Christian intellectual, restoring Protestantism to "a Christian virility."[18] In *Witness*, Chambers called his *Time* articles on Niebuhr and Anderson an "indictment of the modern mind." This they obviously were. More telling, however, was Chambers's admission that the articles comprised "a statement of my own religious faith at the time."[19] Niebuhr himself liked "Faith for a Lenten Age," saying that "only a man who has deeply suffered could have written it."[20]

Trilling read Chambers's pieces in *Time* and *Life* and found their style vulgar, their message a mess of platitudes. A prose stylist of complexity and reserve, Trilling had nothing so direct as a message; an emphatic message could even be construed as illiberal by Trilling's standards, an end rather than an invitation to reflection. In a 1975 essay, Trilling recalled that Chambers "achieved a degree of at least economic security and even a professional reputation of sorts with the apocalyptic pieties of his news-stories for *Time* and the sodden profundities of his cultural essays for *Life*."[21] Yet Trilling shared Chambers's conception of politics as spiritual and of Stalinism as a grave threat to the human spirit. In a 1946 letter, Trilling commented on the inner meaning of Stalinism: "what interests me in it [Stalinism]," Trilling wrote, "is the death of the spirit which it requires for its success." Trilling and Chambers were surprisingly similar in the cause they ascribed to Stalinism and its degradation of the spirit— modern, bourgeois society. "This death of the spirit is what modern society demands of us all," Trilling wrote: "Stalinism I see as not the opposition to but the projection of modern society. The acceleration of modern bourgeois culture in most of its manifestations." Chambers pushed the origins of Stalinism back to the Enlightenment and to the rise of secularism, both of which invited the death of the spirit. Trilling was not as drastic or as radical. The acceleration of modern bourgeois culture had to be slowed down, and for this the Left that had come out of Marxism-Leninism would have to be destroyed. Trilling had no patience with Stalinists or Trotskyists, but he could "imagine moving with some socialist party." He was terribly uncertain: "I am not sure that I am, in any sense of the word, a leftist; put it, not a leftist except ultimately."[22]

Alienation from the Stalinist Left helped Trilling show some intellectual sympathy for Christianity, as he did with T. S. Eliot. An Anglican monarchist, Eliot's verse was discordant, enchanting music for a modern era, and his social thought a forceful rejection of all things liberal, progressive, and radical. To be educated was to be familiar with T. S. Eliot, but the educated classes were on the Left, and there was a "gulf between our educated class and the best of our literature," Trilling thought. Communism had helped to widen this gulf, with the American Communist Party failing to produce "a single work of distinction or even high respectability" since the 1920s.[23] The Left has not yielded much by way of culture, and to the greatest writers of the twentieth century "the liberal ideology has been at best a matter of indifference." Either the liberal educated class would have to change its relation to art, or it would have to change its relation to politics. Otherwise, artists would simply continue to find their bearings elsewhere, many of them in religion and in conservatism, with liberals stuck finding their literary bearings in illiberal art. Trilling's disaffection with the liberal educated class was advanced enough for him to serve as a moderator between it and Eliot's message. Trilling recommended Eliot's ideas "to the attention of readers probably hostile towards Mr. Eliot's religious politics. I say no more than recommend to the attention," Trilling continued, "I certainly do not recommend Mr. Eliot's ideas to the allegiance."

The bridge between Trilling and Eliot was Matthew Arnold. Trilling placed Eliot in "the tradition of Coleridge and after Coleridge, of Newman, Carlyle, Ruskin and Matthew Arnold—the men who, in the days of reform, stood out, on something better than reasons of self-interest, against the philosophical assumptions of materialist liberalism."[24] Materialist liberalism had accelerated in the twentieth century. It was the dominant political ethos of the 1920s, horribly inadequate to the crises of the 1930s, and, in the 1930s, materialist liberalism accelerated haphazardly, although perhaps inevitably, into Stalinism. In Eliot's battle with materialist liberalism, he was reactionary and modern; as such, he was congenial to Trilling. Eliot could convincingly speak out against materialist liberalism in his literature and poetry in a language that was arrestingly contemporary—he had much to teach the radical and the liberal, much to teach the Left. Trilling came close to taking Eliot's side, defending Eliot against radical criticism: "when Mr. Eliot is accused of 'faith,' or of the 'surrender' of his intellect to 'authority,' it is hard to see, when the accusers are Marxist intellectuals, how their own action was always so very different." Marxist intellectuals had displayed faith in Marxism; they had surrendered to the authority of the Party; and they, too, had willingly abandoned reason and skepticism, treating morality as "something to be cultivated after the particular revolution they want is accomplished, but just now it is on the way; or they think of it as whatever helps to bring the revolution about."[25]

Although Stalin's name was absent from Trilling's essay on Eliot, Stalin's presence was everywhere. To postpone morality until the realization of socialism is to condone the lie, the purge, and, eventually, the *gulag*, provided that these moral wrongs can one day be righted by the march of history. Such was the moral history of Stalin's Soviet Union and the sympathetic intellectuals it attracted. Yet the anti-Stalinist Trilling was no partisan of the Christian society. Christianity could very well be better than Marxism without itself being true. Why should one believe in the idea of a Christian society? And why, for the past one hundred years, had so many thoughtful Christians dispensed with their religion, creating the conditions in which a secular ideology such as Marxism could flourish? Trilling presented this second question as one inherent to Christianity. Chambers would have blamed an abstraction—modernity, industrial society, the Left, the twentieth century—for the loss of faith in Christianity, while Trilling wondered what it was "in the nature of Christianity which brought it to the condition in which men and nations, trained in a wholly Christian culture, felt constrained to discover the inadequacy of the dogma which are now expected to save the world"—expected by Christian thinkers such as T. S. Eliot.[26] Trilling's critique of Eliot was gentle. Mostly, Trilling tried to break down a presumed hostility toward Eliot among his non-Anglican readers, giving no indication that, as a Jewish critic, he was obligated to condemn Eliot's anti-Semitism or even to mention it when anti-Semitism was at its world-historical apex. Trilling, the American critic, existed in no great degree of alienation from the Anglican Eliot.

Trilling's alienation was from the Jewish community in America, to which he did not feel, or wish to feel, attached. Trilling formulated his alienation in 1944 in a remarkable, eight-paragraph essay published in the *Contemporary Jewish Record*, the precursor to *Commentary*. It was one part of a symposium titled "Under Forty," in which successful American Jews under the age of forty disclosed their thoughts about being Jewish. In his entry, Trilling's candor was awesome, as was his refusal to flatter the American Jewish community. The terrible circumstances facing European Jewry figured in Trilling's essay, although in general his tone was one of emotional chill.[27] America had never visited "prejudice or persecution" on him, and his good fortune was not unique.[28] The social and cultural adjustment of the American Jews has been a success. Still, in those areas that mattered most to Trilling—in the affairs of the mind and of culture—Judaism and the Jewish community were a debit, a hindrance to be bypassed. Trilling would not deny being Jewish: but this was the most he would concede. He would take "no pride in seeing a long tradition, often great and heroic, reduced to this small status in me." Moving from himself to the American Jewish community, Trilling's attitude hardened. The question was not whether but why this community had reached "its impasse of sterility." Modern Jewish religion is mediocre, lacking "a single voice with the note of authority—of philosophical, or poetic, or even of rhetorical, let alone of religious, authority." Furthermore, a penchant for ritual self-praise obscures the low level of American Jewish culture. The point Trilling wished to make, beyond simply being critical, was that assimilation offered far more than the American Jewish community ever could. Adjustment was to be adjustment to America as Americans, although not as Americans who evaded the Jewish label. Trilling's conclusion was grim: "as the Jewish community now exists, it can give no sustenance to the American artist or intellectual who is born a Jew."[29] The easier assimilation became, the more American Jews should melt into the larger world around them.

One year after Trilling published "Under Forty," *Commentary* came into being, a Jewish magazine intended to fulfill the cultural promise of the *Menorah Journal*. Trilling remained friends with Elliot Cohen, his old mentor from the *Menorah Journal* and *Commentary*'s new editor, and Trilling would write many essays for *Commentary*. But Cohen's mission for the magazine had little to do with Trilling's own cultural and political mission. Cohen's mission statement for *Commentary*, "An Act of Affirmation," was grounded in the "faith that, out of the opportunities of our experience here, there will evolve new patterns of living, new modes of thought, which will harmonize heritage and country into a true sense of at-home-ness in the modern world."[30] Cohen was affirming both the Jewish heritage and America, with the possibility of domesticating the Jewish heritage on American soil. By 1945, Trilling was cut off from his Jewish heritage, a condition that made Cohen's affirmation meaningless. Trilling was indeed at home in America, but a sense of at-home-ness in the modern world eluded him. He found no otherworldly home in religion and had no great interest in the secular jargon of alienation then being spun in Existentialist thought. He was afraid that the modern mind might still succumb to Stalinism, a fear that distanced Trilling from Cohen's optimism. Perhaps the modern world demanded the death of the spirit, Jewish or otherwise; if so, it was no place to seek a home. Trilling, like Chambers, had reservations too deep for him to delight in the modern world, and his unease about this world turned his eyes from the present back to the past, which, for Trilling, was European rather than Jewish or American. There was instruction, and perhaps some solace, in history. Immersion in history could imbue newly anti-communist arguments with authority, serving as intellectual armor against the recurrent political fallacies.

Trilling sought to destabilize the radicalism and progressivism of the Left by bringing it into conflict with the past. His mood resembled that of many around *Partisan Review*, which in the fall of 1942 republished Henry Adams's 1894 address to the American History Association, echoing many of Trilling's arguments about history. Trilling was echoing

Adams, who decried the naïve optimism of his fellow historians, based on the false premise that science ensures progress. Adams underscored the gloom of fin-de-siècle artists and philosophers, noting that recent "European thought has been distinctly despondent among the classes which were formerly most hopeful." Science is a harbinger of crisis, Adams declared, and "The Tendency of History"—Adams' title for the address—was toward disaster, not progress. This is the truth about science and history that progressives refuse to accept. If, Adams argued, "the new science required us to announce that the present evils of the world—its huge armaments, its vast accumulations of capital, its advancing materialism, and declining arts—were to be continued, exaggerated over another thousand years, no one would listen to us with satisfaction."[31] The *Partisan Review* editors who republished Adams's essay were ready to listen with attention. The despairing mood of the 1920s resurfaced once again, inspired by the 1930s and its terrible epiphanies; 1942 was not the best year for contemplating the tendency of history. Like Adams, Trilling wanted his readers to listen to history's depressive music. Trilling's liberal "we" was yet again in need or reform.

In "Tacitus Now," a 1942 essay, Trilling's very title reflected tension between past and present. Tacitus had been a historian in ancient Rome where he was a witness to extreme historical crises—crises on par with those of the 1930s and 1940s. With the Nazi ascendancy in Europe at its highest point, the political upheaval of ancient Rome did not seem abstract or distant to Trilling, who touched on Nazi and Soviet references: "dictatorship and repression, spies and political informers, blood and purges and treacherous dissension have not been part of our political tradition [in America] as they have been of Europe's. But Europe has now come very close to us, and our political education of the last decades fits us to understand the historian of imperial Rome." Tacitus was an honorable historian to the extent that he was not a progressive. He possessed "no notions of historical development to comfort him." In his histories, Tacitus described "the grotesque career of the human spirit" behind the ephemera of Roman politics. This was disturbing enough, if not reason to indulge in progressive illusions of improvement or in the illusion that the human spirit was destined to have an illustrious career. At the very best, one could emulate Tacitus by aspiring to his "power of mind and his stubborn love of virtue maintained despite desperate circumstances."[32] Trilling offered up Tacitus as an intellectual hero.

Whether Roman or British, the past was a provocation to modern ethics, to which virtue was largely alien. In "Mr. Eliot's Kipling," an essay on intellectual manners, Trilling focused on his generation's disregard for Victorian England, which could also be a disregard for virtue. A poet and a writer who publicized the virtues of the British empire in verse and story, Kipling was expansive in his attitude toward virtue, as befits an imperialist, "the first to suggest what may be called the anthropological view, the perception that another man's idea of virtue and honor may be different from one's own but quite respected." Yet Kipling had led the next generation of readers to hate the anthropological view and to hate virtue. "Kipling was an honest man and he loved the national virtues," Trilling explained. "But I suppose no man ever did more harm to the national virtues than Kipling did."[33] Trilling did not praise Kipling's literary prowess; literature and poetry were secondary concerns in this as in so many of Trilling's essays—as, one is tempted to say, in Trilling's criticism in general.[34] The primary issue was the cultural and moral history of Trilling's own generation, from which the theme of communism was never far removed. A reconsideration of Kipling was a quasipolitical act. If it was useful, it was because the Soviet Union stood across from the British empire, introducing a new moral calculus.

Trilling tracked the errant ways of his generation through its reception of Kipling. Recent disgust with Kipling's literature of empire is politically portentous: "our rejection of him [Kipling] was our first literary-political decision," Trilling recalled. For readers on their way to socialism, Kipling symbolized a sick bourgeoisie, false in its ideals, craven in its politics, childish in its style. In reviling Kipling, the bourgeois imperial sentimentalist, the socialist, and the modernist might join hands: "the new movements in literature came to make Kipling seem inconsequential and puerile, to require that he be dismissed as official as, as one used to say, intending something aesthetic and emotional rather than political, 'bourgeois.' " As "we" became more radical, it was not simply the literary facets of imperialism and capitalism—both of which Kipling represented—that were repudiated but imperialism and capitalism themselves and, with them, the civic virtues to which Kipling was dedicated. Although Trilling made no underhanded argument for imperialism and capitalism in his essay on Kipling, he was clearly defending the civic virtues and lamenting the fact that "the idea of courage and duty has been steeped for them [Kipling's twentieth-century readers] in the Kipling vat and they rejected the idea with the color."[35] Trilling wanted his liberal readers to realize what ideas had been rejected along with the imperialist finery of the Victorian age.

In an essay titled "The Sense of the Past," Trilling mounted a defense of history against radicalism and, more than anything, against the moral self-congratulation that he considered a radical character trait, contrasting the a-historical bent of progressives to the self-criticism of the historically aware. Trilling was unraveling the wishful thinking of his generation, which began with Marx, "for whom history was indeed a sixth sense, [who] expressed what has come to be the secret hope of our time, that man's life in politics, which is to say man's life in history, shall come to an end." Trilling continued in the vein of unmasking, as if he were the analyst and "we" the analysand: "with all the passion of a desire kept secret even from ourselves, we yearn to erect a way of life which shall be satisfactory once and for all, world without end, and we do not want to be reminded by the past of the considerable possibility that our present is but perpetuating mistakes and failures and instituting new troubles."[36] History opens up conservative vistas; Trilling felt strongly that they not be overlooked. Matthew Arnold had famously labeled art a criticism of life and Trilling claimed that "the historical sense . . . is to be understood as the critical sense, as the sense which life uses to test itself." To inculcate this historical sense would be to measure the extent of "our own bad thinking," which does "not stay in the academy." Intellectuals "make their way into the world, and what begins as a failure of perception among intellectual specialists finds its fulfillment in policy and action." Marx is responsible for Lenin and Stalin. Trilling was urging a political style that could be fashioned in dialogue with the past. The ensuing sobriety might purchase political wisdom: "without the sense of the past we might be more certain, less weighted down and pessimistic. We might also be less generous and complete, and certainly we would be less aware."[37] Liberals should accept the burden of history so that they can be more aware.

The anti-communist Chambers was similarly preoccupied with history, although he sought something more specific in the past than wisdom. He sought a basis for political action and, specifically, for American conservatism. No denizen of uncertainty, Chambers delved into history to reinforce his certainty about Christianity in religion and conservatism in politics. He set forth his views on history—his sodden profundities—in a series for *Life* magazine grandly titled "The History of Western Culture." The surveys were well-conceived pieces of a conservative argument about history and politics. Faith or spirit was the impetus for historical change, in Chambers's eyes, not class conflict. Capitalism was not the prison house of the Marxist imagination, although it was no vehicle of liberation. If Marx's *Das Kapital* led to some glorious communist future and Edmund Wilson's history of Marxism led to the Finland Station, to the Russian Revolution, Chambers's "History of Western Culture" led to Plymouth Rock and Philadelphia in 1787, to the promise of Christian emancipation. America is the keystone of Western history, the magical place where the Protestant Reformation and democracy met, joining faith and freedom. This is where conservatives should find inspiration for their battles with the modern world. American history is wonderfully rich in conservative resources, and it was to these that Chambers dedicated his series on Western culture.

Chambers was one of many ex-communist intellectuals working towards an ex-communist interpretation of culture. In a *Partisan Review* article "The Case of the Baffled Radical," the art critic Harold Rosenberg went so far as to identify a new literary genre created by the postradical. For a discussion of literary anti-communism, his pretext was a review of Arthur Koestler's *Arrival and Departure*, an early memoir of the journey from communism to anti-communism. Rosenberg recognized "the tragedy of the left intellectual in the past decade," of which Koestler was a prominent example. Koestler had joined the German Communist Party in the 1930s only to experience a Kronstadt around 1937. Since then, his eloquent anti-communist advocacy had earned him Chambers's esteem. Rosenberg had two points to make about Koestler's memoir, both of which could be applied to Chambers's anti-communist writing: it was a modern form of writing, and it was a regrettably popular new kind of literature, "the literature of conscience of the ex-Communist." Rosenberg maintained that "the work of the de-converted Red belongs to the main stream of doubt and negation which has occupied the first place in literature for the past 100 years." More interesting than Rosenberg's loathing for Koestler the anti-communist was the suggestion that fashion favored Koestler: "for all its fashionableness, the conclusion of *Arrival and Departure*, with its assertion of the necessary failure of the modern mind in face of historical problems and its call for a new deity, is intellectually gross."[38]

Fashion favored Chambers, too. His "History of Western Culture" series was "among the most popular ever published in the Luce Press."[39] It was Chambers's effort to inspire the American mind in face of historical problems and to relate these problems to the old Christian deity.

In total, Chambers wrote seven articles for his "Western Culture" series. The order in which they were published was not chronological: "The Protestant Revolution" was the last to appear on June 14, 1948, while "The Age of Enlightenment" came out on September 15, 1947, and "The Edwardians" on November 17, 1947. The final paragraph of the series completes the general argument, the story of religion formalized in the Middle Ages, of religion challenged in the Enlightenment and successively diminished in the nineteenth century, ending with the story of religious awakening in the sixteenth century, revived in Europe with Luther and Calvin, and then again in the Massachusetts Bay Colony. The rise of the middle class and of capitalism, which was also Chambers's story, was thus modified to deny that secular modernity, the product of science and technology, is the endpoint of history. Civilizations thrive only when people believe in them—religious faith might wax and wane, dark ages might put a temporary end to civilization, but faith could also be regained and civilization restored. A Protestant revolution could supplant a Russian revolution. If so, America might continue to stand at the center of modern history.

Because Christianity organized Chambers's portrayal of Western culture, he ended with the Protestant Reformation and began with the Middle Ages. The reduction of Western culture to its Christian centuries gave coherence and polemical energy to the series as a whole: the West at war with communism was not the West of Hellenic arts and liberties, struggling to defeat a latter-day Persia, but the West of Christian zeal.[40] So, at least, it would have to be, in Chambers's judgment, were the West to vanquish Soviet communism. The spirit of the Middle Ages, as Chambers presented it, was not martial or stern but creative and sweet, its "singular sweetness," stemming from faith in God. To aspire to sweetness, the medieval Europeans had at their disposal "that *caritas* (St. Paul's loving charity) which Thomas Aquinas declared to be inseparable from the right understanding of God." Faith created civilization, and in the Middle Ages it created a civilization of awesome achievement. To preserve faith, conservatism was necessary, and so medieval man "implemented his creed in law and, in so far as erring man can, practiced it in his civil

conduct. With it, he sanctified the indissoluble union of the family."
Such solicitude for the Christian creed yielded the intellectual and cultural wealth of the later Middle Ages, when the "medieval mind burst
into creativity in its three ultimate glories: the Gothic cathedrals, the philosophy of Aquinas, and the poetry of Dante." In "Medieval Life," a more
sociologically oriented essay than "The Middle Ages," Chambers noted
that "the peasants' desperate condition led to desperate outbreaks." Their
outbreaks did not undo the medieval order; it was the crusades to reclaim
the Holy Land that hastened the end of the Middle Ages. By stimulating
movement between Europe and Asia, the crusades initiated "a brisk new
trade . . . between East and West," and very slowly trade would bring
modernity.[41]

Chambers placed the origins of modernity in Venice, which had a mer-
cantile elite who were the ancestors of Europe's middle class. For them,
the pre-Christian world of Athens and Rome was a lovely "lost world of
light, reason and luxury." The Renaissance model was not mind in the
service of piety, as it had been for Aquinas or the medieval architect, but
mind in the service of the individual or of itself. Chambers concluded
that "this violent enfranchisement of the mind and the prowess of the individual man was the meaning of the Renaissance."[42] Commerce and the
emancipated mind blossomed into the political enfranchisement of the
middle class, which set the stage for democracy. The serf was no longer
under the lord's control, and in the nineteenth century both serf and
slave would be emancipated. Jean-Jacques Rousseau's sovereign people
were, in essence, the middle class. Here one could detect a Marxist echo:
in the eighteenth century, "the middle class, which controlled the new
sources of wealth, began to challenge the once dominant aristocracy for
overt power in the state which they as bureaucrats were already adminis-
tering." If the Enlightenment cracked open the age-old feudal hierarchies, it also debased Western culture with its caustic, critical spirit. It was
a dissolvent of piety and faith, of the Medieval sweetness; it was "the intellectual chemistry whose gradual precipitate was the modern mind—
secular, practical and utilitarian."[43]

In "The Edwardians," Chambers dwelt on the irony—unbeknownst to
Henry Adams in 1894 when he wrote his address to the American Historical Association—that "progress" would land Europe and the United States
in World War I. "In science the age was one of the most portentous in history," and the material surfeit of the moment convinced many that better

things were still to come—more speed, more power, more wealth. The Edwardians became intoxicated with "the vision of peace and progress." The dream of the utopian capitalists was a Marxist dream as well: "the machine would free millions from the drudgeries inseparable from organizing and servicing a civilization which was growing ever more massive and complex." Such utopian optimism was not a transient episode in Western culture. Its early impetus was the Enlightenment, its finest hour the French Revolution, at least until the Terror, and in the relative peace that followed the Napoleonic wars "the vision of peace and progress" took root. The "realization of the Enlightenment in the idea of progress," so widely held in the nineteenth century, was not simply an illusion. It was Promethean and sinful: the false lure of progress worked against faith in God, encouraging undue faith in the market and the machine. One who did intuit the hollow stability of the Edwardian age was Vladimir Ilich Lenin, "a short, pale fanatic with the face of a Mongol,"—who would capitalize on the chaos of World War I to establish the first communist state.[44] In the fall of 1947, when "The Edwardians" was published, Americans had no reason to sit comfortably and wait for postwar prosperity. They had to realize exactly how vulnerable the edifice of Western civilization was if they were to be the guardians of it.

A subheading, "America is heir and hope of the West's civilization," laid bare the series' Cold War significance.[45] The Pilgrims had the faith that elevated the Middle Ages to high civilization, and they had the freedom of modernity, a happy synthesis of old and new. With the Pilgrims, Chambers burst into purple prose, sententious writing of the sort that irked Trilling. Whether it irked Life's readers is hard to say. Perhaps the popularity of the entire series rested on its sentimental passages, such as Chambers's comparison of the Pilgrims with Christopher Columbus. The Pilgrims discovered a truth as entrancing as Columbus's first glimpse of land: "that it is better to die if that must be the price of freedom, but it is better yet to have the resolution and strength to live that freedom may endure."[46] The Protestant revolution contained the ingredients of an anti-communist conservatism in America. These were Christian piety, love of liberty, and capitalism. With the Protestant revolution, "capitalism had been born," and its birth was in the middle class. Calvinism, in particular, gave religious and economic purpose to middle-class life: it "sanctioned enterprise and set a tone of religious and ethical dealing that, whatever the lapses from it, became the standard for this great creative energy of men." Chambers praised "the spirit of freedom," which "found its religious expression in Protestantism [and] found its secular calling in commerce." America perfected the best of European culture. The spirit of freedom, unleashed by the Protestant revolution, "leaped the Atlantic Ocean and prepared to clear a continental forest, eliminate the remnants of stone-age man and make an appropriate space where the new dignity of the individual, safeguarded by his new freedom of faith could, under God, build a citadel, an arsenal and an altar."[47] In this rhetorical finish to his survey, the historical and the normative were one.

Chambers's "History of Western Culture" proclaimed America and the West to be a good home, evading the "doubt and negation" that Rosenberg regarded as the modernist signature of the "de-converted Red." Chambers had converted to Christianity in order to avoid hopelessness. The "History of Western Culture" series was self-confident and affirmative, not nostalgic or alienated. Chambers was not writing at all like Henry Adams, and he was writing for a big American audience. Perhaps conservatism, of the kind articulated in this pro-Western, pro-American series, had a claim on the future.

In the mid-1940s *Partisan Review* contained countless references to the death of radicalism or, put differently, the birth of conservatism. This was, as Richard Chase wrote in 1944, "our religious time." The war aims of the United States, Dwight Macdonald lamented, are not progressive. They are "an opportunistic adoption to a reactionary status quo." Macdonald's declaration that "we can no longer believe in the inevitability of socialism" was hardly a novel insight in 1943; it was close to being the conventional wisdom at least for the *Partisan Review* set. Arthur Koestler made the point in sociological terms: "the once revolutionary urban bourgeoisie has become a conservative force. No more a sensitive membrane, but an inert sticky glue which holds the social body together." The radical intellectual was rapidly becoming an artifact of the past, a historical figure "whose demise was as sudden and mechanical as its birth," according to William Phillips. Intellectuals were only one part of a vast social montage in which conservatism was gaining in prominence. "Conservative man," a term used by Günter Reimann in a *Partisan Review* essay of that title, was paradigmatic of the contemporary bourgeois order. Conservative man became "the typical representative of Western Civilization once the era of bourgeois revolutions in Europe came to an end, and bourgeois society was firmly established," Reimann wrote.[48]

A resurgent conservatism was partially the work of conservative intellectuals. Even the radical Macdonald granted the "conservative liberal" intellectual an impressive flexibility and power in face of recent crises. Macdonald used a term that would later enjoy common currency but was an unexpected neologism in 1943; he had discovered the neo-conservative. A useful word, it described those who were new to conservatism, as so many were in the 1940s. "The neo-conservative of our time," Macdonald wrote, "rejects the propositions on materialism, Human Nature, and Progress." Like Chambers, the neo-conservatives enjoyed the benefits of pessimism, benefits that were legion in the mid-twentieth century. Referring to such neo-conservatives as Gaetano Mosca, Robert Michels, Vilfredo Pareto, and James Burnham, Macdonald charitably observed that "their freedom from the optimistic illusions of their period allowed them to foresee the catastrophes in store for bourgeois and socialist democracy." The Euro-American neo-conservatives were unlike Chambers in their moderation. They retained something from their years on the Left and were conservative liberals or vice versa, "attempting to combine progressive values and reactionary concepts." Better to be a neo-conservative, Macdonald suggested, than to be a "modern obscurantist" like Jacques Barzun, whose understated Catholicism bothered Macdonald. The modern obscurantism of intellectuals had its counterpart in the obscurantism of mass culture, compelling "the American masses [to] read pulp fiction and [to] listen to soap operas on that triumph of technology, the radio, [while] the German masses are more easily indoctrinated with a lying and debased official culture."[49]

For intellectuals in the 1940s, conservatism had a generational appeal. This was a natural, if depressing, claim for members of the *Partisan Review* circle to make. *Partisan Review*'s editors had begun as communists under the official auspices of the Communist Party. As they grew older, communism was associated in their world with reckless youth. The illusions of youth faded with age and with anti-communism. Arthur Koestler implied that communist intellectuals were childish, writing that "the intelligentsia of the Pink Decade was irresponsible, because it was deprived of the privilege of responsibility. Left in the cold, suspended in a vacuum, they became the decadents of the bourgeoisie."[50] Leslie Fiedler captured the transformation in words edged with sarcasm: "the generation brought up to the heresies of optimism and Progress have compulsively to assert hell, and our being in it, over and over." Fiedler might have had Whittaker

160

Chambers or T. S. Eliot in mind when he added that "our hells are inevitably urban."[51] In a review of Saul Bellow's first novel, *Dangling Man*, Delmore Schwartz beautifully defined the dilemma of his generation.[52] First came the dilemma: "it is one thing to have lost one's faith; it is quite another to begin with the sober and necessary lack of illusion afforded by Marxism, and then to land in what seems to be utter disillusion, only to be forced, stage by stage, to ever greater depths of illusion." Then came the history of the dilemma: "this is the experience of a generation that has come to maturity during the depression, the sanguine period of the New Deal, the days of the Popular Front and the days of Munich, and the slow, loud, ticking imminence of a new war."[53]

Again and again, the conservative intellectual, devoid of Marxist illusions or disillusionments, intruded on the fragmenting radicalism of *Partisan Review*. The seriousness with which the question of conservatism was handled in *Partisan Review* implied a crisis of radicalism in the 1940s. Whatever radicalism was, radicals no longer had the same confidence in radical change that had created the Red Decade. In 1944, T. S. Eliot published "Notes towards a Definition of Culture" in *Partisan Review*, proposing conservative arguments with untrammeled confidence. Eliot's disgust with the modern world was so categorical that it was almost comic. He asked "whether the modern world is hostile not merely to any particular and antiquated form of culture, but to culture in any form." Modernity was culturally bankrupt because of its atheism, for "without religion there can be no culture."[54] Eliot was clearly a marginal figure with his religious arguments, as opposed to his poetry, but *Partisan Review*'s irreligious editor, William Phillips, adopted the rudiments of Eliot's position in his essay, "The Intellectuals' Tradition." Intellectuals, in Phillips's essay, are the new clerics: "in their role of intellectual conservation and in their tightly knit traditions, [they] perform for modern times a function that an institution like the church, for instance, had in the medieval period." Modernity, however, has given intellectuals very little to conserve, making alienation the birthright of the twentieth-century intellectual. "If any one figure can be said to be a symbol of our entire culture," Phillips contended, "it is Henry Adams," who symbolized "the discontinuity that is the mark of our inability to form a complex intellectual tradition."[55] Eliot laid down the challenge, accusing the modern world of emptiness, and to this challenge Phillips had no answer. To concede that Henry Adams was the representative figure of American culture was a terrible concession for a former communist.

The anxiety of conservative influence was palpable in the pages of *Partisan Review*. One could almost sense the different writers looking over their shoulders to see whether another's deradicalization was actually a move to the Right. Phillips saw such a move in Ignazio Silone, whose 1936 novel *Bread and Wine* was about the loss of socialism and the return to a presocialist past. *Bread and Wine* was, in Phillips's view, a novel in which the hero attempts "to recapture those ethical values he had found lacking in socialist practice—or was it socialist theory, too?" Behind the novel's program Phillips detected an implicit conservatism. Silone was notable for "his religious turn" and for "his repudiation of city culture," Chambers-esque qualities indeed. Phillips praised Silone for his insight into the present moment, for writing novels that "have cut so deeply into the cross-currents of faith and skepticism that marked the deterioration of the socialist ideal." Yet Silone had retreated too far from the contemporary scene in his break with socialism. Phillips did not directly denigrate Silone for his "religious turn," but he did make it clear that Silone was turning away from the energy and vitality of "city culture." "If one looks behind Silone's new faith," Phillips wrote, "one can discern the immemorial passivity of the village, with its instinctive faith in the great mysteries of life and death and salvation."[56]

This conservative turn in American and European letters was not met with passivity. Sidney Hook was *Partisan Review*'s most vigorous enemy of conservatism because he was so consistently hostile toward religion. The collapse of radical politics in the 1930s has retrospectively confirmed "Dostoevsky's reactionary genius," Hook wrote in a *Partisan Review* essay on Catholic theologian Jacques Maritain. Hook was disturbed by Maritain's claim that atheism "is nothing else than the non plus ultra of bourgeois humanism." When bourgeois humanism metastasized into Marxism, atheism became "the root of Marxian fallacy in theory and Marxian inadequacy in practice," exactly what Chambers believed about Marxism and the Soviet Union.[57] The tragedy of recent history, Hook implied, was that obscurantism had changed hands. The Bolsheviks had stolen obscurantism from the Right and to continue the Bolshevik repudiation of science and democracy by encouraging a religious revival would be to condemn oneself yet again to the totalitarian model. For Hook, there was "a new failure of nerve in Western civilization." At fault were the newly popular enthusiasts of religion such as Reinhold Niebuhr, whose theology "breathes a defeatism more congenial to Toryism than his own political progressivism." Hook's summary of the conservative mood could be applied to Niebuhr or to Chambers: "a recrudescence of belief in the original depravity of human nature; prophesies of doom for Western culture . . . the frenzied search for a center of values that transcends human interests . . . posturing about the cultivation of spiritual purity." Hook lamented "a veritable campaign to 'prove' that without a belief in God and immortality, democracy—or even plain moral decency—cannot be reasonably justified."[58]

Trilling's stark disassociation from radicalism, his affection for the middle class and his sympathy for religion, distinguished him from Sidney Hook, William Phillips, and most of the intellectuals gathered around *Partisan Review*. His political status was unclear.[59] He was respectful enough toward conservatism to be approached by conservatives of various stripes, such as Robert Maynard Hutchins and Willi Schlamm. Schlamm was a colleague of Chambers's at *Time*, yet another ex-communist intellectual well on his way to the Right. The president of the University of Chicago, Hutchins was a stalwart academic conservative, protecting Western civilization with an ambitious great books program.

Hutchins invited Trilling to serve on a committee for St. John's College charged with creating a curriculum of only great books. Trilling was not a fellow traveler of Hutchins's academic conservatism: the "intellectual life must necessarily be lived on an axis between practicality and the imagination," Trilling wrote to Hutchins in September 1944. As an undergraduate, Trilling had found John Dewey incomprehensible. He mounted no formal attack on Hutchins in the theoretical language of John Dewey, although some echo of Dewey could be heard in the notion that "adult education . . . is [not] rightly served by the inclusion of so large a number of difficult, special and technical books as the committee seems to feel necessary."[60] In the spring of 1945, Schlamm was looking to found a conservative journal of ideas, a *Partisan Review* of the Right, and he sent Trilling a "(Confidential) Memorandum," outlining the journal's mission. Its dual ideals were Christianity and American republicanism, faith in God, and faith in democracy. Political rights, Schlamm argued in his memorandum, must be "derived from a set of more-than-personal values that are true . . . we feel that the standards we have inherited from the Scriptures and the Declaration of Independence are pretty good guesses of what decent people will accept as self-evident truths in another 200 years." Schlamm's wording was infelicitous. Could one honestly make "pretty good guesses" about self-evident truths? Additionally, Thomas Jefferson, the primary author of the Declaration, was not a political thinker who anchored republicanism in the Scriptures. Trilling's dissatisfaction with Schlamm's memorandum was basic. In a marginal note on his copy of the memorandum, Trilling expressed his skepticism: "if liberal relativism is discarded I must know your absolute, and the Scriptures and the Declaration of Independence do not seem specific enough." In an oblique turn of phrase, Trilling wrote Schlamm that "you have all our good wishes for the success of the venture."[61]

Rather than endorsing absolutes of a religious or secular sort, Trilling used the absolutes of others to tame liberal relativism. He hinted at his method in a review for the *Nation*, "John Henry Newman," an appreciation of the Catholic dissenter from nineteenth-century English liberalism. Trilling celebrated Newman's relevance: "of the great figures of the Victorian past there is none that stands the years so well as Newman." Newman was relevant for his modern preoccupation with psychology, something in which non-Catholic readers, like Trilling, could share. Trilling thought that Newman's "sense of the world is so subtle and coherent, and his psychological perception is so complex and shrewd that any reader who takes pleasure in endangering his own fixed ideas must be grateful for the exhilaration that Newman can give."[62] This, for Trilling, was a high pleasure, the supreme activity of the liberal mind. Another specialist in endangering fixed ideas was Alexis de Tocqueville, who was liberal enough to see beyond democracy and to see the dialectic between progress and reaction as a useful tension. De Tocqueville's dialectical imagination was rare, as "few [other] men have understood the nature of democracy, paying it the high, free compliment of supposing that it is not a mere piety, but a restless, changing organic thing, likely to produce contradictions and even dangers."[63] Such was the insight of someone drawn both to aristocracy and democracy, not entrusting liberty to the elites or to the masses but to the unending dialogue between them.

In a liberalism of balance, politics and culture might complement each other via tragedy, the tragedy of irreconcilable opposites. Religion was valuable to Trilling insofar as it was tragic, and tragedy was a gift that art could give to politics.[64] Trilling developed this theme in essays on Wordsworth and Freud in which he explored the secular possibilities of tragedy. Both Wordsworth and Freud impressed Trilling with their maturity, which was based on their acceptance of tragedy. Trilling devoted a long essay to

Wordsworth—"Wordsworth's Ode: Intimations of Immortality"—in which he called Wordsworth a poet endowed with "double vision," a poet skilled at "seeing man both in his ideal nature and in his earthly activity." Earthly activity alludes to earthly destiny, and in Wordsworth's poetry "the knowledge of man's mortality . . . replaces 'glory' as the agency which makes things significant and precious." In Wordsworth's poetry, glory yields to wisdom. His ode is a tribute to the mature man, who faces "the relation of man to his fellows in the moral world of difficulty and pain." With this poem, Wordsworth consecrated his own maturity, bidding "farewell to the characteristic mode of his poetry, the mode that Keats called the 'egotistical sublime' and a dedication to the mode of tragedy."[65] As with Wordsworth, "the idea of the reality principle and the idea of the death instinct form the crown of Freud's broader speculations on the life of man." Freud and Wordsworth were mature precisely because they were uninvolved in facile progressivism. The errors of politics mirror the errors of art: when "we think of the simply humanitarian optimism which, for two decades, has been so pervasive, we must see that it implies, in the smallness of its view of the varieties of human possibility a kind of check on the creative faculties." Freud saw man as containing "a kind of hell within him from which rise everlastingly the impulses which threaten his civilization."[66] This hell was a necessary assumption for intelligent political thought, an assumption disastrous for communism and congenial to anti-communism. "We are ill," Trilling wrote in paraphrase of Freud, "but we are ill in the service of health, or ill in the service of life, or, at the very least, ill at the service of life-in-culture." Trilling worried that the dark mood of the 1940s would allow too great a cultural acceptance of neurosis and ill-health, something bad for culture and politics. "Our grim, late human presence," as Trilling termed it, might merely inspire grim art and grim culture. Trilling was already a skeptic where much of modern art and culture was concerned and had been since the 1920s. In Freud, Trilling saw an intellectual capable of analyzing, without falling into, the abyss of the modern. Freud was an analyst of the twentieth-century crisis who did not succumb to the false promises of communism or religion.[67]

On Freud's hard truths a fine, complicated art could be wrought and, more importantly, a powerful liberal polity might be built.

For Trilling, British novelist E. M. Forster put Freud's wisdom about human nature into literary practice, doing so with a laudable political seriousness and maturity of attitude.[68] Communism was not a theme in

Trilling's 1943 study of Forster, titled simply *E. M. Forster*, nor was anti-communism its explicit theme. The theme of the study was, rather, the moral history of the middle class, its career in Western culture—exactly what Chambers had written about for *Life*. Trilling got to anti-communism through the middle class, and his lesson was not complicated or abstruse: Forster encapsulates in his literature the virtues middle-class liberals need to survive in a world of fascist menace and communist temptation. By Trilling's own admission, *E. M. Forster* was a book endowed with "the special energies that attend a polemical purpose."[69] One aspect of this purpose was to write an appreciation of Forster's novels and of "a difficult feat in an age tortured by anxiety and inevitably haunted by the sense of guilt," in the words of Newton Arvin, a literary critic writing in *Partisan Review* in 1942. Forster's feat was "to remember and assert the claims of imagination and irony, of taste, of the 'hilarity' that Emerson credited to the hero."[70] Trilling matched Arvin almost exactly in his adjectives of praise for Forster, but his critical ambitions exceeded praise. Through Forster, Trilling sought to explain the intellectual and to relate the intellectual to the liberal middle class, thereby reconfiguring the relationship between the two. The intellectual cannot be a false prophet, indulging the fantasies of the middle class. The intellectual must be a moral teacher, a secular educator of the middle-class spirit.

Forster was especially unlike the masters of modernism in his proximity to liberal politics. In part, it was Forster's modesty, his lack of a grandiose social or political agenda, that gave Trilling his "polemical purpose." At a time of extremism, Forster's commitment to the small detail was salutary. His powers of careful observation made him immune to sweeping intellectual programs, and Trilling complimented Forster by calling him "one of the thinking people who were never led by thought to suppose they could be more human and who, in hard times, will not become less." The thinking people of Trilling's generation were, by comparison, prone to wild and unhealthy mood swings, to crimes of exaggeration. The bad times to which Trilling was referring were among the bleakest days of World War II, and Trilling made clear from the outset of his book that "a consideration of Forster's work is, I think, useful in a time of war." Forster was read by "we of the liberal connection," by those immersed in "the liberal tradition, that loose body of middle-class opinion which includes such ideas as progress, collectivism and humanitarianism." Like Trilling, Forster was a doubting liberal, giving "a reluctant and qualified assent to the notion of human improvement—for it is a generous faith. But clearly he has no confidence in it."[71] His assent to human improvement saved Forster from conservatism; his doubts about progress made him a serious liberal. Although not a Christian, Forster retains something of religious intuition. Forster has a mystical bent, in Trilling's critical evaluation of him, one that encompasses both religion and mortality. Without actually being religious, Forster "has a tenderness for religion because it expresses though it does not solve, the human mystery," Trilling wrote. Mysticism encourages Forster to explore what others leave unexplored, and his mysticism is, at heart, "his sense of life being confronted with death. A money civilization chooses not to consider this confrontation." Trilling's own affection for Forster could at times seem mystical. He lauded Forster's "acceptance of the human fact as we know it now."[72] Freud and Forster were both mature, having accepted the immutable limits that biology and history describe. Of these limits the most severe is death, the very opposite of progress and an undying affront to liberal progressivism.

Forster's wisdom, his melancholy, and his self-doubt were a challenge to the liberal middle class. Trilling appreciated Forster's "understanding of the part played by art in the life of the middle class." The kind of art Forster himself created was critical, not of the middle class per se—what major twentieth-century novelist was not critical of the middle class?—but of the moral pieties to which liberalism had accustomed the middle class. In Forster's novel *Where Angels Fear to Tread* "the life of self-complacency has been confronted with the life of self."[73] Indirectly, a novel replacing the certitudes of self-complacency with the complexities of selfhood serves a worthwhile political function. It deflates the pretensions of the liberal intelligentsia, which in turn reflect the self-indulgence of the middle class for which the intelligentsia speaks. The middle class stands assured in the moral righteousness of its liberal ideals. If this moral righteousness coalesces with political righteousness, as it did in the 1930s, it can induce blindness even to the horrors of Stalinism, provided that Stalinism is couched in the ideals of liberalism. The writers of the Popular Front dedicated their art to such self-righteousness, while literary critics worked to unite the art and politics of the pro-Soviet Left. Forster put his art to different use, and, as a critic, Trilling reversed the Popular Front equation. An art that was morally complex and free from self-righteousness would express the spirit of political anti-communism.

Without mentioning anti-communism, Trilling made a long digression about the history of the intellectual in *E. M. Forster*. It was a foreshortened history of Western culture and the chronicle of a wrong turn. The Protestant Reformation had created or been created by the first intellectuals, figures such as Erasmus and Milton who broke free from the hold of the Catholic Church. The modern intellectual arrived on the scene in the eighteenth century, which "witnessed such a notable breaking up of religious orthodoxies and such a transference of the religious feelings to secular life that it is surely the true seed-time of the intellectual as we know him." From the very beginning, the modern intellectual existed in an adversarial relationship to society; in a condition of bourgeois self-hatred. The intellectual cannot be other than middle class, Trilling argued, and "because the intellectual, whatever his social origin, always becomes a member of the middle class, he is obviously aware of how dependent is his existence upon the business civilization he is likely to fear and despise." With regard to the masses, the intellectual "vaguely supposes himself to be in a benevolent superior relation, paternal, pedagogic, even priestlike. He believes it necessary to suppose that they are entirely good; the essential goodness of the masses is for him as much a certainty as the essential badness of the business class." Such are the moral foundations of the intellectual and of the Left, a naïve faith in the masses and a hardened dislike of capitalism. The wrong turn consisted of the intellectual's vanity, and Forster's literature underscores "one of the truly new things in human life in the last two centuries . . . the politics of conscious altruism." Though *of* the middle class, the intellectual does not speak *for* the middle class. Since the eighteenth century, intellectuals have sincerely spoken "of politics in terms of freedom and privilege of groups less advantageously placed than their own; the word 'underprivileged' is a key to the nature of the intellectuals' political attitude . . . consequently, liberal intellectuals have always moved in an aura of self-congratulation."[74]

It was Forster's gift to elude such self-congratulation, and, since writing *A Passage to India*, Forster had "the increasing sense of possible doom," a doom imminent enough in 1943. Instead of enhancing the moral hubris to which liberals were susceptible, Forster's novels exhibit "a dignity which comes from . . . being truly involved in moral choice," Trilling wrote.[75] In his art, Forster infused liberalism with a conservative grace. What Forster and Freud brought to liberalism had made Chambers a conservative. Forster and Freud, as Trilling explicated them, kept alive older notions of moral judgment—sin, evil, tragedy—in a twentieth century that had countless examples of evil doing but an uncertain language for discussing them. Trilling relied on the afterglow of religion to contend with the subject of evil. He seemed to hope that liberalism could express the best of religion, as it became a moral force capable of fighting communism. American liberals might need a British author to guide them, communism might still attract some or many intellectuals, but a corner had already been turned. On this account, Chambers was more pessimistic. The communist disease was far advanced, and only conservatism and religion, frankly and vigorously pursued, could keep the old moral sentiments alive and the modern wickedness at bay. Chambers felt himself to be a lonely voice among a socialist multitude and a wayward conservative minority. He was confident, however, that religion connected him to the American people as much as it alienated him from intellectuals. The people's Christianity was still uncorrupted by secular intellectuals in an America that was Christian by definition; Trilling's America was liberal by definition, committed to a West that was no longer Christian. Whether liberal or Christian or both, America was fertile soil for anticommunism. Americans could be led to understand communism as evil, and they could be helped along by intellectuals who spoke and wrote well about communist evil. On this Trilling and Chambers might agree.

Evil was on the march in the mid-1940s. Trilling and Chambers both addressed the subject of evil directly while responding to the same book, *The Devil's Share* by Denis de Rougement, a Swiss intellectual living in exile in New York City during World War II.[76] De Rougement's book spoke to religious and nonreligious readers alike. Hannah Arendt, a refugee from Nazi terror who was living in New York, found the book startlingly relevant. Arendt was not a religious woman, but she greeted *The Devil's Share* warmly, writing in *Partisan Review* that "among recent publications, I know of very few that come so close to the experience of modern man." It was evil in its Nazi and Soviet variants that made the devil such a close companion to modern experience, which means that "the problem of evil will be the fundamental question of post-war intellectual life in Europe."[77] America had so far been spared the worst of modern history—the *gulag*, the Holocaust, and total war—but it was not disconnected from these horrors. American intellectuals were no less free from the question of evil than their European counterparts. The popularity of Reinhold Niebuhr was evidence enough of the power intellectuals could have when they thought creatively about evil. In *Partisan Review* and elsewhere, the conservatism of the years during and shortly after World War II was a persistent refrain, one that masked an anxiety on the intellectual Left. Could the Left deal with loss of progress, with evil, with the devil?

Trilling found *The Devil's Share* worthwhile but misguided, acceptable as a modern myth, while false in its attempts at theology. Trilling adversely compared de Rougement with Cardinal Newman, "a modern man who did not believe in the modern way, and knew it." Therefore, "we can always read the *Apologia* with instruction—and exhilaration," wrote Trilling, referring to Newman's autobiography, *Apologia pro Vita Sua*. By Trilling's standard of judgment, de Rougement failed to find a modern language for religion as Chambers must also have failed. De Rougement confused myth and religion, "recklessly involving his mythical devil with a plea for religious belief, recognizing no distinction between the kind of credence we give a modern myth—the willing (and even, in this case, slightly facetious) suspension of disbelief—and the kind of belief we must presumably give to religion." Hence, the dismissive title for Trilling's 1945 review, "A Derivative Devil." The mythic is more accessible to the modern reader than the religious; and the literary is most accessible of all. Dostoevsky's "Grand Inquisitor" passage from *The Brothers Karamazov* is about the evils of socialism and it begins with a visit from the devil. In Trilling's judgment, Dostoevsky's "Grand Inquisitor" was "perhaps the greatest moral-political document of our time."[78]

At the behest of Henry Luce, Chambers wrote an essay on the devil in which he treated de Rougement with far more respect. The enthusiastic popular response to "The Devil"—which Chambers published in *Life*—inspired him to comment in *Witness* on the gulf between the media and the American people. "The Devil" was, Chambers wrote, "a religious essay the responses to which astonished *Life*'s editors, who, like so many others, did not know that the American people is, above all, a religious people."[79] The essay was a short story of sorts, a fictionalized version of the argument Chambers had presented in "The History of Western Culture" series. The devil meets a lone pessimist on New Year's Eve at the Plutonium Room, a New York nightclub situated somewhere in Rockefeller Plaza, where the atomic bomb is material for a song and dance routine.[80] This was a satiric touch, on Chambers's part, for *The Devil's Share* began with a discussion at New York's Cosmopolitan Club.

Urban decadence is such that no one recognizes the devilish stranger sitting in the audience "with a rich Miami tan," except for the pessimist, who is remarkably like Chambers himself. The devil explains that "for the last 250 years all Hell has been underground," a word that resonated with Chambers's past in the Soviet underground. The devil—an admirer, apparently, of Joseph Stalin—succeeded in instituting his "Five Hundred Year Plan," a scheme by which reason, progress, and science will hide the devil from view. For the purpose of stealth, "hell must write Progress on its banners and Science in its methods."[81]

This diabolical plot, of which communism is but one manifestation, has so far elicited scant opposition. Lulled into complacency by progress and science, most have forgotten the power of evil, shown by science and progress with the invention of nuclear weapons. Only a handful of intellectuals have not been deceived. The pessimist mentions " 'Reinhold Niebuhr at the Union Theological Seminary . . . In *The Nature and Destiny of Man* I believe that he found traces of your [the devil's] work. And C. S. Lewis has had some fun with you in *The Screwtape Letters*. Denis de Rougement has devoted a whole book to your existence." Echoing Harold Rosenberg, who complained that the literature of ex-communists was fashionable, the devil says of these twentieth-century analysts of evil that "I'm already making plans to turn their findings into a fad." The devil is self-confident: "Oh, how well I know the rationalist and liberal mind," he exults. And history has already shown the mark of the modern mind: "Do you doubt my triumph when you stop to think that the mind of man conceived the concentration camp? Then came the atom bomb."[82] The essay concluded with a rousing defense of Christianity. The devil has destructive powers, but the faithful have the power to create. The pessimist, it turns out, is a Christian. It is precisely because of his Christian pessimism that he can recognize the devil and dispel his arguments. "The Devil" was among the last pieces Chambers wrote for Luce.

By February 1948, when the article was published, the search for devils was not limited to de Rougement, Arendt, Trilling, or Chambers. It had begun in earnest in Washington, D.C. Since 1939, Chambers had left a trail of information about communist subversion in the government bureaucracy. Throughout the 1940s HUAC was eager to exorcise the demons of communism from the U.S. government, but by October 1947 the Committee had reached its "lowest point."[83] Discussions were under way about dismantling HUAC altogether, but HUAC was not disbanded

and it would be greatly aided in its struggle for survival by a junior representative from California, Richard Nixon. If Alger Hiss was devilish in his
espionage for Stalin's Soviet Union, then Nixon was either pessimistic or
shrewd enough to see a devil where most people saw a brilliant and promising civil servant. Nixon put his considerable energy behind the supposition that Hiss was a communist. Several years later, when Senator Joseph
McCarthy presided over the search for ever more communists in government, the language of premodern superstition would return. Time and
again, McCarthy's enemies would accuse him of prosecuting a witch
hunt. McCarthy's supporters countered the charge by arguing that the
witches were real. But until 1948, when the Hiss case began, the devils and
witches of American communism, occupants of a "haunted wood," were a
matter of speculation and debate.[84] Until 1948, the anti-communism of
Trilling and Chambers was not yet implicated in the power politics and
ideological ferocity of the Hiss case. Until 1948, the devils of communism
existed most vibrantly on paper.

6

FICTIONAL ANTI-COMMUNISM

Lionel Trilling's *The Middle of the Journey*

The Middle of the Journey is an uncommonly interesting novel of ideas—a searching and compassionate account of the liberal's dilemma of conscience in a world of absolutes. All liberals should read it.

— ARTHUR SCHLESINGER JR., proposed blurb for
The Middle of the Journey

L ionel Trilling combined history and prophecy in *The Middle of the Journey*, which he published in 1947. The novel's subject is Kronstadt, the break with the Communist Party: the journey begins in communist enthusiasm and culminates in anti-communist maturity, with Kronstadt in the middle. The novel is set in the late 1930s at the time when Trilling and Whittaker Chambers were embroiled in their own Kronstadts and in those of others. Yet, in a mysterious way, the novel also points to the future. Its correlations with postwar American history have long associated the novel with the Hiss case, which began a year after it was published. Trilling consciously based one of the novel's main characters, Gifford Maxim, on his college classmate, Whittaker Chambers. Two of the novel's other main characters, Arthur and Nancy Croom, could be said to resemble Alger and Priscilla Hiss in their angular, fellow-traveling progressivism. As late as 1975, Trilling had to explain the timing of his novel, written before he had ever heard of the Hisses or the Hiss case.[1] More than the Hiss case, Trilling's novel of ideas anticipated the ideological fault lines of the postwar era, the kaleidoscopic spectacle of radicalism, conservatism, and liberalism as each was transformed by the Cold War. The end of the journey will be anti-communist, the novel implies, but it will be reached in separate, conflicting ways by the liberal and the conservative, and possibly never reached at all by the radical.

Trilling arrived at his literary program for *The Middle of the Journey* by writing short stories and by commenting on the anti-communist fiction of others, a genre coming into its own in the 1940s. An early opportunity came with *Adventures of a Young Man*, an anti-communist novel written by John Dos Passos and published in 1939. Trilling titled his review "Determinist and Mystic," and he criticized a penchant for determinism and mysticism in Dos Passos, which led Dos Passos to neglect the nuances of the individual and the Communist Party; the moral texture of communism as modified by history, class, and character. Behind this critique of Dos Passos stood an agenda for *The Middle of the Journey*, a novel subtly in favor of agency and enlightenment. "When he [Dos Passos] omits the tragic scope of world-events to which the members of the Communist Party have had to accommodate their minds and their morals," Trilling wrote, "when he omits, too, the impulses which first turned them to the party and the tragic irony of men who are certain of their perfect virtue yet who act with the cynical opportunism of machine politicians, Dos Passos tells a story far short of what the truth demands."[2] Fiction is the midwife of political truth, and Trilling's review of Dos Passos flags the self-critical role fiction can have in a time of ideological extremism, fiction serving the truth when it investigates the moral plight of an individual, a group, a political party, a generation. Through fiction, writers can be instruments of truth and bringers of enlightenment rather than mysticism. To do so responsibly after the 1930s they have to tell the truth about communism; Dos Passos was admirable for trying but unsteady in his achievement.

Several years later, in 1946, Trilling vented his frustration with the absence of the communist theme in American literature. Eleanor Clark's novel, *The Bitter Box*, was a pleasant exception to this absence. The themes of *The Bitter Box* are "freedom and salvation," Trilling wrote in "The Life of the Novel," but Trilling's concern, in this review, was not so much *The Bitter Box* as the resistance of America's "liberal" culture to a vibrant anti-communist literature. Trilling wrote with disdain about a liberal readership likely to be irritated by the protagonist's "continuing moral growth that leads him to break with the Party," and Trilling sharply criticized the contemporary moral and political climate to which communism remained essential. At the same time, his criticism gave the modern novelist a mission to accomplish: "If we want to understand what has been going on in our moral life to deteriorate our fiction, we could not do better than to begin with this fact: that although the Communist Party has been in existence in this country for more than a quarter-century, it has not appeared in our novels except as a figment."[3] The critical judgments in "Deterministic and Mystic" and in "The Life of the Novel" indicate the scope of Trilling's ambitions for literature and for an anti-communist literature in particular. Trilling's largest ambition was neither literary nor political. It was moral, the dual aim of examining communism as a moral phenomenon and of using fiction to correct communism's moral errors. "We," the educated middle class, who had earlier fallen in love with communism, had no more urgent responsibility and this responsibility, if honored, will contribute to a politically enlightened anti-communism.

Trilling began the task of moral investigation in "Of this Time, of that Place" and "The Other Margaret," short stories that are studies in conservatism more than anti-communism, stories that anatomize the minds and morals of Trilling's generation. In the earlier of the two, "Of this Time, of that Place," Trilling presented three types of conservatism: a romantic intellectual conservatism, an Arnoldian cultural conservatism, and the conservatism of professional ambition. All three types of conservatism are in conflict with each other. The story's protagonist, Joseph Howe, could be described as a young man no longer entirely young: "at twenty-six Joseph Howe had discovered that he was neither so well off nor so bohemian as he had once thought." Howe is in conflict with an older professor, Frederick Woolley, an exemplar of old-fashioned or Victorian cultural criticism and the first openly conservative character in Trilling's fiction. Woolley edits *Life and Letters*, where "he had carried on the defense of what he sometimes called older values." He is a conservative in a country without a conservative tradition, an observation about America that Trilling would memorably repeat in the preface to *The Liberal Imagination*.[4] Trilling writes of Woolley that "in France, even in England, he would have been connected with a more robust tradition of conservatism, but America gave him an audience not much better than genteel." One cannot help but think of Professor Trilling in short-story-writer Trilling's description of Woolley, whose name suggests Anglophilic backwardness: "all his literary life Woolley had been concerned with the relation of literature to morality, religion and the private and delicate pieties, and he had been unalterably opposed to all that he had called 'inhuman human-itarianism.'" In a literary journal, Woolley attacks Howe's poetry, indict-ing its "precious subjectivism" and forcing Howe, the self-styled bohemian, to realize that he does not want "to be marked as the poet of a willful and selfish obscurity."[5]

In "Of this Time, of that Place," Howe does not yield to Woolley's old-fashioned conservatism, but he does give in to the conservatism of bu-reaucratic institutions. The conflict with Woolley proves far less climactic than the conflict that develops between Howe and a gifted but troubled student, Tertan. Tertan has no discipline and no self-restraint, yet he is ex-ceptionally sensitive to ideas; his original essays bespeak a precious sub-jectivism. As if refuting the humanist Professor Woolley, Tertan dismisses humanism as "my nomenclature for making a deity of man." He writes "numerous essays on science, combating materialism." Tertan is a roman-tic figure, solitary, brilliant, touched by madness and unsuited for society. His improbable doppelgänger is Theodore Blackburn, a dutiful student who understands nothing of literature and art. Academic protocol re-quires that Howe fail Tertan and assist in his expulsion from the college, while giving Blackburn an undeserved passing grade that will allow him to graduate. In giving Blackburn a passing grade, Howe knows that he "was carefully and consciously committing a cowardice." By betraying Ter-tan, Howe himself graduates from his own youthful idealism and romanti-cism to an uncertain maturity. Such maturity is unavoidable. "Society" demands that Tertan fail and that Blackburn succeed; the college as an in-stitution certainly makes this demand. Nevertheless, "it would always be a landmark of his life that, at the very moment he was rejecting the official way, he had been, without will or intention, so gladly drawn to it."[6]

In "The Other Margaret," Trilling deepened his exploration of conser-vatism. Its protagonist, Stephen Elwin, is fifteen years older than Joseph Howe, but at the story's outset he, too, has not reached full maturity. El-win is not a poet or a bohemian; he is a liberal, whose immaturity consists of his liberalism. He does not discard his liberalism throughout the course of the story, but step by step he revises his liberal convictions, ren-dering them more conservative. Although no mention is made of com-munism, the political dilemma that Trilling explores in "The Other Margaret" reflects the Kronstadts of his generation, tracing the cultural details and implications of this reverse in nonideological terms. In the con-text of the story, conservatism is less a matter of politics than of personal disposition, connected to taste, aging, and fatherhood. The conservative disposition completes the mature man, even if the necessity of conservatism is sad, perhaps even tragic. The protagonist of "The Other Margaret" is nearing the middle of his journey, leaving youth behind with considerable pain and regret.

"The Other Margaret" begins with a symbolic act—the purchase of a painting. Elwin, an editor who lives in the Upper East Side of Manhattan, has been feeling a new quality of maturity in himself: "more and more, in the last few months, Elwin had been able to experience the sensation of being wise, for it was indeed a sensation, a feeling of stamina, poise and illumination." He is buying a reproduction of Rouault, "one of Rouault's kings. A person looking at it for the first time might find it repellent, even brutal or cruel. It was full of crude blacks that might seem barbarically untidy." Elwin admires the appropriateness of the king as king, his "fierce quality that had modulated, but not softened, to authority." The king has suited himself to power such that power suits him: "one could feel of him— it was the reason why Elwin had bought the picture—that he has passed beyond ordinary matters of personality and was worthy of the crown he was wearing. Yet he was human and tragic . . . In his right hand he had a spray of flowers." Having established the virtue of kingly authority, Trilling proceeds to intertwine it with two other themes: the moral power of acknowledging one's own mortality and the moral uncertainties of contemporary culture, its manners and class structure in disarray. A sentence Elwin learned in adolescence recurs in his mind, challenging his modern insouciance about death. It is a sentence of Hazlitt—"No young man believes he shall ever die"—instilled in his memory by a high school teacher. Elwin recalls that "the chalky familiar classroom had been glorified by this moment of Mr. Baxter's," by the high school teacher quoting Hazlitt.[7] It was Elwin's good fortune to have partaken of Hazlitt's wisdom, to have it in his past. Elwin's "sensation of being wise" is subconsciously associated with Hazlitt's pronouncement on the folly of youth.

Contemporary New York is troubled by a new kind of rudeness. On a bus, the conductor humiliates a middle-class child, a clear instance of class conflict that, for Elwin, is exemplary of modern times. "In the past it could not have happened," he observes to himself. Then the bus was more expensive. Consequently, "the bus was particularly safe. The people who rode in it paid a dime after they had taken their seats were known to be nicer than the people who rode in the subway for a nickel which they paid before admission." The bourgeoisie is less cruel than the proletariat and money can purchase good manners, frankly illiberal thinking. Another affront to the Popular Front ethos was the notion that the older world, with its accepted hierarchy, was benevolent. In it, bus conductors "were known for their almost paternal kindness." In the present tense, some time during the World War II, almost the opposite is the case. The conductor "had outlived his fatherhood, which had once extended to all the bus-world of children." A decent liberal, "he [Elwin] at once brought into consideration the conditions of life of the old man, especially the lack of all the advantages that he himself has had—the gentle rearing and the good education that made a man like Stephen Elwin answerable for all his actions." In the story's cardinal transformation, Elwin's attitude toward the intemperate conductor changes from liberal indulgence to illiberal anger. Unexpectedly, Elwin's liberal superego dissolves under the pressure of an illiberal id. "It was bewildering that he should feel anger at a poor ignorant man, a working man," Elwin thinks to himself. "It was the first time in is life he had ever felt so. It shamed him."[8]

The episode with the conductor anticipates the story of the other Margaret, the Elwins' black maid—"other" because the Elwins' daughter is also named Margaret. Margaret Elwin is thirteen, no longer quite a child and anything but an adult. She has begun to question paternal and patriarchal authority, and for this reason she dislikes the Rouault painting. Premodern and modern, child and adult, confront one another uncomfortably: "it was to Elwin strange and funny, this confrontation of the black, calm, tragic king and this blonde child in her sweater and skirt, in her moccasin shoes . . . but Margaret, with her grave, luminous brow, was able to meet it head on. And not in agreement either." Margaret regards her parents and their relation to the other Margaret with similar consternation. Their previous black maid had been cheerful and efficient; the other Margaret is rude and reckless. Lucy, Elwin's wife, is frankly upset by the other Margaret. Lucy is generally predisposed "to get angry with simple people when she thought they were not behaving well. And lately she had been full of stories about the nasty and insulted temper that was being shown by the people one daily deals with." To this the other Margaret is no exception, and Lucy "had shocked Elwin by giving, just like any middle-class housewife, a list of the precious things Margaret had broken."[9] Lucy is a middle-class housewife and Elwin's attitude a liberal affectation informed by self-hatred.

Elwin must choose between Lucy's dislike of the other Margaret and his daughter's strong will to defend the family's black maid. Trilling's assault on the progressive psyche went far enough to include its racial as well as its class ideals. Not only is the bus conductor an objectionable figure, but so, too, is a black working-class woman. Moreover, the progressive argument in the maid's favor is made by an immature child. Just as Elwin's high school teacher, Mr. Baxter, had left the Hazlitt quote about mortality to linger in Elwin's adult mind, Margaret's schoolteacher is trying to instill wisdom in Margaret. Only Margaret's teacher, Miss Hoxie, is a political progressive, whose pedagogy has stimulated Margaret's concern for the other Margaret. In the child Margaret's words: " 'She's not responsible,' she said desperately, 'It's not her fault. She couldn't help it. Society—' But at that big word she halted, unable to handle it. 'We can't blame her,' she said defiantly but a little lamely.' " Margaret compares the other Margaret to the Elwins' previous maid, Millie, who had been hardworking and polite: " 'Oh, Millie has a slave-psychology,' she said loftily." Listening to his daughter's words, Elwin hears the tutelage of Miss Hoxie, which he strongly rejects. Elwin "wondered if Margaret had submitted the question of Millie to Miss Hoxie. If she had, and if this was the answer she had been given, his daughter had been, yes, corrupted." The parallel structure Trilling sets up is careful: the Hazlitt quote cancels out the liberal sentiment of Miss Hoxie. "It seemed to him [Elwin]—not suddenly, for it had been advancing in his mind for some hours now—that in the aspect of his knowledge of death, all men were equal in their responsibility." Yet this is a conclusion that Elwin must graft onto his liberal self, without jettisoning this self: "as much as Margaret, he believed that 'society is responsible.' He believed the other truth too."[10]

The climax of "The Other Margaret" is also its political moral, which is that progressivism stands in the way of maturity. According to radical ethics, society—or, alternately, history—renders the proletariat less morally responsible than the bourgeoisie. In defending the aptly named "other Margaret," the thirteen year-old Margaret is defending herself and rejecting the authority of her parents at the same time. As Elwin comes to realize about his daughter, "with the foolish phrases derived from the admired Miss Hoxie, she [Margaret] was defending herself from her own impending responsibility. Poor thing, she saw it moving towards her through the air at a great rate, and she did not want it. Naturally enough, she did not want it. And he, for what reason he did not know, was forcing it upon her." The liberal stands between two contradictory truths: that society is responsible and that the individual is responsible. When the other Margaret smashes a clay lamb of Margaret's, symbolically destroying the child's innocence, the child Margaret is shocked and then furious. She had created a sentimentalized image of the other Margaret, with help from Miss Hoxie, an image that is an extension of her childhood self. Having witnessed the other Margaret's willful destructiveness, Margaret "had with her own eyes seen the possibility of what she herself might do, the insupportable fact of her own moral life."[11] Such is Elwin's interpretation, and with it he completes the path to wisdom, which is also the path away from liberal orthodoxy. The story is clearly written in praise of Elwin's path. It is not a polemic against liberalism or the Left but a polemic within liberalism. In "The Other Margaret," Trilling extended, once again, a cautious sympathy to conservatism, derived from reflections on mortality, support for moral absolutes, and the tacit acceptance of hierarchy.

The conservatism of "The Other Margaret" did not go unobserved among contemporary readers. It elicited a harsh response from novelist James Farrell, who had been a literary star in the Popular Front firmament, remaining politically radical well into the 1940s. In the socialist *New International*, Farrell interpreted "The Other Margaret" not just as an ugly attempt to smuggle conservative politics into literature but as a representative example of the conservative turn at *Partisan Review*, where the story was published. Dwelling on the question of class, Farrell upbraided Trilling for reversing the moral bias of socialist realist fiction, for creating sympathetic middle-class characters and unsympathetic working-class characters. "The cultivated intellectual of the middle class is presented as a thoughtful man," Farrell wrote, "a tolerant man, and his conscience is penetrated by the author." Farrell lamented "the very selectivity of the story. The rude lower classes are described by conversation, or else they are seen in action, offending children." Conservative was too mild a term of rejection for Farrell. "The Other Margaret" is "cleverly organized in such a way as to persuasively present a reactionary moral view," to propel the reader away from the side of the worker and over to the side of the king or at least to the side of the father. The fact that the story appeared in *Partisan Review* struck Farrell as sadly meaningful, an indication of an ugly zeitgeist, "of the moods, the retreat from Marxism, the growing moral snobbery of the advanced and cultivated New York intellectual. As such, it is a revealing account of the escape of what we might here call the *Partisan Review* intellectual."[12]

Trilling detailed the anti-communist fervor behind his fiction in private correspondence. In March 1946 he wrote that "I live with a deep fear of Stalinism at my heart." Fascism was another fear, but with fascism the instruments of opposition were obvious—"in one's fantasies one can imagine going out to fight one's Fascist enemies quite simply." The problem with fascism's totalitarian cousin was its appeal, not among enemies but among friends. Even before being usurped by Stalin, communism "has taken all the great hopes and all the great slogans." When Trilling reflected on the degree to which Stalinism "has recruited the people who have shared my background and culture and corrupted them, I feel sick. I am willing to say that I think of my intellectual life as a struggle, not energetic enough, against all the blindness and malign obfuscations of the Stalinoid mind of our time."[13] This statement is remarkable for its intensity and scope: it covered Trilling's whole intellectual life. "The Stalinoid mind of our time" was no less current when Trilling surveyed the American scene in March 1946 than it had been in the late 1930s. The neat demarcation according to which the Popular Front began in 1935 and ended in 1939 had no meaning whatsoever for Trilling. Through a kind of cultural Stalinism, the Popular Front continued apace long after 1939 in his view, and so, too, must the fierce opposition to it. As a consequence *The Middle of the Journey*, Trilling's novel of the Popular Front, was anything but an exercise in antiquarianism. The Popular Front was local color for a story of sweeping historical and contemporary significance, and Trilling criticized reviewers for reading the book as a period piece. "The book really has nothing to do with the Thirties," Trilling wrote, "but with right now and with the whole 20th century. I put it in the thirties to take away some topicality, some too-much-closeness." With this technique of chronological displacement, Trilling had the modernist masters in mind: "the scene of particular time, of what people said and did is just for fun and color, and is some kind of way of making characters. *Ulysses* is set in 1905 on a particular day. Proust writes in particular time: in both books the relation of people to minor events, slang, etc. is interesting and significant." At issue, however, was not the question of literary modernism but of communism or, rather, anti-communism. "So far from trying to refute communism by saying it belonged to the thirties and is now passé, I hoped to imply that it and its derivations are in the very genes of our culture. I don't think that many readers mistook my intentions in these two matters, although I was surprised at the number of reviewers who emphasized the thirties aspect, as if it weren't a common device of novelists to shift a little out of the present for the purpose I mentioned above." As late as 1955, Trilling could write that "the cultural-political situation is very similar to that of the time when the novel was written."[14]

Some indeterminate part of *The Middle of the Journey*, an uncompromisingly personal venture for Trilling, came from his own life. John Laskell, the novel's liberal hero, seems to speak for Trilling, who did not shy away from making this connection. To a student interested in *The Middle of the Journey*, Trilling wrote that it "is autobiographical in only a very limited sense. I once had scarlet fever (which used to be, as I believe it isn't anymore, a dangerous disease) and I had for a time more or less the political attitudes of John Laskell, whose feelings in general are, I suppose, more or less what mine were likely to be at his age."[15] Trilling also made this point in public in a 1947 *Picture News* article succinctly titled "Novelist Trilling on the Liberal Dilemma." "*The Middle of the Journey* is a novel picturing what he [Trilling] believes is the dilemma of liberals today," *Picture News* reported. " 'By liberal, I [Trilling] mean me, first of all,' he [Trilling] explained. 'My position is one of criticizing liberalism from inside the family.' "[16] Trilling qualified the connection to Laskell with reference to time; he was like Laskell "at his age." For Diana Trilling, John Laskell and Lionel Trilling simply resembled one another: "Laskell is Lionel's voice in the novel: his political moderation and the quiet humanity which he counters to the fiery emotions of a Gifford Maxim or a Nancy Croom closely approximate Lionel's own temperament and approach to politics."[17]

If Laskell is like Trilling, the Crooms are Popular Front archetypes. Writing about the Crooms, the literary critic Irving Howe noted "their doctrinaire attachment, not so much to the Communist Party, as to the political and cultural styles created in its ambiance." Trilling had never been a Party member, and Howe is surely right to emphasize that the Crooms were not communists per se. The middle-class Crooms lived in the ambiance of the Party, as Trilling had in the early 1930s. The Crooms may have had a slight autobiographical resonance for Trilling, the ex-communist, but they are too unpleasant to be self-portraits. David Caute deems Nancy "one of the most repellent progressives in modern fiction."[18] The Crooms' progressivism is pronounced, as it never was for

Trilling, who came of age with the cultural pessimism of the 1920s—indeed, with the literary culture of the late nineteenth and early twentieth century, which limited the power radicalism could have over him. He had never ceased to be immersed in the writings of Matthew Arnold, Henry Adams, and T. S. Eliot, a list to which he eventually added Freud, the pessimist's pessimist. The Crooms, on the other hand, have faith in the superiority of modern culture, in a trajectory of economic and cultural progress that communism will fulfill; their culture is an exclusively modern culture. To this mindset Stalin has a fatal appeal. From abroad, the Soviet experiment validated the self-confidence of progressive American intellectuals. In May 1946, Trilling had referred to Stalinism as the "acceleration of modern bourgeois culture in most of its manifestations." Trilling wrote à propos the Soviet Union that he expects "a quantum of injustice in any imperium, [I] expect contradictions as the price of order—what brings me to the puking-point is the fine feelings."[19] The Crooms espouse these fine feelings. They are seamlessly bourgeois and modern and progressive and, hence, pro-Soviet.

The ex-communist Chambers had unique qualifications for appearing in *The Middle of the Journey*. One was obviously that the author knew him. Chambers was also a well-known figure in Trilling's intellectual circle, someone whose biography was at once fantastic and representative, a life that cried out for fictionalization. Trilling mentioned in private correspondence that he did "have my relation with Chambers and there were sources of information about him other than Solow." Trilling was referring here to Herbert Solow, who had befriended Chambers in the late 1930s, circulating the tale of Chambers's break with communism.[20] For William Shiver, a journalist at the *New York Herald Tribune*, Trilling provided further details of his relationship with Chambers. In an article that served as publicity for *The Middle of the Journey*, Shiver wrote that "the last time he [Trilling] saw him [Chambers] was about seven years ago. They had lunch together." "He [Chambers] was trying to get me to take a job in the literary section of 'Time Magazine,'" Trilling recounted, an intriguing sign of Chambers's esteem for Trilling. Asked whether Chambers had told Trilling the story of his life, Trilling's response was negative: "He [Chambers] never actually told it to me at all. But it was pretty well going the rounds among people I used to know and was pretty much talked about. That is, he never kept it very dark. I've found that almost everybody who worked with him at *Time* knew his story. That's one reason I felt free to use it. It was very public property, and I thought there was no reason for not using it."[21] Chambers's story was sufficiently familiar to be public property long before the Hiss case.

The public nature of Chambers's story, of his epic break with communism, was less the material of literature than was Chambers's journey from communism to Christianity and conservatism. Gifford Maxim, the character inspired by Chambers, frames the question of religion in *The Middle of the Journey*, and he is the novel's conservative voice. As did many intellectuals in the 1940s, Trilling believed that religious fervor was on the rise, a force with a serious claim on the future. Trilling had no single attitude toward religion: he respected it, he was alienated from it, he was attracted to it, and he was afraid of it. The same was true of Trilling's attitude toward Maxim, the outspoken Christian conservative. Trilling could admire Maxim, expending enormous empathy on him in *The Middle of the Journey*; yet Trilling's distaste for Maxim is no less palpable than his admiration. Perhaps the real-life model for Maxim was not religious enough, in Trilling's eyes. Chambers's Christian essays for *Time* and *Life* struck Trilling as overdone, almost ridiculous. Maxim has a quality of bathetic intensity similar to the one Trilling perceived in Chambers, whom he once described as a "tragic comedian."[22] Whatever Trilling's opinion of it, Chambers's conservatism completes the political spectrum in *The Middle of the Journey*, just as Maxim's flight from the Communist Party heightens the theme of mortality, and this was the theme that had inspired Trilling to write *The Middle of the Journey* in the first place. Communists can kill, and all people live among death. Such are the moral realities with which the novel's sensitive, intellectual characters must grapple, with or without religious faith. Maxim, "a portrait of Whittaker Chambers as George Eliot might have drawn him," in the words of Leon Wieseltier, concentrated the theme of mortality for Trilling, binding it to questions of communism and anti-communism.[23]

Trilling combined fidelity and selectivity in his attitude toward his sources. The critic John Bayley gently reproached Trilling for "achieving almost too conspicuously at times an Anglican or Episcopalian fragrance" in *The Middle of the Journey*. The critic Robert Warshow, who was a friend of Trilling's, made the same point more directly, focusing on the lack of Jewish characters in the novel. For Warshow, the problem was one of historical accuracy, as "not one of the characters [in *The Middle of the Journey*] is, incredibly, a Jew—though much of the flavor of the

Communist experience in America is their flavor." Trilling's careful dissection of the American middle class lacks the relevant ethnic particularity. Warshow felt that Trilling had ignored "the fact that the middle class which experienced Stalinism was in large part a Jewish middle class, driven by the special insecurities of Jews in addition to the insecurities of the middle class in general."[24] Warshow's criticism explains the disembodied, unemotional quality of *The Middle of the Journey*, the weight Trilling's characters have as intellectuals and their relative weightlessness as people. Trilling's brief discussion of Jewishness in 1944 (in the "Under Forty" symposium) could be read as a rationalization of the missing Jewish dimension in *The Middle of the Journey*. No novel, he argued in 1944, is better because it is a Jewish novel. Jewish writers shine when they enter into the world, not when they remain in some Jewish province of it. Trilling's province in *The Middle of the Journey* was an educated middle class of unmentioned, but presumably WASP, background.

Incorporating Jewishness and Judaism would have complicated Trilling's primary affiliation with liberalism, an affiliation that transcended religious and ethnic particularity. Trilling infused *The Middle of the Journey* with his vision of liberalism in America, what it was and what it should be, offering an unusually candid explication of the novel's liberalism to a French student, Madame Duvette-Navez, who wrote to him in 1953 with a charming question. "Will you accept to tell me, as precisely as possible, what you mean by liberalism," she queried the elusive author of *The Liberal Imagination*. Trilling separated his answer into several parts. One part concerned the classic liberal tradition. Another was American liberalism in the 1930s under the communist star. The third part of Trilling's answer to Madame Duvette-Navez connected *The Middle of the Journey* to the radical 1930s. The classic liberal tradition included the Enlightenment and the romantic movement in literature; it began with Michel de Montaigne and continued on to Matthew Arnold and William Morris, British social critics of the late nineteenth century. It was as much a matter of culture as of political economy. Hence, classical liberalism was, for Trilling, far more than "Manchester liberalism," the doctrine of economic laissez-faire and the convocation of parliaments: "if you take the best ideas of [Jeremy] Bentham—I mean Bentham as he really is, not Bentham as most people represent him—and John Stuart Mill, and [John] Ruskin, and Matthew Arnold, and William Morris, and involve them with the temperament of the English romantic poets, and connect them with Montaigne . . . and much of Rousseau, and much of Stendhal, you will get some notion of the intellectual constellation to which I refer."[25]

This liberalism is by no means a static ideology. It is the possession of living beings caught up in history and culture. In the United States, liberalism belongs to "people who have any pretensions to education." In their eyes, liberalism "is meant to imply thoughtfulness, a belief in the possibility of progress by political means, an open mind, and a resistance to conservative or reactionary ideas." The liberal impetus had two undercurrents in the 1930s, one that belonged with "the Roosevelt administration" and another that was communist. Trilling granted greater significance to the communist impetus: "I should observe of the liberal mind in actuality that it was inclined to give Communism an unreasoned and un-intelligent sympathy, sentimental in its first impulse, though often very hard and bitter in its tenacity. And this may suggest to you," Trilling wrote to his French correspondent, "the sort of cultural error that I have perceived the liberal mind likely to fall into."[26] "The liberal mind in actuality" is a key to communism's sway over liberals, for liberal high-mindedness is not so easy to maintain in practice or in actuality. Hostility to conservatism and belief in the inevitability of progress may combine to foster sentimentality on the one hand and a bitter, hard tenacity in favor of left-wing causes on the other. The Soviet Union was the left-wing cause par excellence in the 1930s, and it was the focal point of the cultural error to which the liberal mind is prone. The liberal shortcomings are not chronic in this description, grave as the error of supporting communism had proven. They are shortcomings that the right kind of liberalism might redress.

In this 1953 letter, Trilling fit *The Middle of the Journey* into the equation he had established for liberalism, which, for him, was hardly the doomed ideology that Chambers considered it to be. "I think of the tendency of that [liberal] culture as on the whole a good thing, but likely to corrupt itself all too easily," Trilling maintained, "and I look at it with some fear (as well as irony) because it seems to me that nothing in our time is more dangerous than the corruption of idealism." *The Middle of the Journey* documents "our time," which belongs only in part to liberals. Liberalism, as Trilling defined it, "will tell you something of the intention of *The Middle of the Journey*, which you can think of as a natural history of the intellectual liberal class as I understand it—its movement to Communism, its wish to deny variousness and complexity in life, or indeed, almost any free emotion, or to admit that life has any depth of mystery (Nancy Croom); or, on the other hand, the movement to false spirituality (Gifford Maxim)."[27] Trilling's task was to return liberalism to the likes of Matthew Arnold and John Stuart Mill and to place it beyond the reach of communists and other false prophets, including the false prophets from the Right who were just then appearing on the horizon.

In *The Middle of the Journey*, the protagonist Laskell has a liberal mind, and he experiences first-hand the cultural error of communism.[28] Although not without its limits, Laskell's initial commitment to communism is very deep. Like Joseph Howe in "Of This Time, of That Place," Laskell had literary aspirations in his youth: "until he was twenty-four he had planned a literary career. He wrote quite well and he had been in revolt against the culture of his affectionate and comfortable Larchmont family." The bohemian-literary leanings faded, and what came to replace them was not bourgeois conformity but communism. In a rough draft of *The Middle of the Journey*, "A Story of Summer," Trilling wrote a note to himself about his protagonist's "turning towards communism, suggesting its connection with the loss of his wife." Communism begins, as it did for Chambers, in despair. Under the influence of communism, which was indirect in Laskell's case, he "had committed himself to the most helpful and progressive aspects of modern life, planning their image in public housing developments, defending them in long dull meetings of liberals and radicals."[29] He becomes "a sort of minor Lewis Mumford," as one reviewer of *The Middle of the Journey* put it.[30] The further Laskell travels from literature and the closer he comes to communism, the more he compounds the cultural error of the liberal mind, its excessive deference to all things progressive and modern.

A sympathizer with communism, Laskell is not a member of the Communist Party. He is a fellow traveler, as Trilling himself had been. In the heyday of the Popular Front, Laskell is "known as a 'sincere liberal,' " sincere in his admiration for the Soviet experiment. For him, "the Party had represented what he would reach if he ever developed in intelligence, virtue, and courage, and the Crooms had pointed the way he must travel to reach this high estate." Laskell is not truly radical. He feels guilty, however, for not being radical enough, for the distance between himself and the Communist Party. This is because "Laskell was not really a political man. The picture of the world that presented itself to his mind was of a great sea of misery, actual or to come. He did not think of it as forces in struggle." Hard-fought struggle is left to Laskell's friend, Gifford Maxim, who is not merely in the Party but working in its underground. Although Laskell involves himself more with ideas than with action, he helps out Maxim when Maxim is a spy for the Soviet Union. He helps Maxim— thereby helping the cause of Soviet espionage in America—"with the sense that, although he did not wholly agree with Maxim and Maxim's political party, he wanted them to exist because of their clear relation to the future. When he said yes to Maxim's requests, he had a strong feeling of hope." Communism played on the liberal's desire for hope at a time of matchless desperation. Laskell's hunger to contribute to the helpful and progressive aspects of life has as its context an economic crisis at home and the rise of fascism abroad.[31]

At first, Laskell is sufficiently radical to abhor Maxim's newfound anti-communism. Laskell rejects Maxim's claims about the Party, which are in part political (that it is murderous) and in part theological (that it is evil). Laskell also questions Maxim's sanity, as if anti-communism could not be the product of a rational mind. Laskell finds himself repulsed by "Maxim's madness and treachery," madness for criticizing the Communist Party and treachery for leaving it. Maxim's reports of Communist Party perfidy cannot be true and must amount to "Maxim's lies about the Party." Maxim states that the American Communist Party takes its orders from the Soviet Union. For Laskell, this is an allegation worthy of reactionaries such as William Randolph Hearst or Henry Luce: "people of liberal mind understand that the belief in Moscow's domination of the Party in America had been created by the reactionary press, and they laughed at it." This sentence carries a heavy weight of irony: what the liberal mind should investigate it dismisses with a self-congratulatory laugh. Even though Laskell participates in this liberal hubris, he has certain doubts. Maxim's change of heart was symptomatic of the 1930s, a small piece of much larger cataclysms: "so far as he [Laskell] believed in Maxim's insanity, it expressed his full sense of the tragic bitterness of the world, the deep confusion of our times, that had distorted a life and mind so fine as Maxim's, despite all the great protection of Maxim's ideas."[32]

To a greater extent than Laskell, the Crooms are people of progressive mind. In the heady 1930s, their progressivism has boiled over into radicalism, a radicalism that is communist in essence, if not always in name. Nancy Croom is the more ardent communist of the two. Her husband, Arthur, is a social scientist, and, more than political dreams, he has professional ambition. He is twenty-eight years old and nowhere near the middle of his journey. He is a man of the twentieth century such that "Henry Adams would have understood Arthur Croom and envied his chances."[33] Nancy is a romantic communist, convinced that communism will bring progress and create a new humanity. In a discussion of Arthur Spengler, whose *Decline of the West* had contributed to the fashionable pessimism of Trilling's and Chambers's youth, Nancy reveals her progressive creed. " 'History,' she says, 'shows that man is dialectically developing and improving himself all the time. There is no limit to his potentialities.' " The air of Marx and Trotsky hangs over this statement, and it is natural that Nancy is " 'considering it [becoming a Party member], I'm so tired of this liberal shilly-shallying talk. I mean to do something real.' " Arthur works in tandem with Nancy, demonstrating how one can be a New Dealer and a communist, for Arthur "needed Nancy's absolute intransigence and ardor . . . as support to his own cooler idealism: it was as if his concern with fact and practicality was then a collection or correction of her excess rather than a limitation of his own moral vision."[34] The story of Alger and Priscilla Hiss has yet to be written. It may be that Trilling captured something of it in *The Middle of the Journey*, without ever having known them personally.[35]

Laskell, Maxim, Nancy, and Arthur had been close friends as communists, but anti-communism breaks their circle apart. At the novel's outset, Maxim has had his Kronstadt. Laskell's Kronstadt begins slowly, imperceptibly, and as with Stephen Elwin in "The Other Margaret," Laskell discovers that he has an illiberal id at war with his liberal superego. This illiberal id acts on him as he sees the Crooms with new eyes. Laskell has suffered through a serious illness. He almost dies, and when he arrives at the Crooms' summerhouse, they are ill at ease with the subject of illness, not to mention death. Once this disturbs Laskell, many other aspects of the Crooms' cultural style begin to disturb him, most of all their reverent attitude toward their handyman, Duck Caldwell. Laskell notices that the Crooms have unwittingly invested political arguments in Duck's character, and Laskell "noted a brooding solicitude for Duck which seemed to him inappropriate." "Duck was an almost obsessive subject of conversation for his friends," Laskell observes. What the Crooms cherished was "Duck's quality of reality," a phrase that evokes one of Trilling's early broadsides against the American Left, republished in *The Liberal Imagination* as "Reality in America." The Crooms are confused in their relationship to reality, because they have succumbed to an ideology dedicated to the remaking of reality. As philo-communists or communists, "the final reality that the Crooms wanted was one of application and hard work and responsibility. And all they ever reported of Duck, apart from his manual skill, suggested only anarchy and evasion."[36] In permitting himself to criticize the working-class Duck, Laskell is retracing the steps taken by Stephen Elwin in "The Other Margaret," who permits himself to criticize a bus conductor and then a black maid. Like Elwin, Laskell has begun to detach himself from liberal orthodoxy without ever intending to do so.

As someone opposed to the Left, Maxim is intent on taking Laskell with him over to the Right. Maxim had previously succeeded in taking Laskell over to communism. In Laskell's imagination, Maxim's communist devotion was almost Christ-like, combining compassion and power.[37] Laskell had a vivid mental image of the communist Maxim, a kind of 1930s mural: "on one side of Maxim stood the figure of the huge, sad, stern morality of all the suffering and exploited men in the world, without distinction or color or creed. On the other side of Maxim stood the figure of power, noble, fierce, indomitable." Maxim stands on the side of suffering men; they stand on his side. Less melodramatically, Maxim stood by Laskell's side after his girlfriend's death. At this time, "it was Gifford Maxim who gave him what companionship he looked for. Laskell found that Maxim's presence, his great, scarred face, gave him fortitude and comfort." As a communist, Maxim was also a gentleman, insisting "on the code of delicacy and politeness, bourgeois though it was." Even as they argue the question of Soviet communism, with Laskell defending and Maxim attacking, Laskell cannot help but admire Maxim's moral candor and his sincerity. "His simplicity was unexpected," Laskell thinks to himself. "It threw into a very strange light the certainty and skill of the answers he had made to Laskell when Laskell had asked him to explain the Moscow trials and the rumors about the actions of the Party in Spain." Maxim's certainty and skill as a communist had their intended effect, pushing Laskell to admire the Soviet Union. Despite the fantastic accusations and convoluted evidence of the Moscow trials, the "guilt [of the accused], after some doubt, had become quite clear to Laskell."[38] Maxim's sincerity as an anti-communist also has its effect.

It is Nancy who inspires Laskell's transformation from communist to anti-communist. Nancy provokes Laskell into realizing his affinity for

Maxim, the anti-communist. Laskell tries unsuccessfully to speak to Nancy about his illness and about the death of his girlfriend, Elizabeth. Thinking of death makes him think of Maxim. "Had he not," Laskell wonders, "in some way, wanted to tell her just what Maxim had wanted to tell him, that people really do die?" Like Stephen Elwin, Laskell has a new sense of his own maturity, and this maturity is precisely what he cannot share with Nancy. Nancy bears a resemblance to the girl Margaret in "The Other Margaret." In ethics, she has remained a child, "the well-loved child of the middle-class taught about the future by means of promises made to him. . . . And all the promises and their fulfillment are symbolic of the great promise, made to him by everyone,—that he will grow and change for the better." The promise of communism is, thus, a natural fit for the middle-class intellectual and not at all an ideological aberration. For Laskell, however, it has become aberrant, following as it does from a childish vision of the world. Laskell concludes "that you could not live the life of promises without yourself remaining a child . . . maturity itself means that the future and the present were brought together, that you lived your life now instead of preparing and committing yourself to some better day to come." Laskell's disagreement with Nancy is not trivial: "he felt a bitter anger at Nancy Croom."[39]

Laskell increasingly adopts the role of conservative against Nancy the radical. Nancy and Laskell diverge in their interpretation of the children's story, *Ferdinand the Bull*, to which "a good many political feelings became attached." In the story, a young bull flees the bullring in a pacifist rejection of violence. Laskell finds himself disgusted with the story, which Nancy adores. With the story's sympathetic readers in mind, Laskell complains that "'they seem to like the idea of a bull going against the nature of bulls.'" Nancy objects to Laskell's criticism: "'Oh no, that's not it. The moral is that if people just refused to fight there would be no more wars. I suppose Ferdinand is just simple human reason, the reason of simple people refusing to cooperate in their own exploitation and slaughter.'" Ferdinand is the downtrodden Russian proletariat refusing to fight in World War I, Ferdinand is an antifascist, Ferdinand is the other Margaret. To Laskell this is nothing more than sentimentality, a facile evasion of nature, which demands that bulls be bulls and that bulls be recognized as bulls. Suddenly, Laskell is horrified by the culture of the Left as outlined in *Ferdinand the Bull*. To Nancy he says, "'I wonder if we're not developing a strange ambivalent kind of culture, people like us. I wonder if we don't rather like the idea of safety by loss of bullhood. A kind of kingdom-come by emasculation.'" Laskell is the cultural conservative in this discussion. Again, the theme of childhood is crucial. *Ferdinand the Bull* is not simply a children's story; it is written from a childish point of view. For the first time, Laskell questions whether a progressive culture—one that transcends the polarities of masculine and feminine, life and death, good and evil—is truly a desirable culture, better than its more traditional alternatives. Shortly after their dispute over *Ferdinand*, Laskell registers another complaint about Nancy: "You talk about morbidity and living in the past—as if you thought death was politically reactionary."[40]

Laskell's most consequential disagreement with Nancy is over Duck Caldwell, whom Laskell and Maxim believe to be evil. Laskell overhears Duck mocking the Crooms and instantly he sees Nancy in his mind's eye "in an aura of self-deception," the political side of which he will soon uncover. What Nancy cannot see, or deceives herself into not seeing, is Duck's malice, which "was emptiness masking itself as mind and desire." Maxim, on the other hand, is quick to see nihilism and evil in Duck. Maxim divines Duck's theft of whiskey, commenting on Duck that he knows "the type—the criminal personality with the strong, narrow streak of intellect." Laskell's perception of evil does not end with Duck; it expands to include Nancy. Nancy could murder for the sake of her ideals, Laskell comes to feel: "the summer had shown him a kind of passion in Nancy Croom . . . the ultimate consequence of which might logically be just such an act of destruction as Maxim feared himself [murder]." Laskell must contend with "his fresh full knowledge of what he had to escape in Nancy, of what this charming and moral woman friend of his could do to him, and was willing to do until he exerted his own will consciously against her intention of which she had no awareness."[41]

Nancy Croom substantiates Laskell's Kronstadt. In the novel's climactic scene, Maxim and the Crooms confront one another. Laskell stands between them, between Left and Right, although he is closer to Maxim. When Laskell tells Arthur of Maxim's conversion to the Right, Arthur is so crestfallen and horrified that he "had probably looked not much different at the moment he learned of the Reichstag fire." In this scene, Laskell is Maxim's ally, although Laskell has not formally changed sides. Indeed, he is a liberal, as he had been when he was a communist. Only now he is an anti-communist liberal, for he concedes Maxim's criticism of the Party. He has also given himself free reign to criticize the Left. Therefore, "even as he told her the story [of Maxim's Kronstadt]—or, rather, as the Crooms put their question to him afterward—he had to resist the feeling that he was telling a story on himself rather than about Maxim." When he tries to explain his position, he slips inadvertently into Maxim's position, which is that liberals are not facing up to the Party's brutality. "We pretty much limit ourselves to ideas—and ideals," Laskell says of his fellow liberals, including the Crooms. "When we act, if we can call it action, it's only in a peripheral way. We do have sympathies with the Party, and even, in a way, with its revolutionary aims. But maybe, sympathetic as we are, we prefer not to think out what the realities of such a party are." Laskell's explanation—which is, really, a justification of Maxim—strikes the Crooms as equivocation. And so, "in the Crooms' eyes he [Laskell] was touched with Maxim's guilt."[42]

Laskell's character is at the complicated heart of the novel, as is his relation to Gifford Maxim. Laskell's relation to the Crooms is simpler to determine. He comes to despise them, and, with them, the whole world of radical politics. They lack culture and a sense of history. They have little empathy for the suffering of individuals, although their empathy for humanity is boundless. They misconstrue virtue and ignore evil, fundamentally misreading Duck's character. They become vivid examples of how not to live. Maxim is far more ambiguous. A man of integrity and intelligence, Maxim cannot be dismissed as Laskell dismisses the Crooms. Yet Maxim is passionately illiberal. He has converted to Christianity, adopting political conservatism because he considers liberalism the first step toward radical corruption. In this, Maxim was no different from the living person on whom he had been based. Maxim calls for the destruction of liberalism, and Laskell must defend himself from this agenda. Critics have failed to resolve the question of whether Laskell succeeds. Some have interpreted Laskell as evidence for an enfeebled liberalism; others, like Arthur Schlesinger Jr., have discovered an honorable "dilemma of conscience" in the novel's liberal protagonist. Trilling's intention was to write a novel that expressed his hopes for an anti-communist liberalism, although the reader may draw other conclusions. Trilling was uncomfortable with open advocacy, which was part of what it meant for him to be a liberal.

Laskell's challenge is to learn from Maxim's conservatism without becoming like Maxim. Maxim first expresses his conservatism to Laskell and the Crooms in a book review. (Trilling the literary critic could not resist turning book reviews into events in his fiction.) The text Maxim has chosen to review is Herman Melville's novella, *Billy Budd*. Maxim organizes his review around the subject of law, penning an indictment of the modern mind for which "Billy Budd will be nothing more than an oppressed worker, and a very foolish one, an insufficiently activated one. . . . And Captain Vere will seem at best a conscience-ridden bourgeois, sympathetic to a man of the lower orders but committed to carrying out the behests of the established regime." Billy Budd has killed a man, and Captain Vere sentences him to death. The Marxist might interpret this as exploitation in the name of the established regime. Maxim interprets the story as "the tragedy of Spirit in a world of Necessity." The Spirit would like to set Billy Budd free: law demands that he be sentenced to death. Spirit is radical, while law is conservative. Maxim's elevation of law above spirit is predicated on the recognition of evil: "as long as Evil exists in the world, law must exist, and it—not Spirit—must have the rule."[43] Evil is the enemy of progress and revolution; it is also the best argument for an established system of law. If he was not repudiating communism with his review, Maxim was certainly condemning Bolshevism, which arrogated to itself the right to make or break the law.

Maxim's conservative reading of *Billy Budd* generates three separate, although equally telling, responses from Arthur, Nancy, and Laskell. Arthur is repulsed: "'that mystical nonsense, it's disgusting,'" he remarks, waving away Maxim's entire argument. Nancy responds to Maxim's inversion of communist thinking and ingeniously justifies the Moscow trials with Maxim's review. In the Moscow trials, she notes that the accused "'may have had to be executed for the sake of what he calls law in the world of Necessity. And you remember how they all concurred in their punishment and seemed almost to want it. Certainly before they died they had a proper appreciation of Law. They realized that the dictatorship of the Proletariat represented Law.'" Laskell is partially disgusted and partially impressed by Maxim's musings on Law and Necessity. Maxim's repetition of these two words induce "an intellectual nausea," but they also speak to Laskell's gradually unfolding anti-communism: "one sentence, in particular, in which Maxim spoke of the reign of the spirit being in the everlasting future, while modern man though they could establish it now, suited what Laskell has been thinking about the future."[44] Arthur accepts no link between politics and religion. Nancy appreciates the theological categories of Maxim's review. Her affiliation with radicalism is religious, although she does not know this. Laskell can follow Maxim. He is not disgusted, but the categories—Law, Necessity, Spirit—are too absolute for him. They can exist as necessary principles in the background. To foreground them, as Maxim so blatantly does, is to risk making them disgusting. Better to put intelligence, culture, and forgiveness in the foreground.

Maxim's conservatism is inseparable from his Christian piety. This piety stirs up horror in Arthur and Nancy and something less than horror in Laskell, something closer to fear. To Maxim's professions of Christian faith Arthur says, "'you can't possibly believe all that business.'" Laskell does not share Arthur's hostility to religion, but he is shocked by Maxim's religiosity; he is startled, for example, "to hear Maxim saying it [a prayer] out beside him in a full loud voice." The novel's narrative voice, which is closest to Laskell in sensibility, places Maxim's piety against liberal Protestantism's debasement in the 1930s. Even Protestant divines are parroting intellectual fashion by sympathizing with the Soviet Union. Of this Reverend Gurney, the local minister, is a symbol: "when he spoke of welfare he emphasized its social and material aspects. Nowadays, he knew, advanced people identified the good with social effort." Therefore, Reverend Gurney "was sympathetic to what he called the Great Experiment that was going on over one-sixth the Earth's surface." His confrontation with the anti-communist Maxim is comic. "'In short, you do not believe in God,'" Maxim tells him, "'in short, sir, you believe in society and social justice and sociology, but you do not believe in God.'" The narrative voice clearly sides with Maxim, sponsor of "Mr. Gurney's first encounter with an intelligent man who seemed to blame him for not believing in God." Maxim has the integrity and courage to disregard fashion, but, for Laskell, he embodies a sinister political potential, a future of strife and intolerance. In Laskell's eyes, "Gifford Maxim was the man of the far future, the bloody, moral, apocalyptic future that was said to come."[45] Laskell fears not so much Maxim's religious faith as the opportunism in Maxim, which might lead him to exploit the faith of others in a coming age of religious passion.

Against Maxim, Laskell appears weak and Maxim is impolite enough to say this directly to Laskell. Maxim's language is comically Marxist: "'Like any bourgeois intellectual,'" he says to Laskell, "'you want to make the best of every possible world and every possible view. Anything to avoid commitment, anything not to have to take a risk . . . You are proud of that flexibility of mind. But it won't last, John, it's diminishing now. It's too late for that—the Renaissance is dead.'" Not only is Laskell weak, according to Maxim, but the entire liberal movement in Western culture, which Laskell represents, is dead. Critics from both the Left and the Right have concurred in Maxim's low opinion of Laskell. Arthur Schlesinger Jr. seemed to surprise himself with his response to *The Middle of the Journey*: "curiously enough," he wrote to Trilling, "Maxim is so much more vital and vigorous a creation than Laskell that his questions, rather than Laskell's answers, remain in the reader's—or at least in my—mind. That, I would say, is the weakness of the book—or perhaps a source of unconscious strength."[46] Reviewing *The Middle of the Journey* in the *National Review*, John Braine condemned Laskell. Braine was less concerned with Maxim's vigor and vitality than he was with Laskell's weakness, which Braine took to be emblematic of the liberals who control American politics: "it is the Laskells with their ingrown belief in the middle way, in the possibility of dialogue . . . with the Crooms, in the continuation of those aspects of capitalism they approve of and the discontinuation of those they don't, who are still in the saddle in the West. And because they acquiesce in the fact of their own extinction, the rest of us will be dragged down to ruin with them." For Robert Boyers, who reviewed *The Middle of the Journey* in the late 1960s, Laskell's weakness suffuses the novel as a whole. Trilling's novel, in Boyers's view, "manifests a sense of bleakness and futility."[47]

Laskell is politically weak because he is culturally alive. Unlike Maxim or the Crooms, who abound with political strength and self-confidence, Laskell is sensitive to beauty, culture, and love. It is as if his very ambivalence and receptivity to doubt keep his eyes open, and with open eyes he sees the loveliness of the world around him. Laskell is Hellenic, while his more doctrinaire adversaries, Maxim and the Crooms, are Hebraic—to borrow terms from Matthew Arnold's *Culture and Anarchy*.[48] In the terminology of *The Middle of the Journey*, Laskell is of the 1920s despite his devotion to communism. The Crooms are of the 1930s, and Maxim is of the future, destined to go "where worldly power lies waiting for men to pick it up." The future that awaits everyone will be conservative. This was "because the intellectual power had gone from that system of idealism [that of the Left], and much of its power and drama had gone. The time was getting ripe for a competing system. And it would be brought by the swing of the pendulum, not by the motion of growth. Maxim was riding the pendulum." The 1920s, by contrast, were a time of freedom and creativity, unencumbered by the drive for power or the burden of guilt. Just as ambition moves Arthur, guilt drives Maxim and Nancy, the novel's two religious characters.[49] Nancy and Arthur give off no impression of romantic love. Maxim has no wife, no lover, no libido for anything but politics. Laskell alone is driven by love, by the love of beauty and by romantic love. In a modest way, he is a bohemian of the 1920s whose bohemianism has been dulled by growing older, by his commitments to communism, and by the ideological era closing in around him.

Laskell has two romances, both of which confirm his capacity for love. His first love is Elizabeth, who was bohemian enough to live in Greenwich Village in the 1920s. Elizabeth "was taken to be modern although she did not write or paint or hold a job." Together, Laskell and Elizabeth are half-bohemians, willing to consider getting married because they are middle class, "but both were sufficiently of their time to be astonished at their being in love." Theirs is a happiness achieved against the logic of "modern times." Even if they are living in the Jazz Age, they had been given "a lucky chance snatched away from the way things were in the stern modern world, a piece of feeling unfortunately left over from the gentler past." Laskell's misfortune is that he does not marry Elizabeth, that he does not formalize their lucky chance. When she dies unexpectedly, Laskell is left with "his comfortable willingness not to be married to her, not to have that responsibility, which, in turn, meant that when she died there had been no way to realize and express his grief, for he had not realized his relation to her." With Elizabeth's death, Laskell travels toward radical politics, entering the stern modern world by default and abandoning whatever plans he had of becoming a writer. Only when he becomes ill and himself almost dies does his sense for beauty return, and he "falls in love" with the rose at his bedside in the hospital. Altered by his serious illness, Laskell sees only the flower: "Laskell, gazing at it [the flower], had known something like desire, but it was a strange desire which *wanted* nothing, which was its own satisfaction."[50] In the novel, only Laskell is privy to such experiences of beauty. Ideology has destroyed the sensitivity to beauty in Maxim, Nancy, and Arthur, an ideology that may be of the Left or of the Right.

Laskell's second affair is with Emily Caldwell, a provincial bohemian and woman of the 1920s who happens to be living in the 1930s. The 1930s have passed her by, and she wears a "bright dress, cut in the 'peasant' style that had been so popular among the women of the painting colony of

Provincetown." Trilling associates Emily with Laskell's Hellenism. When Laskell first sees Emily and her daughter, he thinks to himself that "the pair had the quality that, vague and no doubt pointless, people call Greek." Nancy holds Emily in contempt because they are the inverse of each other. Nancy expresses her contempt along the lines of cultural history, complaining that Emily is "cheap Village, cheap Provincetown, quaint tearoom . . . she was born in 1912—spiritually, I mean—and she died in 1930, and she doesn't know it yet."[51] Laskell and Emily consummate their affair outdoors by a river, leaving aside politics and giving themselves up to nature. At the end of the novel, Emily forgives Laskell for the affair and its disastrous consequences by kissing him. This forgiveness, rather than Maxim's brooding and endless guilt, is associated in *The Middle of the Journey* with the grace of art, with Mozart and Shakespeare, whereas guilt is associated with the heavy hand of religion or of a spiritualized politics. The narrator refers to the concluding moments of Mozart's *The Marriage of Figaro*, when the Countess forgives the adulterous Count, as "the magical last scene where farce moves to regions higher than tragedy can reach." Likewise, nothing Hamlet "says rings with a sweeter and graver note of masculinity than his 'Give me your pardon, sir. I have done you wrong.' "[52]

In addition to being unfashionable, Emily is willing to forgive. She can love, she can love culture, and she has none of the ideological estrangement from death and tragedy that mars Nancy's character. To sharpen the contrast between Nancy and Emily, Trilling emphasized an important book of the 1920s, Oswald Spengler's *The Decline of the West*. Emily has just read Spengler's pessimistic book, and she is enamored of it. "Don't you think it's wonderful?" she asks Laskell, who knows that any right-thinking— which is to say antifascist or left-leaning—intellectual cannot praise Spengler. This is the mid-1930s, and "for all intelligent people of good will, this book, once seductive in its vision of tragedy, now existed only as a curiosity or bad example, the early symptom of a disease which was now a terrible reality." The voice here is Laskell's liberal super-ego, which is challenged by a nebulously conservative id. He reviews the cultural history of *The Decline of the West* in such a way as to flatter those, like Emily, who do not read in order to be right-thinking: "there had been a time when it [*The Decline of the West*] had been attractive because it expressed the modern alienation in the largest possible way, but now it was known to be entirely reactionary because it cut off all hope for the future . . . And yet, he thought, perhaps we hate the book because it has too hideous a possibility of being true, and we hate the man who wrote it as in our hearts we would blame the physician who told us of our unknown but suspected disease." It is to Emily's credit that she reads Spengler with appreciation. Emily and her naïve bohemianism are an example to Laskell, whose health is restored by Emily's love and forgiveness.[53]

With Emily's emotional help and Maxim's political influence, Laskell grows in strength. He makes a forceful rejection of the Crooms' radicalism. Less forcefully, he turns away Maxim's conservatism. Becoming an anti-communist is, for Laskell, a step forward or, perhaps, a step back to the man of culture he had been in the 1920s. It is an awakening: "now that he had lost the vague rebelliousness which he once attached to his notion of the life of the mind, he found that he enjoyed his mind far more and used it much better." This subtle indictment of communism is at the same time a celebration of liberal (anti-communist) maturity. In a 1947 letter, Trilling explained what he wished to achieve with Laskell, who is "not the least bit interested in 'being good.' It's simply that two sources of authority have been destroyed for him: he's invested a good deal of his not enormous emotional capital in them. He sees that it's been a bad investment—he's sore and bruised and enlightened and says what has always been a good, bitter, angry thing to say, 'A plague on both your houses'—and strikes bottom, as he thinks, on a solid modest position, an acceptance of humanness that isn't self-debasing." Laskell's story is one of enlightenment: he "isn't very full when he leaves, or very heroic but he's reasonably undeceived and direct."[54] Trilling had set himself a difficult task, the literary rendering of "a solid modest position." It was not the stuff of Whittaker Chambers or Thomas Mann. This elevation of modesty may have flattened Trilling's novel in comparison with a great antiradical novel like Dostoevsky's *The Devils*. Moderation, however, is a classically Hellenistic virtue, and in making moderation the leitmotif of his anti-communist novel, Trilling was willing to run the risk of a less than overwhelming literary venture.[55]

Trilling risked failure with *The Middle of the Journey*, and in the end his achievement fell short of his aspirations. Trilling's aim was to "refute communism" and to reconfigure the "very genes of our culture." The result, for many readers, was a novel "about as emotionally contagious as a solution to a problem in geometry," as Orville Prescott wrote in the *New York Times Book Review*.[56] Trilling himself was not convinced of the novel's value: "it was that I specifically wanted to avoid tragedy that I petered out in the current job; I thought tragedy would avoid the intellectual issue. But of course I ought to avoid the intellectual issue and throw the whole damn business into the emotional pot."[57] The problem with *The Middle of the Journey* was not that its author wrote without political energy. Trilling's drama of the educated is a twentieth-century variation on an old theme in American literature, an antiradical gesture reminiscent of Nathaniel Hawthorne's A *Blithedale Romance* and Henry James' *The Princess Cassamassima*. All are novels of deft political insight and political caution, and *The Middle of the Journey* captured in literature "the turn in politics toward an increasingly conservative kind of liberalism," words used by Irving Howe to describe the immediate postwar years.[58] The problem with *The Middle of the Journey* was the right calibration of emotion and intellect. Too often Trilling let intellect suppress emotion. Had *The Middle of the Journey* not been a roman à clef, weirdly prescient of the Hiss case, it would probably have gone from its initial cool reception to outright neglect. One might say that Whittaker Chambers saved *The Middle of the Journey* from oblivion.[59]

The Middle of the Journey failed in two respects. It failed to gain a wide readership, and it failed to orient debate during the Hiss case, to which it was in so many ways related. An article in the *Herald Tribune*, "Novel Written in 1947 Parallels Much of Hiss-Chambers Story," inspired no avalanche of publicity and no controversy, even among intellectuals preoccupied by the case. Lionel and Diana Trilling believed that Viking Press, which published *The Middle of the Journey*, "did not like the book," as Diana Trilling put it in her memoirs. In a 1955 letter, Trilling speculated somewhat abstractly on Viking's attitude toward *The Middle of the Journey:* "it always seemed to me that Viking took a rather bearish view of this novel, I think for political and cultural reasons that they aren't aware of." In 1955, the left-wing leanings that might have dampened Viking's enthusiasm for *The Middle of the Journey* were, in Trilling's view, subconscious. Later, Lionel and Diana Trilling came to believe that Ben Huebsch, an editor at Viking, suppressed the reissue of *The Middle of the Journey* during the Hiss case. They were convinced that Huebsch, a fellow traveler, did not want to release any evidence that might favor Chambers over Hiss: in *The Middle of the Journey*, Maxim is unquestionably telling the truth. Whether fault lay with Huebsch and Viking or with a reading public that simply did not respond to the novel, *The Middle of the Journey* played no role in the controversy surrounding the case.[60] An FBI agent took extensive notes on the novel, in search of clues to Chambers's character, and dismissed the book as irrelevant to the Hiss case.[61] On the other hand, the critic John Bayley described *The Middle of the Journey* as a cult book at the time of its publication. Through these readers—enthusiasts of *The Middle of the Journey* such as Arthur Schlesinger Jr. and Daniel Patrick Moynihan—the book would succeed in promoting liberal anticommunism beyond literary circles. According to Trilling himself, however, *The Middle of the Journey* "was met with a kind of awkward silence."[62] Trilling acknowledged this silence by never again publishing a literary work, though he did do extensive work on a second novel, which he never completed; it was published posthumously in 2008.[63]

Even if *The Middle of the Journey* failed, Trilling did not fail himself in writing it. He would go on to promote Laskell's position—his solid modest position—as an indispensable intellectual of the 1950s. In essays, he would do what he could not do in his novel. Writing *The Middle of the Journey* had satisfied Trilling: "my novel was, for me, only a very, very modest success and yet it gives me the only satisfaction I can get out of years of writing," he wrote to John Crowe Ransom in 1948. Trilling's letter to Ransom was confessional: "I don't like my relation to literature. I don't, I think, like myself in the critical and pedagogic role." These were astonishing disclosures for a famous critic and teacher. "I find that I don't any longer have critical detachment," Trilling continued, as if answering those who thought he was retreating from politics. "I think of words as attacking me or being my allies—and I want to fight back and with them. You've always known me to be ideological: I've never known how ideological I really am: I find myself becoming increasingly a religio-political person, I suppose rather crudely so." This was a possible explanation for Maxim's appearance in *The Middle of the Journey* and for his appearance as a partially sympathetic character. Being a religiopolitical person strengthened the bond between Trilling and Ransom, who was a devout Christian and a cultural conservative: "I seem to be alienated from so many of the figures of recent art and thought and alienated from them in this respect," Trilling wrote, "my sense of a strong intimacy between your person and your life in art and thought that accounts for the admiration and affection I have for you."[64]

The divided author of *The Middle of the Journey* was as well suited to understanding the world of the Hiss case as Chambers was to making political capital out of it. Chambers had always wanted to act on the historical stage. He had bit parts in the 1920s as a communist magazine editor, then a more significant role in the cloak-and-dagger world of Soviet espionage. With the Hiss case, the historical stage was no longer a metaphor. The eyes and cameras of America were upon Chambers, and he did not pass up the opportunity to bear witness in the many senses of the phrase. Chambers gave voice to the conservative energies that the Hiss case unleashed, codifying these energies in *Witness*, a book Gifford Maxim might have written, and Trilling was not wrong to detect a hunger for power in Maxim/Chambers. Trilling's ambitions were more purely intellectual, although shaped by the religiopolitical person he privately knew himself to be. Trilling was suited to understanding the Hiss case because he had such a deep knowledge of its contradictory sources in American life.[65] Like Hiss, Trilling had been a communist, and in *The Middle of the Journey* he had applied the force of his imagination to creating a New Dealer of communist convictions. He also worked hard to convey Chambers's ideas and motivations when Chambers was merely an ex-communist intellectual writing for *Time* and *Life*. Trilling was no Old Testament prophet, no Jeremiah decrying the political sins of his fellow Americans, but, modest and unread as his novel was, *The Middle of the Journey* foretold something of the nation's anti-communist journey, which the Hiss case would do a great deal to begin.

7

WITNESS

The Trial of Whittaker Chambers

"Behold, you have loved the truth" (Psalms 51:8), for he who "does the truth comes to the light" (John 3:21). This I desire to do, in my heart before you in confession, but before many witnesses with my pen.

—AUGUSTINE, *Confessions*

The whole world ringing out with Psalms.
Who bears witness to Mahomet? Himself.
Jesus wants his witness to be nothing.
The quality of witnesses is such that they must exist always, everywhere and wretched. He is alone.

—BLAINE PASCAL, *Pensées*, I.1

I can hear now the epithets which will be directed against it [*Witness*] in the drawing rooms, around the dinner tables, and during the cocktail hours among the "better people"—"too emotional," "long and repetitious," "one of those anti-Communist things."

—RICHARD NIXON, "Plea for an Anti-Communist Faith"

Whittaker Chambers, who died in 1961, retained a posthumous power to generate controversy. Shortly before his own death in 1975, Lionel Trilling wrote a passionate letter about the Hiss case to Morris Dickstein, a literary critic and scholar. As a communist spy, Chambers had been morally comfortable with treason, Trilling claimed, and then came his Kronstadt "when he underwent a change of belief—which, I need scarcely say, is not a dishonorable event in a man's life—it was no longer possible for him to take this position" of complicity with Stalin's Soviet

Union.[1] Trilling was standing up for his own past by standing up for Chambers. At the height of the Hiss case, Trilling had refused to testify as a character witness against Chambers. To one of Hiss's lawyers, Trilling went so far as to call Chambers a "man of honor."[2] If Chambers was a man of honor, then his fight against Hiss had to be honorable: "he [Chambers] now gave his loyalty to his country," Trilling wrote of the anti-communist Chambers, "and could not be indifferent to what does it harm. This being so, would you say that it was the part of honor for him to keep silent about the acts of espionage against the United States which his former comrades, some of whom were his friends, persisted in committing?" One might put friends before country, Trilling granted "that position has, of course, been taken—E. M. Forster took it, laying down as an unquestionable rule that one should betray one's country rather than one's friends. I find this reprehensible and contemptible."[3] The arguments for Chambers still had to be made. Decades after it had begun, the Hiss case was not yet closed.

Chambers won the Hiss case in court. His adversary, Alger Hiss, was convicted of perjury, sent to jail, and then to a kind of professional purgatory. The Ware circle that Chambers had helped to assemble in Washington, D.C. was devastated by the Hiss case. After World War II, American communism broke up for good, not just as a party but also as a political movement. A strenuous anti-communism advanced in tandem with the careers of senators Richard Nixon and Joseph McCarthy, both of whom Chambers knew personally. The Hiss case lent domestic or internal immediacy to the Cold War, distinguishing it from World War II, which could easily be construed in nationalist terms, as us versus them, whether "they" were the Germans or the Japanese. The Hiss case revolved around the figure of Alger Hiss, who was not simply an American citizen accused of treason but a prince of the American meritocracy. The list of those who believed in his innocence was awesome: Franklin and Eleanor Roosevelt, Dean Acheson, Adlai Stevenson, Supreme Court Justice Felix Frankfurter, and many other luminaries. Even as resolute an anti-communist as Richard Nixon was, according to his own description, inclined to believe Hiss because he knew so many people who were friends with both Hiss and Hiss's brother Donald.[4] Chambers was a willfully marginal figure with his low voice, his potentially foreign accent, his suits—invariably described as rumpled—and his memorably bad teeth. To triumph in the Hiss case, Chambers had to upend the established symbolism of success and failure, insider and outsider. To banish Hiss from political life, which the Hiss case effectively did, was potentially to banish anyone from political life.

In winning the Hiss case, Chambers became a national figure, and his autobiography, *Witness*, had a national audience; bearing witness would be the cardinal act of his life. In the Hiss case, Chambers's audience was enormous, expanded by the new technology of television; but the Hiss case had many voices in addition to Chambers's. Chambers would have to wait until the trial was over in January 1950 to write *Witness*, a work in which he could express himself at length. The book was serialized in the *Saturday Evening Post* and included in the Book-of-the-Month club. *Witness* succeeded in reaching ninth place on 1952's best-seller list.[5] Such popular interest may have been inevitable, given the controversial tenor of the Hiss case, but it was atypical for a book modeled on Augustine's *Confessions*, the journal of a seventeenth-century Quaker George Fox, and on the novels of Dostoevsky. Much of *Witness* has a film noir or spy-novel quality—a book of shadows, urban gloom, and cultural despair. Yet Chambers structured it to serve an affirmative Christian program. At its heart is a simple conversion narrative, the story of a soul seeking, losing, and then finding God. The political response to communism was an assertively anti-communist polity, Chambers believed, for faith in the West would compel the defense of the West, which was equivalent to American leadership in the Cold War. Chambers would have felt vindicated to learn that Ronald Reagan knew passages of *Witness* by heart.[6]

Through the Hiss case and through *Witness*, Chambers participated in the rebirth of American conservatism. One arena of this rebirth was in party politics. The Republican Party gained ground in the 1948 Congressional elections. In 1952, it claimed the White House, making Richard Nixon—Chambers's champion in the Hiss case as well as his personal friend—vice president at the age of thirty-nine. The Republican Party had learned to use anti-communism to its political advantage, and where domestic communism was concerned, the Republican Party appeared to be setting the political agenda. After all, Alger Hiss had worked under a Democratic administration. His conviction for perjury in 1950 damaged the Democratic Party and, more broadly, the activist Left in America.[7] Chambers himself played less of a role in high politics than he did in the rise of a conservative movement, and *Witness* was among the major books of the postwar conservative intellectual movement, an intellectually serious endeavor and a mass-market success at a time when conservative books were anything but established in the American publishing scene. The Hiss case won Chambers a wide reading audience to which he could introduce his conservative ideas. Reviews from influential intellectuals such as Hannah Arendt, Arthur Schlesinger Jr., and Irving Howe spoke to a new salience for conservative intellectuals, even among those hostile to conservatism. Perhaps there was a readership in search of conservative intellectuals. Very few liberal or radical intellectuals had the kind of numerical triumph Chambers enjoyed with *Witness*.

Publishing data notwithstanding, Chambers was pessimistic about the future of anti-communist conservatism in the 1950s. Indeed, the Hiss case deepened Chambers's pessimism about the direction of Western culture and of the American polity within it. He had convinced the requisite number of jurors, he had convinced anti-communist liberals such as Lionel Trilling and Arthur Schlesinger Jr., and he had convinced politicians such as Richard Nixon that he was telling the truth.[8] Chambers's conservatism, a conservatism of the future, was far less convincing. Conservative intellectuals were often uninterested in day-to-day politics, and liberal intellectuals like Trilling wanted little to do with Chambers's religious conservatism. The Republican politicians who revered Chambers did so with their own ambitions in mind. In Chambers's opinion, Nixon was an impeccable anti-communist, but he was a dubious conservative. Senator McCarthy was a bumbling opportunist, doing necessary work, perhaps, but lacking all the qualities of a conservative statesman. President Eisenhower got Chambers's vote but not his intellectual sympathy. If those who believed Chambers disappointed him, Chambers was maddened by those who thought him a liar. Hiss would title one of his memoirs *In the Court of Public Opinion*, for in this court Hiss fared relatively well and Chambers did not.[9] From Chambers's perspective, the simple American people sided with him, while the elites—in government, in the media, in academia—sided overwhelmingly with Hiss. Chambers was convinced that Hiss's defense team, whose claims were widely disseminated by the intellectual elite, had swayed the court of public opinion. Hiss went to jail only to emerge a martyr persecuted by the likes of Chambers, Nixon, and McCarthy. In many circles, Chambers was persona non grata during and after the Hiss case, a "moral leper," as one of Hiss's lawyers described him. *Witness* was Chambers's counter attack in a living, ongoing political argument.

For Chambers, the Hiss case exposed America's political immaturity, its woeful incomprehension of twentieth-century politics. Americans did not know what communism was.[10] Common Americans, living away from cities, had no idea of the menace in their midst, no grasp of communism as an ideology or as an international movement. If the American people could be counted on to oppose communism, educated Americans were far less dependable. They had succumbed en masse to the communist ideals of the 1930s, and their rush to defend Hiss indicated how little they had learned since that time. They could not fathom the existence of underground revolutionaries, practicing espionage by night and working for the New Deal by day. Other leftists were so enraptured by the ideals of communism, radicalism, or progressivism—often merged together in the heady 1930s—that they adopted Hiss as one of their own. To punish Hiss would be to punish political progress itself and to oppose Hiss was to side with capitalist reaction. Chambers thought that American intellectuals had not yet contended with the nightmare of the twentieth century, which extended from the Siberian *gulag* to Poland's Katyn forest to the Nazi concentration camps. Secular ideology turned fanatical—rootless cities, mass dislocation, total war, the vast darkness of modernity—had not registered among American intellectuals, and it was these catastrophes that had rendered progressivism obscene. America's intellectuals averted their eyes from the world around them, succumbing to a baseless optimism or to the jargons of socialist theory. Chambers wrote *Witness* in order to teach his readers the true story of the twentieth century, the "real Twentieth Century," as the Russian poet Anna Akhmatova called it.

The Hiss case broke in the summer of 1948, but its origins dated back to the 1930s.[11] Among other things, the Hiss case was a debate about the 1930s and the meaning of this decade in American history. Chambers was one representative of the period, an ex-communist like no other: as a communist, he had been a spy; as an anti-communist, he was a farmer. His homosexual liaisons in the 1930s were a part of his biography that he wished to keep hidden, although they hovered at the margins of the Hiss case. Chambers was not an ideal conservative icon for the 1950s because of who he had been two decades prior. Alger Hiss had a similarly complicated relationship to the Red Decade. There was his communist involvement, to which he never confessed. There was his open affiliation with the New Deal, with the brain trust of young lawyers and academics who lived in Georgetown, as Hiss and his family had. There was also Hiss's social status, won in the 1930s, which guaranteed professional success in postwar America—until he was charged with perjury. Hiss belonged to a new elite, the left-liberal intelligentsia that came of age in the 1930s. Trilling had scrutinized this intelligentsia in *The Middle of the Journey*, hoping that self-criticism and self-improvement would purge it of its philo-communism, although the subtleties of *The Middle of the Journey* were lost on the Hiss case, a high-stakes political battle that brought out the zeal and venom of its participants. Chambers and Hiss could only advance by destroying each other. The same was largely true of their advocates. One could keep the spirit of the 1930s—of the Popular Front—alive by declaring Chambers a dupe of the FBI and the powers that be. Or one could leave the 1930s behind by branding Hiss a traitor, a twentieth-century Benedict Arnold.

Two circumstances converged to precipitate the Hiss case. The first was the intensifying significance of Chambers's 1939 meeting with Assistant Secretary of State Adolph Berle, written up as a memo and then deposited in FBI files. Already in 1942, the FBI had questioned Hiss about his relationship to communism; and Chambers himself went to the FBI in 1943, without much result.[12] A series of spectacular defections and confessions were furnishing an ever more disturbing image of Soviet espionage activities in the United States. In May 1945, the FBI questioned Chambers at length. In the summer of 1945, a raid by the Office of Strategic Services (OSS), the precursor to the CIA, on the office of *Amerasia*, a journal dealing with Asian affairs, yielded a cache of stolen government documents. This prompted the dismissal of the journal's editor from his State Department post. The *Amerasia* case drew attention to the question of Soviet espionage in the United States. Then, in September 1945, Igor Gouzenko, a code clerk at the Soviet embassy in Ottawa, defected. When he handed over documents pertaining to an espionage ring, the Canadian government arrested twenty-two alleged Soviet agents in February 1946. The Gouzenko incident raised the question of espionage in North America, and, for those privy to Chambers's accusation, the arrests in Canada could be connected to the rumors about Hiss. One month after Gouzenko's defection, Elizabeth Bentley came forward as the former head of an espionage circle, a parallel apparatus to the Ware circle; she had already gone to the FBI in August 1945.[13] The *New York Sun* implicated Chambers in the Bentley case. A kind of noose—one part evidence, one part suspicion—was tightening around the Ware circle.

The second circumstance responsible for the Hiss case was Alger Hiss's professional advancement. In August 1944, he attended the Dumbarton Oaks conference; he was special assistant to FDR at the Yalta conference. In the spring of 1945, he served as temporary assistant general, helping to organize a conference in San Francisco at which the United Nations was chartered. When the Hiss case began, Hiss was president of the Carnegie Endowment for International Peace, where he worked with John Foster Dulles. Given what the FBI knew and given who he was, Hiss's appearance before HUAC was hardly surprising. It was more surprising that he came before the committee as late as he did, which may be explained by a detail Chambers omitted from his report to Berle.[14] This detail was espionage. This espionage was significant because the Ware circle functioned smoothly when it was in operation, and the web of connections it had in Washington, D.C., was vast. According to G. Edward White, Hiss requested "confidential information from the Office of Strategic Services on postwar atomic energy policy and the internal security of Britain, France, China, and the Soviet Union. In this period Hiss had the sponsorship, with the State Department, of . . . [Secretary of State] Stettinius, and Assistant Secretary of State Dean Acheson." White argues that Hiss's espionage activity was of direct use to Stalin, that his position in government in the 1930s, followed by the spying of British Soviet agent Donald Maclean in the 1940s, gave Stalin valuable information on British and American foreign policy before the Yalta conference.[15]

Chambers complicated the Hiss case by withholding the accusation of espionage, neglecting to mention it to Adolph Berle and to HUAC. In his opening statement to HUAC, he described the Ware circle as a sleeper cell, gathering strength in Washington for future revolutionary action.[16] In March 1948, Chambers pleaded with HUAC not to testify, and when he was subpoenaed on August 2, 1948, "Chambers agitatedly expressed a complete repugnance to the whole idea [of being a witness]," according to Chambers's friend, the journalist Ralph de Toledano.[17] Chambers perjured himself in his early testimony by denying espionage, precisely the charge that would dominate the later phases of the Hiss case. Why he did so remains a core mystery of the Hiss case, one that has inclined many to distrust Chambers, who later explained his strange conduct as an expression of Christian mercy. He wanted Hiss and the other members of the Ware circle to have the same experience of Kronstadt that he had.[18] In *Witness* Chambers equated his reluctance to incriminate Hiss with his Christian faith: "the source of what at least made it possible for me to bear witness against Communism, as a power of evil, lay close to the source of what made it necessary to bear a witness of mercy for the Communists as men."[19] Were they to have Kronstadts of their own, Hiss and his comrades would not need Chambers or HUAC to denounce their communist past.

However reluctant, Chambers was in Washington, D.C. to testify before HUAC on August 3, 1948. He addressed his opening statement to the nation at large, accenting the drama of his autobiography. "I had become convinced that the society in which we live, Western civilization, had reached a crisis, of which the First World War was the military expression, and that it was doomed to collapse or revert to barbarism," he told the Committee. He then detailed his change of heart. In the ten years since his Kronstadt, Chambers had "sought to live an industrious and God-fearing life. At the same time, I have fought Communism constantly by act and written word. I am proud to appear before this Committee." Once he was finished, newspaper reporters "bounded for the telephones like rabbits for their burrows," astounded to hear the names of Alger Hiss, Harold Ware, Nathan Wit, John Abt, and Lee Pressman—New Dealers of midlevel prominence—in connection with "the greatest conspiracy in the nation's history." When called, Hiss presented himself before the Committee with extreme self-confidence. He was not and had never been a communist; he had never known a man by the name of Whittaker Chambers. He was ready to stand by patiently as HUAC cleared up this grotesque misunderstanding. Under pressure, a disparity emerged between the ample detail Chambers volunteered and Hiss's legalistic sparring with the Committee. Hiss's version of events proved difficult to reconcile with documentary evidence. Slowly, the momentum shifted to Chambers, at least for HUAC. HUAC's session of August 25 was televised and before a national audience Chambers likened himself to Martin Luther, proclaiming that " 'I could not do otherwise.' "[20]

In the fall of 1948 the Hiss case became even more dramatic. Hiss challenged Chambers to publicly identify him as a communist. So long as Chambers confined his testimony to HUAC, he could not be sued for libel. On August 27 Chambers went on *Meet the Press* (then a radio program) and called Hiss a communist.[21] Hiss waited a month and then filed suit, using a private detective to investigate Chambers's past, including his sexual history, in hopes of finding evidence that would discredit Chambers.[22] In November, the case took its most spectacular turn. According to *Witness*, Chambers went to the Brooklyn apartment of his nephew and picked up his "lifesaver," a cache of documents and microfilm he had hidden away to inhibit the Communist Party from killing him, secreting this material one last time in the pumpkin patch of his Maryland farm. On November 17 he turned over the "pumpkin papers," as they were soon dubbed, to the government. For the media, the pumpkin papers were a marvelous compliment to the Hiss case, contributing symbolically to the sense of confused motivations, of past secrets exposed in unlikely ways, of abnormal conduct and abnormal evidence. In the words of British journalist Alistair Cooke, the pumpkin papers "seemed to add the final bathos to the Communist's [Chambers's] gift for melodrama."[23] The pumpkin papers elevated the Hiss case from a dispute between an accomplished bureaucrat and a *Time* editor, putting their reputations in jeopardy, to an affair of state. As if to credit the seriousness of the Hiss case, in December Chambers and Hiss both resigned their jobs, putting an end to the first phase of the case. The second phase would last roughly a year, and it would consist of two trials. The first ran from May 31, 1949, to July 8, 1949. The second ran from November 17, 1949, to January 21, 1950.

On September 23, 1949—midway through the Hiss case—President Truman announced that the Soviet Union had detonated an atomic bomb.

The Hiss case reflected the growing power of anti-communist sentiment in America. Alger Hiss as communist traitor was virtually unthinkable in August 1948, even to hardened anti-communists such as John Foster Dulles, Harry Truman, and to HUAC members other than Nixon.[24] The Hiss case, in tandem with an anti-communist or Cold War spirit, rearranged the borders of the thinkable. These borders were bound up in the personalities of Hiss and Chambers, which dominated the first trial. Alistair Cooke, an eyewitness to the trial, captured the difference in appearance between the two men. Hiss projected an image of belonging, although in Cooke's view he did not quite belong to midcentury America. As Cooke put it, "here [in Hiss] was a subject for Henry James: a product of New World courtesy, with a gentle certitude of behavior, a ready warmth." Hiss, the former law clerk for Oliver Wendell Holmes Jr. who used to read T. S. Eliot's poetry to Justice Holmes, "represented the breeding, the graceful probity, the plain living and high thinking, of a waning New England tradition," Cooke observed.[25] Hiss was privately a communist and publicly a New Dealer, but he was never a populist. Hiss's defenders could point to his less than polished enemies—Chambers, Nixon, and later McCarthy—and suggest that *they* did not belong, that they were political imposters upsetting the natural order of things. Anti-communism forged no unity in American political or intellectual life; often it intensified latent disunities.

Never a man to unify, Chambers was an uncertain variable in the Hiss case. He was direct and open in his testimony, but he was also a "fat, sad-looking man in a baggy blue suit," in Cooke's words. Richard Nixon remembered Chambers as "one of the most disheveled-looking persons I had ever seen."[26] If Hiss was composed and self-confident, Chambers had about him the aura of defeat and tragedy. Cooke describes him vividly: "to the end, this bulky, pale man with the expressionless, translucent eyes had told what he knew in the manner of one long resigned to a life of profound error and disillusion and the hope perhaps of a little peace and quiet before the end came." Chambers's speech could easily sound fantastic with its exotic details of underground life. He had built up an "apparatus" in Washington, D.C.; his colleagues and superiors were a shadowy group of international communists, many with assumed names. The eminently respectable Alger Hiss, sitting in court and denying everything with such self-assurance, was supposed to have been an accomplice and friend of Chambers. Cooke neither believed nor disbelieved Chambers, although he was captivated by Chambers's "circumstantial epic touched with just that fragmentary and repetitive color which gave it the quality of a dream, or of a compelling fiction, or the true sound of a dread experience dredged up from a sensitive memory."[27] It was an epic that could inspire great enmity. Arthur Schlesinger Jr. named "the anti-Chambers whispering campaign . . . [as] one of the most repellent in modern history."[28]

Chambers's persona, in all its mystery, was the centerpiece of the first trial, the focal point for Hiss's lawyer, Lloyd Stryker, "the Johnnie Cochran and Alan Dershowitz of his day."[29] Stryker offered a memorable characterization of Chambers on the first day of the trial. Cooke described the scene by quoting Stryker: "In the warm southern countries, you know, where they have leprosy," Striker exclaimed, " 'sometimes you will hear on the streets among the lepers a man crying down the street.' Mr. Stryker lifted his eyes and his voice into a plaintive wail. 'Unclean, unclean' at the approach of a leper. I say the same to you at the approach of this moral leper.' " Stryker humiliated Chambers's wife, Esther, trying to goad her into suggesting that Chambers was a psychopath. He cited Chambers's poetic juvenilia to bolster the argument for pathology. Chambers's atheist play, "A Play for Puppets," from his Columbia days, elicited yet another negative review, this time from Stryker who labeled it "a filthy despicable play." Atheism was hardly a terrible charge against Chambers, who had extensive Christian credentials by 1949. Far more powerful was the charge of homosexuality, which the Hiss defense offered as proof of Chambers's abnormal psychology. Stryker had Chambers's homoerotic poem, "Tanderadei," read to the court.[30] The Hiss defense hired a psychologist, Dr. Carl Binger, to prove Chambers's pathology, but Dr. Binger was not allowed to testify in the first trial. The Hiss defense had two Supreme Court Justices, Felix Frankfurter and Stanley Reed, testify as character witnesses on behalf of Hiss, making the contrast between Hiss and Chambers as stark as possible.[31]

The strategies of Stryker and Thomas Murphy, Chambers's lawyer, were asymmetrical. Stryker appealed to middle-class decency, Murphy to populism. This was how it appeared to Cooke: "where Mr. Stryker had adopted an attitude of nauseated contempt for Chambers, Mrs. Chambers and [Julian] Wadleigh, Mr. Murphy conveyed the subtler imputation that the Hiss witnesses were sentimentally united in a rather snobbish plot to prove that the defendant was altogether too charming a type . . . to be capable of associating with such low characters as the Chamberses and Wadleighs of this world."[32] Both lawyers inadvertently made the Hiss case a referendum on elites. Elites were inherently trustworthy, according to Stryker, and they were neatly aligned on Hiss's side. Elites were inherently untrustworthy, according to Murphy, and it was to Chambers's credit that he did not belong to the East-Coast establishment. Murphy's arguments against Hiss and the coterie of snobs around him persuaded eight out of twelve jurors, not enough to convict Hiss. The first trial ended without a final verdict.

The evidence remained the same for the second trial, but the context around the case was new. The Soviet Union had gone from ally to enemy in the years between 1945 and 1949, and espionage among allies was not the same as espionage among enemies. As more cases involving communist espionage broke out, the charges against Hiss seemed more believable.

Writing about the second trial, Alistair Cooke noticed an "interesting difference from the summer in the prevailing vogue of prejudice. Droves of prospective jurors had been excused in the First Trial when they allowed that they had very likely harbored prejudice against any witness who had been a Communist." These jurors would have been prejudiced against Chambers. "By the autumn of 1949 the reformed Communist was in some places the most trustworthy of American patriots," Cooke continued. "In the courtroom evidently he had lost his threat for the common man." The change in mood was reflected in the demeanor of Chambers. Often glum, soft-spoken, and hopeless in the first trial, Chambers "was spruce and confident" in the second trial.[33]

Even Dr. Binger, the psychiatrist who testified to Chambers's "abnormal sexuality" could not save Hiss. Dr. Binger employed the might of science for the Hiss defense, and only after the case did the FBI learn how far the Hiss defense team was willing to go with its accusations of homosexuality. In a memo to the director, the following rumor was reported: "that Hiss's forthcoming appeal [regarding the guilty verdict in the second trial] is based on new evidence alleging Chambers is a sexual pervert and that he once blackmailed the son [of Priscilla Hiss] into stealing secret documents from Alger Hiss' study for delivery to Chambers, these being the papers later found in the pumpkin."[34] In a 1950 essay on the Hiss case, Diana Trilling noted that allegations of homosexuality were one of several failed attempts to incriminate Chambers: "some of these specific charges either backfired or threatened to backfire if used in court—the homosexual charge, for instance, of which Hiss's lawyers made so much in their pre-trial investigations."[35] The courtroom turned against Dr. Binger with the help of Thomas Murphy's sarcastic populism. This was Alistair Cooke's recollection of Dr. Binger's testimony: "when a psychiatrist is in the offing hell hath no fury like a layman scorned."[36] The Hiss defense suffered under a fundamentally weak argument: that Chambers had concocted his story, most likely with the FBI, and gathered the evidence of espionage by some government-assisted slight of hand. This thesis failed to convince the jurors, and the Hiss case ended with Alger Hiss's conviction for perjury.

The Hiss case was a catalyst and a turning point. It was a turning point in public perception, making domestic communism supremely suspicious and tarnishing the New Deal elite. The guilty verdict in the Hiss case "galvanized the country into a bitter realization of the native American types who might well be dedicated to betrayal from within," as Cooke put it. Senator McCarthy ruthlessly associated the potential guilt of liberal elites with the perfidy of communism. McCarthyism was a repetition of the Hiss case ad nauseum, carried along by a longing on the part of Mc-Carthy and his followers to disbar the Alger Hisses of American life from civil society. The Hiss case was certainly a necessary catalyst in the creation of McCarthyism.[37] It was also a catalyst in the evolution of American conservatism. "The Hiss case forged the anti-Communist element in resurgent conservatism," writes historian George Nash.[38] It did so as much through its iconography as through its legal fine points. To conservatives, Alger Hiss was a symbol of liberal corruption. His status as a liberal, and his popularity among liberals, exposed liberalism for what conservatives thought it was, powerful and treasonous. On the other hand, conservatives had a spokesman and a martyr in Chambers. Chambers was—awkwardly perhaps—a martyr whose side had won in the Hiss case, but he retained the demeanor of a martyr. Chambers was deeply unpopular. He suffered visibly and was the victim of an anti-Chambers whispering campaign, while no such campaign was waged against Hiss. Chambers thought he was on the losing side of history, as many conservative intellectuals believed themselves and their cause to be. It was Chambers himself who formalized this iconography, not in his testimony per se, but in his autobiography *Witness*. If the Hiss case was a gift to conservative politicians, *Witness* was a gift to the conservative intellectual movement.

Witness was published by Random House on May 21, 1952, several months before a presidential election, in which the Democrats lost a White House they had possessed since 1932. Chambers desperately wanted Eisenhower to win the 1952 election, which had many connections to the Hiss case. Both Adlai Stevenson, the Democratic presidential candidate, and Richard Nixon, the Republican candidate for vice president, had figured in the Hiss case. Stevenson was the darling of liberal elites, reason enough for Chambers to revile him, but Stevenson had also supported Hiss. In 1933, Stevenson worked at the Agricultural Adjustment Agency with Hiss and several other members of the Ware circle. Stevenson appeared as a character witness for Hiss during the case. Nixon owed his presence on the ticket in part to the tough anti-communist image he created for himself during the Hiss case. Nixon attacked Stevenson for his role in the Hiss case, and Stevenson counterattacked, accusing Eisenhower of tacitly supporting Hiss at the beginning of the case.[39] In an editor's note to a series of essays on *Witness* published in May 1952 in *Saturday Review*, the editor situated *Witness* "at the core center of one of the most important public debates in American history. Far from ending a celebrated controversy, this book may reopen and encourage it, coming as it does in the middle of a presidential campaign."[40] *Witness* was part of the campaign to get Eisenhower elected, and moments after voting for Eisenhower, Chambers collapsed on the polling-station steps in Westminster, Maryland; he suffered a heart attack, a final step in the ordeal of writing *Witness*.[41]

If Trilling's *The Middle of the Journey* foreshadowed the Hiss case in some strange way, *Witness* was an extended retrospective of the case, even a continuation of it. *Witness* was Chambers's final brief in the unfinished case, unfinished in the sense that many continued to believe Hiss, to revile Chambers, or simply to stand undecided, lost in the labyrinth of details surrounding the case. In *Witness*, Chambers hoped to show himself the master of these details, the one who furnished the most credible version of events. The book's length, eight hundred pages, was part of its agenda. Such a wealth of detail—subject to the scrutiny, rebuttal, and cross referencing of critics—must be the work of a truth teller.[42] How could one invent a fiction of this length in this context? The mystery of Chambers's character had haunted the Hiss case, delaying Hiss's conviction. Chambers was decidedly un-American in character, with an un-American set of ideological passions and an un-American résumé—one of the case's many ironies.[43] In *Witness*, Chambers could relate his character to American history and American culture, bearing witness to his life in politics and using his spiritual autobiography to clarify the case, to transform its shadows and fog into a warm light, clearing the way to a Christian renewal of Western culture.

Chambers's highest ambition for *Witness* was to weave his life story into the history of Western culture.[44] In this ambition, his three models were Augustine, George Fox, and Henry Adams. Christianity united these three figures, who were otherwise far apart in historical moment and sensibility. They were Christian writers who wrote about themselves in part to confess their own sins and the sins of those around them. Augustine titled his book *Confessions*; Fox confessed his inmost thoughts to his diaries.[45] In *The Education of Henry Adams*, Henry Adams confessed that he had never received an education adequate to his needs in life. In addition to confession, Augustine, Fox, and Adams used autobiography to map historical crises. Augustine depicted the dissolution of the Roman empire with civilization imperiled by barbarians from without and by pagan barbarism from within. Augustine intended his own conversion to Christianity to be exemplary, a means to rebirth for a dying civilization. Fox was a spiritual progenitor of Quakerism, whose appeal to the "inner light" was especially powerful in the wake of the English Civil War. In Augustine as in Fox, Christianity was the tool of redemption, a social message enlivened by the travails of the individual soul. Henry Adams may have believed this message, but he did not imbue his memoir with it. Rather, he used his disappointments and melancholy to expose the depravity of modern times, the dangerous notion of progress to which his contemporaries were addicted. Chambers referred to Adams as "my great friend," for Adams was the Christian autobiographer to whom Chambers was closest. "I am not Augustine and I don't like Rousseau, and the times and problems differ," Chambers wrote in September 1951. These times and these problems Adams had intuited, Adams who was "a historical seer such as few peoples have produced."[46]

Witness was an early attempt at a literary genre that would flourish after World War II.[47] The name for this genre is the "literature of witness," most often associated with the crimes of Stalin and Hitler.[48] Around the time Chambers was writing *Witness*, Primo Levi was writing *If This Is a Man* (completed in 1946, although first published in English in 1959) and Czeslaw Milosz was writing *The Captive Mind*, published in the United States in 1959. Levi was an Italian Jew who survived Auschwitz. *If This Is a Man* and *Witness* follow a similar rhythm, the oscillation from the depths to the heights, from the barbarism of the twentieth-century inferno to the paradise of civilization. In *If This Is a Man*, Levi wrote that "precisely because the Lager [concentration camp] was a great machine to reduce us to beasts, we must not become beasts . . . to survive we must force ourselves to save at least the skeleton, the scaffolding, the form of civilization." In a letter to William F. Buckley Jr., Chambers wrote about the "mountains of shoes, men's, women's, children's—children's—which an eyewitness described to me as he saw it before the Nazi crematorium at Polish Maidanek." Chambers did not confine himself to national borders when considering the mass crimes of the twentieth century. "You perhaps do not remember the Katyn forest," Chambers wrote, once again to Buckley. The Soviets had massacred thousands of Polish officers in the

Katyn forest. "It is not just those bodies that lie heaped there. It is that we lie, smothering alive, under the heaps."[49] This was a "we" that encompassed Primo Levi's "I."

The Captive Mind was written by Czeslaw Milosz, a Polish poet and intellectual, and it closely resembles *Witness*. Like Levi and Chambers, Milosz wrote in the name of bearing witness. Milosz survived World War II in Poland—in Warsaw, "the most agonizing spot in the whole of terrorized Europe." This agony was Milosz's birthright as a writer.[50] "Had I then chosen emigration, my life would certainly have followed a very different course," Milosz wrote. "But my knowledge of the crimes which Europe has witnessed in the twentieth century would be less direct, less concrete than it is."[51] Of these crimes, Soviet communism was the most recent and immediate. Milosz wrote *The Captive Mind* as Poland and Lithuania, his place of birth, were being incorporated into the Soviet empire. Milosz was no less convinced than Chambers that the Cold War was a battle for heart and soul on a global scale. "The world today is torn asunder by a great dispute; and not only a dispute, but a ruthless battle for world domination," Milosz wrote in the preface to *The Captive Mind*. Chambers and Milosz agreed that the Cold War battle was poorly comprehended: "many people still refuse to believe that there are only two sides, that the only choice lies between absolute conformity to the one system or absolute conformity to the other."[52] Milosz and Chambers believed that bearing witness to the crimes of the past was a civic duty for both writers and intellectuals, whose responsibility it was to push against a general tendency toward amnesia and denial. As Chambers wrote in *Witness*, "the twentieth century has put out of its mind, because it can no longer cope with the enormity of the statistics, the millions it has exterminated in its first fifty years."[53]

Chambers's challenge in writing *Witness* was to connect abstract arguments about history and civilization to the concrete details of the Hiss case. The book's abstract argument could be summarized as follows: the rational and secular Enlightenment prepared the way for modernity, which has proven to be a disaster. Capitalist modernity, although unappealing, is better than socialism, but only a return to religious faith can truly liberate modern man and embolden him to defend political liberty from communism. Chambers presented himself as living proof of this argument. He had once inhabited the prison house of socialist modernity, from which he had freed himself by becoming a Christian. In *Witness*

Alger Hiss is no less powerful an example of Chambers's abstract argument. His espionage for the Soviet Union demonstrates an equivalence between socialist and capitalist modernity, so long as capitalist modernity is irreligious. To explain Hiss, Chambers went back to the Enlightenment. Hiss the New Dealer, Hiss the liberal, Hiss the progressive, Hiss the communist, Hiss the American success—these were all variations on the theme of Hiss the man of the Enlightenment. Chambers put the point very bluntly in a 1956 letter to Ralph de Toledano: "with Alger [Hiss] the justification of the entire age stands or falls—technology, votes for women, UN, noble experiment, food made from plastics; it's all of a piece, and Alger is one with it; gives it, in fact, precisely the physiognomic form such a one-way trip to Hell must have."[54] The images here are an odd combination—women's suffrage, the United Nations, pro-Soviet sympathies, and fast food—a composite of conservative dislikes. By 1956, the pro-Soviet sentiment no longer seems to fit on the list. The images Chambers gathers here might just as well describe the target audience of *Time*'s advertisements in 1956. However accurate or inaccurate, Chambers's selection of modern bric-a-brac only heightened the symbolism of the Hiss case. Chambers saw himself on the side of America's rustic patriots and Hiss on the side of its enlightened, treasonous, and inauthentic elites.

Chambers placed Hiss in America's enlightened middle class, which Chambers considered secular and left-leaning. Hiss had settled into this elite in the 1940s, Chambers believed, with an eye to protecting himself. If the accusation of communism surfaced, Hiss could rely on the murkiness of Chambers's past and on the quality of his own credentials. Chambers suspected that he "put down roots that made him one with the matted forest floor of American upper class, enlightened middle class, liberal and official life. His roots could not be disturbed without disturbing all the roots on all sides of him." As a communist, Hiss knew the corruption of the bourgeoisie. As a member of the social elite desperate to keep his communist past hidden, Hiss could avail himself of this very corruption. Chambers argued that Hiss "had only to refrain from pressing extreme views, or drawing ultimate conclusions from views very widespread among enlightened people, to find himself saying what all his set was saying, only, perhaps, saying it a little more radiantly, so that he drew a bonus of intense sincerity."[55] Chambers the anti-communist conservative was furious with the American middle class for protecting Hiss, while Hiss—whose sincere political views at the time of the Hiss case are unfathomable—was an upper-class hero of sorts.[56] The adjective "enlightened" is a sinister refrain in *Witness*, used when Chambers writes about Hiss and his devotees. It is also an ironic refrain because the self-professed enlightened are colluding in a lie, a charade, a hoax. Chambers sought to damn the Enlightenment by showing what had become of its children.

Witness was a spirited attack on America's liberal middle class, the carrier of the Enlightenment.[57] Chambers traced his conflict with this sociopolitical entity back to 1939 when he first informed the government of the Ware circle. In doing so, Chambers came up against "the forces of that great socialist revolution, which, in the name of liberalism, spasmodically, incompletely, somewhat formlessly but always in the same direction, has been inching its ice cap over the nation for two decades." Liberalism was a Trojan horse carrying within it socialist warriors. Chambers thought it was an old story: liberal fronts had done the work of the Communist Party in the 1930s, and the Ware circle had staffed important agencies and departments during the New Deal. Chambers persistently exaggerated the interdependence of socialism and liberalism, arguing too narrowly from his personal experience as a Soviet spy, making too much of theoretical abstractions such as socialism and liberalism, at times conflating them; his explanation of the Hiss case was too reductive.[58] According to Chambers, "the forces of this [socialist] revolution . . . had smothered the Hiss case (and much else) for a decade, and fought to smother it in 1948. These were the forces that made the phenomenon of Alger Hiss possible." By erasing the differences between Hiss and his defenders, Chambers erased the border between liberalism and treason. All those on the Left suffered from "the same inability to grasp the character and reality of communism."[59] Only the extreme Left mattered to Chambers: the moderate Left was merely its servant. Alger Hiss was the rule to which there were no meaningful exceptions. "To satisfy his conscience," wrote Kingsley Martin, "Chambers is compelled wildly to exaggerate the influence of Hiss and Communism in the United States."[60]

Chambers exaggerated communism's hold on the American Left, but he had no need to exaggerate the degree of liberal sympathy for Hiss, and Chambers, who knew Hiss was lying, was prone to interpret sympathy for Hiss as delusional.[61] From Chambers's vantage point, "the most articulate section of public opinion was bitterly aroused against me and persistent in its attacks, none of which was checked in the whole course of the Hiss case by even one intelligent effort to talk to me personally and arrive at a first-hand impression of what I might think I was doing."[62] Eleanor Roosevelt declared it "rather horrible" that Hiss lost the case.[63] Prominent journalists from Walter Lippmann to James Reston sided with Hiss.[64] Chambers's friend Ralph de Toledano referred contemptuously to Hiss's "Harvard cheering section."[65] Sympathy for Hiss made Chambers feel persecuted, and Richard Nixon had a similar sense of persecution at the hands of the media and of liberal elites. The Hiss case cursed Nixon, transforming him, in his own words, from "a relatively popular young congressman, enjoying a good but limited press, into one of the most controversial figures in Washington, bitterly opposed by the most respected and influential liberal journalists and opinion leaders of the time."[66] The hostile relationship between Chambers and Hiss, or between Nixon and the liberals, helped set the tone for the conservative movement of the early 1950s. Although President Eisenhower was too secure to feel persecuted, many more ardent conservatives had to deal with liberals like Hiss, whose social status was superior to their own. The Hiss case looked ahead to the "paradoxical combination of respectability and rebelliousness" common to 1950s conservatism.[67]

In *Witness*, the intellectual and political aspects of the Hiss case reinforce each other, the cumulative "effect of a man [Whittaker Chambers] to hurl himself against the rationalism which must destroy the world, and seems to be on the point of doing so."[68] Chambers's battle against the Enlightenment framed *Witness*, determining a great deal of its form and structure. The abstract philosophico-political arguments of the book—of which there were many—began and ended with the witness of a single voice. Convinced that politics depends on the faith of individual citizens, Chambers put the details of his faith on display in *Witness*, dramatizing the subjective self in relation to politics, with the hope that this drama would expose the poverty of rationalism. In addition, *Witness* was a challenge to Hiss to do the same, to discuss his political faith and the motivations that shaped it. Chambers's constant association of politics and religion favored a religious approach to politics—politics as a matter of faith, confession, and witness, and Chambers wanted his book to repudiate the comfortable secularism and the detached style of the educated middle class.[69] Chambers thought that only "the people" would respond cordially to his ideas, which is why Thomas Murphy understood the Hiss case "in its fullest religious, moral and historical meaning," Chambers believed. So, too, did Richard Nixon, for both Nixon and Murphy "came from the wrong side of the rail-road tracks."[70]

Those from the wrong side of the tracks were less likely to be secular and more likely to have faith. "Economics is not the central problem of this century," Chambers argued. "It is a relative problem which can be solved in relative ways. Faith is the central problem of this age." Should one have faith in the Soviet Union or faith in Western civilization? This was the most vital question, the question raised by the Hiss case, which asked on-lookers "whether this sick society, which we call Western Civilization, could in its extremity still cast up a man whose faith in it was so great that he would voluntarily abandon those things which men hold good, includ-ing life, to defend it." A good political idea was one for which people would be willing to die: Chambers wanted no connotation of Enlighten-ment rationalism or liberal moderation in *Witness*.[71] When Chambers and Hiss had been communists, they had seen communism as the only remedy for a sick civilization. Later, Chambers acknowledged Hiss as an adversary "whose equal faith it was that this society is sick beyond saving, and that mercy itself pleads for its swift extinction and replacement by an-other." Hiss and other communists were powerful adversaries precisely be-cause of their faith in the Soviet Union: "their power, whose nature baffles the rest of the world, because in large measure the rest of the world has lost that power, is the power to hold convictions and to act on them."[72] The rest of the world—and Western civilization especially—did not have faith in itself. In Nixon's reading of it, *Witness* "pleads eloquently and effectively for a counter-faith to combat the Communist idea—a faith based not on materialism but on a recognition of God."[73]

By working the Hiss case into an existential quest, Chambers lent grandeur to the conservative movement, reaching in *Witness* his highest rhetorical flights in the introduction "Foreword in the Form of a Letter to My Children." The message of the letter was one of conversion. Cham-bers's conversion to Christianity had enabled him to raise his children as Christians, thereby eliminating the communist temptation in them, and his letter was not in any sense either private or general. Abstract intellec-tuality was valuable only insofar as it helped one to live the good life, to abandon the Enlightenment for the Christian pastoral. Beyond abstrac-tion was the singular, unique, particular soul.

Chambers's "Letter to My Children" takes its readers to the Christian pastoral, a key to Chambers's political vision, to his notion of the well-lived anti-communist or conservative life.[74] The farm shows the wonder of life and death. Chambers tells his children that, on the farm, they encountered the wonders of the universe "with reverence and awe—that reverence and awe that has died out in the modern world and been replaced by man's monkeylike amazement at the cleverness of his own inventive brain." The power of nature is sanctified by a "reverence and awe for life and the world, which is the ultimate meaning of Beethoven and Shakespeare." Nature and culture culminate in Christian piety: "on summer Sundays, you sat between Papa and Mama in the Quaker meeting house. Through open doors, as you tried not to twist and turn in the long silence, you could see the far, blue Maryland hills and hear the redbirds and ground robins in the graveyard behind." Chambers closed the letter to his children with imagery from Dante and the New Testament. He was leading his readers "up and up a narrow defile between bare and steep rocks." Like the journey into the inferno, "it will be dark," but "if I have led you aright, you will make out three crosses, from two of which hang thieves. I will have brought you to Golgotha—the place of skulls. This is the meaning of the journey."[75] (Alexander Solzhenitsyn would write in *The gulag Archipelago* of "the Golgotha of Lubyanka Square," the Lubyanka being Moscow's main prison, the Soviet Bastille.)[76] After Golgotha comes the resurrection of Christ, just as inferno precedes paradise in *The Divine Comedy*. The program Chambers hoped to enact was the Christian redemption of America and, with America, of Western civilization as a whole.[77]

In *Witness*, Chambers's conversion is exemplary. In the chapter "The Faith and Hope of the World," Chambers delves into his faith in communism, which he treats in *Witness* as a secular religion. Finally, in "The Division Point," Chambers recounts his conversion to Christianity, which is followed by "The Tranquil Years," a more extensive discussion of the Christian pastoral than the one sketched in "A Letter to My Children." Micro and macro play off of each other in the final part of *Witness*, which deals with the Hiss case. Chambers had found redemption, absolving himself of the sin of communism by becoming a Christian: William F. Buckley Jr. would describe Chambers's witness as "expiation for ten years' complicity with communism."[78] The Hiss case held out the chance for redemption on a national scale. Hiss's failure to tell the truth about the past, and to accept the consequences, mirrored a failure of understanding on the part of many Americans who pitied Hiss as an innocent victim. The work of redemption had only just begun. *Witness* was a piece of the ongoing effort, but America would be fully redeemed only when a conservative movement had beaten back communism and righted the many wrong turns of Enlightenment and modernity. This personal story mitigated the overarching pessimism of Chambers's magnum opus. What he had done others could also do; what he had done America and the West could do as well.

By cloaking communism in the mantel of religion, Chambers mocked the secularism of communist doctrine. The very power of communism—its romantic appeal to the human spirit—would prove its undoing because it had little other than revolution to offer.[79] The case study in this dilemma was none other than Chambers himself, who was drawn to communism because it "demanded of me those things which have always stirred what is best in men—courage, poverty, self-sacrifice, discipline, intelligence, my life and, at need, my death." This romantic revolutionary élan had pushed Chambers to "commit the characteristic crimes of my century, which . . . is the first century since life began when a decisive part of the most articulate section of mankind not merely ceased to believe in God, but has deliberately rejected God."[80] The terms in which Chambers wrote in *Witness* about his "communist faith" presage his eventual conversion to Christianity. He devoted chapter six, "The Child," to his observation of his daughter's ear, a passage Ronald Reagan would commit to memory. Its complexity had theological significance for him: the human ear could only be God's creation. Leaving the Communist Party and finding God were the result of a "wrenching effort of the soul to seek relief from the death in which it lives." Once Chambers did convert to Christianity, he tried to convert each member of the Ware circle, if not to Christianity then at least away from communism. Most dramatic was Chambers's final meeting with Hiss—something only described in *Witness*—during which Hiss did not yield to Chambers's Christian arguments. The meeting took place in 1938 shortly before Christmas. It was the first Christmas Chambers celebrated with his family, and "for the first time in our lives, I tried to tell my children the Christmas story." The conversion to Christianity was an explicitly conservative act: "the secret springs of my life, which had been lost so long ago in the desert of modernity, joined their impulses, broke free and flowed unchecked." A step forward, Chambers's conversion was presented in *Witness* as a return to his authentic self. "I became what I was," he declared in a classic trope of the conversion narrative.[81]

Chambers's conversion to Christianity was both a repudiation of the Enlightenment and a rediscovery of himself as a common American. He related his conversion back to the abstract argument of *Witness*: when the scales fell from his eyes, "what fell was the whole web of the materialist mind . . . that modern intellectual mood which gives birth to Communism, and denies the soul in the name of the mind, and the soul's salvation in suffering in the name of man's salvation here and now."[82] Converting to Christianity placed him closer to the American people, turning Chambers into a new kind of conservative intellectual. With intellectuals in mind, Norman Podhoretz has written that "American conservatives were the heirs of a long tradition of hostility to their own country."[83] This was a tradition that many conservatives wished to challenge in the 1950s. Chambers thought that farm work and religious devotion joined him to the American people, who were "my people" in *Witness*. "Even when they did not understand," he wrote of the Hiss case, "my people were always about me. I had only to look around me to see them—on the farms, on the streets, humble people, strong in common cause, in common goodness, common forgiveness, because all felt bowed together under the common weight of life."[84] The middle class was inauthentic, hypocritical, and uncomprehending of history, similar to the bourgeoisie of Marxist-Leninist fame; the people were united in their common goodness. This image of the common man resonates with the socialist-realist fiction Chambers published in the *New Masses* in 1932, a thread of continuity in the convert's life story.

Chambers created a stylized image of the people in *Witness*, and to some extent he created a stylized image of himself. In a letter to Ralph de Toledano, Chambers touched on the selectivity of *Witness*. "I left out the step by step progression whereby events (bouncing off me like atoms) moved me to act—seizure of Czechoslovakia, Berlin blockade," he wrote. Chambers highlighted religion when he wrote in *Witness* about his Kronstadt, and the omission of his sexual history had a dramatic effect on *Witness* because his sexual past was bound up with his work as a Soviet spy and with his conversion to Christianity. Although the omission is hardly surprising, it foreshortened the story of his conversion. Yet Chambers's goal in *Witness* was never unfettered confession. *Witness* was a manifesto as much as it was an autobiography, a manifesto for a new conservative movement in America as well as a provocation to the American Right.[85] Chambers was urging conservatives to abandon the isolationist impulse in American foreign policy and to embrace a populist conservatism. Conservatives had to exploit the "jagged fissure" that the Hiss case revealed between liberal elites and the conservative American people, as Chambers believed them to be. American culture was a battleground between its rural Christian masses and a secular, liberal, and urban elite. American conservatives had to struggle against capitalism, modernity, and the middle class, a program that could be reconciled with the call for a populist conservatism. It could be woven into the rhetoric of anticommunism without distortion. Still, an enormous distance separated the ideal from the practical. Chambers's hostility to all things middle class, capitalist, and modern militated against the basic constituents of America's geopolitical power, against capitalism and technology. As a consequence, Chambers's conservatism demanded compromise at best and self-contradiction at worst. Chambers was able to compromise because his priorities were very clear. The Cold War had to be won at all costs and no antimodern dreams were to get in the way.

Chambers sought a conservatism of the future, as was clear from his "Letter to My Children." His children would grow up in a different America, and perhaps they and their compatriots would honor the conservative calling. *Witness* was a blueprint for doing so, a book written to invite the appetite for conservatism. In the final sentence of *Witness*, Chambers returned to the subject of children, writing this time not about *his* children but about *our* children, leaving his readers with an apocalyptic choice to be made before "our children shall be grown, when the witness that was laid on us shall have lost its meaning because our whole world will have borne a more terrible witness or it will no longer exist."[86] The final chapter of *Witness* is titled "Tomorrow and Tomorrow and Tomorrow," an obvious appeal to the future. The future was war with the Soviet Union and with communism. In this war liberals were either on the wrong side or too weak-willed to fight; conservatives would have to be the ones to fight evil, and "evil can only be fought," Chambers exhorted.[87] Given the power of the Left in the United States and abroad, the conservative cause was precarious and unlikely to succeed, unless the future held out potential for a new conservative movement. The conservatism of the present did nothing to assuage Chambers's fears. "Republican [Party] isolationism remained strong in the 1950s," according to Paul Gottfried, and isolationism, for Chambers, betrayed an utter incomprehension of the Cold War.[88] Conventional American conservatives had not made sense of the revolutionary twentieth century, and *Witness* derived much of its energy from this circumstance, from a conservative mind in desperate conflict with the status quo—including the conservative status quo.

Chambers was a radical among conservatives, and he sensed an almost immediate disapproval from the Right once *Witness* appeared in print. "Even before *Witness* was published, when the first few SEP [*Saturday Evening Post*] pieces had appeared, I listened to the assault of the Right on me," Chambers observed in a letter to Buckley. The anti-communist message found a receptive audience, but the conservative ideas Chambers grafted onto it were not especially welcome. This was a problem with *Witness* that manifested itself on the Right and on the Left. "How odd that most of the world seems to have missed the point of *Witness*," Chambers wrote: "that it seems to suppose I said: 'Destroy Communism and you can go back to business as usual.'" Business as usual was American capitalism and the American dream, the pursuit of property and happiness. Chambers was frustrated by the failure of *Witness* to genereate outrage, the outrage he had wanted to stimulate among complacent bourgeois readers: "if the bourgeoisie understood *Witness* outright, they would raise the warcry of their revolutionary heyday and rush me 'to the lantern.' Of course, this is precisely what the socialists confusedly sense; hence, as the perpetrators of the bourgeois dream, their foam and fury."[89] In his laments over *Witness*'s reception on the Right and elsewhere, Chambers may not have been self-critical enough. The United States needed its bourgeoisie to fight the Cold War, generate the requisite capital, staff the bureaucracies, and provide the intellectual leadership. The common people were not in a position to do this job. More prosaically, the Republican Party depended on the bourgeoisie to get elected. Chambers's sympathizers largely accepted the need to "destroy communism," without always accepting the more radical, less pragmatic arguments of *Witness*.

Chambers was sensitive to the contradictions in his conservative position. To wage the Cold War he had to make peace with modern America; other conservatives would have to shake up the status quo in order to meet the geopolitical imperatives of the Cold War. With this dilemma in mind, Chambers distinguished between conservatism and counterrevolution, as Walter Krivistky had taught him to do. "Counter-revolution and conservatism have little in common," Chambers wrote in *Witness*. "In the common struggle against Communism the conservative is all but helpless. For that struggle cannot be fought, much less won, or even understood, except in terms of sacrifice; he wishes to conserve, above all, what he is and what he has." Chambers might have preferred to be a conventional conservative—tilling the soil, tending to his family, adoring his civilization—but the Cold War forced him and everyone else to be active counterrevolutionaries. The counterrevolutionary would have to match the radicalism of the Bolshevik revolution, although the counterrevolutionary had no love of revolution; the counterrevolutionary's radicalism was directed toward restoration. And so, the need to disrupt the status quo—imposed on the counterrevolutionary—was tragic. Chambers was fond of tragedy (so was Lionel Trilling), and Chambers overlaid *Witness* with tragic tones and connotations. Quite often he overdid the tragic mode, achieving a hyperbolic pathos rather than the Shakespearean tragedy to which he aspired.[90] Easy as it is to dismiss "the tragic" in *Witness* as a stylistic affectation, it sheds light on the theoretical problems of an anti-communist conservatism. Tragedy was the one way, even if only aesthetic, to resolve what for Chambers was a bitter paradox. The United States would have to undergo a revolution in its political and cultural life in order to reverse the progress of the Bolshevik revolution.

The contradictions of the conservative position circa 1952 were not entirely theoretical for Chambers. They were also highly practical, crystallizing in the figure of Joseph McCarthy, whose career as an anti-communist crusader began a few weeks after the Hiss case ended. McCarthy owed an enormous debt of gratitude to Chambers. Not only had Chambers's testimony opened up the Hiss case, resulting in a guilty verdict for Hiss, but Chambers had forged an anti-communist language—touched by a "conspiratorial rhetoric"—specifically designed to implicate liberals in communist subversion.[91] As a phenomenon, McCarthyism was an extension and exploitation of Chambers's witness, a reduction of *Witness* to conspiratorial rhetoric. McCarthy indiscriminately targeted the liberal elites who had either defended Hiss, such as Dean Acheson, or who in some way resembled Hiss, such as China specialist Owen Lattimore. McCarthy represented two elements of the new conservatism to which Chambers had dedicated *Witness*. He was an anti-communist and a populist. Chambers refused to condemn McCarthy outright, although he understood McCarthy as a problem for the Right, an inadequate anti-communist. Chambers described McCarthy vividly as "a raven of disaster."[92]

The Hiss case was the specter that haunted McCarthyism, and it was the specter McCarthy used to haunt his opponents. In a book on McCarthy, Roy Cohn, counsel to McCarthy's Government Operations Committee and McCarthy's close associate, made a direct connection between the Hiss case and McCarthy's career. Cohn explained the anticommunist enthusiasm of Senator McCarthy as the reversal of past negligence. Cohn argued that when FDR and Truman had been in power, they neglected to pursue the leads that Chambers and other ex-communist witnesses had given them. The Democratic Party and its liberal supporters had tried to dismiss the Hiss case, which, according to Cohn, was "first aired in 1939 [with Chambers's testimony to Adolph Berle], but no action was taken." Inaction in 1939 set the pattern that Chambers broke against the most formidable of odds. "Later, the House Committee on Un-American Activities looked into the Hiss case," Cohn continued, "but President Truman was not only unimpressed—he denounced the Committee's probe into the Hiss and other cases as 'red-herring diversions.'" Truman never saw the light, Cohn argued, and he never lent his support to Chambers. Cohn's claim was that McCarthy wanted to undo the mistakes of the past. No potential Alger Hiss was to be given the benefit of the doubt, and McCarthy was increasingly generous in his notion of who resembled Hiss—New Dealers, State Department employees, liberals, intellectuals, and, eventually, anyone at all, including Army generals and the president. Everywhere Cohn and McCarthy looked they saw, or wanted to see, the visage of Alger Hiss. When they put William Remington before the Committee, they knew, for example, "that in Remington we had a defendant at least as bright as and probably more cunning than Alger Hiss," Cohn wrote.[93] When McCarthy tried to implicate Adlai Stevenson with accusations of communist subversion, McCarthy repeatedly mispronounced Stevenson's name, "Alger—I mean Adlai."[94]

Chambers was a participant in McCarthy's investigations.[95] He instructed McCarthy on the history of American communism, serving as an unofficial consultant.[96] Chambers willingly participated in an investigation into O. Edmund Clubb Jr., a Foreign Service officer of long standing. Chambers recalled a visit by Clubb in 1932 to the New Masses office, and this recollection helped McCarthy execute a two-year probe into Clubb's past, which resulted in Clubb's suspension from the State Department and finally in the end of his diplomatic career. Chambers grew increasingly doubtful that there was any meaningful connection between Clubb and the Communist Party, doubts that did not stop McCarthy from ruining Clubb's career.[97] Chambers participated unwillingly in another McCarthyite escapade, involving diplomat and Russia expert Chip Bohlen, which Chambers described as the episode "which estranged the Senator and me." By 1957, Chambers was willing to equate the Bohlen episode with the entirety of McCarthy's career, for with McCarthy "the rest was as bad as the Bohlen business, which was outrageous."[98] McCarthy visited Chambers's farm in a staged visit, and "as soon as he stepped inside our door, the telephone rang. That was the *Washington Post*." The telephone call from the *Post* left "the terrifying impression that McCarthy had come to see me about [Chip] Bohlen (in fact we had a long talk on the subject) and that I knew something damaging about Bohlen." McCarthy's theatrics upset Chambers so much that he made a public denial concerning Bohlen and communism: "it was pushing noon on Monday before I discovered the position I had been left in with respect to Bohlen. Hence the statement [denying secret knowledge of Bohlen's past]. Esther [Chambers's wife] tried to restrain me, point out that I would seem to be letting the Senator down."[99]

If Chambers considered McCarthy outrageous in 1957, he was more ambivalent between 1950 and 1954 when the senator was in his heyday. Chambers believed that McCarthy, unlike most American politicians, recognized the internal threat communism posed to state and society. McCarthy was brusque to the point of violence, and in letters that remained unpublished during his lifetime, Chambers repeatedly likened McCarthy to someone throwing punches. Chambers appreciated the political about-face from the early Hiss case, when Chambers had been an object of calumny. At the same time, slugger McCarthy's brute power as an anti-communist was his greatest weakness. He exaggerated and lied; he was a bully when attacking the innocent. Worst of all, McCarthy sullied the cause of anti-communism, encouraging liberals in their self-righteousness. Rather than critically examining the scandal of their communist affiliations in the 1930s—a scandal reiterated in liberal sympathy for Hiss—liberals could point to McCarthy in self-serving horror, fancying themselves the victims of a repressive anti-communist agenda. Chambers was constrained on two sides. If he openly supported McCarthy, he might retroactively validate the claim that the Hiss case was the first McCarthyite hoax. If he openly criticized McCarthy, he bolstered

McCarthy's left-leaning enemies, who were also Chambers's enemies. Chambers chose to remain silent.

In private correspondence Chambers outlined an assessment of McCarthy that was one part admiration and two parts disgust. In March 1953, Chambers wrote to Ralph de Toledano, lamenting McCarthy's opportunism: "I do not think a speech by Senator McCarthy would help anybody except Senator McCarthy," Chambers declared.[100] Several months later Henry Regnery, the editor of a conservative press, sent Chambers the galleys of a book written in praise of McCarthy. *McCarthy and His Enemies* would be published in 1954 and it was written by William F. Buckley Jr. and L. Brent Bozell, young conservative intellectuals. McCarthy himself had read the galleys and found the book too critical. Regnery wanted Chambers's opinion. Chambers dated his response to Regnery January 14, 1954. "In my opinion, the Senator hasn't got a leg to stand on," Chambers wrote. According to Chambers, McCarthy was a fool of sorts: "I said long since that the crucial question about Senator McCarthy was not whether his aims are ultimately good or bad, but whether his intelligence is equal to his energy." It clearly was not, in Chambers's judgment. Low in intelligence, McCarthy also had a low character: "with time," Chambers predicted accurately, "the repeated dull thud of the low blow may prove to be the real factor in his undoing." Despite such grave criticism, Chambers liked *McCarthy and His Enemies*, which was an unashamed argument on McCarthy's behalf. The two sides of Chambers's letter to Regnery were difficult to reconcile. After excoriating McCarthy, Chambers informed Regnery that "I should not hesitate to tell the Senator that I think his book a real job in his behalf and that he owed the author a loud well-done and thank you."[101]

Chambers's letter favorably impressed Buckley, who considered it flattering enough to prevail "on the promotion manager to wire Whittaker Chambers to ask whether he would be willing to write a blurb on the book for promotional use." Chambers declined Buckley's request but not out of any dislike for Buckley. Chambers wrote a letter to Buckley explaining that McCarthyism was a distraction from the Hiss case, which Chambers defined as "still the heart of the anti-Communist fight here, and by it most of the rest stands or falls." The Hiss case had not been won and therefore could still be lost: "the forces and money behind the enemy effort are formidable. In my opinion, we shall not know how formidable until Alger Hiss leaves prison." In a war of ideas, McCarthy was a terrible ally. "It is more and more my reluctant opinion," Chambers confessed, "that he [McCarthy] is a tactician, rather than a strategist; that he continually, by reflex rather than calculation, sacrifices the long view for the short pull."[102] McCarthy could frighten the Hiss camp and hamper the careers of those who belonged to it; but he could not persuade them to revise their image of the 1930s. If anything, McCarthy cast a forgiving light on the 1930s, that decade of progressive idealism so distant from the cynicism and nastiness of the McCarthy era. To the extent that McCarthy created a host of martyrs for the Left, one might simply add another name to the list.

In his letter to Buckley, Chambers equated the war against Hiss with the Cold War, in which Chambers was "scarcely an individual man. I am the witness on whom, to a great degree, it still all swings." His character was still on trial: "the enemy is tirelessly seeking to discredit me. How I conduct myself, what I say and do, what forces and people I publicly associate myself with, are matters to be governed by no whim of mine. My reactions are a kind of public trust." Chambers was exaggerating his public importance in 1954, but he was right to think that McCarthy and Nixon shaped public perceptions of Chambers's own credibility. It was the fate of HUAC, and not merely the status of his personal reputation, that spurred Chambers to guard his credibility so jealously. Chambers felt that the Hiss case had to be correctly understood if Americans were to fight the Cold War with adequate resolve. Even McCarthy's allies "have slowly come to question his judgment and to fear acutely that his flair for the sensational, his inaccuracies and distortions, his tendency to sacrifice the greater objective for the momentary effect, will lead him and us into trouble." The stakes were characteristically high, as Chambers sketched them: "one way whereby I can most easily help Communism is to associate myself publicly with Senator McCarthy; to give the enemy even a minor pretext for confusing the Hiss case with his activities, and rolling it all into a snarl with which to baffle, bedevil and divide opinion." McCarthy might discredit Chambers, thereby discrediting "the whole anti-Communist effort for a long time to come."[103]

McCarthy did one service for the Right. He alerted the masses to the power of the Left, described by Chambers as "the socialist Apparat," a loose coalition of those on the Left, linked by connotation to the Soviet espionage "apparatus," to which Chambers had formerly belonged.[104] McCarthy is to be admired because he "repeatedly calls attention to the antisocialist masses to the fact that the socialist Apparat exists," Chambers wrote to Buckley in April 1954. Whatever the Right will gain from Mc-Carthy, however, the "socialist Apparat" will gain more. "Now, the Communists recognized at once . . . that Senator McCarthy is a political godsend." McCarthy serves two major political functions, both of them bad for the Right: "not only does Senator McCarthy unite through fear the socialist Apparat and its far-flung free-masonry of fellow travelers . . . Equally important, Senator McCarthy divides the ranks of the Right." McCarthy has no sense of himself as a conservative leader, which is why he divides the Right with his demagogic opportunism. Chambers did not believe "that the Senator has what it takes to win the fight for the Right. I believe that Richard Nixon may have some of what it takes. I believe it the more readily because the Left also believes it." In light of later U.S. history, Chambers's prognosis for Nixon and the Left is richly comic: "never suppose that the Left has finished with Nixon. But the Senator has proved a more valuable target."[105]

After McCarthy's political demise in 1954, Chambers continued to argue for a right-wing unity that did not yet exist. As late as the summer of 1954, Chambers was willing to consider a compromise with McCarthy. He could accept "as a working premise, the possibility of compromise within the areas you [William F. Buckley, Jr.] mention—the [Eisenhower] Administration, the Senator." Yet Chambers could not honestly make good on a compromise with McCarthy: "I fear this more in the case of the Senator than of the Administration." By 1955 any such compromise was unthinkable. McCarthy was outstanding in his "bilious ineptitude," Chambers wrote to Buckley in August 1955, by which time McCarthy's career was over. By maligning Eisenhower McCarthy "meant to provoke a split in the Republican Party. If so, his appraisal of the real situation differs so radically from mine as to make talk pointless." The Right could make no compromise with McCarthy: "for the Right to tie itself in any way to McCarthy is suicide." In Senator McCarthy's career Chambers discerned the breakdown of Western civilization, which was doomed if it had nothing better to offer by way of anti-communist leadership. If McCarthy is the best there is, Chambers reasoned, then "the West must have lost that creative virtue, the loss of which spells doom for those who have lost it."[106] As for decent anti-communist statesmen, there are "half a dozen men, if so many, tottering towards their graves. That is the chart of the abyss."[107] The Right had not yet assimilated Chambers's witness, and Senator McCarthy's career had proven to be a perversion of it.

Some liberals did a better job of assimilating Chambers's witness, even while they wrestled with its illiberal substance. Arthur Schlesinger Jr. labeled *Witness* "one of the really significant American autobiographies" and predicted that the "weight and urgency [of *Witness*] as a personal document are likely to win acceptance for its politics and its philosophy. But the politics and philosophy, in my judgment, raise basic issues which deserve independent and critical examination." Schlesinger objected to the connection Chambers made throughout *Witness* between Alger Hiss and the New Deal. Chambers errs, Schlesinger argued, "when he identifies the Popular Front mind, which was a psychosis of the New York intellectual, with the New Deal mind, which was essentially concerned with trying to hold the American system together against economic crisis." Within the world of American liberalism, Alger Hiss was the traitorous exception to a virtuous rule, and with this objection in mind, Schlesinger criticized Chambers for insisting on religion as an anti-communist weapon; Schlesinger saw no role for religion in American political life. Despite a new vogue for religion in the 1950s, "it is notable that the word God does not appear in the Constitution of the United States." The moral import of Christianity can be communicated in a secular version of Reinhold Niebuhr's theses: "the essential issue is not belief in God. It is rather the sense of human limitation, of human fallibility, of what he [Chambers] himself calls the 'mortal incompleteness' of man."[108] One could read Augustine or Chambers sympathetically and still conclude that a secular anti-communist liberalism is the best approach to politics.

Diana Trilling believed Chambers's witness, making her and Chambers allies of sorts, although she regretted any "enforced alignment between anti-Communist liberals and reactionaries [as] particularly open and distasteful." The Hiss case must not unite anti-communist liberals with anti-communist conservatives: "the anti-Hiss liberal must insist on his right not to be labeled a reactionary just because reactionaries agree with him on this case." Liberals must salvage "a better notion of liberalism" from the Hiss case, changing liberalism by making it unequivocally anti-communist. Diana Trilling hoped that the Hiss case would permanently "detach the wagon of American liberalism from the star of the Soviet Union . . . [giving] liberals a sounder insight into the nature of a political idea." If the proper lessons are learned, liberals may avoid "the tragic confusion in liberal government which leaves the investigation of such important matters to the enemies of liberal government." If they were to defeat communism and reactionary conservatism, liberals would have to accept "the task of persuading the liberal who is not afraid of Communism that he should be afraid of it . . . [this task] involves chang-ing a climate of opinion and feeling over the whole of our culture," a project in the future tense.[109] It was a project in which Diana Trilling's husband, Lionel, was still engaged in 1975 when he wrote his letter to Morris Dickstein, struggling to persuade the liberal Dickstein that Hiss was someone to fear and Chambers someone to respect. Lionel Trilling was a liberal witness to the integrity of Chambers's anti-communism.

8

CONSERVATISM AND THE ANTI-COMMUNIST SELF

O born in days when wits were fresh and clear,
And life ran gaily as the sparkling Thames;
Before this strange disease of modern life,
With its sick hurry, its divided aims,
Its heads o'ertaxed, its palsied hearts, was rife—

—MATTHEW ARNOLD, "The Scholar Gypsy"

Opposition is among the joys of youth, a commonplace of radical politics that took on unexpected force when an unknown youth, William F. Buckley Jr., published *God and Man at Yale* in 1952. His book was an exposé of the establishment, ensconced in elite universities, close to the higher circles of government, comfortable with agreed-upon rules of culture and thought. The establishment spread out from institutions such as Yale to Washington, D.C., a seamless web of ideas and attitudes— culture reinforcing politics, politics shaping culture. Undergraduate Whittaker Chambers attacked the powers that be at Columbia when he unveiled his atheist play, "A Play for Puppets," earning the censure of his university. As a professor, Lionel Trilling watched multiple generations of radicals come of age at Columbia, opposing themselves to the official ethos of the university and the moneyed establishment behind it. William F. Buckley Jr. was neither a radical nor even a man of the Left. He was a self-described conservative, a conservative youth whose cause for rebellion was the liberal establishment housed and perpetuated at Yale. His Yale education had been tacitly liberal, tacitly skeptical of Christianity, tacitly hostile toward capitalism, and imbued with the spirit, not of the radical Left but of some amorphous liberal essence.[1]

God and man were under assault at Yale. This was Buckley's alarming message to the nation at large, his book a triumph of opposition and a conservative call to arms. A revolution in manners had made socialism and atheism, to use Buckley's terms from *God and Man at Yale,* the unspoken orthodoxy of the Yale curriculum. Yale's departure from Christianity and capitalism foreshadowed a new kind of American elite already visible at the university, "the nerve center of civilization," in Buckley's words.[2] Liberal Yale was a microcosm of American civilization in disarray. Yale's professors showed a "widespread academic reliance on relativism, pragmatism, and utilitarianism," their patron saint philosopher John Dewey.[3] Buckley's evidence was impressionistic: atheists were self-confident, standing as they did on the cusp of progress and fashion, while Christian undergraduates were embarrassed and confused about their piety. Proponents of liberal tolerance felt justified in their intolerance of religion, and Yale was letting their intolerance cohere into orthodoxy. Buckley mocked official university rhetoric about the marketplace of ideas. Yale's institutional culture demonstrated, he believed, a marketplace for liberal ideas alone, fenced in by the exclusion of conservative ideas. *God and Man at Yale* "sounded the clarion call," Buckley's biographer John Judis has written, "of revolution, calling upon the conservative majority to rise up and overthrow the intellectual elite."[4]

Trilling was an archetypal liberal cleric, his very name associated with the word liberal, only in part because he had published *The Liberal Imagination* to considerable acclaim in 1950. Trilling was liberal in many ways: he voted Democrat and wrote with an eye to the secular politics of reform, which for him was a precondition for American politics and for liberalism. Trilling was an expert in the liberal intellectual tradition, going back to the eighteenth century and coming to fruition in his area of scholarly expertise, Victorian Britain, which was the pioneer of liberal economics, of a liberal polity and a liberal culture, more self-conscious and philosophical in its liberalism than nineteenth-century America. In Britain liberalism was only one of several possibilities and not the "sole intellectual tradition," as Trilling believed it to be in America.[5] Trilling and Buckley could agree on the power of liberal intellectuals in the 1950s, although Buckley was chipping away at this power and Trilling wanted liberal power to be used to good effect, responsibly and creatively. Since his Kronstadt in the early 1930s, the liberal Trilling had been fighting a titanic struggle against the radical Left, trying to draw it toward the liberal imagination. By 1952 this struggle was largely over. The anti-communist intellectuals that huddled around *Partisan Review* had graduated to positions of influence in the 1950s, riding the zeitgeist of the early Cold War.

The liberal anti-communist program was having a satisfying effect on politics. After two trial runs with Adlai Stevenson, the darling of liberal intellectuals, one might find a John F. Kennedy, whose Harvard was not so different from Buckley's Yale or Trilling's Columbia and whose liberal anti-communism had a cultivated intellectual aura. The 1950s was justifiably a decade of liberal self-confidence.

Acknowledging this self-confidence, William F. Buckley Jr. struggled to inaugurate a new conservative age, to upend the liberal status quo, creating a center for conservative ideas and thinkers at the magazine *National Review*, the first issue of which appeared on November 19, 1955. "To a very substantial degree," writes historian George Nash, "the history of reflective conservatism in America after 1955 is the history of the individuals who collaborated in—or were discovered by—the magazine William F. Buckley founded."[6] Buckley, a man of considerable wealth and charm, created a social center for conservative intellectuals in New York City, the fabled Mecca for liberal and radical seekers, and in the pages of *National Review* Buckley tried to unify anti-communism, libertarianism, and traditionalism into what Nash calls fusionism. Anti-communism had to be worked into American conservatism, drawing a line between the isolationist past and the Cold War present. Traditionalists favored religion over secular liberalism and hierarchy over egalitarianism, pledging themselves to defending the older traditions of Western culture. Libertarianism was the American element in the equation, combining a Jeffersonian rhetoric of liberty with nineteenth-century "Manchester" liberalism or laissez-faire. Buckley was a living embodiment and eloquent spokesman of the so-called fusionist idea. Crucial to Buckley's enterprise were ex-communists such as Willi Schlamm, the émgigré intellectual who had tried, and failed, to enlist Trilling in an early *National Review*-like venture. An Austrian Jew, Schlamm escaped Hitler's Europe by coming to the United States in 1938, working as a foreign-policy advisor to Henry Luce before joining up with Buckley at *National Review*.[7] A European ex-communist, Schlamm threw himself into the creation of an American conservatism, sturdy and persuasive enough to tip the Cold War in a Western direction.

Whittaker Chambers, America's most conspicuous ex-communist, was no stranger to the ordeal of conservative self-definition by 1955. Ever since they had met in the early 1950s, Buckley looked up to Chambers as a historic figure and an intellectual mentor, although on its surface their friendship was improbable. Buckley was a cosmopolitan patrician who had been a conservative since childhood. Chambers, the ex-communist, was living in rural isolation when he got to know Buckley. Yet between them grew a vital friendship, anchored in the many letters they exchanged with each other. Chambers and Buckley were conservatives connected by a rebellious streak. When Yale's enfant terrible wrote an admiring book about Senator Joseph McCarthy, *McCarthy and His Enemies* (1954), Chambers was unconvinced by the book's arguments but he relished the liberal outrage it provoked. Chambers had been a communist long before communism was in vogue; he had been a spy when many American communists were radicals of the magazine and the meeting; he had been an embattled anti-communist editor at *Time*. As Christian conservatives fiercely hostile to the Left, Chambers and Buckley did not have to rebel against each other. They were partisans of the Christian West at the height of the Cold War, and Buckley did his best to secure this leonine Cold Warrior as an editor for *National Review*. Chambers could never make up his mind about the job. His relationship to *National Review* was contentious, but much of his published writing after *Witness* appeared in *National Review*. For the magazine, as for postwar American conservatism in general, Chambers was a patron saint. A twenty-three-year-old Gary Wills was hired at *National Review* when Buckley heard that Wills was "a practicing Catholic, [and] admired Chambers's *Witness*."[8]

Chambers, an opposing self par excellence, was a complicated conservative. He could oppose enemy and friend, heresy and dogma. The political pragmatist—seeking party-political advantage and caught up in campaigns, policy detail, and presidents—cohabited with the communicant of Western civilization, in thrall to existential despair. As Chambers said many times and in various ways: "in a larger sense, I believe that the bigger battle is lost in advance."[9] Yet pessimism was not what Chambers wanted to impart to the conservative movement or to the Republican Party. His occasional journalism in the years between the publication of *Witness* in 1952 and his death in 1961 was focused on political action, as was much of his correspondence. In addition to Buckley, Chambers frequently exchanged letters with Ralph de Toledano, a conservative journalist who befriended Chambers during the Hiss case and published in 1950 (with Victor Lasky) a pro-Chambers account of the case, *The Seeds of Treason*. Chambers confided in de Toledano.[10] In the privacy of letters,

Chambers could discuss the distance between his political strategizing and his deep-seated conservatism since he was "a conservative, not first for political reasons—the political position follows logically." Any political position must accord with reality, Chambers believed, before it accords with personal ideals and fantasies, and Chambers had yet to determine the right relationship between the ideal and the real. "If I had to raise a slogan for the Right," Chambers wrote to de Toledano, "it would be: Study. We must go to school; we do not know enough."[11]

Chambers worried about the future of conservatism, whether it could be fused and whether it should be fused. This was one reason to study. The appearance of Russell Kirk's *The Conservative Mind* in 1953 deepened Chambers's doubts about the coherence of American conservatism. In 1953 Kirk was a new star in the conservative firmament, not an ex-communist but an intellectual youth from rural Michigan, schooled in European culture and eager to nurture the conservative mind in America. His first book, *Randolph of Roanoke: A Study of Conservative Thought*, his masters thesis at Duke, was a study of indigenous American conservatism in Virginia.[12] *The Conservative Mind*, the book that made him famous, was an argument for conservative consistency, an effort to prove that there was a conservative caste of mind, formed in the Middle Ages, but available in America as well. Less vivid than Kirk's synthesis of ideas was Kirk's self-confidence: conservatism was viable, it was intellectual, it was European, it was American, it could be defended by a young man. Although Chambers deemed *The Conservative Mind* "the most important book of the twentieth century," he was not especially impressed by Kirk's magnum opus; his praise may have been more an indictment of the twentieth century's thin achievements. Kirk attempted to arrange three centuries of American intellectual history into a single conservative pattern. What struck Chambers was the confusion "brewed by slamming into one pot John Adams, John Randolph, John Calhoun, James Russell Lowell, Henry Adams and George Santayana."[13] *The Conservative Mind* neglected the urgent conservative problems. Initially titled *The Conservative Rout*, the book did not offer a way forward; it could be read as a journey back to Edmund Burke, and for Chambers this was too scholastic an approach to American conservatism.

Throughout the 1950s, Chambers did not cease writing about the troubled conservative mind. If he was a fusionist, it was only a fusion of tradition and anti-communism that he genuinely supported. His predispositions were more in line with Dostoevsky, Heidegger, or Burke than with the midcentury Republican Party. Burke worried about a vulgar modern spirit that would outlast the French Revolution; Dostoevsky used literature to argue that the modern personality was sick, the modern hero an underground man, his spiritual health shattered by a cold, materialist, godless society; and Heidegger inveighed against technology (and, often enough, against America) as a vehicle of modern barbarism. Burke, Dostoevsky, and Heidegger were all trying to conserve some spiritual principle *from* modernity. To the extent that a modern American conservative—and a Republican, for that matter—had to celebrate capitalism, Chambers was only grudgingly a modern conservative.[14] "I am a man of the Right," Chambers wrote in a letter to Schlamm, "because I mean to uphold capitalism in its American version. But I claim that capitalism is not, and by its very nature cannot conceivably be, conservative." This was no small dilemma. Chambers was discouraged by the many confusions of modern conservatism, not just by the tension between conservatism and capitalism. Chambers perceived a "sense of unreality and pessimism on the Right, running off into all manner of crackpotism," as he wrote to Buckley some four years before the John Birch Society, a venue for anti-communist fanaticism, was founded in 1958. In the same letter, Chambers noted a liberal bent among prominent industrialists, "the singular manifestation (or so it seems) of prime capitalists (a Rockefeller, a Harriman or Mennan Williams) turning, as we say, left."[15]

Chambers confronted conservative dilemmas directly by working on a book, a study of Western civilization provisionally titled *The Third Rome*. The drafts and letters ultimately published as *Cold Friday* document Chambers's unsteady search for conservative coherence in the declining West of the 1950s.

Witness loomed behind *The Third Rome*. *Witness* was personal testimony and a bestseller because of the Hiss case, but *Witness* was no handbook for American politics. Political ideologues or politicians might dip in and extract a ringing anti-communist citation, or they might spin variations on the theme of liberal treason, as they would for decades after the Hiss case. Beyond this, however, no high-ranking Republican could act on the religious intensities of Chambers's sharply antimodern book or tell Americans, thereby confessing to the world, that theirs was a "sick society." *The Third Rome* suffered from a similar problem. Chambers could write astutely about tactics, and over time his allegiance to the Republican

Party, rather than to some third-party alternative, would become the norm among conservative intellectuals. Yet, unlike Kirk, Chambers could not find a vital connection between American politics and Western civilization. The distance between aspiration and reality was not a spur to irony for Chambers, as it had been for Henry Adams—who was similarly gloomy about the future of Western civilization—but a spur to blank pessimism and political depression. Chambers was sure he would lose the cultural fight to secular progressive intellectuals, "the enlightened, articulate elite which, to one degree or another, has rejected the religious root of the civilization—the roots without which it is no longer Western Civilization, but a new order of beliefs, attitudes and mandates," as Chambers wrote in 1954 to Buckley.[16]

A pastiche of letters, autobiography, and political-cultural ruminations, *The Third Rome* is an unfinished book. The book has a discernible argument or, if not quite an argument, a single unifying problem: the waves of revolutionary change emanating out from the Enlightenment, of which the Bolshevik Revolution is only a more recent example.[17] Chambers was at a loss to see any alternative to the Enlightenment's dominance. One can only win small battles when "the whole world is unsettled by revolution because, for the first time in human history, the whole world is enmeshed in the same civilization—the technological civilization of the West. It is really one world, where everyone suffers from the same sickness and disorder, whose original focus of infection came from the West—that is, Europe and North America."[18] The dilemma, then, is not the protection of a civilized West from a barbarous East. The dilemma at the heart of *The Third Rome* involves a revolutionary West devastated by a technological civilization that is its own creation. If Chambers had little faith that the West could ever reverse the devastation, he had a genuine faith in ideas, taking inspiration from the European literature of anti-communism—from Arthur Koestler's *Darkness at Noon* (1941) and *The Invisible Writing* (1954), Czeslaw Milosz's *The Captive Mind* (1953), Abbè Lubac's *The Drama of Atheist Humanism* (1950), and Manès Sperber's *The Burned Bramble* (1951).[19] This was the genre to which Chambers wished to add *The Third Rome*. Koestler, Milosz, and Sperber were all ex-communists, preoccupied with the ethics of anti-communism. Chambers claimed that behind the lure of communism is nihilism, the imprint of a civilization that has lost touch with its religious past; these European books were supporting evidence. Nihilism creates an intellectual or spiritual proletariat, and "the forces of the revolution in the West are an intellectual proletariat, disinherited, not in the world's goods, with which they are often incongruously replete, but disinherited in the spirit. This is the answer to the fatuous, reiterated question why men like Arthur Koestler and Whittaker Chambers become Communists," Chambers wrote in *The Third Rome*.[20]

In *The Third Rome*, Chambers was more original in his analysis of communism and the West than in his prescriptive anti-communism. Chambers continuously tried to move beyond the personal data of *Witness*, and the difficulty he encountered may explain the project's many false starts and dead ends. What Chambers did achieve in *Cold Friday* was a portrait of continuous crisis, coextensive with a life severed into communist and anti-communist halves. *Cold Friday* was a retelling, at times a repetition, of *Witness*, as Chambers himself admitted: "Hateful home truths! For they invite the West to stop looking at Communism and look into itself. Hateful home truths! (I said them all in *Witness*.)" In *Cold Friday*, Chambers was forcing renewal on the West, struggling all the while with the old revolutionary desire to be *against*, the old joy of opposition. Chambers was not the typical Eisenhower Republican in his intuition that "the West is swayed by a profound will to die." This intuition forced Chambers to move away "from the vapors of the perishing West," even to "stand against it in its corruption (in this my instinct was never wrong and has never changed) even though one is not at war with it, is even committed to its defense."[21] The title *Cold Friday* evokes the day in the Christian calendar on which Christ is buried, a death that precedes resurrection: faith could promise what reason could not. Jeffrey Hart, a professor of literature and an editor at *National Review*, notes the element of existentialist despair in Chambers's Christian faith: "Whittaker Chambers, on the evidence of *Witness*, was some kind of Kierkegaardian Protestant, his faith a chime heard in the midnight of nihilism—though he called himself a Quaker."[22] The same is true for *Cold Friday*.

In *Cold Friday*, the Cold War is not being fought on an East-West axis. It is a Miltonian battle between the forces of good and the forces of evil— the forces of spirit and the forces of materialism—waged in the individual soul. The West is the author of materialism, both in the mechanics of its political economy, its technological civilization that has conquered the globe, and in the Enlightenment ideas that rationalize its materialist ethos. Karl Marx was nothing if not a nineteenth-century European, and communism, coming as it did out of Marxism, was a European ideology: "Communism is a way of thought and action, a way of reading history and its forces, which was developed in the culture capitals of the West," Chambers wrote at the beginning of *Cold Friday*.[23] Atheism paved the way to communism and to the creation of the Soviet Union, the first officially atheist state. The West itself had fostered "the climate of materialism which breeds revolutionists," even if, by the 1950s, the majority of revolutionists were to be found outside the culture capitals of the West.[24] Materialism is in fact a bridge between the communist East and the anti-communist West. The West preferred some mixture of socialism and capitalism to full-blown communism, but in its love affair with material abundance the West may be easing itself toward a communist future. Communism is the realization of the "materialist view of life," and in this regard the Soviet Union has an advantage over the West. Moscow can camouflage its materialism in the colorful dress of revolution, in a fighting faith for a better future. The West has made materialism an end unto itself, and, for this reason, Chambers believed the West would lose the Cold War. Societies dedicated to "the pursuit of abundance and comfort . . . soon cease to be societies. They become prey. They fall to whatever power can rally the starving spirit of man even though the rallying faith [i.e., communism] is demonstrably worse than the soft complacency that would suffocate the spirit in abundance."[25]

In *Cold Friday*, the tragedy of the Cold War is less the geopolitical weakness of the West than the steady encroachment of materialism in the East and the West. While converting to communism, Chambers had seen the West as a haunted house; a haunted house it remained, and Chambers did his best not to live in it. He had his farm, and his errand into the wilderness only confirmed that Western culture was sick, devoid of roots and of sustaining ties to nationhood. The long journey to anti-communist truth—a traumatic but open-ended journey in *Witness*—could well be futile. Such was the fate of the disillusioned communist who "does not return to the world because he believes that it is morally healthy or capable of solving the crisis which is in fact deeper than when he left it," Chambers wrote in *Cold Friday*. "He returns because he believes Communism is evil. The crisis remains and the world remains unable to solve it." Chambers could not adequately title the manuscript *The Third Rome* because Western civilization, moving from Rome to Constantinople, had reached its nadir in Stalinist Moscow. America might be the Cold War leader of the West, but it was no Rome. Chambers hated New York City— Henry Adams's Babylon—a crude, capitalist city that reflected no grand principle of civilization: "New York City I loathe with an unabatable loathing."[26] "New York, supposing itself the center of the universe, is actually the capital of the entertainment industry," Chambers wrote to de Toledano. There was no other capital city that could orient and refine the civilization of the West. With the future in peril, one could only look back on the past, to the cultural monuments that predated the West's twentieth-century twilight. A sad Chambers praised poems such as Matthew Arnold's "The Scholar Gypsy"—"one of the age's two great defeatist images," whose despairing music had so captivated Lionel Trilling in the 1930s.[27]

When *Cold Friday* was published in 1964, Herbert Solow contacted Lionel Trilling, a recognized authority on Matthew Arnold's sadness, about reviewing the book. Solow, Chambers, and Trilling had a long history together, beginning at Columbia, and to Trilling Solow described *Cold Friday* as "a posthumous book by Whit, more or less autobiographical bits and reflections thereon." Several times before, Trilling had unintentionally presented himself as an intellectual diplomat, able to navigate between respectable liberal opinion and the unruly world of conservative ideas. Duncan Norton-Taylor, editor of *Cold Friday* and a conservative, wanted Trilling to review the book for the preeminent journal of the American Left, the *New York Review of Books:* "Norton-Taylor is concerned," Solow wrote, "about the sort of review the book will get in the *New York Review of Books,* and while he realized that you may be as anti-metaphysical as I am (and he ain't), he'd be happy to think that you might be interested in reviewing the book. I said that you might be interested in reviewing the book. I said I'd not hesitate to suggest that you put in for it at the *NYRB.*" Tantalizing as the prospect of a Trilling review for *Cold Friday* was, it was not to be. Trilling politely and somewhat ambiguously refused the offer. "I'd like to do something about Whit's book [*Cold Friday*]—this is not just a way of speaking: I really would—but I'm afraid I can't," Trilling wrote to Solow in May 1964.[28] Trilling had a low opinion of Chambers's anti-communist writing, and he may not have wanted to denigrate Chambers in print. Nor was Trilling eager to have his name associated with conservatives such as Chambers. The sympathy Norton-Taylor assumed between Trilling and Chambers was a sympathy that Trilling wished to keep within certain borders.

Theirs was not a superficial sympathy, and it was more than biographical. Trilling and Chambers both approached the West as an object of almost spiritual veneration: as Chambers aspired to be, Trilling was, in the words of the historian Alexander Bloom, "a leading figure in the reassertion of the Western tradition and Western values."[29] A love of the West united Trilling's dissertation on Matthew Arnold, which encompassed nineteenth-century European culture as a whole, with his last book, *Sincerity and Authenticity*, a survey of a West rent asunder by competing cultural drives.[30] In an April 1960 letter to a professor at Cambridge University, Trilling issued a Chambers-esque statement about the West, expressed with donnish lightheartedness: "I *do* like the West," he wrote, "and wish it would stop declining."[31]

Similar to Chambers, Trilling saw the West as a spiritual entity in crisis. In June 1953 he published an essay "A Portrait of Western Man," in which his language was more psychosocial than religious: the problem of Western man was his divided self. This self had a history, as the modern self was created out of "a concern with the quality of being, with personality, [that] is the active, moving principle of life today, not merely in the West but all over the world." In Trilling's view, "the political and social unrest of the world today" followed from a hurried democratization of the spirit, "the enormous development of *Geist* [spirit], of personality, of self-consciousness, in places and among people and classes to which it had never before penetrated." The modern self is not seeking God. Its search is for "being, which is most simply conceived as status. Checked and thwarted, it shows itself as hate."[32] Modern literature, as Trilling understood it, testified to disgust with the modern self in all its bourgeois self-preoccupation and status seeking. Chambers worried about the West's lack of confidence; Trilling wrote about a West that was at war with itself. Chambers wrote about the soul without God; Trilling wrote about the psyche out of balance. Chambers sought spiritual health in the common man and in rural places; Trilling asked for spiritual guidance from the educated middle class, very often the middle class of New York City.

In 1948, four years before Chambers published *Witness*, *Partisan Review* printed Trilling's essay "Art and Fortune," an outburst of cultural pessimism about a shattered West. Trilling's concern throughout the essay is "the state of soul in which the novel becomes possible." The state of the West's soul is dire because the bourgeoisie had "ceased some time ago to be the chief source of political leaders; its nineteenth-century position as ideologue of the world had vanished before the ideological strength of totalitarian communism; the wars have brought it to the point of economic ruin." The novel is well suited to registering moral travesties, fostering the "representation, secular and not religious, of man's depravity and weakness." The twentieth century took travesty too far, however, for the novel to contend with the material of its moment. John Dos Passos had created the "camera eye" to document twentieth-century chaos and confusion, but his novelistic innovation—any novelistic innovation—is inadequate to an era of mass murder. "The simple eye of the camera shows us, at Belsen and Buchenwald," Trilling wrote in a rare reference to the Holocaust, "horrors that quite surpass Swift's powers, a vision of life turned back on its corrupted elements which is more disgusting than any Shakespeare could contrive, a cannibalism more literal and fantastic than that which Montaigne ascribed to organized society." No literary genius could take the moral measure of the Holocaust. No intellect can do so either: "before what we now know the mind stops; the great psychological fact of our time which we all obscured with baffled wonder and share is that there is no possible way of responding to Belsen and Buchenwald." A civilization that commits such crimes cannot undo them. The West is therefore lost in the context of its own history, which "may help to explain the general deterioration of our intellectual life."[33]

"Art and Fortune" was a study of the Western imagination devastated by its own environment. In negative it affirmed "the restoration and the reconstruction of the will." The immensity of the challenge lay in the fact that "the religious will, the political will, the artistic will—each is dying of its own excess." By restoration and reconstitution of the will Trilling meant a rebirth of culture, one that can take into account the horrors of fascism and communism without wallowing in self-pity, passivity, and the clichés of received wisdom. Trilling lamented "those desperate perceptions of our life which are current nowadays among thinking and talking people . . . They sink our spirits not merely because they are possible but because they have become so obvious and cliché that they seem to close for us the possibility of thought and imagination." Intellectuals and novelists have peered into the abyss only to grow fond of the abyss, together with their own horrified gaze. They try to "advance further and further into the darkness, seeing to it that the will finally exhausts and expands itself to the end that we purge our minds of the old ways of thought and feeling, giving up all hope of reconstituting the great former will of humanism." As an example, Trilling held up the French existentialist thinker Jean-Paul Sartre, who erred in his "banishment of the author from his books, the stilling of his voice, [which] have but reinforced the faceless hostility of the world and have tended to teach us that we ourselves are not creative agents and that we have no voice, no tone, no style, no significant existence." Instead of the death of the author, Trilling wrote, "what we need is the opposite of this, the opportunity to identify ourselves with a mind that willingly admits that it is a mind and does not pretend that it is History or Events of the World."[34] Trilling's essay could be read as an appeal for books such as *Witness*, for the personal testimony of those adrift in a century of disaster.

In a disastrous century, America might sponsor renewal, and Trilling's aim was to encourage a high culture in America that could offer moral guidance and criticism, polishing the ideas that inform a well-balanced polity. For the West to stop declining, it would have to reach a cultural and geopolitical balance. In the passage of political time between Eisenhower's election in 1952 and Kennedy's election in 1960, Trilling was cautiously optimistic about the achievement of this balance. The advance of liberal anti-communism, with an accompanying style of high culture, showed Trilling that the West could refresh itself after the cataclysms of the 1930s and 1940s. The lows that Stalin and Hitler had reached, dragging the West with them, were so low that the political trajectory could only be upward in the immediate postwar era. The university, the nerve center of civilization, could do much to reverse the West's decline, and rarely did a president admire universities as much as Kennedy did, a man who claimed citizenship in West Berlin as a gesture of Cold War defiance.

An alien to conservatism proper, Trilling entertained plans for America and the West that were often congenial to conservatives. In a 1951 *Atlantic Monthly* essay "The Moral Challenge of Communism," journalist Barbara Wood singled out Trilling for his efforts to revive a beleaguered Western civilization. The light of Western civilization began to fade in the 1920s, she believed, as the West's "faith in the franchise was shaken by the workers' hostility to the liberal state. Its universal education wasted itself in comics and yellow press and produced intellectuals and scientists to denounce the West as a bourgeois sham." Wood turned to Trilling for the right words, for an answer to the dilemma of the West. With approval, Wood wrote that "the artist can in the words of Lionel Trilling, give himself to 'the great work of our time,' which is 'the restoration and reconstitution of the will'—in other words, of the sense of freedom." The West was a sufficiently unspecific entity for Wood's quasireligious or quasi-Christian purposes. It did not matter whether its advocates were Jewish or Christian: advocacy itself was enough. "Faith will defeat no faith," and if Trilling never recommended faith as an anti-communist force, his name could be attached to a revitalization of Western culture without distorting his words or his intentions.[35] The renewal of the West was not necessarily a conservative aim in 1951, although Wood's language in "The Moral Challenge of Communism" was an implicitly conservative language, which Trilling had helped to shape.

Trilling was not wholly uninvolved in questions of faith. Trilling's West was secular, but it was not necessarily atheist. If Trilling could not publicly endorse faith, neither could he privately reject it. In public, he might circle around the question of faith. "There is always enough truth in the idea that disaster follows upon the excess of humanistic pride to make us listen when the social philosophers of orthodox Christianity tell us so," Trilling wrote in a 1949 book review of *Religious Trends in English Poetry*, in which he extolled the benefits of Christian faith. He posed the conflict between secular humanism and orthodox Christianity in terms that were blandly polite: "Professor [Hoxie Neale] Fairchild's attack upon modern humanism is a remarkable piece of writing which, however mistaken in its premises, raises passionately and brilliantly the questions which every serious modern man must confront." Trilling the modern man kept his confrontation with faith private. As his friend, the poet Irving Feldman, wrote to Trilling in 1965, "I can see why you were struck by my chance remark at our last lunch that the limitation of criticism is that it can't be religious." Trilling agreed that criticism could not be religious, and he did so with regret. In an undated letter to Feldman, Trilling vented his frustration with the secular imperatives of his profession and of his own character. He wrote of his new book—presumably his 1965 essay collection, *Beyond Culture*—and "the hole it leaves unfulfilled." The hole was religion: "the concluding sentence had to be 'Come now, let us talk together like serious religious men.' But this I could not say. There isn't any conceivable actual religious formulation I can give credence to." The letter is remarkable in the longing for religion it expresses. "I don't have the power to propose—and probably fully to conceive—the secular attitudes that are proximate to the religious position and that might suit me almost as well. At least not, as you say, in criticism. But it will please you to know that I mean to begin a new novel in a few months. It has at least death, and fathers."[36]

Trilling's mournful incapacity for religion was also his alienation from Judaism, to which he could give no meaningful assent. Trilling's entry into the culture of the West was, at its core, a departure from Judaism, a subject scattered throughout his private correspondence. In 1959, Trilling wrote to Rabbi Isador Hoffman to explain his refusal to speak at Columbia's Menorah Society: "I should like to urge you to believe that it is my respect for the Jewish tradition that has dictated my refusal of your invitations. I am not learned in that tradition and there is nothing I might say about it that would conceivably be worth hearing. My own relation to it is private and personal and not susceptible of discussion on a public occasion." In a 1964 letter, Trilling observed that "I found myself wanting to say kaddish" after his mother's death. A few days later, Trilling wrote about his mother's funeral, performed by Max Kadushin, who "did the service in the old orthodox way, which has considerable reality in it and which I have always thought necessary as against the genteel emphasis of the modern Jewish fashion."[37] Trilling harbored no Freudian hatred of religion: "I don't have his [Freud's] conscious hostility to religion—quite the contrary, I should say," Trilling wrote in 1961 to Ursula Niebuhr, who had asked him to speak at Barnard College on religion. Instead of hostility Trilling had ambivalence: "whenever I try to carry my animal feelings up the intellectual path, I reach a point from which I am driven back. And yet whenever I turn to think about the matter that your course addresses itself to, I find that the concepts (and even the language) of religion force themselves upon me." As with Irving Feldman, Trilling suggested to Niebuhr that his intellectual work followed indirectly from his "animal feelings," which were religious: "because I stand in so unremittingly ambivalent relation to those concepts (and even this language), I have always avoided making statements about 'meaning,' and 'meaning to life,' even approximate or tentative ones, although I must suppose that my involvement with the question shows through what I write."[38] Trilling was a case study in the opposing self.[39]

Conservatives who saw only the conservative side of Trilling's opposing self had a hard time collaborating with him. Or he had a hard time collaborating with them. Russell Kirk believed that Trilling could open his mind to conservatism only when conservatism was as marginal as it appeared to be in 1950. In the preface to *The Liberal Imagination*, Trilling wondered whether there was such a thing as intellectual conservatism. In 1953, after Kirk published *The Conservative Mind,* conservative intellect was robust enough to threaten Trilling, at least in Kirk's opinion. According to Kirk, *The Conservative Mind* was "a rock tossed into the stagnant pond of American intellectualism, [which] made waves not to Trilling's liking." Kirk saw Trilling retreating into his liberalism after 1953, a wholly untrustworthy ally for anyone on the Right:

> In *The Liberal Imagination,* he [Trilling] had suggested that a renewal of the conservative imagination might healthily stimulate the decayed liberal imagination . . . But after the publication of *The Conservative Mind* and its friendly reception, Trilling no longer professed to welcome a conservative challenge; he even deleted a commendatory reference to Burke that had appeared in the first printing of the book. The liberal trumpet had blown; the challenged had appeared, surprisingly; the liberal sword stuck in its scabbard.[40]

Peter Viereck was one of several conservatives who failed to forge an alliance with Trilling. A moderate conservative, Viereck was upset with the fashionable orthodoxies he perceived among liberals; he saw a kindred spirit in Trilling. In June 1950 Viereck sent Trilling an essay he had published in the *Harvard Alumni Bulletin* titled "Babbit Revisited." On it he appended a note to Trilling: "For Lionel Trilling, with the very highest admiration for your non-'Gaylord' brand of uncorrupted liberalism and integrity, respectfully, P. Viereck."[41] The essay was an ironic reinterpretation of Babbitry. Whereas the vulgar middle class of the 1920s was drawn to country-club, small-businessman conservatism, epitomized in the character of George Babbit in Sinclair Lewis' 1922 novel, *Babbit,* Babbit Jr. was by 1950 "always so liberal and avant-garde." Viereck argued that "leftism and the cult of revolt claims for itself the virtue of freshness and independence; instead, it has its own jargon and old-fogy dogmatisms without ever admitting it." This was the loose paraphrase of a sentiment that had informed many of Trilling's essays. Viereck isolated a conservative strain of Western culture—"the accumulated habits of restraint"—for only "this moral heritage of the West can halt Stalinist fascism and can prevent the revival of that Hitlerite fascism against which our generation fought in World War II."[42] Viereck's overture elicited little approval from Trilling. Perhaps Trilling was irritated to see his ideas so lavishly praised—and reiterated—by someone who was not a self-proclaimed liberal. Perhaps Trilling did not especially like Viereck. In 1953 Trilling wrote (in private correspondence) that Viereck is "generally on the right side of things and I like him, though I should not like to have to be in his company for long."[43]

American politics violated the "accumulated habits of restraint" only a few years after World War II, with the campaign to eradicate communism led by Senator McCarthy, a hard-line anti-communist but a questionable conservative. One reason why McCarthy had so little appeal to either Trilling or Chambers, despite their intense anti-communism, was that McCarthy did not reflect the ideals of Western culture or simply of culture in general, as these two Columbia alumni understood them.[44] In his own eyes, McCarthy may have been defending the West from communism, but this ill-educated, provincial man, who spent his evenings carousing and playing poker, had no intellectual commitment to an anti-communist West.[45] His cultural commitment to anti-communism ran through the Catholic Church, no small matter in McCarthy's biography or political career, although a circumstance of greater interest to the Catholic Buckley—who was friends with McCarthy—than to either Trilling or Chambers. At best, McCarthy's thuggish qualities were necessary for suppressing a thuggish movement built on espionage and the allure of revolutionary violence: unlike John F. Kennedy, however, McCarthy was not a Catholic anti-communist with much appeal to intellectuals. McCarthy was at war with the Eastern establishment; he often targeted intellectuals in his investigations. T. S. Eliot refused to write for *National Review* because of the magazine's support for McCarthy.[46]

Trilling was of two minds about McCarthyism. He deplored McCarthy and McCarthyism, but he also responded critically to the anti-McCarthy zeal of fellow liberals. Trilling sought a balance between McCarthy's reckless anti-communism and the self-righteousness of anti-McCarthy liberals, who, Trilling felt, derided McCarthy and applauded themselves for a sudden amnesia. McCarthy's misdeeds encouraged liberals to forget their past infatuation with Soviet communism, and Trilling's response to McCarthy was not notably different from Chambers's, with the important qualification that Trilling cared about McCarthy as a threat to liberal anti-communism, while Chambers cared about him as a threat to conservative anti-communism. For both Trilling and Chambers, McCarthy retarded the evolution of a mature anti-communism in America. In 1953 Chambers published a piece in *Life* magazine titled "Is Academic Freedom in Danger?"—a subtle critique of McCarthy as well as an attack on liberals. In criticizing McCarthy, Chambers upheld a distinction that he himself had blurred in *Witness* and elsewhere, the distinction between liberals and communists: "liberals are not Communists, and a mind would have to be grossly undiscriminating, or inflamed by a passion for absurdity, if it supposed that they were."[47] Nor was academic freedom, which McCarthy clearly imperiled, a small-minded concern. Chambers listed academic freedom as a reason to fight the Cold War: "those thousands quietly watching the congressional hearings by their TV screens . . . [care most about their] sons [who] have gone directly from college into the armed services . . . to fight a war against Communism in the name of freedom, which also includes academic freedom."[48] The subtitle to Buckley's *God and Man at Yale* was *The Superstitions of Academic Freedom*. Buckley argued that the university should forego academic freedom and actively instruct students in the excellence of Christianity and capitalism. In his attachment to academic freedom, Chambers stood closer to the liberal Lionel Trilling.

Whatever liberal flourishes Chambers allowed himself as a conservative, he had no sympathy for McCarthy's liberal critics. In the cries of witch hunt Chambers heard "the voices of liberal neurosis." Liberals minimize the difference between themselves and the communists by their identification with the communist victims of McCarthy: "at every move against Communism, liberal nerves still come unglued, and liberal voices go shrill, fearing that, by design or error, the move may be against themselves." Worst of all, liberals exploit McCarthy's demagogic persona to hone the myth—or, rather, the lie—of their own innocence. The liberals called to testify were not innocent, Chambers believed, with "no connection with the matters under scrutiny," with "no contribution whatever to make to the record while his presence [at HUAC hearings] was a gratuitous inconvenience and humiliation to him."[49] The liberal who hated HUAC most likely also hated Chambers.[50] While openly condemning McCarthy and McCarthyism, Trilling shared in Chambers's critique of anti-McCarthyite liberals. Trilling preferred self-criticism to self-praise and was acutely sensitive to the appearance of orthodoxy among liberals. In December 1952, Trilling wrote to *New Republic* editor Michael Straight, turning down Straight's offer to participate in a tribute to Adlai

Stevenson. Trilling was uncomfortable with the elevation of Stevenson to the status of hero or, after his loss to Eisenhower in 1952, the status of martyr. Trilling liked Stevenson and was glad to vote for him, but he believed that liberals, in idolizing their leader, were in fact idolizing themselves. "I don't want to reduce my politics to this sort of personal congratulation," Trilling wrote, "especially because I have the unhappy feeling that it may deteriorate, as we liberals reiterate it, into a form of *self*-congratulation."[51] The liberal response to McCarthy dismayed Trilling for exactly this reason. Taking the rejection of McCarthy for granted, Trilling deplored the movement from easy rejection to self-congratulation among McCarthy's enemies, who were evading self-criticism. Liberal self-deception had its share in the creation of McCarthyism, and the McCarthyite thesis about American politics, when stripped of its demagogic distortions, was not entirely false.[52] Instead of helping liberals clarify the border between a responsible and an irresponsible anti-communism, McCarthy was dulling liberals to their checkered political past.

Thinking back on the McCarthyite period of the early 1950s, Trilling later equated it with the decline of liberal anti-communism in the intellectual community. In 1967 Trilling argued that "the position of liberal anti-communism, as I understand it, has never been influential, quite the reverse; at least in the section of the country that I inhabit, the climate of opinion has been created by people whose winds of doctrine, or sensibility, blow in the other direction," distinguishing between himself and the typical liberal academic or typical New York liberal. Conventional political wisdom opposed those who "had an adverse opinion of [Owen] Lattimore's conduct—as I did," Trilling wrote in a 1957 essay. McCarthy managed to make communism respectable once again for liberals, whom Trilling described as "not unwilling to take the view that Communism was in essence an intellectual position like another and that there was in it no taint of conspiracy." Liberals cherished the idea of Hiss's innocence, while Trilling was convinced of his guilt. Pro-Hiss liberals were the proponents of a "false position [that] found its simple and glib formulation in the phrase 'anti-anti-communism.' It was proudly enunciated by a good many liberals," Trilling wrote in 1957, "and it had the effect of bringing to an end all thought about the actuality of Communism and of making intellectually unrespectable any really adverse attitude to Communists." It was as if liberals were waiting to unlearn the anti-radical lessons forced on them in the 1930s. Disgust with McCarthy's abuse of power thus legitimated a return to innocence and immaturity. An anti–anti-communist consensus confirmed "the supposition [of the liberal American public] that there is a kind of essential intellectual virtue in expressing 'permissible' judgments on certain subjects, no matter how inadequate to the facts these judgments may be."[53]

In the years between 1950 and 1954, Trilling put his unease with liberal anti-McCarthyism in writing. In 1951, Trilling criticized the defensive mood among liberals, the self-deceiving and ugly pleasures of anti–anti-communism. In a tone of disappointment, Trilling wrote that many educated Americans "are likely to believe that the essence of all liberalism is what has come to be called 'anti-anti-Communism.'" Liberals decry McCarthy's assault on civil liberties and assume that communists would put their civil liberties only to decent use. Even worse, they consider communists a chimera, a figment of the paranoid reactionary imagination, unable to admit "that some people actually are Communists and that, although some of these may be misguided and 'gentle,' some are malign and all are under the direction of a malign power which has a principled hostility to liberty."[54] The issue, for Trilling, was never the merits of McCarthy as an enemy of the Soviet Union, that "malign power." It was the quality of liberal judgment where communism was concerned. Tellingly, Trilling threw his energy into the education of liberals and not into public protest of McCarthyism. Either Trilling felt that the battle for liberal anti-communism was more important or that it was the battle he was best equipped to fight. (He was also a liberal with a communist past, a fellow traveler whom Chambers had asked to assist in Soviet espionage.) Trilling's fight with liberals had an analogue in Chambers's fight with pro-McCarthy conservatives. Conservatives needed to defy McCarthy and impress the need for a responsible anti-communism on the nation, Chambers believed. He was convinced that liberals could not do this job. When Trilling tried to enlist liberals in the practice of an engaged anti-communism, he was frustrated by their resistance.

Trilling's encounter with McCarthyism was not just theoretical. In April 1953, Gene Weltfish, an anthropologist at Columbia, took the Fifth Amendment before a congressional committee. She had publicly accused the United States of using chemical weapons in Korea, drawing attention to herself as a critic of the Cold War. Grayson Kirk, Columbia's president, effectively engineered her departure. In response to McCarthyism on campus, Columbia created a committee on communism in academic life, which Trilling chaired.[55] Trilling tried and failed to strike a balance. He wanted to condemn McCarthy's tactics without overlooking the possibility that there might be communists in academia and that some or all of them had no right to teach. In November 1953, Trilling and the committee worked on a statement about McCarthyism, part of which was a condemnation of the entire McCarthyite approach.[56] Another part of the statement was the recognition that communists might indeed exist; if so, they could and should be investigated. When a *New York Times* article reported only on the anti-McCarthy part of the statement, Trilling was outraged. "Had the statement been truly represented by the *Times* story, I should have voted against it," Trilling wrote in a private letter on November 23, 1953. The next day, Trilling wrote to the editors of the *New York Times*, clarifying the intentions behind the committee statement, which he felt had been misrepresented by the *Times* article. The statement was meant to suggest that "a refusal to testify [before HUAC] must not be automatically condemned but also that a refusal to testify must not be automatically condoned." The authors of the statement had not accepted the right of communists to teach at Columbia: "in the same way, were the question a real one, we should not be concerned to affirm the right of fascists to teach." Subservience to the Communist Party was incompatible with the intellectual freedom of the academic vocation: "membership in the Communist organizations almost certainly implies a submission to an intellectual control which is entirely at variance with the principles of academic competence as we understand them."[57]

In the fight against McCarthyism, Trilling grew estranged from his natural allies, from fellow liberals. In December 1953, Trilling wrote about the myopia of liberals who indulged their loathing of McCarthy, reducing the problem of communism and anti-communist to the condemnation of the Wisconsin senator. Liberals zealously opposed to McCarthy imply "that there cannot possibly be a security problem, that everyone who claims the privileges of the First Amendment is innocent and a hero, that Hiss is an innocent martyr and [Owen] Lattimore a disinterested scholar, etc. This is the tendency of most liberals in the academic life and it seems to me to be very dangerous—it does just what McCarthy hopes for." Another irritant for Trilling was the response to his anti–anti-McCarthyism. Not only did Trilling fail to persuade liberals to be stalwart liberal anti-communists, he also convinced them that his own liberal credentials were suspect.

Trilling's forceful anti-communism placed him to the Right of the liberal mainstream and—to Trilling's chagrin—he was faced with the charge of being a conservative. An opponent of Hiss might well be a friend of Chambers's. "I think I shall not soon forget the animosity that was directed towards me last spring by many of my liberal colleagues who were quite sure that my opposition to the A.A.U.P. statement was the sign of my black reactionary impulses," Trilling wrote.[58]

Trilling's black reactionary impulses were becoming a subject of concern in the 1950s. When Trilling wrote in the first person plural, as he often did, the "we" he employed was the voice of educated American liberalism.[59] Yet he was not—like the historian Arthur Schlesinger Jr., for example—to the manor of the Democratic Party born. Trilling had arrived at liberalism and the Democratic Party from Marxism and communism, even if he had been moderate or a-political back in the 1920s. Having moved to the Right between 1935 and 1952, Trilling left a number of questions unresolved. Where did his shift to the Right end? Where might it end in the future? Why did he show resistance to progressive or radical ideas and sympathy to conservative ideas?[60] Why did Trilling dress and behave like a bourgeois, when the splendors of bohemian New York were only a few subway stops away from his uptown office and home? Why did his writing refer to nineteenth-century traditions, limiting the space available for new beginnings and avant-garde explorations? The very surface of Trilling's liberalism was genteel, mannered, and cool, a liberalism of balance, large and imaginative enough, ideally, to absorb the best of the Left and the Right. One could ask, however, whether this dialectical liberalism was an elaborate subterfuge. Did Trilling's re-radicalized and later antiradical essays constitute a veiled conservatism? Was the reconstitution of the West a conservative endeavor?

Conservative ideas are everywhere in evidence in *The Opposing Self*, Trilling's 1955 book composed of nine essays in literary criticism, with subjects ranging from George Orwell's politics to Jane Austen's novels to the poetry of John Keats. Of the nine authors discussed, five were British, two American, one French, and one Russian: Western culture was, for Trilling, a large tapestry. *The Opposing Self* is the sequel to *The Liberal Imagination*, not to *Matthew Arnold*. It is a book without footnotes or any visible scholarly apparatus, written for a highly educated reader but not at all limited to academics. *The Opposing Self* carried forward the agenda of *The Liberal Imagination*, reworking it into something less overtly anti-communist. The liberal imagination had been freed from the lies of Stalinism, but maturity was still elusive. Horror had inundated Western culture in the 1930s and 1940s—*gulags*, concentration camps, total war, atomic weaponry—leaving the West in disarray. Trilling sought evidence of the imagination at work in *The Opposing Self* and of the West put back together again.[61] Placed in its immediate political context, *The Opposing Self* could be read as a commentary on liberalism from the 1930s to the 1950s. The radical excesses of the 1930s had led to the conservative excesses of the 1950s. Only an agile, intelligent, self-doubting yet self-confident liberalism could navigate such dangerous political shoals, managing to be critical of McCarthy and Stalin and arising out of a healthy self-criticism, not from the authorless, defeatist existentialism of a Jean-Paul Sartre. To achieve health, the liberal imagination demanded the right kind of internal opposition.

In *The Opposing Self*, the path to wisdom leads through conservative self-questioning, preferably in the realm of literature, the school of the political imagination. Conservatives might rely on scripture for doctrine, traveling the straight lines of their faith: liberals, who live on the edge of secularism, need literature, not for a "yes" or "no" to political questions but to study the interplay of character, choice, and fate. The self Trilling had in mind in *The Opposing Self* was modern—emerging, he believed, in the late eighteenth century—and it was defined by its "intense and adverse imagination of the culture in which it has its being." In the preface, Trilling describes the Arnoldian sadness of the modern self, which he contrasts with "the modern imagination of autonomy and delight, of surprise and elevation, of selves conceived in opposition to the general culture. This imagination makes, I believe, a new idea in the world," one that is ebullient and melancholy.[62] *The Opposing Self* is gently pedagogic, emphasizing the modern possibilities of autonomy and delight rather than the modern reality of despair. The conflict between delight and despair is democratic in its oppositions, and the modern culture it affirms is not a catastrophe, as Chambers supposed: Western culture has within it the means of health, if not of progress. It is both better than the culture of communism and capable of excellence in its own right. In *The Opposing Self*, Trilling celebrated health and the Western culture heroes who can bring "us" health.

The jewel of *The Opposing Self*, emphatically the first essay in the book, is "The Poet as Hero: Keats in His Letters." It is a joyous evaluation of Keats's poetry, Keats's love of life, of Keats as "the last image of health at the very moment when the sickness of Europe began to be apparent." As he would throughout *The Opposing Self*, Trilling prefaces sentences with "nowadays," reinforcing the distance between "us," his liberal middle-class educated readers, and the literary figure at hand. "We" play a considerable role in "The Poet as Hero," and Trilling, as usual, is the Vergil leading us back into the past, the knower of us, one of us, who also knows "them," our cultural ancestors. If Keats is the last healthy man in Western history, then we are sick: "we cannot respond to the justification of life by the heroic definition of self." We even seem to celebrate sickness: "nowadays our theory of poetic creation holds that the poet derives his power from some mutilation he has suffered. We take it for granted that he writes out of a darkness of the spirit or not at all." Keats is recognizably our ancestor because of his opposition to culture and society. "We are all naturally not satisfied by the society around us. It never really lends itself to our purposes and expectations. Of Keats this was especially true," Trilling writes. This drove Keats to write about evil, to ponder negation, and in this he showed his premodern heroism: "he was sure that negation was not of his essence, and that it must pass for him to be himself again." Heroism is not made from negation; it is made from confronting negation. One senses something of Trilling's ideal (for us) in the following sentence: "He [Keats] believed that life was given for him to find the right use of it, that it was a kind of continuous magical confrontation requiring to be met with the right answer."[63]

As Trilling portrays him, Keats derives his health from religion and translates it into the secular language of culture. Trilling makes frequent reference to the Book of Job and the Book of Genesis in his essay on Keats. In the nineteenth century, "when religion seemed to be no longer able to represent the actualities of life," the problem of evil confronted Keats "in the theological or quasi-theological form in which alone it has any meaning." A sensitivity to evil made Keats into a liberal rather like Reinhold Niebuhr, a liberal anti-communist before his time, as "for all his stubborn partisanship with social amelioration, he had no hope whatever that life could be ordered in such a way that its condition might be anything but tragic." Without the aid of religion, Keats has succeeded in "his heroic attempt to show how it is that life may be called blessed when its circumstances are cursed." The result is a theology beyond theology, since Keats "writes with an animus against Christian doctrine, but what he is giving, he says, is a sketch of *salvation*."[64] In his balancing act, Keats is both close to us and far away: "the spiritual and moral health of which he seems the image we cannot now attain by wishing for it. But we can attain it by not wishing for it, and clearly imagining it. 'The imagination may be compared to Adam's dream—he awoke and found it truth.' " With Keats, the opposing self is the model self.[65] The essays that follow "The Poet as Hero" are beads on a Keatsian necklace and *The Opposing Self* in its entirety is a tribute to the balancing power of culture. Communism is the object of rejection, liberalism the object of desire, and conservatism the attitude or tradition that smoothes the oscillation.

In "George Orwell and the Politics of Truth," Trilling roots the opposing self in the rocky soil of recent history. Orwell is virtuous for his honesty, which exceeds his anti-communism, "the personal confession of involvement and then disillusionment with Communism," an honesty that resides in his commitment to Victorian middle-class values, a commitment so expansive that "it shocks and dismays us when Orwell speaks in praise of such things as responsibility, and orderliness in the personal life, and fair play, and physical courage—even of snobbery and hypocrisy because they sometimes help to shore up the crumbling ramparts of the moral life." Trilling makes it clear that with Orwell conservatism is at issue: Orwell's "feeling for the land and the past simply seemed to give his radicalism a conservative—a conserving—cast, which is in itself attractive, and to protect his politics from the ravages of ideology." The conservative radical is superior to the radical, whose radicalism is unexamined, who could bury the murderous truths of Stalinism in a haze of self-congratulatory abstraction. "The gist of Orwell's criticism of the liberal intelligentsia was that they refused to understand the conditioned nature of life," conditioned by biology and other limitations. By contrast, the 1930s intelligentsia "who now, in their love of abstractions . . . could not conceive of directing upon Russia anything like the stringency of criticism they used upon their own nation." Orwell's contribution to the literature of anti-communist witness is one of truth resonant with "personal fact," which can be conservative fact, and personal fact is the ultimate enemy of totalitarianism.[66]

In "William Dean Howells and the Roots of Modern Taste," Trilling broadened the personal fact to the facts of family, class, and society, contrasting a quotidian conservatism to the unconditioned spirit so congenial to modern taste. Recent history—the Holocaust above all—has imbued modern taste with extremism. We, the carriers of modern taste, "are all aware of evil; we began to be aware of it in certain quasi-religious senses a couple of decades or so ago; and as time passed we learned a great deal about the physical, political actuality of evil, saw it expressed in the political life in a kind of gratuitous devilishness which has always been in the world but which never before in Western Europe had been organized and, as it were, rationalized." The organization and rationalization of evil has precipitated "our revived religious feelings or nostalgia for religious feelings," which are, in turn, connected to our respect for writers, such as Kafka, who appear to command the subject of evil. Perversely, "evil has for us its own *charisma*." The danger is not an outright attraction to evil but alienation from the civic, from the small personal facts that make up normal, conditioned, real life when "the extreme has become the commonplace of our day." Evil in all its fascinating extremity has a reality above other realities, leading Trilling to pose "the question of why we believe, as we do believe, that evil is the very essence of reality." Consequently, "the very word *civil*, except as applied to disobedience and disorders, is unknowable in our ears." By contrast, the modest pleasures, quotidian quests, and commonplace status questions that permeate Howell's fiction "will at least serve, in Keats's phrase, to bind us to the earth, to prevent our being seduced by the godhead of disintegration."[67]

Trilling's critique of the modern in "William Dean Howells and the Origins of Modern Taste" begins with taste and ends with politics. The dilemma of the modern "we" verges on self-hatred: "we are little satisfied with the idea of family life—for us it is part of the inadequate bourgeois reality." The bourgeoisie, who had once championed the family and promoted the civic dimension in culture, had lost faith in its own core convictions, such that the horrors of modern literature, elevated by modern taste, are strangely reassuring. Thus, "when conditions become extreme enough there is sometimes a sense of deep relief, as if the conditioned had now been left quite behind, as if spirit were freed when the confining comforts and the oppressive assurances of civil life are destroyed." This hallowed sense of alienation is, if taken seriously, an alienation from the civic and therefore from politics per se. Modern literature provides little inspiration for liberal anti-communism, which is a civic initiative, and provides no inspiration for liberalism or democracy, which rely on civic action. The cultural sway of modern taste illustrates "our growing disenchantment with the whole idea of political life . . . we do not consent to live in a particular society of the preset, marked as it is bound to be by a particular economic system, by disorderly struggles for influence, by mere approximations and downright failures." A robustly anti-communist culture would honor the conditions of liberal democracy, and the right high culture could educate liberalism in "the knowledge of the antagonism between spirit and the conditioned—it is Donne's, it is Pascal's, it is Tolstoi's—[which] may in literature be a cause of great delight because it is so rare and difficult; beside it the knowledge of pure spirit is comparatively easy."[68]

In "The Bostonians," an essay on the Henry James novel, *The Bostonians*, Trilling pegs the dangerous modern hunger for unconditioned freedom, not on communism, but on feminism. Trilling presents James as an ideological writer in that "virtually all his fiction represents the conflict of two principles, of which one is radical, the other conservative." In James' novel, the radical element is feminism and the conservative a Southern traditionalism. Trilling's context for the novel is anything but neutral. He characterizes "the movement for female equality which became endemic in America and in the Protestant countries of Europe in the nineteenth century [and] was predominantly social and legal in its program and even had—although not always—an outright anti-erotic bias which exposed it to the imputation of mawkishness and morbidity." In James's purview, feminism is unnatural, as are the implications of its theories, "the sign of a general diversion of the culture from the course of nature." The feminists in *The Bostonians* are in conflict with a Southern gentleman, as if James were anticipating the conflict between a liberal or radical northeast and the southern agrarian intellectuals of the 1930s and 1940s, "the group of gifted men who, a half-century later [after James wrote *The Bostonians*] were to rise in the South and to muster in its defense whatever force may be available to an intelligent romantic conservatism." What many twentieth-century men fear, not just the southern agrarians, is "the loss of manhood, which we are familiar with in Yeats, in Lawrence, in *The Waste Land*." This fear "is given reason for its existence everywhere in *The Bostonians*," carried by James toward misogyny in his "rather unpleasant sense of the threatening sordidness of almost all women except those in their first youth."[69]

The Bostonians is, therefore, a cautionary tale, "the story of the parental house divided against itself, of the keystone falling from the arch, of the sacred mothers refusing their commission and the sacred fathers endangered."[70] Modern taste may be feminist or communist: at the heart of feminism and communism, and of much modern literature, is a repudiation of the middle-class family in its nineteenth-century form.[71]

The other great modern repudiation concerns religion. It was to this repudiation that Trilling addressed his bizarre essay, "Wordsworth and the Rabbis," an amalgam of autobiography, cultural criticism, and literary analysis.[72] By placing Wordsworth next to the Rabbis in the title of his essay, Trilling brought the essay's Jewish connotations into full view. It was as if Trilling wished to write about a Jewish subject and happened to find the opportunity with Wordsworth.[73] The willed rabbinic comparison in "Wordsworth and the Rabbis" runs against the grain of Trilling's intellectual career as a whole, which he dedicated to either the culture of the Christian West or the culture of the secular West. In honor of his Jewish subject in "Wordsworth and the Rabbis," Trilling stepped out from behind the "we" of his narrative voice, emerging as a Jewish "I," whose Jewish education it was that suggested the parallel between Wordsworth and the Rabbis. Wordsworth's Judaic quality is Trilling's Judaic quality—their shared isolation from the modern. While describing his Jewish education, Trilling mentions a specific text, the *Pirke Aboth*, a compendium of sayings from the second-century fathers and a gathering of rabbinic wisdom. It was a significant part of Trilling's education: "my intimacy with the *Pirke Aboth* comes from my having read it many times in boyhood," which may explain why "my early illicit intimacy with them [the Rabbis] had had its part in preparing the way for my responsiveness to Wordsworth, that between the Rabbis and Wordsworth an affinity existed."[74]

Wordsworth shares with the Rabbis a kind of moral calm, which is both premodern and outside the mainstream of Western culture. The mainstream of Western culture is aggressive and confrontational, animated by "the predilection for the powerful, the fierce, the assertive, the personally militant." It flourished in the 1930s, one gathers, for one finds this predilection "in the liberal-bourgeois admiration for the novels of Thomas Wolfe and Theodore Dreiser. On a lower intellectual level we find it in the long popularity of that curious underground work [Ayn Rand's] *The Fountainhead*. On a higher intellectual level we find it in certain aspects of Yeats and Lawrence."[75] Having demonstrated our distance from Wordsworth, Trilling concludes the essay by showing how close we can still be to Wordsworth and the Rabbis. We know horrors that Wordsworth did not know: "we really know in our times what the death of the word can be—for that knowledge we have only to read an account of contemporary Russian literature. We really know what the death of the spirit means—for we have seen it overtake whole peoples." The horrors of modern history have deprived us of "the 'beatitude' which Wordsworth thought was the birthright of every human soul," but good literature cannot do without this beatitude, without the actualities of common life and family life. The healthy quietism of Wordsworth and the Rabbis is there to be discovered in modern literature, in Leopold Bloom, the Jewish protagonist of Joyce's *Ulysses*, who is rabbinic: "if we speak of Wordsworth in reference to the Rabbis and their non-militancy, their indifference to the idea of evil, their acceptance of cosmic contradiction, are we not to say that [Leopold] Bloom is a Rabbinical character?"[76]

Cosmic contradiction echoes the motif of the opposing self; the opposing self must live amidst cosmic contradiction. The phrase, "opposing self," has various meanings in *The Opposing Self*. It can mean a self out of order and out of harmony. Or the opposing self can refer to something more desirable, the lyric self of John Keats, for example, who drew poetry from the "negative capability" of his sensual self in conflict with evil. In "Wordsworth and the Rabbis," the opposing self can be taken to mean modern culture as a whole, which may be closer to sickness but still has the resources of health. These resources are bound up with the God-loving quietism of Wordsworth *and* the Rabbis, representatives of health at a cultural moment when unbalanced extremes are in vogue. Hence, "in our literature, at its most apocalyptic and intense, we find the impulse to create figures who are intended to suggest that life is justified in its elemental biological simplicity." Having praised the affirmative powers of Wordsworth and the Rabbis, Trilling concludes, paradoxically perhaps, with an affirmation of modern culture, a medium for "the will seeking its own negation—or, rather, seeking its own affirmation by its rejection of the aims which the world sets before it and by turning its energies upon itself in self-realization."[77] In the preface to *The Opposing Self*, Trilling wrote, with the Bastille in mind, that "the modern self . . . was born in a prison."[78] If the oppositions of the modern self are correctly balanced, the body of the book implies, it might be freed from physical and mental imprisonment, moving closer to the promised land of self-realization. Bastilles could be built up and torn down; the actual Bastille had been stormed.

Literary critic Joseph Frank did not see anything of the French Revolution in *The Opposing Self*. He was startled by its subtle conservatism. In

"Lionel Trilling and the Conservative Imagination," Frank characterized American conservatism circa 1956 as withdrawal, a stepping back from action—the literal opposite of 1930s communism, which sought to make the world anew through revolution. In Frank's essay, conservatism flowed from the deradicalization that had come to characterize Trilling's generation: "the pervasive disillusionment with politics was given its most sensitive, subtle and judiciously circumspect expression in the criticism of Lionel Trilling—and this is the real answer to the anomaly of his success." Conservatism is a-political, and Trilling's conservatism amounts to "a rejection of the political imagination as a whole." Frank was especially struck by Trilling's essay on Howells, reading it as an affront to the Left and a negation of the radical will, which "finds itself enjoined to treat the most casual conventions of the family life of the middle class as the sacrosanct conditions of life itself."[79] Frank's image of conservatism was not of a movement or a body of ideas, fused or otherwise. It was the intellectual equivalent of the Eisenhower administration, a conservatism of accommodation and stasis. Frank pictured conservatism as the absence of radicalism, and by this criterion Trilling was indeed writing and thinking as a conservative.

According to Frank, Trilling's path to conservatism led through the seminal writings of Sigmund Freud, with whom Trilling's name was often linked in the 1950s. *The Opposing Self* betrayed a Trilling who "now feels that his urgent task is to defend not freedom but the virtues of acknowledging necessity." Necessity, for the avid reader of Freud, might well lie in nature, in the conditions of biology, from which there is no escape. Frank's essay had its own psychological bent, shrewdly analyzing Trilling's anger at being read as a conservative thinker. "One suspects that Freud's sympathy for socialism," Frank writes, "his battle against sexual obscurantism, and his general aura of radicalism, may well have enabled Mr. Trilling to adopt an essentially conservative position under Freud's aegis without feeling it as self-betrayal."[80] Frank charted the distance Trilling had traveled from political radicalism, his dramatic transformation "from a critic of the liberal imagination . . . into one of the least belligerent and most persuasive spokesman of the conservative imagination." Trilling was a spokesman for the conservative imagination in *The Opposing Self*, not a spokesman for conservatism, and his use of the conservative imagination stemmed from his cherished ambitions for American liberals. In Trilling's hands, the conservative imagination was a means not an end. The end was, as the book's title indicated, the opposing self, which would only be a better liberal self.

Frank's essay was more provocative than accurate. However conservative his imagination, Trilling penned no words of praise for conservative causes and offered no encouragement to the Republican Party. He showed no interest in the conservative subculture of the 1950s and wrote no religious polemics in the style of a T. S. Eliot. Trilling believed that liberalism was only first rate when it contained progressive and conservative ideas, while retaining its ability to function, and he maintained a scrupulous distance from the conservative intellectual movement. The publication date for *The Opposing Self* coincided with the founding of *National Review*, and there was, by 1955, a small shelf of conservative books with which any intellectual conservative (in America) was in dialogue: Buckley's *God and Man at Yale*, Chambers's *Witness*, and Kirk's *The Conservative Mind*. Trilling read and disliked *Witness*. If he read *God and Man at Yale* and *The Conservative Mind*, he devoted no attention to them in his published writing or private correspondence; Kirk criticized Trilling for precisely this indifference to postwar American conservatism. Although Trilling was respectful of conservatism, especially European conservatism, his engagement with American conservatism stopped with Henry Adams and George Santayana, somewhere in the 1930s, even if he did not, like fellow New York intellectuals Irving Howe and Dwight MacDonald, mock or lash out at conservative publications.[81] Conservatism, for Trilling, was a part of the opposing self and a part that was there to be transcended, if the liberal self were ever to gain maturity. *National Review* conservatism was of little interest to him.

Yet Trilling was conservative in a way that neither Buckley nor Chambers wished to be in the 1950s. Trilling's opposing self could, through its oppositions, be accommodated to the status quo. Trilling "was exactly in tune with the temper of a period [the 1950s] which found Tocqueville a more reliable guide than Marx to the American reality and whose cultural home was moving from Greenwich Village to an address as yet unspecified but definitely to the north of Fourteenth Street," Trilling's former student Norman Podhoretz observed.[82] Meanwhile, Buckley and Chambers were aligned against the status quo. Buckley would proceed from his youthful rebellion to a central position in the conservative movement, shedding some of his rebellious spirit as the movement became an establishment. *The Third Rome* was so radically a rejection of the status quo that nothing much could be built on it. Chambers may have feared that its publication would somehow undermine the conservative movement, pointing up its intellectual disarray and depriving it of the will to act. Chambers himself would go back to college in the late 1950s, as if to acquire a more useful education; he was frightened by the hole in the middle of his political life, by a will to oppose that was greater than the ability to create. Chambers's opposing self was best channeled, as he knew, into a movement, a modern conservative movement that would act on conservative principle. For Chambers, *The Third Rome* may have been unobtainable, but the vote for Eisenhower still mattered, as did the founding of *National Review* and the publication of polemical books such as Kirk's *The Conservative Mind*.[83] In politics opposition could be creative, if it was intelligently organized; there was energy and passion and will (not just joy) in opposition. Trilling's opposing self was Promethean in its own right, just as it was subtly anti-communist, a lesson learned in the vineyard of anti-Stalinist letters. This was the lesson that Spengler might be wrong; that the West was not lost to the inevitability of decline; that the despair of a literary youth, the tougher despair of the Great Depression, and the final despair of Stalinism were only one tributary of Western history and culture. If *gulags* and concentration camps could be folded into a negative capability, realistic and imaginative, a Keatsian health might still be accessible, the West redeemable, and the high culture of liberal anti-communism an agent of political virtue.

9

THE ESTABLISHMENT OF
AN ANTI-COMMUNIST INTELLIGENTSIA

Who passed through universities with radiant cool eyes
hallucinating Arkansas and Blake-light tragedy
among the scholars of war

—ALLEN GINSBERG, "Howl"

Joseph Stalin died on March 5, 1953. He had seized power in the late
1920s, one of history's greatest tyrants, terrorizing his subjects through
random violence and imprisonment. He annexed what territory he
could, moving populations from one place on the map to another,
spreading circles of misery. Stalin's policies issued in slave labor and mass
murder, although this was not so well known in the 1930s and 1940s.[1]
Similar to World War II, the Cold War had deep connections to the person of Joseph Stalin, to his postwar anxieties about Eastern Europe; to his
vision of the West as foreign and hostile; and to his sense that Soviet
blood, spilled with such abandon in World War II, had confirmed the Soviet Union's status as a great power. Stalin's methods, and his sway over
international communism, grew into "Stalinism," a style of politics, political thought, and cultural action related to the needs of the Party—and
subordinated, when Stalin was still alive, to the whims of the dictator.
Chambers had served this Party, and this dictator, as a spy. In 1930,
Trilling wrote in praise of Alexander Fadeyev, a Stalinist writer and bureaucrat whose fiction was helping build a socialist future.[2] Stalinism had
its intellectual component, and the attraction Trilling and Chambers felt
toward communism in the early 1930s was not separable from Stalinism.
As if recognizing this fact, the Soviet Union had from its inception employed intellectuals in ideological warfare.[3] It would endeavor to fight the
Cold War on the plane of ideas, as much as on the plane of military strategy and confrontation.

If the United States hoped to prevail in the Cold War, it would need its own intellectuals. Not all intellectuals obliged, but an anti-communist intelligentsia gradually solidified in the 1950s. Lionel Trilling and Whittaker Chambers were two of its most talented members. Stalin the mass murderer made more enemies, over time, than he was able to kill: the liberal intellectual who wrote *The Vital Center* (Arthur Schlesinger Jr.) and the conservative intellectual who wrote *Witness* (Whittaker Chambers) agreed on little, but they did agree on the moral outrage of Stalinism and on the political responsibility of containing it, by military force if necessary. What had disappeared by 1953 was the communist intelligentsia in America. The Nazi-Soviet pact of August 1939 disrupted American communism, and the Soviet Union's annexation of Poland, Finland, Lithuania, Latvia, Estonia, Czechoslovakia, Hungary, and other sovereign states made for further moral difficulties. Those who remained within or near the communist fold faced the postwar wrath of Senator McCarthy, who toppled an already weakening edifice. In their 1960 campaigns, Kennedy and Nixon competed to show off their mastery of anti-communist argumentation. Behind them was a vast array of books, articles, magazines, professors, scientists, journalists, and ideologues, an anti-communist intelligentsia as expansive as it had been amorphous in the 1930s. It would survive the death of the monstrous Joseph Stalin, claiming the center, vital or otherwise, of American culture and politics in the 1950s.[4]

This anti-communist intelligentsia was not at all monolithic. Opposition to communism, coupled with the will to weaken or defeat Soviet communism, could reflect an infinity of ideas. Literary critic Irving Howe was an anti-communist and a radical. He would step away from the liberal anti-communism of *Commentary*, and of the Democratic Party, and found the magazine *Dissent* in 1954. At *Dissent*, Howe and others, including Chambers's old friend Meyer Schapiro, defended a radical socialism from the Stalinist Left as well as from the conformist mainstream of American politics. Radical proponents of the avant-garde at *Partisan Review*, like art critic Clement Greenberg and poet Delmore Schwartz, were anti-Stalinists, but they disliked the middle-class aura of liberal anti-communism, and they loathed the populist red baiting of McCarthy, for which they held naïve anti-communists accountable. Trilling was to their Right. A Democrat happy to vote for Adlai Stevenson in the 1950s and then for John F. Kennedy in 1960, and a fierce anti-communist who considered Western civilization a shield to be held up against the communist temptation, Trilling criticized both McCarthy and McCarthy's critics. Howe and his allies at *Dissent* dissented from the status quo, not because it was anti-communist but because anti-communism had been exploited to justify capitalist inequality and to smother dissent in cheap patriotism. Trilling did not rush to celebrate all things American in the 1950s, but neither was he an intellectual devoted to dissent; he thought America could be a force for the cultural and geopolitical good and that intellectuals could augment this force. Liberal and conservative anti-communists operated in parallel political worlds. As a generalization, anti-communism helped unify the Right while it encouraged disunity on the Left. The extended effort to moderate the Left, to furnish it with a liberal imagination and to school it in the dialectics of the opposing self, had succeeded for a time; in the years after 1955, it was succeeding less and less. Liberal anti-communism was prevalent, almost ubiquitous in the 1950s, but beneath its ubiquity was a certain hollowness, which Trilling would come to know well in the years after Stalin's death.[5] Howe's political criticism and Greenberg's cultural criticism, directed at liberal anti-communists such as Trilling, would gain ground on the Left.

To the Right of *Partisan Review, Dissent,* and Trilling was not a placid sea of conservatism. On the Right, the collision of libertarian, traditionalist, and anti-communist sentiments did not coalesce into harmony. Many conservatives worried about the distance between real conservatism and the Eisenhower administration, seeing Eisenhower and his Republican Party as impossible vehicles for true conservatism. With some reluctance, Chambers did what he could to connect *National Review* conservatism to the Republican Party, and in 1960, the politician most closely involved with the Hiss case ran for president. Richard Nixon was not Chambers's beau ideal of a politician, but he was someone on whom Chambers had a degree of influence; Chambers refused to be chief editor of *National Review* because William F. Buckley Jr. and others were insufficiently pro-Nixon and insufficiently anti-McCarthy.[6] Even if Nixon paid nominal attention to *National Review* and publicized his admiration for Russell Kirk, Nixon was not the one to fashion unity out of conservative disunity, although his narrow loss to Kennedy in 1960 obscured a new proximity between the Republican Party and the conservative intellectual. When Barry Goldwater ran for president in 1964, he had a battery of conservative intellectuals behind him, including Buckley, Russell Kirk, and many who read and wrote for *National Review*. For conservatives, the intellectual turbulence of the 1950s would bear political fruit.

Chambers, no less than Buckley, wanted to construct an anti-communist intelligentsia that was by definition conservative. Chambers tried to foster a unity of interest between the American people and the Republican party, between a conservative intelligence that resided in the people and the fortunes of America's only relevant conservative party, drawing hope from history, which illustrated "that the rock-core of the Conservative Position, or any fragment of it, can be held realistically only if conservatism will accommodate itself to the needs and hopes of the masses," as he wrote to *National Review* editor Willi Schlamm in 1954. In turn, Chambers recommended a populist conservatism to the Republican Party, although he doubted that a unified movement would be conservative in the way that he was conservative. Although the needs and aspirations of the masses bolstered the conservative cause, the conservative cause could not avoid contact with a highly industrialized, mechanized society, and regardless of what the political theorist might devise on paper, the American masses would be unwilling to march back to the preindustrial age: "our fight, as I think we said," Chambers wrote to Schlamm, "is only incidentally with socialists or other heroes of that kidney. *Wesentlich* [essentially], it is with machines." Or, as Chambers histrionically put it to Schlamm, "the 40-horsepower tractor is only one turn on the road to the H-bomb and beyond."[7] Nevertheless, a successful conservatism would depend on the production, advertising, and sale of 40-horsepower tractors. This was an intractable—and, at times, an enervating—dilemma for Chambers.

Chambers refused to resolve this dilemma in any way that would endorse libertarian economics. It was better to leave the dilemma of a machine civilization unresolved than simply to equate conservatism with capitalism. Chambers had no grand illusions about the popularity of his particular conservative ideas. "The significant socializing force in the United States is science and technology; the rest is wind," he wrote to Ralph de Toledano in 1956. Science and technology abet the capitalist mentality, which has been wreaking havoc in America since the early nineteenth century. As if anticipating the counterculture of the 1960s, Chambers wrote that "America always destroys its men because it makes truth so expensive and half-truth so profitable: bottled gas. Only two, as far as I can recall, ever beat the game: Thoreau . . . [and] Whitman."[8]

Chambers, similar to the Beat poets whom he admired, recoiled from the increasing commercialism of American culture in the 1950s.[9] Musing on the television show *The Price Is Right*, Chambers wrote in *Cold Friday* that the show's implicit message, its smiling celebration of capitalist pleasure, was un-Christian, for "Christianity, rightly understood . . . is a tragic faith, and must be since life is a tragic experience. It cannot be otherwise since men die." *The Price Is Right* might just as well be Soviet propaganda, substituting capitalist for socialist realism: "the West believes that man's destiny is prosperity and abundance of goods. So does the Politburo." Chambers condemned liberals for allowing abundance and prosperity to determine their social vision. They had willingly abrogated "the duty of the intellectuals of the West to preach reaction." What distressed Chambers was that conservatives did not realize "why the Enlightenment and its fruits were a wrong turn in man's history." In 1954, Chambers told de Toledano that "too many who suppose themselves conservatives have forgotten, or never knew, that the chain of spirit alone has binding force."[10]

Libertarian economists were a choice example of those who had forgotten or never known that the chain of spirit has binding force.

In 1953, Chambers identified the libertarians as a threat to the Right when he wrote about Ludwig von Mises's ominous arrival on the intellectual scene. Born in the Austro-Hungarian empire, von Mises was an academic economist and an early critic of socialism, producing a body of economic ideas at odds with both Marxism and Keynsianism, with communism and with social democracy. Von Mises was a child of the Enlightenment and a committed rationalist who was uncomfortable with the conservative label, but, in America, von Mises was popular in conservative circles, and this popularity was precisely what frightened Chambers. "I think this is very important," Chambers wrote to de Toledano about a possible alliance between von Mises's business-oriented libertarianism and the conservative agenda. Chambers, who despised the world of business, wrote that the businessman "fears the mind: for the mind is the host of the spirit. His [the businessman's] function is anti-spirit. He would like to liquidate it in the interest of efficiency."[11] When a book by von Mises was condensed and published in the mass-circulation magazine *U.S. News and World Report*, Chambers called it "one of the most pernicious pieces of writing that the Right has produced . . . by pernicious I mean the effect that follows when a mind, which speaks with authority in a special field (economics), uses that authority (but not the field it is based in), to offer a false study of our dilemma."[12] Our dilemma, as understood by Chambers, was spiritual and political, a combination of economic woes, a loss of religious faith, and anarchic mass politics that could easily explode into fascism or communism. With von Mises, the problem was that "this grossly shallow man has left the field of economics for the field of mass psychology. He has proclaimed, rather than declared, that the anti-capitalist mood of our time is the result of 'envy and ignorance.' I, for one, have never envied a capitalist in my life. Quite the contrary."[13]

Chambers worried about the materialist bridge between communism and capitalism, falling back on the language of communism to condemn von Mises's love of capitalism. Chambers contended that "socialism is simply capitalism continued in other forms . . . I see why Lenin said . . . that capitalism at the peak of development is the absolute precondition for socialism." As for capitalists, Chambers wrote (with a wink) to de Toledano that "I do not want to liquidate them; I want to get away from them. They seem to me the death of the mind and the spirit." Von Mises had only capitalism to offer a world in crisis. To Chambers he seemed "never to have a waking moment from 1929 onwards; never to have heard of economic crises. Alas, the envious masses have. I should be happy indeed if Dr. Von Mises would shed kindly light on that matter, which, as a conservative, I hold to be the troubling crux of much."[14] Von Mises was no cloistered intellectual: he had access to a sizable reading public. When Ayn Rand published *Atlas Shrugged* in 1957, she reached millions of readers, discovering or creating a readership that was desperate to undo the ethics of the New Deal. Born in Saint Petersburg in 1905, Rand came with her family to the United States in 1926; she would eventually settle in New York. Under the influence of Nietzsche and of libertarian economic doctrine, she fashioned an anti-communist literary corpus, publishing *We the Living* in 1936 and *The Fountainhead* in 1943, novels that attracted a mass audience. These novels dramatized the conflict between the creative ego, which generates wealth and progress, and the perfidy of collectivism, which exploits the ressentiment of the weak so it can subdue the will of the strong. If allowed, leftist ressentiment would impoverish the West as surely as Bolshevism was impoverishing Soviet Russia. Rand commanded little respect from literary critics with her novels, but a large and avid readership made her a towering figure in the anti-communist intelligentsia. True to her philosophy, she was made powerful by the market.

Chambers titled his review of *Atlas Shrugged* "Big Sister Is Watching You," posing Rand as an Orwellian villain, and it appeared in *National Review* in December 1957. Rand represented several of the intellectual trends that Chambers most disliked. That she did so as an enemy of the Left unsettled Chambers in his relationship to the Right. Her fiction proved that "the world, as seen in the materialist view from the Right, scarcely differs from the same world seen in the materialist view from the Left." Rand's novel illustrated a dispiriting axiom: that "the pursuit of happiness, as an end in itself, tends automatically and widely, to be replaced by the pursuit of pleasure with a consequent general softening of the fibers of will, intelligence, spirit."[15] Without religion, the pursuit of happiness is a travesty, and "Randian man, like Marxian man, is made the center of a godless world." Rand's was a conservatism of machines, an agent of the modernity that had already devastated the twentieth century: "she means, almost exclusively, technological achievement, supervised by such a [technocratic] managerial political bureau . . . this can only lead into a dictatorship, however benign, living and acting beyond good and evil, a law unto itself (as Miss Rand believes it should be), and feeling any restraint on itself as, in practice, criminal and, in morals, vicious—as Miss Rand clearly feels it to be." Chambers distrusted Rand's lack of confusion, the straight-arrow dogmatism of her style, in which he detected a totalitarian signature. And so, "from almost any page of *Atlas Shrugged*, a voice can be heard, from painful necessity, commanding: 'To a gas chamber—go!' "[16]

"Big Sister Is Watching You" was scandalously polemical, rendering impossible any alliance between the libertarian Buckley and the Randians. Ayn Rand never talked to Buckley after Chambers's review came out in *National Review*. She would not even enter a room if she knew that Buckley was in it. Future chairman of the Federal Reserve Alan Greenspan, an admirer and acolyte of Rand's, wrote to Buckley to express his sheer disgust: "this man [Chambers] is beneath contempt and I would not honor his 'review' of Ayn Rand's magnificent masterpiece by even commenting on it."[17]

Chambers was so far from being a libertarian that he contemplated scenarios of economic equality. In "Foot in the Door," a 1959 article for *National Review*, Chambers emphasized the domestic incentive for alleviating poverty outside of Europe and the United States, welcoming the fact that "there will be no peace for the islands of relative plenty until the continents of proliferating poverty have been lifted to something like the general material levels of the islanders." Chambers's assessment of global poverty and politics was uncharacteristically blithe: "it is a perfectly practical challenge, abetted by sound self-interest, which must engross the energies of mankind, and more and more, inspire it to a perfectly realizable vision." To this role Americans are very well suited. Chambers thought that the plight of the global poor "would inspire Americans, who, in a sense, invented abundance; and who appear to feel what other nations have felt as a sense of destiny, only in the generous act of bringing their abundance and the know-how behind it, to less fortunate breeds."[18] Here Chambers was foreshadowing President Kennedy's creation of the Peace Corps—or the humanitarian language of Jimmy Carter—more than the Republican Party mantras of small government and self-reliance. The mention of self-interest was a nod perhaps to the libertarian gurus, but here self-interest was the spur to doing good, not to private gain or happiness narrowly pursued.[19]

Chambers was a conservative intellectual with limited patience for intellectuals. He did not want to burden the Republican Party with a cacophony of political ideas. He resolved the many confusions of intellectual conservatism, apparent enough in his magazine journalism and letters, by foregrounding the need for an effective political movement, with a program more than a philosophy, a strategy more than a theory. Chambers was not the professorial type: "though Chambers was a passionately literary man . . . in the last analysis it was action, not belletrism, that moved him most deeply," Buckley wrote in a 1961 obituary. An active program required pragmatism from conservatives, which was not a virtue Chambers associated with the 1950s Right. At the beginning of their friendship, Chambers wrote to Buckley about a modern conservatism that might be aligned with political power. It was self-defeating to rage against modernity: "a conservatism that cannot face the facts of the machine and mass production, and its consequences in government and politics, is foredoomed to futility and petulance. A conservatism that allows for them has an eleventh-hour chance of rallying what is sound in the West."[20] Chambers's pragmatism was something he wanted to impress upon Buckley because he sensed that Buckley was inclined to put principle above praxis.[21] Chambers reassured Buckley of the potential for success on the Right. "The Right can muster great forces," Chambers wrote to Buckley in 1954. "Potentially, it has a base of masses of Americans; potentially it has all the brains, money and other resources it needs. But it can never mobilize them, because it lacks one indispensable: it has no program." The Right is unable to move forward politically because "it will not face historical reality."[22]

Chambers was fighting for leadership of the conservative anti-communist intelligentsia at a time of widespread political redefinition. His fellowship with the libertarian Buckley was possible because Buckley was a Catholic and a lover of Western civilization. Any fellowship with Ayn Rand was impossible because there was nothing of Christian civilization in her literature, no nourishment for the third Rome. There was only the hard-edged talent and unfettered self-interest that could erect the skyscrapers of a modern city, a vision of Wall Streets without end. If Randian conservatism threatened the cultural essence of the Right, an anti-communist liberalism threatened the radical soul of the Left, as defined by those outside the liberal center. The 1950s Left could be variously labeled the reformist wing of a capitalist superpower; a socialist alternative to capitalism; or a reservoir of the radical spirit, opposed to conformity and the oppressive mediocrity of middle-class American life.[23] Lionel Trilling sketched the ideal of a moderate anti-communist liberalism in *E. M. Forster, The Middle of the Journey, The Liberal Imagination,* and *The Opposing Self.* He supported reform, the New Deal, the Civil Rights Movement, and the vigorous application of American power in the Cold War; imbalances on the Left could be corrected by listing to the Right from time to time. Trilling's critics doubted that he was even on the Left, accusing him of a mild or not-so-mild conservatism, of catering to the powers that be, of sacrificing social criticism on the altar of anti-communism, of flattering the new American Caesars bestriding the globe, and of celebrating bourgeois convention in a decade of middle-class melancholia. Trilling's critics disagreed with him about the merits of an anti-communist intelligentsia and about its association with liberalism or the Left.

After Trilling's death in 1975, Irving Howe recalled him as the symbol of an inadequate Left, his popularity in the 1950s a sad commentary on the state of the American Left. "Trilling's intellectual adversaries—among whom, at least in earlier years, I was one—felt that his work had come to serve as a veiled justification for increasingly conservative moods among American intellectuals," Howe wrote. The conservative moods were multiple. One was "a growing uneasiness with literary modernism," with its radical critique of society. Another aspect was Freudian, a Freud-inflected distaste for the self-indulgence of postwar American and Western culture. Through Freud's eyes, Trilling saw simultaneously "the large possibilities of our private selves and the dangers and betrayals which the modern obsession with self has brought." Where politics per se was concerned, Howe lapsed into vagary, allowing that Trilling's writing could be read as "an inducement for a somewhat conservative liberalism," a conservatism he could not quite define because the conservative and the radical commingled in Trilling: "I cannot wholly believe that his conservatism, real or alleged, was the major reason for his influence," Howe wrote. "What drew serious readers to his work was something else which, at risk of being perverse, I want to call a 'radical' approach to culture."[24] Trilling was the teacher of Allen Ginsberg. For a while, Trilling was the esteemed colleague of radical sociologist C. Wright Mills, as he would be of literary scholar Edward Said later in life; Trilling and Said had an affinity for each other, ranging from their taste in literature to a fascination with Freud.[25] Ginsberg, Mills, and Said are all giants of the Left in American intellectual history. Trilling was also the teacher of Norman Podhoretz, the friend of Midge Decter, Irving Kristol, and Gertrude Himmelfarb, who would take his liberal anti-communism in a more conservative direction. As Howe himself wrote to Trilling in 1972—when Kristol and Himmelfarb were prodding their fellow New York intellectuals to vote for Richard Nixon—"I find myself wondering whether the New Left phase of the last 6–7 years wasn't a minor interruption of a major trend— that is, of a trend toward conservatism among American intellectuals from the World War II years onward."[26]

The New Left defined itself against figures like Trilling, and the transition from 1950s liberal anti-communism to the New Left of the mid-1960s had an early precedent in the relationship between Ginsberg and Trilling. (Trilling also taught Beat poet Laurence Ferlinghetti.) When Trilling and Ginsberg exchanged letters in the 1940s and 1950s—debating literary culture and, by proxy, Western civilization—Ginsberg was well on his way to becoming "the richest possible emblem of that whole cultural period," by which literary scholar Morris Dickstein means the 1960s. The letters that Ginsberg wrote to Trilling between 1945 and 1948 show a student throwing off his teacher's language and, with the language, the ethical substance of the teaching. Ginsberg wrote of "cultural decline," but by this he did not mean the decline of the West. The West was an agent of decline; it was reason for "the conflict between the anarchic impulses of the individual psyche and its needs, and the mores of a categorized Protestant civilization which is crippled because it conceives of pleasure as evil." Writing about French poet Rimbaud, Ginsberg declared that Western civilization "offers no hope of personal salvation, no way of life within its accepted structure. His creative powers are not realized in the usual activities of the citizen—at the machine, in the office." Ginsberg's sentiment resonates with the conclusions of *The Third Rome*, but Christ and Rimbaud were not compatible heroes. Rimbaud, the prophet of Ginsberg's generation, wrote poems that signaled "the shift in vision of society from the simple idealism of Sinclair Lewis to the whole camp of post World War II writers . . . his *idée*, his sociological approach rather [than] moral, has already prevailed," as Ginsberg wrote to Trilling, suggesting the failure of his Arnoldian teacher.[27]

By Ginsberg's standards, *The Middle of the Journey* was stillborn, a literary anachronism as soon as it was published in 1947. The postwar novelists who understood the temper of their times were Raymond Chandler, James McCain, and John O'Hara because their heroes were not intellectuals trying to serve civilization but rather holy murderers placing themselves outside the borders of civilization. "There is an interest in the psychopath," Ginsberg informed Trilling, to whom this was surely news, "who moves in his pattern unaffected by moral compunction, by allegory to the confused standards of the age."[28] Ginsberg wrote this letter in 1945. Two years later, Ginsberg wrote an extraordinary letter to Trilling, describing his life as a Beat poet, while stressing in almost pathetic tones the bond between avant-garde student and neo-Victorian teacher. Ginsberg left Columbia's neoclassical campus behind, journeying into a wholly different America and discovering a bohemian cosmos that began in lower Manhattan and opened out to the West Coast, far away in space and time from the decaying, bourgeois culture of the East Coast. Ginsberg was on the road with his fraternity of Beat poets and writers, looking for new registers in American culture, exchanging mainstream for margin, and following an antinomian hunger he had felt as a Columbia student. Writing to Trilling, Ginsberg was candid about "our mutual distrust," but in Ginsburg's view distrust was not cause for animosity. Ginsberg described to Trilling the environment of his life and art, a lived experiment that made poetry out of rebellion: "I am all tangled up with unresolved tableaux of drugs, pool halls, homosexuality, aesthetic theories and quasi-psychoanalytic introspection which is the lot, alas, of my hero."[29]

In 1947, Ginsberg was still writing to his teacher when he wrote to Trilling. Ginsberg used the words complexity and responsibility as evidence of the tie between himself and Trilling: "the final problem and perhaps the virtue of what I am writing is the attempt to resolve all dramatic complexity, and put down the complicated whole; this in turn leads to moral questions (so dear to your heart) in terms of personal 'responsibility.' I think you know the kick I am on, and I am not, as usual, unwilling to accept advice." The letter culminated in a modest proposal—namely, that Trilling tutor Neal Cassady, future hero of the Beat poets and role model for 1960s rebels. There is no hint of irony in Ginsberg's proposal, a mockery of the straight lines that order cultural history. First, Ginsberg mentions "one of Denver's dissolute young bucks (his name is Neal Cassady) whose education, for the time, I am superintending." Perhaps Professor Lionel Trilling could help to make a good citizen of him: "he strikes me as the wisest and most powerful personality I have run across, in school or out, among the young, and since he seems to be assuming finally some 'personal responsibility' I think all will be well for him." Then the punch line: "if you are interested in that sort of thing, you would be in a position to help him in a while as far as school is concerned."[30] Either Trilling would have transformed Neal Cassady, prototype for Dean Moriarty in Jack Kerouac's *On the Road*, into an icon of personal responsibility or Trilling himself could have figured in the Beat epic, tutor extraordinaire to a generation of countercultural rebels.

Intellectual cooperation among Trilling, Ginsberg, and Cassady was not to be. In December 1948, Ginsberg wrote once again about the dissonance between his ambitions and those of his teacher: "I distrust this passion for found structure and coherence," Ginsberg wrote. "This is why I've never taken to your idea of 'order,' which I assumed you always had—because it did not mean anything to me."[31] Ginsberg's letters are remarkable for the good-natured proximity they document, given who Ginsberg and Trilling were at the time.[32] Trilling and Ginsberg had enjoyed the precarious intimacy of teacher and student and once Ginsberg ceased to be Trilling's student, they were likely to be adversaries. Trilling was not so much a defender of the social order—although he was no ideologue of disorder—as he was a seeker of balance. Throughout the 1950s, Trilling was working to balance the many opposing selves of American culture. Ginsberg would largely do the opposite: he would take the tableaux of drugs, pool halls, homosexuality, aesthetic theories, and quasipsychoanalytic introspection and, through his art and his life, try to extend these tableaux, remaking American culture in their image. To the extent that Ginsberg was the leader of a new cultural movement, Trilling was the leader of its established antithesis.[33] Neither teacher nor student would weaken their resolve or compromise their priorities. With the failure of American communism and the increasing moderation of the political Left, Ginsberg's cultural opposition to Trilling was the most potent opposition that Trilling faced (from the Left at least). In winning the fight against 1930s radicalism, Trilling was setting the stage for a later fight between the revolutionary pupils of Rimbaud and the liberal caretakers of Western civilization.

The anti-communist caretakers of Western civilization channeled their "passion for found structure and coherence" into two institutions of impeccable Cold War vintage—the Congress for Cultural Freedom (CCF) and the American Committee for Cultural Freedom (ACCF), each a backbone of the anti-communist intelligentsia. Sidney Hook, Trilling's friend and political mentor, had been a prime mover in the various committees for cultural freedom, the first of which, the Committee for Cultural Freedom, was formed in 1939. Next came the CCF in 1950, an association of intellectuals intended to bridge the worlds of European and American anti-communism. By helping to organize the CCF, Hook was reacting not to philo-communism but to "the emergence of neutralism and anti-Americanism in European intellectual circles." Frances Saunders, a historian of the CCF, has described its purpose as "the winning over of the western intelligentsia to the American proposition."[34] For the CCF, anti-communism was not neutrality and Western civilization was not an abstraction: "the West" signified political and cultural freedom for both the CCF and the ACCF, and these were institutions ensconced in the power structures of Western Europe and the United States, a "state-private network that was to a great extent built on shared values," according to Hugh Wilford, another historian of the CCF.[35] What NATO would do by force of arms, they could do by force of ideas. One institutional link between arms and ideas was the CIA, which was so eager to support an anti-communist intelligentsia that it financed the CCF and several of its European publications; Michael Josselson, who ran the CCF from 1950 to 1967, was a CIA agent. At the height of the Cold War, it was in the American national interest to foster "the development of a nucleus for a Western community of intellectuals, who . . . felt embattled against the virus of neutralism that was spiritually disarming the West against Communist aggression." This was the aim of the CCF in Sidney Hook's words.[36] Whether it was in the interest of intellectuals to be spending the CIA's money, knowingly or unknowingly, was another question.

The ACCF boasted a chaotic array of anti-communist talent, its list of members a social register of the anti-communist intelligentsia. *Partisan Review* editor William Phillips and *Commentary* editor Elliot Cohen worked alongside James Burnham, who was soon to become William F. Buckley Jr.'s close colleague at *National Review*. Conservative intellectual George Schuyler joined forces with Arthur Schlesinger Jr., the liberal par excellence. Trilling's friend, poet W. H. Auden, was there with novelist Ralph Ellison. Reinhold Niebuhr lent his formidable name to the roster. Chambers's old boss at *Time*, Henry Luce, was an enthusiast of the ACCF. Working in its milieu, he even helped to save *Partisan Review* from bankruptcy (despite having been called a Wehrmacht general by William Phillips in an earlier era), quite possibly with CIA money as part of the deal.[37] *Time* has been described as "the right wing of the CIA's covert network," such that "it was difficult to tell precisely where the Luce empire's overseas intelligence network ended and the CIA's began."[38]

The ACCF was weakened by its diversity, even if the names of its members proclaimed artistic and intellectual distinction. Either the ACCF never recovered from the divisions of the McCarthy period, or the ACCF was too weak to survive for very long. Conservatives such as Schuyler, Burnham, and Max Eastman believed that McCarthyism and anti-communism were basically synonymous. Others, such as Diana Trilling, a committed member of the ACCF who would become its national chairman in 1956, wanted the ACCF to condemn McCarthy as a practical and a moral threat to anti-communism. Because of this dispute, Eastman, Burnham, and Schuyler all resigned from the ACCF. The anger ran in both directions, as "some of the more liberal members of the committee were more intolerant of its few conservative members than vice versa," in the recollection of Sidney Hook.[39] By 1957, the ACCF had fallen apart. When the CCF's ties to the CIA were publicized in 1967, they retrospectively tainted the CCF and ACCF as well as those New York intellectuals involved with one or both of the committees. Questions of CIA involvement notwithstanding, the connection to government was itself unremarkable for the anti-communist intelligentsia.[40]

One critic of a system that aligned intellectuals with government action was C. Wright Mills. Mills thought that power corrupts and that anti-communist intellectuals were ensuring their own corruption by cooperating with government and financial power. Although Mills and Trilling would clash over exactly this issue, their relationship began with Mills's admiration for Trilling the author. Mills sent a fan letter to Trilling in 1943. He had read Trilling's short story, "Of this Time, of that Place," and in a rush of enthusiasm told Trilling that "you have made little episodes in my own life into portentous happenings." In 1943, Mills was a twenty-seven-year-old sociologist on the make; by 1955 he was a well-known intellectual of the Left, a radical voice in the 1950s wilderness. In Trilling's recollection, from a letter written in 1974, he "was conscious of his [Mills's] good will toward me" when they first got to know each other. "Some odd, subtle, unhappy change occurred in my feelings towards him—there was a time when I liked and admired him very much, but then I came to think his judgment of things wrong and rather coarse, I came to regard him with a certain patience and even asperity."[41] In a 1955 essay, Mills attacked Trilling for praising the coalition of knowledge and power, tacit praise for the Cold War intellectual.[42] Mills rejected the liberal anti-communists en masse. Their mild-mannered complicity with big business and with the Cold War national security state is repugnant; they give power to the powerful by explaining, justifying, and accommodating themselves to the status quo. Because they dominate public intellectual life, "a conservative mood—a mood quite appropriate for men living in a political vacuum—has come to prevail [among public intellectuals]." Conservatism is, in this context, the politics of the vacuum, almost a withdrawal from politics—similar to the conservatism Joseph Frank had attributed to Trilling. However withdrawn, the liberal anti-communist intelligentsia was political in its contribution of cultural glamour to the Cold War effort. What America lacks abroad, Mills argued, is "cultural prestige. This simple fact has involved those of the new gentility in the curious American celebration."[43] New York was fulfilling Washington's production orders, manufacturing the prestige on which winning the Cold War battle of ideas depended.

Mills stigmatized intellectuals for gracing a Cold War agenda with their gifts, naming his Columbia colleague directly in a footnote: "Mr. Lionel

Trilling has written optimistically of 'new intellectual classes,' and has even referred to the Luce publications as samples of high 'intellectual talent.' What lends his view his optimistic tone, I believe, is less the rise of any new intellectual class than (1) old intellectual groupings becoming a little prosperous" and (2) a technocratic sense of what knowledge is.[44] In a letter to Mills, Trilling accused Mills, the self-proclaimed radical, of aristocratic aloofness: "from the point of view which you express in your essay— a point of view as-it-were aristocratic, and very strict and traditional and ideal—there is nothing to be done with this new class . . . I continue to think that this isn't so." Earlier in the 1950s, Trilling underscored the agency of intellectuals in an ideological age, an age receptive to ideas, even if it was prone to exploiting them. The optimistic message had failed, in Trilling's opinion, because "the intellectual had so far failed in any effect he might have upon the new class—failed because he cultivated his characteristic pathos of powerlessness and isolation and superior personal virtue." Trilling concluded on a note of pessimism: "I now think there is very little chance for the American intellectual to be a power in our general life, not in any direct way. It has come to seem to me that the moment arrives in the life of any American intellectual when he elects either torpor or feckless attitudinizing."[45] Mills, it was safe to assume, had opted for the latter.

Joseph Frank had heard a conservative quiescence in Trilling's prose; Mills scented the will to power; and poet Delmore Schwartz found something worse than either, a love song to the bourgeoisie. Schwartz feared that Trilling was making the bourgeois order respectable once again, undermining the intellectual's responsibility to serve the modern, the avantgarde, and the critical. Such was the poverty of Trilling's cultural anti-communism. In his memoirs, William Barrett, a long-standing *Partisan Review* editor, recalled Philip Rahv as he came "into the office one day after running into [art critic] Harold Rosenberg, who, witty and waspish as ever, had asked where *Partisan Review* was heading when it kept printing somebody like Trilling, who was simply making a case for 'bourgeois values.'" Trilling had placed himself beyond the pale of bohemian respectability. Schwartz agreed with Rosenberg, according to Barrett, and dismissed Trilling as a "reincarnation of the Genteel Tradition."[46] Trilling was sensitive to his alleged conservatism. At a cocktail party, Trilling met up with William Phillips, Rahv's editorial partner at *Partisan Review*, who told Trilling that "he [Trilling] was being read as a conservative thinker . . . He became agitated and indignant, and in an angry voice I rarely heard him use, he insisted that he wrote what he believed and didn't care what people thought."[47]

Schwartz deputized himself to tell the sad truth about Trilling, publishing his exposé of a bourgeois—"The Duchess' Red Shoes"—in January 1953. The Duchess' red shoes of the essay's title referred to Proust's *Remembrance of Things Past*, in which the Duchess Geurmontes sacrifices human decency to manners (she rushes her time with a dying friend so she can dress for a party). This, Schwartz indicated, was how the bourgeoisie put its fine manners to use. The Duchess' red shoes, as a symbol, were a necessary corrective to "Mr. Trilling's doctrine of manners in literature." Schwartz laid bare Trilling's agenda: "what Mr. Trilling is trying to do as a critic of literature and society is to salvage some of the lost or hurt pride of the middle class in its human inheritance." Trilling wrote about class out of his own perfidious class-consciousness: "it is of the [educated] class that he is, at heart, the guardian and the critic." In Schwartz's view, the educated class or the middle class carried no liberal humanizing message. They were snobs, and Trilling was flattering their snobbery. Trilling had read Shakespeare only to conclude that "snobbery is no illusion; that for Shakespeare the illusion, delusion, and insanity, is to imagine a human being ever becoming somewhat free of his social status." Trilling uses literature as a proxy for conservatism, entertaining "social views (and misgivings) which would be intolerable if they were presented nakedly, as social criticism or political programs, instead of being united with literary considerations."[48]

Schwartz, Ginsberg, and Mills seemed not to know about the anti-communist intelligentsia's right wing. If they did, it was not worth their time to criticize it. Trilling was on the conservative side of the world that interested them, and they were disgusted by his betrayal of the Left, by the alchemy of a typical Trilling essay that could transform the seemingly liberal or the seemingly radical into something illicitly conservative. Among New York intellectuals such as Schwartz and Mills, Chambers-esque conservatives had disappeared from view after the Hiss case; Chambers himself had disappeared into a kind of political abyss. The dismissal of out-and-out conservatives by New York intellectuals like Schartz or Mills recalls a 1952 letter from Mary McCarthy to Hannah Arendt, in which McCarthy wrote that "the final word certainly remains to be said about [Whittaker] Chambers; his [*Witness*] can't be treated simply as a book, among other books, to be reviewed. The great effort of this new Right is to get itself accepted as *normal,* and its publications as a *normal* part of publishing—and this, it seems to me, must be scotched, if it's not already too late."[49] One could defer the normalization of the new Right by declaring Trilling a conservative and behaving as if the political spectrum ended with his kind of liberal anti-communism. Had Schwartz, Ginsberg, and Mills directed their attention to Chambers in the late 1950s, and to the new Right in search of normalcy, their horror would only have intensified. The anti-communist intelligentsia was much larger than they allowed, and, as adversaries, the conservative anti-communists were more formidable and more aggressive than Professor Trilling. They sought power more than they sought normalcy, and they voted Republican.

Chambers tried to guide these conservative anti-communists by example. The conservative intellectual had multiple tasks, each of which informed Chambers's writing in the late 1950s: to comment on domestic politics, to relate domestic politics to developments in international affairs, to speculate on the ideals of political economy, to track trends in culture (good and bad), and to promote Western civilization not only as a tool in Cold War struggle but also as the largest and best reason for this struggle. One can see the precedent of Henry Adams in many of these qualities. Adams had lived directly across from the White House, he was masterful at mapping international historical patterns, and he went to the Chicago World's fair of 1893 to encounter the new and to write about it. All of this Adams did on the highest intellectual level. Yet he was an intellectual recluse who published *The Education of Henry Adams* privately, as if there was no public for his refined conservatism. Chambers was a man of the public sphere, whose progression from communism to conservatism was a matter of public record, and this public political life did not fade away, at least among his fellow conservatives. Throughout the 1950s and into the 1960s, *Witness* was woven into the fabric of American conservatism, grassroots as well as elite, something unthinkable for a writer like Adams. In his study of conservative activist Phyllis Schlafly, Donald Critchlow describes her "Reading List for Americans," a list of recommended conservative titles, as an effort to put the masses in touch with new ideas in the 1950s: "the most widely read book on the list was Whittaker Chambers's *Witness.*"[50]

After *Witness*, Chambers's published writing was mostly on politics, only fleetingly on culture, and very rarely on religion. In all three areas Chambers repeated the same thesis: America and the West were moving toward confusion and stasis, moving in circles around a deteriorating status quo. Almost all his *National Review* and other pieces from the 1950s convey conservative pessimism. Khrushchev's 1956 speech at the Twentieth Party Congress, denouncing Stalin, was not a sign of moral renewal, as Chambers interpreted it. It was a sign that communism might be renewing itself politically under "those Bolshevik businessmen, Khrushchev and Bulganin." Khrushchev was dangerous precisely because he had rejected Stalin's legacy. He might do what Stalin no longer could by 1953, which was to inspire belief in the communist dream: "with the smashing of the dark idol of Stalin, Communism can hope to compete again for the allegiance of men's minds, especially among the youth where its influence had fallen to zero," breaking up the "ice that froze and paralyzed the messianic spirit of Communism during the long but (in Communist terms) justifiable Stalinist nightmare." Soviet strategy was not to evangelize the West through communism, this being a lost cause, but to exploit Western pacifism. Hence, Khrushchev's promise of "no third world war." Although communist rulers categorically rejected détente, their calculated rhetoric of relaxation might loosen Western resolve. Soviet talk of peace could lead to Western temporizing, buying time "for mainland China to emerge as a new Communist industrial massif."[51]

Communism was dying out in the West, but outside the West—in Asia, Africa, and Latin America—its future might yet be bright. Poverty and communism would reinforce each other, and outside the West poverty is rampant: "the road to Washington runs through Rio de Janeiro and Mexico City," Chambers argued in a 1957 *National Review* essay titled "Soviet Strategy in the Middle East," "but first it runs through Damascus, Cairo and Algiers."[52] Soviet strategy in the Middle East is to gain access to Arab oil and to assert Soviet influence in the region, consolidating "Communism's advance along the North African land-bridge." One lever of influence is "Arab fear of Israeli expansion."[53] Another is the state of the Arab world, where "an illimitable poverty is the norm, a poverty made sodden by endemic disease, dark by endemic illiteracy and by an absence of hope that may best be called hereditary." Soviet power is a new presence in a region where Western financial and military power evokes an imperialist past. Unlike the West, the Soviet Union will not be seen as "the niggard banker, whose prudent doles serve to replace a political imperialism, of which the memory is green, by an economic imperialism which the Arabs fear is the other side of the political coin." For those Arabs living in poverty, Western influence has an aura of corruption about it, which Chambers conveyed through metaphor: "the dusty flash of a royal Cadillac, steaming past the mud huts, to the $90 million palace which King Saud has conjured up from unirrigated sands."[54] The American contribution is tantamount to the Cadillac.

America can bring modernization to the Middle East, and if it can stem the tide of "an incipient social revolution" it may succeed in checking Soviet influence. After the Suez crisis of 1957, the United States has eclipsed Britain and France as the dominant Western power in the region, "regardless of what anybody might want or the quality of the leadership." A somewhat unsavory Cold War recipe joins the Arab world to the United States. This is the Arab nationalism that "is constrained to work with the West." Because of the Western appetite for oil, and because of the anti-communist imperative, "the West is constrained to work with Arab Nationalism." Here Chambers recommends what he laments in America, an industrialization of the Arab economy that will undo the region's poverty. Chambers writes as if he were Lyndon Johnson enthusing about the Great Society or Franklin Roosevelt promoting the Tennessee Valley Authority. Foreign aid can help to build "the irrigation ditch, the factory, and the damn that supplies the ditch and powers the factory, and all the enterprise the factory feeds and stands for." Chambers does not write about Islam as a political factor, except as it might alienate Arabs from the Soviet Union, which was ruling over millions of Muslims, suppressing their religious freedoms just as it suppressed those of Christians and Jews. Chambers wonders whether "those wretched Arabs heard, too, that in Soviet Siberia several million of their co-religionists exist in a misery not much different from their own? Possibly they have heard. Radio has put everybody in the next room from everybody else."[55] If so, the West is in luck.

Elsewhere, the West was not in luck, and in Chambers's eyes the thwarted Hungarian uprising of 1956 only confirmed the West's weakness. By the time Chambers weighed in on the Hungarian uprising (in *National Review*) it had been put down by Soviet tanks. In the United States there had been no serious discussion of using either conventional or nuclear means to assist the Hungarians; but the uprising dramatized Soviet hegemony, as it did the association of anti-communism with liberation—it was a propaganda victory for the West. For so long, Soviet crimes had gone unnoticed and had failed to arouse the moral indignation of Americans and Western Europeans. Chambers wrote that "millions of Russians (let us remember) have already been destroyed, defying Communism. Their struggle and their cries were lost in the distances of Euro-Asia. But we *heard* the Hungarians, and they tore at least at our nerves." (The metaphor of hearing, in this sentence, recalls the 1931 short story Chambers had written as a communist, "Can You Hear Their Voices?") The bleaker story of the Hungarian uprising, however, was the story of Western indifference, all the more depressing if you believe that "the defeated almost never revolt twice—not in quick succession," a judgment that can verified against later history. Czechoslovakia would have its failed uprising in 1968; and, in the late 1970s, Polish dissidents began to press against Soviet power, a seemingly hopeless endeavor at the time. Not until 1989 would Hungarians take to the streets again, in hopes of destroying communism. The West's inaction in 1956 convinced Chambers of what he already knew, "that the will and intelligence of the West are still unequal to what besets them."[56]

Chambers thought that the West was adrift in the 1950s together with the Republican Party, the only political force that might restore the West to greater health. In 1958, Chambers described the G.O.P. (Grand Old Party) at the midpoint of Eisenhower's second term: "the Republicans had lost touch with reality in all directions, and in all groupings, until domestic policy resembled irresolution tempered by expediency, and foreign policy more resembled something like eccentricity." The disaster of Stevenson and the Democrats has been averted, which may have been Eisenhower's greatest accomplishment. Otherwise, it had been "six years of 'middle of the road' (or twilight sleep)," precisely what the West could not afford at a time of all-consuming Cold War crisis.[57] Chambers's advice to conservatives—that they only work through the Republican Party—was neither easy nor obvious, even in Chambers's own terminology. By affiliating oneself with Eisenhower's Republican Party, one might simply deepen the twilight sleep of America in the 1950s. Chambers witnessed twilight sleep, not just in party politics but also in the grey-flannel-suit drabness of 1950s America. If Trilling celebrated balance and health and observed some evidence for both in Eisenhower's America, Chambers saw balance as boredom, a balanced, rational society that, in its avoidance of choice, was killing off its own spirit. In 1957, the year the Soviets successfully launched the Sputnik satellite into space, Chambers wrote in puzzlement about

> a late and tired habit of mind [in America], which we seek to glorify by twining about it the rather dry and lifeless vine-leaves called: reasonableness, the calm view, common sense, the injunction never, under any circumstances, to feel strongly about anything (which, among other things, is blighting the energy of youth at the source) . . . it is a positive will not to admit or permit greatness in events or men . . . it takes form as a vague distaste, discomfort, distrust, relieved by a preference for the commonplace, the conforming, the small, the minutely (hence safely) measurable, the quantitative—method and dissection replacing life and imagination.

This was the diminishing spirit—diminishing spiritedness—of the West under American leadership. It amounted to a Cold War riddle. Even if the West could project its stupendous wealth outward, rescuing an impoverished world from the communist temptation, it did not necessarily have a worthwhile civilization to project along with its wealth. The West might lend a tired mind to an ignorant world. Unless "the general level of mind" can be raised along with "the level of material well-being," the crises that blazed across the twentieth century in its terrible first half will not abate for long. Unless the general level of mind is raised, "we shall all risk resembling those savages whom, within living memory, civilizers introduced to the splendor of top hats and tight shoes, for the greater glory of their extremities, leaving unredeemed the loin-cloth of their middle zones, and the wits between their ears"—imperialists bringing more barbarism than civilization.[58]

At best, the West could regroup and prepare itself for some future golden age. This was the subject of a 1952 essay Chambers wrote for *Commonweal*, the terminal point of his public thinking and the subject of *The Third Rome*, his unfinished sequel to *Witness*. The title of his *Commonweal* essay was "The Sanity of St. Benedict," and its themes took him back to Columbia College in the early 1920s, back to the university, which Chambers, like Buckley and Trilling, understood as a "repository of the culture of the West."[59] He recalled the Contemporary Civilization course taught at Columbia by "disillusioned veterans of the First World War, and a conscientious objector who refused to take part in it. One day, the objector, staring at some point far beyond the backs of our heads, observed that 'the world is entering upon a new Dark Age.' " This observation was the summa of Chambers's undergraduate education, "one of the few things I carried away from Contemporary Civilization, required for all freshmen." The gloom reverberated with Chambers's formal education, which labeled the middle ages "a thousand years of darkness from which the spirit of man had begun to liberate itself (intellectually) first in the riotous luminosity of the Renaissance, in Humanism, in the eighteenth century, and at last (politically) in the French Revolution."[60] Communism fulfilled the philosophical program taught to the undergraduate Chambers, connecting the lines of civilization that had been etched onto his generation's intellectual map. Liberation and light, as approached by the French Revolution, passed into the idealism of nineteenth-century Western culture, into the music of Beethoven and the political fantasies of Karl Marx, taking the undergraduate Chambers to communism, a means of contesting the coming dark age of capitalist aggression. And then, the liberation and light of Lenin's revolution, of the new Soviet dawn, revealed themselves to be a swindle, a mass of rhetoric falsely illuminating the Stalinist cellar. Chambers the communist revolutionary was not contesting a dark age. He came to believe that he, a servant of the Red Army, was spreading it.

Chambers's Kronstadt posed an old question anew. "What, in fact, was the civilization of the West?" It was not what he had been taught at Columbia. The civilization of the West was the heritage of Christian thought and experience, the culture that Benedict, the creator of Benedictine monasticism, had inaugurated, laying the foundation for Christian learning and practice, for an enduring Christian civilization. Benedict's *Rules*, his rules for monastic life—and, by extension, for the construction of a Christian civilization—answered the question of alienation. Marx's power had derived from his sensitivity to alienation, the alienation of class from class, of bourgeoisie from proletariat, and the alienation implicit to capitalist labor, which forced workers to expend themselves in the production of goods for distant markets and distant masters. The modern proletariat was alienated because it could not enjoy the fruits of its labor. To this profound problem, profoundly grasped, Marx had directed all the wrong spiritual solutions. By contrast, Benedict's *Rules* "ended three great alienations of the spirit . . . the alienation of the spirit of man from traditional authority; his alienation from the idea of traditional order; and a crippling alienation that he feels at the point where civilization has deprived him of the joy of simple productive labor." From Benedict came the answer that was the essence of Chambers's Kronstadt: "about the Benedictine monasteries what we, having casually lost the Christian East, now casually call the West, once before regrouped and saved itself."[61] What we have lost we might regain by virtue of historical precedent and an individual piety meant to serve the cause of civilization.

Some twenty years after Chambers had been an undergraduate, another young man, Norman Podhoretz, was inducted into the mysteries of Western civilization at Columbia. He wrote, in language similar to Chambers's, about his particular conversion experience in "Humanities and Contemporary Civilization," a course with institutional origins in the honors program John Erskine, the teacher of Trilling and the critic of Chambers's atheist play, had helped to create. In Podhoretz's recollection:

> it was the heritage of Western civilization to which we were
> being introduced. And yet the idea of Western civilization
> seemed so broad and generous, so all-embracing of whatever
> might be important or good or great in the world, that most of
> us thought of the adjectives as merely a polite tautology, a kind
> of elegantly liberal nod at the poor old Orient. To our minds,
> this culture we were studying at Columbia was not the creation
> or possession of a particular group of people; it was a repository
> of the universal, existing not in space or time but rather in some
> transcendental realm of the spirit.

Podhoretz had been born into a Jewish working-class family in Brooklyn and had entered Columbia on a scholarship. His talent had brought him to Columbia, where he was supposed to become "a reasonable facsimile of an upper-class WASP." At issue were manners and style and learning, but not religion per se; Chambers had attended a more Christian university. At Columbia, Podhoretz was struggling to assimilate "the heritage of what was, after all, a Christian civilization, and one which had up until—how long? a minute before?—been at literally murderous odds with the heritage, not to mention the bodies, of my own people."[62] The Western civilization Podhoretz studied at Columbia was not the possession of a particular group or people, not even of Christians; it was broad and generous; it could be traced back to Saint Benedict or Aristotle or Homer; and it was liberal, as in its generous acknowledgement that the Orient, too, had a civilization.

As a Columbia senior in the fall of 1949, Podhoretz was ready to study with Trilling, the high priest of America's liberal civilization and the author of *The Liberal Imagination* and *The Opposing Self.* Trilling would complete Podhoretz's anti-communist *Bildung.* Podhoretz had arrived at Columbia with pro-Soviet sympathies, which preceded his ascent to liberal anti-communism, the most advanced of political attitudes: "by the time I had graduated from Columbia four years later, I had been converted into a passionate partisan of the new liberalism—the kind that was at once pro-American and anti-Communist."[63] Both literally and figuratively, Podhoretz was the student of the liberal anti-communist intelligentsia. To Podhoretz this intelligentsia offered light and liberation, a thrilling affirmation of culture, responsive to the most urgent political dilemmas:

> reading Trilling on the liberal imagination, [Sidney] Hook on Marxism, Hannah Arendt on totalitarianism, [Reinhold] Niebuhr and [Hans] Morgenthau and [George] Kennan on political realism, [Dwight] Macdonald on Henry Wallace, [Daniel] Bell on ideology, [Leslie] Fiedler and [Robert] Warshow on the thirties . . . was as liberating in its own fashion to someone like me who had been raised politically on *PM* and the *New York Post* as the earlier discovery through "culture" that all possible ways of looking at the world were not exhausted by the opinions and views of Brownsville [Brooklyn].[64]

Diplomats and literary critics were read as progenitors of a single intellectual current. What began in literature ended in politics and vice versa. Bright Columbia students worshipped "the [literary] critics on the Columbia faculty . . . the late Andrew Chiappe, the late Richard Chase, F. W. Dupee, and especially Lionel Trilling—who became our mentors, our models, our gods. In the classroom as on paper, the critics were not only our guides to the secret riches of literature, they were our guides to philosophy, theology, and politics as well."[65] The anti-communist intelligentsia had made its own high culture, of which a younger generation—consisting of students such as Podhoretz—was the product.

Podhoretz was the product of a distinctly liberal anti-communism, which he found "more persuasive than the cruder and often ill-informed anti-Communism of the Right." Podhoretz's early literary criticism, as he recalled in his memoir *Breaking Ranks*, upheld the virtue of liberal anti-communism, and it was "as a liberal that I did something else in those pieces, which was to defend the secular spirit of contemporary middle-class society against conservative attack." Podhoretz, who had done coursework in the Jewish Theological Seminary while a Columbia undergraduate, was not committed to secularism but to politics as a secular pursuit. If the West was not necessarily Christian, the conflict between communist East and non-communist West was not necessarily, or even significantly, a theological conflict, as Chambers so strongly believed. As an enemy of the Right, Podhoretz attacked a "corollary of the antisecularist position (held, for example, by Whittaker Chambers and William F. Buckley), which was that the main difference between the Western and the Communist worlds was that they were godless and we were not."[66] By rejecting the "extreme right-wing sentiments of a Whittaker Chambers," and doing so as a stalwart anti-communist, Podhoretz was a flawless student of Lionel Trilling's. Diana and Lionel Trilling disapproved of Chambers's "association with Buckley and Richard Nixon, and their own secularist interpretation of what the cold war was about differed sharply from his [Chambers's] basically religious conception," Podhoretz later recalled.[67]

Trilling was Podhoretz's mentor, his intellectual father, and he would assist Podhoretz in his (American) dream of "making it," of becoming an intellectual and professional success. Theirs was not a simple a relationship, however, and in its tensions could be felt the movement of change. Podhoretz was charged with the responsibility of perpetuating a liberal anti-communist heritage.[68] In Jewish American terms, this was a mission Podhoretz could better accomplish than could the luminaries who had lent him their anti-communist wisdom. No less Jewish, Podhoretz was more American than they were. Consciously or subconsciously, his prose would incorporate the rhythms of American speech and not the cadence of European high culture; there is very little of American speech in Trilling's gentle, highly structured, and somewhat mannered prose. About the New York intellectuals (most of them Jewish) who had grouped themselves around *Partisan Review*, Podhoretz made the following claim: *"They did not feel that they belonged to America or that America belonged to them* [italics in the original]."[69] Not only was Podhoretz born later and in some intangible way further from Europe, he was also born into a post-war America more open to ethnic difference, even if Columbia wanted its students to be at least "facsimile WASP's." The barriers to assimilation that had almost prevented Trilling from becoming a full professor at Columbia were gradually weakening. Podhoretz could be a pioneer, going further into America. In other respects, liberal anti-communism was a burden for Podhoretz. It was a burden not to rebel against Trilling as had Allen Ginsberg, whom Podhoretz knew at Columbia.[70] With liberal anti-communism, Podhoretz could not share in the joy of creation, and by adopting a sober anti-utopian creed as his own, Podhoretz was bypassing the radicalism of youth, the enriching mistakes of youth, while he was still young.

By 1960, Podhoretz became the editor of *Commentary*, a magazine at the center of the liberal anti-communist intelligentsia. He owed his good fortune to Trilling.[71] In 1951, Podhoretz had sent his Columbia teacher a letter from Israel, recounting his impressions of the new Jewish state. Trilling sent the letter on to Elliot Cohen, Trilling's old friend and the editor of *Commentary*. The letter did its work, as Irving Kristol, an editor under Cohen, got in touch with Podhoretz and asked him to write for *Commentary*.[72] Kristol was not a student of Trilling's, but, like Podhoretz, his sensibility had been shaped by Trilling's writing and by the Kronstadts of a somewhat older generation.[73] Born to a working-class Jewish family in 1920, Kristol traveled through Trotskyism to the upper reaches of the anti-communist intelligentsia: managing editor at *Commentary* from 1947 to 1952; editor of *Encounter*, an anti-communist magazine in Britain, financed by the CCF and by the CIA, from 1953 to 1958. Gertrude Himmelfarb, Irving Kristol's wife, was another apprentice of Trilling's. An intellectual historian working in Trilling's field—Victorian Britain—Himmelfarb's scholarly and intellectual career was that of the opposing self, a continual critique of the modern and the liberal by comparison with nineteenth-century tradition. Himmelfarb and Kristol were not simply admirers of Trilling, who welcomed his ideas in their own work; they were friends with both Lionel and Diana Trilling. *Commentary* was a center of ideas and a social world, a magazine, a sensibility, and a milieu, a "transatlantic anti-Stalinist community of intellectuals."[74] With Kristol, Himmelfarb, Podhoretz, and *Commentary*—all points that connected with the career of Lionel Trilling—the outlines of the anti-communist intelligentsia intersect with the origins of the neo-conservative movement.

Podhoretz's editorship at *Commentary* confirmed Trilling's influential position within the liberal anti-communist intelligentsia. Trilling had scouted out a young anti-communist talent and placed him in "the *Commentary* office [where] I [Podhoretz] was surrounded by people who were, if anything, even more passionate cold warriors than I myself had become."[75] Much of Podhoretz's writing in the 1950s bore the telltale signs of the teacher's style, with subjects blossoming out from the present moment, tracing culture's historical arc, and moving between culture and politics. As with Trilling, critical evaluation of a novel or short story could be a referendum on liberal anti-communism, on communism, and on radicalism. In 1958 Podhoretz outdid his teacher with a polemical essay titled "The Know-Nothing Bohemians," a review of Jack Kerouac's *On the Road* among other novels, in which he defended liberalism, in all its splendid rationality, from the radical onslaught. "Allen Ginsberg's poetry," Podhoretz wrote, "with its lurid apocalyptic celebration of 'angel-headed hipsters,' speaks for the darker side of the new Bohemianism." The fiction of the Beat generation negates all that Trilling had labored to construct with his literary criticism. It would replace a culture of refined sentiment and incandescent intelligence with one of cheap thrills and under-the-surface brutality: "the Beat Generation's worship of primitivism and spontaneity is more than a cover for hostility to intelligence; it arises from a pathetic poverty of feeling as well."[76] Neal Cassady had missed his chance to carry Trilling's teaching forward into the new generation. Podhoretz acted upon Trilling's teaching by using it as a weapon against the Beats and their outsized irresponsibility.

Podhoretz had a powerful mentor, a well-reasoned creed, and a good job, all of which was in exquisite harmony at *Commentary*. The harmony was excessive, and Podhoretz began to struggle with the creed and the mentor. When Khrushchev gave his 1956 speech, attempting to exorcise the Stalinist ghost, Podhoretz could not help "feeling that the world had become a different place since the death of Stalin and that possibilities now existed which hadn't been there before." In his literary criticism, Lionel Trilling praised variousness and possibility, his fighting words in the contests of the 1930s and 1940s, but "there was very little sense of 'variousness and possibility' in the way Lionel talked about the Soviet Union and Communism, and none at all in the way Diana did," Podhoretz wrote of the Trillings in the 1950s. At this time, the American Committee for Cultural Freedom was splitting into two factions with Diana Trilling on the Right side of the debate. On the Left were the anti–anti-communists, who felt that anti-communism had invited political reaction and cultural mediocrity in America, while needlessly antagonizing the Soviet Union. By 1957, Podhoretz, too, "was beginning to grow restless with the general outlook on life that [he] had absorbed from Lionel (though not from him alone)." Podhoretz and the Trillings understood their disagreement to be more than personal: "though both Lionel and Diana strongly disapproved of the radicalization I was undergoing in those years, they (especially Lionel) also took it seriously as a sign of a general change in the cultural climate and tried very hard to understand what it was all about."[77]

Podhoretz had absorbed more than a political doctrine from Trilling. He had absorbed a metapolitical conservatism, a reverence for sobriety and maturity, and by 1956 Podhoretz was seeking alternatives to this style. In Podhoretz's first memoir, *Making It*, published in 1967, he generalized about the decade after World War II, arguing that in "the imagery of American writing from 1946 and 1956 on subjects as diverse as psychoanalysis, theology, politics, and literature . . . the idea of youth came to be universally associated . . . with the idea of neurosis . . . and the idea of maturity with mental and spiritual health." To this generalization about art and culture Podhoretz adds a political judgment: that "the causes of this fascinating development were closely tied up with the cold war." The Cold War demanded maturity and sobriety from those working toward victory. For the generation that came of age before the Cold War, support for the American side demanded a repudiation of radical youth. These cold warriors were perennially at the middle of the journey, in an adult terrain that avoided, simultaneously, the passivity of old age and the follies of youth. It was a maturity close to intellectual patriotism. To indulge in criticism of America was "to give aid and comfort to the totalitarian enemy," or so believed *Commentary*'s editor, Elliot Cohen, Podhoretz's boss. Podhoretz made no distinction between Lionel Trilling and Elliot Cohen in this regard: "when Lionel was accused of being a 'conservative' (and in those circles in those days this was indeed an accusation), he would sometimes acknowledge that in certain respects he was."[78]

For a devout Trilling student, forbidden fruit was not so much the conservatism of a Chambers or a Buckley—this could comfortably be considered eccentric and marginal in the 1950s—but radicalism of any kind.

Radicalism had not vanished with the 1930s, and in the late 1950s radicalism was newly alluring to Podhoretz. For him, the vehicle of the new radicalism was Norman Mailer, a novelist whose radical youth was the inverse of Trilling's stylized maturity. It was Mailer's radical attitude toward culture and toward sex as well as literature that attracted Podhoretz to him: "bored with my own sensibly moderate liberal ideas, but with Marxism and all its variants closed off as an alternative, I saw in Mailer the possibility of a new kind of radicalism—a radicalism that did not depend on Marx and that had no illusions about the Soviet Union," Podhoretz writes in his memoirs. Another radical prophet, for Podhoretz, was Norman O. Brown, a psychologist whose 1959 book, *Life against Death*, was a polemic against Freudianism, as it had been absorbed into American intellectual life. Brown questioned the conservative imagination that Freud was sanctioning in America, with Trilling as one of the leading "conservative" interpreters of Freud. In Podhoretz's paraphrase, conservative Freudians like Trilling thought that "evil was not imposed from without by institutions or caused by unnecessary restraints: it came from within and it had to be repressed, which meant . . . there could be no civilization without discontent." Brown and Mailer worked together in Podhoretz's mind: just as Mailer "encouraged me to think that my own personal restlessness was worthy of respect and demanded to be acted upon . . . [Norman O. Brown] provided me with grounds for believing that such action could, at least theoretically, be taken. Despite the absence of Marx and the presence of Freud, radicalism was still possible."[79]

In conversation, Trilling referred to Norman Mailer, Norman O. Brown, and Norman Podhoretz as " 'the Norman invasion.' "[80] They were invading his kingdom.

The writing of Mailer and Brown trumpeted radical excitement, and so did the writing of Paul Goodman, a radical who was sui generis. Goodman's books and articles would connect the clenched radicalism of the 1930s to the ebullient radicalism of the 1960s. When Podhoretz began working for *Commentary* in 1955, Goodman was "one of the writers I sought out and tried to publish." Goodman swam in the radical undercurrents around him, not so far beneath the surface of the 1950s, and tried to move 1950s radicalism in a political direction. In Podhoretz's words, he "gave the new radicalism a *political* potential it had previously lacked," not philo-communism or social democracy but a political mentality liberated from Cold War polarities and Cold War worries. Goodman challenged the rigidities of liberal anti-communism, its habits of restraint, sobriety, and maturity, its affirmation of adulthood and impatience with adolescence. If the liberal anti-communist said "you cannot," for fear of giving aid and comfort to the totalitarian enemy, Goodman said "you can," investing his "yes" with spiritual force and with an enjoyment of the absurd. "By making so convincing a case for the connection between the spiritual and the social, Goodman also made the entire enterprise of rad- ical social criticism seem intellectually viable once again," in Podhoretz's view. Podhoretz the *Commentary* editor was undermining the *Commen- tary* of his elders.[81]

Radical ideas about culture intertwined with radical ideas about politics, resulting in the break-up of established Cold War taboos. Schooled in the grave imperative of anti-communism, Podhoretz won- dered whether it was worth perpetuating Cold War hostilities in the post- Stalin era. The Cold War may have been a fact of nature in the late 1940s and early 1950s, when Stalin was alive and when, with the Korean War, cold turned to hot. However, by the late 1950s not only had Khrushchev replaced Stalin, with little adjustment from American cold warriors, but the United States was also without a viable strategy for winning the Cold War. A decade into the conflict, there was only a strategy for continuing it. The same stagnation applied to the Soviet Union: "after ten years the cold war had reached a point of stalemate," Podhoretz recalled of the late 1950s, "with neither side being able to look forward to a significant turn- ing of the tide. Under these circumstances it began to seem possible that the cold war could be brought to an end, and a small movement made its appearance in the United States to encourage just such a development." This was Chambers's exact fear circa 1956: that the West would opt out of the Cold War, not because it accepted the logic of Marxism- Leninism but because it was succumbing to an insidious pacifism, which Khrushchev's Soviet Union was eager to encourage and exploit. Cham- bers felt that General Secretary Khrushchev had ideological weapons that were unavailable to Stalin, and Podhoretz would have been a case in point. By a small movement of like-minded intellectuals, Podhoretz had figures such as sociologists David Riesman (a friend of Trilling's) and Nathan Glazer in mind, liberals then testing the conventional wisdom of Cold War strategy. This was hardly a group of impassioned radicals. The Trillings considered the new development an obvious wrong turn; Pod- horetz found its suggestions intriguing. Perhaps nuclear disarmament could ease a Cold War tension that had scarred international politics, depleting the treasuries and the spirits of the two Cold War combatants. By 1960, Podhoretz was "raising dangerous doubts about the continuing viability of liberal anti-Communism, doubts reaching all the way back to its belief that the sole cause of the cold war was Soviet expansionism and all the way forward to its conviction that Soviet domination of the world was the greatest of all possible evils."[82] Cultural and political radicalism engendered each other, and at the heart of both was the question of America's health in the 1950s. It was intellectually oppressive to assume health where there might be sickness and wisdom where there might be solipsism and error. For denizens of the Norman invasion, the health of America, the balance of its culture, and the purpose of its foreign policy, were better treated as open questions, as questions that could be answered in the negative. For the author of *The Opposing Self*, the Norman invasion could not have come as a complete surprise.

Podhoretz was at the middle of his own, and of his generation's, political odyssey. At a time when conservatives were inventing their tradition in books such as *The Conservative Mind* and *Witness*, liberals such as Trilling were waging an ever more difficult campaign to pass their tradition from one generation to the next. Podhoretz's first editorial for *Commentary*, published in February 1960, was a study in ambiguity, a postscript to the 1950s that posed an implicit question about the 1960s. "The 50's, in short, undertook to demonstrate that the Protestant-liberal-bourgeois synthesis had *not* broken down," Podhoretz wrote, "that, in fact, our civilization was proving itself capable of adapting to new circumstances without losing form or identity. In this undertaking, *Commentary* was an important participant." The editorial's ideological lines were very clearly drawn. Protestant was the inverse of atheist; liberal was the inverse of autocratic; and bourgeois was the inverse of classless. Anti-communism, thus defined, was resolutely American, given the centrality of Protestantism, liberalism, and property rights in American history and culture. (This claim was basically the same as that advanced by Chambers in his "History of Western Culture" series for *Life* magazine.) Yet liberal anti-communism was already an ideology in the past tense. "*Commentary* under my [Podhoretz's] predecessor Elliot E. Cohen had been a major participant in the effort to demonstrate that Western civilization was not falling apart, as so many of its critics from the Marxist Left and the cultural Right had been proclaiming. This defense had seemed plausible for a while. But it had begun to wear thin in recent years," Podhoretz wrote of the late 1950s in his memoir *Breaking Ranks*.[83] Podhoretz himself—circa 1960—was increasingly ambivalent about Western civilization and especially ambivalent about the price being paid, in spirit, by its most rigorous defenders.

Podhoretz's editorial was both prescient and inaccurate. By 1960, the Protestant-liberal-bourgeois synthesis was certainly wearing thin, and avant-garde voices from C. Wright Mills to Allen Ginsberg were there to intone its demise, while exploring other syntheses—a socialist-radical-egalitarian synthesis or a bohemian-sexually liberated-poetic synthesis. "What I for one knew [in 1960] was that the intellectual community was moving back toward radicalism," Podhoretz writes in *Breaking Ranks*, and his first editorial for *Commentary* codified this knowledge.[84] The moderation of the Left, after the 1930s, had come full circle, arriving at a synthesis of nineteenth-century coloration, a synthesis that was not doing much to inspire the young; but there was ample evidence to refute Podhoretz's editorial. The Protestant-liberal-bourgeois synthesis described only one wing of an anti-communist intelligentsia that did (in aggregate) dominate the intellectual life of the 1950s. *Commentary* magazine—sponsored as it was by the American Jewish Committee—illustrated the open space between liberalism and Protestantism. Podhoretz's own assaults on the cultural Right, throughout the 1950s, suggested that secularism and liberalism were natural partners, just as much as liberalism and Protestantism. The reigning synthesis could be rearranged: a defense of religion and of social hierarchy, with an implied hierarchy of taste, might well be conservative, leading back to the bible of modern conservatism, to Edmund Burke's *Reflections on the Revolution in France*, in which Burke indicted French radicals for an atheism and an egalitarianism that went against human nature. Perhaps the Bolsheviks had made a similar mistake, and the proper response to their experiment was a Protestant-conservative-bourgeois synthesis or a Protestant-conservative-populist synthesis, as Chambers would have preferred.

By rebelling against the Protestant-liberal-bourgeois synthesis, Podhoretz was trying to throw off the enormous weight of the anti-communist intelligentsia. Anti-communism had been too successful: one could not credibly argue for Stalin or Khrushchev—for the Soviet version of revolution—as one could in 1932. Too often, anti-communism had the sound of one hand clapping, a symptom of its intellectual triumph. David Riesman, Nathan Glazer, Allen Ginsberg, C. Wright Mills, and Delmore

Schwartz were anything but Communist Party members; they had their own hostility to Soviet communism, and the object of their dissent, the anti-communist intelligentsia, was not simply dominant in terms of raw numbers but embedded in countless institutions. Some of them—like the American Committee for Cultural Freedom and the Congress for Cultural Freedom—would prove transient. Others, like the universities, would not remain anti-communist forever. The major trend, however, was of influence through institutionalization: both *Commentary* and *National Review* would continue in the elaboration of anti-communist arguments well into the 1970s and 1980s. Ties formed between anti-communist intellectuals and government, whether official, as in George Kennan's case, or covert, as in the CIA's funding of anti-communist magazines and networks, would persist until the end of the Cold War. Nixon had his Henry Kissinger and Carter his Zbigniew Brezinski. Under Ronald Reagan, a new set of anti-communist intellectuals, many of whom had come of age in the 1950s, would put their talent at the service of the White House, the State Department, and the Pentagon. The anti-communist intelligentsia was an enduring element of postwar American politics, fundamental to America's prosecution of the Cold War; its influence would remain in Washington long after the Cold War had ended.

The scholars of war, who inspired Ginsberg's lament in "Howl," constituted a vast, powerful army without much esprit de corps. By 1960, when Podhoretz was questioning the liberal anti-communism of his elders, Trilling and Chambers, his former Columbia classmate, were no longer friends. They had too little in common to be personal friends and too much in common, perceived differently, to be political friends. They had no interest in creating an anti-communist intelligentsia. The term would have been too bland, too lifeless, too far from the vital questions of what anti-communism was, what it meant for Western civilization, and what political order it dictated. Trilling considered Chambers's conservatism mawkish and retrograde in its religious intensities. To his mind, there was danger in the political forces arrayed behind this yeoman farmer in Westminster, Maryland, a night of reaction that would descend, were his ideas truly to become the pattern of American politics. Chambers, having discovered the sanity of Saint Benedict, must have found little sanity in the elliptical, moderate, secular, liberal essays of Trilling, if he bothered to read them at all; they were reports from a New York that was doing more harm than good to Western culture, the record of a mind that knew despair and crisis and communism, without knowing that all three were matters of faith, not to be grasped by the secular mind alone. Trilling and Chambers may have been scholars of war, only theirs was not the same war, and there was no ultimate victory for one, no victory in the Cold War, that would not have been defeat for the other.

EPILOGUE

Whittaker Chambers's death elicited an extraordinary obituary from Columbia University, where Chambers's journey to the Communist Party had begun in the early 1920s. This college obituary echoed the "whispering campaign" waged against Chambers during the Hiss case and portrayed Chambers as "relatively humble, he had the stuff that made Hitler and Stalin, and he had the wit to put himself in line for such a role should opportunity offer." Chambers was faulted, above all, for his influence: "he [Chambers] was an ugly man, but for a while American [sic] looked like Whittaker Chambers. It has not been sufficiently noted that his great book, *Witness*, ranks with *Mein Kampf*, though it is much better written and funnier." Chambers—the McCarthy-era Hitler—was a pathological man, and his college obituary reflected a liberal tendency to associate conservatism with psychological disorder. Columbia historian Richard Hofstadter detected a "paranoid style" on the Right; Columbia sociologist Daniel Bell emphasized the connection between McCarthyite conservatism and "status anxiety."[1] The obituary writer for the "Class of 1924 Newsletter" vulgarized this liberal suspicion of the Right, offering psychological jargon as explanation for Chambers's life and career. "Whittaker's immense personal achievement," the obituary declared with mock intimacy, "was to transfer his own sublimated hysteria to large sections of the American people."[2] Chambers had already been banished from Columbia for his atheist "A Play for Puppets." After his death, Chambers's memory was expelled for the conservative anticommunism of the adult man.

One outraged reader of the Columbia obituary was Chambers's friend, William F. Buckley Jr., and, Buckley wrote to a Columbia faculty member to lament the insulting obituary. In July 1962, Buckley wrote to Lionel Trilling, asking if Trilling had "seen the newsletter of the class of 1924 and its obituary on Whittaker Chambers? It is the most sickening piece of prose I think I have ever read. I call it to your attention because I remember Whit's references to your kindness and integrity, and thought you might want to protest it." Trilling protested the obituary, and his protest assuaged Buckley's outrage. "I knew you would respond in that way and am most grateful to you," Buckley wrote some ten days after his initial letter to Trilling, implying a bond of respect between Buckley and Trilling on the one hand and between Trilling and Chambers on the other.[3] If intellectuals on the Left objected to Trilling's "conservative imagination," intellectuals on the Right admired Trilling precisely because he was generous to conservatives.

Trilling's modulated perspective did not inform Chambers's *New York Times* obituary. The *Times* identified Chambers as an important historical figure, worthy of a long obituary, and it presented Chambers as someone who may have told the truth, without commemorating Chambers's work as a conservative intellectual. Chambers was invisible in his own most conspicuous obituary. This "confessed former spy currier" was trapped in the Hiss case, which William Fitzgibbon—the author of this obituary—deemed "one of the most dramatic and anger-provoking affairs in the country's history." The case remained so contentious and the details so murky that "differences of opinion about the Hiss case would not disappear." Rather than defining the Hiss case, as he had aspired to do in *Witness*, Chambers was defined by the case—"Chambers Is Dead; Hiss Case Witness."[4] Fitzgibbon listed several consequences of the Hiss case: it "convinced many that a Communist spy had obtained access to the most confidential documents," it "provided the Republicans with ammunition to attack the Roosevelt and Truman Administrations," and "it started Richard M. Nixon of California on the road that took him to the Republican nomination for President in 1960." The Hiss case did not alert Americans to a spiritual crisis, to a lack of confidence in Western civilization that was inhibiting the fight against Soviet communism, the message Chambers had tried so desperately to broadcast when he had the nation's attention. Fitzgibbon's paraphrase of *Witness* resembled the diagnosis of pathology devised by Hiss's legal defense team. With regard to Chambers's early life, "the complicated neuroses that beset the family were set down in detail in Mr. Chambers's book, 'Witness.' " After noting the suicide of Chambers's brother, Fitzgibbon also wrote that "a woman member of the family menaced her sleeping kin with an axe." He then added—an absurd detail in context—that "there were also intellectual

treats—much reading of good books and visits to the theater when there
was money." Even Chambers's conversion to Christianity seemed furtive
and strange: "he had been 'secretly reached' by the inner life of Quakerism, as he put it."[5] Chambers's *Times* obituary was the obituary of a historical curiosity. Over time, one might imagine, this historical curiosity
would fade from memory.

Faith in Alger Hiss's innocence has been slow to fade. "One of the successful spies in American history," Hiss was released from prison in the
fall of 1954, an unemployable man believed by many to be a traitor. Yet in
1956 Hiss was invited by students to speak at Princeton University, a year
before he published his memoir and interpretation of the case, *In the
Court of Public Opinion*. In 1958, Fred Cook published *The Unfinished
Story of Alger Hiss*, a title that told its own story. By this time, Hiss was being interviewed by Meyer Zeligs, an acquaintance of Carl Binger, the
psychologist who had testified to the psychoses of Whittaker Chambers
during the Hiss case. Zeligs would eventually devote a book to the psy-
chotic Whittaker Chambers, *Friendship and Fratricide: An Analysis of
Whittaker Chambers and Alger Hiss*. By the late 1960s, Hiss was a familiar
speaker on college campuses, audacious enough to say, in a 1972 *Life*
magazine profile of him, that "by the time I am 80, I expect to be respected and venerated." Another pro-Hiss book came out in 1976, John
Chabot Smith's *Alger Hiss: The True Story*. Given that Hiss was guilty,
there was no empirical argument to be made for his innocence, but the
longing for his innocence was such that, in the words of G. Edward
White, "after '67 all the subsequent twentieth-century books on the [Hiss]
case took as their central premise not that Hiss was innocent, but that the
American public could not make up its mind." When Hiss died in 1996,
ABC news anchor Peter Jennings spoke definitively of Hiss's innocence.[6]
To this day, New York University's Tamiment Library maintains a Web
site honoring Hiss's memory.[7]

A reversal of Chambers's historical legacy began long before 1996. In a
1984 *New York Times* article titled "White House Freedom Medal Set for
Whittaker Chambers," Chambers emerged as a hero to some. The political distance between 1961 and 1984 was immense. A conservative movement gathered force after Chambers's death, contributing decisively
to the 1980 election of Ronald Reagan. Reagan drew inspiration from
Chambers, and the president's anti-communism was Chambers-esque,
more so certainly than the détente-oriented anti-communism of the

Nixon administration.[8] In 1984 Reagan posthumously awarded Chambers a White House Freedom Medal, and in 1988 he turned Chambers's Maryland farm into a national historic landmark. Chambers was a "professed Soviet agent who became a celebrated anti-Communist 35 years ago." The later article acknowledged what the obituary failed to recognize—namely, Chambers's stature as a conservative intellectual: "Mr. Chambers became a hero of the conservative movement and an anti-Communist writer."[9] It was none other than President Reagan who claimed Chambers as a conservative of note. According to the article, "Mr. Reagan has regularly praised Mr. Chambers over the years as a patriot." In addition, Reagan "has often referred to Mr. Chambers's account of turning from communism and finding belief in God the day he pondered the intricacies of nature represented by 'the sight of his infant daughter's ear.' "[10]

President Reagan viewed Chambers as a historic figure, "the tragic and lonely Whittaker Chambers," as Reagan put it in his autobiography, and he honored Chambers as a truth teller who had laid the intellectual foundation for the Reagan presidency.[11] Reagan characterized Chambers as someone whose influence gradually increased over time. " 'He [Chambers] was not believed at first,' the President said of Mr. Chambers's testimony. 'But the inexorable power of truth was slowly felt and overwhelming evidence led a jury to convict one of the former officials [Alger Hiss] of perjury.' " In a speech at Eureka College, Reagan's alma mater, the president placed Chambers's truth telling about Soviet communism in a historical trajectory: the journey from the socialist lie to the laissez-faire, anti-communist truth. Reagan's career demonstrated the political side of the journey, while Chambers was crucial to the intellectual journey of American conservatism: " 'Chambers's story represents a generation's disenchantment with statism and its return to eternal truths and fundamental values,' Mr. Reagan declared then [February 6, 1984], in hailing what he called a current 'counter-revolution of the intellectuals' that was 'predated by one of the most vivid events of my time [the Hiss case].' "[12]

If Ronald Reagan was the president closest to Chambers, John F. Kennedy was the president closest to Trilling. Kennedy never gave Trilling a White House Freedom Medal, and the Democratic Party never turned Trilling's Claremont Avenue apartment in New York City into a national historic landmark; but in April 1962 Kennedy did invite Lionel and Diana Trilling to the White House.[13] Chambers had cautiously predicted Kennedy's election in 1957, but Chambers was hardly the sort of urban liberal sophisticate to whom Kennedy appealed.[14] In the 1950s urban liberal sophisticates had a longstanding romance with Adlai Stevenson and certainly not with Nixon or Eisenhower. Although Kennedy may not have been quite as intelligent, witty, or urbane, he did what Stevenson never could, winning back the White House for the Democratic Party. Kennedy appealed greatly to liberal anti-communist intellectuals. He had written a book before becoming president, he liked intellectuals and wanted their support, and he could speak their language. One might say that Kennedy appealed to the vanity of liberal intellectuals, but Kennedy's appeal was also bound up with his political power. He projected toughness, and with communism he did not waver. He promised to marshal America's energy, intelligence, and power to combat Soviet tyranny. Both Diana and Lionel Trilling were susceptible to Kennedy's political charm, and when they received an invitation to a White House dinner for Nobel Laureates, they were thrilled. In a 1997 *New Yorker* essay, Diana Trilling lovingly recounted the details of their evening with the Kennedys. Without irony, she called her essay "A Visit to Camelot."[15]

The Trillings' visit was the culmination of their liberal anti-communism and a validation of Lionel Trilling's conservative turn. With Trilling's circle in mind, Norman Podhoretz wrote that "all of us in the family [of New York intellectuals] knew and were even friendly with members of the White House staff; they read our magazines and the pieces and books we ourselves wrote, and they cared—it was said the President himself cared—about what we thought. Would Roosevelt have cared? Would Truman? Would Eisenhower?"[16] With Kennedy, the intellectual need not brood on the margins. There was now the chance to converse with and perhaps even educate politicians. Podhoretz has written that "intellectuals were recognized [by the Kennedy administration] as an occupational grouping that mattered in American life: from having carried a faint aura of disreputability, the title 'intellectual' all at once became an honorific, and much began to be made in Washington as elsewhere of leading representatives of this particular class."[17] The intellectual could be someone of social standing, steeped in the social graces, properly tailored, with good manners—a member of "society," to use a term from Trilling's literary criticism. Trilling often challenged the modern impulse to flee from society, which he understood as the constraints, hierarchies, civilizational contents, and discontents that order human interaction. Diana Trilling's *New Yorker* essay featured the Trillings' delight in society, not excluding the high society assembled at the White House. In the spring of 1962 the Trillings had everything they wanted: a sense of their own political integrity and intellectual seriousness, recognition for these traits from an American president, and the feeling that the president was in harmony with the nation. Kennedy lent political equilibrium to the liberal anti-communist position. In an essay published in 1963, shortly after Kennedy's assassination, Diana Trilling wrote that Kennedy had done much to restore "America to its appropriate moral rank among nations."[18]

During their evening at the White House, Diana Trilling studied the calculus of social rank. She paid close attention to clothing as an index of society, to which some belonged and others did not. An old woman at the White House definitely belonged, as she "looked exquisite, with beautiful jewelry that had probably been in their family forever." Both Diana and her husband were attached to refinement. "With our old-fashioned notions," Diana recalled, "we decided that I should wear the simplest possible short evening dress, black, if I could find one, and covered up, not bare." They worked hard to belong to society. Without question, the Kennedys belonged, and they belonged in part because they looked so good—"the President was handsome and exuded energy." Lyndon Johnson, alas, did not belong, and he dressed the part. At the White House, he "had on the most awful dinner jacket. I think it was gray, and I don't know what it was made of, but it seemed to shimmer, as if he were master of ceremonies in some cheap night club." Richard Nixon must have stood somewhere near and quite possibly beneath Lyndon Johnson in the essay's implied social system. In conversation with Diana Trilling, Jacqueline Kennedy recalled the bad taste of the Eisenhower White House. Jacqueline said, in Diana Trilling's paraphrase: "It was just unbearable. There would be Mamie in one chair and Ike in another . . . everybody stood, and there was nothing to drink."[19]

On their way to the White House, the Trillings had not entirely escaped their communist past. On the train from New York to the White House, they met up with "a very seedy-looking man carrying a suitcase and a large raggedy bulging briefcase . . . It was James Farrell," an emissary from the radical 1930s, it seemed.[20] Author of the Studs Lonegan trilogy, novels about working-class life in Chicago, Farrell had traveled in the same radical circles as the Trillings back in the early 1930s; he had courageously recommended that "the 1935 session of the American Writers Congress be closed with the singing of 'The International.' "[21] The seedy-looking man with the suitcase evoked the Trillings' own transformation from youthful communists to respectable adults. In 1946, Farrell had criticized Lionel Trilling's short story "The Other Margaret" for abetting "the moods, the retreat from Marxism, the growing moral snobbery of the advanced and cultivated New York intellectual."[22] In 1962, Farrell was still resisting the image of the advanced and cultivated New York intellectual: "he [Farrell] was wearing a suit that I think was supposed to be brown, but it was so shabby that you could no longer tell its color," Diana Trilling wrote. "His necktie was under his ear and a button was missing from his shirtfront." In a comic irony, however, Farrell had reserved a more expensive seat on the train to Washington than had the Trillings. When this dawned on Lionel, Diana "could feel humiliation racing through every inch of my husband's body. He [Lionel] was riding in a coach while this poor, bedraggled devil who looked as if he had not had a bed to sleep in for a year or a change of underwear in a month was traveling in a chair." Irony followed irony, and at the White House dinner the Trillings once again encountered Farrell. Now he "was transformed. He had on an absolutely clean shirt, his suit was pressed and sparkling clean, every shirt stud was in place. He looked dreamy."[23]

A man not transformed was physicist J. Robert Oppenheimer, whose presence at the White House dinner was interpreted by Diana as "a nice gesture on the part of President Kennedy, wanting publicly to rehabilitate Oppenheimer after he had been treated as a security risk for nearly a decade. But his appearance was that of a spectre, a *momento mori*."[24]

That evening the White House was gorgeous, a meeting of power and intellect not mingled in such magnitude since the New Deal. James Farrell was only one of many artists and intellectuals gracing the Kennedy White House. Others in attendance were Robert Frost, William Styron, James Baldwin, Katherine Anne Porter, and John Dos Passos, whose own conservative turn was complete by 1962.[25] Liberal anti-communist intellectual Arthur Schlesinger Jr. was part of the Kennedy entourage, standing so close to power that he could not be as light-hearted as the rest of the dinner guests. Schlesinger, who had recommended *The Middle of the Journey* to "all liberals," was now an intellectual muse of sorts to the president. When Schlesinger saw Diana Trilling, he "waved and came over.

He greeted me and introduced his wife, but he didn't seem relaxed or friendly, like everybody else. He appeared to be self-conscious, as if borne down by his official White House connection." If Schlesinger was self-conscious, it was because his role as intellectual at the Kennedy court was so important. Kennedy distinguished himself among the intellectuals not just by the power he possessed but by speaking well to intellectuals. After dinner, he gave what would become a famous toast: the White House had not seen such a gathering of intellect beneath its roof since Thomas Jefferson dined there alone. With these words, Kennedy "at once had the place in his hands. Everybody loved it."[26]

The Kennedys also worked their magic on Lionel Trilling. When he was first introduced to Kennedy, the president recognized him as a familiar face. " 'Oh, it's you,' the President exclaimed. 'I'm so glad to see you.' Lionel beamed, of course, and said, 'Thank you.' Jacqueline Kennedy went a step further in welcoming Lionel to the White House: "You know, I have a step sister who won't have an idea in her head unless you tell her it's right to have it. She never says anything unless you say it's all right to say it." The first moment Diana and Lionel were alone together he confessed: "I'm going to die—I've never been so flattered in my whole life." The flattery continued after dinner when Lionel and Diana were invited upstairs to a smaller party away from the official reception halls. For a while, Lionel sat with Jacqueline, and the two discussed literature. As Diana Trilling observed, "she [Jacqueline Kennedy] and Lionel were getting on so splendidly—Lionel really liked her, and she really liked him."[27] Jacqueline Kennedy wanted to talk about D. H. Lawrence with Trilling. She asked his opinion of Lawrence's oeuvre, at one point jumping up to check a quote in her private library. John F. Kennedy cut the literary soirée short, Diana Trilling felt, because he wanted to get back to work. Even Camelot had its limits, and the Trillings had only this one evening in their Camelot. The beauty of the evening—like the political equilibrium of liberal anti-communism itself—was fleeting.[28]

In politics victory can be as transient as defeat. John F. Kennedy's assassination in 1963 opened a new and turbulent era in American history, and Lyndon Johnson—his awful dinner jacket notwithstanding—took Kennedy's place.[29] Over the course of the 1960s, intellectuals moved steadily away from the White House because of Johnson and the Vietnam War, which put immense strain on the liberal anti-communist position, prompting many to abandon liberalism and many to abandon anti-communism. In 1968, the Democratic nominating convention could not contain all the radical passion on the Left. Protestors and police clashed in the streets of Chicago. The 1968 assassinations of Martin Luther King Jr. and Robert Kennedy left instability in their wake. The adversary culture developed into a counterculture, a widespread rejection of a conservative status quo associated with the 1950s. In the 1960s, revolution vied with reform, causing the Left to splinter into fragments. "Never suppose that the Left has finished with Nixon," Whittaker Chambers had cautioned in 1954, and in 1968 Richard Nixon—long-term nemesis of the Left—won the contest he had lost to Kennedy in 1960; Nixon had yet to finish with the Left.[30] The Nixon administration's subsequent collapse into scandal was spectacular, but it was not the death knell of American conservatism. Nor did Nixon's tawdry demise help in the rebirth of the American Left. To the contrary: Nixon's resignation marked the end of moderate, Eisenhower conservatism in American politics. Four troubled years of the Carter presidency preceded the Reagan Revolution, Reagan the most vociferously anti-communist of all postwar American presidents. A mere twenty-two years after the Trillings' charmed White House dinner, a Republican president bestowed a Freedom Medal on Whittaker Chambers.

The Trillings' evening at the White House yielded a moment of political bliss that Chambers never experienced. Because of his friendship with Nixon, Chambers enjoyed some proximity to presidential power during the Eisenhower era. At one point, Vice President Nixon invited Chambers to dinner at the White House, but Chambers was too sick to attend.[31] With or without a White House dinner, there was no conservative Camelot for Chambers, who would surely have preferred his farm to any Washington "society." As an anti-communist, Chambers dressed as badly as James Farrell on his way to Washington, D.C. In the 1950s, Chambers still looked like a 1930s man of the people, a Steinbeck protagonist keeping close to the soil. Chambers was suspicious of fashionable success, and success was Camelot's elixir. Unlike the Trillings, Chambers had no political heroes as an anti-communist. The anti-communist conservatives he knew were all imperfect: McCarthy was a demagogue, Nixon an opportunist, and Eisenhower hardly a conservative at all. The conservative movement had only a handful of intellectuals behind it in 1961, when Chambers died, and it had no political leadership for the foreseeable future. Chambers had helped set in motion a movement that would take decades to mature, but he had no prophetic insight into its destiny. He was convinced that the communists would win the Cold War.

In the long term, Chambers's pessimism was no more judicious than the Trillings' jubilation after meeting the Kennedys. The Trillings made little attempt at prophesy once their intoxicating evening was over.[32] They left the White House for Union Station, and "we could have danced our way, Lionel and I were so giddy," Diana Trilling wrote in her *New Yorker* essay. "In fact, we did dance into the train station . . . It was a kind of minuet we performed the length of Union Station all the way to our train and to our compartment." They could not have known that they were dancing as well into the traumatic 1960s, which brought a touch of revolution through the gates of Columbia University. In the spring of 1968, student protest washed over the campus where Trilling and Chambers first met. The animosity toward Chambers in the "Class of 1924 Newsletter" included Trilling in 1968, when radical students denounced their liberal sage as a corrupt defender of the status quo. Trilling belonged among "establishment critics who preached the necessity of order, myth, stability, a conservative tradition," in the words of Jonah Raskin, a former student of Trilling's and a participant in the uprising at Columbia.[33] Without accepting the conservative label, Trilling did what he could to defend the university from the revolutionaries.[34] Neither of these two Columbia alumni—neither Trilling nor Chambers—was a stranger to revolutionary changes of heart. In their political youth, they had given their hearts to communism only to spend the majority of their adult lives reflecting on the imperative of anti-communism. They knew firsthand the connection between a radical and a conservative turn.

NOTES
INDEX

NOTES

Introduction

1. It is unclear whether Nixon knew much, or anything, about Alger Hiss before encountering him in the House Un-American Activities Committee (HUAC) hearings in the summer of 1948. Irwin Gellman argues that Nixon had no such knowledge. *The Contender: Richard Nixon the Congress Years, 1946–1952* (New York: Free Press, 1999), 222–223.
2. Historians disagree on the question of anti-communism and continuity on the American Right. Ellen W. Schrecker notes "that anticommunism in its modern form as a consciously organized campaign against the left began in the 1870s." *Many Are the Crimes: McCarthyism in America* (Princeton, N.J.: Princeton University Press, 1999), xiii. David H. Bennet also sees the origins of the twentieth-century Right in the nineteenth century: "the old antialienism, the source of the early right-wing movements, was replaced by the new, the fear of communism." *The Party of Fear: From Nativist Movements to the New Right in American History* (Chapel Hill: University of North Carolina Press, 1966), 13. Paul Gottfried disagrees, pointing to the "increasing irrelevance of the prewar, especially non-American, traditionalist thinking for the postwar Right." *The Conservative Movement* (New York: Twayne, 1993), xi. Gottfried details the "rich, indigenous American conservative traditions—Southern Agrarian, Taft Republican and Brahmin individualist—that did not fit into the procrustean synthesis created in the fifties." Ibid., ix.
3. Anti-Stalinism is a subspecies of anti-communism. The danger of subsuming everything under the anti-communist rubric is that one can miss the Marxism to which some intellectuals—such as radicals Dwight Macdonald and Philip Rahv—adhered as anti-Stalinists. This was an important distinction on the Left. It does not apply to the Right, for which communism, whether Stalinist or not, was ipso facto reprehensible.
4. Leo Ribuffo offers a cogent description of the conservative turn: "while centrists expelled Popular Front liberals and 'anti-anti-Communists' from the 'vital center,' the new conservatives repudiated the 'isolationists' and anti-Semites who had been *their* unseemly allies during the 1930s. This parallel

315

ideological restructuring by movements that remained, through a process of stringent elimination, the only respectable Left and Right, pushed the whole political spectrum rightward." "Why Is There So Much Conservatism in the United States and Why Do So Few Historians Know Anything about It?" *American Historical Review* 99, no. 2 (April 1994): 444.

5. Gerald Sorin describes the two alcoves in *Irving Howe: A Life of Passionate Dissent* (New York: New York University Press, 2002), 17.

6. This is according to conservative activist Ann Coulter, *Treason: Liberal Treachery from the Cold War to the War on Terror* (New York: Crown Forum, 2003), 17.

7. Whittaker Chambers, *Witness* (Washington, D.C,: Regnery, 1997), 4.

8. Coulter, *Treason*, 201–202, 292, 292.

9. Jacques Barzun, ed., *A Company of Readers: Uncollected Writings of W. H. Auden, Jacques Barzun, and Lionel Trilling from the Readers' Subscription and Mid-Century Book Clubs* (New York: Free Press, 2001). Barzun outlines the aspirations of the Readers' Subscription and Mid-Century book clubs in a short foreword to *A Company of Readers*, "Three Men and a Book," ix–xvii.

10. Peter Steinfels traces neoconservatism back to the 1930s. "The political reality that loomed over these years [from the 1930s to the 1950s], and that provided the formative political experiences for these men [the neoconservatives] was the rise of totalitarianism and the failure of socialism in the face of that threat. The experience was to determine their attitudes and give all their later work its moral impetus." *The Neoconservatives: The Men Who Are Changing America's Politics* (New York: Simon and Schuster, 1979), 26. Murray Friedman argues that Trilling, together with Elliot Cohen (the first editor of *Commentary*) and Leo Strauss, a political philosopher, "formed the nucleus of the emerging Jewish conservatism" in the 1950s. *The Neoconservative Revolution: Jewish Intellectuals and the Shaping of Public Policy* (Cambridge: Cambridge University Press, 2005), 36.

11. Norman Podhoretz, "Prologue: A Letter to My Son," in *Breaking Ranks: A Political Memoir* (New York: Harper and Row, 1979), 3–20. The political rhythms in this letter are Chambers-esque: "if you want to understand my own political development," Podhoretz writes to his son, "the first thing you have to bear in mind is that it was on these attitudes towards Communism on the one side and America on the other that I cut my teeth as a young intellectual. It was from here that my odyssey to radicalism began, and it was back to a remarkably similar set of attitudes that my gradual revulsion from radicalism eventually took me." Ibid., 16.

12. David Horowitz, *Radical Son: A Journey through Our Times* (New York: Free Press, 1997), 2. Horowitz continued the motif of parents and children in a book coauthored with Peter Collier, *Destructive Generation: Second Thoughts on the*

Sixties (New York: Summit Books, 1989). Midge Decter, the wife of Norman Podhoretz, writes in a similar vein in her book *Liberal Parents, Radical Children* (New York: McCann & Geoghehan, 1975).

13. See, for example, the title of Norman Podhoretz's memoir, *My Love Affair with America: The Cautionary Tale of a Cheerful Conservative* (New York: Free Press, 2000). Gertrude Himmelfarb looks back with appreciation to the American Enlightenment in *The Roads to Modernity: The British, French and American Enlightenment* (New York: Knopf, 2004).

14. Norman Podhoretz has devoted a book to analysis of the Bible, *The Prophets: Who They Were, What They Are* (New York: Free Press, 2002). Will Herberg made an early journey from Left to Right after which he wrote extensively about religion. See *Judaism and Modern Man* (Philadelphia: Jewish Publication Society of America, 1951) and *Protestant, Catholic, Jew: An Essay in American Religious Sociology* (Garden City, N.J.: Doubleday, 1955).

15. Jeffrey Hart writes that *National Review* "would steer overall, with occasional lurches toward purist ideology, in the 'strategic' direction favored by [Whittaker] Chambers and [James] Burnham: toward the conservative side of mainstream American politics." *The Making of the American Conservative Mind: National Review and Its Times* (Wilmington, Del.: ISI Books, 2005), 363.

16. John Diggins attributes errors of judgment made by Ronald Reagan and the neoconservatives to Whittaker Chambers. The collapse of the Soviet Union "was a refutation of his [Reagan's] political philosophy . . . Whittaker Chambers convinced many neoconservatives that communism was the winning side of history and anticommunists would be the losers." *Ronald Reagan: Fate, Freedom and the Making of History* (New York: Norton, 2007), 336.

17. David Horowitz, "Marx's Manifesto: 150 Years of Evil," *Eutopia* 3, no. 3 (March-April 1999): 1. In a biographical sketch of Horowitz, Scott Sherman writes that "by 1989 Horowitz was comparing himself to Gifford Maxim, the Whittaker Chambers character in Lionel Trilling's novel *The Middle of the Journey*, an ex-communist who confronted the radical tendencies of his time with what he knew, from his experience, of the reality which lay behind the luminous words of the great promise. Horowitz had arrived at the final destination of his journey." "David Horowitz's Long March," *The Nation*, July 3, 2000. Available at http://www.thenation.com/doc20000703/sherman/5. July 1, 2007.

18. Ruth R. Wisse, *The Modern Jewish Canon: A Journey through Language and Culture* (New York: Free Press, 2000), 17. Cornel West argues that Trilling's "brand of liberalism blended into a tempered conservatism." "Lionel Trilling: Godfather of the Neoconservatism," *New Politics* new series 1 (Summer 1986):

240. West's essay rests on a critical attitude toward neoconservatism, supporters of which, in his opinion, "moved to the forefront of the already polemicized and politicized intellectual life—only to further contribute to its debasement." Ibid. West continues his analysis of Trilling in *The American Evasion of Philosophy: A Genealogy of Pragmatism* (Madison: University of Wisconsin Press, 1989), 164–181. According to Jacob Heilbrunn, Trilling "privately sympathized with it [neoconservatism] on narrow cultural grounds." *They Knew They Were Right: The Rise of the Neocons* (New York: Doubleday, 2008), 42.

19. Gertrude Himmelfarb, *On Looking into the Abyss: Untimely Thoughts on Culture and Society* (New York: Knopf, 1994), 6.

20. Diana Trilling, *The Beginning of the Journey: The Marriage of Diana and Lionel Trilling* (New York: Harcourt, Brace, 1993), 404. Norman Podhoretz disagreed with the drift of Diana Trilling's judgment. He recalled a conversation with Diana (after Lionel's death) in which he expressed the "great irony that even those few of my ex-friends who were still strongly anti-Communist (especially Diana herself) should have been so hostile to the very president [Ronald Reagan] whose election and whose policies in office owed so much to the idea that they themselves in their turn had done so much to nurture. In this connection, it is instructive to remind ourselves that Reagan— who was entirely at one with the pre-Vietnam family in stressing the moral aspects of the cold war over considerations of realpolitik . . . began his life on the Left." *Ex-Friends: Falling Out with Allen Ginsberg, Lionel & Diana Trilling, Lillian Hellman, Hannah Arendt, and Norman Mailer* (New York: Encounter, 2000), 224.

21. Michael Denning argues for the longevity—and dubious value—of anti-Stalinist lessons: "the 'lessons' of the dangers of fellow traveling remained a leitmotif in the attacks on left-wing solidarity movements from the 1960's to the 1980's." *The Cultural Front: The Laboring of American Culture in the Twentieth Century* (New York: Verso, 1998), 12.

22. Robert Service, *Stalin: A Biography* (London: Macmillan, 2004), 369; Irving Howe, "The New York Intellectuals," in *Irving Howe: Selected Writings, 1950–1990* (New York: Harcourt, Brace, Jovanovich, 1990), 245.

1. Sons of the Bourgeoisie

Epigraph: Lionel Trilling understood "Dover Beach," which he included in an anthology of great literature, to be a portrait of "modern life, which has seen the ebbing of the sea of faith. We assume that he [Arnold] means religious faith, and this assumption is borne out by other of Arnold's poems in which the diminution of religious faith is a reason for melancholy. But Arnold felt that the lessening of religious faith went hand in hand with the lessening of personal energy, vitality and confidence, of that happy unquestioning attachment to life which William James called 'animal faith.' " Lionel Trilling, *Prefaces to the Experience of Literature* (New York: Harcourt, Brace and Jovanovich, 1979), 252.

1. "Columbia Magazine Play Stirs Strike," *New York Evening Post* (November 7, 1922), p. 4; "Sketch of Christ's Life Causes Editor to Resign," *New York Tribune*, November 7, 1922; "Columbia Magazine Play Stirs Strike," p. 4; "Sketch of Christ's Life Causes Editor to Resign." John Erskine does not mention "A Play for Puppets" in his memoirs. *My Life as a Teacher* (New York: J.B. Lippincott Co., 1948).

2. Lionel Trilling, "Faculty Critic Maintains 'Review' Is Greatly Changed in Viewpoint," *Columbia Spectator*, December 9, 1932, p. 4. A hatred of vulgarity was a common aspect of literary modernism. One example would be Edmund Wilson's analysis of T. S. Eliot's 1922 poem, "The Waste Land": "Never have the sufferings of the sensitive man in the modern city chained to some work he hates and crucified on the vulgarity of his surroundings been so vividly set forth." Edmund Wilson to John Peale Bishop, September 5, 1922, in *Letters on Literature and Politics, 1912–1972* (New York: Farrar, Straus, and Giroux, 1977), 94.

3. Trilling, "Faculty Critic Maintains 'Review' Is Greatly Changed in Viewpoint," p. 4.

4. Later in life, Trilling attributed an upward mobility of the spirit to Columbia's influence: "the Columbia *mystique* was directed to showing young men how they might escape from the limitations of their middle-class or their lower-middle-class upbringings by putting before them great models of thought, feeling, and imagination, and great issues which suggested the close interrelation of the private and personal life with the public life, with life in society." "Some Notes for an Autobiographical Lecture" in *The Last Decade: Essays and Reviews, 1965–1975*, ed. Diana Trilling (New York: Harcourt, Brace, Jovanovich, 1979), 229.

5. François Furet sees frustration with bourgeois options as a determining circumstance of twentieth-century intellectual life: "the bourgeois have provided a common quarry for all modernity's malcontents—those who incriminate the mediocrity of the bourgeois world, as well as those who denounce its lies." *The Passing of an Illusion: The Idea of Communism in the Twentieth Century*, trans. Deborah Furet (Chicago: University of Chicago Press, 1999), 10.

6. Trilling, "Faculty Critic Maintains 'Review' Is Greatly Changed in Viewpoint," p. 4.

7. Trilling observed that "though vexed by financial worry, [my family] was firmly and programmatically middle-class. Both parents were devoted not merely to the idea of education as a means of social advancement, which was of course characteristic of Jewish immigrants, but also to the idea of 'culture.' " Lionel

Trilling to John Vaughn, December 15, 1972, Lionel Trilling Papers, Special Collections, Butler Library, Columbia University, Box 28 (hereafter cited as Trilling MSS).

8. As Trilling pointed out, "City College, with no expense at all, was out of the question for my parents as being socially inferior [to Columbia]." Lionel Trilling to John Vaughn, December 15, 1972, Trilling MSS, Box 28. Trilling shared his parents' disdain for public universities. As Diana Trilling recalled of the time he taught at Hunter College (between 1927 and 1929): "he regarded the experience as only a degrading one and afterward did not wish to speak of it." Diana Trilling, "Lionel Trilling: A Jew at Columbia," in *Speaking of Literature and Society*, ed. Diana Trilling (New York: Harcourt, Brace, Jovanovich, 1980), 420.

9. Lionel Trilling to John Vaughn, December 15, 1972, Trilling MSS, Box 28; Lionel Trilling, "Memoirs." Trilling MSS, Box 36 (Folder 396); Lionel Trilling to John Vaughn, December 15, 1972, Trilling MSS, Box 28; Lionel Trilling, "Memoirs." Trilling MSS, Box 36 (Folder 396).

10. Lionel Trilling to John Vaughn, December 15, 1972, Trilling MSS, Box 28.

11. Lionel Trilling, "Memoirs." Trilling MSS, Box 36 (Folder 396); Lionel Trilling to John Vaughn, December 15, 1972, Trilling MSS, Box 28; Lionel Trilling, "Memoirs." Trilling MSS, Box 36 (Folder 396).

12. Lionel Trilling to John Vaughn, December 15, 1972, Trilling MSS, Box 28.

13. Lionel Trilling to John Vaughn, December 15, 1972, Trilling MSS, Box 28; Lionel Trilling, "Memoirs." Trilling MSS, Box 36 (Folder 396).

14. Thomas Bender writes that "the formative influences of the young Trilling were the Greenwich Village intellectuals of the World War I era (especially Randolph Bourne, Van Wyck Brooks, and Edmund Wilson); Columbia College with its commitment to liberal humanism; and the group of Jewish writers associated with the *Menorah Journal.*" "Lionel Trilling and American Culture" *American Quarterly* 42, no. 2 (June 1990): 330–331. To this one should add the Judaism and Anglophilia of Trilling's parents, which preceded and reinforced the liberal-humanism Trilling absorbed at Columbia: "he retained his father's intellectual grammar," argues Susanne Klingenstein, "but expressed himself in the vocabulary of his consent [American] culture." *Jews in the American Academy, 1900–1940: The Dynamics of Intellectual Assimilation* (New Haven: Yale University Press, 1991), 141. Writing about his birthday, Trilling claimed that "my being born on the day of the great Republic's acutest fit of self-consciousness did much to determine the process of my own self-consciousness." "Memoirs." Trilling MSS, Box 36 (Folder 396).

15. In his essay for *The God that Failed*, Arthur Koestler presents both the radical Right (fascism) and the radical Left (communism) as deformed children of a

declining bourgeoisie: "the pauperized bourgeoisie became the rebels of Right and Left; Schickelgrueber [Hitler] and Diagashivili [Stalin] shared about equally the benefits of the social migration." *The God that Failed*, ed. Richard Crossman (New York: Harper, 1949), 19. Malcolm Cowley associates "modern" morals with the children of the middle class: "one might say that the revolution in morals [of the 1920s] began as a middle-class children's revolt." *Exile's Return: A Literary Odyssey of the 1920s* (New York: Norton, 1934), 64.

16. Whittaker Chambers, "Personal History of Whittaker Chambers." Alger Hiss Defense Files, Harvard Law School Special Collections, Box 49 (Folder 2) (hereafter cited as AHDF).

17. Whittaker Chambers, *Witness* (Washington, D.C.: Regnery, 1997), 105, 92.

18. Ibid., 105, 155, 148.

19. Ibid., 104, 102, 109–110, 91, 117.

20. Ibid., 135, 134, 135–137, 148. The adolescent Stalin also responded warmly to Victor Hugo: "Joseph Dzhughashvili was fond of Victor Hugo's *The Year Ninety-Three.*" Robert Service, *Stalin: A Biography* (London: Macmillan, 2004), 40.

21. Three such poems are: "To a Young Man, H.R.B," *The Nation*, July 25, 1924; "Lothrop, Montana," *The Nation*, June 30, 1926; and "Tandaradei," *Two Worlds*, June 1926. All other evidence on Chambers's homosexuality comes from his "Statement" to the FBI. AHDF, Box 46 (Folder 13). The question of Chambers's homosexuality is complicated by an extreme thinness of documentary evidence. The existing evidence consists almost exclusively of Chambers's own homoerotic poetry and a brief FBI statement.

22. Whittaker Chambers to Meyer Schapiro, circa September 15, 1924, Meyer Schapiro Papers, Special Collections, Butler Library, Columbia University, Box 1 (Folder 1924) (hereafter cited as Schapiro MSS). Chambers was not necessarily writing about homosexuality in this letter, although the letter clearly indicated Chambers's fear of sensuality as disruptive and dangerous, a cause for worry.

23. In one example among many, Chambers wonders to Schapiro "whether I can conquer the complex of my own maladjustments and excesses before they conquer me." Whittaker Chambers to Meyer Schaprio, June 2, 1927, Schapiro MSS, Box 1 (Folder 1926–1927).

24. Diana Trilling, *The Beginning of the Journey: The Marriage of Diana and Lionel Trilling* (New York: Harcourt, Brace, 1993), 98.

25. Trilling, "Lionel Trilling: A Jew at Columbia," 417.

26. Edmund Wilson to Seward Collins, circa 1927, in *Letters on Literature and Politics*, 240. John Erskine, the creator of Columbia's great books program, described its objects of study as "the great books of Western Europe for the last two or three thousand years." *My Life as a Teacher* (New York: J.B. Lippincott

Co., 1948), 171. Trilling recalled Erskine in 1974 in the following words: "he believed that the best way to make oneself intelligent and thus to prepare oneself to function well as a citizen or as the practitioner of one of the professions was through a happy and intimate acquaintance with the great intellectual and artistic works of the past, books chiefly, but music and the visual arts as well." "The Uncertain Future of the Humanistic Ideal," in *The Last Decade*, ed. Diana Trilling, 164. Trilling referred to Erskine's great books program as "that enchanting General Honors course that Erskine had devised." Ibid., 164. In his anthology of Trilling essays, Leon Wieseltier selected an essay title of Erskine's, "The Moral Obligation to Be Intelligent," to characterize the style and substance of Trilling's work. *The Moral Obligation to Be Intelligent: Selected Essays*, ed. Leon Wieseltier (New York: Farrar, Straus and Giroux, 2000).

27. See H. L. Mencken, *The Philosophy of Friedrich Nietzsche* (Boston: Luce, 1908), an early introduction of Nietzsche to an American reading audience.

28. In context, the phrase refers to Henry Adams: "at once the last representative of our classic literature and the inaugurator of our immediate modernity of explicit despair." Lionel Trilling, "Dreiser, Anderson, Lewis, and the Riddle of Society," *The Reporter* 6 (November 13, 1951): 40.

29. Quoted in Timothy P. Cross, *An Oasis of Order: The Core Curriculum at Columbia College* (http://www.college.columbia.edu/core/oasis/). Trilling would teach in the General Honors program from 1937 onward, long after he "became prominent." The core curriculum at Columbia still bears Trilling's stamp in that, currently, the "last required reading is Freud's *Civilization and Its Discontents*." *An Oasis of Order*. In the words of Daniel Bell, "the intention in reading the 'great books' [in the general honors program] was to inculcate in the student a humanistic rather than a professional orientation; to force him to confront a great work directly, rather than treat it with the awe reserved for a classic, and, in the contemporary jargon, 'to acculturate' a student whose background and upbringing had excluded him from the 'great traditions.'" *The Reforming of General Education: The Columbia College Experience in Its National Setting* (New York: Anchor Books, 1966), 13–14. For more on the great books emphasis at Columbia in the 1920s and 1930s see Justus Buchler, "Reconstruction in the Liberal Arts," in A *History of Columbia College on Morningside*, ed. Irwin Edman (New York: Columbia University Press, 1954), 48–135.

30. Lionel Trilling, "The Van Amringe and Keppel Eras," in A *History of Columbia College on Morningside*, 19. Trilling writes that the university's bucolic setting, when it first moved uptown in 1987, "must have substantiated the feeling of many students that they were pioneers of an American Acropolis." Ibid., 22.

31. Trilling, "Some Notes for an Autobiographical Lecture," in *The Last Decade*, 233, 233.

32. This is not to suggest that Erskine neglected the problem of vulgarity. Vulgarity was, in fact, a concept that the humanists and the avant-garde shared: "the idea of the 'vulgar' sums up a great deal of what [John] Erskine, and Trilling after him, wanted to overcome," Mark Krupnick writes, providing a conceptual link between Erskine and *The Morningside* circle. *Lionel Trilling and the Fate of Cultural Criticism* (Evanston, Ill.: Northwestern University Press, 1986), 50.

33. Lionel Trilling to John Vaughn, December 15, 1972, Trilling MSS, Box 28. Trilling would include one of Shaw's plays, "The Doctor's Dilemma," in his anthology of great literature. See *Prefaces to the Experience of Literature*, 37–33.

34. Lionel Trilling to John Vaughn, December 15, 1972, Trilling MSS, Box 28. Trilling referred to Dewey's influence more positively in 1933. For Columbia undergraduates of the mid-1920s, Trilling wrote, Dewey was a "symbol of the reality we were seeking—but to most of us still a literary reality." Trilling [with Milton Rugoff], "Columbia '25—Columbia '33," *Modern Youth* 1 (May–June 1933): 9. In an essay on the history of Columbia, Trilling was respectful but a bit cool toward Dewey: "John Dewey was of course the great name. To some College students who heard him in his graduate lectures he was a personal inspiration, and he gave to philosophy at once an immediacy and a prestige that were of great account in the intellectual tone of student life." "The Van Amringe and Keppel Eras," 29.

35. Trilling, "Memoirs." Trilling MSS, Box 36 (Folder 396).

36. Lionel Trilling to John Vaughn, December 15, 1972, Trilling MSS, Box 28.

37. To say that *The Education of Henry Adams* appealed to Trilling is not to say that Trilling liked Henry Adams: "I did not like Adams on my first acquaintance with him and I did not like him better in later years, when I knew more about him." "Memoirs." Trilling MSS, Box 36 (Folder 396).

38. T. J. Jackson Lears writes that Adams in "his life and work embodied all the major themes of antimodernism." *No Place of Grace: Antimodernism and the Transformation of American Culture, 1880–1920* (New York: Pantheon, 1981), 262. Antimodernism can be a confusing term because the object of rejection is almost never modernist literature but rather some idea of modernity or modern society, most often industrial capitalism.

39. Lionel Trilling, "Memoirs." Trilling MSS, Box 36 (Folder 396).

40. Regarding Adams's antimodern contemporaries, T. J. Jackson Lears writes that "above all, the fault [of the modern world] lay in the complacent belief in progress" held by the bourgeoisie. *No Place of Grace*, 289. Those reared on *The Education* in the 1920s were well prepared for the Marxist arguments of the 1930s, arguments in which the failure of the bourgeoisie figured with similar prominence.

41. Lionel Trilling, "Memoirs." Trilling MSS, Box 36 (Folder 396). Adams's failure was culturally representative. As T. J. Jackson Lears observes, Adams endeavored "to link his own retrospective sense of failure with the failures of bourgeois culture." *No Place of Grace*, 286.

42. Lionel Trilling's grandfather was named Israel Cohen. The correspondence with *The Education* concerns two famous sentences. They read: "Under the shadow of the Boston State House, turning its back on the house of John Hancock, the little passage called Hancock Avenue runs, or ran, from Beacon Street, on the summit of Beacon Hill; and there, in the third house below Mount Vernon Place, February 16, 1838, a child was born, and christened later by his uncle, the minister of the First Church after the tenets of Boston Unitarianism, as Henry Brooks Adams. Had he been born in Jerusalem under the shadow of the Temple, and circumcised in the synagogue by his uncle the high priest, under the name of Israel Cohen, he would scarcely have been more distinctly branded, and not much more heavily handicapped in the races of the coming century, in running for such stakes as the century was to offer." "The Education of Henry Adams," in *Henry Adams* (New York: Library of America, 1983), 723.

43. Trilling's ruminations on Henry Adams bring to mind Norman Podhoretz's *Making It*, a far more effusive celebration of the bourgeois ethos than anything Trilling ever wrote and an association that occurred to Trilling himself. In a marginal note on the draft of his memoirs (circa 1974) he writes: "Young men of the present time would not know what Adams is talking about. They wouldn't because they don't have the imagination of society (ha!)/ of American society as a source of honor/ But I did/ the son of Jewish immigrants thought the same way the Boston Brahmin, the scion of presidents// making it." "Memoirs." Trilling MSS, Box 36 (Folder 396).

44. Trilling, "Memoirs." Trilling MSS, Box 36 (Folder 396).

45. Ibid. One gets an image of Trilling caught between *The Morningside* circle and the genteel aspirations of his family in Mark Van Doren's essay, "Jewish Students I Have Known": "something fastidious in his [Trilling's] gentle nature kept him from irony and rendered him incapable of satire, though he was by no means unaware of absurdities." *Menorah Journal* 13, no. 3 (June 1927): 367.

46. Whittaker Chambers, "Statement: January 3, 1949," AHDF, Box 48 (Folder 19). The leftist political orientation of *The Morningside* circle was especially important in Chambers's intellectual development because at Columbia "the words Communism and Communist were almost never heard" in the early 1920s, as Chambers remembered. *Cold Friday*, ed. Duncan Norton-Taylor (New York: Random House, 1964), 93.

47. Van Doren. "Jewish Students I Have Known," 367. Van Doren's passage on Chambers is intriguing: "perhaps the best one of them all was a young man

whom I found in the first class, seven years ago; and he was unmistakably a Gentile." Ibid., 268. Van Doren noticed Chambers's penchant for bringing together thought and action, writing that Chambers was "interesting for a quality intensely expressed through all of his words and deeds." Ibid., 268.

48. Chambers, *Witness*, 164.

49. In 1920, Chambers even helped out with the Coolidge campaign. Sam Tanenhaus, *Whittaker Chambers: A Biography* (New York: Modern Library, 1998), 25.

50. Chambers, *Cold Friday*, 99, 104, 92, 99, 114.

51. Whittaker Chambers, "Personal History of Whittaker Chambers." AHDF, Box 49 (Folder 2). As an advisee of Van Doren's, Chambers was bothered by Van Doren's indifference to politics: Van Doren played with ideas, while "for me [Chambers], an idea was a starting point of an act." *Cold Friday*, 15.

52. "It was the ernste Menschen who shaped Chambers's idea, never altered, of the intellectual life," writes Sam Tanenhaus. *Whittaker Chambers*, 22.

53. Chambers, *Cold Friday*, 125, 126. This new culture was secular. *The Morningside* circle helped make Chambers irreligious: "before I found it in Communism, I assimilated from them [*The Morningside* circle] that vision of man who has repudiated God, by his own intelligence creating a new world order, peace and plenty." Ibid., 130.

54. Ibid., 127, 127. One might compare Chambers's reaction to the modernist writers—whose "cry echoed in my soul"—to the clichéd response to modernist literature that Trilling observed among his Columbia students of the early 1960s. These were students who "move through the terrors and mysteries of modern literature like so many Parsifals, asking no questions at the behest of wonder and fear. Or like so many seminarists who have been systematically instructed in the constitution of Hell and the ways of damnation or like so many *readers*, entertained by moral horror stories. I asked them to look into The Abyss, and both dutifully and gladly, they have looked into The Abyss, and The Abyss has greeted them with the grave courtesy of all objects of serious study, saying: 'Interesting, am I not? And *exciting*, if you consider how deep I am and what dread beasts lie at my bottom. Have it well in mind that a knowledge of me contributes materially to your being whole, or well-rounded men." "On the Teaching of Modern Literature," *Beyond Culture: Essays on Literature and Understanding* (New York: Viking, 1968), 27.

55. Ibid., 92, 127.

56. Lionel Trilling, "On the Death of a Friend," *Commentary* 29, no. 2 (February, 1960): 93; Norman Podhoretz, *Making It* (New York: Random House, 1967), 207; Trilling, "On the Death of a Friend," 94.

57. In a letter to Alan Wald, Trilling shed some light on his movement away from Judaism: "to speak of the *Menorah Journal* as a response to Jewish 'isolation'

isn't nearly enough—you must make the reader aware of the shame that young middle-class Jews felt; self-hatred was the word that later came into vogue but shame is simpler and better." Lionel Trilling to Alan Wald, June 10, 1974, Trilling MSS, Box 29. One feels this shame in Trilling's 1929 letter to Elliot Cohen about the *Menorah Journal*: "believe me, this was perhaps the first Jewish manifestation of which I could say that [it was not clumsy or vulgar]." Lionel Trilling to Elliot Cohen, December 2, 1929, Trilling MSS, Box 7.

58. Lionel Trilling, "A Novel of the Thirties," in *The Last Decade*, 14. The essay first appeared in *Commentary* 41 (1966): 43–51.

59. Susanne Klingenstein observes that Trilling's "frame of reference in the reviews [written between 1926 and 1929] is never Jewish culture." *Jews in the American Academy, 1900–1940*, 169.

60. Perhaps one should say that Elliot Cohen, more than the *Menorah Journal*, was the catalyst: "there are many of us who, if we live our intellectual lives under the aspect of a complex and vivid idea of culture and society," wrote Trilling in his obituary of Cohen, "owe that idea not to the social sciences but to Elliot Cohen." "On the Death of a Friend," 94.

61. Lionel Trilling, "A Novel of the Thirties," 14–15.

62. Mark Krupnick uses the term, "Jewish booboisie," in relation to the *Menorah Journal*'s satirical inspiration. "The *Menorah Journal* Group and the Origins of Modern Jewish-American Radicalism," *Studies in Jewish-American Literature* 5, no. 2 (1979): 63. Diana Trilling repeats Krupnick's allusion to Mencken: "Although [Mencken's] *American Mercury* was an essentially conservative magazine addressed to middle-class readers, much of its claim to seriousness could be traced to its derisive view of the American bourgeoisie . . . the *Menorah Journal* breathed the same cultural air as the *Mercury*." *The Beginning of the Journey*, 139.

63. Max Eastman, *Love and Revolution: My Journey through an Epoch* (New York: Random House, 1964), 466.

64. Trilling, "Columbia '25—Columbia '33," 10.

65. Oswald Spengler, *The Decline of the West* (New York: A. Knopf, 1926).

66. Lionel Trilling, "Cities of the Plain," review of *Cities of the Plain* by Marcel Proust, trans. C. K. Scott Moncrieff, *New York Evening Post*, January 21, 1928, sec. 3, p. 14.

67. Lionel Trilling, "A Gobineau Novel of Rare Vintage," review of *Pleiads* by Count de Gobineau, *New York Evening Post*, October 27, 1928, p. 9, 9, 9.

68. Lionel Trilling, "What Price Jewry," review of *The City without Jews* by Hugo Bertauer, trans. Salomea Neumark Brainia, *Menorah Journal* 13 (April 1928): 219.

69. Ibid., 145.

70. Lionel Trilling, "Another Jewish Problem Novel," review of *The Disinherited* by Milton Waldman, *Menorah Journal* 16 (April 1929): 377, 377.

71. Lionel Trilling, "A Novel of the Thirties," in *The Last Decade*, 11. The editorial crisis of 1929 at the *Menorah Journal* also concerned questions of Zionism. Responding to the 1929 tensions between Jews and Arabs in Palestine, Herbert Solow asked in a series of articles why Jews and Arabs did not align themselves as a single proletariat against the bourgeoisie. Klingenstein, *Jews in the American Academy, 1900–1940*, 173. Solow's anti-Zionism, as opposed to the indifference toward Zionism that had characterized the attitude of Trilling and others in the 1920s, presaged the turn toward communism most *Menorah Journal* contributors would undergo in the 1930s.

72. Lionel Trilling to Elliot Cohen, December 2, 1929, Trilling MSS, Box 7.

73. Trilling, "Notes on an Autobiographical Lecture," in *The Last Decade*, 237.

74. Lionel Trilling, "Of Sophistication," review of *Roman Summer* by Ludwig Lewisohn, *Menorah Journal* 14 (April 1928): 106.

75. Lionel Trilling, "Stendhal Made Valiant War on Vulgar Boredom," review of *Stendhal* by Paul Hazard, trans. Eleanor Hard, *New York Evening Post*, April 20, 1929, p. 11, 11.

76. Lionel Trilling, "Despair Apotheosized," review of *Labyrinth* by Gertrude Diamant, *Menorah Journal* (October 17, 1929): 92, 93, 94.

77. Lionel Trilling, "The Necessary Morals of Art," review of *and Co.* by Jean-Richard Bloch, trans. C. K. Scott-Moncrieff, *Menorah Journal* 18 (February 1930): 183, 182, 183, 183.

78. Lionel Trilling, "D. H. Lawrence: A Neglected Aspect," *Symposium* 1 (July 1930): 362.

79. Lionel Trilling, "Portrait of the Artist as American," review of *Portrait of the Artist as American* by Matthew Josephson, *Symposium* 1 (October 1930): 558–559.

80. Lionel Trilling, "The Promise of Realism," *Menorah Journal* 18 (May 1930): 480, 483.

81. Trilling, "Portrait of the Artist as American," 560, 560, 561, 561, 561, 561.

82. Trilling, "Some Notes on an Autobiographical Lecture," in *The Last Decade*, 235; Trilling, "Portrait of the Artist as American," 562.

83. Diana Trilling, "Lionel Trilling, A Jew at Columbia," in *Speaking of Literature and Society*, 421.

84. Trilling, "Some Notes on an Autobiographical Lecture," in *The Last Decade*, 238.

85. Mark Shechner writes that Trilling "deserted [that] cultural enterprise [of the *Menorah Journal*] and its efforts at cosmopolitan Jewishness in 1930 for the riptides of the intellectual mainstream." *After the Revolution: Studies in the Contemporary Jewish-American Imagination* (Bloomington: University of Indiana Press, 1987): 56. Elinor Grumet dates the break from the *Menorah Journal* to autumn of 1931, when "Trilling divorced his literary career from

Jewish cultural interests. That divorce was a thoughtful and conscious act."
"The Apprenticeship of Lionel Trilling," *Prooftexts* 4 (May 1984): 153. It was
conscious because, in Grumet's view, he "found Jewish cultural nationalism an
intellectual dead-end." Ibid., 167.

86. Lionel Trilling to Elliot Cohen, December 2, 1929, Trilling MSS, Box 7.

87. Lionel Trilling, "The Changing Myth of the Jew," in *Speaking of Literature
and Society*, 67.

88. Trilling, "Columbia '25—Columbia '33."

89. Arthur Schlesinger Jr. paraphrased his father with these words. *A Life in the
Twentieth Century: Innocent Beginnings, 1917–1950* (Boston: Houghton Mifflin,
2000), 17.

90. Whittaker Chambers, "Statement," January 3, 1949, AHDF, Box 48
(Folder 19).

91. Chambers, *Cold Friday*, 134, 91–92. The cataclysm of World War I was
something that Chambers associated with the "message" of modernist
literature: "the first rumblings of catastrophe had been uttered by a generation
of giants by contrast with whom we could trace the decline of the human
condition and the deepening of the crisis. Ibsen, Tolstoy, Nietzsche,
Strindberg, Hauptmann, Shaw, Hardy, Matthew Arnold, Tennyson had
foretold us." Ibid., 140.

92. Chambers, *Cold Friday*, 140, 141.

93. Chambers, "Statement," January 3, 1949, AHDF, Box 48 (Folder 19).

94. Chambers expressed this hatred in a 1923 book of poetry, *Defeat in the Village*,
which he never published. His artistic aim was "to preserve through the
medium of poetry the beautiful Long Island of my boyhood before it was
destroyed forever by the advancing City. I wished to dramatize the continual
defeat of the human spirit in our time, by itself and by the environment in
which it finds itself." *Witness*, 165.

95. Whittaker Chambers to Meyer Schapiro, circa September 15, 1924, Schapiro
MSS, Box 1 (Folder 1924).

96. Chambers never enjoyed college. "I was at college much against my will. It
seemed to me the strangest, most unreal place I could imagine," he later wrote.
"Personal History of Whittaker Chambers," AHDF, Box 49 (Folder 2). His will to
leave followed from his will to act: "I became disgusted with the faculty and
student body as being rather unrealistic. I decided to quit school and join the
Communist Party." "Statement," January 3, 1949, AHDF, Box 48 (Folder 19).

97. Chambers, "Statement," January 3, 1949, AHDF, Box 48 (Folder 19). Sorel's
endorsement of violence helped Chambers to support a revolutionary
movement: "with reference to the use of violence on the part of the American
Communist Party to overthrow the Government, I have no personal
recollection of any published statement to that effect, nevertheless it was

universally understood." "Statement," January 3, 1949, AHDF, Box 48 (Folder 19).

98. One could substitute Chambers for Sorel in the following passage: "cherishing heroic values, usually in what he thought of as their rugged, peasant or proletarian forms, Sorel contemplated the contemporary world with the distaste of the moral aesthete: it was dead, gray, spiritless, tame, rotted with humanitarianism and pedantry." John Burrow, *The Crisis of Reason: European Thought, 1848–1914* (New Haven, Conn.: Yale University Press, 2000), 142.

99. Chambers, "Statement," January 3, 1949, AHDF, Box 48 (Folder 19). That Chambers's interest in communism intensified in 1923 is ironic when one considers Daniel Aaron's observation that "most American writers, even the rebellious ones, had lost interest in Russia and Communism and in proletarian culture by 1923." *Writers on the Left: Episodes in American Literary Communism* (New York: Avon Books, 1961), 120.

100. The progression Chambers followed was not unique. Polish poet Czeslaw Milosz, born in 1911, describes the radicalization of his fellow students at the university in Vilnius in the following words: "disputes over the significance of metaphor in poetry yielded to discussions of the theories of George Sorel, and later Marx and Lenin." *The Captive Mind*, trans. Jane Zielonko (New York: Vintage, 1981), 145.

101. Lenin "not so sure of the controls of society as the engineer was of the engine that was taking him to Petrograd, yet in a position to calculate the chances with closer accuracy than a hundred to one, stood on the eve of the moment when for the first time in the human exploit the key of a philosophy of history was fit in a historical lock." Edmund Wilson, *To the Finland Station: A Study in the Writing and Acting of History* (New York: Farrar, Straus, and Giroux, 1972), 546. The title of Wilson's study, *To the Finland Station*, echoes that of Virginia Woolf's *To the Lighthouse*. Wilson's title made for a subtle polemic: Lenin reached the Finland Station, while Woolf's characters mostly contemplated reaching the lighthouse.

102. Chambers, "Statement," January 3, 1949, AHDF, Box 48 (Folder 19).

103. Chambers, *Witness*, 196. Ignazio Silone draws attention to the martyrdom that attracted young bourgeois to the Communist Party, one that evokes Christian martyrdom: "the links which bound to the Party grew steadily firmer," Silone wrote for *The God that Failed*, "not in spite of the dangers and sacrifices involved, but because of them. This explains the attraction exercised by Communism on certain categories of young men and women, on intellectuals, on the highly sensitive and generous people who suffer most from the wastefulness of bourgeois society." *The God that Failed*, 99.

104. David Caute presumes a bond between communism and the Enlightenment in his book on Western intellectuals and communism. For Western

intellectuals sympathetic to communism, Caute argues, the Soviet Union embodied the ideals of the Enlightenment: "the Enlightenment, having been betrayed and deformed in its own Western cradle, was now reborn [in the Soviet Union] on virgin soil." *The Fellow Travelers: A Postscript to the Enlightenment* (New York: Macmillan, 1973), 71. For an analysis that places the origins of communist revolution in romanticism rather than the Enlightenment see: James Billington, *Fire in the Minds of Men: Origins of the Revolutionary Faith* (New Brunswick, N.J.: Transaction Publishers, 1999).

105. Chambers, *Cold Friday*, 182, 183.

106. Ibid., 183.

107. The term *narodniki* refers to a late nineteenth-century movement among young Russian intellectuals who left the cities to go back to "the people" (*narod* in Russian means both the people and the nation). Martin Malia's study of Russia's image in Western thought suggests that Chambers was not as anomalous as he thought. Malia describes a common variety of Russophilia (characteristic, for example, of the young Thomas Mann) that closely resembled Chambers's own: "to those disillusioned with [European] civilization, [Russia's] archaic rural society seemed an oasis of 'Slavic soul,' a spiritual quality rapidly disappearing in the industrial, urban world of the West." *Russia under Western Eyes: From the Bronze Horseman to the Lenin Mausoleum* (Cambridge, Mass.: Harvard University Press, 1999), 165. Western attraction to the "Slavic soul" predated the Russian Revolution. Chambers understood "the spirit of the Narodniki [as] all that was soldierly and saintly in the revolution . . . I need scarcely underscore the point at which this strain of the revolutionary spirit blends with a Christian élan." *Cold Friday*, 78.

108. Chambers, *Cold Friday*, 78.

109. By 1924, Chambers had left Calvin Coolidge far behind: "The silk-workers have carried another factory outside of Patterson," he wrote to Meyer Schapiro, "15,000 hard-coal workers are workless; the miners and families are being evicted in West Virginia. My blood boils left. Calvin Coolidge has addressed the Boy Scouts." Whittaker Chambers to Meyer Schapiro, August 23, 1924, Schapiro MSS, Box 1 (Folder 1924).

110. Whittaker Chambers, "Personal History of Whittaker Chambers," AHDF, Box 49 (Folder 2), 160.

111. Chambers, *Cold Friday*, 143, 143.

112. Chambers, "Personal History of Whittaker Chambers," AHDF, Box 49 (Folder 2).

113. Whittaker Chambers to Meyer Schapiro, November 3, 1926, Schapiro MSS, Box 1 (Folder 1926–1927). The hopelessness he expressed in private correspondence anticipated the hopelessness he would vent in letters to Ralph de Toledano and William F. Buckley Jr. in the 1950s, two friends and allies in the conservative

movement. One might take two quotes as examples. "The score, as the points are chalked up, clearly and boldly, more and more convinces me that the situation is hopeless, past repair, organically irremediable." Whittaker Chambers to William F. Buckley Jr., February 25, 1954, in *Odyssey of a Friend: Whittaker Chambers' Letters to William F. Buckley, Jr., 1954–1961*, ed. William F. Buckley (New York: Putnam, 1969), 53. "Nobody can save a society that cannot save itself." Whittaker Chambers to Ralph de Toledano, in *Notes from the Underground: The Whittaker Chambers–Ralph de Toledano Correspondence, 1949–1960*, ed. Ralph de Toledano (Washington, D.C.: Regnery, 1997), 79.

114. Whittaker Chambers to Meyer Schapiro, April 24, 1927, Schapiro MSS, Box 1 (Folder 1926–1927); Whittaker Chambers to Meyer Schapiro, February 27, 1927, Schapiro MSS, Box 1 (Folder 1926–1927); Whittaker Chambers to Meyer Schapiro, April 24, 1927, Schapiro MSS, Box 1 (Folder 1926–1927); Lionel Trilling, "Portrait of the Artist as American," 558–559.

115. Whittaker Chambers to Meyer Schaprio, April 24, 1927, Schapiro MSS, Box 1 (Folder "1926–1927").

116. Whittaker Chambers, "March for the Red Dead," *Daily Worker*, May 23, 1927, p. 6, 6.

117. Whittaker Chambers, "Before the End," *Daily Worker*, July 9, 1927, p. 3.

118. Whittaker Chambers to Meyer Schaprio, April 24, 1927, Schapiro MSS, Box 1 (Folder 1921–1927).

119. Chambers, *Witness*, 227; Whittaker Chambers to Meyer Schapiro, April 24, 1927, Schapiro MSS, Box 1 (Folder 1926–1927); Chambers, *Witness*, 277; Whittaker Chambers to Meyer Schapiro, April 24, 1927, Schapiro MSS, Box 1 (Folder 1926–1927).

120. Sam Tanenhaus notes that Chambers's "position at the *Daily Worker* afforded him an unimpeded view of the Party's destructive intrigues." *Whittaker Chambers*, 60.

121. Furet, *The Passing of an Illusion*, 131.

122. Whittaker Chambers, "FBI Interview," May 10, 1945, AHDF, Box 48 (Folder 10).

123. Chambers, *Witness*, 237, 238, 239.

124. Ibid., 251; Whittaker Chambers, "Statement," January 3, 1949, AHDF, Box 48 (Folder 19). Sam Tanenhaus writes that "rumors of closet Trotskyism were to dog Chambers during his entire thirteen years in the Party." *Whittaker Chambers*, 61. Whatever Chambers's admiration for Trotsky, he never took the Trotskyite movement very seriously. He did not consider it a viable alternative to the Soviet Union under Stalin: it may have been right in theory, but, once Trotsky was in exile, the movement aligned with his name was irrelevant.

125. Chambers, *Witness*, 259.

2. Red Years in the Red Decade

Epigraph: Leon Trotsky, *Literature and Revolution*, trans. Rose Strumsky (London: Red Words, 1991), 284.

1. Its full title was *Culture and the Crisis: An Open Letter to the Writers, Artists, Teachers, Physicians, Engineers, Scientists, and Other Professional Workers of America* (New York: Workers' Library Publishers, 1932). The publication's primary author was Lewis Corey, the "American Antonio Gramsci," in Michael Denning's words. *The Cultural Front: The Laboring of American Culture in the Twentieth Century* (New York: Verso, 1996), 99.

2. French writer André Gide could have been summarizing this argument when he wrote about his attitudes circa 1936 that "the fate of culture was linked, in my mind, with the future of the Soviet Union." André Gide, in *The God that Failed*, ed. Richard Crossman (New York: Harper, 1950), 176.

3. The 1932 alliance between American communists and bohemians was tenuous. "Since 1912," writes Daniel Aaron, "a polarizing process had been under way which divided the Bohemian from the revolutionary." *Writers on the Left: Episodes in American Literary Communism* (New York: Avon Books, 1961), 91. The process was powerful but never total. Malcolm Cowley described 1930s intellectuals as unified by the "notion that capitalism and its culture were in violent decay and on the point of being self-destroyed." *The Dream of the Golden Mountains: Remembering the 1930s* (New York: Viking, 1930), 315.

4. *Culture and the Crisis*, 29, 27, 29.

5. Daniel Aaron notes that "probably a good many who [signed the letter] voted communist, not because they expected or even wanted the communists to win, but out of protest." *Writers on the Left* (New York: Columbia University Press, 1992), 214.

6. *Culture and the Crisis*, 30.

7. Aaron, *Writers on the Left*, 384.

8. Whittaker Chambers, *Witness* (Washington, D.C.: Regnery, 1997), 261.

9. Lincoln Steffens to Whittaker Chambers, June 18, 1933, Alger Hiss Defense Files, Harvard Law School Special Collections, Box 2 (Folder 13) (hereafter cited as AHDF).

10. Murray Kempton, *Part of Our Time: Some Ruins and Monuments of the Thirties* (New York: Simon and Schuster, 1955), 132.

11. Chambers, *Witness*, 263, 263.

12. Quoted in *From Furmanov to Sholokhov: An Anthology of the Classics of Socialist Realism*, ed. Nicholas Luker (Ann Arbor, Mich.: Ardis, 1988), 19. Officially sanctioned socialist realism was to rest on three qualities: *partiinost'* (party feeling), *narodnost'* (national feeling or feeling for the people), and

klassovost' (class feeling). Chambers's socialist realist fiction rested only on two of the three qualities, *narodnost'* and *klassovost'*.

13. Chambers, *Witness*, 263.

14. Whittaker Chambers, "Can You Make Out Their Voices?," in *Ghosts on the Roof: Selected Journalism of Whittaker Chambers, 1931–1959*, ed. Terry Teachout (Washington, D.C.: Regnery, 1989), 6, 15, 15. Bagheot's name recalls the most famous nineteenth-century editor of the *Economist*, Walter Bagehot, and, as such, would have been yet another sign of the terrible reality hidden behind the façade of laissez-faire economics.

15. Ibid., 5, 8, 9.

16. Whittaker Chambers, "You Have Seen Their Heads," in *Ghosts on the Roof*, 22, 22, 25, 29, 29.

17. Whittaker Chambers, "Our Comrade Munn," in *Ghosts on the Roof*, 36, 37, 39.

18. Allen Weinstein, *Perjury: The Hiss-Chambers Case* (New York: Random House, 1997), 95.

19. Aaron, *Writers on the Left*, 384. In 1932, Chambers was on the road to intellectual prominence and not just among the Party faithful. He was described by Sidney Hook as "quite well known [in the early 1930s] for his contributions to the *Daily Worker* and the *New Masses*." Sidney Hook, *Out of Step: An Unquiet Life in the Twentieth Century* (New York: Harper and Row, 1987), 277.

20. Chambers, *Witness*, 276.

21. Arthur Koestler, in *The God that Failed*, 37.

22. Christopher Andrew and Oleg Gordievsky, *KGB: The Inside Story of Its Foreign Operations from Lenin to Gorbachev* (New York: Harper Collins, 1990), 231. Even in Moscow, Chambers was not fully obedient to Party discipline, sending a postcard back to America that bestowed a "Soviet blessing" on a friend's newborn baby. Ibid., 231.

23. Allen Weinstein argues that Chambers "welcomed and relished the new assignment as an opportunity to demonstrate his talents while serving as a front-line 'soldier of the revolution.' " *Perjury*, 99.

24. Chambers, *Witness*, 280. Ann Douglas notes Chambers's "romantic penchant for the psychic and political underground." "Whittaker Chambers, a Biography," http://www.english.upenn/~afilreis/50's/chambers-review.html.

25. Whittaker Chambers, "Chambers, Whittaker—Homosexuality," AHDF, Box 46 (Folder 11); Whittaker Chambers, "Chambers, Whittaker—Homosexuality," AHDF, Box 46 (Folder 11); Ibid. Chambers's statement on homosexuality to the FBI suggests that his conversion to Christianity related both to his communism and to his sexual behavior as a communist: "with reference to my homosexual activities and my other immoral relations with women, mentioned heretofore, I might point out that up to the year 1938 I had absolutely no religious training,

nor had there been any in my family." "Statement," February 15, 1949, AHDF, Box 46 (Folder 13).

26. Chambers, *Witness*, 291, 292, 293, 293, 293. Sam Tanenhaus describes Ulrich and Elena as "deeply cultured." *Whittaker Chambers: A Biography* (New York: Modern Library, 1998), 84.

27. Tanenhaus, *Whittaker Chambers*, 86.

28. Chambers, *Witness*, 325, 325, 326.

29. Ibid., 214, 38. "I did not know then that Ulrich was a type of the past, and that Herman was the Stalinist of the future," wrote Chambers in *Witness*, 315.

30. Ibid., 312, 313.

31. Hook describes Chambers at the time of the lunch as "a Communist who piously accepted the Party line but whose vestigial political common sense left him uneasy about it." *Out of Step*, 277.

32. Diana Trilling, *The Beginning of the Journey: The Marriage of Diana and Lionel Trilling* (New York: Harcourt, Brace, 1993), 207.

33. Their discussion of "social fascism" was hardly accidental: they had been "brought together at lunch by Lionel Trilling for the purpose of debating the Communist tactics that had boosted Hitler into power in Germany." Tanenhaus, *Whittaker Chambers*, 141. As Tanenhaus describes the scene: Hook "demolished the Communist theory of 'social fascism' while Chambers, not bothering to defend his masters, had sat by imperturbably." Ibid.

34. Hook, *Out of Step*, 277.

35. Diana Trilling thought "it highly improbable that this meeting took place. Lionel was never much interested in the debate in Communist theory and his connection with Chambers was not of a sort to have suggested this kind of social arrangement." *The Beginning of the Journey*, 271. In an exchange with Hook, she described the distance between Chambers and Trilling in stronger language: "I find it inconceivable that the [Lionel Trilling] would have been so concerned with Chambers's view of what was meant by Social Fascism as to initiate an occasion to enlighten Chambers on this score." "Remembering Whittaker Chambers: An Exchange between Diana Trilling and Sidney Hook," *Encounter* 46, no. 6 (June 1976): 94.

36. Hook, *Out of Step*, 277–278.

37. Lionel Trilling to Eric Bentley, February 13, 1946, Lionel Trilling Papers, Box 1 (hereafter cited as Trilling MSS).

38. Lionel Trilling, "Product of the Revolution?" *The Griffin* (July 1955): 5, 5, 5.

39. Edmund Wilson, *Axels' Castle: A Study in the Imaginative Literature of 1870–1930* (New York: Scribner and Sons, 1931).

40. Lionel Trilling "A Transcendental Prude," review of *Philene: From the Unpublished Diaries* by Henri Frederic Amiel, trans. Van Wyck Brooks, *Nation* 130 (June 11, 1930): 682, 683.

41. Luker, *From Furmanov to Sholokhov*, 27, 28.

42. Lionel Trilling, "The Social Emotions," review of *The Nineteen* by Alexander Fadeyev, *New Freeman* 1 (July 6, 1930): 429, 430, 429, 430.

43. Lionel Trilling, "Genuine Writing," review of *By the Waters of Manhattan* by Charles Reznikoff, *Menorah Journal* 19 (October 1930): 89.

44. Lionel Trilling to William S. Gamble, February 6, 1959, Trilling MSS, Box 16.

45. This is exactly the word François Furet would use in his history of communist infatuation in the West, *The Passing of an Illusion: The Idea of Communism in the Twentieth Century*, trans. Deborah Furet (Chicago: University of Chicago Press, 1999).

46. Sigmund Freud, *Civilization and Its Discontents*, trans. James Strachey (New York: W.W. Norton, 1961), 70, 71, 73. Trilling would paraphrase this argument in 1971, this time as an enthusiast of *Civilization and Its Discontents*, which "may be supposed to stand like a lion in the path of all hopes of achieving happiness through the radical revision of the social life." "Authenticity and the Modern Unconscious," *Commentary* 52, no. 3 (September 1971): 43.

47. Hook, "Remembering Whittaker Chambers," 95.

48. Diana Trilling recalled that "in the course of the summer [Sidney Hook] converted several of us, including Lionel and me, to Communism." *The Beginning of the Journey*, 179.

49. One is not quite sure whether Diana Trilling had herself and Lionel in mind when she wrote that "it was from the supposed friendship between Communism and liberalism that most intellectual sympathizers with Communism drew their sense of moral validation." *The Beginning of the Journey*, 196. In 1972, Trilling wrote that he "never had more than a superficial knowledge [of Marxist doctrine], although I suppose that what I did have was as profound as that of most of my friends: we almost all worked on hearsay." Lionel Trilling to John Vaughn, August 10, 1972, Trilling MSS, Box 28. One read literature closely; one absorbed Marx's arguments by osmosis.

50. Hook, *Out of Step*, 155.

51. Lionel Trilling, "The Youth of Arnold," review of *The Letters of Matthew Arnold to Hugh Clough* ed. Howard Foster Lowry, *Nation* 136 (February 22, 1933): 211.

52. If there was any connection between Trilling's revolutionary aspirations for culture and his interest in Arnold it was in the concept of the "classical." As he wrote in 1933, "for Arnold the charm of the classical ideal lay in the sense of human serenity that it gave; the basis of his criticism of the romantic poets was their inability to be secure." Ibid.

53. Lionel Trilling to Elliot Cohen, summer 1931, Trilling MSS, Box 31.

54. In his notebook Trilling wrote that the Victorians "make my *parent* literature, the reading with which I was most cozily at home—I could feel their warmth

and seemed always to know my way among them." "From the Notebooks of Lionel Trilling," *Partisan Review* 1 (1984): 497.

55. Lionel Trilling, with Milton Rugoff, "Columbia '25—Columbia '33," *Modern Youth* 1 (May–June 1933): 8.

56. Inevitably, the undergraduate of 1925 came off as superficial by comparison. Yet, in assessing the literature of the 1932 undergraduates, this alumnus of *The Morningside* circle could not help point out that "the purely literary contributions [to the *Columbia Review*, the 1932 version of the *Morningside*] are not very good." Trilling, "Columbia '25—Columbia '33," 44.

57. "It was from the Sinclairs that Lionel and I had our first instruction in the truth of Soviet Communism," recalled Diana Trilling. "Lionel and I dismissed her and David's report as a deficiency of imagination." *The Beginning of the Journey*, 202. The taboo on outright criticism of the Soviet Union was a common feature of New York intellectual life in 1932. Max Eastman wrote of himself in 1932 that "privately and in little esoteric meetings or publications I was warning against Stalin as an enemy of the faith, but in public lectures I was still defending the Soviet system and defending the Bolsheviks." *Love and Revolution: My Journey through an Epoch* (New York: Random House, 1964), 549. On the general subject of Americans traveling to the Soviet Union see Paul Hollander, *Political Pilgrims: Travels of Western Intellectuals to the Soviet Union, China and Cuba, 1928–1978* (New York: Oxford University Press, 1981), 102–176.

58. Hook, *Out of Step*, 179.

59. Quoted in Aaron, *Writers on the Left*, 243.

60. Lionel Trilling, "Sainte-Beuve," review of *Sainte-Beuve: A Literary Portrait* by William Frederick Giese, *Nation* 134 (April 20, 1932): 472.

61. Lionel Trilling, "Carlyle," review of *Carlyle* by Emery Neff, *Modern Quarterly* 6 (Summer 1932): 110, 110.

62. Ibid., 109, 109, 111.

63. Ibid., 109.

64. Lionel Trilling, "Forced Labor," review of *Forced Labor in the U.S.* by Walter Wilson, *Modern Monthly* 7 (June 1933): 314, 314, 314, 314, 314. Trilling is probably referring here to *Soviet Russia Today*, a magazine first published in 1932. Whittaker Chambers also read *Soviet Russia Today*. He described it with considerable irony as "a magazine of facts and figures (taken impartially from Soviet sources) and adding up to a paean of Soviet progress, beamed monthly, toward the unthinkingly enlightened American middle class." *Witness*, 333. Trilling's view of *Soviet Russia Today* was almost identical, although his "we" is more capacious: "for many years the hero of our moral myth was that worker-and-peasant who smiled from the covers of *Soviet Russia Today*, simple, industrious, literate—and grateful." "Elements that Are Wanted," review of *The*

Idea of a Christian Society by T. S. Eliot, *Partisan Review* 7, no. 4 (July–August 1940): 375.

65. Trilling, "Forced Labor," 314.

66. Diana Trilling, "Remembering Whittaker Chambers: An Exchange between Diana Trilling and Sidney Hook," *Encounter* 46, no. 6 (June 1976): 94; Diana Trilling, *The Beginning of the Journey*, 216; Lionel Trilling to Eric Bentley, November 28, 1947, Trilling MSS, Box 1; Trilling, *The Beginning of the Journey*, 210.Whittaker Chambers watched their departure from the NCDPP with apparent interest. After their exit from the committee, he called Diana to say that "he supposed he now knew what my answer [to his request for assistance] must be." Diana Trilling, "Remembering Whittaker Chambers," 94. Chambers was right: Diana was not interested. This one small episode at the NCDPP proves the larger point made by Judy Kutulas that "long before the 1935 People's Front, the CPUSA had effectively alienated a substantial percentage of its most logical allies." *The Long War: The Intellectual People's Front and Anti-Stalinism, 1930–1940* (Durham, N.C.: Duke University Press, 1995), 77.

67. Trilling, *The Beginning of the Journey*, 212. Alan Wald observes that Diana Trilling "was much more involved in the episode than her husband." "The Menorah Group Moves Left," 301. Lionel Trilling confirmed this judgment (he may have inspired it) in a letter to Wald, noting that Diana "had a much more intimate and actual involvement with the political activities of the *Menorah Journal*." Lionel Trilling to Alan Wald, June 10, 1974, Trilling MSS, Box 29.

68. Sidney Hook to Lionel Trilling, December 6, 1933, Trilling MSS, Box 7.

69. Lionel Trilling, "Ruskin: A Career of Error," review of *John Ruskin: An Introduction to Further Study of His Life and Work* by R. H. Wilenski, *Nation* 137 (October 25, 1933): 488.

70. Lionel Trilling, "Kultur in Eclipse," review of *Germany—Twilight or New Dawn?* by Anonymous, *Brooklyn Eagle Sunday Review* (November 19, 1933): 17.

71. Lionel Trilling, "The Comic Genius of Dickens," review of *Charles Dickens: His Life and Work* by Stephen Leacock, *The Nation* (February 7, 1934): 161.

72. Lionel Trilling, "The Coleridge Letters," review of *The Unpublished Letters of Samuel Taylor Coleridge*, ed. Earl Leslie Griggs, *The Nation* (December 27, 1933): 738, 739. Warren Susman would later make a similar argument about the tangled communalism and individualism, conservatism and radicalism, of the 1930s. See Warren Susman," *Culture as History: The Transformation of American Society in the Twentieth Century* (New York: Pantheon Books, 1984), 150–183.

73. Lionel Trilling to Meyer Schapiro, December 14, 1933, Trilling MSS, Box 7.

74. Hook, "Remembering Whittaker Chambers," 95.

75. Alfred Kazin recalled this episode as an antidote to a retrospective nostalgia for the 1930s: "unlike Michael Denning, whose optimistic radical thinking is based on a nostalgia for what he really believes was a form of CIO-created 'social democracy' in the Thirties, I at eighty-two still tremble when I remember myself as a young socialist in 1934. A memorial was being held in New York's old Madison Square Garden to honor the Austrian Socialists who had risen up against Dollfuss' clerical Fascist regime and were slaughtered with the active aid of Mussolini. The memorial was broken up by Communists throwing chairs down on us from the upper balconies. People ran out of the Garden screaming." "Rewriting the Thirties," *Intellectual History Newsletter* 19 (1997): 50.

76. Kutulas, *The Long War*, 72–77.

77. Hook, "Remembering Whittaker Chambers," 95.

78. Chambers, *Witness*, 349.

79. Ibid., 332.

80. Weinstein, *Perjury*, 118, 118.

81. Tanenhaus, *Whittaker Chambers*, 92.

82. John Hermann was a signatory of *Culture and the Crisis*. *Culture and the Crisis*, 32.

83. Quoted in Allen Weinstein and Alexei Vassiliev, *The Haunted Wood: Soviet Espionage in America—The Stalin Era* (New York: Random House, 1999), 39.

84. Weinstein, *Perjury*, 86.

85. Allen Weinstein writes that "Priscilla's Socialist commitment seemed much stronger than Alger's at the time . . . [although] Alger and Priscilla had already been considerably 'radicalized' . . . long before the election of a Democratic reform administration caused the couple to move from New York City to Washington." *Perjury*, 86–87.

86. Alger Hiss, *Recollections of a Life* (New York: Arcade, 1988), 57, 42. Hiss's first love was literature, not politics: "throughout Johns Hopkins and Harvard Law School he had been largely apolitical, his primary interests being in avant-garde literature and the arts." G. Edward White, *Alger Hiss's Looking Glass Wars: The Covert Life of a Soviet Spy* (New York: Oxford University Press, 2004), 28.

87. Chambers, *Witness*, 71

88. Josephine Herbst to William A. Rueben, October 26, 1968, AHDF, Box 117 (Folder 6). Chambers thought that the Ware circle considered him Russian. *Witness*, 330. Indeed, he tried to pass himself off as central European or Russian. Many of his underground contacts "believed that he was either a German or a Russian because of the slight accent and foreign intonation he affected." Weinstein, *Perjury*, 102.

89. Weinstein, *Perjury*, 182.

90. Allen Weinstein makes this point about the Ware circle in general: its members "mixed easily with New Dealers of their own generation and with older, more influential figures in the Roosevelt Administration." Weinstein and Vassiliev, *The Haunted Wood*, 41.

91. Chambers, *Witness*, 336. Tony Hiss, Alger's son, recalls a different attitude toward Franklin Roosevelt held by Alger and Priscilla Hiss: "I was still three when President Roosevelt died. Both my parents were shattered. I can remember sitting very still; I had never seen grief so powerful or so jagged, hadn't known that such an immense force existed and that it could overwhelm strong, self-composed people from one moment to the next." *The View from Alger's Window: A Son's Memoir* (New York: Knopf, 1999), 139.

92. Chambers, *Witness*, 336, 336, 343, 338.

93. White, *Alger Hiss's Looking Glass Wars*, 45, 46.

94. Ann Douglas speculates about a possible homosexual relationship between Chambers and Hiss, noting that "Chambers referred to a 'mince' in his [Hiss's] walk, and Richard Nixon, a staunch Chambers ally, always believed the two had been lovers." "Whittaker Chambers, a Biography," available at http://www .english.upenn/~afilreis/50's/chambers-review.html. Meyer Zeligs alleges homosexual attraction to Hiss on Chambers's part but does not believe that it was reciprocated. (Apart from the documentary material it contains, Zeligs's study is little more than a paraphrase of the Hiss defense, laced with bizarre psychoanalytic conjecture.) *Friendship and Fratricide: An Analysis of Whittaker Chambers and Alger Hiss* (New York: Viking, 1967). Any analysis of Chambers's homosexuality should be left open until there is more and better evidence.

95. Chambers, *Witness*, 312.

96. Ibid., 360. The friendship between Hiss and Chambers, and between their families, was yet another violation of underground protocol, regardless of whether the friendship had the qualities Chambers ascribed to it in *Witness*. On the basis of evidence from the Hiss case and from Soviet archives, Allen Weinstein and Alexander Vassiliev conclude that "Chambers's Soviet overseers would have been appalled at the strong personal friendship, . . . had they known of this blatant indifference to normal, cautious rules of tradecraft related to meetings between couriers and sources." *The Haunted Wood*, 43.

97. What upset Chambers was the logic of the purges because the accused were Communist Party faithful, many of them heroes of the October Revolution: "if the charge [against them] was true, then every other Communist had given his life for a fraud. If the charge was false, then every other Communist was giving his life for a fraud." *Witness*, 78.

98. Ibid., 79. The next sentence in *Witness* reads: "the Purge caused me to re-examine the meaning of Communism and the nature of the world crisis." Ibid. The passage in *Witness* implies that the Purge provoked an immediate

reexamination of communism for Chambers, whereas extant letters from 1936 show no such thing. A serious reexamination probably began some time in 1937.

99. Ibid.

100. Whittaker Chambers to Meyer Schapiro, summer 1936, Meyer Schapiro Papers, Box 1 (Folder 1936–1937) (hereafter cited as Schapiro MSS).

101. Whittaker Chambers to Meyer Schapiro, circa July 1936, Schapiro MSS, Box 1(Folder 1936–1937); Whittaker Chambers to Meyer Schapiro, July 31, 1936, Schapiro MSS, Box 1 (Folder 1936–1937).

102. The term "equivocal commitments" comes from the title of Eric Homburger's book, *American Radicalism, American Writers and Radical Politics: Equivocal Commitments, 1900–1939* (New York: St. Martin's, 1986). Chambers could see radicalism only in the light of extreme commitments.

103. Furet, *The Passing of an Illusion*, 279.

104. Michael Denning refers to the period between 1929 and 1959 as the "age of the CIO." *The Cultural Front*, xviii. He argues persuasively that the working class exerted greater cultural influence in the 1930s than it had before 1929. At the same time, the Left began to attract middle-class intellectuals in record numbers during the 1930s, which would in turn change the nature of the American Left, making it less foreign and less marginal.

105. Alfred Kazin wrote that "after 1935, the Communists rode to new influence on the United Front, and hated no one so much as intellectuals like Hook, Eastman, and Calverton who still preserved revolutionary ideas in the form of honest personal judgments." *New York Jew* (New York: Knopf, 1978), 73.

106. Hook, *Out of Step*, 220.

107. Ibid., 218.

108. Referring to the Moscow trials, Judy Kutulas writes that "the year 1935 was a dismal one for the intellectual left, one where reality finally caught up with their earlier dreams." *The Long War*, 218.

109. Mary McCarthy, *Intellectual Memoirs: New York, 1936–1938* (New York: Harcourt, Brace, Jovanovich, 1992), 18, 16. In his diaries of the 1930s, Edmund Wilson described a fashion show with "Depression names for dresses." *The Thirties: From the Notebooks and Diaries of the Period*, ed. Leon Edel (New York: Farrar, Straus and Giroux, 1977), 318. There was the "Five Year Plan" (cotton voile nightgown with Rodier Cotton plaid jacket), the "People's Choice" (Decharne crepe suit, conturier moire blouse), and the "Revolt of the Masses" (Amerin Freudenberg lace evening dress). Not all of the names had left-wing connotations. There was also the "Nazi" (chatillon faconne street dress). Ibid., 318.

110. On the generational tensions between the Popular Front and the New York intellectuals see Judy Kutulas, *The Long War*.

111. Lionel Trilling, "Politics and the Liberal," review of *Goldworthy Lowes Dickenson* by E. M. Forster, *Nation* 139 (July 4, 1934): 24, 24–25.

112. Lionel Trilling, "Studs Lonigan's World," review of *Guillotine Party* by James T. Farrell, *Nation* 141 (October 23, 1935): 484, 484, 484. Chambers shared Trilling's high opinion of *Man's Fate*: "*Man's Fate*, Malraux's novel about the Chinese revolution," he wrote in *Witness*, "excited me tremendously." *Witness*, 361. Chambers was writing about himself before his break with communism.

113. Trilling, "Studs Lonigan's World," 485.

114. William Phillips, *A Partisan View: Five Decades of the Literary Life* (New York: Stein and Day, 1983), 35.

115. Ibid., 38.

116. In his notebook (on May 6, 1936) Trilling lamented the "art for art's sake" position of his adviser, Emory Neff: "my last conversation with him about poetry brought out the opinion that ideas do not matter in poetry—the music was everything. Interpretation obvious: in 1924 it was OK to write about Carlyle Mill & the factory conditions. But now it was getting near and real and he is running for cover into 'music.' " "From the Notebooks of Lionel Trilling," 501.

117. Lionel Trilling to Malcolm Cowley, May 5, 1935, Trilling MSS, Box 2 (Folder Cowley, Malcolm).

118. Ibid. Trilling had reflected in his notebooks (circa 1931–1932) on the conservatism of great writers: "Aristophanes was a Tory & hated Socrates' seriousness with the usual Tory's hate of it. The fabliaux were not discouraged by the Church (see the Church in Heaven). Cervantes was far from revolutionary. Rabelais defended an aristocratic ideal." "From the Notebooks of Lionel Trilling," 497.

119. Lionel Trilling to Alan Brown, July 16, 1936, Trilling MSS, Box 7; Lionel Trilling to Alan Brown, December 13, 1936, Trilling MSS, Box 13. Trilling liked Santayana's assault on American optimism, "his objection to the characteristic mode of American thought . . . its refusal to recognize the hard, intractable nature of the world, its non-human quality which must painfully appear as an anti-human quality." Lionel Trilling to Richard Sennett, November 16, 1963, Trilling MSS, Box 20.

120. Lionel Trilling, "Eugene O'Neill," *New Republic* 88 (September 23, 1936): 176. Trilling had inside knowledge of O'Neill's dramaturgy, having served as an extra in the Broadway production of O'Neill's *The Fountain*. Nathan Abrams, *Commentary Magazine, 1945–1959: "A Journal of Significant Thought and Opinion"* (London: Vallentine Mitchell, 2007), 13.

121. Ibid., 179, 177, 177.

122. Ibid., 178, 177. One enthusiast of the Theater Guild's productions of Eugene O'Neill was the undergraduate Alger Hiss. He "would sit in the top balcony for

Theatre Guild production of the avant-garde art of the period—George
Bernard Shaw *(Saint Joan)*, Ferenc Molnar *(The Play's the Thing)*, Luigi
Pirandello *(Six Characters in Search of an Author)* and Eugene O'Neill *(All
God's Chillun Got Wings* and *Desire under the Elms).*" John Chabot Smith,
Alger Hiss: The True Story (New York: Penguin, 1976), 51.

123. Trilling, "Eugene O'Neill," 177, 179, 179.

124. James Gilbert argues that "unlike European radicalism, it [American radicalism]
has been largely isolated from its traditional constituency, the proletariat and,
perhaps more importantly, from the working-class party. Thus isolation and the
recurring attempt to end such estrangement became one of the characteristic
sources of energy in literary-political movements." *Writers and Partisans: A
History of Literary Radicalism in America* (New York: Wiley and Sons, 1968), 4.

125. William Phillips, "How *Partisan Review* Began," *Commentary* 62, no. 6
(December 1976): 42.

3. Kronstadt

Epigraph: Sigmund Freud, *Civilization and Its Discontents*, trans. James Strachey
(New York: W.W. Norton, 1961), 70.

1. Diana Trilling, *The Beginning of the Journey: The Marriage of Diana and
Lionel Trilling* (New York: Harcourt, Brace, 1993), 220; Sidney Hook, *Out of
Step: An Unquiet Life in the Twentieth Century* (New York: Carol and Graf,
1987), 286; Trilling, *The Beginning of the Journey*; Hook, *Out of Step*, 286.
Chambers did not leave his own description of this event.

2. Trilling, *The Beginning of the Journey*, 220, 220. Herbert Solow to Lionel and
Diana Trilling, circa 1938. Lionel Trilling Papers, Special Collections, Butler
Library, Columbia University, New York, Box 6 (Folder Solow, Herbert)
(hereafter cited as Trilling MSS).

3. Both Diana Trilling and Sidney Hook later contended that the Halloween
party was a key psychological experience for Chambers. Hook wrote that
"[Herbert] Solow was to argue with me and others that this event played a
great and symbolic role in Chambers's mind as an act of political resurrection,
indeed that the Halloween décor then [in 1938] was the real clue to his
selection, ten years later, of a hollowed-out pumpkin within which to conceal
the microfilm evidence that incriminated Hiss!" *Out of Step*, 287. Diana
Trilling had a similar impression to Solow's: "it occurred to me during the
trial that there was a ready explanation for Chambers having chosen a
pumpkin in which to hide his microfilm. Unconsciously this had no doubt
been suggested to him by the decoration at Anita Brenner's Halloween party."
The Beginning of the Journey, 220. Regardless of whether pumpkins
represented rebirth for Chambers, the anger he would later feel toward the
Trillings and Solow must have begun with this Halloween fiasco. In 1950, he

wrote that "before the Purge, the Trillings were happy fellow travelers, and the place to find them was around the edge of the C.P. [Communist Party]. After the Purge, or perhaps a little earlier, they switched to Trotsky. Herbert Solow . . . also a gifted, if subjective, poputchik [fellow traveler] in his day, takes the same high tone among the tea cups that Diana Trilling takes. It never ceases to annoy me." Whittaker Chambers to Ralph de Toledano, May 16, 1950, in *Notes from the Underground: The Whittaker Chambers-Ralph de Toledano Correspondence, 1949–1960*, ed. Ralph de Toledano (Washington, D.C.: Regnery, 1997), 24.

4. Louis Fischer, in *The God that Failed*, ed. Richard Crossman (New York: Harper, 1950), 204.

5. As Judy Kutulas notes, "[Popular] Front politics were never mass politics, but 1937 marked their apex." *The Long War: The Intellectual People's Front and Anti-Stalinism, 1930–1940* (Durham, N.C.: Duke University Press, 1995), 105.

6. William Barrett, *The Truants: Adventures among the Intellectuals* (Garden City, N.J.: Anchor Press, 1982), 76.

7. William Phillips, *A Partisan View: Five Decades of the Literary Life* (New York: Stein and Day, 1983), 42; Mary McCarthy, *Intellectual Memoirs: New York, 1936–1938* (New York: Harcourt, Brace, Jovanovich, 1992), 22.

8. "Editorial Statement," *Partisan Review* 4, no. 1 (December 1937): 3, 3. Lionel Trilling to editor of the *New Republic*, circa 1938, Trilling MSS, Box 7.

9. The two central *Partisan Review* editors also had their Kronstadt in 1936, according to Terry Cooney: "at the end of December 1936, [William] Phillips and [Philip] Rahv came to see [James] Farrell and declared themselves through with the Stalinist movement." *The Rise of the New York Intellectuals: Partisan Review and Its Circle* (Madison: University of Wisconsin Press, 1986), 98.

10. Lionel Trilling to Alan Brown, August 26, 1936, Trilling MSS, Box 7. Trilling himself suggested the connection between Marx and Freud in his intellectual development: "I began to be skeptical of Marxist doctrine [around 1931] . . . I suppose it could be said that my diminished—but never wholly extirpated—responsiveness to Marxism gave Freudianism its chance. I came to know much more about psychoanalytic theory than I had ever known about Marxist theory and such knowledge as I had led me to reject the facile and often vulgar Freudian interpretations of most literary men of the day." Lionel Trilling to John Vaughn, August 10, 1972, Trilling MSS, Box 28. Interestingly, Tony Hiss, the son of Alger Hiss, recalls a similar leaning in the mind of Alger. "There are recurrent references," Tony Hiss recalled, "especially in the Lewisburg [the prison where Alger served out his term] letters, to a nineteenth-century European thinker who changed the world—but the man Alger had come to admire so greatly was Sigmund Freud, not Karl Marx." *The View from Alger's Window: A Son's Memoir* (New York: Knopf, 1999), 39.

11. Lionel Trilling to the editors of the *New Republic*, April 4, 1937, Trilling MSS, Box 7; Lionel Trilling, "Marxism in Limbo," review of *Europa in Limbo* by Robert Briffault, *Partisan Review* 4 (December 1937): 71, 71.

12. Reason and skepticism were Trilling's terms: "I feel as much as you do at the manner in which reason and skepticism are being washed aside," he wrote of the Popular Front. Lionel Trilling to James Farrell, July 31, 1937, Trilling MSS, Box 2.

13. Trilling, "Marxism in Limbo," 72, 71.

14. Lionel Trilling to Alan Brown, March 28, 1937, Trilling MSS, Box 7.

15. Lionel Trilling to the editors of the *New Republic*, April 4, 1937, Trilling MSS, Box 7.

16. Such was Trotsky's argument. He stated it in greatest depth in his history of the Russian Revolution, translated by Max Eastman and made accessible to an English-language audience in 1937: *The Revolution Betrayed: What the Soviet Union Is and Where Is it Going*, trans. Max Eastman (Garden City, N.Y.: Doubleday, Doran, and Co., 1937).

17. Lionel Trilling, "Hemingway and His Critics," review of *The Fifth Column and the First Forty-Nine Stories* by Ernest Hemingway, *Partisan Review* 6 (Winter 1939): 59, 55.

18. Ibid., 59.

19. Edmund Wilson, "Flaubert's Politics," *Partisan Review* 4, no. 1 (December 1937): 20; André Gide, "Second Thoughts on the U.S.S.R.," *Partisan Review* 4, no. 2 (January 1938): 25.

20. This Quarter, *Partisan Review* 6, no. 1 (Fall 1938): 10; Philip Rahv, "Two Years of Progress," *Partisan Review* 4, no. 3 (February 1938): 25; This Quarter, *Partisan Review* 6, no. 2 (Winter 1939): 10.

21. This Quarter, *Partisan Review* 6, no. 3 (1939): 10, 10. Lionel Trilling to Alan to Brown, September 1940, Trilling MSS, Box 7. Philip Rahv, This Quarter, *Partisan Review* 4, no. 3 (February 1938): 62.

22. Lionel Trilling, "Realism and the Old Order," review of *The Brothers Ashkenazi* by I. J. Singer, trans. Maurice Samuel, *The Jewish Record* (January 4, 1937): 21–22.

23. Ibid., 22. Regarding "racial hatred" in the Soviet Union, and the general lack of response to it among Jewish American intellectuals, Sidney Hook emphasized the paucity of information. "At that time [1939]," Hook wrote in his memoirs, "the full dimensions of the cultural and religious oppressions of the Jews in the Soviet Union and its satellite nations had not yet been revealed." *Out of Step*, 353. To this one might add the reluctance of *Partisan Review* intellectuals to involve themselves with Jewish questions in general. Even where information was far more plentiful—i.e., in the case of the Nazis' persecution of European Jews—the *Partisan Review* intellectuals rarely moved beyond their instinctual

antifascism to the espousal of specifically Jewish causes (agitation, say, for greater acceptance of Jewish refugees in the United States).

24. Trilling, "Realism and the Old Order," 22.

25. Chambers expressed his fear in a 1938 letter to Meyer Schapiro, telling Schapiro in German that he would go to the American authorities if threatened: "I said at the first sign of monkey-business on their part, I would seek protection *bei einem amerikanischem Festungsgefängnis, kostet was das persönlich mag, den wir haben eine Krise der Verzweiflung erreicht* [by the American authorities, whatever the personal cost might be, for we've reached a crisis of despair]." Quoted in Allen Weinstein and Alexei Vasiliev, *The Haunted Wood: Soviet Espionage in America—The Stalin Era* (New York: Random House, 1999), 46. Weinstein mentions Otto Katz in conjunction with Chambers's fear. Katz was a contract killer for the Comintern "known for his role in tracking down and assisting the murder of key Soviet intelligence defectors in Europe." Ibid.

26. Chambers, *Witness*, 75.

27. Ibid., 439, 414.

28. Sidney Hook mentions this episode in his memoirs. "Sometime during 1937," Hook recalled, "Meyer Schapiro made some pointed remarks to me to the effect that Chambers had strong doubts about the Moscow trials on the basis of the official transcript then available in English." *Out of Step*, 281.

29. Ibid., 26, 284. In a letter to Eric Bentley about Whittaker Chambers, Trilling wrote, referring to Carlo Tresca and Juliet Poyntz, that "intimate friends of his [Chambers] are old friends of mine." Lionel Trilling to Eric Bentley, November 28, 1947, Trilling MSS, Box 1. Both Tresca and Poyntz were assumed to have been murdered by the Soviet underground.

30. Sam Tanenhaus, *Whittaker Chambers: A Biography* (New York: Modern Library, 1998), 275. The summons to Moscow was certainly dangerous. In *The Gulag Archipelago* Alexander I. Solzhenitsyn writes about "our own real spies abroad. (These were often the most dedicated Comintern workers and Chekists . . . They were called back to the Motherland and arrested at the border. They were then confronted with their former Comintern chief . . . who confirmed that he himself had been working for one of the foreign intelligence services—which meant that his subordinates were automatically guilty too. And the more dedicated they were, the worse it was for them.)" *The Gulag Archipelago, 1918–1956: An Experiment in Literary Investigation*, trans. Thomas P. Whitney (New York: Harper and Row, 1974), 72.

31. Ann Applebaum, *Gulag: A History* (New York: Doubleday, 2003), xvi, xvii.

32. Robert Service, *Stalin: A Biography* (London: Macmillan, 2004), 339.

33. Allen Weinstein endorses Hook's argument: "Chambers escaped, in short, for the most basic of reasons: self-preservation." *Perjury: The Hiss-Chambers Case*

(New York: Random House, 1997), 273. Weinstein elaborates: "Chambers decided, as did several leading Soviet operatives in the United States at the time to stall and disregard the summons [to Moscow] to return to certain arrest and (minimally) imprisonment." Allein Weinstein and Alexei Vasiliev, *The Haunted Wood*, 45. "He had left the underground," Weinstein continues, "still a devoted Marxist." *Perjury*, 281. The break was slower than Chambers presented it in *Witness*, but the evidence is too spotty for definitive conclusions.

34. Whittaker Chambers, "Statement," January 3, 1949, Alger Hiss Defense Files, Harvard Law School Special Collections, Box 48 (Folder 19), p. 121 (hereafter cited as AHDF).

35. The full citation is: Vladimir Vyzcheslavovich Tchernavin, *I Speak for the Silent Prisoners of the Soviets*, trans. Nicholas Oushakoff (New York: Hale, Cushman and Flint, 1935).

36. Chambers, *Witness*, 80, 444.

37. Ibid., 35; Whittaker Chambers, "Chambers, Whittaker—Homosexuality," AHDF, Box 46 (Folder 11), p. 122; Chambers, *Witness*, 82.

38. Whittaker Chambers, "Chambers, Whittaker—Homosexuality," AHDF, Box 46 (Folder 11), p. 122; Whittaker Chambers, "Chambers, Whittaker—Homosexuality," AHDF, Box 46 (Folder 11).

39. James Cannon, *The Militant*, June 9, [year unknown], AHDF, Box 2.

40. Chambers, *Witness*, 84; Cannon, *The Militant*, June 9, [year unknown], AHDF, Box 2. Depending on the content of the meeting, it could indeed have reflected a post-Kronstadt Marxist orientation for Chambers. Hook, *Out of Step*, 281.

41. Chambers had a knack for inspiring distrust. Such was Hook's excuse in his memoirs, his explanation for the rather fantastic chain of reasoning that led him to prevent Chambers from seeing Dewey. "Everything I knew about Chambers," Hook explained, "was compatible with the possibility that he might be involved in an intrigue of this sort." *Out of Step*, 282.

42. Ibid., 283.

43. Chambers, *Witness*, 459, 453. Once again, the only evidence for these meetings is *Witness* and Chambers's own FBI testimony. André Gide had exactly the same realization in 1937. He noted in his journal that "the Communist spirit has ceased being in opposition to the Fascist spirit, or even differentiation itself from it." *The God that Failed*, 171.

44. Chambers, *Witness*, 473, 471, 471.

45. Ellen Schrecker identified a "concerted campaign by a loosely structured, but surprisingly self-conscious, network of political activists" as the 1930s precursor to McCarthyism. *Many Are the Crimes: McCarthyism in America* (Princeton, N.J.: Princeton University Press, 1999), xiii. Schrecker dates the origins of McCarthyism all the way back to the nineteenth century: "anticommunism in

its modern form as a consciously organized campaign against the left began in the 1870s." Ibid., 48.

46. Richard Gid Powers, *Secrecy and Power: The Life of J. Edgar Hoover* (New York: Free Press, 1987), 239. Powers argues that "Hoover at this time [early 1940s] was less than convinced the threat of Communist espionage was as great as claimed by the radical right." Ibid., 239.

47. M. J. Heale, *American Anticommunism: Combating the Enemy Within, 1830–1970* (Baltimore: Johns Hopkins University Press, 1990), 103, 112.

48. With the Dies Commission, the problem of anti-communism in government began to have some resonance with the general public: "public opinion polls revealed that most American were familiar with, and sympathetic to, the committee's work." David Oshinsky, *A Conspiracy So Immense: The World of Joe McCarthy* (New York: Free Press, 1983), 93. Some seventy-four percent of those who had heard of the Dies Committee wanted it to continue its work, according to a 1938 Gallup poll. Walter Goodman, *The Committee: The Extraordinary Career of the House Committee on Un-American Activities* (New York: Farrar, Straus, and Giroux, 1968), 53.

49. David Caute, *The Great Fear: The Anti-Communist Purge under Truman and Eisenhower* (New York: Simon and Schuster, 1978), 111.

50. In *The Red Network*, a self-published exposé of communist subversion in the United States, the undeniably conservative Elizabeth Dilling did not see Republicans as the inevitable foes of communism. As she wrote in warning, "Americans who are alarmed at the present socialist administration, labeled as 'Democratic,' may easily turn out 'Democrats' and vote in Republicans at the next election, but how many of the elected 'Republican' officials will be radicals of the same stripe?" *The Red Network: A Who's Who and Handbook of Radicalism for Patriots* (Kenilworth, Ill.: Elizabeth Dilling, 1934), 74. Nor did she propose that Republicans had to be the ones to promote the anti-communist cause: "we need a rockbound old American or an anti-Marxian Democrat (with a Congress to match) to lead America." Ibid., 91. Dilling's eccentric book further illustrated the low intellectual level of much anti-communist advocacy in the 1930s, the equivalent in letters of Father Coughlin and Huey Long in politics. She listed Freud as a "sex psychologist," Marx as a "German Jew," and H. L. Mencken as a dangerous radical. Ibid., 282, 204, 206. Chambers appeared on her list of radicals, but she mentioned no other member of the Ware circle or second apparatus.

51. Whittaker Chambers to Meyer Schapiro, circa 1938, Schapiro MSS, Box 1 (Folder 1936–1937). Whittaker Chambers to Meyer Schapiro, July–August 1938, Schapiro MSS, Box 1 (Folder 1938).

52. Whittaker Chambers to Meyer Schapiro, July–August 1938, Schapiro MSS, Box 1 (Folder 1938).

53. Chambers, *Witness*, 88; Whittaker Chambers, *Cold Friday*, ed. Duncan Norton-Taylor (New York: Random House, 1964), 41.

54. Chambers, *Witness*, 481; Whittaker Chambers," Intelligence Report," review *The Menacing Sun* by Mona Gardner, in *Ghosts on the Roof: Selected Journalism of Whittaker Chambers, 1931–1959*, ed. Terry Teachout (Washington, D.C.: Regnery, 1989), 491; Whittaker Chambers, "Night Thoughts," review of *Finnegan's Wake* by James Joyce, in *Ghosts on the Roof*, 54. Whittaker Chambers, "The New Pictures: Ninotchka," in *Ghosts on the Roof*, 56.

55. Whittaker Chambers to Meyer Schapiro, circa 1938–1939, Schapiro MSS, Box 1.

56. Tanenhaus, *Whittaker Chambers*, 157. The three essays were: "Stalin's Hand in Spain" (April 15, 1939), "Why Stalin Shot His Generals" (April 22, 1939), and "Stalin Appeases Hitler" (April 29, 1939). In these detailed and often personal essays, Krivitsky argued that the Popular Front was a sham, used in the end only to augment the power of Stalin himself: "obedient members of the Communist Party dropped their opposition to the ruling government, and, in the name of 'democracy,' joined forces with the other political parties. The technique was to elect, with the aid of their 'fellow travelers' and their dupes, national administrations friendly to the Soviet Union." "Stalin's Hand in Spain," *Saturday Evening Post* (April 15, 1939): 6.

57. The full citations are: *In Stalin's Secret Service: An Expose of Russia's Secret Policies by the Former Chief of the Soviet Intelligence in Western Europe* (New York: Harper and Bros., 1939) and *I Was Stalin's Secret Agent* (London: H. Hamilton, 1939).

58. Editor's Note in "Stalin's Hand in Spain," *Saturday Evening Post* (April 15, 1939): 5; Chambers, *Witness*, 462, 462.

59. "All of the major Humanists found inspiration in Matthew Arnold, who more than any single person shaped the Humanists' point of view." J. David Hoeveler Jr., *The New Humanism: A Critique of Modern America, 1900–1940* (Charlottesville: University Press of Virginia, 1977), 25. Both Arnold and the New Humanists had a conservative aura about them. As a critical movement, New Humanism influenced several prominent conservative intellectuals. Among these were T. S. Eliot, Peter Viereck, Austin Warren, and Russell Kirk. Paul Gottfried, *The Conservative Movement* (New York: Twayne, 1993), 22.

60. Edmund Wilson, *The Twenties: From Notebooks and Diaries of the Period*, ed. Leon Edel (New York: Farrar, Straus and Giroux, 1976), 352; Lionel Trilling, *A Gathering of Fugitives*, ed. Diana Trilling (New York: Harcourt, Brace, Jovanovich, 1977), 55, 55. Mark Shechner refers to Trilling's study of Matthew Arnold as "deliberately unfashionable in its ideas." *After the Revolution: Studies in the Contemporary Jewish Imagination* (Bloomington: University of Indiana Press, 1987), 78.

61. Diana Trilling, *The Beginning of the Journey*, 267. David Hollinger writes that "the appointment of Lionel Trilling as assistant professor in 1939 [at Columbia] was a breakthrough so striking that its story is still told by aging English professors around the country, in tones that Civil War buffs reserve for describing the battle of Gettysburg." *Science, Jews, and Secular Culture: Studies in Mid-Twentieth-Century American Intellectual History* (Princeton, N.J.: Princeton University Press, 1996), 139.

62. Sidney Hook to Lionel Trilling, July 12, 1938, Trilling MSS, Box 7; Jacques Barzun to Lionel Trilling, June 1937, Trilling MSS, Box 1.

63. William Barrett, *The Truants: Adventures among the Intellectuals* (Garden City, N.Y.: Anchor Press, 1982), 163–164.

64. Lionel Trilling, "Matthew Arnold Poet," in *Major British Writers*, ed. G. B. Harrison (New York: Harcourt, Brace and World, 1954), 426. Matthew Arnold was surely a poet of modern loss, but he was to be valued, in Trilling's estimation, for his moderation and health and for not succumbing to the tragedy of lost faith and beauty. "If Arnold perceived a sickness in the life of his time," Trilling wrote in praise of Arnold, "he was not perversely and sentimentally attracted to it." High praise from Trilling. Ibid., 429.

65. Ibid., 427–428, 428, 431. In another review, Trilling touched on the plight of the Victorians, who, "deprived of so many of the comforts of religion . . . put upon literature the conscious responsibility for man's spiritual guidance." "Evangelical Criticism," review of *Towards the Twentieth Century* by H. V. Routh, *New Republic* 95 (June 20, 1938): 314. Mark Shechner connects Trilling's relationship to England (and especially to the Victorians) with his Jewish pieties: "Trilling's anglophilia was wholly consistent with his rabbinism, its fulfillment rather than its contradiction, and he became more the Jew by becoming more the Victorian." *After the Revolution*, 78.

66. Lionel Trilling to Alan Brown, September 1938, Trilling MSS, Box 7. Ludwig Feuerbach wrote a critique of Christianity important to the development of Marxism, *The Essence of Christianity*, which he published in 1841. See Leszek Kolokowski, *The Main Currents of Marxism: Its Origins, Growth and Dissolution*, vol. 1, trans. P. S. Falla (Oxford: Oxford University Press, 1981), 114–119.

67. Trilling, *Matthew Arnold* (New York: W.W. Norton and Co., 1939), 254, 188. Trilling adopted this point from T. S. Eliot, who "tells us that Arnold was not a revolutionary and not a reactionary . . . he tried to make the past of Europe march with its future." Ibid., xiii.

68. Ibid., 13, 13.

69. Ibid., 114, 79, 102, 104. Trilling's description of Arnold's "The Scholar Gypsy" would probably have appealed to Chambers: a "threnody for the lives of men smirched by modernity." Ibid., 112.

70. Ibid., 205, 207, 221.

71. Ibid., 342.

72. Arnold's career was an "exploration of two modern intellectual traditions which have failed him and his peers, the traditions of romanticism and rationalism . . . Each alone, he feels, is insufficient, but together they promise much." *Matthew Arnold*, 79.

73. Ibid., 301, 224.

74. Ibid., 384, 232, 232, 384.

75. Ibid., 342, 279, 387.

76. Ibid., 252, 291, 342, 343, 152, 159.

77. Ibid., 221, 62. Trilling wanted readers to remember that Matthew and Thomas Arnold's views were exceptional for their time: "to many men of his century there seemed an irreconcilable conflict between democracy and order, between freedom and organization, between populace and State." *Matthew Arnold*, 62.

78. Ibid., 221, 272–273, 277, 277.

79. Irving Kristol, "Arnold and Trilling," review of *Matthew Arnold* by Lionel Trilling, *New Leader* (July 2, 1949), Trilling MSS, Box 59.

80. Irving Howe, "Reading Lionel Trilling," *Commentary* 56 (August 1973): 68–71; Trilling, *Matthew Arnold*, 56; Irving Kristol, "Arnold and Trilling," *Enquiry* 2 (April 1944): 20–23.

4. First Steps in an Anti-Stalinist World

Epigraph: Henry R. Luce, *The American Century* (New York: Farrar and Rinehart, 1941), 3.

1. See Leslie Fiedler, *An End to Innocence: Essays on Culture and Politics* (Boston: Beacon Press, 1955).

2. Kevin Smant, *How Great the Triumph: James Burnham, Anticommunism and the Conservative Movement* (Lanham, Md.: University Press of America, 1992), 23–63.

3. Martin Malia makes this point emphatically: "for the duration of the war, to all the liberal West Stalin became respectable, and the Russian people admirable." *Russia under Western Eyes: From the Bronze Horseman to the Lenin Mausoleum* (Cambridge, Mass.: Harvard University Press, 1999), 335.

4. Stephen J. Whitfield refers to a "wartime suspension of anti-Stalinism" at *Partisan Review. The Critical American: The Politics of Dwight Macdonald* (Hamden, Conn.: Archon Books, 1984), 46. This suspension, which broke down toward the end of the war, was not the same as pro-Soviet conviction.

5. Daniel Bell, *The End of Ideology: On the Exhaustion of Political Ideas in the Fifties* (Glencoe, Ill.: Free Press, 1960), 310. Daniel Aaron uses the same date in stating that "the communist literary movement ceased to have much importance

after 1940." *Writers on the Left: Episodes in American Literary Communism* (New York: Avon Books, 1961), 396. John Patrick Diggins cites an anecdote from Max Eastman's memoirs, dated 1939, showing the decline in intellectual sympathy for the Soviet Union. Eastman described a cocktail party at which he was asked if he still believed in the "socialist idea," to which he said, " 'No,' and I could not have said it with more conviction if I had made the decision months before." *Love and Revolution: My Journey through an Epoch* (New York: Random House, 1964), 632. From this anecdote and other evidence Diggins concludes that "by 1939 a considerable section of the American intellectual community seemed to be following Eastman's path . . . turned against communism of all varieties and had begun to question all political strategies that derived from Marxist premises." *Up from Communism: Conservative Odysseys in American Intellectual History* (New York: Harper and Row, 1975), 177.

6. François Furet points out a growing divide between American and European intellectuals over the question of communism in the 1940s: "As the American intelligentsia was converting en masse to anti-Communism, most European intellectuals were wondering why they could not agree that the price to pay for the defense of liberty against Stalin was to extend their blessing to the American cult of free enterprise . . . Cold War pro-Communism [in Europe] was less and less protected by anti-Fascism, but it relied more and more on the anti-capitalist alibi in the almost a ideal form provided in the United States." *The Passing of an Illusion: The Idea of Communism in the Twentieth Century*, trans. Deborah Furet (Chicago: University of Chicago Press, 1999), 429.

7. Whittaker Chambers, *Witness* (Washington D.C.: Regnery, 1997), 459.

8. Lionel Trilling to Eric Bentley, January 29, 1946, Lionel Trilling Papers, Special Collections, Butler Library, Columbia University, New York, Box 9 (hereafter cited as Trilling MSS).

9. Lionel Trilling, "The Situation in American Writing: A Symposium," *Partisan Review* 6 (Fall 1939): 109.

10. Ibid. Trilling did not fear menaces from without when he thought of war. He worried about subversion from within, not communist subversion but that of the business elite. Trilling wrote of his "very strong belief that if Roosevelt is elected there may well be war and the most enormous sabotage by the manufacturing class." Trilling thought the pressures of war would be too much for a Democratic administration: "Almost, I wish Wilkie would get elected if war must come." Lionel Trilling to Alan Brown, September 3, 1940, Trilling MSS, Box 7.

11. Lionel Trilling to Bruce Bliven, August 8, 1941, Trilling, MSS, Box 1.

12. Neil Jumonville, *Critical Crossings: The New York Intellectuals in Postwar America* (Berkeley: University of California Press, 1991), 50.

13. Diana Trilling, *The Beginning of the Journey: The Marriage of Diana and Lionel Trilling* (New York: Harcourt, Brace, 1993), 322.

14. James Burnham, "Lenin's Heir," *Partisan Review* 12, no. 1 (Winter 1945): 70, 71.

15. "The Liberal 'Fifth Column,' " *Partisan Review* 13, no. 3 (Summer 1946): 293, 292, 293, 292.

16. Ann Applebaum, *Gulag: A History* (New York: Doubleday, 2003), 441, 441–442, 442, 443.

17. Lionel Trilling to Eric Bentley, February 14, 1946, Trilling MSS, Box 31.

18. Sidney Hook, "The Future of Socialism," *Partisan Review* 14, no. 1 (January–February 1947): 372, 374, 374.

19. Irving Howe, "Europe's Long Night," review of *The Long Dusk* by Victor Serge, trans. Ralph Mannheim, *Partisan Review* 14, no. 1 (January–February 1947): 93, 94; Granville Hicks, "On Attitudes and Ideas," *Partisan Review* (March–April 1947): 123, 123.

20. Quoted in Whitfield, *The Critical American*, 15.

21. William Barrett, "Talent and Career of Jean-Paul Sartre," *Partisan Review* 13, no. 2 (Spring 1946): 244; Claude-Edmonde Magny, "French Literature since 1940," *Partisan Review* 13, no. 2 (Spring 1946): 148; Hannah Arendt, "What is Existenz Philosophie," *Partisan Review* 13, no. 1 (Winter 1946): 42.

22. Granville Hicks, "On Attitudes and Ideas," *Partisan Review* 14, no. 2 (March–April 1947): 126.

23. William Phillips, "The Resistance," *Partisan Review* 8, no. 4 (September–October 1946): 488. Comparing Luce to a Nazi was something of a trope among left-leaning intellectuals in the 1940s. Freda Kirchway compared "The American Century" with *Mein Kampf*, as did Oswald Garrison Villard. Robert E. Herzstein, *Henry R. Luce: A Political Portrait of the Man Who Created the American Century* (New York: Scribner's, 1994), 182.

24. "Krivitsky's death," writes Allen Weinstein, "persuaded Chambers that he should cease efforts to expose his former underground associates in government. The talk with Berle convinced him that the effort would be futile and perhaps fatal." *Perjury: The Hiss-Chambers Case* (New York: Random House, 1997), 294.

25. An atomistic conservatism would last for some time. George Nash argues that as late as 1945 "no articulate, coordinated, self-consciously conservative intellectual force existed in the United States." *The Conservative Intellectual Movement, Since 1945* (New York: Basic Books, 1979), xiii.

26. M. J. Heale notes that with HUAC "for the first time, anticommunism was being fueled by party politics." *American Anticommunism: Combating the Enemy Within, 1830–1970* (Baltimore: Johns Hopkins University Press, 1990), 121.

27. The "Old Right," the Taft Republicans, "were anti-Communist without being cold warriors." Paul Gottfried, *The Conservative Movement* (New York: Twayne, 1993), 5.

28. Sam Tanenhaus writes that "this was the job he had coveted since 1939." *Whittaker Chambers: A Biography* (New York: Modern Library), 179.

29. Robert E. Herzstein writes of Chambers convincing Luce that "communists, manipulated by Stalinists, were at war with decent men in many countries, especially America and China." *Henry R. Luce*, 349, 178.

30. Chambers, *Witness*, 497, 499.

31. Whittaker Chambers, "Anatomy of Fascism," review of *As We Go Marching* by John T. Flynn, *American Mercury* (April 1944): 97, 97.

32. Richard H. Pells, *The Liberal Mind in a Conservative Age* (New York: Harper and Row, 1985), 11.

33. Quoted in Patricia Neils, *China Images in the Life and Times of Henry Luce* (Savage, Md.: Ronwar and Littlefield Publishers, 1990), 231.

34. Quoted in Ibid., 146.

35. Quoted in Robert T. Elson, *The World of Time, Inc.: The Intimate History of a Publishing Enterprise*, vol. 2, ed. Duncan Norton-Taylor (New York: Athenaeum, 1968–1986), 108.

36. Whittaker Chambers, "Area of Decision," in *Ghosts on the Roof*, 98.

37. Sam Tanenhaus notes the impact Burnham's *Partisan Review* essay, "Lenin's Heir," had on Chambers in 1944. Tanenhaus argues that this influence is most visible in a piece written between "Area of Decision" and "The Ghosts on the Roof" on Stalin (February 5, 1945). *Whittaker Chambers*, 189.

38. Chambers, "Area of Decision," 102.

39. Robert Herzstein, *Henry R. Luce*, 356–357.

40. Theodore White was not a communist, and he was not pro-communist. He had been briefly affiliated with the left-leaning Institute of Pacific Relations and he was acquainted with Owen Lattimore, who would be at the center of considerable McCarthyite controversy in the 1950s. White's perspective was, in Robert Herzstein's words, "that of a liberal antifascist, skeptical of Communists but willing to work with them against an evil enemy [like the Japanese." *Henry R. Luce*, 196. In 1944, White "saw the Communists as a *possible* force for positive change." Ibid., 300.

41. "Crisis" was "drafted by Fred Guin and 'sewn together' by Chambers," according to Sam Tanenhaus. Chambers went to a source other than Theodore White, drawing material for his rewrite from Lin Yutang's *The Vigil of a Nation* (New York: J. Day, 1945).

42. Whittaker Chambers, "Crisis," *Time* (November 13, 1944): 108.

43. Whittaker Chambers, "The Ghosts on the Roof," *Time* (March 5, 1945): 111.

44. Czeslaw Milosz, *The Captive Mind*, trans. Jane Zielonko (New York: Vintage Books, 1955), 135. Chambers's argument resonated with Russian intellectuals arrested by Stalin: "In their own countries Roosevelt and Churchill are honored as embodiments of statesmanlike wisdom. To us in our Russian prison

conversations," writes Alexander Solzhenitsyn, "their consistent shortsightedness and stupidity stood out as astonishingly obvious. How could they, in their decline from 1941 to 1945, fail to secure any guarantees whatever of the independence of Eastern Europe? How could they give away broad regions of Saxony and Thuringia in exchange for the preposterous toy of a four-zone Berlin, their own future Achilles' heel? And what was the military or political sense in their surrendering to destruction at Stalin's hands hundreds of thousands of armed Soviet citizens determined not to surrender? They say it was the price they paid for Stalin's agreeing to enter the war against Japan. With the atom bomb already in their hands, they paid Stalin for not refusing to occupy Manchuria, for strengthening Mao Tse-tung in China, and for giving Kim Il Sung control of half Korea! What bankruptcy of political thought!" Alexander I. Solzhenitsyn, *The Gulag Archipelago, 1918–1956: An Experiment in Literary Investigation*, trans. Thomas P. Whitney (New York: Harper and Row, 1973), 259–260.

45. Here, too, the *Partisan Review* circle was not so far from Chambers in its evaluation of the political situation. Hook retrospectively described his opinion of Roosevelt in his memoirs, recalling that "Roosevelt was profoundly ignorant about the nature of communism, not only as an ideological system but as a functioning totalitarian society." *Out of Step: An Unquiet Life in the Twentieth Century* (New York: Harper and Row, 1987), 312.

46. Robert Service, *Stalin: A Biography* (London: Macmillan, 2004), 335.

47. Chambers, "The Ghosts on the Roof," 112–113, 114.

48. Ibid., 114, 114, 114, 115.

49. Tanenhaus, *Whittaker Chambers*, 191, 193.

50. Ellen Schrecker dates the origins of McCarthyism back to 1946. She argues that "the crucial developments that brought McCarthyism to the center of American politics occurred between 1946 and 1949, when the nation's political elites, preoccupied with the issue of communism, took up the tools that the anti-communist network had so conveniently forged." *Many Are the Crimes: McCarthyism in America* (Boston: Little, Brown, 1998), xvi–xvii. Chambers may well have been used as a tool by ambitious anti-communist politicians such as Richard Nixon, but he was not a self-conscious member of an anti-communist network; nor was he ever a hero to most of the nation's political elites. He felt himself an embattled minority among the nation's intellectual elites, even at a mainstream, nonradical magazine such as *Time*.

51. Allen Weinstein writes that "both FBI and State Department counterintelligence officials had begun earlier in 1945 to scan Chambers's depositions and the Berle memo, reacting uneasily to the rise of Hiss [to ever higher positions in government]." *Perjury: The Hiss-Chambers Case* (New York: Random House, 1997), 307.

52. Sam Tanenhaus points to this irony: "at just the moment when the country at large was awakening to the 'Red Menace,' Chambers had lost his zeal for Red hunting." *Whittaker Chambers*, 207. By some accounts, 1945 was the year in which the tide began to turn (according to Daniel Bell, the year was 1940). Arthur Schlesinger Jr. recalls that "Arthur Koestler's critique of Soviet communism in *The Yogi and the Commissar* had a far more sympathetic audience [in 1945] than it could have had two years earlier." *Innocent Beginnings: A Life in the Twentieth Century* (Boston: Houghton Mifflin, 2000), 355.

53. Schlesinger Jr., *Innocent Beginnings*, 398, 399, 399.

54. Whittaker Chambers, "The Challenge," review of *A Study of History* by Arnold J. Toynbee, *Time* (March 17, 1947): 142, 141. For an analysis of Toynbee in relation to notions of Western decline see Arthur Herman, *The Idea of Decline in Western History* (New York: Free Press, 1997), 256–294.

55. Tanenhaus, *Whittaker Chambers*, 198.

56. William Phillips, *A Partisan View: Five Decades of the Literary Life* (New York: Stein and Day, 1983), 17.

57. Ibid., 39, 41, 48–49, 49.

58. Lionel Trilling, "The America of John Dos Passos," *Partisan Review*, no. 5 (April 1938): 27, 28, 29, 28.

59. Lionel Trilling, "Hemingway and His Critics," *Partisan Review* 6, no. 2 (Winter 1939): 53, 59.

60. Ibid., 60, 60.

61. Lionel Trillling, "Parrington, Mr. Smith, and Reality," review of *Main Currents in American Thought* by V. L. Parrington, and *Forces in American Criticism* by Bernard Smith, *Partisan Review* 7, no. 1 (January–February 1940): 9, 31, 32.

62. The essay to which Trilling referred was: "Literature and Power," *Kenyon Review* 2 (Autumn 1940). Archibald MacLeish published his essay in book form as *The Irresponsibles: A Declaration* (New York: Duell, Sloan and Pearce, 1940).

63. Lionel Trilling, "Sherwood Anderson," *Kenyon Review* 3 (Summer 1941): 26, 30. Anderson had been connected to the communist front, the NCDPP, to which Trilling had belonged. Trilling's friend Elliot Cohen had recruited Anderson. Nathan Abrams, *Commentary Magazine, 1945–1959: "A Journal of Significant Thought and Opinion"* (London: Vallentine Mitchell, 2007), 24.

64. Lionel Trilling, "An American Classic," review of *Let Us Now Praise Famous Men* by James Agee and Walker Evans, *Mid-Century* 16 (September 1960): 3–10.

65. Lionel Trilling, "Artists and the 'Societal' Function," review of *Writers in Crisis* by Maxwell Geismar, *Kenyon Review* 4 (Autumn 1942): 428, 428.

66. In *The End of Ideology*, Daniel Bell linked the appeal of Freudianism with that of Protestant neoorthodoxy, linking, as it were, the anti-communist mood of Trilling with the religious mood of Chambers. He described an intelligentsia "skeptical of the rationalist claim that socialism, by eliminating the economic

base of exploitation, would solve all the social questions; and to a great extent this anti-rationalism is the source of the vogue of Freudianism and neo-orthodox theology." Ibid., 311.

67. Lionel Trilling, "The Progressive Psyche," review of *Self-Analysis* by Karen Horney, *Nation* 155 (September 12, 1942): 216.

68. Lionel Trilling, "The Lower Depths," review of *Dark Wedding* by Roman Sendor, trans. Eleanor Clark, and *Men from Nowhere* by Jean Malaquais, *Nation* 156 (April 24, 1943): 603, 602, 604.

69. Sidney Hook, "The Failure of the Left," *Partisan Review* 10, no. 2 (March–April 1943): 174.

70. Lionel Trilling, "Last Testament," review of *The World from Yesterday: A Biography* by Stefan Zweig, *Contemporary Jewish Record* 6 (August 1943): 428.

71. Lienel Trilling to Eric Bentley, November 2, 1947, Bos 1, Trilling MSS.

72. Whittaker Chambers, "The Old Deal," review of *The Age of Jackson* by Arthur Schlesinger Jr., *Time* (October 22, 1945). In his memoirs, Schlesinger remembered Chambers's review as "curious but shrewd." *Innocent Beginnings*, 359.

73. Chambers, "The Anatomy of Fascism," 58.

74. Tanenhaus, *Whittaker Chambers*, 172.

75. Whittaker Chambers, "The Revolt of the Intellectuals," in *Ghosts on the Roof*, 61, 60.

76. Mark Shechner makes a similar point in broader and somewhat disparaging terms, describing the turn away from communism among Jewish intellectuals as "a mass exodus from the ghettos of revolutionism toward the condos of individualism. The single enabling condition that allowed Jewish writers in our time to emerge as serious modern authors was the emergence of a demanding and intricate self, a self that was an idea before it could become a social possibility." *After the Revolution: Studies in the Contemporary Jewish-American Imagination* (Bloomington: Indiana University Press, 1987), 7. Michael Denning holds the Cold War responsible for a retreat from politics among intellectuals: "as the Cold War constricted the wide-ranging political, social, and cultural debates of the 1930s and 1940s, literary intellectuals turned increasingly inward." *The Cultural Front: The Laboring of American Culture in the Twentieth Century* (New York: Verso, 1998), 434.

5. Toward an Anti-Communism of the Left and an Anti-Communism of the Right

Epigraph: Lionel Trilling, "The Sense of the Past," *Partisan Review* 9, no. 3 (May–June 1942): 237.

1. Chambers did not even have a concerted anti-communist movement on which to draw. In the words of George Nash: "for all the disillusionment

generated in the 1930s, the intellectual impact of the early revolt against the Red Decade remained decidedly marginal in 1945." *The Conservative Intellectual Movement: Since 1945* (New York: Basic Books, 1979), 88. Chambers was only one of several lonely conservatives circa 1945 with high ambitions. Nash lists "the Olympian [Albert] Nock, [Friedrich] Hayek in war-torn London, [Frank] Chodorov on a meal a day, [William F. Buckley] seemingly alone at Yale—these and others seem especially noteworthy for their refusal to abandon what frequently appeared to be a doomed position." Ibid., 34–35.

2. Daniel T. O'Hara associates Trilling with liberation in the title of his study, *Lionel Trilling: The Work of Liberation* (Madison: University of Wisconsin Press, 1988).

3. In 1942, Chambers wrote a memo to Henry Luce about the essential difference between the Left and Right. Belief in God, Chambers argued, is "the real line of clearage in the modern world between conservatism and revolution, cutting across all lines of economic class and political party; binding together proletarian and capitalist in a common belief in the primacy of God, just as they inexorably throw together those who believe in the primacy of secular man no matter what their superficial differences or pseudo-religious trappings." Quoted in Sam Tanenhaus, *Whittaker Chambers: A Biography* (New York: Random House, 1997), xxi.

4. Quoted in Richard Wightman Fox, *Reinhold Niebuhr: A Biography* (New York: Pantheon, 1985), 273. Asked by literary scholar Nathan Scott whether Niebuhr had influenced him, Trilling replied " 'we must talk about that some time.' " Charles Brown, *Niebuhr and His Age: Reinhold Niebuhr's Prophetic Role in the Twentieth Century* (Philadelphia: Trinity, 1992), 243.

5. Whittaker Chambers to Meyer Schapiro, circa 1943, Meyer Schapiro Papers, Butler Library, Columbia University, Box 1 (Folder 1939–1953) (hereafter cited as Schapiro MSS).

6. Whittaker Chambers, *Witness* (Washington, D.C.: Regnery, 1997), 517.

7. Whittaker Chambers, writing under the pseudonym John Land, "Literary Autolysis," *American Mercury*, 58, no. 242 (February 1944): 247. For a discussion of authorship in Chambers's unsigned articles and articles written under pseudonyms see Terry Teachout, "Editor's Note" in *Ghosts on the Roof: Selected Journalism of Whittaker Chambers*, ed. Terry Teachout (Washington, D.C.: Regnery, 1989), xi. See also Tanenhaus, *Whittaker Chambers*, 153–199. Chambers's article was a combined review of P. Alter Waring and Walter Magnes, *Roots in the Earth: The Small Farmer Looks Ahead* (New York: Harper, 1943); Arthur Koestler, *Arrival and Departure* (New York: Macmillan, 1943); and G. A. Borgese, *Common Cause* (New York: Duell, Sloan and Pearce, 1943). *American Mercury* was edited by Eugene Lyons, author of an early

anti-communist tract about communist subversion in America, *The Red Decade: The Stalinist Penetration of America* (New York: Bobbs-Merril, 1941).

8. Chambers, "Literary Autolysis," 247, 247.

9. Whittaker Chambers, "In Egypt Land," *Time* (December 30, 1946): 64.

10. In "In Egypt Land," Chambers cited Arnold Toynbee, who wrote about Syrian slaves bringing Christianity to Rome. African Americans had the same capacity to civilize a potentially pagan American populace. Chambers's hopes for African Americans melded empathy, flattery, and condescension. He reviewed the constraints racial prejudice had imposed on Marian Anderson, noting that in the South Anderson "avoids Jim Crow by traveling in drawing rooms on night trains" and "even in New York she could not until recently stay at most good hotels." Ibid., 60. The flattery derived from putting black Americans in the role of Christian missionaries, and the condescension, was in the citation from Toynbee's *A Study of History* with which Chambers concluded his piece: "with their [African Americans'] childlike intuition and their genius for giving spontaneous esthetic expression to emotional religious experience, they may be capable of rekindling the cold grey ashes of Christianity." Ibid., 64.

11. Chambers, "In Egypt Land," 64. Chambers's piece on Anderson was very popular, bringing "in a deluge of reader mail." Tanenhaus, *Whittaker Chambers*, 197.

12. "Chambers kept four books in the top drawer of his desk at *Time*," writes Terry Teachout. They were "Kafka's *Parables and Paradoxes*, Burke's *Reflections on the Revolution in France*, Dostoevsky's *The Possessed* and Coriolanus." *Ghosts on the Roof*, ix.

13. Whittaker Chambers, "The Tragic Sense of Life," *Time* (April 28, 1947): 104, 106. The article was a review of Max Brod's *Franz Kafka: A Biography* (New York: Schocken, 1947). It is not entirely certain—although it is both plausible and likely—that Chambers wrote "The Tragic Sense of Life." See Terry Teachout, "Editor's Note" in *Ghosts on the Roof*, ix.

14. Arthur Schlesinger Jr., *Innocent Beginnings: A Life in the Twentieth Century* (Boston: Houghton Mifflin, 2000), 513.

15. Whittaker Chambers, *Cold Friday*, ed. Duncan Norton-Taylor (New York: Random House, 1964), 227.

16. Whittaker Chambers, "Faith for a Lenten Age," *Time* (March 8, 1948): 70, 70, 70, 70–71.

17. Chambers did mention Niebuhr's liberalism, writing that "most U.S. liberals think of Niebuhr as a solid socialist who has some obscure connection with Union Theological Seminary that does not interfere with his political work." Ibid., 79.

18. Chambers, "Faith for a Lenten Age," 76, 76. Richard Wightman Fox argues that "Henry Luce, Whittaker Chambers and other conservatives did their best to turn his [Niebuhr's] thought to their advantage. If man was fundamentally

flawed, liberal reformers ought to quit struggling with the free-enterprise system and make way." *Reinhold Niebuhr: A Biography* (New York: Pantheon, 1985), 202.

19. Chambers, *Witness*, 505, 506.

20. Quoted in Fox, *Reinhold Niebuhr*, 233–234.

21. Lionel Trilling, "Whittaker Chambers and 'The Middle of the Journey,' " *New York Review of Books* 22, no. 6 (April 17, 1975): 22. Trilling had once held Chambers's writing in high esteem. In the years that Chambers contributed to the *Morningside* (1924–1925), Chambers wrote, according to Trilling, "with an elegant austerity." "Later, beginning with his work for the *New Masses*, something went soft and 'high' in his tone and I was never again able to read him, either in his radical or in his religiose phase, without a touch of queasiness." Ibid.

22. Lionel Trilling to Eric Bentley, May 12, 1946, Lionel Trilling Papers, Butler Library, Columbia University (hereafter cited as Trilling MSS).

23. Lionel Trilling, "Elements that Are Wanted," review of *The Idea of a Christian Society* by T. S. Eliot, *Partisan Review* 7, no. 5 (September–October 1940): 375. Ibid., 375.

24. Ibid., 368.

25. Ibid., 369, 373.

26. Ibid., 370.

27. William Chase, analyzing Trilling's "Under Forty" entry, writes that Trilling presented himself as "one for whom the facts of his own Jewishness figure only as a reality *against* which he defines himself, never *within* which he finds his definition." *Lionel Trilling: Literature and Politics* (Stanford, Calif.: Stanford University Press, 1980), 10.

28. Lionel Trilling, "Under Forty: A Symposium on American Literature and the Younger Generation of American Jews," *Contemporary Jewish Record* 6 (February 1944): 3–36.

29. Ibid.

30. Elliot Cohen, "An Act of Affirmation: Editorial Statement," *Commentary* 1, no. 1 (November 1945): 2. *Commentary* was profoundly anti-communist. Nathan Abrams writes that "by 1949 the State Department had published and broadcast over Voice of America no less than twenty *Commentary* articles in the German occupation zone." *Commentary Magazine, 1945–1959: "A Journal of Significant Thought and Opinion"* (London: Vallentine Mitchell, 2007), 67.

31. Henry Adams, "The Tendency of History," *Partisan Review*, 9, no. 5 (September–October 1942): 375, 377.

32. Lionel Trilling, "Tacitus Now," review of *The Complete Works of Tacitus* trans. Alfred John Church and William Jackson Broadlibb, ed. Moses Hadas, *Nation* 155 (August 22, 1942): 153–154, 187, 190, 192, 192. It was these qualities of Tacitus

(power of mind, love of virtue) that Trilling most admired in the intellectual. The stoic Roman was superior to the modern intellectual insofar as modern intellectuals dramatized their responsibility. "The writer with the conscious sense of responsibility," Trilling wrote to Eric Bentley, "is the symptom of the mass-state—he believes in readers who are less good than he is. He acts like a pedagogue, but already he is merely the demagogue of mass-state moralism." Lionel Trilling to Eric Bentley, May 17, 1946, Trilling MSS, Box 9.

33. Lionel Trilling, "Mr. Eliot's Kipling," review of *A Choice of Kipling's Verse* by T. S. Eliot, *Nation* 57 (October 16, 1943): 116.

34. On Trilling's indifference to the "non-paraphrasable" elements of poetry see Helen Vendler, "Lionel Trilling and the *Immortality Ode*," *Salmagundi* 41 (1978): 66–85.

35. Lionel Trilling, "Mr. Eliot's Kipling," in *The Liberal Imagination: Essays on Literature and Society* (New York: Viking Press, 1950), 113, 117, 121.

36. Lionel Trilling, "The Sense of the Past," in *The Liberal Imagination*, 195.

37. Ibid., 233.

38. Harold Rosenberg, "The Case of the Baffled Radical," review of *Arrival and Departure* by Arthur Koestler, *Partisan Review*, 9, no. 1 (Winter 1944): 103, 100, 103. Chambers called Koestler an "ex-revolutionist and perhaps the best mind writing fiction in Europe." "Literary Autolysis," 249. Despite Rosenberg's disdain for the ex-revolutionist, *Partisan Review*'s editor, William Phillips, approached Chambers about writing an essay for *Partisan Review*. In a letter to Chambers, Phillips wrote "we think it valuable for a magazine like *Partisan Review* to explain to its public that behind the sensational headlines lies a human and political story involving the tragedy of a lost cause—a tragedy that has moral, political and personal repercussions." Quoted in James Gilbert, *Writers and Partisans: A History of Literary Radicalism in American* (New York: Wiley and Sons, 1968), 272.

39. Tanenhaus, *Whittaker Chambers*, 198.

40. Chambers constantly blended the history of Western culture with the practice of anti-communism. He wrote, for example, of his friend Walter Krivitsky, the ex-communist defector from the Soviet Union turned anti-communist: "there was something about his death that suggested the great Bishop of Hippo, St. Augustine, dying at the close of the Roman world to the echo of vandal swords against the city gates." "Silence, Exile, and Death," *Time* (February 10, 1941): 63. Chambers was also prone to using biblical allusions when writing about himself, comparing himself, in the first sentence of *Witness*, to Lazarus: "In 1937, I began, like Lazarus, the impossible return." *Witness*, 25.

41. Whittaker Chambers, "The Middle Ages," *Life* (April 7, 1947): 69, 70, 70, 101; Whittaker Chambers, "Medieval Life," *Life* (May 26, 1947): 66, 67, 68.

42. Whittaker Chambers, "The Glory of Venice," *Life* (August 4, 1947): 46–77.

43. Whittaker Chambers, "The Age of Enlightenment," *Life* (September 15, 1947): 75–116.

44. Whittaker Chambers, "The Edwardians," *Life* (November 17, 1947).

45. Whittaker Chambers, "The Age of Exploration," *Life* (March 22, 1948): 73.

46. Ibid., 101, 101, 101.

47. Whittaker Chambers, "The Protestant Revolution," *Life* (June 14, 1948): 58–129.

48. Richard Chase, "History vs. the City of God," *Partisan Review* 11, no. 1 (Winter 1944): 53; Dwight Macdonald, "The Future of Democratic Values," *Partisan Review* 10, no. 4 (July–August 1943): 325; Arthur Koestler, "The Intelligentsia," *Partisan Review* 11, no. 3 (Summer 1944): 270; William Phillips, "The Intellectuals' Tradition," *Partisan Review* 8, no. 6 (November–December 1941): 490; Günter Reimann, "The Fate of Conservative Man," *Partisan Review* 7, no. 4 (July–August 1940): 396. George Orwell sadly affirmed "the apathy and conservatism of people everywhere," adding that a "socialist today is in the position of a doctor treating an all but hopeless case." "Toward European Unity," *Partisan Review* 14, no. 3 (May–June 1947): 348, 346.

49. Dwight Macdonald, "The Future of Democratic Values," 327, 329, 328. The neo-conservative, combining progressive and reactionary concepts, was an intellectual type explored in *Partisan Review* from various perspectives. Nicola Chiaromonte wrote of French Catholic writer Georges Bernanos that Bernanos was antielitist, Christian and republican, adjectives that could just as easily have been applied to Whittaker Chambers. "Bernanos and Christian Liberty," *Partisan Review* 11, no. 3 (Summer 1944): 343.

50. Koestler, "The Intelligentsia," 273.

51. Leslie Fiedler, "The World as Inferno," review of *The Tower of Babel* by Elias Canetti, trans. C. V. Wedgewood, *Partisan Review* 14, no. 3 (May–June 1947): 316.

52. Bellow's title was itself a commentary on the intellectual mood of the 1940s. *Dangling Man* (New York: Vanguard, 1944).

53. Delmore Schwartz, "A Man in His Time," *Partisan Review* 11 no. 3 (Summer 1944): 348–349.

54. T. S. Eliot, "Notes towards a Definition of Culture," *Partisan Review* 11, no. 2 (Spring 1944): 148, 156.

55. Phillips, "The Intellectuals' Tradition," 488, 489.

56. William Phillips, "The Spiritual Underground," review of *The Seed beneath the Snow* by Ignazio Silone, trans. Frances Frenaye, *Partisan Review* 9, no. 6 (November–December 1942): 531, 531, 529, 531.

57. Sidney Hook, "The Integral Humanism of Jacques Maritain," *Partisan Review* 7, no. 3 (May–June 1940): 214, 223, 204. Hook's description of Catholicism as totalitarian was intended to be inflammatory. Even some of *Partisan Review*'s

readers were bothered by his hostility toward religion. R. W. Flint, for example, wrote in to *Partisan Review* decrying Hook's "failure, often merely pettish and perverse, to take the specifically Christian inheritance of European thought seriously." "Letter: Reply to Sidney Hook," *Partisan Review* (June 1948): 734.

58. Sidney Hook, "The New Failure of Nerve," *Partisan Review* 10, no. 1 (January–February 1943): 2, 17, 8, 3, 3.

59. Mark Krupnick argues that by 1946 "there was not a great deal to distinguish the liberal conservatism of [Robert Penn] Warren from the increasingly conservative liberalism of Trilling." *Lionel Trilling and the Fate of Cultural Criticism* (Evanston, Ill.: Northwestern University Press, 1986), 55.

60. Lionel Trilling to Robert Maynard Hutchins, September 19, 1944, Trilling MSS, Box 7. On Hutchins's educational aspirations in the 1940s see Mary Ann Dzuback, *Robert M. Hutchins: Portrait of an Educator* (Chicago: University of Chicago Press, 1991), 208–230.

61. Willi Schlamm to Lionel Trilling, July 5, 1945, Trilling MSS, Box 9; Lionel Trilling, marginal note on "(Confidential) Memo," Trilling MSS, Box 9; Lionel Trilling to Willi Schlamm, May 24, 1945, Trilling MSS, Box 9.

62. Lionel Trilling, "John Henry Newman," review of *John Henry Newman* by John Moody, and *John Henry Newman* by Charles Frederick Harrold, *Nation* 162 (February 2, 1946): 132, 132.

63. Lionel Trilling, "The Writer and His Responsibilities," *American Scholar* (Autumn 1945): 503.

64. Ted Solotaroff writes that for younger readers Trilling "was reassuring politically. Reading him you felt that you hadn't betrayed your heart by abandoning your radicalism, which was suspect anyway, for 'the tragic sense of life' and 'moral realism.'" "The New York Publishing World," in *Creators and Disturbers: Reminiscences by Jewish Intellectuals of New York*, ed. Bernard Rosenberg and Ernest Goldstein (New York: Columbia University Press, 1984), 409.

65. Lionel Trilling, "Wordsworth's Ode: Intimations of Immortality," *English Institute Annual* 3 (New York: Columbia University Press, 1942): 1–28.

66. Lionel Trilling, "The Legacy of Sigmund Freud: An Appraisal," *Kenyon Review* 2 (Spring 1940): 171, 172. "The Legacy of Sigmund Freud" has three parts. Alexander Reid Martin wrote on "The Therapeutic"; Eliseo Vivas wrote on Freud's "Philosophical Legacy"; and Trilling took the "Literary and Aesthetic." In her memoirs, Diana Trilling noted Lionel's lifelong "admiration for Freud. But it was Freud the man of ideas, Freud the witness to the tragedy of civilization, whom he esteemed. He was not primarily concerned . . . with psychoanalysis as a medical practice." Diana Trilling, *The Beginning of the Journey: The Marriage of Diana and Lionel Trilling* (New York: Harcourt, Brace, 1993), 256.

67. Resolutely secular, Freud was, however, a thinker who, in Trilling's view, assimilated something of religion into a secular context. Trilling made this

point parenthetically: "we are all ill: the statement is grandiose, and its implications—the implications, that is, of understanding the totality of human nature in terms of disease—are vast. These implications have never been properly met (although I believe that a few theologians respond to them)." "A Note on Art and Neurosis," *Partisan Review* 12, no. 1 (Winter 1945): 167.

68. Diana Trilling suggests the antiprogressive appeal Forster had for Lionel Trilling: "he [Forster] has the knowledge of good-and-evil, a brave knowledge which we do not often encounter in our progressive culture." *The Beginning of the Journey*, 400.

69. Lionel Trilling, *E. M. Forster*, rev. ed. (New York: New Directions, 1964), ix.

70. Newton Arvin, "Two Cheers for Forster," review of *E. M. Forster* by Lionel Trilling, *Partisan Review* 10, no. 5 (September–October 1942): 451.

71. Trilling, *E. M. Forster*, 16, 2, 9, 7, 133.

72. Ibid., 12, 32, 14. European writers who confronted death, such as Forster, were more likely to attract Trilling. In the words of Carolyn Heilbrun, who studied with Trilling, he "was wont to sneer at America's attitude to death." *When Men Were the Only Models We Had: My Teachers Barzun, Fadiman, Trilling* (Philadelphia: University of Pennsylvania Press, 2002), 84.

73. Trilling, *E. M. Forster*, 55, 55.

74. Ibid., 92, 93, 93.

75. Ibid., 92, 58.

76. Jeffrey Mehlmann describes de Rougement as "the most ubiquitous French-speaking intellectual of the postwar emigration." *La part du diable* was first published in 1942; it was published in English as *The Devil's Share* in 1944. Its immediate inspiration came from Christian thinkers Reinhold Niebuhr and Jacques Maritain. "The aspect of America that most troubled him [de Rougement]," Mehlmann explains, "was an inability to believe in evil. He mentioned this one evening at the home of the theologian Reinhold Niebuhr, editor of the journal *Christianity in Crisis*. But it was at the Cosmopolitan Club, a few days earlier, in conversation with Jacques Maritain, that the project of the book took shape." *Émigré New York: French Intellectuals in Wartime, 76. Manhattan, 1940–1944* (Baltimore: Johns Hopkins University Press, 2000), 45.

77. Hannah Arendt, "Nightmare and Flight," review of *The Devil's Share* by Denis de Rougement, *Partisan Review* 12, no. 2 (Spring 1945): 259, 259.

78. Lionel Trilling, "A Derivative Devil," review of *The Devil's Share* by Denis de Rougement, *Kenyon Review* 7 (Summer 1945): 500, 499, 498.

79. Chambers, *Witness*, 508.

80. The atom bomb was, for Chambers, final proof that technology had not brought progress. In a cover story for *Time*, he wrote of an atom-bomb test in the Bikini Island as evidence of the way "in which the most progressive of centuries would write in one blinding stroke of disintegration the inner meaning of

technological civilization: all matter is speed and flame." "Crossroads," *Time*
(July 1, 1946): 126. Chambers offered no extensive discussion of Hiroshima, only
a dramatization of the event, one that humanized the agency behind it: "then
the Enola Gay will take off on its fourth and final run. The bomb bay will open.
The bombardier Major Harold Wood, before World War II a grocery clerk of
Bordentown, N.J., will release the bomb." "Crossroads," 52. Trilling did not
write about Hiroshima or Nagasaki.

81. Whittaker Chambers, "The Devil," *Life* (February 2, 1948): 78.
82. Ibid.
83. Tanenhaus, *Whittaker Chambers*, 213.
84. Allen Weinstein used this phrase for the title of a book on communism, taking
it from a poem by W. H. Auden, *The Haunted Wood* (New York: Random
House, 1999).

6. Fictional Anti-Communism

Epigraph: Arthur Schlesinger Jr. to Pascal Covici, August 27, 1947, Lionel Trilling
Papers, Special Collections, Butler Library, Columbia University, Box 5 (hereafter
cited as Trilling MSS).

1. Lionel Trilling, "Whittaker Chambers and 'The Middle of the Journey,' " *New
York Review of Books* 22, no. 6 (April 17, 1975): 18–24. This essay has recently
been republished as the introduction to *The Middle of the Journey* (New York:
New York Review, 2002).
2. Lionel Trilling, "Determinist and Mystic," review of *Adventures of a Young
Man* by John Dos Passos, and the *Bridegroom Cometh* by Waldo Frank, *Kenyon
Review* 2 (Winter 1940), 95.
3. Lionel Trilling, "The Life of the Novel," review of *The Bitter Box* by Eleanor
Clark, *Kenyon Review* 8 (Autumn 1946): 659, 658.
4. Lionel Trilling, "Of this Time, of that Place," in *Of this Time, of that Place,
and Other Stories* (New York: Harcourt, Brace Jovanovich, 1979), 79. Trilling's
famous words are: "in the United States at this time [1950] liberalism is not
only the dominant but even the sole intellectual tradition. For it is the plain
fact that nowadays there are no conservative or reactionary ideas in general
circulation. This does not mean, of course, that there is no impulse to
conservatism or to reaction. Such impulses are certainly very strong, perhaps
even stronger than most of us know. But the conservative impulse and the
reactionary impulse do not, with some isolated exceptions, express themselves
in ideas but only in action or in irritable mental gestures which seek to
resemble ideas." Lionel Trilling, *The Liberal Imagination: Essays on Literature
and Society* (Garden City, N.Y.: Doubleday Anchor Books, 1967), vii.
5. Lionel Trilling, "Of this Time, of that Place," 80. William Chase sees Trilling
in Howe: "this immensely conservative ambivalence on Howe's part, toward

science, toward collective human judgment, toward the expensive process of human socialization, and toward rational and calculating modes of thought is characteristic of Trilling. He shares that ambivalence. It is what will grow to define him as a critic of literature and society." *Lionel Trilling, Criticism and Politics* (Stanford, Calif.: Stanford University Press, 1980), 28.

6. Trilling, "Of this Time, of that Place," 84, 94, 96.

7. Lionel Trilling, "The Other Margaret," *Partisan Review* 12 (Fall 1945): 488, 481, 481, 481, 484.

8. Ibid., 486, 486–487, 487, 487. Trilling associates Elwin's illiberalism with his newfound maturity, giving a kind of implicit sanction to Elwin's loss of liberal reflexes. It "occurred to him [Elwin] to think that perhaps he had felt his anger [toward the conductor] not in despite of his wisdom but because of it. It was a disturbing, even horrifying fancy." Ibid., 487.

9. Ibid., 489, 491, 491.

10. Ibid., 496, 498, 498, 498, 499. In a newspaper interview, Trilling made clear the tie between communism and an atrophied sense of individual responsibility: "He [the liberal] has put increasing emphasis on the responsibility of society and taken the emphasis off the responsibility of the individual. This is where he gets drawn to authoritarianism and, by a transference of that idea, where he begins to dull his emotions." "Novelist Trilling on the Liberal Dilemma." Trilling MSS, Box 59.

11. Trilling, "The Other Margaret," 499, 501.

12. James Farrell, "A Comment on Literature and Morality: A Crucial Question of Our Times," *New International* 12 (May 1946): 145, 145.

13. Lionel Trilling to Eric Bentley, Typed Letter Signed (TLS), March 7, 1946, Trilling MSS, Box 1. The Popular Front was an ethos as well as a moment in time; the ethos outlived its moment. "For many liberals, as Trilling observed at the time," writes Mark Krupnick, "it [the Popular Front] provided an ethics and a culture." *Lionel Trilling and the Fate of Cultural Criticism* (Evanston, Ill., Northwestern University Press, 1986), 61.

14. Lionel Trilling to Eric Bentley, November 4, 1947, Trilling MSS, Box 1; Lionel Trilling to Herbert Feinstein, September 20, 1955, Trilling MSS, Box 13.

15. Lionel Trilling to John Allen, February 17, 1975, Trilling MSS, Box 30.

16. Lest this self-description appear too simple for the politically elusive Trilling, he went on to attach ambiguities to it. "I have never felt myself to be a political active person," Trilling explained, in part because the United States has no equivalent of the British Labor Party. "I would be very glad if there were [such an equivalent]," Trilling continued. "Some years ago, it was perhaps the American Labor Party. It isn't now . . . I would call myself—I think I am a socialist—in that vague sense that I call myself a liberal." "Novelist Trilling on the Liberal Dilemma," in *Picture News*, Trilling MSS, Box 59.

17. Diana Trilling, *The Beginning of the Journey: The Marriage of Diana and Lionel Trilling* (New York: Harcourt, Brace, 1993), 387.

18. Irving Howe, "On The Middle of the Journey," review of *The Middle of the Journey* by Lionel Trilling, *New York Times Book Review* (August 22, 1976): 31; David Caute, "Summer People," review of *The Middle of the Journey* by Lionel Trilling, *New Statesman* (April 11, 1975): 486.

19. Progressives also betray the connection "between modern politics and a loss of the sense of the past," according to Trilling. Lionel Trilling to Robert Flint, May 17, 1946, Trilling MSS, Box 9. Trilling's low opinion of progressivism did not abate with time. In a 1963 letter to Norman Podhoretz, a former Trilling student who was then the editor of *Commentary*, Trilling elaborated on his argument about the progressive misuse of fine feelings: "I like your piece very much indeed. How could I not, my exasperation with the clichés of liberal-progressive sentiment being what it is? Against the dreadful liberal-progressive-no-feeling, which eventually establishes itself as no-thought and no-action, the only antidote is personal testimony of such honesty as yours has." Lionel Trilling to Norman Podhoretz, January 5, 1963, Trilling MSS, Box 4.

20. Lionel Trilling to Alan Wald, June 10, 1974, Trilling MSS, Box 29. Trilling was ambivalent about Chambers from the beginning: "I hesitate to say that I disliked him and avoided his company," Trilling wrote in 1975, "there was indeed something about him that repelled me, but there was also something that engaged my interest and even my respect. Yet friends we surely were not." "Whittaker Chambers and 'The Middle of the Journey,' " 19.

21. William Shiver, *New York Herald Tribune* (October 1947) in Trilling MSS, Box 5. Trilling repeated this claim in 1975: Chambers's "underground activity . . . was one of the openest secrets while it lasted." Perplexingly, Trilling wrote to William A. Reuben that "the character of Maxim was wholly my creation and was drawn without consultation of any document or person." Lionel Trilling to William A. Reuben, February 26, 1969, Trilling MSS, Box 25. John Diggins stresses the accuracy of Trilling's portrait: "Chambers's psyche, as revealed in his own confession, *Witness*, and in Lionel Trilling's treatment in his novel, *The Middle of the Journey*, represented a curious mix: Christian terror approaching the inexorability of death, communist determinism acknowledging the inevitability of history." *Ronald Reagan: Fate, Freedom and the Making of History* (New York: Norton, 2007), 115.

22. Trilling, "Whittaker Chambers and 'The Middle of the Journey,' " 23. Trilling saw absurdity and pretentiousness in Chambers's religious persona: "He [Chambers] had a sensibility which was all too accessible to large solemnities and to the more facile paradoxes of spirituality, and a mind which, though certainly not without force, was but little trained to discrimination and all too

easily seduced into equating portentous utterance with truth." "Whittaker Chambers and 'The Middle of the Journey,' " 23.

23. Leon Wieseltier, "Introduction," in *The Moral Obligation to Be Intelligent: Selected Essays* (New York: Farrar, Straus, Giroux, 2000), x. In *The Middle of the Journey,* according to William Chase, Maxim's "experience as a communist revolutionary has brought him sharply to the recognition that people do die, that at times they die violently." *Lionel Trilling, Criticism and Politics,* 39. Perhaps Trilling meant to suggest something of Reinhold Niebuhr or the religious tenor of the age by naming him Gifford Maxim—"maxims of the Gifford lectures [a lecture series that Niebuhr had been asked to deliver]?" asks Richard Wightman Fox. *Reinhold Niebuhr* (New York: Pantheon, 1985), 234.

24. John Bayley, "Middle-Class Futures," review of *The Middle of the Journey* by Lionel Trilling, *Times Literary Supplement* (April 11, 1975): 399. Robert Warshow, "The Legacy of the '30's: Middle-Class Mass Culture and the Intellectuals' Problem" *Commentary* (December 1947): 543, 543. Warshow's cogent critique is more compelling for Trilling's weak response to it. "The suppression [of Jewish context]," Warshow writes, is "made all the more obvious by the inclusion of one minor character in a stock role." "The Legacy of the 1930's," 543. Ibid. Trilling did not answer Warshow directly, but he did write back to David M. Kleinstein, the director of a Jewish community center, who was, like Warshow, perturbed by the absence of Jewish characters in *The Middle of the Journey.* Referring to the "minor Jewish character in a stock role," Trilling writes that "Dr. Graf, a Jew, just walks into my novel . . . You ask what difference it makes whether he is Jewish or not. It makes none—in this connection no more than that he is bald or owns a bulldog . . . don't you think it might be useful to have Jews just walking around in fiction, not certified as good or suffering or significant, but just like everybody else." Lionel Trilling to David M. Kleinstein, March 20, 1948, Trilling MSS, Box 10. For a discussion of Jewishness and *The Middle of the Journey* see Michael Kimmage, "Lionel Trilling's *The Middle of the Journey* and the Complicated Origins of the Neo-conservative Movement," *Shofar* 21, no. 3 (Spring 2003): 48–63.

25. Madame Duvette-Navez to Lionel Trilling, January 5, 1953, Trilling MSS, Box 11; Lionel Trilling to Madame Duvette-Navez, May 29, 1953, Trilling MSS, Box 11.

26. Lionel Trilling to Madame Duvette-Navez, January 5, 1953, Trilling MSS, Box 11.

27. Lionel Trilling to Madame Duvette-Navez, May 29, 1953, Trilling MSS, Box 11.

28. Laskell must disprove what in Leslie Fiedler's words was "the implicit dogma of American liberalism during the past few decades [the 1930s and 1940s], piling up a terrible burden of self-righteousness and self-deceit for the day when it would become impossible any longer to believe that the man of good will is identical with the righteous man, and the liberal is, per se, the hero." "Hiss, Chambers, and the Age of Innocence."

29. Trilling, *The Middle of the Journey* (New York: Viking Press, 1947), 32. Lionel Trilling, "A Story of Summer," Typed Manuscript (Tms), circa 1947, Trilling MSS, Box 36 (Folder 398). Lionel Trilling, *The Middle of the Journey*, 26.

30. Walter Allen, "New Novels," *The New Statesman and Nation* (November 6, 1948): 401.

31. Lionel Trilling, *The Middle of the Journey*, 56. Laskell has only a cloudy notion of Maxim's involvement with espionage. This corresponds to the sense Trilling himself had of Chambers's underground work in the 1930s: Chambers's "foreign connection [to Moscow] required that I admit into consciousness the possibility, even the probability, that he was concerned with something called military intelligence, but I did not equate this with espionage—it was as if such a thing had not been invented." "Whittaker Chambers and 'The Middle of the Journey,' " 19.

32. Trilling, *The Middle of the Journey*, 126, 127.

33. Compare this with Leslie Fiedler's observations about Alger Hiss: "How strangely the Marxist ideal and the dream of Horatio Alger blended into the motives of treason." "Hiss, Chambers and the Age of Innocence," 63.

34. Trilling, *The Middle of the Journey*, 185, 233, 234.

35. Trilling may have encountered Priscilla Hiss at Columbia, where she completed a M.A. in literature in 1929. She was also a member of the Morningside Heights branch of the Socialist Party. Had he known her well, he would surely have mentioned it. Elizabeth Bentley, another figure at the margins of the Hiss case, received a Master's degree at Columbia in 1935, before embarking on a career of Soviet espionage. Irwin Gellman, *The Contender: Richard Nixon the Congress Years, 1946–1952* (New York: Free Press, 1999), 194.

36. Trilling, *The Middle of the Journey*, 10, 94, 95, 96.

37. Late in life, Trilling would recall the charisma Chambers had possessed as an undergraduate, his "moral authority," which, when Chambers was a radical, was connected with his infamously bad teeth. Chambers's teeth, in Trilling's words, "annihilated the hygienic American present—only a serf could have such a mouth, or some student in a visored cap who sat in his Moscow garret and thought of nothing save the moment when he would toss the fatal canister into the barouche of the Grand Duke." "Whittaker Chambers and 'The Middle of the Journey,' " 120. Trilling's delightful set of Slavic associations reinforce the common perception of Chambers as un-American.

38. Trilling, *The Middle of the Journey*, 120, 37, 135, 128, 145.

39. Ibid., 110,139, 139, 24.

40. Ibid., 107, 112.

41. Ibid., 193, 226, 233, 186.

42. Ibid., 141, 141–142, 144, 144.

43. Ibid., 155, 155, 156.

44. Ibid., 158, 158, 157, 157.

45. Ibid., 285, 246, 247, 247, 55. The critic Nathan O. Scott attributed Laskell's fear of Maxim to an impoverished liberalism. Scott lamented the secular liberal's critique of the Christian and the charge that Maxim is an opportunist. In suggesting that Maxim "is simply riding the pendulum," Scott writes, "Mr. Trilling is not quite fair . . . he has too much capitulated to the occupational suspicion of the [liberal] ideologue." Scott also noted Maxim's effect on Laskell, the moral education he gives Laskell, whose "response to the transformed [anti-communist] Maxim has to be seen as part of a gnostical dialectic the other part of which is his final comprehension of the Crooms." Trilling's difficulty in comprehending a character like Maxim, Scott believed, stemmed from his "intelligence," which is deep enough to see through the problems of liberalism, while remaining "radically, though perhaps not incorrigibly, secular." "Lionel Trilling's Critique of the Liberal Mind," *Christianity and Society* 16, no. 2 (1966): 18.

46. Trilling, *The Middle of the Journey*, 301; Arthur Schlesinger Jr. to Lionel Trilling, August 26, 1947, Trilling MSS, Box 5.

47. John Braine, "Lionel Trilling's *The Middle of the Journey*," review of *The Middle of the Journey* by Lionel Trilling, *National Review* (November 2, 1969): 1228. Braine's paraphrase of the novel is ironic in his rewording of it. He borrows words from Maxim, who is speaking about liberals and religion. The extinction to which Maxim refers is that of the liberal mind and not of humanity. Maxim sarcastically describes "the supreme act of the humanistic critical intelligence—it perceives the cogency of the [religious] argument and acquiesces in the fact of its own extinction." Trilling, *The Middle of the Journey*, 305; Robert Boyers, "*The Middle of the Journey* and Beyond, Observations on Modernity and Commitment," review of *The Middle of the Journey* by Lionel Trilling, *Salmagundi* 1, no. 4 (1966–1967): 8–18.

48. The relevant chapter is "Hebraism and Hellenism," chapter four in Arnold's *Culture and Anarchy*. In Arnold's words: "as the great movement of Christianity was a triumph of Hebraism and man's moral impulses, so the great movement which goes by the name of the Renascence was an uprising and re-enstatement of man's intellectual impulses and Hellenism." *Culture and Anarchy*, ed. J. Dover Wilson (Cambridge: Cambridge University Press, 1932), 139.

49. Trilling, *The Middle of the Journey*, 300. Maxim makes this point cogently, linking himself and Nancy: "my sense of guilt as a human being drove me to the Party," he tells Laskell, "and my sense of guilt as a member of the Party drove me to work that was special and secret . . . John, I will get out of the system by admitting my guilt." Ibid., 273.

50. Ibid., 35, 36, 36, 267, 15.

51. Ibid., 16, 78. The novel's bias obviously favors Emily, whose "silliness and attempts at culture are so much more worth having than Duck's 'genuineness,' " in the words of the critic John Bayley, "Middle-Class Futures," 398. Bayley's observation neatly inverts Nancy's comparison of Duck, who "is so *real*—just as Emily is unreal." Trilling, *The Middle of the Journey*, 19. Trilling spelled out his personal bias in a letter to a reader curious about Emily. Trilling wrote that Emily's "foolishness has about it, I believe, a kind of innocence and sweetness and gaiety, and it seems to me that the people who condemn her for lack of taste are, though justified, deficient in generosity." Lionel Trilling to Patricia Fudold, May 10, 1960, Trilling MSS, Box 16.

52. Trilling, *The Middle of the Journey*, 68, 187.

53. In a *National Review* essay on *The Middle of the Journey*, John Braine dwelt on Emily's forgiveness of Laskell, which, in Braine's view, had religious overtones. Her forgiveness "rises into the higher love, *agape*, the love of God. And this ultimately he [Laskell] must put in the place of Communism . . . During his illness and convalescence he has learned something about love. The achievement of *The Middle of the Journey* is that we learn with him." "Lionel Trilling's *The Middle of the Journey*," *National Review* (November 2, 1969): 1228. Frank S. Meyer, a conservative intellectual and editor at *National Review*, had sent Trilling Braine's essay. Trilling wrote back to Meyer, politely distancing himself from Braine's review: "thank you for sending Mr. Braine's essay on *The Middle of the Journey*. I read it with an interest not diminished by my strong reservations about its interpretations of the novel's political import." Lionel Trilling to Frank S. Meyer, December 15, 1969, Trilling MSS, Box 25. Braine was not the only critic to see religious themes in *The Middle of the Journey*. In the *New Yorker*, J. M. Lalley wondered whether "because of the repeated mentions of Saint Paul . . . the journey has anything to do with the road to Damascus." "Two Journeys and Pastoral," review of *The Middle of the Journey*, *When the Mountain Fell* by C. F. Ramuz, and *One Fine Day* by Mollie Painter-Downes, *New Yorker* 23 (October 25, 1947): 126–132.

54. Lionel Trilling to Eric Bentley, November 4, 1947, Trilling MSS, Box 1.

55. In a heart-felt obituary of Trilling in the *New York Times Book Review*, Irving Howe also wrote in praise of Laskell, who "comes to believe that men must accept the 'givens' of nature and history which they inherit with their first breath. Perhaps, as some of Trilling's critics have charged, this subtly conveys a message of social conservatism. But what it clearly seeks to check is the fanaticism that would force history on behalf of a program, even at the expense of living men and women." "On 'The Middle of the Journey,' " *New York Times Book Review*, August 22, 1976, 31.

56. Orville Prescott, "Books of the Times," *New York Times Book Review* (October 12, 1947): 8.

57. Lionel Trilling to Eric Bentley, November 28, 1947, Trilling MSS, Box 1.

58. Irving Howe, "The New York Intellectuals," in *Selected Writings, 1950–1990* (San Diego, Calif.: Harcourt, Brace, Jovanovich, 1990), 251.

59. Trilling hinted at this in the title of his *New York Review of Books* essay on *The Middle of the Journey*: "Whittaker Chambers and 'The Middle of the Journey.' " The 2002 reissue of *The Middle of the Journey* had little to do with the Hiss case. It was also re-released in 1966 and 1976: *The Middle of the Journey* (New York: Avon Books, 1966) and *The Middle of the Journey* (New York: Scribner, 1976). Nevertheless, the most recent publication of Trilling's 1947 novel may be related to the reevaluation of Chambers, which began in 1978 with Allen Weinstein's *Perjury: The Hiss-Chambers Case* (New York: Knopf, 1978), consolidated with Sam Tanenhaus's biography *Whittaker Chambers: A Biography* (New York: Random House, 1997), and continued with *Venona: Decoding Soviet Espionage in America* (New Haven: Yale University Press, 1999) by Harvey Klehr and John Earl Haynes and *The Haunted Wood: Soviet Espionage in America—The Stalin Era* (New York: Random House, 1999) by Allen Weinstein. The more interesting Chambers becomes as a man—and not just as a participant in the Hiss case—the more interesting *The Middle of the Journey* becomes.

60. Michael Wreszin points out that there is no hard evidence showing Huebsch prevented *The Middle of the Journey* from getting reprinted. It may or may not have happened. In Wreszin's opinion it did not: "Diana Trilling claimed to have learned of Huebsch's Communist past during an interview with the bookseller and bibliographer Walter Goldwater, who is now dead. Thus the source for the smear can be traced from Goldwater to Trilling to [Sam] Tanenhaus to [Hilton] Kramer. None offered any evidence; they just repeated the accusation." See http://www.historycooperative.org/journals/jah/87.3/letters.html.

61. In an FBI "Office Memorandum," the following sober verdict was expressed: "this book [*The Middle of the Journey*] has been reviewed and it is not believed that any information contained in this book is of any value in this investigation although there is some similarity to Chambers's activities after he had broken from the Communist Party in 1938." Alger Hiss Defense Files, Harvard Law School Special Collections, Box 75 (Folder 10).

62. Lionel Trilling to Henry F. Thoma, March 1, 1956, Trilling MSS, Box 14. John Bayley, "Middle-Class Futures," 398; Daniel Patrick Moynihan made *The Middle of the Journey* the centerpiece of his 1972 address to incoming students at Harvard College, subsequently published in *Commentary* as "An Address to the Entering Class as Harvard College," *Commentary* 54 (December 1972): 55–60; Lionel Trilling to Henry F. Thoma, March 1, 1956, Trilling MSS, Box 14.

63. Lionel Trilling, ed. Geraldine Murphy, *The Journey Abandoned: The Unfinished Novel* (New York: Columbia University Press, 2008).

64. Lionel Trilling to John Crowe Ransom, September 21, 1948, Trilling MSS, Box
10. Trilling was touching here on the "dissociation of sensibility," a key phrase
of the New Criticism with which Ransom was associated: "the Western world is
in decay [since the scientific and secular revolutions of the seventeenth
century], but some hope seems to be held out for the reconstitution of the
original wholeness. The total man, the undivided 'unified sensibility' which
combines intellect and feeling, is the ideal that requires a rejection of
technological civilization, a return to religion or, at least, to a modern myth
and, in the Southern critics, allowed a defense of the agrarian society surviving
in the South." *American Criticism, 1900–1950*, vol. 6, in *A History of Modern
Criticism, 1750–1950* (New Haven, Conn.: Yale University Press), 148–149.
R. W. Flint notes Trilling's "unique alienation from the revolutionary
complacencies of the avant-garde of which he is an obvious leader by force of
talent." "From Vertigo to Tears," *New Leader* 30 (October 1947), 10.

65. Leslie Fiedler's essay, "Hiss, Chambers and the Age of Innocence," was a
paraphrase (conscious or unconscious) of *The Middle of the Journey*. Fiedler's
essay could almost be read as a summary of Trilling's "message": "It is not
necessary that we liberals be self-flagellants," Fiedler wrote. "We have desired
good, and we have done some; but we have also done great evil. The
confession in itself is nothing, but without the confession there can be no
understanding, and without the understanding of what the Hiss case tires
desperately to declare, we will not be able to move forward from a liberalism
of innocence to a liberalism of responsibility." "Hiss, Chambers and the Age
of Innocence," 119. Fiedler's Judeo-Christian language here—good, evil,
confession—is closer to Chambers than to Trilling.

7. *Witness*

Epigraphs: Saint Augustine, *Confessions*, trans. Henry Chadwick (Oxford: Oxford
University Press, 1991). Blaine Pascal. *Pensées*, trans. A. J. Kreilsheimer (London:
Penguin Books, 1966), 33. Richard Nixon, "Plea for an Anti-Communist Faith,"
Saturday Review, May 14, 1952, p. 12.

1. Lionel Trilling to Morris Dickstein, April 28, 1975, Lionel Trilling Papers,
Special Collections, Butler Library, Columbia University, Box 30 (hereafter
cited as Trilling MSS).

2. Trilling described this event in a 1975 essay, "Whittaker Chambers and *The
Middle of the Journey*": "when 'a Hiss investigator' tried to induce me to speak
against him in court, I had refused and said, 'Whittaker Chambers is a man of
honor.' " It was not an opinion that Trilling ever revised: "Whittaker Chambers
had been engaged in espionage against his own country," Trilling continued in
this essay; "when a change of heart and principle led to his defecting from his
apparatus, he had eventually not only confessed his own treason but named the

comrades who shared it, including one whom for a time he had cherished as a friend [Alger Hiss]. I hold that when this has been said of him, it is still possible to say that he was a man of honor." "Whittaker Chambers and *The Middle of the Journey,*" *New York Review of Books* 22, no. 6 (April 17, 1975), 19.

3. Lionel Trilling to Morris Dickstein, April 28, 1975, Trilling MSS, Box 30. Trilling may have been thinking of Murray Kempton's *New York Review of Books* essay on Chambers, "A Narodnik from Lynbrook," while writing to Dickstein about betrayal and loyalty. Reviewing Chambers's letters to William F. Buckley Jr., Kempton wrote in 1970 that "there are the distasteful associations of the art for which he [Chambers] was best remembered, not the espionage but the naming of his partner in espionage. The second is a kind of betrayal far worse thought of by private men than the first." "A Narodnik from Lynbrook," in *Alger Hiss, Whittaker Chambers and the Schism in the American Soul,* ed. Patrick Swan (Wilmington, Del.: ISI Books, 2003), 169.

4. Irwin Gellman, *The Contender: Richard Nixon the Congress Years, 1946–1952* (New York: Free Press, 1999), 200.

5. Stephen Whitfield sees hypocrisy in the publishing success Chambers enjoyed with *Witness*: "the author presented himself as such a man [a martyr], but so gaunt a martyrdom was not to be his destiny. The *Saturday Evening Post* paid $75,000 for the serial rights to *Witness* and excerpted the autobiography for eight weeks. NBC invited him to read the forward, his 'Letter to My Children,' on both radio and television. *Witness* was a Book-of the-Month Club selection as well as the number nine best seller of 1952." *The Culture of the Cold War* (Baltimore: Johns Hopkins Press, 1991), 18.

6. Lou Cannon writes that "in his politically reformative years during the 1960s [Ronald] Reagan read Barry Goldwater's *The Conscience of a Conservative* and Whittaker Chambers's *Witness,* the seminal work of American anticommunism. While Reagan was resistant to the inner despair that pervaded the life of Whittaker Chambers, he could quote from memory the famous passages where Chambers watches his sleeping daughter and decides he can no longer be an atheist. He was impressed that Chambers had abandoned his belief in Communism while still believing that the forces of Marxism-Leninsim would prevail." *President Reagan: The Role of a Lifetime* (New York: Public Affairs, 1991), 252. Stephen Whitfield adds that "Nixon . . . listed *Witness* as one of his three favorite books (along with *War and Peace* and Senator Lafollette's autobiography). John Wayne, the most popular actor of the 1950s, claimed to have reread *Witness* often and to have memorized long sections of it. He gave one of his daughters *Witness* on her sixteenth birthday. Chambers was the only conservative quoted by another film star, Ronald Reagan, in his own autobiography, *Where's the Rest of Me?* (1965)." *The Culture of the Cold War,* 18–19.

7. "The political fallout [of Hiss's conviction for perjury] for the Democratic party—and for the fate of liberalism—was immediate," writes Stephen Whitfield. "Because Hiss had been a New Dealer, the thrust of social reform became discredited, progressives felt beleaguered and Roosevelt's wartime policies towards the Soviet Union and Eastern Europe were open to venomous interpretation." *The Culture of the Cold War*, 28.

8. Richard Pells writes that "Chambers seemed credible to certain anti-Stalinist intellectuals with whom he had maintained a friendship of sorts in the 1930s: Lionel and Diana Trilling, Meyer Schapiro, Sidney Hook." *The Liberal Mind in a Conservative Age: American Intellectuals in the 1940's and 1950s* (New York: Harper and Row, 1985), 272. Pells added other leaders in journalism and intellectual life to the pro-Chambers list: Murray Kempton, Philip Rahv, Harold Rosenberg, Leslie Fiedler, Bruce Bliven, and Richard Rovere. Ibid., 273. Given the facts of the case, Arthur Schlesinger Jr. simply assumed that Hiss was guilty. *Innocent Beginnings: A Life in the Twentieth Century, 1917–1950* (Boston: Houghton Mifflin, 2000), 497.

9. Alger Hiss, *In the Court of Public Opinion* (New York: Knopf, 1957). Hiss asserted his innocence in no uncertain terms. As late as 1994, historian Ellen Schrecker writes that "exactly what Elizabeth Bentley, Alger Hiss, or Julius and Ethel Rosenberg did or did not do may never be known." *The Age of McCarthyism: A Brief History and Documents* (Boston: St. Martin's, 2002), 18. The *American National Biography* entry for Whittaker Chambers does not present Hiss as guilty. Its concluding sentence is tellingly open ended: "In the 1987 Public Broadcasting System (PBS) documentary "The Conservatives," [William F.] Buckley declared that Chambers 'reified the hard spiritual case against Communism more successfully than anyone in that generation.' Others continued to view Chambers in a less than charitable fashion as a pathological liar who was driven by class resentment to destroy Hiss." Robert L. Cottrell in *American National Biography*, vol. 4, ed. John A Garraty and Mark C. Carnes (New York: Oxford University Press, 1999), 648.

10. Political scientist Robert Skidelsky puts the matter in terms that Chambers would surely have endorsed: "Roosevelt was never concerned about who should liberate whom, because he dreamed of a post-territorial condominium with 'Uncle Joe,' exercised through multilateral institutions like the IMF, the World Bank, and the UN. This be can be counted the most spectacular misjudgment in American history, aided and abetted by a network of spies in the Treasury and State Departments." "Hot, Cold and Imperial," review of *1945: The War that Never Ended* by Gregor Dallas and *Among Empires: American Ascendancy and Its Predecessors* by Charles Maier, *New York Review of Books* 53, no. 12 (July 13, 2006): 50.

11. Irving Howe wrote about the Hiss case as a political inevitability. "The Thirties" were bound to produce a Hiss case: "the political course of the thirties made it inevitable that, quite apart from this well-groomed man and this unkempt one, there be a clash between two men, one a liberal who was recruited from the idealistic wing of public service, the other a former Communist who repudiated his past and then, as *Witness* testifies, swings to the politics of the far right. If not these two, then two others; if not their shapes and accents, other shapes and accents." "God, Man and Stalin," *Nation* (May 24, 1952): 81.

12. Gellman, *The Contender*, 198.

13. Gouzenko's and Bentley's testimony alerted J. Edgar Hoover to the possibility that Alger Hiss was a Soviet spy. In November 1945 Hoover arranged for a tap to be placed on Hiss's phone, and in November 1945 Hoover warned Truman about Hiss. Richard Gid Powers, *Secrecy and Power: The Life of J. Edgar Hoover* (New York: Free Press, 1987), 297–298.

14. Allen Weinstein notes that "both FBI and State Department counterintelligence officials had begun earlier in 1945 to scan Chambers's depositions and the Berle memo, reacting uneasily to the [professional] rise of Hiss." *Perjury: The Hiss-Chambers Case* (New York: Random House, 1997), 307. The issue of domestic communism did not move presidential politics, for the Republicans or for the Democrats, in either the 1944 or the 1948 elections. As Ellen Schrecker puts it, "Washington signed on to the anticommunist crusade in a fitful, meandering way." *Many Are the Crimes: McCarthyism in America* (Boston: Little, Brown, 1998), 86.

15. G. Edward White, *Alger Hiss's Looking Glass Wars: The Covert Life of a Soviet Spy* (New York: Oxford University Press, 2004), 46, 45. Writing in 2004, Ellen Schrecker sees little of world-historical value in Hiss's, and others', espionage activities: "if there had been no Harry Dexter White, no Nathan Gregory Silvermaster, or no Alger Hiss, would the history of the world really have been all that different between the 1930s and the 1950s? Would the Soviet Union have collapsed, or Stalin have moderated his policies, or the United States have gained the upper hand in determining the postwar fate of Eastern Europe or China? Nothing revealed thus far in the new sources available in Washington or Moscow establish any credible basis for making such an argument." *Cold War Triumphalism: The Misuse of History after the Fall of Communism*, ed. Ellen Schrecker (New York: Free Press, 2004), 161.

16. Chambers risked losing the attention of HUAC by not mentioning espionage. This was the recollection of Richard Nixon, who was predisposed to believe Chambers: "because his [Chambers's] charges did not include espionage, they left little impression on me or on the other Committee members." *Six Crises* (New York: Simon and Schuster, 1990), 4. Initially, Hiss was the more credible figure to Roy Cohn, who was destined to be an arch-McCarthyite. "I believed

at first that Alger Hiss was innocent," Cohn wrote in his 1968 book, *McCarthy*. "I felt that a sensational press was stampeding our judicial process, and that given his day in court, Hiss would prove himself the victim of a conspiracy headed by Whittaker Chambers." *McCarthy* (New York: New American Library, 1968), 23.

17. Ralph de Toledano, *Seeds of Treason: The True Story of the Hiss-Chambers Tragedy* (New York: Funk and Wagnells, 1950), 149. In Richard Nixon's observation, Chambers was not an eager witness at the beginning of the HUAC sessions: "at first, he [Chambers] seemed an indifferent if not reluctant witness." *Six Crises*, 2.

18. In his very public opening statement (made on August 3, 1948), Chambers appealed to his former comrades to change their ways: "I should like, thus publicly, to call upon all ex-Communists who have not yet disclosed themselves, and all men within the Communist Party whose better instincts have not yet been corrupted and crushed by it, to aid in the [anti-communist] struggle while there is still time." Quoted in Whittaker Chambers, *Witness* (Washington, D.C.: Regnery, 1997), 542.

19. Chambers, *Witness*, 727. Chambers spelled out the same point in more detail: "in my own case, I had been given time to work out a new life. In breaking with the Communist Party, time is a most essential factor. I wanted to give these people the same opportunity I had . . . there was a distinction in my mind between the ultimate perfidy of espionage and the mere fact of Communism. In general, I think there are two kinds of men. One kind believes that god is a God of justice. The other believes that God is a God of mercy. I am so constituted that I will always range myself on the side of mercy." Quoted in de Toledano, *Seeds of Treason*, 124.

20. Chambers, *Witness*, 541, 543, 542–543.

21. Sam Tanenhaus, *Whittaker Chambers: A Biography* (New York: Random House, 1997), 274, 278.

22. De Toledano, *Seeds of Treason*, 222. G. Edward White writes that Hiss's strategy "nearly worked. Hiss's demeanor reinforced the credibility of his denial. Alger Hiss was very good at convincing others of his sincerity. He could project a 'terrible evenness,' an absence of bitterness or outrage, even a sympathy for his accusers. He nearly convinced HUAC." *Alger Hiss's Looking-Glass Wars: The Covert Life of a Soviet Spy* (New York: Oxford University Press, 2004), 240. For a discussion of homosexuality and the political mood of the early Cold War, see Thomas Doherty, *Cold War, Cool Medium: Television, McCarthyism, and American Culture* (New York: Columbia University Press, 2003), 215–230.

23. Alistair Cooke, *A Generation on Trial: U.S.A. v. Alger Hiss* (New York: Knopf, 1950), 92.

24. In *Six Crises,* Nixon underscored a reluctance on the part of the Republican Party to exploit anti-communism in the 1948 presidential election: "domestic Communism was not a significant issue in that campaign. Probably because of the uncertain status of the Hiss-Chambers case, [Thomas] Dewey felt it was not proper to give too much prominence to the issue of Communist infiltration in government during the Truman Administration." *Six Crises,* 45. Ellen Schrecker makes the opposite point: "HUAC's pursuit of Alger Hiss reinforced the Republican Party's campaign against the Truman administration." *The Age of McCarthyism: A Brief History with Documents* (Boston: St. Martin's, 2002), 62.

25. Cooke, *A Generation on Trial,* 108, 11. Richard Nixon situated Hiss in a more contemporary context. Hiss was, in his words, "clearly the symbol of a considerable number of perfectly loyal citizens whose theater of operation are the nation's mass media and universities, its scholarly foundations, and its government bureaucracies." *Six Crises,* 67. Nixon believed this theater of operation to be hostile toward him and toward HUAC: "the *Washington Post,* which was typical of a large segment of the national press and of public opinion, had always taken a dim view of the Committee on Un-American Activities and had launched an all-out assault on its procedures after Hiss first testified." Ibid., 44–45.

26. Cooke, *A Generation on Trial,* 121; Richard Nixon, *The Memoirs of Richard Nixon* (New York: Grosset and Dunlap, 1978), 52–53.

27. Cooke, *A Generation on Trial,* 148, 121, 148.

28. Arthur Schlesinger Jr., "Whittaker Chambers and His 'Witness,' " *Saturday Review,* May 24, 1952, p. 9. Sidney Hook reiterated Schlesinger's observation. The "outrageous screams [of Hiss and his supporters] against his [Chambers's] personal life and that of his wife surpassed in virulence anything known in recent American history." "The Faiths of Whittaker Chambers," *New York Times Book Review* (May 25, 1952): 71. To this Irving Howe added that in *Witness* "Chambers complains bitterly, and with justice, about the smears he has suffered from many Hiss supporters." "God, Man and Stalin," 86. John Dos Passos concurred when he noted "the moral lynching of Whittaker Chambers by the right-thinking people of this country." "Mr. Chambers's Descent into Hell," *Saturday Review,* May 24, 1952, p. 11.

29. Patrick Swan, "Introduction," in *Alger Hiss, Whittaker Chambers and the Schism in the American Soul,* xiv.

30. Cooke, *A Generation on Trial,* 118, 118, 140–141.

31. The notion that character was sufficient to exonerate Hiss and incriminate Chambers remained current long after the Hiss case was over. In 1957 in a review of Hiss's memoir, *In the Court of Public Opinion,* Mark DeWolfe Howe wrote that "if one has any interest in our national taste it is impossible to give credence to such a man as Chambers in preference to such a man as Hiss."

"The Misfortune of a Nation," *Nation* (May 18, 1957): 128. Chambers was a "master mountebank." Ibid., 136; Meyer Zeligs devoted an entire book to the argument that Chambers was pathological. *Friendship and Fratricide: An Analysis of Whittaker Chambers and Alger Hiss* (New York: Viking, 1967). In a sympathetic review of Zeligs's book in the *Nation*, a pro-Hiss magazine to this day, David Cort wrote that "Chambers has been a walking swindle since childhood on; the researcher [Zeligs] could find no falsities in the life story of Hiss." "On Guilt and Resurrection," *Nation* (March 20, 1967): 133. Ellen Schrecker, who is skeptical about Chambers's version of events, describes Chambers as someone "as brilliant as he was unbalanced." *The Age of McCarthyism*, 30.

32. Cooke, *A Generation on Trial*, 258, 183.

33. Ibid., 283–284, 287. Chroniclers of the Hiss case reiterate Cooke's eyewitness observation: "the government was aided by something else [other than new developments in the case in the second trial], a dramatic change in the nation's mood." Tanenhaus, *Whittaker Chambers*, 146. Allen Weinstein makes a similar point: "the American mood had altered dramatically in the four-month interval between the deadlock at Alger Hiss's first trial and the opening of his second. During this period the Cold War heated up within the United States and abroad." *Perjury*, 419.

34. "Chambers, Whittaker—Homosexuality," Alger Hiss Defense Files, Special Collections, Harvard Law School, Box 46 (Folder 11).

35. Diana Trilling, "A Memorandum on the Hiss Case," *Partisan Review* 17, no. 5 (May–June 1950): 32.

36. Cooke, *A Generation on Trial*, 313.

37. Ellen Schrecker sees a political design in the events leading up to McCarthyism: "the crucial developments that brought McCarthyism to the center of American politics occurred between 1946 and 1949, when the nation's political elites, preoccupied with the issue of communism, took up the tools that the anti-communist network had so conveniently forged." *Many Are the Crimes*, xvi–xvii.

38. George Nash, *The Conservative Intellectual Movement, Since 1945* (New York: Basic Books, 1979), 100.

39. Richard Fried, *Men against McCarthy* (New York: Columbia University Press, 1976), 233–237.

40. "Editor's Note," *Saturday Review*, May 24, 1952, p. 8.

41. Tanenhaus, *Whittaker Chambers*, 472.

42. Sidney Hook felt that "the internal evidence of this book is so overwhelmingly detailed and cumulative, it rings with such authenticity, that it is extremely unlikely that any reasonable person will remain unconvinced by it." "The Faiths of Whittaker Chambers," 70.

43. Chambers described his alienation from his fellow Americans in a 1951 letter: "All my life I have felt weighed down by the burden of communication . . . Everything had to be translated. I rarely have that difficulty with Europeans (we speak within the same frame of reference), and with Europeans I never feel as I do with Americans, or seldom . . . and I suspect that the origins of the uncommunication are religious." Whittaker Chambers to Ralph de Toledano, April 19, 1951, in *Notes from the Underground: The Whittaker Chambers-Ralph de Toledano Correspondence, 1949–1960* (Washington, DC: Regnery, 1997), 38.

44. Some critics have felt that Chambers realized this ambition. An ex-communist himself, literary critic Granville Hicks wrote that "if it would be rash to call it the equal of St. Augustine's *Confessions* or the *Confessions* of Rousseau, it has passages of their quality." "Whittaker Chambers's Testament," *New Leader* (May 26, 1952): 57.

45. Chambers made this point himself in *Witness*: "Fox's *Journal* is still less a book than a voice for those to whom it speaks. It was a voice that spoke peculiarly, as Quakers say, 'to my condition.' " *Witness*, 483.

46. Whittaker Chambers to William F. Buckley, in *Odyssey of a Friend: Whittaker Chambers's Letters to William F. Buckley, Jr., 1954–1960*, ed. William F. Buckley, Jr. (Washington, D.C.: Regnery, 1987), 94; Whittaker Chambers to Ralph de Toledano in *Notes from the Underground*, 62, 169.

47. *Witness* was part of a new American genre, the ex-communist memoir. Titles contemporary with *Witness* include: Louis Budenz, *This Is My Story* (New York: McGraw Hill, 1947); Angela Calmoris, *Red Masquerade: Undercover for the F.B.I.* (Philadelphia: Lippincott, 1950); Elizabeth Bentley, *Out of Bondage: The Story of Elizabeth Bentley* (New York: Devon-Adair, 1951); and Herbert Philbrick, *I Led Three Lives: Citizen, "Communist," Counterspy* (New York: McGraw Hill, 1952). These American books were not the obvious models for *Witness*. As Sam Tanenhaus writes, "*Witness*, lavishly praised on the right as a Bible of patriotic anti-communism, itself stands far outside the normative tradition of American classics. Its influences are almost all European." *Whittaker Chambers*, 466.

48. See Annette Wieviorka, *L'ère du témoin* (Paris: Plon, 1998); and Dominick LaCapra, *History and Memory after Auschwitz* (Ithaca, N.Y.: Cornell University Press, 1998).

49. Whittaker Chambers to William F. Buckley Jr., February 9/10[?], 1957, in *Odyssey of a Friend*, 134, 133.

50. Chambers very much admired Milosz's writing about Warsaw: "Milosz chose to bring his thoughts and recollections of the Warsaw ghetto to one burning point: the image of a young woman, who did not wish to die, trying to outrun the murderers who steadily gained on her while she cried: 'No! No! No!' He

chose to make a single impression of the Warsaw uprising define his notion of reality in our time: it was the sight of the paving, tilting on edge, row by row, under the force of firepower. Truth in our time must partake of the bleakly intimidating reality if it is to be true for us." Whittaker Chambers to William F. Buckley Jr., May 9 [?], 1957, in *Odyssey of a Friend*, 156–157. In a 1991 letter to Sam Tanenhaus, Milosz wrote that "I have always felt great sympathy for [Whittaker Chambers] and thought about his tragic life. He suffered much." Czeslaw Milosz to Sam Tanenhaus, June 18, 1991, quoted in *Whittaker Chambers*, 593n.

51. Czeslaw Milosz, *The Captive Mind*, trans. Jane Zielonko (New York: Vintage Books, 1981), vii–viii.

52. *Witness* and *The Captive Mind* were related in the audience to which they were addressed—namely, an audience that was insufficiently anti-communist. In 1981 Milosz appended a short note to *The Captive Mind*, pointing out that it "was written in 1951/1952 in Paris at the time when the majority of French intellectuals resented their country's dependence on American help and placed their hopes in a new world in the East, ruled by a leader of incomparable wisdom and virtue, Stalin." *The Captive Mind*, v.

53. Chambers, *Witness*, 78.

54. Whittaker Chambers to Ralph de Toledano, January 2, 1956, in *Notes from the Underground*, 208. Richard Nixon published *Six Crises* ten years after *Witness* was published. The portrait he draws of Hiss has much in common with the one Chambers had created in *Witness*. According to Nixon, Hiss "believed in an absolutely materialistic view of the world, in principles of deliberate manipulation by a dedicated elite, and in an ideal world society in which 'the party of the workers' replaces God as the prime mover and the sole judge of right and wrong." *Six Crises*, 67.

55. Chambers, *Witness*, 550, 610.

56. Michael Denning writes that "the three great spy cases [of the early Cold War] offered more than spies: they stood as an inverted image of the alliance that made up the Popular Front. Alger His was immediately recognized as an emblem of the Ivy-League-educated model, from an established Anglo family; Julius and Ethel Rosenberg were the epitome of the young ethnic plebians coming of age in the depression; and Klaus Fuchs embodied the émgiré intellectual." *The Cultural Front: The Laboring of American Culture in the Twentieth Century* (New York: Verso, 1996), 104–105.

57. Chambers was not the only one to connect Hiss's supporters with the liberal middle class. Diana Trilling (writing in 1950) observed that "most of Hiss's supporters are people of the middle and upper middle-class, of education, breeding, professional solidity and distinction, people of great probity; thoughtful and conscientious citizens." "A Memorandum on the Hiss Case," 39.

58. Sam Tanenhaus writes that in *Witness* "Chambers champions American democracy but seems wholly inured to its practical operations—the give-and-take, the bargaining, the pragmatic adjustments, the constant dialogue." *Whittaker Chambers*, 466.

59. Chambers, *Witness*, 763.

60. Kingsley Martin, "The Witness," *New Statesman and Nation* (July 19, 1952): 103. For Judy Kutulas, the exaggeration of the communist menace was common to all anti-communists: "anti-Stalinists always overestimated the size and strength of communism in America." *The Long War: The Intellectual People's Front and Anti-Stalinism, 1930–1940* (Durham, N.C.: Duke University Press, 1995), 125.

61. In his memoirs, Richard Nixon shared Chambers's frustration: "to this day [circa 1978], Alger Hiss has emphatically insisted on his innocence and makes periodic attempts to clear himself. This tenacity, together with the passage of time and the vagaries of memory, has now and then been rewarded with honorable publicity and increasing acceptance." *The Memoirs of Richard Nixon*, 70. Diana Trilling made a similar point in 1950: "perhaps the most striking aspect of the Hiss case is the passion of loyalty that has been roused on Hiss's side, not merely among people who knew him—that is readily understandable—but among men and women who would seem to have no closer connection with him than with Chambers." "A Memorandum on the Hiss Case," 38. Philip Nobile gave some empirical legitimacy to these perceptions in a 1976 poll of one hundred lawyers, journalists, and intellectuals—"the new Hiss jury split down the middle." "The State of the Art of Alger Hiss" *Harper's* (April 1976): 204. Nobile added that circa 1976 Hiss "has remained a Gatsbeyesque figure around New York City, charming guests at celebrity parties and gathering converts without even trying." Ibid., 211.

62. Chambers, *Witness*, 707.

63. Quoted in Peter Andrews and Bert Andrews, *A Tragedy of History: A Journalist's Confidential Role in the Hiss Case* (Washington, D.C.: R.B. Luce, 1962), 221.

64. Sam Tanenhaus writes that "almost everyone in a position to help was loyal to Hiss and remained so for many years to come." *Whittaker Chambers*, 286.

65. De Toledano, *Seeds of Treason*, 279.

66. Nixon, *The Memoirs of Richard Nixon*, 71. Nixon made a similar point in *Six Crises*, noting that the Hiss case "left a residue of hatred and hostility towards me—not only among the Communists but among substantial segments of the press and intellectual community—a hostility that remains even today." *Six Crises*, 69.

67. Jerome Himmelstein, *To the Right: The Transformation of American Conservatism* (Berkeley: University of California Press, 1990), 8. Himmelstein

does not use this phrase in relation to the Hiss case but as a general characterization of 1950s conservatism.

68. Chambers, *Witness*, 791.

69. Hilton Kramer mentions "the great uproar that the publication of *Witness* created in the world of literary and intellectual debate." "Thinking about *Witness*," in *Alger Hiss, Whittaker Chambers and the Schism in the American Soul*, 305. Uproar was not the same as acceptance. According to Kramer, the targets of Chambers's animosity responded in kind: "in the world of the *New Yorker*, which was solidly pro Hiss, the *New Republic*, whose editor in those days [Michael Straight] was subsequently revealed to have been a member, earlier on, of another underground Soviet apparatus, and other such staunch liberal journals, the barriers were created and Chambers was stripped of his literary standing." Ibid., 317.

70. Chambers, *Witness*, 793.

71. Chambers loved using the pedigree of great names to bolster his points. On the depredations of reason, he quoted from Goethe: "man without God is a beast, never more beastly than when he is most intelligent about his beastliness. 'Er nennt's Vernunft,' says the Devil in Goethe's *Faust*, 'und braucht's allein, nur tierischer als jedes Tier zu sein'—Man calls it reason and uses it simply to be more beastly than any beast." Ibid., 13.

72. Ibid., 17, 4, 4, 9.

73. Richard Nixon, "Plea for an Anti-Communist Faith," 12.

74. Rebecca West noted the pastoral motif in *Witness*. As readers of *Witness*, she wrote, "we see through his eyes the miraculous quality of the American landscape which touches and astounds all European visitors." "Whittaker Chambers," *Atlantic Monthly* (June 1952): 116. West connected the pastoral and the Christian elements of *Witness*, describing Chambers as "a Christian mystic of the pantheist school, a spiritual descendent of [Meister] Eckhart and [Jakob] Boehme and Angelus Silesius." Ibid., 117.

75. Chambers, *Witness*, 19, 19, 18, 21, 21–22.

76. Alexander I. Solzhenitsyn, *The Gulag Archipelago, 1918–1956: An Experiment in Literary Investigation*, trans. Thomas P. Whitney (New York: Harper and Row, 1973), 18.

77. The ubiquity of Christian themes repulsed some readers of *Witness*. "If Chambers is right in believing the major bulwark against Stalin to be faith in God, then it is time for men of conviction and courage to take to the hills," wrote Irving Howe. "God, Man and Stalin," 89. Howe's essay title was, presumably, a mocking reference to William F. Buckley Jr., whose book *God and Man at Yale* was published in 1951. Elmer Davis believed that Chambers "substitutes a God who has much in common with Stalin." "History in Doublethink," *Saturday Review*, June 28, 1952, p. 103.

78. William F. Buckley Jr., "The End of Whittaker Chambers," *Esquire* (September 1962): 144.

79. James Billington situates the communist impulse less in the Enlightenment than in the Romantic movement. "The revolutionary faith was shaped not so much by the critical rationalism of the French Enlightenment (as is generally believed)," he writes, "as by the occultism and proto-romanticism of Germany. This faith was incubated in France during the revolutionary era within a small sub-culture of intellectuals who were immersed in journalism, fascinated by secret societies, and subsequently infatuated with "ideologies" as a secular surrogate for religious belief." *Fire in the Minds of Men: Origins of the Revolutionary Faith* (New Brunswick, N.J.: Transaction Publishers, 1999), 3-4.

80. Chambers, *Witness*, 196, 449.

81. Ibid., 35, 25, 75, 82, 83. John Diggins uses a very similar formulation to describe the novelist John Dos Passos's conversion from communism to conservatism. Dos Passos was "a conservative who became what he always was" when he became an anti-communist. *Up from Communism: Conservative Odysseys in American Intellectual History* (New York: Columbia University Press, 1994), 97.

82. Chambers, *Witness*, 83.

83. Norman Podhoretz, *My Love Affair with America: The Cautionary Tale of a Cheerful Conservative* (New York: Free Press, 2000), 93. George Nash argues for a rise in populism among conservative intellectuals in the 1950s, making Chambers a transitional figure. The ex-radicals who moved to the Right in the 1950s began, according to Nash, "to apotheosize Middle America." *The Conservative Intellectual Movement*, 128.

84. Chambers, *Witness*, 794.

85. Peter Andrews notes that "with a queer perversity, it [the Hiss case] challenged both the liberal and conservative mainstreams of American political thought." *A Tragedy of History*, 3.

86. Chambers, *Witness*, 799. Dostoevsky ended *The Brothers Karamazov* with images of children, whose innocence hints at the possibility of redemption in a sinful world.

87. Chambers, *Witness*, 798.

88. Paul Gottfried, *The Conservative Movement* (New York: Twayne, 1993), 15.

89. Whittaker Chambers, *Odyssey of a Friend*, 69, 62, 62.

90. Chambers's pessimism was also intended to mobilize conservatives and to shatter conservative complacency. Chambers was not entirely unsuccessful in this intention. Roy Cohn, for example, approvingly invoked Chambers's pessimism when speaking in 1957 to the Executives' Club of Chicago: "Whittaker Chambers, who left the Communist movement and came on our side, said that he felt in his heart he was leaving the winning side and joining the losing side. I would be less than candid if I did not admit there is much

logic to support the statement of Whittaker Chambers." Quoted in Roy Cohn, *McCarthy* (New York: New America Library, 1968), 263.

91. Tanenhaus, *Whittaker Chambers*, 467.

92. Whittaker Chambers to William F. Buckley Jr., August 2, 1955, in *Odyssey of a Friend*, 78.

93. Cohn, *McCarthy*.

94. David Oshinsky, *A Conspiracy So Immense: The World of Joe McCarthy* (New York: Free Press, 1983), 234.

95. Schrecker, *Many Are the Crimes*, 265. Schrecker describes a kind of political machinery set in motion by anti-communist intellectuals like Chambers and anti-communist politicians like McCarthy: "the professional anti-Communists became disproportionately influential in shaping the political repression of the McCarthy period. They selected its targets and developed the mechanism through which that repression operated. Even more important, they were considered the nation's leading experts about domestic Communism, shaping the ideas that most ordinary Americans, as well as politicians, held about Communism." Ibid., 45.

96. Tanenhaus, *Whittaker Chambers*, 454, 456.

97. David Caute, *The Great Fear: The Anti-Communist Purge under Truman and Eisenhower* (New York: Simon and Schuster, 1978), 311–312. Caute places primary blame on McCarthy, but the McCarthyite assault on Clubb began with Chambers, to whom Caute contemptuously refers as "that archinformer and walking memory bank." Ibid., 311.

98. Whittaker Chambers to William F. Buckley Jr., May 9[?], 1957, in *Odyssey of a Friend*, 159, 159.

99. Whittaker Chambers to Ralph de Toledano, April 6, 1953, in *Notes from the Underground*, 115, 116, 116, 116. In his letter to de Toledano, Chambers launched into a sarcastic diatribe against the media: "one of the recurring oddities of my situation is that the press, which has consistently tried to discredit me and all I may say, clearly believes in its black heart that I know everything abut everybody since time began, and was probably a witness to the even and have, in some pumpkin, a tape recording of those great words: 'Fiat lux.' " Ibid., 116.

100. Whittaker Chambers to Ralph de Toledano, March 1953, *Notes from the Underground*, 109.

101. Whittaker Chambers to Henry Regnery, January 14, 1954, in *Odyssey of a Friend*, 24. In 1950, Chambers conveyed a positive judgment of McCarthy to Richard Nixon: " 'He [McCarthy], for one, knows that you must go forward. You can't stand still, you won't go back—in war, in politics.' " Quoted in Irwin Gellman, *The Contender*, 355.

102. Whittaker Chambers to William F. Buckley Jr., February 7, 1954, in *Odyssey of a Friend*, 26.

103. Ibid., 26, 26, 26, 28.

104. One might compare Chambers's notion of a left-wing apparatus with David Horowitz's notion of a left-wing network. According to Horowtiz, the left "has a long and well-documented history of dissembling about its agendas. In the past, the Communist Party, for example, operated through 'front' groups which concealed the radical agendas of those who controlled them . . . the disingenuous tradition of the political left has continued into the present." See: http://www.discoverthenetworks.org/groupProfile.asp?grpid=7030.

105. Whittaker Chambers to William F. Buckley Jr., August 30, 1954, in *Odyssey of a Friend*, 49.

106. Ibid.; Whittaker Chambers to William F. Buckley Jr., in *Odyssey of a Friend*, 78, 79.

107. When McCarthy died in 1957, Chambers was overcome with melancholy but not with retrospective sympathy for what McCarthy had done. Chambers recalled that "this man [McCarthy] and I fought in the same wars in which he suffered greatly. But he was not my leader." This was because McCarthy "never understood Communism or the war on Communism." Whittaker Chambers to William F. Buckley Jr., May 9[?], 1957, in *Odyssey of a Friend*, 160.

108. Arthur Schlesinger Jr., "Whittaker Chambers and His 'Witness,' " 8, 8, 9, 40, 41, 40.

109. Diana Trilling, "A Memorandum on the Hiss Case," 30, 31, 32, 43, 48, 43. Trilling's essay was an extended review of Ralph de Toledano's pro-Chambers book, *Seeds of Treason*.

8. Conservatism and the Anti-Communist Self

Epigraph: http://www.bartleby.com/101/751.html.

1. Socialism per se was not the aim of Yale liberals, according to Buckley. Rather, the liberal program was "a slow increase of state power, through extended social services, taxation, and regulation." Whatever the program, "the net influence of Yale economics is to be thoroughly collectivistic." *God and Man at Yale: The Superstitions of Academic Freedom* (Chicago: Regnery, 1951), 46, 46.

2. Ibid., 193.

3. Ibid, 25.

4. John Judis, *William F. Buckley, Jr., Patron Saint of* Conservatives (New York: Simon and Schuster, 1988), 86. On the critical reception of *God and Man at Yale*, especially its warm reception in the Midwest and south, see Judis, *William F. Buckley, Jr.*, 92–98. McGeorge Bundy, then still an academic dean, penned a less receptive "Eastern" review, calling Buckley "a twisted and ignorant man whose personal views of economics would have seemed reactionary to Mark Hanna." "The Attack on Yale," *Atlantic Monthly* 188, no. 5 (November 1951): 51. In his reply to Bundy's review, Buckley was no less ad

hominem, excoriating "Mr. Bundy's advocacy of irresponsible, irreproachable education by an academic elite." "The Changes at Yale," *Atlantic Monthly* 188, no. 6 (December 1951): 82.

5. Lionel Trilling, *The Liberal Imagination: Essays on Literature and Society* (New York: Anchor Books, 1950), vii.

6. George Nash, *The Conservative Intellectual Movement in America, Since 1945* (New York: Basic Books, 1979), 231.

7. Communists who went over to the Right, Schlamm and Chambers had parallel backgrounds before coming to *National Review*. Schlamm and Buckley—and Chambers as well—"believed that the way to change politics in a country was to challenge the reigning intellectuals. Both men [Buckley and Schlamm] had come to the conclusion that a magazine was the way to do so." Judis, *William F. Buckley, Jr.*, 116.

8. Ibid., 157.

9. Whittaker Chambers to William F. Buckley, Jr., April 6, 1954, in, William F. Buckley, Jr., ed., *Odyssey of a Friend: Whittaker Chambers's Letters to William F. Buckley, Jr., 1954–1961* (New York: Putnam, 1969), 60.

10. Like Trilling and Chambers, Ralph de Toledano was an undergraduate at Columbia College. One can assume that de Toledano held Trilling in high esteem from a letter he sent to Trilling in 1960, asking for a blurb: "if you like the book, I would be most indebted to you if you wrote a few lines for use by Ferrar, Straus & Cudahy, and the publishers." Ralph de Toledano to Lionel Trilling, January 3, 1960, Trilling MSS, Box 16. The book to which de Toledano was referring is *Lament for a Generation*. He did not get a blurb from Trilling, but Richard Nixon agreed to write the preface for it. *Lament for a Generation* (New York: Farrar, Straus and Cudahy, 1960).

11. Whittaker Chambers to Ralph de Toledano, May 16, 1950, in *Notes from the Underground: The Whittaker Chambers-Ralph de Toledano Correspondence*, ed. Ralph de Toledano (Washington, D.C.: Regnery, 1997), 23; Whittaker Chambers to Ralph de Toledano, June 9, 1956, in Ibid., 274.

12. Russell Kirk, *Randolph of Roanoke: A Study in Conservative Thought* (Chicago: University of Chicago Press, 1951).

13. Whittaker Chambers, *Cold Friday*, ed. Duncan Norton-Taylor (New York: Random House, 1964), 221. As conservative intellectuals, Kirk and Chambers had a great deal in common. For one, they were enemies of the city and enthusiasts of the country: "to counter the spread of industrialization and urbanization, Kirk recommended that conservatives embrace agrarianism," writes W. Wesley McDonald in *Russell Kirk and the Age of Ideology* (Columbia: University of Missouri Press, 2004), 147. In addition, Chambers and Kirk saw themselves as a small civilized minority, living in barbarous times: "there are those (the 'Remnant,' as Kirk liked to call them) doing their best to

stitch together once more the fragments of that serviceable old suit we variously call 'Christian civilization' or 'Western civilization' or 'the North Atlantic community' or 'the free world.' Not by force of arms are civilizations held together, but by the subtle threads of moral and intellectual principle.'" W. Wesley McDonald, *Russell Kirk and the Age of Ideology*, 218–219.

14. In his negative attitudes toward business and capitalism, Chambers retained the attitudes of a literary Columbia undergraduate, attitudes not confined to the early 1920s. As someone who studied at Columbia some twenty years after Chambers, Norman Podhoretz wrote in 1967 that "a young man who studies literature is in effect electing to join a kind of political party within the American cultural order: the party of opposition to the presumed values of the business world." *Making It* (New York: Random House, 1967), 54–55.

15. Whittaker Chambers to Willi Schlamm, September 1954, in *Cold Friday*, 236; Whittaker Chambers to William F. Buckley Jr., September 1954, in *Cold Friday*, 238. Republican Party analyst Kevin Phillips confirms the trend Chambers was lamenting, the leftward drift of affluent Americans from the 1930s to the 1960s. In 1968 Phillips wrote: "who can doubt that today's Establishment—the great metropolitan newspapers, the Episcopal and other churches, the Supreme Court, Beacon Hill and Manhattan's fashionable East Side—to some extent reflects the institutionalization of a successful New Deal, just as the Roosevelt-baiting press lords, industrialists and Supreme Court justices of the Nineteen-Thirties represented a weakening conservative Establishment rooted in the post-Civil War reign of industrial laissez faire and political Republicanism." *The Emerging Republican Majority* (New Rochelle, N.Y.: Arlington House, 1969), 83–84.

16. Whittaker Chambers to William F. Buckley Jr., April 6, 1954, in *Odyssey of a Friend*, 67.

17. Jeffrey Hart notes the popularity of anti-Enlightenment ideas at *National Review*—namely, the notion that liberals and communists were all descendants of the Enlightenment. Hart writes that *National Review* intellectuals "while making the appropriate distinctions, also saw that philosophically, communism and liberalism were both products of the Enlightenment. Both emphasized equality, Communists through force, liberals as a political goal. Though communism could be called 'hard' socialism, liberals, or many of them, were simply 'soft' socialists." *The Making of the American Conservative Mind: National Review and Its Times* (Wilmington, Del.: ISI Books, 2005), 89. In his autobiography, Russell Kirk writes that "the men of the Enlightenment had cold hearts and smug heads; now their successors, as the middle of the twentieth century loomed up, were in the process of imposing upon the world a dreary conformity, with Efficiency and Progress and Equality for their watchwords—abstractions preferred to all those fascinating and lovable

peculiarities of human nature and human society that are the products of prescription and tradition." *The Sword of Imagination: Memoirs of a Half-Century of Literary Conflict* (Grand Rapids, Mich.: Edermans, 1995), 69.

18. For Chambers, twentieth-century revolution included capitalism: "what we commonly overlook, perhaps because most of the [revolutionary] movements are directed against capitalism, is that capitalism is itself a revolutionary force." *Cold Friday*, 210. Despite great differences between Chambers and the Frankfurt School philosophers, Max Horkheimer and Theodore Adorno, they shared a considered suspicion of the Enlightenment and of capitalism. *Cold Friday* and *Witness* bear comparison with two key Frankfurt School texts, published shortly before *Witness*: Max Horkheimer and Theodore Adorno, *Dialektik der Aufklärung: Philosophische Fragmente* (Amsterdam: Querido, 1947) and *Minima Moralia: Reflexionen aus dem beschädigten Leben* (Berlin: Suhrkamp, 1951).

19. Arthur Koestler, *Darkness at Noon* (New York: Modern Library, 1941); Arthur Koeslter, *The Invisible Writing* (London: Collins, 1954); Czeslaw Milosz, *The Captive Mind* (New York: Knopf, 1953); Henri de Lubac, *The Drama of Atheist Humanism*, trans. Edith M. Riley (Cleveland: World Publishing, 1950); this was initially published as *Le drame de l'humanisme athée* (Paris: Éditions Spes, 1945); Manès Sperber, *The Burned Bramble* (Garden City, N.Y.: Doubleday, 1951).

20. Chambers, *Cold Friday*, 44.

21. Ibid., 7.

22. Hart, *The Making of the American Conservative Mind*, 109. Hart also argues that Chambers's was a fighting faith: "Chambers, we know from *Witness*, had experienced the deepest pit spiritually, but he wanted to fight intelligently and prudently, gathering allies." Ibid., 87.

23. Chambers, *Cold Friday*, 13.

24. In *Cold Friday*, Chambers placed the center of revolutionary gravity outside of Western Europe and the United States: "it is well, perhaps, to remember that freedom, in our understanding of the term, has been restricted largely to the United States and the fringe of Western Europe. In the rest of the world it has not accepted currency, and over large areas of Europe the Second World War and the revolutions that preceded it utterly destroyed the conditions of freedom and raised strong questions in many minds whether freedom is practicable in the conditions of our times." Ibid., 78.

25. Chambers, *Cold Friday*, 69, 15.

26. Ibid., 41, 144, 129.

27. Whittaker Chambers to Ralph de Toledano, June 12, 1956, in *Notes from the Underground*, 265; Chambers, *Cold Friday*, 214. In the preface to *The Opposing Self*, Trilling writes that "our habits of feeling have changed since the time when Arnold's poem ["The Scholar Gypsy"] had a special place in the world's

affection—we are no longer quite suited by the large sadness with which it speaks of the loss of peace and joy. And yet there isn't, I think, a more comprehensive and comprehensible delineation of the modern self in its relation to the culture than that which Arnold makes in this elegy for his own youth." *The Opposing Self: Nine Essays in Criticism* (New York: Viking Press, 1955), xiii.

28. Herbert Solow to Lionel Trilling, May 1, 1964, Trilling MSS, Box 5; Lionel Trilling to Herbert Solow, May 10, 1964, Trilling MSS, Box 5.

29. Alexander Bloom, *Prodigal Sons: The New York Intellectuals and their World* (New York: Oxford University Press, 1986), 166.

30. In Trilling's notion of the West, as in Chambers's, Europe occupied the foreground and America the background, although what was valid for Europe was valid for America. In *Sincerity and Authenticity*, the West was the protagonist of a drama, during which "at a certain point in its history the moral life of Europe added to itself a new element, the state or quality of self which we call sincerity." *Sincerity and Authenticity* concerns the value "attached to the enterprise of sincerity which became a salient, perhaps a definitive, characteristic of Western culture for some four hundred years." *Sincerity and Authenticity* (Cambridge, Mass.: Harvard University Press, 1971), 2, 6.

31. Lionel Trilling to Peter [?] St. John's Cambridge, April 18, 1960, Trilling MSS, Box 16.

32. Lionel Trilling, "A Portrait of Western Man," *Listener* 49 (June 11, 1953): 969, 974.

33. Lionel Trilling, "Art and Fortune," *Partisan Review* 15 (December 1948): 1271–1292.

34. Ibid., 253–254.

35. Barbara Wood, "The Moral Challenge of Communism," *Atlantic Monthly* (1951): 41, 41, 39. Wood was quoting from Trilling's essay "Art and Fortune." Wood wrote in glowing terms about Victorian England, going beyond Trilling in her effusive praise of the Victorians: "Solon rescued the Greeks from a confusion of rancor and division. Christian faith carried mankind onward from the wreck of Rome. The Reformation challenged the Church to universal reform. Wesley and the Evangelicals transformed the England of Whig families and Hogarth's Gin Lane into the great age of Victorian piety." Ibid., 41.

36. Lionel Trilling, "Romanticism and Religion," review *Religious Trends in English Poetry* by Hoxie Neale Fairchild, *New York Times Book Review* (September 4, 1949): 13; Irving Feldman to Lionel Trilling, November 2, 1965, Box 22; Lionel Trilling to Irving Feldman, [undated], Trilling MSS, Box 22. William Barrett writes that "the cast of his [Trilling's] mind was the rational, secular, and non-religious one of a classical liberalism." *The Truants: Adventures among the Intellectuals* (Garden City, N.J.: Anchor Press, 1982),

170. Joseph Shoben puts it better: "although secular in conviction and outlook, he [Trilling] invested an informed seriousness in the moral traditions of both Jewish and Christian faith and theology." *Lionel Trilling: Mind and Character.* (New York: Ungar, 1981), 62. To this one can add Leon Wieseltier's point that trilling allowed "sublimities of character and understanding that may not competently be captured by an exclusively naturalistic vocabulary." *The Moral Obligation to Be Intelligent: Selected Essays* (New York: Farrar, Strauss, Giroux, 200), xi.

37. Lionel Trilling to [?], December 1, 1964, Trilling MSS, Box 21; Lionel Trilling to Stanley [?], December 19, 1964, Trilling MSS, Box 21. Writing about the New York intellectuals as a whole, Ruth Wisse argues that "their accelerating distaste for the Jewish community from which they had emerged was only the other side of that same process of acculturation, and every bit as parochial as the ethnocentricity they were attacking. As the Jewish bourgeoisie tried to keep up with the Jones, so they were trying to keep up with the (T. S.) Eliots, and both began to succeed at exactly the same time." "The New York (Jewish) Intellectuals," *Commentary* 84 (November 1984): 37.

38. Lionel Trilling to Ursula Niebuhr, January 16, 1961, Trilling MSS, Box 17.

39. According to Norman Podhoretz, Trilling "was like a man of faith who was constantly assailed by uncertainty and doubt as to whether the works to which he was devoting his life were really all that important." *Ex-Friends: Falling out with Allen Ginsberg, Lionel & Diana Trilling, Lillian Hellman, Hannah Arendt and Norman Mailer* (New York: Free Press, 1999), 65.

40. Russell Kirk, *The Sword of Imagination: Memoirs of a Half-Century of Literary Conflict* (Grand Rapids, Mich.: William B. Eerdmans, 1995), 166, 40.

41. Peter Viereck to Lionel Trilling, June 24, 1950, Trilling MSS, Box 11.

42. Peter Viereck, "Babbitry Revisited," *Harvard Alumni Bulletin*: 716, 719, in Trilling MSS, Box 11.

43. Lionel Trilling to Stephen [Marcus?], December 15, 1953, Trilling MSS, Box 11. Like Trilling, Peter Viereck, and Russell Kirk "agreed that the moral inspiration of great literature nurtures a sense of individual self-awareness and worth that the 'blueprint mentality' of the ideologist cannot understand." McDonald, *Russell Kirk and the Age of Ideology*, 60.

44. *National Review* editor William Schlamm saw McCarthy as a savior of the West: "at the heart of what McCarthy said and did was the very essence of Western Civilization," he argued. Quoted in Ronald Lora and William Henry Longton, "American Conservatism in the Twentieth Century," in *The Conservative Press in Twentieth-Century America* (Westport, Conn.: Greenwood Press, 1999), 13.

45. J. David Hoeveler writes that "to [Peter] Viereck McCarthy represented the kind of anti-intellectual populism that was, he felt, one of the most dangerous

products of democratic culture." *American Conservatism: An Encyclopedia* (Wilmington, Del.: ISI Books, 2006), 888.

46. Hart, *The Making of the American Conservative Mind*, 84.

47. Chambers noted that the communist state and the welfare state "are in direct competition with each other, since each offers itself as an alternative solution for the crisis of the twentieth century: and Fabian Britain has at last supplanted Soviet Russia in the eyes of political liberals when they look abroad." Whittaker Chambers, "Is Academic Freedom in Danger?" in, ed. Terry Teachout, *Ghosts on the Roof: Selected Journalism of Whittaker Chambers, 1931–1959* (Washington, D.C.: Regnery, 1989), 267. Distinguishing between liberals and communists did not prevent Chambers from thinking that liberals and their Democratic Party were subversive. To de Toledano Chambers wrote that an article in *Look*, which directed the attention "for the first time (so far as I know) of a mass readership to the maneuver of the basic Democratic strategy about subversion. As you know, it was to attack the open (and relatively unimportant) CP [Communist Party] and distract attention from the Communists in government." Whittaker Chambers to Ralph de Toledano, January 8[?], 1953, in *Notes from the Underground*, 153.

48. Whitaker Chambers, "Is Academic Freedom in Danger?" 277.

49. Ibid., 267.

50. One senses something of the liberal contempt for Chambers's influence (some forty-five years after the Hiss case) in the words of historian Ellen Schrecker: "Hiss's conviction for perjury legitimated HUAC's activities. In addition, it so thoroughly bolstered the right-wing contention that the New Deal was infested with Soviet spies that by the time Hiss was convicted for perjury in January 1950, it was no longer possible to ignore allegations of Communist subversion, no matter how ridiculous or unfounded." *No Ivory Tower: McCarthyism and the Universities* (New York: Oxford University Press, 1986), 8.

51. Lionel Trilling to Michael Straight, December 1952, Trilling MSS, Box 11. Michael Straight had a history of Soviet espionage. See Roland Perry, *The Last of the Cold War Spies: The Life of Michael Straight, the Only American in Britain's Cambridge Spy Ring* (Cambridge, Mass.: Da Capo, 2005).

52. Trilling often followed the political trail blazed by Sidney Hook, to whom he owed his initial involvement in communism. In his memoirs, Hook wrote sharply about liberals, whose lack of anti-communist initiative left the task of anti-communism to a political fool like McCarthy: "until the outbreak of the Korean war," Hook argued retrospectively, "indifference to the nature of the Communist Party and its penetration into many American agencies of government contributed to creating the climate of opinion in which Senator McCarthy was to win an initial credibility for his demagogic exaggerations."

Out of Step: An Unquiet Life in the Twentieth Century (New York: Harper and Row, 1987), 333.

53. Lionel Trilling in "Liberal Anti-Communism Revisited: A Symposium," *Commentary* 44 (September 1967): 76; Lionel Trilling, "Mind and Market in Academic Life," review of *The Academic Mind* by Paul Lazarsfeld and Wagner Thielens Jr., and *The Academic Marketplace, The Griffin* 7 by Theodore Caplow and Reece McGee (December 1957): 13, 8, 8, 14. Ellen Schrecker writes that "the Fund for the Republic, an offshoot of the Ford Foundation, was concerned about the apparent erosion of civil liberties on American campuses and gave the sociologists Paul Lazarsfeld and Wagner Thielens, Jr., a quarter of a million dollars to find out how college professors were responding to McCarthyism." *No Ivory Tower*, 309.

54. Lionel Trilling, "Some Are Gentle, Some Are Not," review of *The Troubled Air* by Irwin Shaw, *Saturday Review*, June 9, 1951, p. 9.

55. On Gene Weltfish and McCarthyism see Ellen Schrecker, *No Ivory Tower*, 255–256. Schrecker writes that "Columbia's commitment to academic freedom was, in fact, stronger than that of most universities during the McCarthy era." Ibid., 255. But Schrecker is sharply critical of Trilling's Columbia committee. She accuses him of intellectual collaboration with McCarthyism: "many of the nation's leading intellectuals were directly involved with one or another aspect of McCarthyism. The American historian and present [1986] Librarian of Congress Daniel Boorstin named names for HUAC; Lionel Trilling, perhaps the leading literary critic of the day, chaired a Columbia committee that developed guidelines for Congressional witnesses; and Talcott Parsons, whose formal paradigms shaped much of American sociology, participated in HUAC's special survey of Cold War academic freedom cases." Ibid., 339–240. On Trilling and the Columbia committee see Alexander Bloom, *Prodigal Sons: The New York Intellectuals and Their World* (New York: Oxford University Press, 1986), 249.

56. The authors of the statement questioned "the propriety and benefits of investigations which exaggerate results, punish individuals unjustly by publicity, use accusations as charges, prove guilt by association, deny witnesses the procedural rights and privileges for their own defense and for the committee itself to serve as a regularly constituted jury." "Statement: Draft," November 11, 1953, Trilling MSS, Box 11.

57. Lionel Trilling to Rose V. Russell, November 23, 1953, Trilling MSS, Box 11; Lionel Trilling to Editors of the *New York Times*, November 24, 1953, Trilling MSS, Box 11. In his memoir, *Making It*, Norman Podhoretz writes critically of "hard" anti-communists, like Hook and Trilling, and their attitude toward McCarthyism: "there can be little question that hard anti-Communists were more concerned with fighting what they took to be misconceptions of the

nature of Soviet Communism than with fighting the persecution to which so many people were being subjected in the early fifties; and it shames me to say that I shared fully in their brutal insensitivity on this issue." *Making It* (New York: Harper, 1980), 291.

58. Lionel Trilling to Harold Taylor, December 15, 1953, Trilling MSS, Box 11.

59. Trilling's "we" was not synonymous with the Democratic Party or with any political party, although Trilling took it for granted that a liberal was a Democrat and vice versa. Never extensively involved in the Democratic Party, Trilling was loyal to it. In 1954 he wrote a letter to Eleanor Roosevelt, informing her of his "natural sympathy with much of the program of the ADA [Americans for Democratic Action]." Lionel Trilling to Eleanor Roosevelt, February 26, 1954, Trilling MSS, Box 4.

60. Trilling's famous reference to conservatism in the preface of *The Liberal Imagination* was dismissive of conservatism, but it is telling that conservatism is the only alternative to liberalism. Radicalism is beneath consideration.

61. A student of Trilling's who would go on to a career of literary scholarship, Carolyn Heilbrun, wrote of Trilling the teacher: "Trilling's lectures [in the early 1950s] . . . seemed to hold the key to salvation, and salvation, for me as for him, was what I hoped to find in literature. Not religious salvation, of course, but a sense of how to live in a culture I both treasured and wished to overturn. What Trilling provided was an acrobatic balance between 'bourgeois' values and the need radically to affect them. It was in literature that he believed this balance, and profound instruction on how to live, could be found. I always followed him in this." *When Men Were the Only Models We Had: My Teachers Barzun, Fadiman, Trilling* (Philadelphia: University of Pennsylvania Press, 2002), 26.

62. Trilling, *The Opposing Self*, x, xiv.

63. Ibid., 49, 46, 7, 12, 7, 4–5. Irving Howe would title his essay on Trilling's life, written in 1976 shortly after Trilling's death, "Continuous Magical Confrontation."

64. Lionel Trilling, "Keats," in *The Opposing Self*, 39, 39, 42, 45.

65. Ibid., 41, 49.

66. Lionel Trilling, "Orwell," in *The Opposing Self*, 153, 152, 159, 159–160, 163–164, 164, 163.

67. Lionel Trilling, "William Dean Howells and the Origins of Modern Taste," in *The Opposing Self*, 98, 99, 99, 103, 101, 103, 102–103.

68. Ibid., 80, 81, 80, 93. A nineteenth-century writer like Howells might seem irrelevant to Cold War polarities, but for Trilling his novels had contemporary relevance. Communism still appealed to the modern spirit, for it is conceivable as free and unconditioned, when middle-class democratic capitalism is demonstrably conditioned and not fully free. In Trilling's words: "The wide disrepute into which capitalist society has fallen all over the world is justified

by the failures and injustices of capitalism; but if we want to understand the assumptions about politics of the world today, we have to consider the readiness of people to condemn the failures and injustices of Communist society." Lionel Trilling, "Howells," in *The Opposing Self*, 91.

69. Lionel Trilling, "The Bostonians," in *The Opposing Self*, 108, 109–110, 111, 113.

70. Ibid., 114, 116, 117.

71. Carolyn Heilbrun writes critically about Trilling's relation to female students at Columbia, which he treated as if it should remain an all-male bastion: "Columbia was one of the last non-Catholic male schools to become coed, and one of the reasons for this surely was not, as was supposed, the presence of Barnard; it was the powerful protest of Lionel Trilling, which still echoed on our ears." The problem was in part personal: "he seemed to expect them [women] to abjure any consideration of their own moral destinies." But it was also literary, as it were: "his lack of imagination when it came to women, and his failure, or profound disinclination, to sympathize with them and their lot." *When Men Were the Only Models We Had*, 24, 93, 98.

72. "Wordsworth and the Rabbis" was first published as "Wordsworth and the Iron Time" in *Kenyon Review* 12 (Summer 1950): 477–497. It was also published in *Commentary* as "Wordsworth and the Rabbis: The Affinity between His 'Nature' and Their 'Law,' " *Commentary* 11 (February 1955): 108–119.

73. Carolyn Heilbrun (who is herself Jewish) writes about the surprise this essay elicited in her as a close reader of Trilling: "by the time I read 'Wordsworth and the Rabbis,' I was actually startled to find him discussing the Jewish training in his boyhood, and that essay was only published in 1955 . . . I always, without much thought, considered Trilling English—not literally so, but English all the same." *When Men Were the Only Models We Had*, 61. Another Jewish student of Trilling's, Norman Podhoretz conveys a similar surprise when he writes that, in "Wordsworth and the Rabbis," Trilling "was finally able to say something good about something Jewish," *Ex-Friends*, 93.

74. Lionel Trilling, "Wordsworth and the Rabbis," in *The Opposing Self*, 124, 125, 125.

75. Ibid., 133, 133.

76. Ibid., 128.

77. Ibid., xi, 150, 150.

78. Ibid., xi.

79. Joseph Frank, "Lionel Trilling and the Conservative Imagination," *Sewanee* 59, no. 2 (Spring 1956): 254, 256, 266. Thomas Bender makes a similar point about Trilling and "his easy acceptance of a middle-class and business civilization in the 1950s." "Lionel Trilling and American Culture," *American Quarterly* 42, no 2 (June 1990): 339.

80. Mark Krupnick is more balanced than Frank when he writes that Trilling's "idealism, derived from Arnold and Victorian moralism, is at odds with his

realism, derived from Freud and the modernist revolt against Victorian idealism." *Lionel Trilling and the Fate of Cultural Criticism* (Evanston, Ill.: Northwestern University Press, 1986), 63. Mark Shechner writes, more generally, that "especially for Jews, psychoanalysis gave license to self-doubt and ambivalence," a license with which Trilling seems to have been born. *After the Revolution: Studies in the Contemporary Jewish Imagination* (Bloomington, In: University of Indiana Press, 1987), 61. Leon Wieseltier describes Freud, Trilling, and Isaiah Berlin as "rationalists with night vision," an apt contrast— light and dark—for the opposing self. *The Moral Obligation to Be Intelligent: Selected Essays* (New York: Farrar, Straus, Giroux, 2000), xv.

81. Irving Howe wrote vicious reviews of *Witness* and of James Burnham's book, *Suicide of the West:* "God, Man, and Stalin," review of *Witness* by Whittaker Chambers, *The Nation* 174 (May 24, 1952): 21; and "Bourbon on the Rocks," review of *Suicide of the West* by James Burnham, *New York Review of Books* 11 (May 14, 1964): 7. Dwight MacDonald offered a mocking assault on *National Review* in "On the Horizon: Scrambled Eggheads on the Right," *Commentary* 21, no. 4 (April 1956). Chambers wanted to write a rejoinder to MacDonald for *National Review,* but never did. William F. Buckley Jr., "Whittaker Chambers, 1901–1961," in *Miles Gone By: A Literary Autobiography* (Washington, D.C.: Regnery, 2004), 308. Norman Podhoretz writes of his contempt for conservatism, circa 1960, typical for New York intellectuals: "To me—and in this I was representative of the intellectual community—the Republicans were at once the party of stupidity and the party of resistance to change." *Breaking Ranks: A Political Memoir* (New York: Harper & Row, 1979), 95.

82. Podhoretz, *Making It,* 126.

83. As Buckley recalled after Chambers's death, Chambers "would not associate himself with a journal which might oppose Eisenhower's reelection . . . or even be indifferent to his prospects for winning; let alone any magazine that might oppose Nixon's nomination in the event Eisenhower withdrew." William F. Buckley Jr., "The End of Whittaker Chambers," *Esquire* (September 1961): 32.

9. The Establishment of an Anti-Communist Intelligentsia

Epigraph: According to Barry Miles, "scholars of war" in the final text of "Howl" echoes words from an earlier draft of the poem, "post-war cynical scholars," which "refers to some of Lionel Trilling's students, perhaps an inkling of literary 'cold-warrior' Norman Podhoretz." Allen Ginsberg, *Howl: Original Draft Facsimile, Transcript and Variant Versions* (New York: Harper and Row, 1986), 125.

1. As late as 1956, Chambers believed that Stalin's crimes had gone unnoticed, noting "three to six million peasants whom Stalin (that is to say, Stalin and the Communist party) killed as a matter of deliberate policy, by withholding food

from them. What of these dead?" "The End of a Dark Age Ushers in New Dangers," *Life* (April 20, 1956): 289.

2. Trilling's review was "The Social Emotions," review of *The Nineteen* by Alexander Fadeyev, *New Freeman* 1 (July 6, 1930). Fadeyev's career was a lesson in the hard facts of Stalinism. In the words of Ann Applebaum: "after Khrushchev's speech [in 1956], Aleksandr Fadeev, a committed Stalinist and much-feared literary bureaucrat, went on an alcoholic binge. While drunk, he confessed to a friend that as head of the Writers' Union, he had sanctioned the arrests of many writers he knew to be innocent. Fadeev killed himself the following day. He allegedly left a one-sentence suicide letter, addressed to the Central Committee: 'The bullet fired was meant for Stalin's policies, for Zhdanov's aesthetics, for Lysenko's genetics.' " *Gulag: A History* (New York: Doubleday, 2003), 516.

3. Richard Pipes, *Russia under the Bolshevik Regime* (New York: Vintage, 1995), 166–239.

4. Norman Podhoretz notes that the word *Stalinism* survived the death of Stalin, lasting well beyond 1953. He refers to "Communism (or Stalinism, as many of us still called it, even though Stalin was dead and Khrushchev had denounced him)." *Breaking Ranks: A Political Memoir* (New York: Harper and Row, 1979), 63.

5. According to Norman Podhoretz, liberal anti-communists knew "how fragile the liberal anti-Communists consensus really was and conversely how deceptive was the apparent weakness of fellow-traveling liberalism, especially among intellectuals. Intimidated by McCarthyism and discredited by Stalinism, the fellow-traveling liberals had temporarily lost their nerve, but they had by no means been converted or given up." Ibid., 173.

6. Richard Gid Powers, *Not without Honor: The History of American Anticommunism* (New York: Free Press, 1995), 284.

7. Whittaker Chambers to Willi Schlamm, 1954, in *Cold Friday*, ed. Duncan Norton-Taylor (New York: Random House, 1964), 232, 235.

8. Whittaker Chambers to Ralph de Toledano, June 12, 1956, in *Notes from the Underground: The Whittaker Chambers-Ralph de Toledano Correspondence*, ed. Ralph de Toledano (Washington, D.C.: Regnery, 1997), 270; Whittaker Chambers to Ralph de Toledano, January 11[?], 1957, in Ibid., 290.

9. John Judis writes that Chambers and James Burnham—a former Trotskyite *Partisan Review* editor turned hard-line anti-communist conservative—"shared an interest in the work of beat-generation novelist Jack Kerouac." *William F. Buckley, Jr, Patron Saint of the Conservatives* (New York: Simon and Schuster, 1988), 160. Sam Tanenhaus notes Chambers's affection for "Jack Kerouac and Allen Ginsberg, college dropouts and bohemians, as Chambers had been twenty years before." *Whittaker Chambers: A Biography* (New York: Random House, 1997), 505. Chambers had lived as a vagabond before college, traveling from

Long Island to New Orleans. He had also written poetry, including homoerotic poetry, which figured in the Hiss case as incriminating evidence. Some five years after the Hiss case came to an end (in 1950), Ginsberg first performed "Howl" in San Francisco, a new departure in American culture. Ginsberg was a graduate of Columbia College and a homosexual who knew communism from his family.

10. Whittaker Chambers, *Cold Friday*, 228, 212, 217; Whittaker Chambers to Ralph de Toledano, March 17, 1954, in *Notes from the Underground*, 163.

11. Whittaker Chambers to Ralph de Toledano, April 6, 1953, in *Notes from the Underground*, 117.

12. Chambers, *Cold Friday*, 222.

13. Whittaker Chambers to Ralph de Toledano, October 17, 1956, in *Notes from the Underground*, 279.

14. Ibid., 280, 281, 280. Chambers wrote little about economics, but when he did his general ideas were not always at odds with those of Von Mises. In 1957, he wrote that "Keynes is a dialect of Marx not too greatly different than Slovene, say, is from Russian," proceeding to the claim that "socialism still has more in common with Communism than either of these two has with conservatism." "A Westminster Letter: The Left Understands the Left," *National Review* (November 17, 1957): 306, 207.

15. Whittaker Chambers to Ralph de Toledano, October 17, 1956, in *Notes from the Underground*, 281; Chambers, *Cold Friday*, 316.

16. Whittaker Chambers, "Big Sister Is Watching You," in *Ghosts on the Roof*, ed. Terry Teachout (Washington, D.C.: Regnery, 1989), 318, 317.

17. Whittaker Chambers, "Big Sister Is Watching You," in ed. Terry Teachout, *Ghosts on the Roof: Selected Journalism of Whittaker Chambers, 1931–1959* (Washington, D.C.: Regnery, 1989), 317; Judis, *William F. Buckley, Jr.*, 159; Alan Greenspan quoted in John Judis, Ibid., 160.

18. Whittaker Chambers, "Foot in the Door," in *Ghosts on the Roof*, 349. Chambers's anticapitalist views resembled those of fellow conservative Russell Kirk, who sought "to protect the traditional order against the destructive and socially disintegrative consequences of the avaricious pursuit of wealth and rapid industrialization, Kirk unquestionably favored appropriate governmental regulation of market forces," as W. Wesley McDonald writes. *Russell Kirk and the Age of Ideology* (Columbia: University of Missouri Press, 2004), 113–114. Chambers and Kirk shared a larger antimodern ethos: "to counter the spread of industrialization and urbanization, Kirk recommended that conservatives embrace agrarianism." Ibid., 147.

19. Chambers was not a party-line conservative at a time when there was no settled party line among conservatives. Sam Tanenhaus notes Chambers's frequent deviation from conservative conventional wisdom: "having allied himself with the right, he seemed bent on challenging, rebuking, and even outraging its

axioms." *Whittaker Chambers*, 501. Chambers dissented from right-wing orthodoxy when he argued that his nemesis, Alger Hiss, should have the right to travel, "a right of man and of the citizen," as Chambers wrote. "The Hissiad: A Correction," in *Ghosts on the Roof*, 343.

20. William F. Buckley Jr., "The End of Whittaker Chambers," *Esquire* (September 1961): 32; Whittaker Chambers to William F. Buckley Jr., September 7, 1954, in William F. Buckley Jr., ed., *Odyssey of a Friend: Whittaker Chambers's Letters to William F. Buckley, Jr., 1954–1961* (New York: Putnam, 1969), 79.

21. Chambers described the difference between himself and Buckley in a letter to Willi Schlamm: "Bill [Buckley] is a true conservative; I am at best a counter-revolutionist . . . we find ourselves wide apart on matters of great pitch and moment—especially the moment when strategy or tactics arise." Put bluntly, Chambers's "primary interest is to win a war rather than to defend a position." Whittaker Chambers to Willie Schlamm, January 7, 1955, in Ibid., 98.

22. Whittaker Chambers to William Buckley, April 6, 1954, in Ibid., 69.

23. Neil Jumonville charts the intellectual divisions within the anti-communist Left of the 1950s in a chapter titled "Affirmers and Dissenters" in *Critical Crossings: The New York Intellectuals in Postwar America* (Berkeley: University of California Press, 1991), 49–101. The key issue, for Jumonville, is whether intellectuals affirmed or dissented from the "American system."

24. Irving Howe, "Continuous Magical Confrontation," Lionel Trilling Papers, Special Collections, Butler Library, Columbia University, Box 7 (hereafter cited as Trilling MSS).

25. In a letter to Trilling, Edward Said wrote in tones that suggested influence and respect: "If I might, I would add to what you have written: that 'modernism' has had—in America at least—the worst of effects. The nihilism, the despair, the angst all heedlessly taken, and nothing taken—from Nietz-sche for instance—of his (the modernist) joy in the powers of mind and feeling. Surely modernism is at least about the overcoming powers of intellect, plus their constant undermining, and its *constitutive* engagement in reality . . . At Columbia . . . there's a kind of *fainéance*, a wilting permissiveness that makes me feel lonely and even drowning." Edward Said to Lionel Trilling, January 25, 1972, Trilling MSS, Box 28. Said's final sentence recalls Whittaker Chambers's description of liberal Columbia as a "bland, emollient, persuasive climate." *Cold Friday*, 99.

26. Irving Howe to Lionel Trilling, December 3, 1972, Trilling MSS, Box 3. Howe thought of Trilling as someone on whom conservatism intruded, noting "the conservative inclinations that creep in to his liberal persuasions" and Trilling's "falling back with some didactic bravado on the moral assurances of nineteenth-century writers." "Reading Lionel Trilling," *Commentary* (August 1973): 68. In 1968, Howe wrote that "the overwhelming intellectual drift [in the

1950s] was to the right." "New York Intellectuals," in *Selected Writings, 1950–1990* (New York: Harcourt, Brace, Jovanovich, 1990), 257.

27. Morris Dickstein, *Gates of Eden: American Culture in the Sixties* (Cambridge, Mass: Harvard University Press, 1997), 10; Allen Ginsberg to Lionel Trilling, September 4, 1945, Trilling MSS, Box 9. For an analysis that contrasts Ginsberg and Trilling, as cultural figures, while placing both in a Cold War context see Michael Davidson, *Guys Like Us: Citing Masculinity in Cold War Politics* (Chicago: University of Chicago Press, 2004).

28. Allen Ginsberg to Lionel Trilling, September 4, 1945, Trilling MSS, Box 9. From the beginning, Ginsberg knew exactly how contrary his ethical and poetic sensibility was to Trilling's. Long after he was a student, Ginsberg said of Trilling that "in a sense [he] tried to revive the humanistic solidarity and good manners of mid-nineteenth-century England. Mahogany Arnold." Quoted in Barry Miles, *Ginsberg: A Biography* (New York: Simon and Schuster, 1989), 37.

29. Allen Ginsberg to Lionel Trilling, circa 1957, Trilling MSS, Box 10. Todd Gitlin writes about Ginsberg and Trilling as if they occupied two entirely different areas of Columbia University: "at Columbia University, where [Jack] Kerouac and Ginsberg met and where Lionel Trilling's gentility reigned supreme, literary studies emphasized cool distance, teeth-gritting irony, the decorous play of literary reference." Todd Gitlin, *The Sixties: Years of Hope, Days of Rage* (New York: Bantam Books, 1993), 49.

30. Allen Ginsberg to Lionel Trilling, circa 1947, Trilling MSS, Box 10. Paraphrasing William Burroughs, Norman Podhoretz writes "that if Ginsberg were cut open, Lionel Trilling, the Columbia professor to whom he had been closest as a student, would be one of the shaping forces found within him." *Ex-Friends: Falling out with Allen Ginsberg, Lionel & Diana Trilling, Lillian Hellman, Hannah Arendt, and Norman Mailer* (New York: Free Press, 1999), 44.

31. Allen Ginsberg to Lionel Trilling, December 1948, Trilling MSS, Box 10.

32. As teacher and friend, Trilling gave Ginsberg a great deal of support and encouragement. Trilling was enthusiastic about Ginsberg's poetry, and he came to Ginsberg's defense when Ginsberg got in trouble for scrawling "Fuck the Jews" on his dormitory window at Columbia. When Ginsberg was embroiled in a homicide case, Trilling testified on his behalf and recommended psychiatric treatment. Miles, *Ginsberg*, 61, 79, 119.

33. According to Ginsberg's biographer, Barry Miles, Ginsberg "viewed the literary establishment of Lionel Trilling, *Partisan Review, Kenyon Review* and the Southern School as ultimately reactionary." Ibid., 212.

34. Frances S. Saunders, *The Cultural Cold War: The CIA and the World of Arts and Letters* (New York: New Press, 1999). Hugh Wilford argues, against Saunders, that the intellectuals enlisted by the CIA, both directly and indirectly, "were almost impossible to manage." *The Mighty Wurlitzer, How the*

CIA Played America (Cambridge, Mass.: Harvard University Press, 2008), 97. For more on the U.S. government's efforts to create a transatlantic anti-communist intelligentsia, see chapters three and four in Giles Scott-Smith, *The Politics of A-Political Culture: The Congress for Cultural Freedom, the CIA and the Post-War American Hegemony* (London: Routledge, 2002), 58–112.

35. Wilford, *The Mighty Wurlizter*, 254.

36. Sidney Hook, *Out of Step: An Unquiet Life in the Twentieth Century* (New York: Harper and Row, 1987), 432, 440. Historian Richard Gid Powers uses a language similar to Hook's to describe the function of the Congress for Cultural Freedom: it "helped nourish a flourishing anticommunist cultural community." *Not without Honor: The History of American Anticommunism* (New York: The Free Press, 1995), 212. Henry Kissinger got CIA support for a Harvard summer school in international relations by describing his aspiration "to create a spiritual link between a segment of foreign youth and the U.S." Quoted in Wilford, *The Mighty Wurlitzer*, 124.

37. Saunders, *The Cultural Cold War*, 162–163.

38. Wilford, *The Mighty Wurlitzer*, 231.

39. Hook, *Out of Step*, 428.

40. According to Richard Gid Powers, CIA influence "was well known to the Congress's friends and foes alike." *Not without Honor*, 212. Lionel Trilling was appalled by the CIA's involvement in anti-communist intellectual life. "It goes without saying that the CIA's covert backing of cultural and political projects, many of which were admirable in themselves, was a disaster in our national life," Trilling wrote shortly after details of CIA funding had been publicized. "Symposium on Liberal Anti-communism and Vietnam" *Commentary* (September 1967): 76. Hugh Wilford sees CIA funding as a sort of pattern, important to the neoconservative movement: "as strands of the New York intellectual community fed into the neoconservative movement, new sources of institutional support could become available in the shape of conservative corporations and think tanks, and the need for an alliance with secret federal agencies could pass." *The Mighty Wurlitzer*, 98.

41. C. Wright Mills to Lionel Trilling, February 2, 1943, Trilling MSS, Box 4; Lionel Trilling to Dan Wakefield, February 11, 1974, Trilling MSS, Box 29. Trilling criticized Mills for not exercising the liberal imagination. In a memo Mills wrote to himself, paraphrasing Trilling's comments to him on *White Collar*, Trilling's complaint was "too absolute a doctrine. White collar life also has its pleasantries and gratifications. You obscure complexities and qualifications in this thought." Quoted in Irving Horowitz, *C. Wright Mills: An American Utopian* (New York: Free Press, 1983), 252.

42. Mills was responding to Trilling's essay "The Situation of the American Intellectual at the Present Time." *Perspectives USA* 3 (Spring 1953): 24–42.

Philip Rahv pushed Irving Howe to attack Trilling in Howe's 1954 essay "This Age of Conformity," which was similar to Mill's critique. Rahv anticipated that " 'many people—the Trillings, for example, would be annoyed.' " Quoted in Gerald Sorin, *Irving Howe: A Life of Passionate Dissent* (New York: New York University Press, 2002), 137.

43. C. Wright Mills, "On Knowledge and Power," in, ed. Irving L. Horowitz, *Power, Politics and People: The Collected Essays of C. Wrigth Mills* (New York: Ballantine Books, 1968), 599, 603.

44. Ibid., 607. One circumstance behind the Mills essay, which may have provoked its reference to "the Luce publications," is the sociologist Dan Bell's move from *The New Leader* to *Fortune*, a Luce publication. A rival of Mill's, Bell was a liberal anti-communist and a good friend of Trilling's. Horowitz, *C. Wright Mills*, 85.

45. Lionel Trilling to C. Wright Mills, November 22, 1955, Trilling MSS, Box 4. Irving Horowitz interprets the exchange between Mills and Trilling as "the aristocratic literary critic defending mass culture and the populist sociologist defending elite culture." Dissenting from the perception that Trilling was distancing himself from political life in the 1950s, Horowitz rightly observes that "the vigor of Trilling's response is indicative of a triumphal rather than a retreating liberalism." Horowitz, *C. Wright Mills*, 252, 284.

46. William Barrett, *The Truants: Adventures among the Intellectuals* (Garden City, N.Y.: Anchor Books, 1982), 164, 179. Rahv's doubts about Trilling were nothing new, according to Norman Podhoretz, with Trilling "falling under Rahv's glowering but thoroughly justified suspicion as early as the mid-thirties of having more Freud in his system than Marx." Norman Podhoretz, *Making It* (New York: Random House, 1967), 126.

47. William Phillips, *A Partisan View: Five Decades of the Literary Life* (New York: Stein and Day, 1983), 71. One finds a similar response in Trilling's 1957 letter to Leon Edel: "if my dismissal of Fromm, Henry, and Sullivan (and of Jung and Reich) must inevitably create, as you say, 'an impression of conservatism,' then I did indeed 'intend' to create it. But I don't think—and I'm sure you don't really think—that one makes intellectual judgments with an eye to whether or not they will seem 'conservative' or 'progressive.' " Lionel Trilling to Leon Edel, February 25, 1957, Trilling MSS, Box 14.

48. Delmore Schwartz, "The Duchess' Red Shoes," in, ed. Donald A. Dike and David H. Zucker, *Selected Essays of Delmore Schwartz* (Chicago: University of Chicago Press, 1985), 209, 222, 212, 209, 212. Trilling responded with anger: "I was angry with Delmore Schwartz for his essay—amusedly angry— because I perceived a personal cast in his argument, especially, of course, in his ridiculous misinterpretations and misrepresentations," he wrote in a

1957 letter. Lionel Trilling to John Aldridge, March 6, 1957, Trilling MSS, Box 14.

49. Mary McCarthy to Hannah Arendt, December 2, 1952, in *Between Friends: The Correspondence of Hannah Arendt and Mary McCarthy: 1949–1975*, ed. Carol Brightman (New York: Harcourt Brace and Company, 1995), 11–12.

50. Donald Critchlow, *Phyllis Schlafly and Grassroots Conservatism: A Woman's Crusade* (Princeton, N.J.: Princeton University Press, 2005), 40. Critchlow argues that *Witness* and books like it helped to build a grassroots conservative movement: "literature such as *Witness* inspired a large anticommunist movement that emerged in local communities across the nation, where individuals met in study groups to study the nature of communism and address local issues that revealed subversive influences." Ibid., 40. *Witness* was also a key text for a college-educated conservative elite: "for activisits such as [Grover] Norquist, coming of age in the 1970's, the book [*Witness*] was their Rosetta stone, unlocking a language that would give order and meaning to a murky world seemingly controlled by liberals . . . For the generation of conservatives who emerged in the 1970's—and onto the national scene in the '80's and 90's—the personal connection with Chambers was visceral." Nina Easton, *Gang of Five: Leaders at the Center of the Conservative Crusade* (New York: Simon and Schuster, 2000), 79, 81.

51. Chambers, "The End of a Dark Age Ushers in New Dangers," In *The Ghosts on the Roof*, 287, 289, 290, 286. Chambers would continue to worry about Soviet exploitation of Western exhaustion and Western pacifism, writing, in 1959, that "the purpose of the Soviet missiles is to impose on the West a truce of exhaustion, taking form in one or another degree of atomic disarmament." "Missiles, Brains and Mind," in *Ghosts on the Roof*, 337.

52. Chambers dismissed Latin America as a geopolitical backwater: "most of us do not think much or often about Latin America, except, perhaps, as the cut-rate vactionland of the colored airline ads." "Soviet Strategy in the Middle East," in *Ghosts on the Roof*, 294.

53. Ibid., 297. Chambers made a strong appeal for Israel in this essay: "an immense compassion—mere good will is too genderless a term—before the spectacle of Jewish tragedy in our century, must move our hourly understanding of what the State of Israel means in terms of hope fired by such suffering." Ibid., 296.

54. Chambers, "Soviet Strategy in the Middle East," 297, 297, 298.

55. Whittaker Chambers, "A Westminster Letter: To Temporize Is Death," *National Review* (November 17, 1957), 311.

56. Ibid.

57. Whittaker Chambers, "A Republican Looks at His Vote," in *Ghosts on the Roof*, 332, 331.

58. Whittaker Chambers, "The Coming Struggle for Outer Space," in *Ghosts on the Roof*, 302; Whittaker Chambers, "Foot in the Door," in *Ghosts on the Roof*, 349-350.

59. Whittaker Chambers, "Is Academic Freedom in Danger?" in *Ghosts on the Roof*, 265.

60. Whittaker Chambers, "The Sanity of St. Benedict," in *Ghosts on the Roof*, 262, 263, 262.

61. Ibid., 263. When Chambers wrote about Marx and alienation in the 1950s, it was his generation's Marxism that he had in mind. Chambers may have enjoyed the poetry of Allen Ginsberg, but he was no premature child of the 1960s. He did not respond to Herbert Marcuse's reading of the humanist Marx in *Eros and Its Discontents*, the Marcuse for whom "all labor is alienated labor; satisfaction comes only through erotic activity, leisure, or play." Dickstein, *Gates of Eden*, 74.

62. Podhoretz, *Making It*, 43, 49, 44-45. Western civilization, as handed down to Podhoretz, may have been American by default, but it was basically a European concept: "In the context of the idea of Western Civilization to which I had been converted at Columbia—'Western,' as I have already indicated, having for me the force of 'universal'—America was definitely a minor province and definitely to be treated as such." After graduate work at Cambridge University, Podhoretz observed that he "had spent six years at two major universities without ever finding out that America existed as a factor in the history of the West, that it was anything but an inferior and altogether uninteresting offshoot of European civilization." Ibid., 84, 90.

63. Podhoretz, *Breaking Ranks*, 21,

64. Podhoretz, *Making It*, 89.

65. Ibid., 41.

66. Podhoretz, *Ex-Friends*, 223; Podhoretz, *Breaking Ranks*, 26, 27. Podhoretz preferred the secular Sidney Hook to conservatives such as Chambers, believing that "what separated us [in the West] from them [under communism] was that we were free and they were not, that our political system was democratic and that theirs was totalitarian. And I consistently maintained that liberal democracy was itself a value—a value that Americans wanted to live by and that they were even willing to die for." *Ex-Friends*, 70-71.

67. Podhoretz, *Making It*, 288; Podhoretz, *Ex-Friends*, 77n. As for Chambers, Podhoretz mentions the Trillings' strong support for his testimony in the Hiss case: "they believed that he [Chambers] was telling the truth about Alger Hiss's involvement in espionage on behalf of the Soviet Union, and they strongly supported him in the fierce controversy aroused by that charge." *Ex-Friends*, 77n. George Nash writes that "to much of the *Commentary* circle of the mid- and late 1970's, the existing conservative intellectual circle was an unimpressive

lot. In this largely unspoken attitude, *Commentary* may have been influenced by the much-quoted words of its literary patron saint . . . Lionel Trilling [to the effect that America had not real intellectual conservatism]." "Joining Ranks," in *Commentary in American Life*, ed. Murray Friedman (Philadelphia: Temple University Press, 2005), 45.

68. In Podhoretz's recollection, for the Trillings he was "a true disciple, forcefully and articulately carrying their intellectual and political point of view forward into a new generation. So indeed I was. My earliest published writings were pervaded by Lionel's influence." *Ex-Friends*, 69.

69. Podhoretz, *Making It*, 117.

70. The relationship between Ginsberg and Podhoretz began well. "As a freshman, age sixteen, I had submitted a long poem about the prophet Jeremiah to the college literary magazine of which he [Ginsberg] . . . was the editor, and to my great delight he had accepted it for publication," Podhoretz writes. *Ex-Friends*, 23.

71. Podhoretz owed his *Partisan Review* connection to Trilling as well. Phillip Rahv and William Phillips "knew that I was Lionel's protégé, and they . . . invited me to write for them." Podhoretz, *Ex-Friends*, 68.

72. Podhoretz describes the start of his *Commentary* career in *Ex-Friends*, 67, 156n. Cohen had been aware of Podhoretz since 1952, when he read and liked Podhoretz's review of *The Liberal Imagination*. Nathan Abrams, *Commentary Magazine, 1945–1959: "A Journal of Significant Thought and Opinion"* (London: Vallentine Mitchell, 2007), 123.

73. In Kristol's words, "Lionel Trilling I worshiped. His essays in *Partisan Review* were, for me, an event." Quoted in Joseph Dorman, *Arguing the World: The New York Intellectuals in Their Own Words* (New York: The Free Press, 2000), 72.

74. Abrams, *Commentary Magazine*, 103.

75. Podhoretz, *Ex-Friends*, 114.

76. Norman Podhoretz, "The Know-Nothing Bohemians," in *Doings and Undoings: The Fifties and After in American Writing* (New York: Farrar, Straus and Giroux, 1966), 147, 156. Trilling disliked "Howl," Ginsberg's 1955 poem and manifesto. As he wrote to Ginsberg: "I'm afraid I have to tell you that I don't like the poems at all. I hesitate before saying that they seem to me quite dull, for to say of a work which undertakes to be violent and shocking that it is dull is, I am aware, a well known and all too easy device." He continued: "They are not like Whitman—they are all prose, all rhetoric, without any music. What I used to like in your poems, whether I thought they were good or bad, was the *voice* I heard in them, true and natural and interesting. There is no real voice here. As for the doctrinal element of the poems, apart from the fact that I of course reject it, it seems to me that I heard it very long ago and that you give it

to me in all its orthodoxy, with nothing new added." Lionel Trilling to Allen Ginsberg, May 29, 1956, quoted in *Howl*, 156.

77. Podhoretz, *Breaking Ranks*, 40, 40; Podhoretz, *Ex-Friends*, 72, 75.

78. Podhoretz, *Making It*, 281, 281; Podhoretz, *Ex-Friends*, 76, 77. Jacob Heilbrunn has described Podhoretz's critique of Trilling from the Left and then, later, from the Right as "a kind of double patricide." *They Knew They Were Right: The Rise of the Neocons* (New York: Doubleday, 2008), 73.

79. Podhoretz, *Breaking Ranks*, 47, 48, 49. Trilling and Brown were not simple antagonists. Trilling played a role in promoting *Life against Death*, according to Podhoretz: "I even succeeded in getting Lionel Trilling to read it [*Life against Death*] and his subsequent endorsement ensured that attention would be paid to the new edition, which indeed it was." *Breaking Ranks*, 48.

80. Quoted by Podhoretz in *Breaking Ranks*, 49.

81. Ibid., 51, 50, 54. Morris Dickstein also writes of Goodman and Mailer as carriers of the future: "it was prophetic of [Norman] Mailer and Paul Goodman (in *Growing Up Absurd*) to seize on the beat and hip phenomena, as well as the plague of delinquency and youthful anomie, as cracks in the whole system, harbingers of a new spirit they themselves only dimply anticipated." *The Gates of Eden*, 54.

82. Podhoretz, *Ex-Friends*, 81.

83. Podhoretz, "The Issue," *Commentary* 29 no. 2 (February 1960) 183; Podhoretz, *Breaking Ranks*, 84.

84. Podhoretz, *Breaking Ranks*, 86.

Epilogue

1. "Class of 1924 Newsletter," pp. 15–16, Lionel Trilling Papers, Special Collections, Butler Library, Columbia University, Box 1 (hereafter cited as Trilling MSS). Richard Hofstadter, "The Paranoid Style in American Politics," in *The Paranoid Style in American Politics and Other Essays* (New York: Knopf, 1965), 3–41. First titled *The New American Right* and then republished as *The Radical Right* in 1963, Daniel Bell's 1955 anthology is among the earliest and most important scholarly works devoted to postwar conservatism. *The New American Right* (New York: Critereon Books, 1955). When Alger Hiss read *Witness*, he, too, saw paranoia on the Right: "any enlightened layman will realize at once that [*Witness*] is the product of a seriously disturbed psyche," he wrote in a letter to his wife, Priscilla. Quoted in G. Edward White, *Alger Hiss's Looking-Glass Wars: The Covert Life of a Soviet Spy* (New York: Oxford University Press, 2004), 106.

2. "Class of 1924 Newsletter," pp. 15–16; Trilling MSS, Box 1.

3. William F. Buckley Jr. to Lionel Trilling, July 13, 1962, Trilling MSS, Box 1; William F. Buckley Jr. to Lionel Trilling, June 24, 1962, Trilling MSS, Box 1.

4. William Fitzgibbon, "Whittaker Chambers Is Dead; Hiss Case Witness," http://www.nytimes.com/ books/97/03/09/reviews/Chambers-medal.html.

5. See http://www.nytimes.com/books/97/03/09/reviews/Chambers-medal.html.

6. White, *Alger Hiss's Looking-Glass Wars*, 231. "He [Hiss] should be thought of," White writes, "as one of the successful spies in American history, not only because of the quality and duration of his espionage for the Soviet Union, but because of his singular ability, in his successive looking-glass wars, to deceive so many persons about the dimensions of his life." Ibid., 249. Enthusiasm for Hiss, and his version of events, was strong in the 1960s and 1970s: "without any substantial concrete evidence to bolster his campaign for vindication, by the early 1970's Hiss had redirected that campaign along profitable lines. He would partially reinvent himself in the process." Ibid., 141. Arthur Herman argues, in his revisionist book on McCarthy, that Hiss was either being rehabilitated or forgotten in the 1970s: "if McCarthy was guilty, the reasoning goes, then those he tormented must be innocent." *Joseph McCarthy: Reexamining the Life and Legacy of America's Most Hated Senator* (New York: Free Press, 2000), 5. White labels Hiss's long life "an example of the potential consequences of the otherworldliness of the elite intelligentsia," a judgment with which Chambers would have emphatically concurred. *Alger Hiss's Looking-Glass Wars*, 125.

7. See http://homepages.nyu.edu/~th15/home.html.

8. "Reagan's hostility toward liberalism had its origins in the Hiss-Chambers affair," writes John Patrick Diggins, although "Reagan's sense of religion was opposite that of Whittaker Chambers, who condemned America to purgatory. Chambers spoke to our fears, Reagan to our desires." *Ronald Reagan: Fate, Freedom, and the Making of History* (New York: Norton, 2007), 9, 14.

9. For obvious reasons, conservatives have been most likely to credit Chambers with intellectual importance. Chambers is one of only two intellectuals to have multiple entries in William F. Buckley Jr.'s anthology of American conservative thought. *Did You Ever See a Dream Walking: American Conservative Thought in the Twentieth Century*, ed. William F. Buckley Jr. (New York: Bobbs-Merrill, 1970). Chambers has no entry in *The Companion to American Thought*; nor is he mentioned in its section on conservatism, a section that begins with the declaration that "American history has conspired against the flowering of conservative thought." "Conservatism," in *The Companion to American Thought*, ed. Richard Wightman Fox and James T. Kloppenberg (Oxford: Blackwell, 1995), 142. Chambers has only one reference in the index (the French philosopher Jacques Derrida has eighteen), and it is for the entry on William F. Buckley Jr. Although *Witness* is touched on with regard to Chambers, Chambers is described not as a contributor to American thought but as "the accuser of [Alger] Hiss in one of the great controversies of the domestic Cold War." Ibid., 93. Chambers has recently acquired a place in

academic intellectual history. See, for example, "Selection from *Witness*," in *The American Intellectual Tradition: A Sourcebook: Volume II: 1865 to the Present*, ed. David Hollinger and D. Capper (New York: Oxford University Press, 1997), 271–284.

10. "White House Freedom Medal Set for Whittaker Chambers," http://www .nytimes.com/books/97/03/09/reviews/chambers-medal.html. The *Times* article also illustrated the conservative movement's political clout circa 1984: "In reply to a question, the White House said a number of letters of recommendation [for the White House Freedom Medal] had been submitted for Mr. Chambers, including some from conservative groups." Ibid.

11. Ronald Reagan, with Richard Hubler, *Where's the Rest of Me? The Autobiography of Ronald Reagan* (New York: Karz-Segil, 1981), 268. Reagan honored Chambers, and he honored Chambers's intellectual milieu. In the words of Jeffrey Hart, a *National Review* editor, "Reagan was an assiduous reader of *National Review*, had a particularly high regard for [James] Burnham's prudential and realistic foreign policy, was a friend of [William F.] Buckley, and awarded the Presidential Medal of Freedom to both Chambers (posthumously) and Burnham. He attended the magazine's thirtieth anniversary dinner at the Plaza Hotel, as well as the opening of *National Review*'s Washington office at the Madison Hotel." *The Making of the American Conservative Mind: National Review and Its Times* (Wilmington, Del.: ISI Books, 2005), 260.

12. "White House Freedom Medal Set for Whittaker Chambers."

13. President George W. Bush recently bestowed a Presidential Freedom Medal on Trilling's student Norman Podhoretz. See "A Neocon is Honored by a President He Reveres." *New York Times*, June 24, 2004, sec. B, p. 4, col. 3.

14. In 1957, Chambers discussed the 1960 election, mentioning the possibility of a Kennedy victory: "I claim nearly always to be wrong about American politics," he wrote to William F. Buckley Jr. "But, like everybody else, I make my guess. As of this moment my guess would be that, if there is no marked economic bust before 1960 (I find it difficult to believe that there will not be), then the Vice President [Richard Nixon] should have a favoring wind . . . If economic trouble comes, I should guess that it will be neither Nixon nor [Senator William] Knowland, but, more likely John Kennedy of Massachusetts. Senator Kennedy, I mean; perhaps he isn't John. I may change most of this guess a month hence." Whittaker Chambers to William F. Buckley Jr, May 9, 1957, in *Odyssey of a Friend: Whittaker Chambers Letters to William F. Buckley, Jr.*, *1954–1961*, ed. William F. Buckley (Washington, D.C.: Regnery, 1987), 160–161.

15. In an essay titled "The Assassination of President Kennedy," Diana Trilling noted that "the academic and literary intellectuals of New York . . . had been Kennedy supporters if they are ever to be called supporters of anyone in

office." This support had not been immediate: "before the Cuban [missile] crisis the American intellectual class, particularly in its radical wing, was elaborately on guard against Kennedy's pleasure in intellectual company. Was one to forfeit one's right of criticism for the sake of dinner in the White House?" But with Kennedy's success in the Cuban missile crisis, the intellectual class warmed to Kennedy, and "for the first time since the Second World War the American intellectual could admit the existence of an enemy other than his own government and a leadership adequate to the needs of his own nation." "The Assassination of President Kennedy," in *We Must March My Darlings: A Critical Decade* (New York: Harcourt, Brace, Jovanovich, 1977), 4, 6, 7.

16. Norman Podhoretz, *Making It* (New York: Random House, 1967), 313.

17. Ibid., 312.

18. Trilling, "The Assassination of President Kennedy," 6. In a letter to Mary McCarthy, Hannah Arendt offers a fascinating postscript to the Trillings' evening at the White House: "Otherwise—nothing changed. Except of course for regular invitations of intellectuals into the White House. There is a nice story about Diana Trilling buying herself the appropriate outfit, then becoming unsure and calling up the White House, describing her dress in detail, if it would do. I do not want to imply that I think Kennedy is wrong in inviting these people. On the contrary, I think he is more or less right, the trouble is only that he will corrupt everybody without wanting to." Hannah Arendt to Mary McCarthy, May 20, 1962, in Carol Brightman, ed., *Between Friends: The Correspondence of Hannah Arendt and Mary McCarthy: 1949–1975* (New York: Harcourt, Brace and Company, 1995), 132.

19. Diana Trilling, "A Night in Camelot," *New Yorker* (June 2, 1997): 65, 57, 54, 59.

20. Ibid., 56. Back in the 1930s, Farrell had encountered Whittaker Chambers in the offices of the *New Masses*, where he told Chambers "that his child had been stillborn. Farrell remembers best of all from that conversation Chambers' brooding passivity. Eighteen years later [in 1950], Farrell again met Chambers, who said he had never forgotten that day because Farrell's story seemed to him the essence of tragedy. 'And what was tragic about it?' said Farrell. 'I was young; it was life.' " Murray Kempton, *Part of Our Time: Some Ruins and Monuments of the Thirties* (New York: Simon and Schuster, 1955), 130.

21. Ibid., 140.

22. James Farrell, "A Comment on Literature and Morality: A Crucial Question of Our Times," *New International* 12 (May 1946): 145.

23. Trilling, "A Night in Camelot," 56, 56.

24. Ibid., 60.

25. Norman Podhoretz recalls intellectuals both desiring and worrying about evenings at the White House. Under Kennedy, Podhoretz remembers, "writers

and intellectuals, as well as other people I knew, were receiving invitations to dinner at the White House. Those who received such invitations were of course flattered and delighted, and those who did not were dejected and upset, but except for socialites like [George] Plimpton, everyone was disconcerted. What did it mean? Would accepting an invitation to the White House compromise one's freedom to criticize—and in the case of some, to despise— the Kennedy administration?" *Breaking Ranks: A Political Memoir* (New York: Harper and Row, 1975), 105. Diana Trilling does not discuss this worry, most likely because she and Lionel were not troubled by it.

26. Trilling, "A Night in Camelot," 58, 63, 60.

27. Ibid., 59, 65.

28. Diana Trilling repeatedly used the metaphor of balance to describe the Kennedy presidency. American life without Kennedy was out of balance, she implied: "the death of John Kennedy . . . made for a subtle and perhaps a more pervasive disturbance in our historical balance. It affected our sense of ourselves as a people; it deprived us of the promise of a future." "Introduction," in *We Must March My Darlings*, xiv.

29. Diana Trilling saw Kennedy's assassination in 1963 as a turning point in American history: "How more decisively underscore the anger and emptiness of themed- and late sixties and our American self-contempt, earned and unearned, than by reminding ourselves of how acute and actual had been the hope generated in us by the Kennedy presidency?" "Introduction," *We Must March My Darlings*, xiv.

30. Whittaker Chambers to William F. Buckley Jr., April 6, 1954, in *Odyssey of a Friend*, 35.

31. Sam Tanenhaus, *Whittaker Chambers: A Biography* (New York: Random House, 1997), 492.

32. The intoxication was literal as well as figurative. Lionel Trilling drank prodigiously before dinner: "I could see that he wasn't being his shy self. He had had six martinis, I'd been counting," Diana Trilling observed. "An Evening at Camelot," 59.

33. Jonah Raskin, *Out of the Whale: Growing Up in the American Left: An Autobiography* (New York: Links Books, 1974), 192. In Raskin's estimation, "Trilling and [T. S.] Eliot were guilty of creating a conservative, anti-Communist, and often racist perspective. Trilling had been against the student rebellion at Columbia. He denied the existence of black culture and scorned Langston Hughes, a 'neighborhood writer' . . . Trilling was opposed to a gay lounge at Columbia because he thought repressed homosexuals were more neurotic and therefore more creative than gay people who were open about their sexuality." Raskin went so far as to create a "wanted poster for Trilling. I identified my old professor as a 'cultural imperialist,' 'a literary cricket,' a

member of the '*Partisan Review* mob.' His crime was 'brainwashing.' " Ibid., 192, 194.

34. Diana Trilling, "On the Steps of Low Library," in *We Must March My Darlings: A Critical Decade* (New York: Harcourt, Brace, Jovanovich, 1977), 75–154.

INDEX